*A Collection of Fiction and Poetry
by former Fellows of the Stanford Writing Workshop
to celebrate Stanford's Centennial*

THE UNCOMMON TOUCH

THE UNCOMMON TOUCH

◆ ◆ ◆

Fiction and Poetry
from the
Stanford Writing Workshop

Edited by

JOHN L'HEUREUX

Foreword by Wallace Stegner

Stanford Alumni Association
Stanford, California

Library of Congress Catalogue Card Number: 88-63442
ISBN 0-916318-34-6 (case)
    0-916318-33-8 (pbk.)
    0-916318-35-4 (special ed.)

Acknowledgments of previous publication, copyright notices, and permissions to reprint the
selections in this book may be found beginning on page 507.

Jacket, cover and book design: Jeffrey Whitten
Jacket and cover illustration: Gwyn Stramler
Typesetting: Terry Robinson & Co., Inc.

This book is dedicated to

Wallace E. Stegner

on his eightieth birthday

CONTENTS

FOREWORD

Wallace Stegner

When Rip Van Winkle returned to his village after his twenty-year sleep on the mountainside, he found things bewilderingly changed. The faces of the people he met were not faces he knew, the clothes were of a fashion he did not recognize, the children and dogs who followed him into town were unfamiliar. The village itself was much bigger and more populous than he remembered. Old houses were gone, new houses had sprung up, there were strange signs over the doors. His own house, when he found it, stared at him through broken windows from under its collapsing roof. Orators were preaching incomprehensible doctrines in the street, and General Washington, whoever he was, had replaced King George III on the tavern sign. Asked to identify himself, Rip quavered out that he was "a poor, quiet man, a native of the place, and a loyal subject of the King, God bless him," and the villagers clamored for him to be run out of town as a Tory.

My own sleep on the mountainside has not been as long as Rip's—it is only eighteen years since I retired from Stanford—but my feelings are not unlike his. Neither students nor dogs recognize me as I walk on the campus, and however wistfully I look for familiar faces, I see only strangers. The landmarks by which I used to steer are still there, but at every turn I find new, confusing buildings in which I have never set foot and whose purpose I cannot name. People wear funny looking clothes, and facial hair seems to have sprouted on every chin but mine. I get shinsplints walking in from where I am able to park my car.

Reading this anthology of stories and poems written over the years by people who have been students in the Stanford writing program is every bit as acute an experience in recognition and disorientation as is revisiting the campus after long absence.

True, the greatly gifted people from the past are here, or most of them—those who electrified the seminar with the things they wrote, and galvanized their fellow students into competitive efforts. A satisfying number of them have made substantial contributions to contemporary literature, and the names of some of them are household words. I am not going to repeat their names here. To name some would be to overlook others, and I am not in a mood to overlook anybody who took part in the enterprise. Whether they ever made it big or not, they contributed, and they remain part of its history.

In fact, if I had been making the selections, more of the writers from the forties, fifties, and sixties would be here; this would be a fatter book. For the enterprise deserves a maximum memorial, one that credits everyone who took part in it. At its best, it was both competitive and friendly, individual and group-related. It was simultaneously a teaching and a learning, and the currents flowed both ways. Teachers and students, we were all performers and all members of the audience; and those annually re-formed seminars were probably the best audience, the most stimulating and the most critical and the most sympathetic, that any of us ever had.

To find so many old friends and old favorites collected together is to have the past reaffirmed and solidified. But there are also selections in this volume that are entirely new to me, and writers who are known to me only as names, if at all. Of the ninety-eight contributors, I find that I personally know only sixty. Inevitably the work of the others, even when it strikes me as brilliant, is less vivid to me because I have no memory of its making. I was not there when its authors fought it into shape. I do not associate it with the struggling apprenticeship of a longtime friend. Though many of these later writers worked under fellowships bearing my name, and speak of themselves among themselves as "Stegners," they are almost as remote from me as the four-legged Stegners up in Montana who derive from a Red Angus bull that an admirer named for me.

That I never knew them personally, and was not there while they mastered their craft and refined their art, is my loss, just as surely as it is my great gain to number many of the older ones as my good friends as well as my ex-students. But reading the collected works of knowns and unknowns together reinforces my sense of how much has changed during the eighteen years of my absence, and at the same time reassures me that nothing has stopped. The writing program has grown like a coral reef, the present continuing from and building upon and branching out from what we were doing in the forties, fifties, and sixties. Though names and faces change, and literary fashions and literary economics change, and faculty and staff totter toward retirement or out the other side, the purpose of this association remains what it used to be: to provide literary talent with the opportunity to define itself, and grow, and mature, under guidance and in the stimulating company of the like-minded.

It is a very much larger and more comprehensive program than it was back in the forties, when the students were fewer, the selection process more hand-to-mouth, and the headquarters was my office, without even a secretary. The entire staff was then Richard Scowcroft, Yvor Winters, and myself, all of us part time in the writing program, and one or two equally part-time teaching assistants. The fellowships now carry five times the stipend they carried then, and there are more of them. The prize and publication functions have withered, for complex but legitimate reasons. The visitor schedule, always important, has been enlarged by the generosity of Jean and Bill Lane, who endow three major literary visitors annually. There was other, earlier help, first from Dr. E. H. Jones and his family, then from the will of Edith Mirrielees, the beloved teacher who helped give Stanford its first literary reputation, and from Neilma Gantner, who funded a series of Australian fellows. Later still, there have been other donors to the program, and it is currently engaged in an ambitious funding effort that will insure ten fellowships in fiction and ten in poetry each year. Begun as an adjunct of the academic schedules of the English Department, the writing section has moved toward greater autonomy and is now hardly at all degree-oriented.

Those are all changes that I applaud. If I could have achieved them during my tenure as director, I would have; and I have cheered the success of Richard Scowcroft, Nancy Packer, Ken Fields, and especially John L'Heureux as they have expanded our first little universe. Nevertheless, though the independence of the writing section seems to me essential, I do not want to minimize the importance of the academic connection. Stanford has been absolutely essential to the fostering of these writers and has backed the program with enthusiasm even when it threatened, as it did once or twice, to become embarrassing. By its very existence, by the nature of its commitment to the life of the mind, it has made itself the best possible place for a young writer to grow.

For it is unhappily true that many American communities, especially the smaller ones and those without some sort of academy to leaven their lump, are intellectually and culturally and artistically inert. Any college or university, even a modest one, generates a more vigorous life flow, and many towns and small cities take most of their character from the academies they foster. Try to think of Princeton, Chapel Hill, Charlottesville, Amherst, Palo Alto, Berkeley, Cambridge, New Haven, without their intellectual cores: they shrink like Alice at the entrance to the rabbit hole. When the university is a great one, as Stanford is, the suburb or town in which it is set takes on a glow. It offers the best that has been thought and said in the past, and it holds the key to the future. Writers need both tradition and freedom. They have to know where their society has been before they can handle the language and the relationships out of which they will make their fictions and poetry. And minds grow by contact with other minds, the bigger the better, as clouds grow toward thunder by rubbing together.

It is one of the great satisfactions of my life that I was able, at the end of World War II when the campus was suddenly flooded with GI students of a maturity and motivation unheard of on any campus until then, to see an opportunity and help bring it to a group of young writers at Stanford. I was young then myself, no more than ten years older than most of my students, and their enthusiasm was a tonic to me.

Once begun, the thing we had started together grew almost by itself. Not every student got everything from it that he needed or expected, or that we hoped to provide. But most were stimulated, many were encouraged, some even seem to have been instructed. Almost all grew: the evidence is on the pages before us. What is more important, what impresses returning Rip Van Winkle, is that the program itself has demonstrated both durability and flexibility. It did not fall into a rut, it did not petrify. Under new management it adapted itself both to new students and new conditions, and is thriving.

Before I came to Stanford in 1945 I had taught for a half dozen years at Harvard, and all the time I was at Harvard I was impressed—I, a western boy who had never even seen a writer until I was past twenty-one—by how many of the writers I respected and revered had gone through that university and had their wits and their language honed on that fine whetstone. It seemed to me that Harvard had singlehandedly created or sponsored half of American literature.

Looking through this celebratory anthology that records forty-two years of Stanford effort, I have two principal perceptions: that a great university is indeed the best finishing school for literary talent, and that Harvard now is a long way from dominating the field.

PREFACE

John L'Heureux

In my writing workshop, a fairly typical one, twelve people sit around a long table and listen while somebody reads a new and therefore fragile piece of fiction. After the reading the eleven others discuss the story, frankly and sometimes brutally, as if the author weren't sitting there with them. They talk about what the story is trying to do, how it's trying to do it, whether it has used the best means to the desired end, and how well the story succeeds. I sit at one end of the table, the dread thirteenth person, and try to say as little as possible. Occasionally I interrupt with a question or comment that I hope will steer the discussion toward the larger and more important issues. At the end, I summarize, hitting the major points and leaving the rest for a lengthy written report I give to the author. When the workshop meeting goes well, we succeed in creating a kind of critical essay on the story at hand, everybody is satisfied, and the author goes away with a clear sense of how to revise the story to achieve the symmetry and perfection it deserves. When the workshop meeting doesn't go well, nobody feels satisfied, the author goes away hurt and depressed and sometimes vengeful, and I wonder why I didn't become a painter like my father.

What I've described above is the ideal workshop meeting, and it's pretty rare; as rare, I should imagine, as the total disaster. Most workshop meetings are neither miraculous nor hellish; they're located somewhere in between—in a place where comments do not build on one another to form a shapely and intelligent critical essay but stumble over one another in contradiction, exclamation, and often laughter; where I talk altogether too much; where an author, filled with the pride of authorship and blindly defensive, protests against any and all criticism; where one or two comments are meant less to enlighten than to retaliate for what was said last week; where the participants feel they were not nearly so helpful as they might have been; and where the author goes away with a pretty good sense of how to make the story work *despite* what everybody said.

A writing workshop, even the best, is wanton with energy and talent; it can crush the weak and empower the crass; it offers endless opportunity to give and receive injury; it is frequently as frustrating, indeed as maddening, as life itself. Surely the writing workshop is the oddest, most problematic, most dangerous, and least economical route to take on the way to becoming a writer. And yet all the poets and fiction writers in this fat book have taken exactly that route.

They've done so because, when all the bad things about it have been said, the writing workshop finally is the one place where you can be sure you and your work are taken seriously, where your writing intentions are honored, where even in a mean-spirited comment you can divine—if you wish—the truth about your writing, its strength and its weaknesses. It is a place where you are surrounded by people whose chief interest in life is also yours, where talk is never anything but writing and writing well and writing better, where book chat is the primitive calculating talk of writers rather than the civil and judiciary talk of critics, where money is always short but somehow someone always has the latest Carver or Paley or Updike and it's passed around and admired and aspired to. It is where you make friends that last your entire life. It is where they give you a little time and a little money and a lot of emotional and psychological support. It is where somehow you pick up the notion that what you're doing is a good and noble thing, and though you may not write as well as you'd like, it is enough and will suffice.

When Wallace Stegner founded the Stanford Writing Program in 1946, it was with all these things in mind. He knew firsthand how effective a writing program could be because he had studied at the Iowa Writers Workshop in its earliest days and had subsequently taught writing at Harvard. From Iowa he borrowed the notion that the writer's craft can be taught and from Harvard he borrowed the laddered courses of increasing expectation; the idea of having nonmatriculated Writing Fellows was purely and magnificently his own. Iowa was the first degree-granting writing program in the country, and Wally Stegner made Stanford's the second. Since '46, degree programs have proliferated at an unbelievable rate; there are now, according to the Associated Writing Program newsletter, some 350 programs that grant between 7,000 and 8,000 degrees each year. Iowa and Stanford, I'm happy to say, remain at the top of that long list of programs.

I took over direction of the Stanford Writing Program twelve years ago and at that time I carefully studied the founding documents and all the accompanying correspondence. As I set about editing *The Uncommon Touch*, I had the pleasure of rereading that document file, and I was struck and humbled by the energy and enthusiasm and selflessness that leaps from the pages of Wally's eloquent letters: to the deans and provost as he fights for University support and establishes the intellectual and academic legitimacy of the Program, to Dr. Edward H. Jones who gave the first half-million that got the program handsomely off and away, and then to other donors, to interested writers, to teachers in the program, to students, and even to disgruntled applicants who didn't make the final cut. His first concern was to help promising writers; his writing program was the means to that end.

It was his particular genius to add to the Stanford Writing Program something that made it then, and makes it now, unique. From the start a generous sum of money ($1,800 in 1946) was awarded to six Fellows, accomplished but not yet established writers who came to Stanford to work on and complete a project while attending the writing workshop. They did not work for a degree. Their status was anomalous within the University and it still is: they are post-doctoral fellows without the doctorate, professional poets and fiction writers in an academic world. In 1990, recognizing the impressive competence of so many M.A. writing programs throughout the country, Stanford will leave it to them to do what they do so well and will put its own considerable resources into an all-Fellowship program: ten Fellows in fiction and ten in poetry, receiving $10,000 per year for each of two years, plus another $3,500 each year in workshop tuition. It is a bold and very expensive move and it does credit, I think, to Wallace Stegner's original intention in founding the program.

Even while we honor Wallace Stegner with this book, I think it is important to acknowledge Richard Scowcroft who often served as Co-Director of the Program and who succeeded him on his retirement, and to honor also both Nancy Packer and Kenneth Fields who have served the program well both in and out of the Directorship.

I should mention too the extraordinary faculty the writing program has enjoyed; in addition to our colleagues in the English Department who have so often had a profound influence on the workshop and the workshop members, there have been writers whose primary task was leading the graduate workshops: in poetry, Yvor Winters, Donald Davie, W. Simone Di Piero, Denise Levertov, Kenneth Fields; in fiction, Richard Scowcroft, Nancy Packer, Gilbert Sorrentino. Further there have been special writers who have taught here for a year or a single quarter and who, caught up in the workshop, were pleased to return for a second and third time. Albert Guerard and Frank O'Connor come to mind in fiction and Janet Lewis in poetry, and then a long list of eminent writers who have given us their time and talent as teachers: William Abrahams, Alice Adams, Hortense Calisher, Walter Van Tillburg Clark, Henri Coulette, Malcolm Cowley, Bernard DeVoto, Ernest Gaines, Herbert Gold, Richard Jones, Carolyn Kizer, Tillie Olsen, Grace Paley, Katherine Anne Porter, Robert Stone. Short-term visitors have included W. H. Auden, Saul Bellow, Elizabeth Bowen, Robert Frost, Erika Mann, Theodore Morrison, Anais Nin, Stephen Spender, William Styron. More recently, through the munificence of Jean and Bill Lane and their Lecture Series, short-term visitors have included Donald Barthelme, Wendell Berry, Joseph Brodsky, Raymond Carver, E. L. Doctorow, Nadine Gordimer, Thom Gunn, Seamus Heaney, John Irving, Galway Kinnell, Maxine Kumin, Stanley Kunitz, Larry McMurtry, Ved Mehta, James Merrill, Toni Morrison,

Iris Murdoch, Joyce Carol Oates, Octavio Paz, Wallace Stegner himself, Peter Taylor, Eudora Welty, Richard Wilbur. And among us always are the Jones Lecturers: young writers who teach poetry and fiction writing to Stanford undergraduates on a part-time basis and who devote the rest of their time to completion of a major project. Michelle Carter, Tim Dekin, Allan Gurganus, Ron Hansen, David MacDonald, Alan Shapiro, Tim Steele, Scott Turow, Stephanie Vaughn, Tobias Wolff, Al Young, and many many other fine writers have served as Jones Lecturers.

Faced with so many distinguished faculty and students, I made the difficult decision to include the fiction and poetry of workshop participants only, though of course faculty who were once workshop participants have been included. Selections from the work of the Stanford writing faculty, past and present, full-time and part, would make another book altogether, and a very large one indeed.

There are many workshop writers I would like to have printed, but for various reasons I was simply not able to include them. Naturally I consulted Wallace Stegner, Richard Scowcroft, Nancy Packer, Kenneth Fields, and others—lifelong friends of the Program—as I attempted to compile a complete list of workshop participants, but I take full responsibility for the table of contents. And, I confess, I take some pride in it too.

The authors themselves selected the poetry and fiction for this book; at my request, they wrote their own biographies and they introduced their work. These biographies and introductions have been printed as they were composed so that *The Uncommon Touch* is, in every sense, the writers' book.

In his Preface to the first collection of *Stanford Stories*, in 1946, Wally wrote: "Any writing program in a university must justify itself ultimately by its ability to produce professional writers—by which I do not mean commercial writers necessarily. A program to produce professionals cannot afford to be slipshod, self-indulgent, arty, cliquish, local, or long-haired. It cannot be amateur and play-for-fun; it must try constantly to play for keeps, to maintain a standard that needs no apology."

The Uncommon Touch testifies to how well Wally Stegner succeeded when he established the Stanford Writing Program. It is not too rash, I think, to say that without his writing program, the history and nature of contemporary American literature would be different, and perhaps very different, from what it is today. So many good poets, so many good fiction writers have found voice and vision in these workshops. They were given time and encouragement and instruction, and they were given validation as writers.

The Uncommon Touch is dedicated to Wallace Stegner, to honor his eightieth birthday and to celebrate the writing program he founded.

NOTE

I wish to thank the Centennial Committee, the Alumni Association, and the Office of the Dean of Humanities and Sciences for the extremely generous financial support they have given for the production of this book.

And I want especially to acknowledge my friend and assistant Michelle Carter who took time from her own splendid fiction writing to handle the correspondence required in putting together this book—and did it the way she does everything: with energy, wit, thoroughness, and style.

—John L'Heureux

EDWARD ABBEY

Edward Abbey was born in 1927 on a sidehill farm in the Allegheny Mountains of Appalachia. After two years with the U.S. Army in Italy he moved to the American Southwest in 1947. He is the author of some twenty books, including Desert Solitaire, The Monkey Wrench Gang, The Fool's Progress, *and* One Life at a Time, Please. *At present he lives with his wife and two small children on a ranch in southern Utah, sometimes wintering near Oracle, Arizona.*

"Until the publication of *The Monkey Wrench Gang* in 1975, I was not able to make a living by writing alone. To supplement unreliable royalties I worked part time, from 1956 until 1976, as a seasonal park ranger, fire fighter, and fire lookout for the National Park Service and the U.S. Forest Service. These are ideal occupations for any writer without trust fund or academic sinecure and I recommend them to any and all aspiring poets, essayists, storytellers, and philosophers. The following selection will give the reader a hint of the pleasures and the rigors of such a life."

◆   ◆   ◆

Fire Lookout

MEN GO MAD IN this line of work. Read a book called *The Dharma Bums* by Jack Kerouac and you'll see what I mean. He spent a summer as fire lookout in a shack on Sourdough Mountain in the Cascades, a lookout haunted by the spirit of Gary "Japhy Ryder" Snyder who had also worked there. Kerouac never recovered. A few years later the Forest Service offered me the same job at the same place. Trying to maintain their literary reputation. Prudently I turned it down.

Women too go mad in the solitary confinement of a mountain peak, though not so readily as men, being stronger more stable creatures with a lower center of gravity. Perhaps the severest test of a marriage is to assign a man and wife to a fire lookout; any couple who survive three or four months with no human company but each other are destined for a long, permanent relationship. They deserve it.

My career as a fire lookout began by chance. Having injured my knee during the Vietnam War (skiing in Colorado), I was unable to resume my usual summer job as patrol ranger in a certain notorious Southwestern national park. I requested a desk job. The Chief Ranger thought I lacked the competence to handle government paper work. He offered me instead the only job in the Park which required less brains, he said, than janitor, garbage collector or Park

Superintendent. He made me fire lookout on what is called the North Rim, a post so remote that there was little likelihood I'd either see or be seen by the traveling American public. An important consideration, he felt.

The lookout tower on North Rim was sixty feet tall, surmounted by a little tin box six feet by six by seven. One entered through a trapdoor in the bottom. Inside was the fire finder—an azimuth and sighting device—fixed to a cabinet bolted to the floor. There was a high swivel chair with glass insulators, like those on a telephone line, mounted on the lower tips of the chair's four legs. In case of lightning. It was known as the electric chair. The actual operations of a fire lookout, quite simple, I have described elsewhere.

My home after working hours was an old cabin near the foot of the tower. The cabin was equipped with a double bed and a couple of folding steel cots, a wood-burning stove, table, shelves, cupboard, two chairs. It made a pleasant home, there under the pines and aspen, deep in the forest, serenaded by distant coyote cries, by poorwills, and sometimes by the song of the hermit thrush, loveliest of bird calls in the American West.

My father came to visit one day and stayed for the season. He was given the job of relief lookout on my days off. In the evenings after supper we played horseshoes. Whenever I hear the jangle of horseshoes now I think of North Rim, of that forest, that cabin, that summer. My father has powerful hands, hard, gnarled, a logger's hands, very large. In his hand a playing horseshoe looks like a quoit; a horse's shoe can hardly be seen at all. His pitch is low and accurate, the shoe—open end forward—sliding with a soft *chunk* full upon the upright, rigid peg. A firm connection. Top that ringer, son, he'd say. We walked the Grand Canyon from rim to rim that summer, and once again a few years ago. The second time he was seventy-two years old.

The first sensible thing I did at North Rim, before my father appeared, was fall in love with the ranger. Not the Chief Ranger but the one who manned the park entrance station a few miles down the road. Park Ranger Hendrickson (GS-4) was one of those golden Californians from the San Diego area. She wore her sea-bleached hair in a heavy ponytail that fell below her clavicles. Like most girl swimmers she had a well-developed pair of lungs, much admired by the boys. Pretty as a Winesap in September, she looked especially fetching in her ranger suit: broad-brimmed straw hat, white blouse with Park Service pin, the snug skirt of forest green twill that ended, as was the fashion then, a good six inches above her knees. Like most sexual perverts I've always suffered from a fatal weakness for women in uniform—for cheerleaders, majorettes, waitresses, meter maids, prison matrons, etc. On my first meeting with Bonnie Hendrickson (as we shall here name the young woman) I said to her, frankly, "You know— I've always wanted to lift a ranger's skirt."

"You'll need a hiking permit," she replied. A quick-witted girl—with a B.A. in French. We soon became good friends. On my days off I sometimes helped her get through the tedious hours at the entrance station. While she leaned out her little window collecting entrance fees from the tourists, answering questions, chatting about Smokey the Bore and the fire danger, I was kneeling at her feet, unseen from outside, gently rolling down the ranger's pantyhose. We played various such experiments in self control. I experimented, she displayed the self control. An innocent game, like horseshoes, with similar principles. Top that ringer . . .

On her days off she would visit me in the lookout tower, assisting me in *my* duties. As I'd be reporting a fire over the Park Service radio system she was unbuttoning my Levi's. "Fire Dispatch," I said into the microphone, "this is North Rim Lookout."

"Yeah?" The Fire Dispatcher had the weary, cynical voice of a police desk sergeant. "What's your problem now, Abbey?"

"Reporting a smoke, sir."

"Yeah? And where do you think this one is, Abbey?"

"Well sir, I've got a reading of zero-four-two degrees and thirty—oooh, watch those fingernails!—thirty minutes. Near Fredonia."

"Yeah . . ." A long pause. Then the weary voice. "I hate to tell you this, Abbey, but that's the same fire you reported last week. Like I told you then, that's the Fredonia sawmill and it's been smoking away in that same spot for fifty years. Ten four?"

"Yes sir, ten four. Oh Christ . . . oh *yes* . . . !"

"No swearing on the airwaves. These here transmissions are monitored by the Federal Communications Commission."

One cold rainy afternoon Bonnie and I were down in the cabin on the bed, a fire crackling in the stove, when our experiments were interrupted by a banging on the door. Bonnie ducked beneath the covers, I yanked on my pants and cracked the door open. Two Park Service fire fighters stood there grinning at me through the drizzle, their truck snuggled against the plump round rear of Bonnie's little car. "Hey Ed," says one, "we got a report of a hot fire in this area."

"Get out of here." I slammed and barred the door.

But I don't want to give the impression that a fire lookout's life is all work. There was time for play. One night a week we'd drive to the village on the Canyon rim and visit the bar. My Hopi friend would be there, old Sam Banyaca the shaman, and the veteran mule wrangler known only as Walapai, a leathery runt of a half-Indian cowboy who always squatted on top of his barstool, having never learned to sit anything but a horse. Behind the bar was Robert the intellectual bartender, smug smirk on his fat face, about to recite a new limerick. He claimed to be the only living composer of original limericks in America. I still remember two of them. I wish I could forget.

> A modest young fellow named Morgan
> Had an awesome sexual organ;
> It resembled a log
> Dredged up from a bog,
> With a head on it fierce as a Gorgon.

And the other:

> An old Mormon bishop named Bundy
> Used to wed a new wife every Sunday;
> But his multiple matehood
> Was ruined by statehood—
> *Sic transit gloria* Monday.

"*Mundi!*"

"Monday!"

"It's Friday, f'crush sake," says old Walapai, turning his bleary eyes toward us and swaying on his stool. "You honkies drunk already?" He crashed to the floor.

I spent four sweet summers on that sublime North Rim, not always alone in my tower. During the third summer a thing happened which caused me the deepest grief of my life. So far. The pain of my loss seemed unendurable. I called an old friend, Ann Woodin of Tucson, for comfort. She came to my part of the forest bearing apples, a flagon, black caviar and a magnum of Mumm's. We sat on a log under the trees at evening, by a fire, and listened to the birds, and talked, and ate the caviar and drank the champagne and talked some more. She helped me very much. A lady with class, that Ann. A lady *of* class. The same who once rescued me at two in the morning from the Phoenix City Jail down in Goldwater country, where the police had locked me up for what they called "negligent driving." Joseph Wood Krutch, another Tucsonan, dedicated one of his books to Ann Woodin. She is, he wrote, "an ever-present help in time of trouble."

Four summers. Sweet and bitter, bittersweet hilarious seasons in the forest of ponderosa and spruce and fir and trembling aspen trees. The clang of horseshoes in the twilight. The smell of woodsmoke from the cabin. Deep in the darkling pines the flutesong of a hermit thrush. Lightning, distant thunder, and clouds that towered into evening. Rain on the roof in the night.

One day somebody in Park headquarters down on the South Rim of the Canyon, the bad rim, the grim rim, said to somebody else, "Do we really need a fire lookout on North Rim?"

And the other man said, "I didn't know we had one."

The lookout was closed at the end of my fourth season and has never been used since. My father had long before returned to his own woods in Pennsylvania where he still lives and works. He is now eighty-three. And Ranger Hendrickson—sweet witty lovely daring Bonnie—she had gone back to California where, I've heard, she married well, to a man with a steady job, property, money, prospects, a head on his shoulders. Not a fire lookout. Not by a long shot.

KATHARINE ANDRES

Katharine Andres was born in New York City and attended Bennington College, the University of Virginia, and Cornell University. She was a Stegner Fellow, then a Jones Lecturer at Stanford. She has published in The New Yorker, The Iowa Review, *and the* Threepenny Review. *She lives in Palo Alto, California.*

"I wrote 'With the Potters' when I first got to Cornell, where I was in the M.F.A. writing program. The parts of it, its events invented, its characters seized from the edges of my life, quite willingly fit together into what I thought was a funny story. But when I read it to the writing class I was in, no one was amused at all, and I had to say things like, 'Yes, I know isolation isn't really funny.' This was useful and unnerving, this evidence of the distance between writer and reader, one of those things that once you've stumbled on it, you can't ever get it completely out of your head again."

◆　　　◆　　　◆

With the Potters

I HAD FOUND ALL at once that terrible things happened when I went out. As I was driving to work one morning, a car hit mine and one of my headlights was shattered. It made me feel off balance—as though I were seeing through one eye—and I quit my job that day. The next time I went out, I got lost looking for a bookstore in an area of Boston I knew well. Then, during the Christmas rush, a woman, flung against me by the crowd, caused me to drop my bag of groceries, breaking a dozen eggs. "Scrambled," a man with a cigar said. I went back to my parents' house, and for six weeks hardly left my room.

When Walker Potter called, in early March, and asked me to go to a poetry reading, his voice on the telephone was steady and even-toned. I hoped some of that steadiness might be conferred upon me the way when one person in a room yawns the others can't help doing the same.

During that year the Potters' invitations held great power. Saying no to them, it was clear, was saying no to rehabilitation. I'd gone to school with Walker's sister, Victoria, and when she moved to San Francisco I became friends with Walker and their mother as well. I was weak enough to do what they asked as long as the prospect was less painful than the walls of my room. There each wall was broken by a door—to the study, the bathroom, the closet, and the hall. I dreamed I'd be better if those walls were unbroken expanses. The night of the reading, I shut all of the doors as if I had a cat or dog I wanted to be there when I got back, and went out to meet Walker on a rainy street corner by the M.T.A. station.

These were the circumstances: Walker had met Miss Thorndyke, the woman who sponsored these bimonthly poetry readings, at a series of art lectures at the Gardner Museum. Miss Thorndyke had greatly admired the questions Walker asked the lecturer. She had approached him at the end of one of the lectures and told him about these poetry readings that were held in her apartment. She had such interesting people. Wouldn't he come? He had promised. Another month went by and she reminded him. Now it had been half a year, and when Walker saw her at the museum he felt guilty. Though he dreaded the interesting people, he would have to go.

I was at the corner first, but Walker hurried up before I'd even begun to worry that he wouldn't come. He wore his trenchcoat belted and a cap with a bill. He was very thin and tall, and only the skirt of his coat blown out by the wind and the bill of his cap gave him a third dimension. "You're here," he said.

"Yes. I hope this won't be too awful."

"You should try not to worry so much."

"How's your mother?" I asked. "I spoke to her the other day, and she mentioned something about helping with her spring cleaning."

"How fortunate you are," he said solemnly.

When we came out of the train, we were lost. Walker knew Back Bay as little as I did. The rain had picked up and the hem of my dress was damp around my knees. We circled blocks. Walker asked a man if he knew where Locust Street was, but the man only said, "Yes," and hurried on. He looked Japanese.

Then we found it. It was the narrowest building on the block, squeezed between two solid administrative buildings of some secretarial school. "From this we know that secretaries are fat and healthy, while poets starve," Walker said, but I knew he wasn't bitter, because he didn't write poetry himself. His favorite poem began, "Loveliest of trees, the cherry now . . ." I had learned things about Walker from Victoria, and sometimes I had spent the night in his room while he was away at college.

We walked up four flights of stairs. On the fifth floor a door was open and there were sounds of talking. "The poets," I said.

We were drawn into a room where we knew no one. The conversation stopped for a minute and a girl in red clamdiggers and a silk kimono said, "Thorny's in the kitchen making coffee."

Just as she said this, a woman appeared in the doorway. "Dear Walker," she said, as though she were testing the range of her voice. Her hair was impossibly red for a woman in her middle fifties, and it stood out from her head in separate spikes like an artist's rendering of fire. She wore pink toe shoes and a man's oxford shirt tucked into royal-blue stretch pants. Her face, powdered as pink as the toe shoes, was absurdly happy to see Walker. "And you've brought a friend."

"Yes, this is Ruth."

Miss Thorndyke introduced us to a pair of women sitting cross-legged on the floor, a man in a business suit, a boy with a guitar, and some other people, on pillows, in corners, everywhere. Walker and I shared the piano bench and accepted cups of herb tea so strong that I was sure it had some purpose. Miss

Thorndyke took a chair by the fireplace and smiled. "We'll begin. Mona, would you like to read first?"

Mona pulled a piece of paper from her leather bag. Her poem seemed to be about roses and menstruation, and she read it in a shrill, monotonous voice.

When she was done, Miss Thorndyke said, "That was lovely, Mona."

Sitting as we were, side by side on the bench, Walker and I couldn't look at each other without being obvious. If we'd been lovers, I might have squeezed his hand, but it wasn't Walker that I loved. I didn't know whom he loved, though once when we passed a church in Concord he'd told me that he would like to be married there.

Miss Thorndyke chose another woman to read next. She was tense and gray-haired, with eyes that were stretched wide open. I've always wondered about people with very clear blue eyes: do they see more? Her poem was about the spring and I liked it very much, though she read quickly, with a grim smile. Then the businessman read a long prose poem about a trip to Belgium. My back was tired from sitting with nothing to lean against. Walker was still sitting stiffly, hardly moving at all. He lived with his widowed mother in a dark small room at the back of her house. He was almost thirty and had been there since he finished college. I was living at home too, of course, keeping strange hours to avoid my parents in the kitchen or the halls. Now I thought I might take my savings from the bank and go somewhere far away. I wasn't sure where. If I were going to go by boat, all of these people might be my fellow-passengers.

It would be an imposing ship, like the QE 2, whose purser had arranged this evening's entertainment in the blink of an eye. Of course, it was too wet to promenade on the deck, as we had other evenings. We were sailing on this grand ship to another hemisphere for the winter. Walker, I knew, had great respect for tradition and property. I wanted to ask what he thought of the odd passenger list. Though his mother would buy undignified things at the supermarket—pistachio-flavored jello or chicken spread in a can—Walker invariably wore a jacket and tie at the dinner table.

The poem about Belgium ended. The last line, about a pigeon flying into the station "gray as a commuter," reminded me of Boston, and I wondered whether this man had been to Belgium at all. Walker, I knew, must be appalled by all of this; he'd always had a prejudice against strange people. I wondered what the best way for normal people to behave among strange ones was. I didn't want to disappoint Walker, because he might very well tell his mother and sister.

There was a silence, as befits the end of a long, dull poem. Miss Thorndyke stood, her list in her hand. "I think Twenty-seven has something for us."

Twenty-seven turned out to be the young man with the guitar. He had sleek black hair parted in the middle and a crooked scar at the corner of his mouth which did not allow him to stop smiling. He struck a harsh chord and began to intone, "I'm going away on a train. I won't be back again." At the end of every couplet came another chord, each one booming louder in the crowded room. I suddenly had to go to the bathroom. The door was shut, and there was no answer when I knocked. As I opened the door, two cats ran by me. I entered and closed the door behind me and was left with their smell. Through the wall I heard the consternation I'd caused in the next room.

When I came out, Miss Thorndyke was waiting with a gray-and-white spotted cat under one arm and a thin black one under the other.

"I'm sorry," I said. "I didn't know they were there."

"You'll read something for us?" she asked, her eyebrows rising, mobile as a clown's.

"I'm sorry," I said again. "I'm not a writer. I don't have anything." I remembered that in school people used to say "The dog ate it," so now, with a smile to show that I was joking, I said this to Miss Thorndyke. She looked at me quizzically, then at the two cats under her arms.

I wondered how much longer Walker and I would stay. I liked being there better than at home. Though I always wanted to say no when people asked me to do things, once I did them I felt better. Things were improving slowly. I felt I was travelling a long distance, though I wasn't sure in what direction. I liked to think of it as an anatomical journey: first a leg, then perhaps an arm, some other day the torso and a hand, and finally the head. When I had completed the head—rounded the horn—I would be well again. This was much better than the voyage on the QE 2, which, I now realized, would be circular and leave me off at the port where I had embarked.

When the reading was over, we would get on the M.T.A. again and go home. I would have liked to go to Walker's little room, and he could have gone to mine. He would do well taking up my life where I'd left off. He'd wake up in the morning and go down to breakfast with my parents. "Yes, one sunny side up, thank you," Walker would tell my mother. And the pictures in my room wouldn't look crooked, so he would have to jump out of bed to tilt one a little in one direction, and then a few minutes later back the other way.

People began to chat about the rain, mustering courage to go out into it. I always feel sad when I leave a place where people haven't been unpleasant. Of course, it was fine to look at Walker now. How sharp his nose was. My mother once said that it sliced the air in front of him like a knife as he walked. I believed this. When the air was cut into two parts, Walker stepped bravely between, like an explorer into the black mouth of a cave.

On the way home, we were lost again. Looking for the M.T.A., we passed Twenty-seven with his guitar. He held it over his shoulder with no case, and under the street light it glistened in the rain.

"Well, what did you think?" Walker asked, taking great stiff-legged strides over puddles. He began to laugh his high-pitched, hiccupping laugh and I laughed, too, so that my stomach hurt and I had to lean against a lamppost to steady myself. On the space between my hat and coat I felt the wet metal against the skin of my neck, like an unexpected hand. I sprang away from it.

A week later, Mrs. Potter, hunting for some papers in the basement of the building she owned, asked me to move heavy boxes and help her clean up a little. "You'll come," she had said to me on the telephone, and I could hear no question in her voice. I was uneasy about this. I was still mapping out my journey, and I wasn't sure whether I'd gone in the right direction following Walker to the poetry reading. But I trusted Mrs. Potter. She was a very ordinary person, who could no more lose her ordinariness than someone walking down a long straight corridor can lose his way.

Mrs. Potter's five-story building was downtown. Two floors were taken up by a fabric outlet, another by a telephone-answering concern. There was also a deaf-mute who repaired furniture. Mrs. Potter complained that whenever she wanted to get in touch with him she had to send a letter. The fifth floor was empty, and she spent her days trying to rent it.

In the basement were Potter family relics: Victoria's cradle, Walker's stilts, and the overflow of antiques from the Potters' house in Dedham. It was an enormous room, cement-floored, and the ceiling, the same dark gray, was visible through a maze of pipes. Dirt had collected in airy black heaps all over the floor. Mrs. Potter and I stirred the heaps up as we walked, and they clung to the toes of our shoes and attached themselves to our ankles. I moved four heavy cardboard boxes at once, hugging them to me like ungainly fat people. In the bottom box there were little wads of tissue paper. I picked one up and a chip of glass fell back among the others.

"My prisms," Mrs. Potter said. "I collected them for years."

"What for?"

"I thought I'd have a chandelier above the dining-room table and they'd cast rainbows on the tablecloth. You may have this one," she offered, holding it out to me in her narrow hand. It had a flaw, but I took it and put it in my pocket.

She set me to work sweeping up the piles of dirt, while she looked through the boxes I'd lifted down. The noise of bristles on cement gave me gooseflesh. Mrs. Potter, up to her elbows in newspaper, was looking over various pieces of china which cast their poor light back on her face. It was narrow, and her hair, growing stiff from her forehead, had no color at all. It elongated her face so that it was like a rubber mask sagging out of shape.

"Ruth," she said to me abruptly. "I think you're getting well. You seem to be recovering from that young man."

"It's not just that."

"Of course not, but I think it's time you did something with yourself."

"Like what?"

"You might look for a job."

"I hate jobs. Haven't I explained to you, Mrs. Potter, the way I feel about jobs? When there is something I *have* to do in a day, I can't get up in the morning. It spoils everything for me. Every day is like the fifth straight day of hard rain. Please, I'd rather not think about it now."

I remembered how the elevator man at my last job had called me Mary Mope. "And how's Miss Mary Mope this morning?" he would ask as I turned myself over to him for the day's incarceration. In the evenings he would say, "Free at last to run home to her lover's arms."

"Don't," I had begged him. His words had turned the remaining part of the day into the other half of a vault that held me. It shut tight around me with a sharp click.

"I can't bear another job," I said to Mrs. Potter.

She was sitting on a dusty Louis XIV chair, and she gestured to me to sit in its twin. She had a thermos full of brandy. "I didn't know if it would be warm down here," she explained, offering me some damp floury wafers wrapped in tinfoil. "Let me tell you a story."

"It isn't an allegory, is it? I can't bear allegories."

She promised that it wasn't. "You may apply it to your own case as you will.

"When I was a girl—nineteen or twenty—I was still living at home, and very much in love. I had auburn hair then. Can you believe that? One evening I was standing on the fire escape of my apartment building with Kingsley, the man I was engaged to marry, and across the street there was a man at the very edge of the roof.

"'He's going to jump,' Kingsley said.

"I only laughed, but of course he did jump or fall. He fell to the ground faster than you can imagine. I felt sick and dizzy, as if I were going to fall from the fire escape myself. His thud shook me terribly. Later that night I tried to explain to Kingsley how it made me feel different. But this time he laughed and warned me against appropriating other people's tragedies for my own."

"Is that the end?" I asked. I was pleased with the story, because it didn't apply to me. Nothing that applied seemed to help.

"No, there's more. The man didn't die. It was only the third floor. We stood watching, and an ambulance came from the Holy Samaritan. It was two blocks away and there were always ambulances screaming by our house.

"I couldn't stop myself from thinking about him. In a few days I went to see him in the ward.

"'I'm saved from myself now,' he said as I came in. And it was true. He was so weighed down with plaster he couldn't move at all. It encased two broken legs, some cracked ribs, and a dislocated clavicle. Even his head was bound in a space helmet of gauze. I couldn't see his face at all, and since it had been dusk when he jumped, I still had no idea what he looked like.

"'I saw you fall,' I said. 'Fall' seemed more polite than 'jump.'

"'I saw you watching with your husband,' he said.

"'Oh, that wasn't my husband. We're engaged,' I said, and I told him all about Kingsley and me, but what I really wanted to know was why he had jumped. Just being with him made me feel shaky, and I knew I wouldn't feel right until I understood. So I kept going back every couple of days. There was never anyone else visiting him. Then one day he was in a semi-private room.

"'Are you a relation of Mr. Walker's?' the doctor asked as I was going in.

"'A distant one,' I said. I wanted to hear what he had to say.

"'I think you had better notify the family. Mr. Walker is a very sick man,' he said.

"'You mean he's crazy?' I said.

"The doctor looked at me as though I were very stupid. 'What I mean,' he said, 'is that his bones aren't mending properly. We have reason to believe that he has a disease of the bone marrow and won't live more than a few months.'

"I said, 'Oh, yes,' to show that it was perfectly obvious to me that he would never recover.

"I watched Mr. Walker carefully that day. I thought it might be my last chance to find out why he had jumped. To tell you the truth, he seemed to be getting better. In fact, out of the blue, he asked me to marry him. He knew that I was engaged, but Kingsley was sailing to England with his family just then. I'd grown very fond of Mr. Walker, so I agreed. It was the simplest way to make everyone happy. I felt then as if my mind were in order again. That's the end of the story."

"But it isn't. What happened?"

"Mr. Walker did die. From the semi-private they moved him to a private room. At last he was out of his casts, and he held my hand. His hand was thinner and whiter than my own. He left me his mother's jewels, and a year later, when I married Walker and Victoria's father, I named my son for him."

"You married Kingsley?"

"No, George Potter. Kingsley took the slow boat to England."

We'd finished the crackers, but there was still brandy in the thermos. The box at my feet was books. "If there's anything you'd like, take it. Walker and Victoria weren't interested."

There was a collection of poetry at the top, and I chose that.

"Did the story help?" Mrs. Potter asked.

"I don't see how you could have done it."

"I could do anything then."

She sat quietly, with her eyes almost closed, and I looked through the book. There was a poem that reminded me of the one the wide-seeing blue-eyed woman had read at Miss Thorndyke's:

> I know a green grass path that
>   leaves the field,
> And, like a running river, winds
>   along . . .

I imagined Mrs. Potter young, with her auburn hair and her masklike face stretched back to prettiness. I watched her walk partway down a long, dark hall, but she stopped and went through the first door she came to. From there she followed the path until, squinting, I lost sight of her.

PETER S. BEAGLE

Peter S. Beagle is the author of three novels (most recent, The Folk of the Air*) and five books of nonfiction. He has also written many magazine articles and a number of movie and television screenplays. Beagle currently resides in the Seattle area.*

"I wrote this story at Stanford in 1961—in a day and a half—to see if I could sneak a fantasy past Frank O'Connor, who hated the whole genre, among others. He read it to the class in his rolling, wonderful Abbey Theatre style, and then announced grandly, 'This is a beautifully written story. I don't like it.' It's the one story of mine that ever made the O. Henry Award anthology."

♦   ♦   ♦

Come Lady Death

THIS ALL HAPPENED IN England a long time ago, when that George who spoke English with a heavy German accent and hated his sons was King. At that time there lived in London a lady who had nothing to do but give parties. Her name was Flora, Lady Neville, and she was a widow and very old. She lived in a great house not far from Buckingham Palace, and she had so many servants that she could not possibly remember all their names; indeed, there were some she had never even seen. She had more food than she could eat, more gowns than she could ever wear; she had wine in her cellars that no one would drink in her lifetime, and her private vaults were filled with great works of art that she did not know she owned. She spent the last years of her life giving parties and balls to which the greatest lords of England—and sometimes the King himself—came, and she was known as the wisest and wittiest woman in all London.

But in time her own parties began to bore her, and though she invited the most famous people in the land and hired the greatest jugglers and acrobats and dancers and magicians to entertain them, still she found her parties duller and duller. Listening to court gossip, which she had always loved, made her yawn. The most marvelous music, the most exciting feats of magic put her to sleep. Watching a beautiful young couple dance by her made her feel sad, and she hated to feel sad.

And so, one summer afternoon she called her closest friends around her and said to them, "More and more I find that my parties entertain everyone but me. The secret of my long life is that nothing has ever been dull for me. For all my life, I have been interested in everything I saw and been anxious to see more. But I cannot stand to be bored, and I will not go to parties at which I expect to be bored, especially if they are my own. Therefore, to my next ball I shall invite the one guest I am sure no one, not even myself, could possibly find boring. My friends, the guest of honor at my next party shall be Death himself!"

A young poet thought that this was a wonderful idea, but the rest of her friends were terrified and drew back from her. They did not want to die, they pleaded with her. Death would come for them when he was ready; why should she invite him before the appointed hour, which would arrive soon enough? But Lady Neville said, "Precisely. If Death has planned to take any of us on the night of my party, he will come whether he is invited or not. But if none of us are to die, then I think it would be charming to have Death among us—perhaps even to perform some little trick if he is in a good humor. And think of being able to say that we had been to a party with Death! All of London will envy us, all of England!"

The idea began to please her friends, but a young lord, very new to London, suggested timidly, "Death is so busy. Suppose he has work to do and cannot accept your invitation?"

"No one has ever refused an invitation of mine," said Lady Neville, "not even the King." And the young lord was not invited to her party.

She sat down then and there and wrote out the invitation. There was some dispute among her friends as to how they should address Death. "His Lordship Death" seemed to place him only on the level of a viscount or a baron. "His Grace Death" met with more acceptance, but Lady Neville said it sounded hypocritical. And to refer to Death as "His Majesty" was to make him the equal of the King of England, which even Lady Neville would not dare to do. It was finally decided that all should speak of him as "His Eminence Death," which pleased nearly everyone.

Captain Compson, known both as England's most dashing cavalry officer and most elegant rake, remarked next, "That's all very well, but how is the invitation to reach Death? Does anyone here know where he lives?"

"Death undoubtedly lives in London," said Lady Neville, "like everyone else of any importance, though he probably goes to Deauville for the summer. Actually, Death must live fairly near my own house. This is much the best section of London, and you could hardly expect a person of Death's importance to live anywhere else. When I stop to think of it, it's really rather strange that we haven't met before now, on the street."

Most of her friends agreed with her, but the poet, whose name was David Lorimond, cried out, "No, my lady, you are wrong! Death lives among the poor. Death lives in the foulest, darkest alleys of this city, in some vile, rat-ridden hovel that smells of—" He stopped here, partly because Lady Neville had indicated her displeasure, and partly because he had never been inside such a hut or thought of wondering what it smelled like. "Death lives among the poor," he went on, "and comes to visit them every day, for he is their only friend."

Lady Neville answered him as coldly as she had spoken to the young lord. "He may be forced to deal with them, David, but I hardly think that he seeks them out as companions. I am certain that it is as difficult for him to think of the poor as individuals as it is for me. Death is, after all, a nobleman."

There was no real argument among the lords and ladies that Death lived in a neighborhood at least as good as their own, but none of them seemed to know the name of Death's street, and no one had ever seen Death's house.

"If there were a war," Captain Compson said, "Death would be easy to find. I have seen him, you know, even spoken to him, but he has never answered me."

"Quite proper," said Lady Neville. "Death must always speak first. You are not a very correct person, Captain." But she smiled at him, as all women did.

Then an idea came to her. "My hairdresser has a sick child, I understand," she said. "He was telling me about it yesterday, sounding most dull and hopeless. I will send for him and give him the invitation, and he in his turn can give to Death when he comes to take the brat. A bit unconventional, I admit, but I see no other way."

"If he refuses?" asked a lord who had just been married.

"Why should he?" asked Lady Neville.

Again it was the poet who exclaimed amidst the general approval that this was a cruel and wicked thing to do. But he fell silent when Lady Neville innocently asked him, "Why, David?"

So the hairdresser was sent for, and when he stood before them, smiling nervously and twisting his hands to be in the same room with so many great lords, Lady Neville told him the errand that was required of him. And she was right, as she usually was, for he made no refusal. He merely took the invitation in his hand and asked to be excused.

He did not return for two days, but when he did he presented himself to Lady Neville without being sent for and handed her a small white envelope. Saying, "How very nice of you, thank you very much," she opened it and found therein a plain calling card with nothing on it except these words: *Death will be pleased to attend Lady Neville's ball.*

"Death gave you this?" she asked the hairdresser eagerly. "What was he like?" But the hairdresser stood still, looking past her, and said nothing, and she, not really waiting for an answer, called a dozen servants to her and told them to run and summon her friends. As she paced up and down the room waiting for them, she asked again, "What is Death like?" The hairdresser did not reply.

When her friends came they passed the little card excitedly from hand to hand, until it had gotten quite smudged and bent from their fingers. But they all admitted that, beyond its message, there was nothing particularly unusual about it. It was neither hot nor cold to the touch, and what little odor clung to it was rather pleasant. Everyone said that it was a very familiar smell, but no one could give it a name. The poet said that it reminded him of lilacs but not exactly.

It was Captain Compson, however, who pointed out the one thing that no one else had noticed. "Look at the handwriting itself," he said. "Have you ever seen anything more graceful? The letters seem as light as birds. I think we have wasted our time speaking of Death as His This and His That. A woman wrote this note."

Then there was an uproar and a great babble, and the card had to be handed around again so that everyone could exclaim, "Yes, by God!" over it. The voice of the poet rose out of the hubbub saying, "It is very natural, when you come to think of it. After all, the French say *la mort*. Lady Death. I should much prefer Death to be a woman."

"Death rides a great black horse," said Captain Compson firmly, "and wears armor of the same color. Death is very tall, taller than anyone. It was no woman I saw on the battlefield, striking right and left like any soldier. Perhaps the hairdresser wrote it himself, or the hairdresser's wife."

But the hairdresser refused to speak, though they gathered around him and begged him to say who had given him the note. At first they promised him all sorts of rewards, and later they threatened to do terrible things to him. "Did you write this card?" he was asked, and "Who wrote it, then? Was it a living woman? Was it really Death? Did Death say anything to you? How did you know it was Death? Is Death a woman? Are you trying to make fools of us all?"

Not a word from the hairdresser, not one word, and finally Lady Neville called her servants to have him whipped and thrown into the street. He did not look at her as they took him away, or utter a sound.

Silencing her friends with a wave of her hand, Lady Neville said, "The ball will take place two weeks from tonight. Let Death come as Death pleases, whether as man or woman or strange, sexless creature." She smiled calmly. "Death may well be a woman," she said. "I am less certain of Death's form than I was, but I am also less frightened of Death. I am too old to be afraid of anything that can use a quill pen to write me a letter. Go home now, and as you make your preparations for the ball see that you speak of it to your servants, that they may spread the news all over London. Let it be known that on this one night no one in the world will die, for Death will be dancing at Lady Neville's ball."

For the next two weeks Lady Neville's great house shook and groaned and creaked like an old tree in a gale as the servants hammered and scrubbed, polished and painted, making ready for the ball. Lady Neville had always been very proud of her house, but as the ball drew near she began to be afraid that it would not be nearly grand enough for Death, who was surely accustomed to visiting in the homes of richer, mightier people than herself. Fearing the scorn of Death, she worked night and day supervising her servants' preparations. Curtains and carpets had to be cleaned, goldwork and silverware polished until they gleamed by themselves in the dark. The grand staircase that rushed down into the ballroom like a waterfall was washed and rubbed so often that it was almost impossible to walk on it without slipping. As for the ballroom itself, it took thirty-two servants working at once to clean it properly, not counting those who were polishing the glass chandelier that was taller than a man and the fourteen smaller lamps. And when they were done she made them do it all over, not because she saw any dust or dirt anywhere, but because she was sure that Death would.

As for herself, she chose her finest gown and saw to its laundering personally. She called in another hairdresser and had him put up her hair in the style of an earlier time, wanting to show Death that she was woman who enjoyed her age and did not find it necessary to ape the young and beautiful. All the day of the ball she sat before her mirror, not making herself up much beyond the normal touches of rouge and eye shadow and fine rice powder, but staring at the lean old face she had been born with, wondering how it would appear to Death. Her steward asked her to approve his wine selection, but she sent him away and stayed at her mirror until it was time to dress and go downstairs to meet her guests.

Everyone arrived early. When she looked out of a window, Lady Neville saw that the driveway of her home was choked with carriages and fine horses. "It all looks like a great funeral procession," she said. The footman cried the names of her guests to the echoing ballroom. "Captain Henry Compson, His Majesty's Household Cavalry! Mr. David Lorimond! Lord and Lady Torrance!" (They were the youngest couple there, having been married only three months before.) "Sir Roger Harbison! The Contessa della Candini!" Lady Neville permitted them all to kiss her hand and made them welcome.

She had engaged the finest musicians she could find to play for the dancing, but though they began to play at her signal not one couple stepped out on the floor, nor did one young lord approach her to request the honor of the first dance, as was proper. They milled together, shining and murmuring, their eyes fixed on the ballroom door. Every time they heard a carriage clatter up the driveway they seemed to flinch a little and draw closer together; every time the footman announced the arrival of another guest, they all sighed softly and swayed a little on their feet with relief.

"Why did they come to my party if they were afraid?" Lady Neville muttered scornfully to herself. "I am not afraid of meeting Death. I ask only that Death may be impressed by the magnificence of my house and the flavor of my wines. I will die sooner than anyone here, but I am not afraid."

Certain that Death would not arrive until midnight, she moved among her guests, attempting to calm them, not with her words, which she knew they would not hear, but with the tone of her voice, as if they were so many frightened horses. But little by little, she herself was infected by their nervousness: whenever she sat down she stood up again immediately, she tasted a dozen glasses of wine without finishing any of them, and she glanced constantly at her jeweled watch, at first wanting to hurry the midnight along and end the waiting, later scratching at the watch face with her forefinger, as if she would push away the night and drag the sun backward into the sky. When midnight came, she was standing with the rest of them, breathing through her mouth, shifting from foot to foot, listening for the sound of carriage wheels turning in gravel.

When the clock began to strike midnight, everyone, even Lady Neville and the brave Captain Compson, gave one startled little cry and then was silent again, listening to the tolling of the clock. The smaller clocks upstairs began to chime. Lady Neville's ears hurt. She caught sight of herself in the ballroom mirror, one gray face turned up toward the ceiling as if she were gasping for air, and she thought, "Death will be a woman, a hideous, filthy old crone as tall and strong as a man. And the most terrible thing of all will be that she will have my face." All the clocks stopped striking, and Lady Neville closed her eyes.

She opened them again only when she heard the whispering around her take on a different tone, one in which fear was fused with relief and a certain chagrin. For no new carriage stood in the driveway. Death had not come.

The noise grew slowly louder; here and there people were beginning to laugh. Near her, Lady Neville heard young Lord Torrance say to his wife, "There, my darling, I told you there was nothing to be afraid of. It was all a joke."

"I am ruined," Lady Neville thought. The laughter was increasing; it pounded against her ears in strokes, like the chiming of the clocks. "I wanted to give a ball so grand that those who were not invited would be shamed in front of the whole city, and this is my reward. I am ruined, and I deserve it."

Turning to the poet Lorimond, she said, "Dance with me, David." She signaled to the musicians, who at once began to play. When Lorimond hesitated, she said, "Dance with me now. You will not have another chance. I shall never give a party again."

Lorimond bowed and led her out onto the dance floor. The guests parted for them, and the laughter died down for a moment, but Lady Neville knew that it would soon begin again. "Well, let them laugh," she thought. "I did not fear Death when they were all trembling. Why should I fear their laughter?" But she could feel a stinging at the thin lids of her eyes, and she closed them once more as she began to dance with Lorimond.

And then, quite suddenly, all the carriage horses outside the house whinnied loudly, just once, as the guests had cried out at midnight. There were a great many horses, and their one salute was so loud that everyone in the room became instantly silent. They heard the heavy steps of the footman as he went to open the door, and they shivered as if they felt the cool breeze that drifted into the house. Then they heard a light voice saying, "Am I late? Oh, I am so sorry. The horses were tired," and before the footman could re-enter to announce her, a lovely young girl in a white dress stepped gracefully into the ballroom doorway and stood there smiling.

She could not have been more than nineteen. Her hair was yellow, and she wore it long. It fell thickly upon her bare shoulders that gleamed warmly through it, two limestone islands rising out of a dark golden sea. Her face was wide at the forehead and cheekbones, and narrow at the chin, and her skin was so clear that many of the ladies there—Lady Neville among them—touched their own faces wonderingly, and instantly drew their hands away as though their own skin had rasped their fingers. Her mouth was pale, where the mouths of the other women were red and orange and even purple. Her eyebrows, thicker and straighter than was fashionable, met over dark, calm eyes that were set so deep in her young face and were so black, so uncompromisingly black, that the middle-aged wife of a middle-aged lord murmured, "Touch of the gypsy there, I think."

"Or something worse," suggested her husband's mistress.

"Be silent!" Lady Neville spoke louder than she had intended, and the girl turned to look at her. She smiled, and Lady Neville tried to smile back, but her mouth seemed very stiff. "Welcome," she said. "Welcome, my lady Death."

A sigh rustled among the lords and ladies as the girl took the old woman's hand and curtsied to her, sinking and rising in one motion, like a wave. "You are Lady Neville," she said. "Thank you so much for inviting me." Her accent was as faint and as almost familiar as her perfume.

"Please excuse me for being late," she said earnestly, "I had to come from a long way off, and my horses are so tired."

"The groom will rub them down," Lady Neville said, "and feed them if you wish."

"Oh, no," the girl answered quickly. "Tell him not to go near the horses, please. They are not really horses, and they are very fierce."

She accepted a glass of wine from a servant and drank it slowly, sighing softly and contentedly. "What good wine," she said. "And what a beautiful house you have."

"Thank you," said Lady Neville. Without turning, she could feel every woman in the room envying her, sensing it as she could always sense the approach of rain.

"I wish I lived here," Death said in her low, sweet voice. "I will, one day."

Then, seeing Lady Neville become as still as if she had turned to ice, she put her hand on the old woman's arm and said, "Oh, I'm sorry, I'm so sorry. I am so cruel, but I never mean to be. Please forgive me, Lady Neville. I am not used to company, and I do such stupid things. Please forgive me."

Her hand felt as light and warm on Lady Neville's arm as the hand of any other young girl, and her eyes were so appealing that Lady Neville replied, "You have said nothing wrong. While you are my guest, my house is yours."

"Thank you," said Death, and she smiled so radiantly that the musicians began to play quite by themselves, with no sign from Lady Neville. She would have stopped them, but Death said, "Oh, what lovely music! Let them play, please."

So the musicians played a gavotte, and Death, unabashed by eyes that stared at her in greedy terror, sang softly to herself without words, lifted her white gown slightly with both hands, and made hesitant little patting steps with her small feet. "I have not danced in so long," she said wistfully. "I'm quite sure I've forgotten how."

She was shy; she would not look up to embarrass the young lords, not one of whom stepped forward to dance with her. Lady Neville felt a flood of shame and sympathy, emotions she thought had withered in her years ago. "Is she to be humiliated at my own ball?" she thought angrily. "It is because she is Death; if she were the ugliest, foulest hag in all the world they would clamor to dance with her, because they are gentlemen and they know what is expected of them. But no gentleman will dance with Death, no matter how beautiful she is." She glanced sideways at David Lorimond. His face was flushed, and his hands were clasped so tightly as he stared at Death that his fingers were like glass, but when Lady Neville touched his arm he did not turn, and when she hissed, "David!", he pretended not to hear her.

Then Captain Compson, gray-haired and handsome in his uniform, stepped out of the crowd and bowed gracefully before Death. "If I may have the honor," he said.

"Captain Compson," said Death, smiling. She put her arm in his. "I was hoping you would ask me."

This brought a frown from the older women, who did not consider it a proper thing to say, but for that Death cared not a rap. Captain Compson led her to the center of the floor, and there they danced. Death was curiously graceless at first—she was too anxious to please her partner, and she seemed to have no notion of rhythm. The Captain himself moved with the mixture of dignity and humor that Lady Neville had never seen in another man, but when he looked at her over Death's shoulder, she saw something that no one else appeared to notice: that his face and eyes were immobile with fear, and that, though he offered Death his hand with easy gallantry, he flinched slightly when she took it. And yet he danced as well as Lady Neville had ever seen him.

"Ah, that's what comes of having a reputation to maintain," she thought. "Captain Compson too must do what is expected of him. I hope someone else will dance with her soon."

But no one did. Little by little, other couples overcame their fear and slipped hurriedly out on the floor when Death was looking the other way, but nobody sought to relieve Captain Compson of his beautiful partner. They danced every dance together. In time, some of the men present began to look at her with more appreciation than terror, but when she returned their glances and smiled at them, they clung to their partners as if a cold wind were threatening to blow them away.

One of the few who stared at her frankly and with pleasure was young Lord Torrance, who usually danced only with his wife. Another was the poet Lorimond. Dancing with Lady Neville, he remarked to her, "If she is Death, what do these frightened fools think they are? If she is ugliness, what must they be? I hate their fear. It is obscene."

Death and the Captain danced past them at that moment, and they heard him say to her, "But if that was truly you that I saw in the battle, how can you have changed so? How can you have become so lovely?"

Death's laughter was gay and soft. "I thought that among so many beautiful people it might be better to be beautiful. I was afraid of frightening everyone and spoiling the party."

"They all thought she would be ugly," said Lorimond to Lady Neville. "I—*I* knew she would be beautiful."

"Then why have you not danced with her?" Lady Neville asked him. "Are you also afraid?"

"No, oh, no," the poet answered quickly and passionately. "I will ask her to dance very soon. I only want to look at her a little longer."

The musicians played on and on. The dancing wore away the night as slowly as falling water wears down a cliff. It seemed to Lady Neville that no night had ever endured longer, and yet she was neither tired nor bored. She danced with every man there, except with Lord Torrance, who was dancing with his wife as if they had just met that night, and, of course, with Captain Compson. Once he lifted his hand and touched Death's golden hair very lightly. He was a striking man still, a fit partner for so beautiful a girl, but Lady Neville looked at his face each time she passed him and realized that he was older than anyone knew.

Death herself seemed younger than the youngest there. No woman at the ball danced better than she now, though it was hard for Lady Neville to remember at what point her awkwardness had given way to the liquid sweetness of her movements. She smiled and called to everyone who caught her eye—and she knew them all by name; she sang constantly, making up words to the dance tunes, nonsense words, sounds without meaning, and yet everyone strained to hear her soft voice without knowing why. And when, during a waltz, she caught up the trailing end of her gown to give her more freedom as she danced, she seemed to Lady Neville to move like a little sailing boat over a still evening sea.

Lady Neville heard Lady Torrance arguing angrily with the Contessa della Candini. "I don't care if she is Death, she's no older than I am, she can't be!"

"Nonsense," said the Contessa, who could not afford to be generous to any other woman. "She is twenty-eight, thirty, if she is an hour. And that dress, that bridal gown she wears—really!"

"Vile," said the woman who had come to the ball as Captain Compson's freely acknowledged mistress. "Tasteless. But one should know better than to expect taste from Death, I suppose." Lady Torrance looked as if she were going to cry.

"They are jealous of Death," Lady Neville said to herself. "How strange. I am not jealous of her, not in the least. And I do not fear her at all." She was very proud of herself.

Then, as unbiddenly as they had begun to play, the musicians stopped. They began to put away their instruments. In the sudden shrill silence, Death pulled away from Captain Compson and ran to look out of one of the tall windows, pushing the curtains apart with both hands. "Look!" she said, with her back turned to them. "Come and look. The night is almost gone."

The summer sky was still dark, and the eastern horizon was only a shade lighter than the rest of the sky, but the stars had vanished and the trees near the house were gradually becoming distinct. Death pressed her face against the window and said, so softly that the other guests could barely hear her, "I must go now."

"No," Lady Neville said, and was not immediately aware that she had spoken. "You must stay a while longer. The ball was in your honor. Please stay."

Death held out both hands to her, and Lady Neville came and took them in her own. "I've had a wonderful time," she said gently. "You cannot possibly imagine how it feels to be actually invited to such a ball as this, because you have given them and gone to them all your life. One is like another to you, but for me it is different. Do you understand me?" Lady Neville nodded silently. "I will remember this night forever," Death said.

"Stay," Captain Compson said. "Stay just a little longer." He put his hand on Death's shoulder, and she smiled and leaned her cheek against it. "Dear Captain Compson," she said. "My first real gallant. Aren't you tired of me yet?"

"Never," he said. "Please stay."

"Stay," said Lorimond, and he too seemed about to touch her. "Stay. I want to talk to you. I want to look at you. I will dance with you if you stay."

"How many followers I have," Death said in wonder. She stretched one hand toward Lorimond, but he drew back from her and then flushed in shame. "A soldier and a poet. How wonderful it is to be a woman. But why did you not speak to me earlier, both of you? Now it is too late. I must go."

"Please stay," Lady Torrance whispered. She held on to her husband's hand for courage. "We think you are so beautiful, both of us do."

"Gracious Lady Torrance," the girl said kindly. She turned back to the window, touched it lightly, and it flew open. The cool dawn air rushed into the ballroom, fresh with rain but already smelling faintly of the London streets over which it had passed. They heard birdsong and the strange, harsh nickering of Death's horses.

"Do you want me to stay?" she asked. The question was put, not to Lady Neville, nor to Captain Compson, nor to any of her admirers, but to the Contessa della Candini, who stood well back from them all, hugging her flowers to herself and humming a little song of irritation. She did not in the least want Death to stay, but she was afraid that all the other women would think her envious of Death's beauty, and so she said, "Yes. Of course I do."

"Ah," said Death. She was almost whispering. "And you," she said to another woman, "do you want me to stay? Do you want me to be one of your friends?"

"Yes," said the woman, "because you are beautiful and a true lady."

"And you," said Death to a man, "and you," to a woman, "and you," to another man, "do you want me to stay?" And they all answered, "Yes, Lady Death, we do."

"Do you want me, then?" she cried at last to all of them. "Do you want me to live among you and to be one of you, and not to be Death anymore? Do you want me to visit your houses and come to all your parties? Do you want me to ride horses like yours instead of mine, do you want me to wear the kind of dresses you wear, and say the things you would say? Would one of you marry me, and would the rest of you dance at my wedding and bring gifts to my children? Is that what you want?"

"Yes," said Lady Neville. "Stay here, stay with me, stay with us."

Death's voice, without becoming louder, had become clearer and older; too old a voice, thought Lady Neville, for such a young girl. "Be sure," said Death. "Be sure of what you want, be very sure. Do all of you want me to stay? For if one of you says to me, no, go away, then I must leave at once and never return. Be sure. Do you all want me?"

And everyone there cried with one voice, "Yes! Yes, you must stay with us. You are so beautiful that we cannot let you go."

"We are tired," said Captain Compson.

"We are blind," said Lorimond, adding, "especially to poetry."

"We are afraid," said Lord Torrance quietly, and his wife took his arm and said, "Both of us."

"We are dull and stupid," said Lady Neville, "and growing old uselessly. Stay with us, Lady Death."

And then Death smiled sweetly and radiantly and took a step forward, and it was as though she had come down among them from a great height. "Very well," she said. "I will stay with you. I will be Death no more. I will be a woman."

The room was full of a deep sigh, although no one was seen to open his mouth. No one moved, for the golden-haired girl was Death still, and her horses still whinnied for her outside. No one could look at her for long, although she was the most beautiful girl anyone there had ever seen.

"There is a price to pay," she said. "There is always a price. Some one of you must become Death in my place, for there must forever be Death in the world. Will anyone choose? Will anyone here become Death of his own free will? For only thus can I become a human girl."

No one spoke, no one spoke at all. But they backed slowly away from her, like waves slipping back down a beach to the sea when you try to catch them. The Contessa della Candini and her friends would have crept quietly out of the door, but Death smiled at them and they stood where they were. Captain Compson opened his mouth as though he were going to declare himself, but he said nothing. Lady Neville did not move.

"No one," said Death. She touched a flower with her finger, and it seemed to crouch and flex itself like a pleased cat. "No one at all," she said. "Then I must choose, and that is just, for that is the way that I became Death. I never wanted to be Death, and it makes me so happy that you want me to become one of yourselves. I have searched a long time for people who would want me. Now I have only to choose someone to replace me and it is done. I will choose very carefully."

"Oh, we were so foolish," Lady Neville said to herself. "We were so foolish." But she said nothing aloud; she merely clasped her hands and stared at the young girl, thinking vaguely that if she had had a daughter she would have been greatly pleased if she resembled the lady Death.

"The Contessa della Candini," said Death thoughtfully, and that woman gave a little squeak of terror because she could not draw her breath for a scream. But Death laughed and said, "No, that would be silly." She said nothing more, but for a long time after that the Contessa burned with humiliation at not having been chosen to be Death.

"Not Captain Compson," murmured Death, "because he is too kind to become Death, and because it would be too cruel to him. He wants to die so badly." The expression on the Captain's face did not change, but his hands began to tremble.

"Not Lorimond," the girl continued, "because he knows so little about life, and because I like him." The poet flushed, and turned white, and then turned pink again. He made as if to kneel clumsily on one knee, but instead he pulled himself erect and stood as much like Captain Compson as he could.

"Not the Torrances," said Death, "never Lord and Lady Torrance, for both of them care too much about another person to take any pride in being Death." But she hesitated over Lady Torrance for a while, staring at her out of her dark and curious eyes. "I was your age when I became Death," she said at last. "I wonder what it will be like to be your age again. I have been Death for so long." Lady Torrance shivered and did not speak.

And at last Death said quietly, "Lady Neville."

"I am here," Lady Neville answered.

"I think you are the only one," said Death. "I choose you, Lady Neville."

Again Lady Neville heard every guest sigh softly, and although her back was to them all she knew that they were sighing in relief that neither themselves nor anyone dear to themselves had been chosen. Lady Torrance gave a little cry of protest, but Lady Neville knew that she would have cried out at whatever choice Death made. She heard herself say calmly, "I am honored. But was there no one more worthy than I?"

"Not one," said Death. "There is no one quite so weary of being human, no one who knows better how meaningless it is to be alive. And there is no one else here with the power to treat life"—and she smiled sweetly and cruelly—"the life of your hairdresser's child, for instance, as the meaningless thing it is. Death has a heart, but it is forever an empty heart, and I think, Lady Neville, that your heart is like a dry riverbed, like a seashell. You will be very content as Death, more so than I, for I was very young when I became Death."

She came toward Lady Neville, light and swaying, her deep eyes wide and full of the light of the red morning sun that was beginning to rise. The guests at the ball moved back from her, although she did not look at them, but Lady Neville clenched her hands tightly and watched Death come toward her with her little dancing steps. "We must kiss each other," Death said. "That is the way I became Death." She shook her head delightedly, so that her soft hair swirled about her shoulders. "Quickly, quickly," she said. "Oh, I cannot wait to be human again."

"You may not like it," Lady Neville said. She felt very calm, though she could hear her old heart pounding in her chest and feel it in the tips of her fingers. "You may not like it after a while," she said.

"Perhaps not." Death's smile was very close to her now. "I will not be as beautiful as I am, and perhaps people will not love me as much as they do now. But I will be human for a while, and at last I will die. I have done my penance."

"What penance?" the old woman asked the beautiful girl. "What was it you did? Why did you become Death?"

"I don't remember," said the lady Death. "And you too will forget in time." She was smaller than Lady Neville, and so much younger. In her white dress she might have been the daughter that Lady Neville had never had, who would have been with her always and held her mother's head lightly in the crook of her arm when she felt old and sad. Now she lifted her head to kiss Lady Neville's cheek, and as she did so she whispered in her ear, "You will still be beautiful when I am ugly. Be kind to me then."

Behind Lady Neville the handsome gentlemen and ladies murmured and sighed, fluttering like moths in their evening dress, in their elegant gowns. "I promise," she said, and then she pursed her dry lips to kiss the soft, sweet-smelling cheek of the young lady Death.

LESLEE BECKER

Grew up in the Adirondacks. Came to Stanford in 1984 as a Stegner Fellow. Have had stories in The Atlantic, Iowa Review, New Letters, American Fiction 87, *and* Nimrod, *where I won the Katherine Anne Porter Fiction Prize. I have received a James Michener Fellowship and am currently a Jones Lecturer in fiction at Stanford.*

"I was between stories, trying to quit smoking, trying to relieve my cash-flow problems. I went to the Discovery House Resale Shop to sell some things, and found myself buying instead and talking to a salesclerk, telling her all sorts of things. I began a story later, with a character lying to a clerk. The story's changed some since its appearance in Gil Sorrentino's workshop. The Discovery House is gone. I'm still trying to quit smoking, still facing the jaws of indigence, still talking to clerks, and, yes, still hoping to find closets full of stories."

◆   ◆   ◆

Twilight on the El Camino

WHEN I FIRST WENT into the business, my father told me: "Buying a car is one of the most important decisions people have to make." He sold Buicks, had his own dealership, Bahr Motors, a real showcase. On the Fourth of July, he had the whole fleet polished, and I rode with him in the parade in a black Roadmaster. I'd lob candy to kids, wave, and pretend I was a war hero.

My father owns a small wrecking yard now. He's seventy, and he tells people he's in the salvage phase of his automotive career. I work at Del's Auto Mart. I've been there eleven years and wouldn't be sticking it out if it weren't for my family. I want good things for them.

Del's got this ice-cream philosophy about cars. "Imagine you're driving down the road," he tells the new salesmen, "and you get a craving for ice cream. You got it in your mind that a vanilla cone will do, so you pull into the first place you see. Now, once you eye forty flavors and all kinds of extra concoctions, you think vanilla's going to satisfy you?"

So we give the customers trade-in deals no one can match, and all kinds of extras—tape decks, TVs, radials, turkeys, and barbecue grills.

We've got one of the biggest places on the El Camino, one you can spot a long ways off because of the revolving '54 Thunderbird perched above the banners on a tall pole. We needed the Thunderbird because this strip is plastered with car places.

People tend to remember Del's television ads. His latest angle is to pass himself off as an evangelist. He appears in a red robe behind a podium, hollers about time running out, and then, as the car's wheeled in, his voice drops, just like he's in the presence of the vessel of salvation. All of us salesmen wear identical three-piece suits, flanking him as Del's Disciples.

My kids laugh whenever they see the ad, and the first time I saw myself on television, I decided I had to change things. I started on the weight first. I dieted, gave up smoking, and took up running. I imagine winning an important prize at the end of the run, and crowds of cheering people applauding, and my father right there congratulating me.

They say it helps to picture yourself as a nonsmoker, to remember the part of your life before you smoked and to project yourself into the future without seeing cigarettes. I didn't have any trouble with the early part, but as I tried to see my future, a little knot began to fist up in my stomach. It wasn't connected to cigarettes as much as to the image of myself getting farther away from the early and good part of my life, and moving into something sad and probably wrong.

Last night, I was out running and found myself noticing other people's homes—their careful lawns, the landscaping, the shape and condition of the houses. I was outside of one—a big mansion of a place—at dusk. A patch of light from one of the tall windows hit the center of the lawn just as I was approaching the house. I stopped, looked inside, and saw a family sitting at a table under a bright chandelier, a man, woman, and a little boy. That's all. But it held me, and I felt on the edge of something.

This morning I overslept, and because of all the El Camino traffic I got to work late. Del was sitting at his desk, involved on the phone. He looked at me and then his watch, but he left it at that. I got a cup of coffee, looked to see if I had any messages, and started to read the *Chronicle*, an article about a family living in their car. I showed the story to Bill, this guy who's been at Del's almost as long as I have.

"Jesus," he said. "If old Del sees that, he'll try to sell them something bigger. Is that a new suit, Charlie?"

"No, I've had it a while. I took off some weight."

"Wish I could," he said. "Maybe I should join one of those fitness centers."

"You don't need that. Just run. I feel a hundred percent better with that and giving up the cigarettes."

"Yeah," he said, like he was resigned to stay the way he was.

I got up for another cup of coffee, thought about taking a doughnut, but didn't. I was watching the salesmen and the bookkeepers when Del came over.

"Did you call that fellow back, Charlie? The Toyota?"

"Not yet, Del."

He shook his head, went to the window, and thumbed me toward it. I looked out and saw an elderly man in a mulberry leisure suit, work boots, and a western hat.

"Hey," Del hollered across the showroom, "we've got a live one, a real lay down."

The man was inspecting a Datsun pickup. Del grinned as Bill and a couple of salesmen came to the window.

"You know what hemorrhoids and cowboy hats have in common?" Del asked.

Bill rolled his eyes and the other salesmen continued to gawk at the old man.

"Sooner or later every asshole's going to have 'em," Del answered.

The guys laughed. Then one started flipping a coin to see who'd take the man. Del yanked a wad of bills from his pocket, pulled out a twenty, put it on my desk, and smoothed it out.

"Twenty bucks says the old man's looking for . . ."

"A Chevette," one of the salesmen said.

"Whadya say, Charlie?" Del said, sticking his face close to mine.

"He's got a right to look," I said.

I walked outside and stood in the middle of the lot, hearing the plastic banners overhead, flapping. The man was looking at a Cutlass Supreme when I introduced myself. He had to lean toward me, crooking his head in my direction, to hear me over all the noise. He shook my hand.

"A fine automobile," he said.

"It sure is," I said. "Want to get in, get a closer look?"

"Nope," the man said, running his hand over the fender. "It's out of my league."

"We don't get many Cutlasses. People hang onto them."

"Came here with my boy. It's his first car. That's him over there, Mr. Bahr," he said, pointing to a tall, skinny kid eyeing a cherry red Mustang with a "RED HOT" sign propped in the windshield.

I knew this about the car. It had been wrecked. The bearings were blown and the suspension joints were bad, but Del had his boys restore it. They gave it a paint job, body work, and a set of new tires. It was one of Del's specials, and when one of us sells a car like that, we get something extra to sweeten up the commission, usually five or ten percent, under the table.

"Mr. Bahr, this is my son, Roger," the man said as we approached the boy. "He's at the community college, studying Computer Science. Plays basketball too."

"Play a little hoop, huh?" I said, and the kid looked at me a minute and then looked back at the car.

"Sure is flashy looking," the man said.

When I told him the price, he winced.

"Can I take it for a spin?" the kid asked me.

"Why don't you look around, son?" the man said. "You want to take your time on something like this."

"It's my car, Dad. I want to give it a test run, all right?"

"No law against that," I told him. "Just so you know what you're doing."

"I know what I'm doing," the kid said.

I got the keys, and the kid left, leaving me and the man in the lot.

"You sure do have a lot of automobiles here," the man said. "My boy knows all about them. Ford makes that car, don't they?"

"The Mustang? It's one of their best sellers."

"They're reliable," he said, like he was asking me for assurance. "I had a Ford pickup. They got a reputation."

The kid pulled into the lot, banging on the horn and beaming as he got out of the car.

"I want it, Dad."

The man started to press on the fenders to check the shocks.

"McPherson Struts," I told him.

The kid lifted the hood, and his father checked the oil stick. He stared at it, then held it close to his nose. Then he got down on his hands and knees and peered under the car. I glanced back to the showroom to see if anyone was watching, but they weren't. When the man stood up, he took off his hat and wiped his brow.

"It runs fine, Dad," the kid said, staring into the engine.

"Maybe we ought to look around some more, son. Wouldn't hurt to check around," the man said.

"Someone else will get it if I don't."

The man looked at me. "Is that right, Mr. Bahr? Are there other interested parties?"

"Well," I said, and paused a moment. "Cars move in and out of here pretty fast."

"You know anything about the previous owner?" the man asked. "Last thing I want is to get somebody else's headache."

"Last thing anybody wants," I said. "We've got records in the office, and in the glove compartment there's a maintenance log. But I'll tell you this. It's been repainted. The Mustang didn't look like this when we got it."

The man nodded and looked at me as though he appreciated getting privileged information. The kid shook his head and walked away from us.

"That's the one he wants, all right. He's got his mind made up," the man said, and walked over to his son.

"Look," I said, joining them. "Why don't you two take your time, talk things over by yourselves. I'll be inside. There's no rush."

The man thanked me, and I returned to my office. Del's twenty was still on my desk. When I saw the man and the boy heading toward the showroom, I put the twenty in my pocket. They wanted the car, they told me. The man reached into his pocket for his wallet, and started counting out cash.

"You're doing the down payment in cash?" I asked him.

"Doing the whole thing," he said.

"I can knock off a hundred then," I said, which is where I would've started dropping the price anyway if he hadn't gone for it outside. "I can give you that as sales manager," I added, looking to see if any of the other salesmen heard me. "I've been here a long time, and I can tell you it's a rare experience to see cash again. Most people think it's the buyer who gets taken, but we get bad checks, and a couple of times we've gotten stuck with stolen cars."

"Is that a fact?" the man said. Then he stood up, shook my hand, and looked directly into my eyes. "I got the one my boy wanted. It was good doing business with you, Mr. Bahr."

I smiled at the boy, and he and his father headed toward the door. "You have any trouble during the warranty period, even after, you come back and see me," I shouted.

"Del," I said. "I need to leave early. Personal business."

He didn't say a word.

"Toothache," I said. "It's been driving me nuts."

"Okay, Charlie. I'll have Bill take care of the Toyota."

"Thanks, Del," I said and got up to leave. "Oh, I meant to tell you, the kids love the new commercial. They get a real kick out of it."

"Yeah, well some son of a bitch wants it off the air. Claims it's sacrilegious."

I shook my head. "Well, it caught the bastard's attention, so it's doing the job for us."

I got into my car and headed north, and when I saw the sign for 80 East, the possibility of being somewhere else seemed the most important thing. I could go east, maybe to Ashtabula, Ohio, the place my father left during the Depression to come to California. I could take the same route he took, only in the opposite direction, and maybe, by following things back to their source, I could start all over again.

I remembered when I was little how Ohio seemed like a magical place. I almost made it to Akron once. I was a semifinalist in the Soap Box Derby. I built the whole thing myself, the way you're supposed to. My father supervised to make sure I followed the rules exactly. The kid who beat me couldn't have built his machine by himself. I had a hard time not crying when I lost. Then my father gave me one of those talks that only made me madder.

"Charlie," he told me, "you only lost a race. Think of what he lost."

I started to feel very hungry, took an exit, and went into a convenience store. I loaded up with a pack of Marlboros and some snacks, and as I stood at the check-out counter, I knew the clerk and other customers were making assessments about me and my appetite. The woman ahead of me was pretty, well-dressed, tanned, with wheat-colored hair that looked professionally styled. Everything about her had an elegance that spelled money. She looked at what I laid out on the counter, and then she looked at me with a small smile.

"For my kids," I said, gesturing toward my food.

She kept staring at me. "You're one of those TV personalities, aren't you?" she asked me.

I looked away from her and faced the little bleacher of gum and candy by the register. "I've done some spots," I said.

"I thought so," she said, then took her bag and left.

She pulled away, and when I got into my car, I kept saying, "Jesus, Jesus."

I tore into a candy bar, and smoked a cigarette, which made me feel dizzy at first, and then it felt better.

On the drive back, I kept hoping Peg would be home. I rehearsed all the things I wanted to tell her.

She was baking, standing by the oven. "You're home early," she said. "Is anything wrong?"

I went to the liquor cabinet and poured myself some Scotch.

"Want me to fix you something to eat?"

"I'm not hungry," I said, sitting down at the table. "You wouldn't believe what happened to me today, Peg."

She sat down across from me, and I looked at her eyes, a particular blue that never quite comes across in pictures.

"I lied, Peg. What I really wanted to do was tell Del off, but I didn't. I told him I had a toothache. Can you believe it? A grown man making up stories to get out of work?"

She smiled and shook her head. "You're so hard on yourself, Charlie."

"It gets worse," I said, this nervous grin coming over me. "The man I sold this car to. I lied to him too." I waited for a reaction, a sign of disappointment, but she looked more confused than disappointed.

"Del had a hand in it, didn't he?" she said.

"Sure, in a way, but I'm the one who sold the car. Jesus, I even told the customer I was the sales manager."

"Is that all?" she said. When she started to get up from the table, I put my hand over hers.

"Peg, let's just sit still for a second."

She touched my face, ran her fingertips along the edge of my cheek. I closed my eyes for a moment, and we kept quiet for a while.

"God, I'm so sick of that job, Peg. I wish we could get away, a trip, do something different."

She looked at the clock. "I better go and get the kids." She kissed me on the forehead. "You stay here and relax."

After she left, I made another drink and took it and the atlas outside to the lawn chair. It would be secondary roads the whole way, I decided, to give us all the chance, especially the kids, to really see things. And my father would be with us, going over territory he hadn't seen in fifty years. I traced my finger over the route, then lay back in the chair. Some thin clouds threading the edge of the sky were starting to spool and drift toward the center.

When the kids came outside, I was feeling better. "Daddy's got a big surprise for both of you," I said, and Peg smiled with me. "We're going on a trip."

"Oh boy," Ellen said.

"On a plane?" Bobby asked.

"By car. Across the country. See," I said, pointing to the atlas.

"When?" Bobby said.

"How about Christmas?"

"That's a long way off," he said and looked up at his mother.

"Well, how about tonight? How about eating out? Wherever you want."

"Road Runner," Ellen said.

"Okay, Road Runner it is. We'll go over to your grandfather's afterwards. How about that?" I said, getting up from the chair.

"There's nothing to do over there," Bobby said.

The good feeling was wearing off by the time we reached the restaurant. We ordered a large pizza with the works, and when it came, horns and sirens went off. Everyone looked at our table for a minute, then returned to their eating. I burned the roof of my mouth, and some of the sauce dribbled onto my chin and shirt.

"How come we're going on a trip?" Bobby asked. He picked a mushroom off his pizza.

"Because," Peg said, "your father wants us all to see the country."

"We're going to Ohio," I said. "Where your grandfather's from."

"Ohio," Ellen said, making funny shapes with her lips.

"Ohio?" Bobby repeated.

After we left and got home, the kids rushed into the house as if they were glad to get away.

The TV was blaring at my father's house, and he had dozed off in his chair. I punched the set off, and he woke up and looked at me.

"Charlie, I didn't hear you come in." He turned on the light and stared at me with a puzzled expression.

I looked down at my shirt. "Took the kids out to dinner and spilled some food on me," I said.

"You ought to put some water on that before the stain sets," he said and started to get up from his chair.

"I'll get it, Dad," I said, and we both headed toward the kitchen.

I could hear water dripping below when I turned on the faucet. I opened the cabinet under the sink and saw a pan filled with water. I emptied it and took a look at the pipe.

"You should get this fixed. I could call this plumber I know for you."

He shook his head. "You know what plumbers get now? The pan'll do."

When we returned to the living room, he started picking through some mail. "I've got something to show you," he said. "Look at this."

He handed me a brochure that showed a new line of wrecking trucks. I looked at a device named "The Jaws of Life," a huge-toothed contraption for prying smashed cars open.

"This one caught my eye," he said, and pointed to a big truck filled with elaborate machinery. "Of course, it's top of the line, more than what I need."

"It's nice, Dad," I said and lit a cigarette.

"Smoking again, huh?"

"Afraid so."

"How are Peg and the kids?"

"Fine. They ask about you all the time. Want to know when you're coming over again."

"What's that?" he said, cupping his hand behind his ear.

"The kids, Peg, they want to see you again."

He nodded. "So, you went to dinner tonight, you say."

"To Road Runner. The kids love it. We had a great time."

"Good. How's the job going?"

"Real busy, Dad. I must have inherited it from you," I said, leaning toward him. "Del says I'm his number one man. I think he's going to put me in the assistant manager slot."

"I saw him on the TV, you too. Must have cost a bundle for those ads."

"He can afford it. A woman recognized me today from television. At the Quik Trip."

"Is that so? At the Quik Trip? You know, I tried some of those low cholesterol eggs, Charlie. They don't taste right. Say, they're having an antique auto show at the Cow Palace. I'll bet Bobby'd love to see those cars." He looked down at the floor and then at me. "Everything all right, Charlie?"

"I almost made a big commission today, Dad," I said.

"You always liked cars," he said, and both of us kept quiet a minute.

"This fellow came in today, would've gotten stuck with a real lemon, but I wouldn't allow it. I may have lost some money, but I came home with something else."

He nodded. "Is business falling off, Charlie?"

"No, that's not what I mean. I put my foot down, Dad," I shouted. "No more bad deals."

"Good for you, Charlie," he said, slapping his leg.

"Things are going to be different now, starting with a vacation. How'd you like to see Ashtabula again, look up some old friends?"

He pondered it a moment. "I doubt if I'd know anyone there anymore," he said, "and besides, what about my business? Who'd take care of things?"

"I don't know, but we can work something out. Look," I said, getting up. "I better be going. I'll get that pipe taken care of for you, and we'll all go to the auto show."

I went outside, saw the kitchen light go off and the TV come on. I went out back, lit a cigarette, and walked over to his salvage area. The moon was big and under its light, all the cars looked solemn and dignified. I got in behind the wheel of an old Chrysler and looked out through the cracked windshield. I slid my fingertips over the starred lace of cracks and wondered what the person felt right before he crashed.

I leaned back into the upholstery and remembered what it used to be like, lying down in a car, watching crowns of trees and squares of sky glide by when I was a kid, off for a drive, my parents in the front seat and me in the back. Sometimes I'd get carsick, and we'd stop and pull over so I could get air. My mother would take me in her lap, hold me, and tell me to find something solid to look at. I'd focus on the hood ornament or my father behind the wheel, and then I'd forget about being sick and would ride along, pretending I was on an important mission, responsible for reading the maps and the territory. When we got home, I liked believing I had led my family to safety.

I got out of the Chrysler and into my own car. The traffic on the El Camino was moving slowly from one stop to the next. Behind me, and as far ahead as I could see, was a spine of lights, giving everything a yellow flush, shiny and new-looking, like whatever was there under that glow must be worth having.

WENDELL BERRY

I was born in 1934, and have lived most of my life in Henry County, Kentucky, where I still live. I married Tanya Amyx in 1957. We have two children, a daughter and a son, and two granddaughters.

"This poem, 'History,' is an attempt to get what I feel to be the course and burden of my own history, the history of my own part of the country, into one statement. I dedicated it to Wallace Stegner because of his involvement with his history, which I found instructive, and to acknowledge my debt to him."

History

For Wallace Stegner

1.
The crops were made, the leaves
were down, three frosts had lain
upon the broad stone
step beneath the door;
as I walked away
the houses were shut, quiet
under their drifting smokes,
the women stooped at the hearths.
Beyond the farthest tracks
of any domestic beast
my way led me, into
a place for which I knew
no names. I went by paths
that bespoke intelligence
and memory I did not know.
Noonday held sounds of moving
water, moving air, enormous
stillness of old trees.
Though I was weary and alone,
song was near me then,
wordless and gay as a deer
lightly stepping. Learning
the landmarks and the ways

of that land, so I might
go back, if I wanted to,
my mind grew new, and lost
the backward way. I stood
at last, long hunter and child,
where this valley opened,
a word I seemed to know
though I had not heard it.
Behind me, along the crooks
and slants of my approach,
a low song sang itself,
as patient as the light.
On the valley floor the woods
grew rich: great poplars,
beeches, sycamores,
walnuts, sweet gums, lindens,
oaks. They stood apart
and open, the winter light
at rest among them. Yes,
and as I came down
I heard a little stream
pouring into the river.

2.
Since then I have arrived here
many times. I have come
on foot, on horseback, by boat,
and by machine—by earth,
water, air, and fire.
I came with axe and rifle.
I came with a sharp eye
and the price of land. I came
in bondage, and I came
in freedom not worth the name.
From the high outlook
of that first day I have come
down two hundred years
across the worked and wasted
slopes, by eroding tracks
of the joyless horsepower of greed.
Through my history's despite
and ruin, I have come
to its remainder, and here
have made the beginning
of a farm intended to become
my art of being here.
By it I would instruct
my wants: they should belong

to each other and to this place.
Until my song comes here
to learn its words, my art
is but the hope of song.

3.
All the lives this place
has had, I have. I eat
my history day by day.
Bird, butterfly, and flower
pass through the seasons of
my flesh. I dine and thrive
on offal and old stone,
and am combined within
the story of the ground.
By this earth's life, I have
its greed and innocence,
its violence, its peace.
Now let me feed my song
upon the life that is here
that is the life that is gone.
This blood has turned to dust
and liquefied again in stem
and vein ten thousand times.
Let what is in the flesh,
O Muse, be brought to mind.

♦ # THOMAS BONTLY ♦

A *Stegner Fellow at Stanford in 1965–66, Thomas Bontly has published four novels:* The Competitor *(Scribner's, 1966),* The Adventures of A Young Outlaw *(Putnam's, 1974),* Celestial Chess *(Harper and Row, 1979),* Shadow of the Giant *(Random House, 1988). His short stories have appeared in* Esquire, McCall's, Redbook, Boy's Life, *and other magazines. He teaches at the University of Wisconsin, Milwaukee.*

"'Re-Encounter' was occasioned by a summer in Europe and a return to Paris after twenty years. Editors have not liked the story because of its 'surprise ending,' but it seems to me a shrewd reader really ought to see it coming. The story enshrines a romantic episode I had been trying to work into my fiction for twenty years, so of course I find it delightful. The Jamesian tone of the opening also amuses me—but of course that tone couldn't be sustained; it might have been a better story if it had."

♦   ♦   ♦

Re-Encounter

APPREHENSIVE, HIS EYES FIXED on the woman who seemed unaware of his approach, Gerhardt made his way through the maze of tables beneath the striped awning of the sidewalk cafe. The traffic along the Boulevard St. Michel sounded harsh and menacing in his left ear, while with his right he seemed to hear distant music, the sad and sentimental refrain of some well-remembered song from his youth, when all the songs had been sad and sentimental, so easy to remember, so hard to forget.

What an extraordinary coincidence, he thought—he had been thinking of her all afternoon as he browsed among the Left Bank bookstalls, dappled sun and shadow along the Seine, and the splash of water against concrete as the long red-and-white tour boats went by reminded him of that morning over twenty years ago now when they came down to breakfast beside the river, having bought a kilo of dark red cherries from a vendor outside their hotel, and how they sat with the bag on their laps and spit the seeds into the sluggish current—the impudence of youth!—and all these memories of their week in Paris so sharp and vivid that, when he first saw her in the shade of the striped awning, beyond the thick hedge that sheltered her from the clamorous street, he couldn't help wondering if he were hallucinating.

She looked, Gerhardt thought, remarkably as she had twenty years ago, still a sight to catch the eye of any young Frenchman strolling the Boulevard on this mild summer afternoon, whereas Gerhardt himself had grown old, had lost most of his hair, had put on weight around the middle, had gotten used to thinking of himself as an old fox too sly—or was it just too lazy?—to leave his hole. It had taken this return to Europe, and more particularly to Paris, to coax certain memories out of hibernation, so that for these last few days he often found himself attempting to measure his loss—the world, that is, which might have been his, if, twenty years ago, he had had the courage, the integrity, the whatever-the-hell-it-took to claim it as his own.

And there she was. Alone. A coffee cup at her elbow and a small pad of writing paper, a collection of post cards and blue air-mail envelopes on the table before her. She was wearing the rather simple yet sporty clothes he always thought of her as wearing—a white shirt-blouse and plaid skirt, a beige sweater over her shoulders. No jewelry (she'd never worn any), very little makeup, her only adornment that lustrous reddish-brown hair, perhaps a shorter cut than he remembered from the old days, but hadn't she yet produced a single strand of gray? He remembered how she used to fuss over her hair, how she hated for him to see her in curlers yet couldn't stand to let it go unwashed after a day of knocking about dusty old Paris. They were students then, dirt poor, and she wouldn't have dreamed of going to a Parisian hairdresser. He supposed she could go to one now, if she wished, and perhaps the hairdresser would add a touch of something to the rinse to maintain that rich, reddish tint, but no, if he knew her at all (and even after all these years he was sure he did) she would never dye her hair . . . nor was she likely to go to a Parisian hairdresser, even if she had married a rich man.

He was nearly to her table now and still she hadn't seen him. How would she react? What if, out of anger or hurt pride, she simply refused to recognize him, to acknowledge his existence? Gerhardt thought uncomfortably of the quarrel this morning with his wife. The Louvre had been crowded, the kids difficult— it hadn't taken much to start them sniping at one another (it never did, these days!)—and Gerhardt had gone off to nurse all his old grudges and regrets in silence. He wondered if she, his old flame, could be nursing similar grudges against her husband. It wasn't difficult to make up scenarios for their re-encounter. Gerhardt wrote fiction on occasion (slightly more than a hobby and a good deal less than a profession) and, though he always tried to avoid such shopworn themes as the reunion of long-lost lovers, he thought that in this case it wouldn't be difficult to work out the details—if only *she* would cooperate!

He spoke her name, prepared to count his heartbeats until a look of recognition and welcome appeared in her fine dark eyes. At once he saw that it was going to be all right—she welcomed him with one of her large, open, honest smiles—just exactly the sort of smile he remembered from days gone by and had hoped, not with much confidence, to elicit from her now.

He took the chair beside her and said quickly, "What extraordinary luck, finding you here in Paris! Do you live here now?"

With that old facility she once had for catching his mood and accepting his lead (their conversations, he used to think, were like dances—they had made him a verbal Fred Astaire), she said, "Oh, I live here, didn't you know? At least we usually spend the spring and early summer here. When it gets hot we retreat to our cottage in Scotland."

"We?" Gerhardt asked with a foolish grin.

"Oh yes—you mean you haven't heard about my third marriage?"

"Your third? I guess we don't have the same friends any longer. I've often thought about you, wondered how you were doing, but no one seemed to know."

"Well, I've heard about *you*," she said, as if playfully accusing him of not trying hard enough to find out about her. "I know you're a professor at some American university—in the middle west, isn't it?—and you've published several novels—"

"Only three," Gerhardt said modestly.

"Oh, then I've read them all," she said proudly. "I was afraid maybe I'd missed one or two. They're awfully good—but I haven't seen myself in any of them yet."

She *would* look for that, Gerhardt thought. "I've been saving you, our story, for when I had the craft to do it right." He knew that was a lie. He would never have the craft for that—several banished drafts had already told him as much.

"You're looking good, John," she said. "I guess your wife has been taking care of you."

"Oh yes, she takes excellent care of me," he said, thinking how splendidly they were carrying it off. No tears, no accusations, and most of all, thank God, no embarrassment. This is the way, it occurred to him, that departed spirits must meet on the other side—no rancor nor recrimination, no tedious recapitulation of past offenses—simply a joyful recognition of one another. "I'm here, I made it!" "I'm so glad, so did I!"

"So this third husband of yours, he's Scottish?"

"Actually, he's German. We have a castle in Bavaria, but we only go there in the autumn for the hunting and sometimes in the winter for the skiing—on our way to the Grecian Isles."

"Sounds wonderful," he said, thinking that she was putting it on a bit thick just now, but never mind, he'd get the truth out of her later. "And don't you ever go back to the States?"

"Occasionally—to see the children from my second marriage."

"Oh, I see." He wondered if she was counting that week they had spent in Paris as her first marriage. It had been, in every way, a honeymoon. "And how many children do you have?"

She appeared to have to add them up. "Well, there's Godfrey from my first marriage—he's at Oxford now, doing wonderfully well—and then there's the twins, Agatha and Alyoisus, from my second marriage—"

Gerhardt laughed. "You didn't name your son Alyoisus!"

"It was my second husband's idea. He had a vicious sense of humor."

"You always did tend to get mixed up with mean men," Gerhardt said, venturing into dangerous territory.

"Oh, no," she said, "*most* of them were very nice. But you, as I recall—you had a fatal attraction to a certain mousey type of *hausfrau*. Did you find the wife you were looking for?"

"I'd hardly call her 'mousey,'" Gerhardt said, "although sometimes she exhibits certain cat-like qualities. We're quite happily married—at least, I always *thought* we were."

"But lately you're inclined to have doubts?"

"Ah, well, I guess we're both starting to get a bit old and crotchety and set in our ways . . . and then, too, this trip has brought back a lot of memories—things I might have done differently, if only I'd known—"

"But why should that prove a problem?" she wickedly asked, as if she didn't know!

He decided to hold back, to try for an easier angle.

"Oh, you know how it is when you travel with your family—dragging suitcases through train stations, trying to find a decent hotel, keeping track of the kids—it does get to be a hassle. But I gather you don't have those problems?"

"Gunther and I usually travel without the children—it's so much easier that way. If we do bring one or two of them with us, there's usually a nanny to look after them."

"Must be nice. I always said you deserved a rich husband."

She looked surprised. "Did you say that? I don't remember you saying that."

"Maybe I didn't say it out loud, but it was one reason, you know, why—"

A waiter had approached. Gerhardt, whose French was no better now than it had been twenty years ago, looked to her for assistance.

"I bet you'd like a cocktail," she said. "You see, I still remember your American tastes. I think they could make you a passable martini here—without ice, of course."

"Ask them to try," Gerhardt said. "And join me, please, if you will."

In brisk, expert French she ordered them both gin martinis. He looked at her fondly. It was hard to believe she could still look so young and attractive—he almost believed her stories!

"It's really great to see you again," he said, after the waiter left. "Is your husband meeting you here?"

"No, he's at the races. He won't be back until this evening. And your family—?"

"I left them at the hotel. My son's got a nasty cold and my daughter—she's ten—got worn out this morning at the Louvre. I don't know what my wife's doing."

"Probably out spending your money," she teasingly suggested.

"I never worry about that. Liz is very economical."

"Oh, one of those! You make her sound like a little Japanese car!"

He saw that she was determined to make fun of him and he began to weary of the game they were playing. It had been all right—had been, in fact, a Godsend—as a means of easing the initial awkwardness of their meeting. But now he wanted to get behind her teasing. He wanted to probe deeper. Most of all, he wanted to find out if she too heard that distant music, that well-remembered song.

"Have dinner with me this evening," he said.

"What, just the two of us?"

"My family won't mind. There's a small cafe just across from the hotel where they can eat. The kids don't appreciate French cuisine anyway."

"And your wife?"

"I'll give her an oil change tomorrow."

She laughed. "You're still a bastard, aren't you?"

"It's so good to see you again," he insisted. "I can't help being selfish. I'd like to have you all to myself—just for one evening?"

He realized he was pleading. All right, then, to hell with it, he'd plead. This was something he'd never expected would happen to him. How many second chances did a man get?

She looked at him seriously, thoughtfully, and he remembered the first time she looked at him like that, when he proposed they spend a week together in Paris. They had met in London, two American students on the loose, and though they made a show of being freethinking, free-living vagabonds, she had responded to his half-serious invitation with that same sober, solemn gaze, as if reading in his face the moral labyrinth into which, given half a chance, he might lead her. It had given him pause, that serious look of hers, and it did now, but he had persisted that first time and gotten what he wanted; he felt sure he could do so again.

"We're not children," he said, using the line he'd used then.

"All the more reason why we shouldn't act like children," she said, countering in similar fashion.

"We're not exactly doddering fossils, either," he said, adding a new element to the argument.

"Have we been acting as if we were?"

"I think we've been having a splendid time," he said, "but now I want more."

"You always did," she replied, with a touch of irony.

The waiter returned with their martinis. Gerhardt sipped his and decided that, though it was a bit heavy on the vermouth, it was just what he needed in order to wage a final assault on her scruples.

"Do you remember that little place on the Quai—just across from Notre Dame? It's still there—I passed it this afternoon. I could take you there."

Her dark eyes warmed to the memory. "And will you want me to order for you again?"

"You did all right on the martinis," he said.

"I've had twenty years to study the language."

They were both silent for a moment and Gerhardt remembered how it had happened—their first quarrel. It was on their second visit to the restaurant, the first having proved an utter delight when they gambled on their inadequate French and had each been rewarded by an elegant entree—his beef and hers chicken. On the second night they planned to switch; she would order what he'd had, he would order her dish. But at the last moment, the waiter hovering over their candlelit table, she had faltered: "Oh, John—I'm not *sure* what I had last night!"

"Take a guess," he urged her, embarrassed in front of the waiter, "I'm sure everything here is good."

But what he got, when their dinners were served, was a plate of gray glop, accompanied by an evil-looking greasy green sauce. Brains, guts, puke from the kitchen cat? Gerhardt was appalled. She was penitent and offered to take it for herself; he could have the beef dish he'd enjoyed last night. No, he said, he wouldn't dream of asking her to eat that mess. They had neither the money nor the courage to tell the waiter to take it away. Gerhardt forced it down, ugly forkful by ugly forkful, as she pleaded with him to spare her. He took great and perverse pleasure in not sparing her. He would eat the stuff if he choked. She began to cry. He told her to shut up, for God's sake, people were staring. She said she didn't give a damn—she said he and the whole city of Paris could go to hell. They finished their dinner in silence.

Walking out into the lingering dusk of a summer evening, seeing the sky glowing violet behind the spires of Notre Dame and rippling violet in the ruffled river, Gerhardt reflected that it was well he found out in time what an impossible creature she was. Yet the memory of the afternoon they had just spent in their Left Bank hotel room rose up to rebuke and torment him. How sweetly her slim young body had come to his bed, how tenderly, with what depth of love, her dark eyes had looked up at him from the pillow. How could he be so cruel to the woman who had given him the treasure of her love? Could he really harden his heart against her over such a silly misunderstanding?

It appeared that he could. Not that he wanted to prolong the quarrel, but he knew no way to end it. Even to say he was sorry would only open the hostilities once again. She did not accept apologies gracefully, seemed to find in them some hidden rebuke. Well, he'd be damned if he would say he was sorry this time—let *her* find a way to end the quarrel!

They were walking up the Boulevard St. Michel and he saw the bright lights, the gleaming shop windows, the little cubicles full of tourist junk; he saw Paris as a gaudy, garish midway like those of the second-rate carnivals that used to visit his hometown, three balls for a quarter kid, there's a sucker born every minute, *what am I doing here with this woman?*—when suddenly, on a crowded corner, she seized his arm and spoke desperately, her breath warm against his neck: "Oh John, let's go back to bed! Nothing bad ever happens there!"

Instantly, his anger left him. A crust fell from his heart. He kissed her on the lips right there on that crowded corner (the French had seen it all) and, arm in arm, as if fleeing bootless apologies that now would never have to be made, they hurried back to their hotel. And the night was full of music . . .

"Are you *sure* you want to go back to that particular restaurant?" she asked him, twirling a pair of sunglasses.

"I've dreamed of it for twenty years," he said. "It was the happiest night of my entire life."

"There's been nothing as good since?"

This was a hard question. He thought for a moment. "There's never been anything quite the same . . . it was special."

"You were beastly to me, you know."

"And you were sweet to me. Listen, I'll eat gray glop until it comes out of my ears. I'll even let *you* eat it, if you want to so much."

She laughed. "Now I'm convinced you're sincere! Isn't it wonderful, our meeting like this? I'm so glad . . . but what about your family? And my husband?"

"To hell with 'em," he said forcefully. "Now that I've found you again, I'm not giving you up."

"But—couldn't we all be friends?"

"What, me and Gunther? You and Liz?"

"Gunther can put up with you, if Liz can put up with me."

That struck Gerhardt as an elegant idea. "She'd better put up with you, or I'll trade her in on a Honda."

She put on her sunglasses, hiding her eyes from Gerhardt and turning herself, on the spot, into a stranger. But he knew her now—oh yes, he certainly knew her!

"I do have to go back to the hotel," she said. "I want to change into something more romantic."

Though he liked her just the way she was, he supposed it would be a good idea to check up on the kids. "I'll walk you back," he said, "unless you're staying on the Right Bank now."

"No—Gunther and I prefer the Left; it's still the real Paris, as far as I'm concerned."

He dropped some francs on the table and followed her out of the little maze of tables. They walked up the Boulevard to the Rue Cardinal, then another two blocks to the Rue des Grandes Ecoles. He was struggling a bit with his conscience. Perhaps he had been *too* impetuous. What would the kids say? Didn't they have some rights?

Ah, but it was just as it had been twenty years ago, he thought, when his tedious conscience, his curiously conventional cast of mind, had required him to return to the States (to a career, to duty, to discipline) when he might have accepted her offer to stay on in Europe, to live off her meager earnings for a year, to give his writing a chance, et cetera. What might their life have been? What fabulous things might they have done?

Yet nothing, he saw, was ever really lost. Discovering her here in Paris this afternoon he seemed to have filled those twenty intervening years with a romance, a happiness of their own. She hadn't changed. Nor had he. Apologies were still difficult for both of them, but somehow, thank God, they got made.

They came to a small gate in a discolored white wall. She led the way down a narrow cobbled lane to a large courtyard where a single chestnut tree spread its boughs and a variety of weeds and flowers blossomed in its rock-ledged shade. They entered a door in a tall white house with green shutters, passed through a small lobby, climbed a flight of creaking stairs, followed a dark and treacherously sloping corridor. She took out a key and, giving him a temptress's smile over a flirtatious shoulder, unlocked a door.

Two children looked up at their entrance. The boy was sprawled on one of the two beds, sniffing air up a stuffy nose and reading a science fiction paperback. The little girl was playing with paper dolls at the desk.

"Hi, Mom. Hi, Dad—where ya been?" the boy asked.

"Oh, just having a drink," Liz said. "Timothy, can you take your sister across the street for dinner this evening? Your father has something planned—for just the two of us."

"Kee-rumm," Timothy said, but not as if he meant to make an issue of it.

Gerhardt went over to the window to look down into the courtyard and off across the rooftops of Paris. He thought for a moment that he caught a strain of familiar music on the warm summer breeze, but it was only a TV from the house across the court.

EDGAR BOWERS

Edgar Bowers came to Stanford in 1947, to study with Yvor Winters; he received the M.A. degree in 1947 and the Ph.D. in 1953. Since 1958, he has lived on the Miramar Beach in Santa Barbara.

"These poems were written for Yvor Winters's class in the Writing of Verse: 'The Stoic' in 1948 and 'Tyndale' in 1950."

◆   ◆   ◆

The Stoic: for Laura von Courten

All winter long you listened for the boom
Of distant cannon wheeled into their place.
Sometimes outside beneath a bombers' moon
You stood alone to watch the searchlights trace

Their careful webs against the boding sky,
While miles away on Munich's vacant square
The bombs lunged down with an unruly cry
Whose blast you saw yet could but faintly hear.

And might have turned your eyes upon the gleam
Of a thousand years of snow, where near the clouds
The Alps ride massive to their full extreme,
And season after season glacier crowds

The dark, persistent smudge of conifers.
Or seen beyond the hedge and through the trees
The shadowy forms of cattle on the furze,
Their dim coats white with mist against the freeze.

Or thought instead of other times than these,
Of other countries and of other sights:
Eternal Venice sinking by degrees
Into the very water that she lights;

Reflected in canals, the lucid dome
Of Maria dell'Salute at your feet,

Her triple spires disfigured by the foam.
Remembered in Berlin the parks, the neat

Footpaths and lawns, the clean spring foliage,
Where just short weeks before, a bomb, unaimed,
Released a frightened lion from its cage,
Which in the mottled dark that trees enflamed

Killed one who hurried homeward from the raid.
And by yourself there standing in the chill
You must, with so much known, have been afraid
And chosen such a mind of constant will,

Which, though all time corrode with constant hurt,
Remains, until it occupies no space,
That which it is; and passionless, inert,
Becomes at last no meaning and no place.

◆　　　◆　　　◆

From William Tyndale to John Frith*

The letters I, your lone friend, write in sorrow
Will not contain my sorrow: it is mine,
Not yours who stand for burning in my place.
Be certain of your fate. Though some, benign,
Will urge by their sweet threats malicious love
And counsel dangerous fear of violence,
Theirs is illusion's goodness proving fair—
Against your wisdom—worldly innocence
And just persuasions' old hypocrisy.
Making their choice, reflect what you become;
Horror and misery bringing ruin where
The saintly mind has treacherously gone numb;
Despair in the deceit of your remorse
As, doubly heretic, you waste your past
Recanting, by all pitied, honorless,
Until you choose more easy death at last.
Think too of me. Sometimes in morning dark
I let my candle gutter and sit here
Brooding, as shadows fill my cell and sky
Breaks pale outside my window; then the dear
Companionship we spent working for love
Compels me to achieve a double portion.
In spite of age, insanity, despair,
Grief, or declining powers, we have done
What passes to the living of all men
Beyond our weariness. The fire shall find

Me hidden here, although its pain be less
If you have gone to it with half my mind,
Leaving me still enough to fasten flesh
Against the stake, flesh absolute with will.
And should your human powers and my need
Tremble at last and grow faint, worn, and ill,
Pain be too much to think of, fear destroy,
And animal reluctance from the womb,
Endurance of your end's integrity,
Be strong in this: heaven shall be your tomb.

*John Frith, Tyndale's most loyal disciple, returned to England from the continent in 1533, when he was thirty years old. He was arrested and burned at the stake. This letter would have been written to Frith in prison from Tyndale in Holland, where, not long after, he too was imprisoned and burned at the stake for heresy.

BLANCHE McCRARY BOYD

Blanche McCrary Boyd has written two novels, Nerves *(1973) and* Mourning the Death of Magic *(1977). A collection of her autobiographical journalism,* The Redneck Way of Knowledge, *appeared in 1982. Her stories and essays have appeared in* Esquire, Vogue, Vanity Fair, *and* The Village Voice. *She is currently Writer-in-Residence at Connecticut College.*

"During a ten-year hiatus from writing fiction, I accidentally became a journalist, and, as a journalist, I had to learn to write in the first person. This technique, which previously escaped me, has proven quite useful; nevertheless, I was astounded when an editor asked why I wasn't presenting my new short stories as memoirs. Because they're not, I finally said."

◆   ◆   ◆

My Town

ACT I: A Typical Day

WHEN I WAS IN 11th grade, my English teacher, Mr. Harrison, dropped his college ring down Jimmie Lucas's shirt, then reached inside to retrieve it. Mr. Harrison had been to military college and perhaps thought such behavior could be passed off as horseplay.

He'd been reading *Our Town* to us out loud. Most students at Plaxton High School majored in Home Economics or Agriculture, and Mr. Harrison had been teaching there for 15 years. At some point in his career he had probably discussed literature and assigned papers, but by the time I was in his class, we diagrammed sentences or else he read to us. There was no point in giving assignments, because we didn't do them.

In the first act of *Our Town*, one typical day in Grover's Corners, New Hampshire, is described, and I was as bored by Mr. Harrison's droning as everyone else when Jimmie Lucas raised his hand. "Bill," he said, "are you sure you went to VMI? Do they even *have* English majors at VMI?" Jimmie smiled winningly, baring his large white teeth. We were not allowed to call Mr. Harrison by his first name.

Jimmie had a blond waxed flattop and the most attractive collarbones I'd ever seen. He'd ridden in the back seat with me the week before, on the way home from a basketball tournament. My friend Marla arranged it. Jimmie wasn't sexually interested in me, but at certain ages certain invitations are irresistible. He'd kissed me several times, and I was so thrilled to have my fantasy fulfilled that I couldn't actually feel anything. "I don't much want to do this," he kept saying, nibbling wetly on my neck, "I've got to play again tomorrow night." I kissed him back woodenly, worried about what to do with my tongue. "Jesus," he groaned after a while, leaning back and pointing to the crotch of his warm-up pants. "You've done it to me now. This is your fault."

"What?" I said, refusing to look down.

"I *knew* this would happen," he said. "*Look* at it."

I stared hard at the couple in the front seat, who were pretending to be deaf. "Jimmie," I said, inspired, "what do you think of Mr. Harrison?"

"He's a queer," Jimmie snarled at the fogged window beside him. "Everybody knows that."

"But what do you think of him?"

"I think he's a queer."

I tried a different approach. "If you could have anything in the world you wanted, what would it be?"

He looked darkly hopeful. "I'll show you," he said, grabbing my wrist.

I snatched my hand away. "I mean really, Jimmie. What would you want?"

"A Corvette," he said, folding his arms across his chest. He shut his eyes and pretended to be asleep.

Outside the other back window, which was unfogged by Jimmie's distress, I watched the South Carolina landscape go by. Or, rather, I watched the dark and caught glimpses of Spanish moss in live oak trees, stands of scrub pine, the shacks where black people lived. White people's houses were few. The Low-country was mostly black in the rural areas, and the schools had not yet been integrated. Our district was over 30 miles long, and the trips to ball games were tedious. I was disappointed about Jimmie, so I composed a new note for Mr. Harrison:

> *When you're driving your car*
> *and relief seems too far*
> *remember that suffering is always random*
> *But you are protected by your friend*
> *The Phantom.*

I had begun these notes a few weeks ago, scribbling them on Mr. Harrison's blackboard before class. One I even left on the dashboard of his car. He seemed very happy about them.

Mr. Harrison was a tall, masculine man, but his buttocks were a bit thick, probably from sitting down for 15 years, and he had a generous mouth that the boys took to be an indication of his homosexuality. "I know what he does with those rubber lips," I once heard Jimmie's friend Cliff say.

In English class Jimmie flirted contemptuously with Mr. Harrison, both to entertain the rest of us and to stall the readings. Mr. Harrison always fell for Jimmie's insolence, stopping whatever he was doing to smile and chat.

"VMI was tougher than the army," he said. "I promise you it was tougher than playing basketball."

"Why weren't *you* in the army?" Cliff asked. Cliff was a burly boy with little, blinky eyes.

Mr. Harrison smiled. "Somebody had to bring y'all some culture."

Perhaps this is why I liked Mr. Harrison: I had never heard the word *irony*, but I was attracted to it.

"Cliff," Mr. Harrison said, "you aren't by any chance the Phantom, are you?"

"Nah," Cliff said, "it's Jimmie."

I was hurt by this exchange. Neither Cliff nor Jimmie was smart enough to rhyme anything, even partially.

"Let me see your ring," Jimmie said.

Mr. Harrison hesitated, then rose from his desk and walked toward Jimmie. Maybe he just wanted to stand next to him. I could understand that. He handed Jimmie his ring.

Jimmie examined it and threw it to Cliff, who was sitting beside me.

Mr. Harrison didn't know what to do, so he just stood there. After a few seconds, Cliff threw it back, and Mr. Harrison's hand snatched it out of the air right in front of Jimmie's.

Jimmie grabbed Mr. Harrison's wrist and they struggled. "Here, you want it so much," Mr. Harrison said, and he dropped the ring down the back of Jimmie's shirt.

The class was very quiet except for the sound of their breathing. No one quite knew what to do. It was English class and something wrong had happened.

"I'll get it," Mr. Harrison said in his grown-up teacher's tone, reaching his hand matter-of-factly inside Jimmie's shirt.

Jimmie leaped from his seat. I could see him trembling. He pulled out his shirt tail and the ring hit the linoleum floor with a brief, metallic sound. It rolled toward me and stopped right by my penny loafer. I picked it up. It was a heavy gold school ring with a blue stone.

Mr. Harrison looked grateful as I handed it to him. He went back to his desk and took up reading *Our Town*.

It's hard to explain what happened next. The class was tense, unhappy, unnerved, and so we began to listen desperately to *Our Town*.

Dr. Gibbs was chastising his son George for not doing his chores and leaving his mother to chop wood. The play was set in 1900 and it was 1962, but I didn't think that could account for all the differences. My father had died at work when a cinder block fell on him; Jimmie's father was a butcher at Mack's Meats. Cliff's father was our town doctor, and, as everyone knew, he beat Cliff: that's where the scars on Cliff's back came from.

The play continued. Dr. Gibbs was disgruntled because Mrs. Gibbs was staying too long at choir practice. I began to giggle. The women, on the way home from choir practice, stopped on the corner to gossip about the town drunk: "Really, it's the worst scandal that ever was in this town!"

I was trying to stop giggling when Mrs. Gibbs arrived home and Dr. Gibbs complained, "You're late enough," and Mrs. Gibbs replied, "Now Frank, don't be grouchy. Come out and smell my heliotrope in the moonlight."

I began to laugh out loud. I didn't know what heliotrope was, and this remark struck me as hilariously off-color.

Mr. Harrison stopped reading. I had my head down on the desk but I knew he was looking at me. "Try to get hold of yourself," he said. The irony was back in his voice.

But this laughter was like nothing that had ever happened to me, except grief.

My face felt hot, my contact lenses were floating off my eyes. I gripped the edges of my desk as Mr. Harrison continued to read. The laughter was worse than hiccups. It wasn't even funny.

A few minutes later Mr. Webb, Dr. Gibbs's neighbor, went up to his daughter's room to see why she wasn't in bed. "I just can't sleep yet, Papa," she said. "The moonlight's so *won*-derful. And the smell of Mrs. Gibbs's heliotrope. Can you smell it?"

A howling noise escaped me. I began to pound on my desk.

"My dear," Mr. Harrison said, "heliotrope is a flower."

I stood up, squinting to hold my lenses in place. I could hardly breathe, much less speak. The laughter was brutalizing me with its terrible release. I was no longer sure if I was laughing or crying.

Now Mr. Harrison sounded concerned. "Do you want to go home?"

I pulled my books against my chest, nodding.

"Go by the office," he said.

I struggled down the hallway, still laughing, my face soaked. In the principal's office I couldn't speak so I wrote a note to the secretary and pushed it across her desk: "GOING HOME. CAN'T STOP LAUGHING."

ACT II: Love and Marriage

Nine years passed.

Jimmie married Marla's other friend, Janine. He inherited Mack's Meats, and he and Janine had two children. Soon after birth the girl died of spinal meningitis; the boy is peculiar and timid.

Right out of high school Cliff surprised everyone by marrying Marla. Through luck and accidents he became a successful antique dealer in Charleston, 30 miles away from Plaxton. Cliff has learned to talk comfortably and grammatically about Edwardian, Victorian, or antebellum, but on Sundays he remains content to watch ball games on TV with Jimmie while Marla and Janine make chili or fried chicken and pies with Cool Whip on top.

Mr. Harrison developed a hearing problem and had to leave teaching. He has become a furniture restorer, a job he can do in his own garage. Sometimes he does freelance work for his former student Cliff.

I moved to California and became enmeshed in a number of pursuits I considered revolutionary and beautiful. I have returned to South Carolina to tell my mother that, like Mr. Harrison, I am homosexual.

The action begins.

"It makes me want to throw up," my mother says.

We are driving in her Mercedes to the country club to have dinner and play bingo. My mother does not really like her Mercedes, so she is letting me drive it. She bought it because she can afford it, but a Datsun, she has decided, is a superior car.

"You don't like this car because you've gained too much weight to be comfortable under the steering wheel." We are pulling out of the driveway past the guardhouse.

"The steering wheel is too large and it is incorrectly placed."

"I think the steering wheel's all right."

My mother is wearing a red jersey dress and lots of gold jewelry. She will limp tomorrow from her high heels. I am wearing a black dress and high heels to prove to her that I still like being a woman. My feet will hurt tomorrow too.

We pull into the country club parking lot and park under the moss-draped arms of a huge live oak tree. When I come around the car to open her door and help her out, I kiss her on the cheek. "Does that make you want to throw up?"

My mother is shorter than I am, and much heavier. The woman I have changed my life over is taller and angular, and when I embrace her, it is nothing like kissing my mother on the cheek.

She hugs me miserably. "Honey, I'm just afraid people will try to hurt you about this."

"I'm afraid too, Momma."

"Couldn't you change your mind?"

"I don't think so." Over her shoulder, beyond the smooth green fairway, I watch the Ashley River slide turbidly by.

Cliff and Jimmie are watching the same slow-moving river through the plate-glass window in Jimmie's den. "I always wanted to live on this river," Jimmie says. He says this every Sunday, but today there is something vague in his voice, something about loss.

"You did it, Bo." This is what Cliff always says too. Cliff has just closed a deal on an 18th century house in Charleston, and his voice is as wistful as Jimmie's.

Jimmie does not want Cliff to move away from Plaxton. It's one thing to work in Charleston, but moving there is another.

"It's too far from my store out here, Bo. Ain't nobody in Plaxton gonna buy my anty-cues."

Jimmie closes the curtain. He is thinking about butchers' wounds. Butchers are always slicing toward their abdomens, and sometimes they get cut. His father cut himself once in 20 years, perforating his intestine, but it was lung cancer that killed him. Janine hates the duck pattern on the curtains, but Jimmie insisted. "My daddy always wanted to live on this river," he says.

My mother is winning at bingo. She plays so many cards she has to put some on an extra chair beside the table. She mumbles for the caller, an adenoidal, bored young woman, to slow down. "Honey, why don't you tell her to slow down." My mother is too polite to complain to anyone directly.

"I'm too well brought up to do any such thing." But when I go up to collect one of my mother's $25 prizes, I convey her request. The girl gives me a bovine look and nods. Southerners are as polite as cattle, except when they're not. When they're not, they might shoot you or chase you around the yard with a hatchet.

"Thank you, honey," my mother whispers when I have reseated myself at the table.

Later, at home, she will tie a pair of underpants around her head. "It just works better than anything to protect my hairdo. I know it looks silly."

In pajamas we will have a nightcap, bourbon for her, brandy for me, and keep the television running in the background. On the news is a picture of Bobby Seale tied to a chair with his mouth taped shut. His trial has been severed from the trial of the rest of the Chicago Eight. They have become the Chicago Seven.

"My father's sister was...," my mother says. "Of course we didn't call it... we didn't call it anything."

"How did you know she was? You can call it gay."

"Well, she lived with another woman who was younger than she was, and she raised her child with her. Also, she was mannish."

"Do you think I'm mannish?"

"And cousin Bryce, when he was going to marry that girl he brought home for Christmas? Then he excused himself from dinner and went upstairs and shot himself? I think he was too."

"Do you think I'm mannish?"

"Gay seems like such an inappropriate word."

"Thank you for trying to give me the family history."

Jimmie and Cliff are watching the same newscast. Their wives have fallen asleep on the sofa. The popcorn has spilled onto the coffee table. "How'm I gonna get her into the car?" Cliff says. He is drunk, and Jimmie is drunk too.

"Look at that nigger," Jimmie says when the picture of Bobby Seale tied to his chair comes on. "I'm glad somebody burned the high school down. So much for going to school with them."

Cliff raises Marla's limp arm and drops it. "I guess she's not driving."

"Remember those pig balls?" Jimmie says. "Only good thing we learned in agriculture. Castrating pigs." He makes a noise that is half whispered but high-pitched like a scream.

Janine stirs on the sofa without waking.

"If I close one eye I see fine," Cliff says, "but I've got to drive with two."

"On Harrison's doorstep. With a note from the Phantom. Old Harrison, old rubber lips. He probably thought it was a compliment. He probably thought that weird girl did it. The one who laughed." Jimmie is dropping more popcorn onto the floor, piece by piece.

Cliff is suddenly angry. He helps Marla to her feet. "Don't be stupid, Jimmie. Of course he knew we did it. Of course he knew that."

Ten months after I return to California, my lover leaves me for a man who wears his shirts half buttoned, exposing a chestful of hair and gold chains. She has grown her nails long and painted them red. "I just couldn't handle it," she says.

"It?" My lover has been an active participant in the women's movement who said the word *lesbian* as easily as my mother said *Republican*. "What about being revolutionaries? What about custody of the cats?"

"My shrink says I was going through a phase. You can keep the cats."

We are standing close to each other, but I am looking at the poster of Emma Goldman on the wall behind her. "Don't you think you could have figured this out about yourself a bit sooner?"

For several months I lie in bed listening to Linda Ronstadt records. Linda Ronstadt, I become certain, understands suffering. Cocaine is financially out of reach, so I drink half gallons of wine, smoke marijuana, and inhale hundreds of hits of laughing gas. Nitrous oxide is the propellant for whipped cream dispensers. Dealers sell the cartridges with a small instrument that empties them into balloons. I don't laugh much, but my lungs develop enough to inhale an entire balloon in one breath.

ACT III: Death

Mr. Harrison liked the mall. It was a safe place to walk, and his doctor had told him to walk. He couldn't go to bars anymore because the music hurt his ears, and going to the Battery to cruise wasn't safe at his age. But in the bright artificial light of the mall he could walk and look. The smooth, careless bodies of the young were a kind of museum, and he felt harmless enough, looking.

When he was tired, he would sit in the center of the mall where the fountain was. The noise of the water was soothing.

My mother and I found him there, eating a cup of frozen yogurt. He was wearing a plaid wool shirt, and his gray hair was combed neatly. His eyes had the dreamy quality the hard of hearing sometimes develop.

"Look," my mother said. "Isn't that your old high school English teacher? Mr. Harrison?"

My mother had recently had a face-lift, and it was too soon for her to be out in public. She still looked bruised and puffy and garish. "Like Frankenstein," she'd said cheerfully, putting on her sweat suit that morning. My mother had 12 identical sweat suits, all in different colors. Today she was wearing powder pink, with dark glasses.

"Yes, it is." I was holding my mother's elbow. When she'd asked me to take care of her during her recovery, I'd been touched, and I was taking my duties seriously.

"Bill!" my mother said gaily, as if they'd been friends for years. "Look who's home!"

Mr. Harrison looked alarmed as my mother seized his hand. He didn't recognize either of us at first. I'd been out of high school 25 years and my hair was streaked with gray; my mother looked as if she'd been beaten up in a barroom fight.

"Ellen?" Mr. Harrison said.

"One and the same," I said.

He fumbled with his yogurt cup. "My stars. I thought you'd never come back to this little town. I thought you were too big for us."

"She is! She is!" my mother said. "She lives in Boston now and works for a publisher! She's just come home to help me with my face-lift. Don't I look like Frankenstein?"

"You remember my mother," I said.

Late the next afternoon I drove out to Plaxton in my mother's vintage Mercedes. The car was 15 years old, seasoned, and comfortable, and, according to my mother, the best car she'd ever had. The offending steering wheel had been replaced by a signed mahogany Nardian she'd ordered from the Beverly Hills Motoring Accessories Catalog and then tried to install herself. "For a hobby. I need a hobby." Luckily, she did the automobile no serious damage.

The road across the marshes had become a divided highway. At Rantowles River, I noticed that the huge oak tree that used to hang into the water was gone. The banks had been cleared, and where the tree once was a small ranch house had been built. The house had a picture window, but the curtains were closed.

Past Rantowles, the road was a familiar two-lane blacktop that the fecund brush crowded toward. In clearings were the same old shacks or small brick houses. A black snake slithered across the pavement. In the distance the road looked shiny, wet. "It's a mirage," my father told me when I was a little girl. "The heat causes it." I loved the word *mirage* and would say it over and over, looking at the end of the road.

In Plaxton, the Chevrolet dealer still looked as if he only stocked two or three cars. The drugstore was boarded up, but a combination convenience store and gas station was new. Mack's Meats had expanded. Instead of being a small cinder block building, it was a larger cinder block building.

I pulled in beside the phone booth near the gas pumps at the convenience store and sat there for a few minutes. It was cool in the air-conditioned car, but I was sweating. Finally I got out and called my apartment in Boston.

Meg's voice, husky and mocking, answered on the tape machine: "This is Tammy Faye Bakker. Jim and I can't come to the phone now, because we're praying over my hairdo, trying to get it to go down . . ."

"Meg," I said after the beep, "I hate these damn phone jokes. I guess I don't have much of a sense of humor when I'm down here. Picture this. I'm standing in a parking lot across from Mack's Meats in Plaxton, South Carolina, and the man I lost my virginity to is probably over there. It's too damn hot down here. I miss you. My mother is too weird. It's all too weird. Tonight I'm going to dinner at my high school English teacher's house. I'll call back tonight. I miss you."

The asphalt was sticky under my tennis shoes.

"Is Jimmie here?" I asked the girl behind the counter. There were no customers in the store. The girl, slight and bored, looked familiar. One of the Glendennings, I decided. She directed me through a doorway to Jimmie's cluttered office.

He was sitting behind a metal desk, punching figures into an adding machine. We'd both aged, but "Ellen!" he shouted, "is it really Ellen?" and hugged me hard.

Behind him, on the wall, hung a cookie tin cover with a reproduction of "Blue Boy" on it. Below Blue Boy was a collection of basketball trophies. Jimmie's body had thickened, but he still felt fine. "You always had the best collarbones," I said into his neck.

"Yeah, well . . ." He pulled away.

"How's Janine?"

"Fine, fine. Did you see my daughter out there? We finally had another daughter. She's on the junior varsity." When he smiled I saw that one of his teeth had been capped. The cap had a bluish cast.

We sat and passed time for a few minutes. There was a map of a steer on the wall, each part labeled with the cuts of meat it provided. Jimmie's daughter brought us coffee. I could see, now, how much she looked like Janine. The fact that there were no customers was misleading. Jimmie did mostly slaughtering, and business was good. "Janine's gotten fat as a house. You wouldn't believe it." He laughed appreciatively, a tone I recognized. A week after I'd ridden home from the basketball tournament with him, I'd gone out to Jimmie's house on some excuse. He'd taken me for a ride in his two-tone green Rambler with the fold-down seats. We'd parked in the woods, and he'd laughed at my trembling in that same exultant way.

"Jimmie, did you used to be taller? When you played basketball?"

He frowned. "I played guard."

Dinner at Bill Harrison's house began awkwardly. He was lonely, he said, and he'd burned the pork chops. Did I like opera?

His house, low-ceilinged and airless, was jumbled with broken antiques. "I don't know much about opera." He turned down the scratchy record he was playing. His stereo was of obviously poor quality, a weekend special from some discount house.

"Cliff loved it. He gave me this record. It's a rare recording. Very rare."

"Cliff from high school? *Cliff?*"

He nodded, smiling. "Cliff died last year, you know."

"Cliff died?" I realized I was beginning to sound stupid. "I'm sorry. It's just that I saw Jimmie today, and he didn't tell me."

"Well, they grew apart."

Over his shoulder I saw a framed 8 x 10 photograph on an end table. Cliff's small, blinky eyes stared out of it. Mr. Harrison turned and picked it up and handed it to me.

I spoke carefully. "I didn't know."

"I worked for him some, restoring furniture. Marla had a bad time, but I think she's all right now. She's a sweet girl."

"What did he die of?"

"Cancer."

We sat down at his kitchen dinette set. Its plastic wood contrasted with the faded antiques in the rest of the house. "Bill," I said, "did you know I'm gay too?"

He was pouring iced tea for us and hadn't heard.

"Bill," I said when he was looking at me, "I wanted you to know I'm gay."

Emotions rushed across his face. "Cliff told me."

"How . . ."

"He was an antique dealer, you know, and he found out these things."

"Cliff was . . . Bill, did Cliff die of AIDS?"

"Of course not," he said quickly, handing me the bowl of red rice. "Cliff was happily married. I worked for him. That was all."

I understood that he was lying to me, and I was sorry. He'd probably made his decision to lie about Cliff long ago. I would have liked for us to talk. I would have liked to tell him about the hard 10 years I'd had, the confusion and self-hatred, before something resembling acceptance had come to me. A treatment center for drug addiction had helped. So had meeting Meg. "It's nice to see you again" was all I said.

He looked grateful, watching my lips. "It's nice to see you too."

I tried to think of a question that wouldn't intrude. "How did you and Cliff get to know each other?"

He clutched his fork, and his faded eyes lightened. "In high school he used to write these notes on my blackboard and sign them The Phantom. Do you remember the Phantom?"

I nodded and looked down, concentrating on cutting my pork chop.

"Well, he wrote me a very mean one and left me something mean, on my doorstep. I won't say what. Then he came to my house to apologize, and we talked."

The pork chops really were burned. The red rice was flavorless, and the broccoli was frozen, served from a boiled plastic bag. I looked Bill right in the eyes. "That's a wonderful story."

After dinner I lay sprawled on his sofa drinking cup after cup of instant coffee while he played his scratchy opera records for me. He sat in a pink Victorian wing chair with his head tilted back, and once tears ran down his face. "Can you hear it?" he kept saying. "Can you hear it?"

"I hear it," I said.

NORΛ CΛIN

Nora Cain (b. 1952) graduated from Gonzaga University in 1974. In 1977, she was a Stegner Fellow in poetry at Stanford. After teaching in the freshman English program for a year, she became a Jones Lecturer in poetry. She has two small daughters, and, for the present, she has traded in technical writing for full-time motherhood, and looks back nostalgically to forty-hour work weeks. She is married to Kenneth Fields and together they are Resident Fellows at Robinson House, a dorm at Stanford. Her poems have appeared in Gramercy Review and Sequoia.

"These poems are taken from a sequence entitled 'A Treasury of Quilts' and are concerned equally with the intricacies of quilting and the attending states of mind that the quilt names evoke."

◆　　　◆　　　◆

Drunkard's Path

This quilt creates a sense of lost balance and perspective by the interplay of curved and straight pieces, set against each other so that no curve is ever fully completed and no straight line meets another straight line. Because of the difficulty in sewing curved pieces together without puckering or buckling, this is considered a pattern for the expert.

She was familiar with the turns
of the heart and mind—the intricate
patterns of light and dark
changing without warning
and back again, as if the block
were set straight to the edge
and had never varied—
she could see them in her sleep.
Cutting along the edge of a pattern,
the familiar truths, manageable
as cotton, shifted under her hand
and the sharp angulations,
difficult to piece, fell into place
and were understood.
She came to feel
that only she could control the treacherous,

snaking design, too full of curves
and odd pieces for the beginner, the uninitiated.

She pierced it again and again,
the needle, sharp as a tongue,
glinted in her hand
taming the chaos, making it all lay
flat and calm and known
as the world had once been.

♦   ♦   ♦

Darting Minnows

The minnows are actually small diamonds that run across the quilt in an open cross-hatch design. Tossed on a bed, or over a sleeping person, the pattern seems to move like small fish.

Sleep children, and dream of the rain,
the steep whisper of the run-off,
the heavy loam settling in the fields,
and the unquenchable green of spring wheat
filling the land.

Sleep, and forget the rasp
of the thistle on the screen, the
hopeless chant of the cricket rising
above the scalded earth.

Sleep, and I'll spread over you this dream of water;
the quilt's shifting patterns
slide like the slow moving river,
and in the darkest blue,
under the shadow of the willow, where you hang your feet,
the tiny diamonds, now white,
now silver, flash like the minnows,
and you feel their curious kisses
before they move upstream.

♦   ♦   ♦

Grief Quilt

This is not a particular pattern but a genre in which the quilt serves as an expression of the seamstress's grief. No two grief quilts are alike but it was popular to appliqué fences along the quilt's borders, creating a cemetery in the center. Coffins and gravestones were cut from the garments of loved ones who had died.

Against this stark ground of white,
the iron fence, webbing of bushes,

and bare trees reach out from the
meticulous order of death.
I keep them here—husband, children, friends—
away from the distractions of summer;
the rank confusion of daylilies, ubiquitous
weeds and wildflowers, cloying honeysuckle.

Nothing grows above the stones, losses
are never blurred or worn from the heart,
and with these stitches I make
a kind of hybrid life, more stable and kind
than any I have known.

At night my hands trace over the border of coffins
and I read once more the stories of my days:
the soft batiste of the baby's gown,
a daughter's party dress crackles under my touch,
and from my husband's best suit,
the fragrance of his pipe.

Under the weight of my grief,
I turn in the dark
honing my losses like the scythe
that will carry me, dreamless and vigilant,
into their midst.

MICHELLE CARTER

Michelle Carter was an undergraduate, a graduate student, and a Jones Lecturer at Stanford. Her first novel, On Other Days While Going Home, *was published by Morrow in 1987 and Penguin in 1988. She has published short fiction in* Playgirl, Grand Street, *and various literary magazines, plus the anthologies* 20 Under 30 *and* The New Generation. *She received an N.E.A. grant in 1987. She is currently an assistant professor of creative writing at San Francisco State University.*

"One day, after a series of brutal assaults on elderly women in her neighborhood, my not-elderly mother announced that she intended to buy a gun. Though her police officer friend Debbie had offered to teach her to use it, the thought preoccupied and worried me. What was it about her getting that gun? I suppose this story came of trying, to use John L'Heureux's words, to 'tighten the circle of mystery' around whatever it is we're all in for."

Sister

WE'RE SITTING ON SISTER'S roof, her brand new gun resting on her lap. Tomorrow her friend Betsy the cop is going to teach her how to use it. Sister probably doesn't have any bullets yet, my only comfort. She brought that thing up here purely to irk me.

We're not roof sitters by nature, Sister and I. This is some new thing we've taken on in our thirties, now that we can scramble onto treacherous places without pretending to be fearless or graceful. We seem to head for the roof when Sister's most frustrated and angry, whenever there's something she can't stand, something she can't do anything about. We dig our heels into the gritty tar, lean back with our elbows on two cushions she keeps in the attic. The slope isn't very steep and the house is only one story high. We can see only the length of this block and a few junk-strewn backyards.

Sister points to one of the houses, the gun still on her lap. The house is a cotton-candy pink, but the curtains are drawn and the windows are dark.

"That's Mrs. Filbert's lawn, there," she says. "See the path to the backyard? That's where they grabbed her. Going out the back door with her basket of laundry."

"Whites?" I say. "Colors? Delicates?"

"Hand washables," she says. "Lingerie." Sister often takes pains to ignore my tone. She says sarcasm is not going to protect me from anything.

Three old women on Sister's block have been robbed this month. Betsy calls her every night with details from the police reports. We've known Betsy the cop since high school, when she was blonde and slim-hipped, and more envied than loved. Who knew anything about the world back then?

"Mrs. Inge was a week ago tonight," Sister says. "To think of her, tied up with a drapery cord, one of her own afghans thrown over her head."

"Hey," I say, "a new touch! Her own afghan. I like it."

I watch her and wait for a wounded look, a flash of anger, a wave of the gun maybe. Nothing. She only stares off toward Mrs. Filbert's lawn. So here I sit, the bad little sister, making light of violence against old ladies. Mrs. Inge even gave me a fruitcake last Christmas. I'm ashamed of myself, then not. There is something behind all this. I look at the gun, just resting there, and Sister half-reclining and unaware, as though it were some knitting she might or might not get to. As if it were binoculars. The remote control for the TV. How do I know there aren't bullets in that thing? I will not give in and ask her about it.

"How's Betsy?" I say.

"Pregnant," she says.

"Again?"

"Sure," she says. "Why not? Four marriages, four babies. She said this morning that she likes to have a baby with every man she marries. Nice hobby, I told her—sort of like stealing an ashtray from every casino you gamble in."

I'm not sure why she sounds so bitter. But then I haven't always understood what makes Sister unhappy.

"Maybe she'll end up staying with this guy," I say, "this Anthony."

"Arthur," she says. "She might stay. Now."

Betsy and Sister had planned to go to Paris next Spring. Betsy had talked Arthur into taking care of the two kids who still lived at home. With the oldest gone and the youngest in junior high, it was looking as if Betsy might be freeing herself up, might be able someday soon to be with a man or not, based on reasons of her own, not just the reasons of a mother. Sister never wanted a husband or kids. She and Betsy had talked about going to Paris as if it stood for something.

"Well," I say. "At least all that talk about Paris got you taking French."

"French," she says. "There's one ridiculous language."

"Come on," I say. "You loved it." There's only so much you can blame a language for things.

"Example," she says. "*Que voulez-vous.*"

I wait, but she just looks at me. "I don't know what you're saying," I say. "Something to do with 'you want.'"

"Maybe," she says. "But you never know. Those three words, in that order, could mean any of four things: 'What do you want?' 'What's to be done?' 'What can you expect?' Or 'It can't be helped.'"

"So," I say. "That's three less phrases you've got to learn."

"No," she says. "That's not the point. The important part is being able to understand what you hear. And how the hell can you understand if a single phrase could mean four different things?"

She's tapping an index finger on the handle of that gun. I let myself look, stare it down: It's not sleek and silver like our old cowgirl six-shooters. It's a flat, dull black; it's smaller than Sister's outstretched hand.

"Okay," I say. "What is that thing doing up here with us?"

Sister laughs. I realize the question surprises her. "I'm just trying it out," she says. "For the feel of it, from up here." She points again to Mrs. Filbert's house. "We're not so far from there, you know."

At first I think she's talking about distance, about how, given a good, strong New England gale and a bottle of burgundy, we could push off from this roof and land square on Mrs. Filbert's lawn. Then I think of how three children passed through Mrs. Filbert's womb, how they probably have their own houses and lawns. That's when I remember the afghan, the drapery cord. Just trying it out, Sister said, for the feel of it. For the feel of what, I'd like to know.

A moving van rumbles by and I feel the house shudder beneath us. Sister sits up, touches her fingertips to the gun to keep it from sliding off her lap.

"A van," she says. "One of the witnesses I.D.'ed a van after Mrs. Filbert's assault. Was there anything written on it? Did you see?"

She's leaning forward, farther, watching the van blink right, stop, turn.

"Damn," she's saying. "Did you see it?"

I see her holding that gun, pressing it to her chest like something dear. Will pregnant Betsy take her out to the practice range tomorrow? Will she show Sister how to fill the chamber, the empty outline of a villain in her sights?

Sister's on her knees now, leaning over the edge of the roof.

"Damn it," I call out. "*Careful.*" I grab her arm, she's startled, she wrestles it from me. The gun drops between her knees and bounces on the tar. Sister slides a bit, tries to slap her foot onto the gun, finally trapping it at the roof's edge. She holds steady there, leaning back to keep her balance, her leg out stiff, the gun under her foot.

We're quiet for a time, neither of us moves. When Sister looks up at me, we break into a laugh. We laugh till we're holding our stomachs, till our eyes are wet; we're loud enough to disturb Mrs. Filbert, though the curtains don't stir. When Sister bends her leg and releases the gun, it remains, secure, at the edge of the roof. We're just as we were, then, no harm has been done us. But when our laughing is over, what then do I hear? What is it I see falling slowly to earth?

RAYMOND CARVER

1939–1988

I can't turn around without seeing some evidence of Raymond Carver's presence in my life, and feeling his absence now. It was Ray who gave me the news that my first son was born, and Ray and Tess who sat up all night with that boy while the second was coming into the world. He found the house I still live in, and, through resolute and cunning machinations, got me the job I still hold. He helped me with my work. He was my dear friend. I will never stop missing him.

But I cannot do justice to Ray by pulling a long face and speaking in pained, lugubrious tones. Ray can't be remembered that way. Instead, whenever I start to talk about Ray with another of his friends, there are a few moments of ritual gravity and then we begin to remember him as he was—smart and funny and kind, boyish, loyal, tough, peasant-shrewd, fragile. We can't talk about Ray without telling stories, recalling things he said and did, not a few of them in the realm of outlawry, and then almost in spite of ourselves a strange joy, even hilarity, comes over us. And that is as it should be, because Ray made us feel this joy when he was alive and we most truly remember him when we let his memory bring it back to us.

Ray was the happiest man I ever knew. He was happy as we can only be happy when we have been brought to the brink of death and then spared for a while. He used to love telling the story about Dostoevsky's last-minute reprieve, and I always had the sense he was talking about himself too. He took nothing for granted. Every new day, every moment with his friends, every new story and poem was an astonishment to him. The good and loving life he shared with Tess Gallagher, the extraordinary respect his work inspired in all kinds of people—to Ray, these were miracles. At moments of particular happiness he would look around with pure wonder. "Things could be worse," he'd say.

He was entirely without pretense. Jim Heynen once told Ray a story about something strange that had happened to him. As Jim was coming out of a bank a bald eagle dropped a salmon bang on the hood of his car, which salmon Jim took home and ate. Not long after Jim told Ray this story he read a poem of Ray's in which an eagle drops a salmon at the poet's feet while he's out taking a walk. Later Jim asked Ray about it, asked if by chance Ray had made use of his story. "Well, Jim," he said, "I guess I must have, because I don't take walks."

Ray had this bedrock honesty about himself, and the effect was that you could be equally honest without fear of being judged. He took you as you were, with as little sanctity or heroism as you owned, so long as you did not pretend to more than you owned. There was absolute freedom in his company. One could, and did, reveal anything—Ray had an insatiable, uproarious appetite for stories on the human scale, stories about the endless losing war our good intentions wage against our circumstances and our nature. He was so greedy for these stories that one day I found myself confessing to something I hadn't done, just for the pleasure of seeing him shake his head and say, "It's a jungle out there, Toby, it's a jungle out there."

Chekhov wrote of his character Vassilyev that "he had a talent for humanity." Ray had that talent. Whatever was human interested him, most of all our struggle to survive without becoming less than human. This struggle shaped his life. His understanding of it, compassionate and profound, made him the great writer that he was, and the great friend.

—Tobias Wolff

RAYMOND CARVER

Raymond Carver was born in Clatskanie, Oregon, in 1939. A Stegner Fellow at Stanford in 1976, Carver received two grants from the N.E.A. and, in 1979, a Guggenheim Fellowship. In 1983, he received the Mildred and Harold Strauss Living Award. He published five collections of fiction, including What We Talk About When We Talk About Love *(1981),* Cathedral *(1983), and* Where I'm Calling From: New and Selected Stories *(1988). Carver died of lung cancer in August, 1988.*

"Errand" is Carver's fictionalized reinvention of Chekhov's final years of life. William Abrahams, who awarded the story first prize in the 1988 O. Henry collection, writes that because Chekhov believed he lacked "a political, religious, and philosophical world view," he chose instead to describe how his characters "love, marry, give birth, die, and how they speak." This has remained the homely task of many important and lasting twentieth-century writers—through Chekhov and Carver and, one expects, well beyond.

◆   ◆   ◆

Errand

CHEKHOV. ON THE EVENING of March 22, 1897, he went to dinner in Moscow with his friend and confidant Alexei Suvorin. This Suvorin was a very rich newspaper and book publisher, a reactionary, a self-made man whose father was a private at the battle of Borodino. Like Chekhov, he was the grandson of a serf. They had that in common: each had peasant's blood in his veins. Otherwise, politically and temperamentally, they were miles apart. Nevertheless, Suvorin was one of Chekhov's few intimates, and Chekhov enjoyed his company.

Naturally, they went to the best restaurant in the city, a former town house called the Hermitage—a place where it could take hours, half the night even, to get through a ten-course meal that would, of course, include several wines, liqueurs, and coffee. Chekhov was impeccably dressed, as always—a dark suit and waistcoat, his usual pince-nez. He looked that night very much as he looks in the photographs taken of him during this period. He was relaxed, jovial. He shook hands with the maître d', and with a glance took in the large dining room. It was brilliantly illuminated by ornate chandeliers, the tables occupied by elegantly dressed men and women. Waiters came and went ceaselessly. He had just been seated across the table from Suvorin when suddenly, without warning, blood began gushing from his mouth. Suvorin and two waiters helped him to the gentlemen's room and tried to stanch the flow of blood with ice packs. Suvorin saw him back to his own hotel and had a bed prepared for Chekhov in one of the rooms of the suite. Later, after another hemorrhage, Chekhov allowed himself to be moved to a clinic that specialized in the treatment of tuberculosis and related respiratory infections. When Suvorin visited him there, Chekhov apologized for the "scandal" at the restaurant three nights earlier but continued to insist there was nothing seriously wrong. "He laughed and jested as usual," Suvorin noted in his diary, "while spitting blood into a large vessel."

Maria Chekhov, his younger sister, visited Chekhov in the clinic during the last days of March. The weather was miserable; a sleet storm was in progress, and frozen heaps of snow lay everywhere. It was hard for her to wave down a carriage to take her to the hospital. By the time she arrived she was filled with dread and anxiety.

"Anton Pavlovich lay on his back," Maria wrote in her "Memoirs." "He was not allowed to speak. After greeting him, I went over to the table to hide my emotions." There, among bottles of champagne, jars of caviar, bouquets of flowers from well-wishers, she saw something that terrified her: a freehand drawing, obviously done by a specialist in these matters, of Chekhov's lungs. It was the kind of sketch a doctor often makes in order to show his patient what he thinks is taking place. The lungs were outlined in blue, but the upper parts were filled in with red. "I realized they were diseased," Maria wrote.

Leo Tolstoy was another visitor. The hospital staff were awed to find themselves in the presence of the country's greatest writer. The most famous man in Russia? Of course they had to let him in to see Chekhov, even though "nonessential" visitors were forbidden. With much obsequiousness on the part of the nurses and resident doctors, the bearded, fierce-looking old man was shown into Chekhov's room. Despite his low opinion of Chekhov's abilities as a playwright (Tolstoy felt the plays were static and lacking in any moral vision. "Where do your characters take you?" he once demanded of Chekhov. "From the sofa to the junk room and back"), Tolstoy liked Chekhov's short stories. Furthermore, and quite simply, he loved the man. He told Gorky, "What a beautiful, magnificent man: modest and quiet, like a girl. He even walks like a girl. He's simply wonderful." And Tolstoy wrote in his journal (everyone kept a journal or a diary in those days), "I am glad I love . . . Chekhov."

Tolstoy removed his woollen scarf and bearskin coat, then lowered himself into a chair next to Chekhov's bed. Never mind that Chekhov was taking medication and not permitted to talk, much less carry on a conversation. He had to listen, amazedly, as the Count began to discourse on his theories of the immortality of the soul. Concerning that visit, Chekhov later wrote, "Tolstoy assumes that all of us (humans and animals alike) will live on in a principle (such as reason or love) the essence and goals of which are a mystery to us. . . . I have no use for that kind of immortality. I don't understand it, and Lev Nikolayevich was astonished I didn't."

Nevertheless, Chekhov was impressed with the solicitude shown by Tolstoy's visit. But, unlike Tolstoy, Chekhov didn't believe in an afterlife and never had. He didn't believe in anything that couldn't be apprehended by one or more of his five senses. And as far as his outlook on life and writing went, he once told someone that he lacked "a political, religious, and philosophical world view. I change it every month, so I'll have to limit myself to the description of how my heroes love, marry, give birth, die, and how they speak."

Earlier, before his t.b. was diagnosed, Chekhov had remarked, "When a peasant has consumption, he says, 'There's nothing I can do. I'll go off in the spring with the melting of the snows.'" (Chekhov himself died in the summer, during a heat wave.) But once Chekhov's own tuberculosis was discovered he continually tried to minimize the seriousness of his condition. To all appearances, it was as if he felt, right up to the end, that he might be able to throw off the disease as he would a lingering catarrh. Well into his final days, he spoke with seeming conviction of the possibility of an improvement. In fact, in a letter written shortly before his end, he went so far as to tell his sister that he was "putting on a bit of flesh" and felt much better now that he was in Badenweiler.

Badenweiler is a spa and resort city in the western area of the Black Forest, not far from Basel. The Vosges are visible from nearly anywhere in the city, and in those days the air was pure and invigorating. Russians had been going there for years to soak in the hot mineral baths and promenade on the boulevards. In June, 1904, Chekhov went there to die.

Earlier that month, he'd made a difficult journey by train from Moscow to Berlin. He travelled with his wife, the actress Olga Knipper, a woman he'd met in 1898 during rehearsals for "The Seagull." Her contemporaries describe her as an excellent actress. She was talented, pretty, and almost ten years younger than the playwright. Chekhov had been immediately attracted to her, but was slow to act on his feelings. As always, he preferred a flirtation to marriage. Finally, after a three-year courtship involving many separations, letters, and the inevitable misunderstandings, they were at last married, in a private ceremony in Moscow, on May 25, 1901. Chekhov was enormously happy. He called Olga his "pony," and sometimes "dog" or "puppy." He was also fond of addressing her as "little turkey" or simply as "my joy."

In Berlin, Chekhov consulted with a renowned specialist in pulmonary disorders, a Dr. Karl Ewald. But, according to an eyewitness, after the doctor examined Chekhov he threw up his hands and left the room without a word. Chekhov was too far gone for help: this Dr. Ewald was furious with himself for not being able to work miracles, and with Chekhov for being so ill.

A Russian journalist happened to visit the Chekhovs at their hotel and sent back this dispatch to his editor: "Chekhov's days are numbered. He seems mortally ill, is terribly thin, coughs all the time, gasps for breath at the slightest movement, and is running a high temperature." This same journalist saw the Chekhovs off at Potsdam Station when they boarded their train for Badenweiler. According to his account, "Chekhov had trouble making his way up the small staircase at the station. He had to sit down for several minutes to catch his breath." In fact, it was painful for Chekhov to move: his legs ached continually and his insides hurt. The disease had attacked his intestines and spinal cord. At this point he had less than a month to live. When Chekhov spoke of his condition now, it was, according to Olga, "with an almost reckless indifference."

Dr. Schwöhrer was one of the many Badenweiler physicians who earned a good living by treating the well-to-do who came to the spa seeking relief from various maladies. Some of his patients were ill and infirm, others simply old and hypochondriacal. But Chekhov's was a special case: he was clearly beyond help and in his last days. He was also very famous. Even Dr. Schwöhrer knew his name: he'd read some of Chekhov's stories in a German magazine. When he examined the writer early in June, he voiced his appreciation of Chekhov's art but kept his medical opinions to himself. Instead, he prescribed a diet of cocoa, oatmeal drenched in butter, and strawberry tea. This last was supposed to help Chekhov sleep at night.

On June 13th, less than three weeks before he died, Chekhov wrote a letter to his mother in which he told her his health was on the mend. In it he said, "It's likely that I'll be completely cured in a week." Who knows why he said this? What could he have been thinking? He was a doctor himself, and he knew better. He was dying, it was as simple and as unavoidable as that. Nevertheless, he sat out on the balcony of his hotel room and read railway timetables. He asked for information on sailings of boats bound for Odessa from Marseilles. But he *knew*. At this stage he had to have known. Yet in one of the last letters he ever wrote he told his sister he was growing stronger by the day.

He no longer had any appetite for literary work, and hadn't for a long time. In fact, he had very nearly failed to complete "The Cherry Orchard" the year before. Writing that play was the hardest thing he'd ever done in his life. Toward the end, he was able to manage only six or seven lines a day. "I've started losing heart," he wrote Olga. "I feel I'm finished as a writer, and every sentence strikes me as worthless and of no use whatever." But he didn't stop. He finished his play in October, 1903. It was the last thing he ever wrote, except for letters and a few entries in his notebook.

A little after midnight on July 2, 1904, Olga sent someone to fetch Dr. Schwöhrer. It was an emergency: Chekhov was delirious. Two young Russians on holiday happened to have the adjacent room, and Olga hurried next door to explain what was happening. One of the youths was in his bed asleep, but the other was still awake, smoking and reading. He left the hotel at a run to find Dr. Schwöhrer. "I can still hear the sound of the gravel under his shoes in the silence of that stifling July night," Olga wrote later on in her memoirs. Chekhov was hallucinating, talking about sailors, and there were snatches of something about the Japanese. "You don't put ice on an empty stomach," he said when she tried to place an ice pack on his chest.

Dr. Schwöhrer arrived and unpacked his bag, all the while keeping his gaze fastened on Chekhov, who lay gasping in the bed. The sick man's pupils were dilated and his temples glistened with sweat. Dr. Schwöhrer's face didn't register anything. He was not an emotional man, but he knew Chekhov's end was near. Still, he was a doctor, sworn to do his utmost, and Chekhov held on to life, however tenuously. Dr. Schwöhrer prepared a hypodermic and administered an injection of camphor, something that was supposed to speed up the heart. But the injection didn't help—nothing, of course, could have helped. Nevertheless, the doctor made known to Olga his intention of sending for oxygen. Suddenly, Chekhov roused himself, became lucid, and said quietly, "What's the use? Before it arrives I'll be a corpse."

Dr. Schwöhrer pulled on his big mustache and stared at Chekhov. The writer's cheeks were sunken and gray, his complexion waxen; his breath was raspy. Dr. Schwöhrer knew the time could be reckoned in minutes. Without a word, without conferring with Olga, he went over to an alcove where there was a telephone on the wall. He read the instructions for using the device. If he activated it by holding his finger on a button and turning a handle on the side of the phone, he could reach the lower regions of the hotel—the kitchen. He picked up the receiver, held it to his ear, and did as the instructions told him. When someone finally answered, Dr. Schwöhrer ordered a bottle of the hotel's best champagne. "How many glasses?" he was asked. "Three glasses!" the doctor shouted into the mouthpiece. "And hurry, do you hear?" It was one of those rare moments of inspiration that can easily enough be overlooked later on, because the action is so entirely appropriate it seems inevitable.

The champagne was brought to the door by a tired-looking young man whose blond hair was standing up. The trousers of his uniform were wrinkled, the creases gone, and in his haste he'd missed a loop while buttoning his jacket. His appearance was that of someone who'd been resting (slumped in a chair, say, dozing a little), when off in the distance the phone had clamored in the early-morning hours—great God in Heaven!—and the next thing he knew he was being shaken awake by a superior and told to deliver a bottle of Moët to Room 211. "And hurry, do you hear?"

The young man entered the room carrying a silver ice bucket with the champagne in it and a silver tray with three cut-crystal glasses. He found a place on the table for the bucket and glasses, all the while craning his neck, trying to see into the other room, where someone panted ferociously for breath. It was a dreadful, harrowing sound, and the young man lowered his chin into his collar and turned away as the ratchety breathing worsened. Forgetting himself, he stared out the open window toward the darkened city. Then this big imposing man with a thick mustache pressed some coins into his hand—a large tip, by the feel of it—and suddenly the young man saw the door open. He took some steps and found himself on the landing, where he opened his hand and looked at the coins in amazement.

Methodically, the way he did everything, the doctor went about the business of working the cork out of the bottle. He did it in such a way as to minimize, as much as possible, the festive explosion. He poured three glasses and, out of habit, pushed the cork back into the neck of the bottle. He then took the glasses of champagne over to the bed. Olga momentarily released her grip on Chekhov's hand—a hand, she said later, that burned her fingers. She arranged another pillow behind his head. Then she put the cool glass of champagne against Chekhov's palm and made sure his fingers closed around the stem. They exchanged looks—Chekhov, Olga, Dr. Schwöhrer. They didn't touch glasses. There was no toast. What on earth was there to drink to? To death? Chekhov summoned his remaining strength and said, "It's been so long since I've had champagne." He brought the glass to his lips and drank. In a minute or two Olga took the empty glass from his hand and set it on the nightstand. Then Chekhov turned onto his side. He closed his eyes and sighed. A minute later, his breathing stopped.

Dr. Schwöhrer picked up Chekhov's hand from the bedsheet. He held his fingers to Chekhov's wrist and drew a gold watch from his vest pocket, opening the lid of the watch as he did so. The second hand on the watch moved slowly, very slowly. He let it move around the face of the watch three times while he waited for signs of a pulse. It was three o'clock in the morning and still sultry in the room. Badenweiler was in the grip of its worst heat wave in years. All the windows in both rooms stood open, but there was no sign of a breeze. A large, black-winged moth flew through a window and banged wildly against the electric lamp. Dr. Schwöhrer let go of Chekhov's wrist. "It's over," he said. He closed the lid of his watch and returned it to his vest pocket.

At once Olga dried her eyes and set about composing herself. She thanked the doctor for coming. He asked if she wanted some medication—laudanum, perhaps, or a few drops of valerian. She shook her head. She did have one request, though: before the authorities were notified and the newspapers found out, before the time came when Chekhov was no longer in her keeping, she wanted to be alone with him for a while. Could the doctor help with this? Could he withhold, for a while anyway, news of what had just occurred?

Dr. Schwöhrer stroked his mustache with the back of a finger. Why not? After all, what difference would it make to anyone whether this matter became known now or a few hours from now? The only detail that remained was to fill out a death certificate, and this could be done at his office later on in the morning, after he'd slept a few hours. Dr. Schwöhrer nodded his agreement and prepared to leave. He murmured a few words of condolence. Olga inclined her head. "An honor," Dr. Schwöhrer said. He picked up his bag and left the room and, for that matter, history.

It was at this moment that the cork popped out of the champagne bottle; foam spilled down onto the table. Olga went back to Chekhov's bedside. She sat on a footstool, holding his hand, from time to time stroking his face. "There were no human voices, no everyday sounds," she wrote. "There was only beauty, peace, and the grandeur of death."

She stayed with Chekhov until daybreak, when thrushes began to call from the garden below. Then came the sound of tables and chairs being moved about down there. Before long, voices carried up to her. It was then a knock sounded at the door. Of course she thought it must be an official of some sort—the medical examiner, say, or someone from the police who had questions to ask and forms for her to fill out, or maybe, just maybe, it could be Dr. Schwöhrer returning with a mortician to render assistance in embalming and transporting Chekhov's remains back to Russia.

But, instead, it was the same blond young man who'd brought the champagne a few hours earlier. This time, however, his uniform trousers were neatly pressed, with stiff creases in front, and every button on his snug green jacket was fastened. He seemed quite another person. Not only was he wide awake but his plump cheeks were smooth-shaven, his hair was in place, and he appeared anxious to please. He was holding a porcelain vase with three long-stemmed yellow roses. He presented these to Olga with a smart click of his heels. She stepped back and let him into the room. He was there, he said, to collect the glasses, ice bucket, and tray, yes. But he also wanted to say that, because of the extreme heat, breakfast would be served in the garden this morning. He hoped this weather wasn't too bothersome; he apologized for it.

The woman seemed distracted. While he talked, she turned her eyes away and

looked down at something in the carpet. She crossed her arms and held her
elbows. Meanwhile, still holding his vase, waiting for a sign, the young man
took in the details of the room. Bright sunlight flooded through the open
windows. The room was tidy and seemed undisturbed, almost untouched. No
garments were flung over chairs, no shoes, stockings, braces, or stays were in
evidence, no open suitcases. In short, there was no clutter, nothing but the usual
heavy pieces of hotel-room furniture. Then, because the woman was still looking
down, he looked down, too, and at once spied a cork near the toe of his shoe.
The woman did not see it—she was looking somewhere else. The young man
wanted to bend over and pick up the cork, but he was still holding the roses
and was afraid of seeming to intrude even more by drawing any further attention
to himself. Reluctantly, he left the cork where it was and raised his eyes.
Everything was in order except for the uncorked, half-empty bottle of champagne that stood alongside two crystal glasses over on the little table. He cast
his gaze about once more. Through an open door he saw that the third glass
was in the bedroom, on the nightstand. But someone still occupied the bed! He
couldn't see a face, but the figure under the covers lay perfectly motionless and
quiet. He noted the figure and looked elsewhere. Then, for a reason he couldn't
understand, a feeling of uneasiness took hold of him. He cleared his throat and
moved his weight to the other leg. The woman still didn't look up or break her
silence. The young man felt his cheeks grow warm. It occurred to him, quite
without his having thought it through, that he should perhaps suggest an
alternative to breakfast in the garden. He coughed, hoping to focus the woman's
attention, but she didn't look at him. The distinguished foreign guests could, he
said, take breakfast in their rooms this morning if they wished. The young man
(his name hasn't survived, and it's likely he perished in the Great War) said he
would be happy to bring up a tray. Two trays, he added, glancing uncertainly
once again in the direction of the bedroom.

He fell silent and ran a finger around the inside of his collar. He didn't
understand. He wasn't even sure the woman had been listening. He didn't know
what else to do now; he was still holding the vase. The sweet odor of the roses
filled his nostrils and inexplicably caused a pang of regret. The entire time he'd
been waiting, the woman had apparently been lost in thought. It was as if all
the while he'd been standing there, talking, shifting his weight, holding his
flowers, she had been someplace else, somewhere far from Badenweiler. But now
she came back to herself, and her face assumed another expression. She raised
her eyes, looked at him, and then shook her head. She seemed to be struggling
to understand what on earth this young man could be doing there in the room
holding a vase with three yellow roses. Flowers? She hadn't ordered flowers.

The moment passed. She went over to her handbag and scooped up some
coins. She drew out a number of banknotes as well. The young man touched
his lips with his tongue; another large tip was forthcoming, but for what? What
did she want him to do? He'd never before waited on such guests. He cleared
his throat once more.

No breakfast, the woman said. Not yet, at any rate. Breakfast wasn't the
important thing this morning. She required something else. She needed him to
go out and bring back a mortician. Did he understand her? Herr Chekhov was
dead, you see. *Comprenez-vous?* Young man? Anton Chekhov was dead. Now

listen carefully to me, she said. She wanted him to go downstairs and ask someone at the front desk where he could go to find the most respected mortician in the city. Someone reliable, who took great pains in his work and whose manner was appropriately reserved. A mortician, in short, worthy of a great artist. Here, she said, and pressed the money on him. Tell them downstairs that I have specifically requested you to perform this duty for me. Are you listening? Do you understand what I'm saying to you?

The young man grappled to take in what she was saying. He chose not to look again in the direction of the other room. He had sensed that something was not right. He became aware of his heart beating rapidly under his jacket, and he felt perspiration break out on his forehead. He didn't know where he should turn his eyes. He wanted to put the vase down.

Please do this for me, the woman said. I'll remember you with gratitude. Tell them downstairs that I insist. Say that. But don't call any unnecessary attention to yourself or to the situation. Just say that this is necessary, that I request it— and that's all. Do you hear me? Nod if you understand. Above all, don't raise an alarm. Everything else, all the rest, the commotion—that'll come soon enough. The worst is over. Do we understand each other?

The young man's face had grown pale. He stood rigid, clasping the vase. He managed to nod his head.

After securing permission to leave the hotel he was to proceed quietly and resolutely, though without any unbecoming haste, to the mortician's. He was to behave exactly as if he were engaged on a very important errand, nothing more. He *was* engaged on an important errand, she said. And if it would help keep his movements purposeful he should imagine himself as someone moving down the busy sidewalk carrying in his arms a porcelain vase of roses that he had to deliver to an important man. (She spoke quietly, almost confidentially, as if to a relative or a friend.) He could even tell himself that the man he was going to see was expecting him, was perhaps impatient for him to arrive with his flowers. Nevertheless, the young man was not to become excited and run, or otherwise break his stride. Remember the vase he was carrying! He was to walk briskly, comporting himself at all times in as dignified a manner as possible. He should keep walking until he came to the mortician's house and stood before the door. He would then raise the brass knocker and let it fall, once, twice, three times. In a minute the mortician himself would answer.

This mortician would be in his forties, no doubt, or maybe early fifties— bald, solidly built, wearing steel-frame spectacles set very low on his nose. He would be modest, unassuming, a man who would ask only the most direct and necessary questions. An apron. Probably he would be wearing an apron. He might even be wiping his hands on a dark towel while he listened to what was being said. There'd be a faint whiff of formaldehyde on his clothes. But it was all right, and the young man shouldn't worry. He was nearly a grownup now and shouldn't be frightened or repelled by any of this. The mortician would hear him out. He was a man of restraint and bearing, this mortician, someone who could help allay people's fears in this situation, not increase them. Long ago he'd acquainted himself with death in all its various guises and forms; death held no surprises for him any longer, no hidden secrets. It was this man whose services were required this morning.

The mortician takes the vase of roses. Only once while the young man is speaking does the mortician betray the least flicker of interest, or indicate that he's heard anything out of the ordinary. But the one time the young man mentions the name of the deceased, the mortician's eyebrows rise just a little. Chekhov, you say? Just a minute, and I'll be with you.

Do you understand what I'm saying, Olga said to the young man. Leave the glasses. Don't worry about them. Forget about crystal wineglasses and such. Leave the room as it is. Everything is ready now. We're ready. Will you go?

But at that moment the young man was thinking of the cork still resting near the toe of his shoe. To retrieve it he would have to bend over, still gripping the vase. He would do this. He leaned over. Without looking down, he reached out and closed it into his hand.

TURNER CASSITY

Turner Cassity was born in Jackson, Mississippi, in 1929, and has always been careful to distance himself from the excesses, the imprecision, the derivativeness of southern writing. Employment in the Caribbean and in South Africa, as well as in that other remove, academia, has aided him greatly in his estrangement. He has worked at Emory University Library since 1962.

"I can hardly convey how little I am interested in 'experiment.' Does anyone know an experimental poem that actually succeeds? In poetry every new subject is an innovation; the art lies in bringing the matter into line—literally—with the inalterable forms."

Why Fortune is the Empress of the World

The insect born of royalty has Marx
And worker housing as a life; has sex
Or clover honey to his pleasure, as
Have we. The parrot speaks. All use: the ant
The aphid and the crocodile the bird.
What then is human wholly? Is it heart?
Fidelity exists in any dog.
Good Doctor who have found your Missing Link,
On your return what will you have him be?
Free agent or a tenant in a cage?

A simple test will serve. It more or less
Is this: can he be taught a game of chance?
It is not possible, you must agree,
To think of animals as gambling. Odds,
Except for us, do not exist. An ape
Assumes always his jump will reach the limb.
For all his skill, he cannot cut his loss.
We, on the other hand, at our most threatened
Turn instinctively . . . to Reason? No.
To Fortune, as a mindlessness of mind.
The random that we create creates us.
In overcrowded lifeboats, we draw lots.

◆　　　◆　　　◆

Carpenters

Forgiven, unforgiven, they who drive the nails
    Know what they do: they hammer.
If they doubt, if their vocation fails,
    They only swell the number,

Large already, of the mutineers and thieves.
    With only chance and duty
There to cloak them, they elect and nail.
    The vinegar will pity.

Judas who sops, their silver his accuser, errs
    To blame the unrewarded.
They guard the branch he hangs from. Guilt occurs
    Where it can be afforded.

MARILYN CHIN

Marilyn Chin is a poet and translator who was a Stegner Fellow at Stanford in 1984–85. She has won other awards for her poetry, namely, a fellowship from the National Endowment for the Arts, the Mary Roberts Rinehart Award, and a Pushcart Prize. Her first book of poems, Dwarf Bamboo, *was nominated for a Bay Area Book Reviewers Award.*

"I chose these poems because they are two of my favorites. They are a little irreverent (especially the one about eating dogs!); however, I think that the form and content work well together in these poems. (I am, of course, using the word 'form' very loosely here.) Also, these two make me chuckle every time I read them."

◆   ◆   ◆

Art Is What Humans Leave Behind, Roberto

Art is what humans leave behind, Roberto,
that greenback burns, this house will crumble,
children grow into accountants, azaleas into weed.
Our beauty fades as does our love;
My breasts sag, your gums recede,
my black hair will turn into grey hanks.
What we dream, tame, fructify, cull
will vanish in the comfort of night.
And what will we have left, Roberto?

(He shrugs: our undying love? Music, stars?
A butterfly dreamt by a guy named Chuangtzu?)

Meanwhile, we drive, 10,000 miles of silicon valley.
I forget what race I am, what sex I am,
why my body no longer feels seventeen.
There are the bridges: the Oakland-Bay,
the S & M, the Dumbarton, the Gate-not-so-Golden.
And the tolls, the damn tolls. My mind is empty,
but my pockets are heavy with change.
My love, this is no philosophical problem.

This is not a meditation on existence.
This is the goddam truth about my existence,
and I don't think I am very fond of it.

(He sighs, balks, sighs again.)

Roberto, what do you think we should do, darling,
exact a minor revolution? Let's say that tomorrow,
should tomorrow ever come, we leave our jobs
and both go home, I mean to our own homes,
you to yours, me to mine and begin again.
You, back to that treehouse of your youth
where I may visit as an honorary member
only on Saturdays for licorice and English tea.
And me, to my grandmother's house filled with
plum candy and ancient Chinese baubles . . . Ooh,
the rank of stinky salt-fish and fermented black beans.

(Look, he points, in the courtyard,
a cardinal in the bottlebrush tree, how remarkable!)

We can't turn the clock hands back,
shovel shit up a cow's ass and have it come out grass.
Look at me now: the April-of-your-life, your April-showers-
bring-May-flowers, my eyes lowered in shame,
my teeth blacken, the pearls of my happiness
hidden within their very shells . . . and you return
every day, every year, every decade,
my great white knight on a piebald horse,
my foe, my love—to save me. Tell me
an old Chinese woman's bitter tale
longer and stinkier than the bandages around her feet.
Emancipation never comes. It winds, unwinds,
but never comes . . . for all escapes are temporary . . .

(But temporary is better than none.)

◆   ◆   ◆

After My Last Paycheck from the Factory

After my last paycheck from the factory,
two thin coupons, four tin dollars,
I invited old Liu for an afternoon meal.
                for the Chinese Cultural Revolution
                and all that was wrong with my life

I ordered vegetables and he ordered dog,
the cheapest kind, mushu, but without the cakes.
I watched him smack his greasy lips

and thought of home, my lover's gentle kisses—
his faint aroma, still with me now.

I confided with a grief too real,
"This is not what I expected"
and bit my lip to keep from crying,
"I've seen enough, I want to go home."
But suddenly, I was seized by a vision

reminding me why I had come: two girls
in uniform, red bandanas and armbands
shouting slogans and Maoish songs,
"the East is red, the sun is rising;"
promises of freedom and a better world.

Trailing them was their mascot of Youth,
a creature out of Doctor Seuss or Lewis Carroll
purplish pink, variegated and prancing.
I stood in awe of its godlike beauty
until the realist Liu disrupted my mirage.

"It's the dog I ordered and am eating still!"
he mumbled with a mouthful of wine.
And as it came closer I saw the truth:
its spots were not of breeding or exotic import,
but rampant colonies of scabies and fleas,

which, especially red in its forbidden country,
blazed a trail through the back of its woods;
and then, its forehead bled with worms,
so many and complex as if *they* did its thinking.
I rubbed my eyes, readjusted the world . . .

Then focused back on his gruesome dish
trimmed with parsley and rinds of orange.
One piece of bone, unidentified which,
stared at me like a goat's pleading eye
or the shiny new dollar I'd just lost.

Old Liu laughed and slapped my back,
"You American Chinese are hard to please."
Then, stuck his filthy chopsticks into my sauce.
"Mmmm, seasoning from Beijing, the best
since opium," then, pointed to a man

sitting behind me, a stout provincial governor
who didn't have to pay after eating the finest
Chinese pug, twenty-five yuan a leg.

He picked his teeth with a splintered shin,
burped and farted, flaunting his wealth.

Old Liu said with wine breath to kill,
"My cousin, don't be disillusioned,
his pride will be molested, his dignity violated,
and he as dead as the four-legged he ate
two short kilometers before home."

EVAN S. CONNELL ✦

I was born in Kansas City, served as a naval aviator during World War II, and attended Stanford in 1947–48. I studied writing with Wallace Stegner and Richard Scowcroft, and since then have published a number of books, including Mrs. Bridge, Mr. Bridge, The Connoisseur, The Diary of a Rapist, *and* Son of the Morning Star. *I am presently at work on "The Alchymist's Journal."*

"I stole the yellow raft from a close friend, a Navy flier. He was a patrol bomber pilot in the South Pacific and on one mission he saw an empty yellow raft in the ocean. After the war, when we both were students at the University of Kansas, he wrote a long, boring, sentimental story that included a mention of the raft. He tried to sell the story, but failed. I asked if I could have the raft. He said yes."

✦　　✦　　✦

The Yellow Raft

FROM THE DIRECTION OF the Solomon Islands came a damaged Navy fighter, high in the air, but gliding steadily down upon the ocean. The broad paddle blades of the propeller revolved uselessly with a dull whirring noise, turned only by the wind. Far below, quite small but growing larger, raced the shadow of the descending fighter. Presently they were very close together, the aircraft and its shadow, but each time they seemed about to merge they broke apart—the long fuselage tilting backward, lifting the engine for one more instant, while the shadow, like some distraught creature, leaped hastily through the whitecaps. Finally the engine plunged into a wave. The fuselage stood almost erect—a strange blue buoy stitched with gunfire—but then, tilting forward and bubbling, it disappeared into the greasy ocean. Moments later, as if propelled by a spring, a small yellow raft hurtled to the surface where it tossed back and forth, the walls lapped with oil. Suddenly, as though pursuing it from below, a bloody hand reached out of the water. Then for a while the raft floated over the deep rolling waves and the man held on. At last he drew himself into the raft where he sprawled on the bottom, coughing and weeping, turning his head occasionally to look at the blood on his arm. A few minutes later he sat up, cross-legged, balancing himself against the motion of the sea, and squinted toward the southern horizon because it was in that direction he had been flying and from that direction help would come. After watching the horizon for a long time he pulled off his helmet and appeared to be considering it while he idly twisted the radio cord. Then he lay down and tried to make himself comfortable. But in a little while he was up. He examined his wound, nodded, and with a cheerful expression he began to open a series of pouches attached to the inner walls of his raft: he found dehydrated rations, a few small luxuries, first-aid equipment, and signal flares. When the sun went down he had just finished eating a tablet of candy. He smacked his lips, lit a cigarette, and defiantly blew several smoke rings; but the wind was beginning to rise and before long he quit pretending. He zipped up his green canvas coveralls to the neck, tightened the straps and drawstrings of his life jacket, and braced his feet against the tubular yellow walls. He felt sick at his stomach and his wound was bleeding again. Several hours passed quietly except for the indolent rhythmic slosh of water and the squeak of rubber as the raft bent over the crest of a wave. Stars emerged, surrounding the raft, and spume broke lightly, persistently, against the man huddled with his back to the wind. All at once a rocket whistled up, illuminating the watery scene. No sooner had its light begun to fade than another rocket exploded high above; then a third, and a fourth. But darkness prevailed: overhead wheeled the Southern Cross, Hydra, Libra, and Corvus. Before dawn the pilot was on his hands and knees, whispering and stubbornly wagging his head while he waited to meet the second day. And as he peered at the horizon it seemed to him that he could see a marine reptile the size of a whale, with a long undulating swan-like neck, swimming toward him. He watched the creature sink into the depths and felt it glide swiftly under the raft. Then the world around him seemed to expand and the fiery tentacles of the sun touched his face as he waited, drenched with spray, to challenge the next wave. The raft trembled, dipped, and with a sickening, twisting slide, sank into a trough where the ocean and the ragged scud nearly closed over it. A flashlight rolled to one side, hesitated, and came rolling back while a pool of water gathered first at the pilot's feet, then at his head, sometimes submerging the flashlight. The walls of the raft were slippery, and the pouches from which he had taken the cigarettes and the food and the rockets were now filled with water. The drawstrings of his life jacket slapped wildly back and forth. He had put on his helmet and a pair of thin leather gloves to protect himself from the stinging spray. Steep foaming waves swept abruptly against the raft and the horizon dissolved into lowering clouds. By noon he was drifting through a steady rain with his eyes closed. Each time the raft sank into a trough the nebulous light vanished; then with a splash and a squeak of taut rubber it spun up the next slope, met the onrushing crest, whirled down again into darkness. Early that afternoon a murky chocolate streak separated the sea from the sky. Then the waves imperceptibly slickened, becoming enameled and black with a deep viridian hue like volcanic glass, their solid green phosphorescent surfaces curved and scratched as though scoured by a prehistoric wind; and the pilot waited, motionless, while each massive wave dove under the bounding yellow raft. When the storm ended it was night again. Slowly the constellations reappeared.

At dawn, from the south, came a Catalina flying boat, a plump and graceless creation known as the PBY—phlegmatic in the air, more at home resting its deep snowy breast in the water. It approached, high and slow, and almost flew beyond the raft. But then one tremendous pale blue wing of the PBY inclined toward a yellow dot on the ocean and in a dignified spiral the flying boat descended, keeping the raft precisely within its orbit until, just above the water, it skimmed by the raft. Except for the flashlight rolling back and forth and glittering in the sunshine the yellow raft was empty. The PBY climbed several hundred feet, turned, and crossed over the raft. Then it climbed somewhat higher and began circling. All morning the Catalina circled, holding its breast high like a great blue heron in flight, the gun barrels, propellers, and plexiglass blisters reflecting the tropical sun. For a while at the beginning of the search it flew tightly around the raft, low enough to touch the water almost at once, but later it climbed to an altitude from which the raft looked like a toy on a pond. There was nothing else in sight. The only shadow on the sea was that of the Navy flying boat moving in slow, monotonous circles around and around the deserted raft. At one time the PBY angled upward nearly a mile, its twin engines buzzing like flies in a vacant room, but after about fifteen minutes it came spiraling down, without haste, the inner wing always pointing at the raft. On the tranquil sunny ocean no debris was floating, nothing to mark the place where the fighter sank—only the raft, smeared with oil and flecked with salt foam. Early in the afternoon a blister near the tail of the Catalina slid open and a cluster of beer cans dropped in a leisurely arc toward the sea where they splashed like miniature bombs and began filling with water. Beyond them a few sandwich wrappers came fluttering down. Otherwise nothing disturbed the surface of the ocean; nothing changed all afternoon except that a veil gathered softly across the sky, filtering the light of the sun, darkening the metallic gleam of the Coral Sea. At five o'clock the PBY banked steeply toward the raft. Then it straightened up and for the first time in several hours the insignia on its prow—a belligerent little duck with a bomb and a pair of binoculars—rode vertically over the waves. The prow of the Catalina dipped when it approached the raft and the pitch of the engines began to rise. The flying boat descended with ponderous dignity, like a dowager stooping to retrieve a lost glove. With a hoarse scream it passed just above the raft. A moment later, inside the blue-black hull, a machine gun rattled and the raft started bouncing on the water. When the gunfire stopped the strange dance ended; the yellow raft fell back, torn into fragments of cork and deflated rubber that stained the ocean with an iridescent dye as green as a rainbow. Then the Catalina began to climb. Higher and higher, never again changing course, it flew toward the infinite horizon.

DEAN CRAWFORD

Dean Crawford's first novel is The Lay of The Land *(Viking, 1987), and he's just completed another. A Mirrielees Fellow in the Stanford Creative Writing Program in 1974–75, Crawford has taught at Stanford (freshman English), Santa Clara University, and North Adams State College; he is now teaching at Vassar. "Bird Shoal" was his second published story.*

"I started this story in the writing program, but it took a few years of tearing parts out and nailing parts in before it was ready to be published. So I put it through a lot of drafts (more than I like to admit) and a few hundred rereadings. Amazingly, though, I still managed to misspell the name of a place where the story is set: Ocracoke, *not* Okracoke. I must have been convinced that the right spelling was Okracoke, reasoning that the name was *okra + Coke,* two of the South's favorite foods and (as anyone who's tried them together knows) a great combo and a potent narcotic when the okra is sliced up and then dissolved in the Coke (it takes about three seconds) like aspirin."

♦ ♦ ♦

Bird Shoal

A letter to my wife, estranged no more

IF I COULD LIVE in Hollywood, among my fellow sleepwalkers, funny folks, costumed shades, I wouldn't want to. If I could have the life of Faulkner beside a kidney pool, chattering at the portable with my shirt off, moneyed and leisured, nude even, I wouldn't have it in a silver bowl. If I could be a barboy, consort, cocaine-head, cavorter with stars, the chorus girls and cocktail waitresses who have "promise" and call me "Rip," I'd run from the temptation. Glamour was never what I yearned for, but the movie version of my dream.

You knew that already, didn't you, Alicia? Once wife-of-mine, you'll tell me when I wander from the point, blur, or fudge the facts. Correct me when I'm wrong. I know you will.

Dreaming, I would take Bird Shoal, to have and to hold a slender stretch of North Carolina's Outer Banks, open to wind and sea and an occasional hurricane for thrills. I'd accept a weathered house with third floor look-out, widow's walk, a rusting bike, three miles of curved beach and one strong dog to run it, a light blue boat, the public eye, and you.

"Me?" you say. "You diddle-headed dildo! You turkey! You didn't want any part of me three years ago when you ran off to California—two years ago when

I agreed to fly out—two months ago! Why now? So why now do you come on with your blue-moon tripe? Dreamer! Moonie! Mick!"

You're right, of course, my noodle. What right have I to ask? Who am I to ask you now, after all these years? Actually, you see, I'm not really asking. Only dreaming.

We used to moon together, past and future. We named the children (even though we could never picture them): Phoebe, Jenny, Seth. And we reenacted the Reconstruction South. You: the southern belle, raven-haired and ranting; a Scarlett, bandanaed, grubbing turnips from the salted soil. Me: a simple gent and carpetbagger in a shiny suit.

"Oh how you do go on . . ." Your voice begins to thaw. "But weren't you talking about Bird Shoal?"

Of course, we'd need a grant, or a patron, or a rent-free situation. And on Thursdays I could sail to the mainland for supplies. The boat would be a tiny thing, sloop rig, eighteen feet or so, wooden and blue, blue like my childhood dinghy. I used to sail it down Eel River, out toward the lighthouse that looked exactly like a spark plug, bobbing out of reach.

I'll splice commas in the mornings and rope in the afternoons. Who says we can't bring back the past? We'll sit in the sun and read to each other: Whitman! Thomas! Yeats! The Lake Isle at Innesfree! I want to hear the wind rustling in the bamboo, whistling through your toes. I'll read you Moby Dick while you gaze significantly out to sea. Call me Ishmael! Call me anything!

Can you get off on it, Alicia? Are you tempted?

Come back, little Sheba. No one knows me like you do. The restless nights of expectations since you went away. I lie awake and dream of your hot body beside me: your soft ass pressed against my belly, or your nose nuzzled into my shoulder and one leg sprawled over both of mine. Every morning we were reborn! Alicia, I need you for my rest. I need you to get me up in the morning.

"But why me?" you ask quite justifiably. "You've had lots of other women. Why not Lisa or Lori or Susu or Peepee, Mumu, Ta-ta, whatever her name is? Or Dotie, the towering whore! Poor boy. Her ass wasn't soft enough for you, after all? What makes mine so special? What do you want from me?"

Hush, and I'll tell you: you're all mixed up with my sexual imagination. And that's not all . . .

"Oh, Christ," I can hear you say. "Not that damn thing again. The male ego, rearing its horny head."

But now I understand it! I kept confusing people with the place. It wasn't the women that I wanted. It was Bird Shoal. Close your eyes, and I'll show you. Once and for all. I'll pit my flights of whimsy against your earthy might. I'm ready now, Alicia (too late! too late!). Come dream with me. Remember with me. Pretend.

♦   ♦   ♦

When we stayed in Beaufort on the Outer Banks, we could see Bird Shoal, glittering in the sun, contoured like a woman, with real birds rising above it. We slept huddled together, the house was so cold, and stretched the covers over our heads while we played with each other's parts. Do you remember the circus tent? The elephant? The chartreuse troupe rippling in the breeze on the beach at Bird Shoal? Wasn't it a magical visitation? How they got there I'll never know.

"By barge," you say. But why? "Circus people are crazy. They're mostly from L.A."

Do you think they were filming a movie? Fellini in North Carolina? For four days, they marched that elephant up and down the beach: a sliver of Sahara between canal and sea. The elephant trumpeted into the wind, then heaved on through the white sand, trailing a procession of tiny-footed dwarfs, brightly costumed, fluting—except we couldn't hear the music. I saw Arabian horsemen crash down the dunes, their loose clothes flapping behind them.

Then, one morning, they were gone. We asked at the bait shop. "Yup," the crabman said. "They come every year to exercise the stock."

I stared again at the unembellished screen of shapely sand and saw a tapered beach rising with conviction up to hips, softly easing down to waist and arms and hanging breasts, her long hair swept like marsh grass in the sea. I saw a woman in repose and wanted her, of course, but only because I didn't know what else to do with such a beautiful sight. You see a purple mountain, you want to put it in your mouth. A perfect blond, you want to ruin her. A rainbow, if only you could suck it like a popsicle.

Tell me again, Alicia, that the circus tent was real.

You don't answer me. The telephone rings, but there's no response. I need your confirmation, and no one else will do: yes, it happened, I remember, it was great, it was grand. A single voice talking, this is lunacy. It takes at least two to make it real.

We had a boat. It's a shame that we never got out to Bird Shoal. You were cold, I remember. I know that you're sensitive to the cold.

"Unfair!" you protest. "The first September frost on the Outer Banks in forty years, and we were staying in a house with no heat."

Yup, that's the kind of house I'd like to have: clapboard, stripped bare and then silvered by the sun, solid and proven sturdy. The house had sustained four hurricanes and surely could withstand four more.

You say, "Because the wind could move so freely through the walls."

But didn't we eat well, Alicia? We had cracked crab and homemade bread, ham and cheese, fried on the grill, steamed clams and roasted oysters. The kitchen was the only warm room in the house. We danced, back-to-back, side-to-side, while we chopped and stirred. We sang "Sweet Georgia Brown," and I thought I heard our voices rattling down the halls, poking our rambunctious human life into those cold unfriendly rooms.

Then, warm after eating and drunk on the sound of our own voices, we made love while the afternoon sun shone on the coverlet. I remember you thought I'd never come. "This isn't normal," you said. I smiled and stuck my finger up your ass. I probed deeper inside you; my two intrusions separated only by a wall, I could feel my own hardness against my fingertip. Your shudders broke in waves inside, and I reached further down both tracts sightless and mindless, stretching for that point where uterus meets anal canal. When your orgasms came like labor pains, only seconds apart, I remember that you screamed "NO!" and the look in your eyes was terror.

"I don't remember that," now you say. "It sounds like a fantasy to me."

(Could it have been a dream? No, no, I think it's true.)

Afterwards, I found you propped diagonally in a window frame. Your finger was on the glass, but only when I walked up beside you did you begin to tap, as though it took a presence to trigger your motion. "Windowpane, counterpane, where does it come from?" you asked. I gently asked, "What happened?" A whimsical smile: "La petite morte didn't seem so petite," you said. I reached inside your robe and ran my hand from knee to neck. The robe fell away, and for a moment, disembodied, we looked together at the stretch of your body, its fleshy forms, its softness out of joint against the sharp etched lines of window sash and glass, the harsh blue of the sky: a joke without the humor.

Then you turned back to the window. I asked if you weren't cold, but you didn't hear me. In another world, you scratched at the bumps on the glass with your fingernail.

That day, I wondered if we might wither away and die, dry up and be blown away by the wind. Being alone together was like standing on one leg: we couldn't do it for very long. There were no normalcies, no standards, no other people, and therefore no way to triangulate our position. Anything could have happened! Alicia, I can tell you now, in print, five years and 3,000 miles from the fact—I was afraid to be alone with you.

"This is news? Wake me, Screwball, when you're getting to the point."

You remember the dead wing of the house in Beaufort—upstairs, unpainted, unlit, unclean? We thought it was haunted. We made jokes. Aunt Minnie Turnsty, the seventy-pound ghost, dragging her chains and shackles, complaining about the weight. Vince and Pam once told us they saw her in that house, just so. You said they were loony as the bird to begin with. Who could be afraid of a seventy-pound ghost? Pam was just wrought with guilt, you said, on account of the shack-up.

It was my duty to check the stove chimney before I went to bed. I hated to go back there, down the dark hall. The only light was behind me. Again and again, I looked over my shoulder to be sure that I hadn't lost sight of the light.

"You were probably stinko."

True, often I was tight and terrified of stumbling. What was I afraid of? I was afraid that if I ever lost sight of the light, my yellow pathway back, I'd be spun around and around and around and I'd never come out. But who could be afraid of little Aunt Minnie Turnsty?

"The spinnies!" Wife-like, you seize on the drunken detail. "Lout! I'm fed up to here with your evasions. You weren't afraid of Aunt Minnie. She sounds like a decoy to me."

All right. I was afraid to suffer alone with you, terrified that alone I wouldn't have the strength to resist if you looked me in the eye and calmly intoned, "Come, sit down, and we'll bleed together. Come bleed with me." I was afraid that I would never clot. I was afraid that once I'd become a blob blubbering on the floor, you might reach out an upturned palm, and say, "Good. Now, come, and we'll slash our wrists together. Open your veins to me."

I can see you shake your head now in dismay. "What a monster you make of me. How you use me. First, a shrew: challenging, shrill, and combative. But, as if that weren't enough—making me a full-bodied, living shrew—you have to make me a disembodied *voice!* Not even a character! Then, such an honor, I'm a warm body in your bed, a flesh without a head, a breast that flops across your chest; someone to get you up in the morning, a glorified alarm clock! My earthy weight, my ass! What people must think of me. And now . . ." You can hardly believe your own ears, eyes, whatever. "A vampire! Worse, a *suicidal* vampire! You're not even making sense."

♦   ♦   ♦

Bear with me. That's what you vowed in marriage, after all.

I wasn't afraid of you on Okracoke Island, honeymoon, when we checked into the little hotel and didn't come out of our room until they knocked on the door, and I wasn't the least bit scared of you, not even of your temper, the day we walked out to the lighthouse at Cape Hatteras.

"Sure, with other people around. Walking in a cold wind was always the kind of thing you were best at, just your cup of tea."

That day, we saw no other people, all afternoon. In California, I see mostly people. They smile, "Far out." Neon in their eyes, freon in their blood. Even the liquor stores sport marquees here: "Help Preserve Wildlife! Throw a Party!" I drink too much and whimsicalize. Some days I don't get out of bed. Afternoons are my prime time for dreaming.

R & R! not B&B, with a glass of water on the side.

"Your boozing metaphors again? You don't want me."

I loved to lie awake and hold you after you'd dropped off to sleep. Alicia, Alicia, your name is like a whisper. You were never like a whisper, except when you were asleep.

"If you want a whisperer, stick with Teetee, Wawa . . . what's her name?"

Nini. And she's as audible as your Hindu cowboy. What's his name? You remember, they named him for a cigarette.

"His name is Kamil." You correct me with a smile. "He's a DJ and speaks quite distinctly."

I want to hear the wind whispering in the eaves, indistinctly. I want to come in from sailing, wearing slicks, and hear you say, "It's so rough, I was worried. You poor baby, it must have been so cold." I want to sit in the evenings beside a wood stove and read to you, hot from the typewriter, the page I've just written.

"You want me fawning at your feet, or in the kitchen baking bread. That's what you want."

Alicia, I want to fall asleep with your fat ass pressed against my belly again. I want us to rub hot against each other in our sleep, moving together in our dreams as though blind in a dance, and wake already inside of you. I want to coil and spring out of bed in the morning, bring you juice before your body begins to stir, straddle you and bounce without fear of morning grumpiness, without a guarded thought in all my mind or heart.

I want it all, I guess, the way the movies promised. Is that where our dreams come from? Your hair shimmering with splendor in the long grass? skyrockets? flames and melting celluloid?

No answer. Who wants to live alone on a sandbar? But, if I had you again, would I still crave Nighttown, the neon reflection on black pavement? If we were good, and good together, would I need the bars, nightlife? Staring at the sand curves of shoal, would I still dream of other bodies? How many watchful eyes would I need to keep it real and airy? How do you keep a love fresh for a lifetime, without refrigeration?

I would build the house myself, laying clapboard over clapboard, shingle upon shingle, and nailing with a steady beat while watching over my shoulder for the storm. Inside I would fix it like a ship: tight and cozy, nooked. But I couldn't build it for myself alone. I'd codify!

"And use your words wrong."

I need you for editorial work. I need you to keep me honest. Ask me a straight question, and I'll give you a straight answer. I always meant to, Alicia. No one else has seen beneath my skin or touched the rancid meat there.

"Not even me," you say.

It's true. But I think you'd do it, if I could let you.

Awake, on Bird Shoal, I thrash my head from side to side to shake a lifetime's sleep and a recurrent nightmare. I'm trembling. What is it? How long have I been asleep?

You ask, "What is it?" Your voice is calm and gentle. "Tell me."

In my dream, I'm running down stairs, the stairwell of a tall building, a skyscraper (someone else's dream?). Footsteps beat behind me on the stairs: coming for me. I check the door on each landing. Locked, locked. I run on. The light dims as I descend. Walls are wetter. Am I underground? I know what's at the bottom, humming in the dark: machinery, furnace, turbine, no more doors. I hear his steps again. How could he be gaining? Fanatically, I run. It's nearly dark, the only light filters from above. Moss creeps in from the sides of the runners. I could slip. I throw myself at a door—locked. He's right behind me now. I can smell his Bowery breath and almost feel his stubble. Twisting, dizzy, I run, slide, nearly fall. Then there's a door, red sign, flashing EXIT. When I throw my body against the bar, it falls away. Sunlight pours in around me. I'm free, free for now at least, on the fire escape.

"Who is he?" you ask.

I don't know. He's tall, skinny, my size, but older. His eyes are narrow, cold, cruel. He hates me, I can feel his hate. But I don't know why he hates me.

"No? Who does he look like?" you ask in a patient tone. "Describe him."

An aging bum, his face swollen shut from self-loathing.

Your finger touches my chest and releases me. "You. He's you."

My body douses itself with sweat, and you rock it in your arms. "Baby," you say. "But why does he hate you?"

Because I'm still young and healthy. Because I'm busy making him.

"Why do you do it?" You don't relent. "Must you become that man?"

I don't know. I can't look him in the eye. So I'm afraid of my own shadow—so what? What can I do about it?

"Know it. Face it. Reveal it to someone, I guess."

I have roommates. I'm scared to live alone. I don't want to be a Jude Obscure. I'm afraid of growing middle aged and creepy, walking on the beach, some beach, in khakis and a straw hat. I'm scared of going gay, the secret deep within me like a gene, germinating in a distant pancreas, even now.

We're slouching in sweaters like college students, reading novels. Beach weekend, a cottage at Kitty Hawk. A near-miss, north of Hatteras. Outside it's storming, but we're safe within, encapsuled, drinking tea. We slump in our chairs with legs entwined. Your feet are in my lap. You work your toes between my legs, rubbing, poking, probing for a hardness as though for a bone. Maybe I won't want to: I don't respond.

I hear your book snap shut. You ask, "What are you afraid to let me see?"

My mass of contradictions. My churning ball of worms.

"What's inside the ball? What do these worms of yours feed on?"

Homosexuality! I spill the beans.

"Even for a college boy, that's too easy."

Alicia, there's a man inside, struggling to wake up in me. Is he a gambler, or a skidrow bum? Faulkner, the topless scriptwriter? A paunchy fag in khakis and a straw hat? A carpetbagger, long past his appointed time? or Dagwood, the weekend sailor-man? Who is it?

I want to pare the fears away, expose each like the layers of a baseball. First, the stitching. Can you see? The wrapper's off. Unwind the sticky string. A golf ball! Inside of a baseball—isn't that a joke? Then, to crack the plastic core, to peel the shell for you to see. Now serious, intent, I want to pierce the inner ball, as a child might pin and slice a wren.

Can you watch?

◆　　　　◆　　　　◆

We walk for miles along the curved beach, an edge of the wedge of land. The sky is gray, overshadowed, overcast. The wind sweeps your auburn hair and heaps it, all on one side of your head. I see that your ear is pink. The wind is cold and blows the water back. Spray lifts from the tops of the waves, then it flies away.

"Where are we going?"

Hatteras Point, the Outer Banks, I don't know when. Way out past the lighthouse, farther than we walked before, farther than we've ever been. Out to the sand-spar tip of the point at Hatteras Cape. It could be any time of the day. Carcasses of dead birds and fish are strewn upon the beach.

"Why do you bring me here, to a place so cold and grisly? Why do you always do this to me?"

This is a primeval place, Alicia, where the sea from the North and South meet nearly head on. The Civil War! We'll settle it once and for all.

"The War Between the States, you mean."

(I smile: the comfort of a familiar fight.)

I won't argue that point, Alicia. The two mad gods who rule the seas bump together here, and right here they rub tushies. Anyway, the decision to come here was out of my hands.

"Turkey! Yankee! Loon! When are you going to start accepting responsibility?"

It's a dream! Who can control their dreams? Was it your fault, in your dream, that I stood by and watched your father beat you?

"That was different. You were horrid in my dream."

And now?

"Now I don't dream of you at all."

That's different. But I'm giving us a chance now in my dream. Let's see what we can change.

Like a girl, you walk with me and look for sea shells, sea shells by the seashore. You find the bones of crabs, a cannibal feast for birds. The gulls rise in mass before us as we walk, and they settle back down to the sand behind. Roller-coaster, they rise and fall. Sandpipers are swept before us on the beach. I watch sand crabs perform the same eternal cartoon act: scurrying into their holes as we approach and peeping back out again when we're past. But I don't point them out to you; you might declare them "creepy" and insist on turning back.

"Even in his dreams, he holds out on me."

All right. We'll see what you can do.

We walk inland, into the wedge, the witch. Scrub oaks form a line of scalp. A shark, shaped like a dinosaur, reclines on the brackish sand. A creature washed ashore—how long ago? With my toe, I prod its belly, obscene white, and feel the dead flesh jiggle.

"A pre-vert?" You surprise me with your zoological humor.

Ahead, I spot a circle of flies clouding. Another body—I motion to you, come see. Half the meat stripped away by crabs, their claws tearing, feeding their mouths, working up and down. They wheel to face us, then scurry away.

"What is it?"

Porpoise, humanoid, a mile from the sea. His meat blood red and raw. His fish eye says, "Come bleed with me." I take a branch . . .

"No," you say. "He doesn't say that. Dead fish eyes don't talk, and when they do, they say 'Look at me.'"

Whose dream is this anyway?

"Yours and mine. You take a branch. What happens next?"

With a branch, I flip his body over. Alive! alive with worms.

I look for your revulsion, but you don't turn away. Instead you stare. "Scrape the worms away," you say.

There's nothing there.

"Scrape the worms away."

The ocean festering at the edge of land, a point of irritation. The waves come marching from two sides, heads bobbing in a crowd; ranked, they smash into each other. The spar of sand points out and down beneath the churning mix of waves. I wade out to my knees, further, waiting for you to call, to whine, "Come back here! Come back *now!*" A game of war: the waves from the south overrun the north, the north chasing back the south. Then they crash head on—a fountain of spray rises into a mist which settles over me. I'm still waiting for your call.

What's that you say? Your voice is weak and fading, as though on a telephone line. You're talking to me through a dream and in my sleep. Alicia, do you want me to wake up now?

You say, "My ears were ringing, the wind was so cold."

◆   ◆   ◆

I'm sitting in the New England Lounge on El Camino Real. *Real* means something different in California. The bar is vinyl but nice, you know, almost royal. Strapless evening gowns and leisure suits. I slump alone at the end of the bar, with no one to notice me except the bartender. He slips me extra cocktail napkins, and I scribble a note to you. I'm drinking Irish whiskey and want the tears to flood my eyes like hot sugar water, but when I look at the mural behind the bar, I can't bring myself to cry. The mural depicts a seacoast scene, a cape, it could be a sandbar. The New England Bar and Shoal: we grab at straws in California. Four weathered houses, pier with eight pilings, twelve clustered fishing boats of expressionist tendencies. The scene is both sparse and distorted, like a dream recollected. Pelican with four gulls, flanked. Buoy with bird, perched. Three running children, distant. I can't make out their faces. Phoebe, Jenny, Seth? Or are these the children from someone else's dream, equally unconceived? They chase a sloop which heels out along the shore toward—you guessed it, Alicia—a lighthouse. I place the call.

I woke you.

"Who is this?"

What a question.

Then you warn me, "I'm not alone . . ."

Who cares? Close your eyes again, one more time. We'll walk back to the lighthouse, the spark plug, bobbing. We'll bring quilts and sweaters and smoked oysters, soup and novels. We'll lug them up the spiral stairs. There's nothing there! Unless we bring it.

You ask, "Have you been drinking?" The static rises in a wave and swirls around your voice before it subsides. I suppress a sob and pretend not to hear the question.

We'll prop our legs up on each other, and you don't even have to mind your toes. Meet me in St. Louie? Hooie? Houston? Mobile? Baton Rouge? Anywhere, we'll have a holiday. And our time together will be as fearless as it was once conceived to be.

Do you have any money, Alicia?

"No," you snap. But then you soften and demur. "Oh, crackpot, dufus, who conceived this fearless rendezvous in the first place?"

I did. Me. I could do it in my sleep.

JOHN DANIEL

John Daniel studied and taught in the Stanford Creative Writing Program from 1982 to 1988 as a Wallace Stegner Fellow, an M.A. student, and a Jones Lecturer in poetry. He and his wife, Marilyn, an environmental engineer, now live in Portland, Oregon. The two poems in this anthology are from his first book, Common Ground, *published in 1988 by Confluence Press.*

"I came to Stanford in 1982 on a fellowship bearing Wallace Stegner's name, and by a second stroke of luck I spent the next five years living a hundred feet from the man himself. The half-wild field we shared as a kind of back yard is the place of my poem 'Of Earth.' Two of the Great Horned Owls in my other poem used to nest in the palm trees of the Inner Quad. Since the Quad's renovation they are gone, but upstairs in Building 50, where we in the workshop tried out our voices as the owls delivered their more accomplished ones outside, the good words go on."

Of Earth

For Wallace Stegner

Swallows looping and diving
by the darkening oaks, the flash
of their white bellies,
the tall grasses gathering last light,
glowing pale gold, silence
overflowing in a shimmer of breeze—
these could have happened
a different way. The heavy-trunked oaks
might not have branched and branched
and finely re-branched
as if to weave themselves into air.
There is no necessity
that any creature should fly,
that last light should turn
the grasses gold, that grasses
should exist at all,
or light.

But a mind thinking so
is a mind wandering from home.
It is not thought that answers
each step of my feet, to be walking here
in the cool stir of dusk
is no mere possibility,
and I am so stained with the sweet
peculiar loveliness of things
that given God's power to dream worlds
from the dark, I know
I could only dream Earth—
birds, trees, this field of light
where I and each of us walk once.

◆　　◆　　◆

A Year Among the Owls

1.
At dusk an owl sits blinking
in the oak
as students walk home, alone
and in pairs
through the silent quad,

lifts its tail, craps white
and flies
to the ridge of the red-tiled roof—
silhouette,
turning its head
one way then the other,

still there
as it grows too dark for me to see.

2.
You can't see the owl at night,
but it sees you.

Sometimes at dusk you can see it,
but it saw you first.

In daylight you can haul yourself up
and peer in its hole. It's asleep.

You're still not important,
even though you've climbed a tree.

3.
With the call of one owl the stillness
of lamplight and desk is changed
to the stillness of forest and night.
From the nest in the pine, the hollow oak,
from barns, mineshafts, seacliff ledges
they glide forth, soundless, seeing and hearing
with a clarity we could not bear, a field
of bright knowing across the dark land.

4.
In the classroom we talk about our poems.
Outside in the rain
the owl in the oak and the owl in the palm
call to each other.

5.
I assumed you were still
when you gave your call.
I didn't know until now,
watching you in the palm,
that your white throat puffs
like a tuba player's cheeks,
and you lean forward
very carefully it seems
placing your voice into air.

6.
I am like the owl in two ways:
I sleep in the day,
I move into homes I did not build.

Some think the owl is lazy.
Some think the owl is smart.

7.
Tired of reading while the owl calls,
I open the door and answer:

hoo hoooo   hoo hoo

It is silent the rest of the night.

8.
When it comes I hope it's at night
in the fields, a sudden shadow
against stars. In the grasp
of that vision much clearer than mine,
I'll rise with my fading light
in the great silent motion of wings.

9.
As I heard the owls in my sleep
I kept drifting to the surface
and downward again.
Toward morning I dreamed of a boy
blowing a song on an empty bottle,
over and over, alone
in the dark but not afraid,
trying to get it just right.

TERRY DAVIS

Terry Davis was born in Spokane, Washington, in 1946. He received an M.F.A. from the Iowa Writers Workshop in 1973, and attended Stanford on a Stegner Fellowship in 1976. His novels are Vision Quest *(1979) and* Mysterious Ways *(1984). He is Writer-in-Residence at Mankato State University.*

"This is an excerpt from *Mysterious Ways,* a novel in the form of a 'found journal.' It's the story of Karl Russell's short life full of misfortune. In these two entries misfortune is taking the form of what appear to be common warts."

Funny Tissue

April 11, 1968

THE WARTS ARE HISTORY now. All that's left of them are little burn holes with tiny, jagged black lips like the edges of steel cut with a torch. The doctor did it with an instrument that looked like an electric ice pick. He'd burn down through the wartmeat and into real flesh, then he'd swirl around in the hole till he burned out the sides. The blood would boil for part of a second, then it would be all burnt up.

The shots hurt a little, the burning tissue stank some, and I'm not crazy about having a bald spot on top of my head. But the hardest thing to endure about it all was the doctor's running commentary.

His name was Havermeyer and he looked as young as I am. His hair was longer than mine, which—thank heaven—is long enough to cover my new bald spot. He worked fast, and he talked as fast as he worked.

First he gave me about half a dozen shots all around the wartpatch on my wrist, then he plugged in the burner and held it up in my face. "We burn 'em out," he said. "Just like the cattlemen and the homesteaders. We," he said, "are the cattlemen."

I was sitting on the examination table in my T-shirt with my forearm resting on my thigh. He bent down and touched the point of the burner to a wart. There was just the faintest sizzling sound, then a tiny bubble of blood, then a little black hole he began to scour.

"When we talk about nature's wonders," Havermeyer said, "one of the wonders we'd better talk about is warts. Absolutely fascinating little buggers. More than fascinating." He looked up at me and I saw the tiny black specks on his thick glasses. He bent down again. "More than fascinating," he said. And he burned more warts. "Their secrets are manifold and prodigious, Russell." He straightened up and shook the burner in my face. "I am talking manifold and prodigious," he said before he bent back down. "The little guys are so neat I hate to do them in like this," he said. "But they'll sprout right up again."

"What!" I said. "Why are we doing this then?"

"Oh, we're probably intimidating these guys sufficiently," he said. "I mean the virus will manifest itself on some other carrier. Might pop up on the family dog or cat, for example. Cat catches a mouse, bats it around with a warty paw, scratches the wart open, keeps on batting the mouse. Mouse escapes with its life, let's say; and it also escapes with warts. Miss Mouse recovers from her minor injuries and steps out one night with Mr. Toad. They do the Funky Broadway by the side of the road—"

I thought the crazy bastard was going to start dancing.

"—Mouse opens up a wart on the lip of a tin can. They slow dance a little, and pretty soon toad finds himself with real warts alongside all those venom glands that look like warts."

Havermeyer glanced up at me. "You *can* get warts from toads, you know," he said before he looked down again.

"A kid comes along, picks up the toad and sets it on the crest of the fender fin of a '58 Caddy. The toad teeters, loses his balance. His little toad fingers stretch over the peak of the fin. Between those fingers lurks a real wart. His back legs flail, struggle for purchase. The waxy surface of the metal militates against adhesion, and the toad falls. The jagged edge of a tiny scratch on the side of the fender catches the wart as the toad descends.

"Toad is just a memory when the junior high coed rests her arm on the Caddy fin as her boyfriend suggests they do their social studies together in his parents' rec room that night. In a couple days the young lady is in her bath when we hear, 'Oooh, Ma! I got a ugly wart under my arm!'"

Havermeyer had moved around so that he was squatting beside me, getting a straight shot at the warts on the side of my wrist.

"And it's not like they need to be passed from carrier to carrier," he said. "They'll just pop up. On a foot, a tongue, on a penis, in a vagina. You ought to get an eyeful of venereal warts sometime. They look amazingly like baby cauliflower."

"I really ought to," I said. "Everybody should."

"We talk about warts as a virus," Havermeyer said as he worked away, "but they aren't actually viruses themselves. They're the media through which the virus reproduces, launches its satellites, establishes its turf. Warts are how the virus tells us hello." He looked up at me with a satisfied smile.

"Tells us hello?" I said.

"That's right," Havermeyer replied. He bent his head back to his work. "Communication. At least it could be communication," he said. "I'm saying maybe, but I'm thinking probably."

I said I wasn't interested in hearing anymore from the wart virus.

"Number sev . . . en . . . teen!" Havermeyer exclaimed as he scoured the last wart on my wrist.

He straightened up, hooked a stool with his foot, and pulled it over to us. I sat on it and he sat above me on the table with his legs hanging down over my shoulders. As his scissors clicked and hair dropped on my shoulders he told me he was cutting a circle I could cover nicely with a yarmulke.

Havermeyer wrapped his legs around my chest and gave me the shots in my scalp. I flinched every time the needle went in, but he held me pretty hard. He unwrapped his legs and poked my bare scalp with his fingernail until I told him I couldn't feel it. Then he started with the burner.

"Consider this, Russell," he said. "You can reason with warts. You can entreat them. You can maybe even fool them. Ever heard the folk-medicine stories where the local shaman gets the carrier to draw a picture of his warts, then burns the picture or sends it out to sea in a bottle or buries it or gets rid of it some other way?"

"No," I replied.

"Eighty percent of the time the warts go away," Havermeyer said. "Hypnosis works too."

"How do you hypnotize a wart?" I asked.

"How do you hypnotize a wart?" he repeated. "I love it. You don't hypnotize the wart, Russell," he said. "You hypnotize the carrier and tell him his warts will be gone in a certain time. And in eight out of ten cases, they are."

"What if they aren't?" I asked.

"Then we get a bunch a the boys and we burn 'em out," he replied. "But eight out of ten times you tell 'em to go away, they go."

He lowered the burner to the level of my shoulder and the smoke curling off the tip went right up my nose.

"Feature this," he said. "Say your shaman or your shamanette gets you to draw just six of your twenty-nine warts on a piece of paper. Eighty percent of the time the six pictured warts go away and the twenty-three others stick around for another sitting."

He paused for a response and I told him I didn't think I got the point.

"The point," he said, "is how the hell did your body cut off the blood to those six warts and not the others? And what mechanism was it in your body—or in your mind of course—that read the images, identified the wart on the tip of your index finger, did it in, and left you the fingertip as original, as smooth, as if it had never suffered an invasion of anything? So smooth that your postwart fingerprints are identical to your prewart?

"What we're talking about here is either a superintelligent mechanism in the body that we can somehow reach through both conscious and subconscious suggestion in the presence of the wart virus. Or—and this is *my* theory—some external intelligence that understands we've taken offense at its overtures, and therefore says 'bye-bye' as mysteriously, as mischievously, maybe, as it said 'hello.'

"Now, the internal mechanism," Havermeyer went on as he continued rooting out my warts, "the internal mechanism idea offers potential fully in the realm of miracle. Say we found out how to get in touch with this mechanism at will, and in the presence of *all* invasionary cells, not just warts. Among other things"—and he reached down over my head and snapped his fingers in my face—"we could cure cancer like that! We could just say, 'Get on outa here, melanoma!' and melanoma would hit the road.

"But," he kept on, "but . . . but! What if warts *are* the communication of an external intelligence? And what if we could get on good terms with it? What if something as immensely complex as cell rejection were child's play to this entity? We could cure everything! We could customize human life like a '49 Merc!"

I felt pressure on my scalp twice more, then Havermeyer lifted a leg over my head and hopped down off the table.

"That'll do it!" he said. "Nineteen of 'em up here. A full baker's dozen plus six. A grand total of thirty-six warts. At two grand a unit, you owe me 72,000 dollars. I hope you're heavily covered by virus insurance, my friend." He laughed and slapped me on the shoulder and started taping gauze on my wrist.

I asked him what it was really going to cost, and he said thirty bucks. "Less than a buck a wart—cheap at twice the price," he said.

"Wha'd you do to the warts on your wrist?" he asked as he started taping gauze over my bald spot.

"I shaved 'em off one time," I replied.

"Do not do that!" he yelled at me. "Do not ever do that," he said more quietly. "That's the one sure way to spread warts. The ones on your wrist were more calloused and more deeply entrenched than the ones on your head because you messed with them. Amateurs in the wart business," he said, "should not perform surgery on themselves. You've got to be subtle with warts. Either that or you've got to burn 'em right down through the roots. Warts don't have a whole lot of respect for half-measures."

I thanked him and told him I'd remember.

May 23, 1968 at Jen's

I was taking a shower this morning, scrubbing my head with Jen's little shampoo brush, when she said something I didn't hear. I opened my eyes, pulled back the curtain, stuck my head out, and asked her what she'd said. She looked at me with her mouth open and her eyes wide and scared.

In the mirror behind her I saw the blood. My head was covered with bloody lather and bright blood dripped down my face and neck.

"Jesus, Russ," Jen said. "What is it?"

I touched around the top of my head carefully. "I don't know," I said.

I closed the curtain and got back under the spray. I set the brush in the soap dish and felt around my head with both hands as I rinsed off the soap. I couldn't feel anything there, and I didn't feel any pain. I turned off the water, asked Jen to get an old towel, and pulled the curtain all the way open.

I looked in the mirror and didn't see any blood. Jen looked me over and didn't see any either. "Turn around," she said.

I started to turn and we both saw the bright blood matting the side of my head.

"Sit down on the edge of the tub," Jen said. She folded the towel across my shoulders and bent to look. I could feel her fingers moving my hair out of the way. I asked what she saw and she said she didn't see a thing. At the top of my head her fingers stopped.

"What is it?" I said.

"Well . . . ," Jen said.

"It's warts," I said. "That's where I had them before."

"I guess they are," Jen said.

She led me into the bedroom as though I were hurt, sat me on a chair, wiped the blood, and dried the rest of me with the clean part of the towel. "Just stay this way a minute," she said. "They've about stopped bleeding."

Out of the corner of my eye I saw her take her watch off the dresser. "Doctors' offices open in fifteen minutes," she said as she stepped into her jeans. "I'm calling your dermatologist and we're getting these things off as soon as we can."

We sat at the kitchen table and drank our coffee. Mine didn't have much taste. I watched Jen talk on the phone and thought how the warts had grown overnight. I knew they hadn't been there when we made love because Jen would have felt them as she stroked my hair. The fucking things had grown in six hours.

"Our appointment's at three-thirty," Jen said walking back from the phone. "By four-thirty they'll be gone."

I nodded my head and tried to smile at her. But all I could think of was how the warts had grown overnight.

My spirits didn't pick up much when Jen and I got to Spokane. Havermeyer was gone and his brother had taken over his practice. The brothers look exactly alike and they both inspire the same amount of confidence. Which is none. "You guys are twins—right?" I said.

"Not on your life," Havermeyer said. "Bernie's just a punk kid. He's eleven months younger. That's why he's so competitive. He concocts theories like this 'viral communications' shtick just to distract me, then he takes a Ph.D. in some other field and lords it over me that he's becoming a Renaissance man.

"'Viral communications!' Can you believe it! I guess Stanford'll award a fellowship to anybody. They think he's gonna talk warts into curing cancer. What the little fart's probably doing is sitting on the beach, writing a children's book about an elephant seal who yearns to dance ballet.

"Two years ago Bernie told me he was taking the Schawlow-Townes Fellowship at Harvard—my old alma mammie, by the way—and you know what he did?"

"What?" I said. I really wasn't in the mood.

"We have an appointment to get warts removed," Jen said.

"Sure," Havermeyer said. "But you'll love this. Bernie had the fellowship all right, but what he mostly spent his time on was taking a Ph.D. in art history and turning his dissertation into a coffee table book on *Epidermal Anomalies as Illustrated in Flemish Portraiture*. He's a sick kid, but you really hafta appreciate his breadth of quirkiness."

Jen stepped up to him. "Look, Doctor," she said. "We'd like to get these things taken off, then we'd like to be on our way."

Havermeyer looked Jen over, then centered his eyes on her breasts. "Well," he said, "whatever you say. But personally I think they look fine on you." He shook his head. "Your time for the hundred will go way down," he said. "But I bet you both end up missing them."

"Oh, Christ!" Jen said. She walked to the window and looked out.

"Come on, Dr. Havermeyer," I said. "The warts are on my head. Start burnin' 'em, please."

"Okay," Havermeyer said. "Just a little derm humor."

He told me to take off my shirt and sit up on the table. Jen walked over and stood beside me.

"You might want to wait outside," Havermeyer said to her. "There are funner things to look at than wart-burnings. You could read my brother's book."

"I'm gonna stay," Jen said. "I'll be fine. I castrate horses," she said. She looked him in the eye.

"All right!" Havermeyer replied. He held his hand out, palm up. Jen slapped it after a second or two.

He looked through my hair, found the warts, and snipped a clear spot around them. "You say my brother did these about a month ago?"

"That's right," I replied.

"Well, the kid didn't go deep enough," he said. "But they're gone for good this time. Mark 'er down," he said. "And we'll send the bill to Dr. Viral Communications, care of Stanford University."

He stood on a stool, gave me the shots, then started burning. Jen held my hand. You could hear them sizzle. Jen turned her head away from the smoke.

"Nasty, ain't it?" Havermeyer said. "Just imagine a whole burning person."

He finished up and told me to put my shirt on. But then he stopped me. "Hold on a sec," he said. "Let's take a gander at these."

"At what?" Jen and I both said.

"At this," Havermeyer said.

He pushed me down on the table on my stomach and he and Jen looked at my lower back. I bent around but couldn't see anything. He held a mirror for me and I saw them. They looked like calluses—like the ones I'd had on my wrist. But these were as big around as nickels.

"You guys wanna leave this patch?" Havermeyer asked. "Grow attached to them, did you?"

"Karl," Jen said, "you didn't have these yesterday?"

"No," I said. Oh, Christ! I thought. "I don't think so," I said.

"Well, whadaya say we excise these babies?" Havermeyer said.

"Do it," I said.

He said he was going to cut these and make sure he got all the roots. He moved me to my side and gave me a shot. When I couldn't feel him pinch me anymore he started cutting.

I felt the pressure of the scalpel, but that was all. Jen had moved to the head of the table and taken my hand. I felt the pressure increase and heard Havermeyer grunting. Jen was looking back with her jaw set. Then I felt the cutting and let out a yell. The pain stopped as soon as Havermeyer did, but I'd already broken out all over in sweat.

Havermeyer whipped around the table and got into his cabinet. "They're deeper than I thought," he said as he worked with his back to us. "I didn't go deep enough with the analgesic. Sorry, Russ," he said.

"It's okay," I said. I was starting to feel a little sick.

Jen got down on her knees so her head was level with mine. "It's okay, Hon," she whispered. "A few minutes more and they'll all be gone."

Havermeyer walked back with a syringe that had a needle on it about four inches long. I flinched every time he put it in, but after a minute or so I couldn't feel anything from my nipples to my knees.

It wasn't long before he exhaled a great "Whew!" "That's it," he said. "All stitched up." He moved in front of me and held out a stainless steel dish. "We got 'em," he said. "And are they whoppers!"

Jen stood up. When Havermeyer showed her what was in the dish her face went the color of bone. "I've grown horseradishes that never got this big," Havermeyer said.

"Let's see," I said.

He lowered the dish. Six white things that did look like horseradishes with the stalks cut off lay in a film of blood. One of them was longer than the needle he shot me with the second time.

He held a gauze pad over the spot and taped it down. He gave a roll of tape and two small boxes to Jen. "They'll seep a little tonight," he said. "Just keep putting pads on until it stops."

He walked to the window and turned and leaned against the radiator. "Russell," he said, "I want you to just lie here a while until you feel like dancing. And I want you to leave your phone number at the desk. I'm going to send these to the lab. Just to make sure we don't have any funny tissue here."

Funny tissue? I thought.

Havermeyer tossed a towel and it landed on my head. "No charge for this one, kids," he said. "We bill this one to Brother Bernie." And he walked out.

Jen dried the sweat off me, then she pulled up a chair and lay her head by mine until I felt okay to get up.

TIMOTHY DEKIN

I am currently teaching in the English Department at Northwestern University. My books of poems are Winter Fruit *and* Carnival. *My fiction has appeared in* TriQuarterly Magazine, *and I am at work on a novel.*

"I have been interested in the renaissance 'confessional' poem (that is, the poem of moral inventory), the best example of which might be Gascoigne's 'Woodsmanship.' 'The Errand' is my attempt to exploit the convention. 'The Plague' is inspired by Defoe's *Journal of the Plague Year.*"

The Plague

London, 1665

The worst of August. By then, death was no
Item at ale to make us cluck our tongues.
We had run dry of tears. I saw a man
One morning step around a man like dung.

I saw a fisherman place two cod, bread,
And shillings on a rock, then back away
Until his wife retrieved them and walked off.
The rich had left, and those who couldn't stayed.

One mother left her children soon enough,
And some said this was evil, some said not:
"Love is a killer," she implored her neighbors,
"It stayed my husband, and now what's he got?"

We were all hoarse from shouting across the street
Or through a door to friends we feared were marked.
The clergy said our plight mimicked our crime;
That we had always guarded heart from heart,

Suspicious, offensive in each other's sight,
And all our charity but to be liked.
Our Father, and our thieving brother Jack,
Both shunned us; our hearts and pockets left unpicked.

The night the Dog Star set, three thousand felt
Its hot breath and the long rasp of its tongue.
One man chased down his wife and kissed her saying,
"E'en now thou hast it and we'll soon be one."

Despair set in. We knew we were all doomed.
But then the streets filled up: those who had waited
Left hope and fear, ran to the market, church,
The stews, the pubs. And then the plague abated.

♦   ♦   ♦

The Errand

After so long, I'd thought my cure was done.
But still I detour by one little bar.
I have re-earned a welcome.
                                        I'd buy one
Small glowing cognac to feel up to par,
Which I could drink one handed now not two
Or leave there, radiating near my change
As it seems most of my new friends can do.
Sipping, I'd take stock. There is stock again
After three years' saved up sobriety,
Though mine's a perishable good I've heard,
Subject to boredom, fear, self-pity, me,
And tallied on a cocktail napkin, blurred
And ringed by the wet impress of my glass,
Adds up to what? A man who won't cause trouble?
Who has a job, friends, credit; whose great task
Is to live normally? Make mine a double.
There's an oasis whose bright waters flash
Chilling reflections of my glistening fur;
Springs leap up from the rocks—I bite at, dash,
And though I keep an eye out on the herd
Slumped in their postures of regret, I meet
My face, amazing in a moon stunned pool,
And sniff my image till my cheeks are wet
Lifting up from the bar. I scrape my stool.
The noose beside my ear has settled full,
Red loop of neon tubing, my old leash
I almost wish someone would tighten, pull,
That I might find direction, or release;
Some keeper, orange emblazoned crossing-guard
To halt the traffic for this wayward dog
Whose master has forgotten.
                                        I regard
The sign until a crowd moves me along;

Then board a bus that shudders and shuts down
For every stop light, each curb's human freight,
While up above me on a bar of chrome
I see that shiny, miniature face—
Which my hand covers when, as more crowd on,
Swaying a little, I offer up my place.

ALISON DEMING

Alison Deming was born in 1946 in Connecticut and has lived mostly in New England. After receiving an M.F.A. from Vermont College, she was a fellow at the Fine Arts Work Center in Provincetown (1984–85) and a Wallace Stegner Fellow at Stanford (1987–88). Her work has appeared in Black Warrior Review, Nimrod, Tendril, Denver Quarterly, *and other journals. Currently she coordinates the writing program at the Fine Arts Work Center.*

"In high school I loved science, especially biology, because it seemed to care intensely about the physical world and to explain how I got to be a part of it. More recently, I wanted to take up that interest in some poems, because that seemed like a good way to dwell in the desire that drives science, rather than in the ruts it leaves behind."

Science

Then it was the future, though what's arrived
isn't what we had in mind, all chrome and
cybernetics, when we set up exhibits
in the cafeteria for the judges
to review what we'd made of our hypotheses.

The class skeptic (he later refused to sign
anyone's yearbook, calling it a sentimental
degradation of language) chloroformed mice,
weighing the bodies before and after
to catch the weight of the soul,

wanting to prove the invisible
real as a bagful of nails. A girl
who knew it all made cookies from euglena,
a one-celled compromise between animal and plant,
she had cultured in a flask.

We're smart enough, she concluded,
to survive our mistakes, showing photos of farmland,
poisoned, gouged, eroded. No one believed
he really had built it when a kid no one knew
showed up with an atom smasher, confirming that

the tiniest particles could be changed
into something even harder to break.
And one whose mother had cancer (hard to admit now,
it was me) distilled the tar of cigarettes
to paint in on the backs of shaven mice.

She wanted to know what it took,
a little vial of sure malignancy,
to prove a daily intake smaller
than a single aspirin could finish
something as large as a life. I thought of this

because, today, the dusky seaside sparrow
became extinct. It may never be as famous,
reads the clipping, as the pterodactyl or the dodo,
but the last one died today, a resident
of Walt Disney World where now its tissue samples

lie frozen, in case someday we learn to clone
one from a few cells. Like those instant dinosaurs
that come in a gelatin capsule—just add water
and they inflate. One other thing this
brings to mind. The euglena girl won first prize

both for science and, I think, in retrospect, for hope.

♦   ♦   ♦

My Intention

What I look for is never what I find
and what I find is always a moment
which wouldn't have arrived if I hadn't
been distracted, mind pacing
from one thought to another that doesn't connect
until I look on the map for the nearest green patch without roads.
Green for the clarity of things that metabolize
standing in one place. So I call up friends
and we drive up the switchbacks past the scorch of summer

to hike off while the sun finds the next ridge west
and we guess a way back with no trailmarkers,
down into the greener basin, redwoods covered with moss
and the air heavy as canvas left out in the rain.
Oaks shell us with acorns and we go farther down
into the mossy air, the trees bigger than steeples,
so many with cores blackened and hollow from lightning strikes,

but solid above, climbing, hardly tapering, up
towards their supper of light.

But whatever we hiked off starts pouring
back over us, driving back down, laundry or work or the argument
that still hangs in the air. Whatever didn't get finished
is waiting, my drifting distraction, which I had hoped
the day would transform into something I could love.
My friend's neighbor stands in the shadow of his driveway
with binoculars. That's Jupiter, he says, the brightest
it will ever be, its orbit and ours at their closest.
Then he brings out a jury-rigged telescope—

eyepiece from a flea market, shaft of plumber's pipe
mounted on a junked record player turntable, pivoting
on little squares of Teflon—but the mirror,
the blessed two hundred dollar mirror, a simple twelve-inch
Newtonian reflector of no ordinary wonder—there,
he shows us, are the moons of Jupiter, four errant darlings,
one so close to the planet it looks like a blister at 10 o'clock,
and casting its shadow at 11. That's when it comes to me,
getting the grey bands at the equator into focus,
that this centering on what drifts was my intention all along.

STEPHEN DIXON

A number of nonacademic jobs since leaving the Stanford Writing Program in '65, before getting a teaching post in the writing seminars at Johns Hopkins University in 1980. Married Anne Frydman and have two daughters, Sophia and Antonia. Ten books published since 1976: four novels and six story collections, the last collection, The Play, *from Coffee House Press (1988), and the last novel,* Garbage, *from Cane Hill Press (1988).*

"As usual, nothing or nothing much to say. The story, in first draft, sort of wrote itself, and when it was over it said so. Then lots of rewriting before I felt satisfied, but always trying to keep the spontaneity of the first draft. I've an idea what I was trying to do with it but the reader might have other ideas."

◆   ◆   ◆

A Sloppy Story

"LISTEN TO THIS," I say. "This guy comes in and says to me and I say to him and he says and I say and the next thing I know he does this to me and I do that to him and he this and I that and a woman comes in and sees us and says and I say to her and he says to me and she to him and he says and does this to her and I say and do that to him and she doesn't say anything but does this and that to us both and then a second time and he says and she says and I say and we all do and say and that's it, the end, what happened, now what do you think?"

"It won't work," a man says. His partner says "It will work, I know it will" and I say "Please, gentlemen, make up your minds. Do you think it will work or not?" The first man says no and his partner yes and I clasp my hands in front of my chest hoping they'll agree it will work and give me money for it so I won't have to be broke anymore or at least not for the next year, when the phone rings and the first man picks up the receiver and says "Yuh?" The person on the other end says something and the man says "You're kidding me now, aren't you?" His partner says "Who is it, something important?" and the man says and his partner says "Just tell him to go fly away with his project, now and forever" and I just sit there and the man hangs up the phone and says to us "Now where were we?"

"I was," I say. "He was," his partner says. "Okay," he says, "Let's continue where we left off from, though quickly, as I got a long day" and we talk and he says "I still don't go for it" and his partner says "I'm starting to agree with you, now and forever" and I say "Please, gentlemen, let me tell the story over.

Maybe it will be more convincing the second time around and I promise to be quicker about it" and I start the story from the beginning: guy coming in, says to me, me to him, does this, I do, woman, what we all said and did and then the partner, not agreeing, phone ringing, call ending, my retelling the story. After I finish I say "So what do you think? Will it work?"

"No," they both say and I say "Well, no harm in my having tried, I guess" and the first man says "No harm is right except for our precious lost time" and sticks out his hand and I shake it and shake his partner's hand and say "Can I use your men's room before I go? It might be my last chance for a while." His partner says "Second door to the right on your way out to the elevator" and I say "Which way is the elevator again, left or right when I get out of your office?" and he says and I say "Thanks" and they say and I leave, wave good-bye to the receptionist, go to the men's room on their floor, take the elevator down, go through the building's lobby to the street. It's a nice day, finally. It was raining heavily when I came in. My umbrella! Damn, left it upstairs, should I go back for it? No. Yes. What the hell, why not, it's not an old umbrella, it's still a good serviceable umbrella. And if I don't get it I'll have to buy a new umbrella at probably twice what the one upstairs cost me three years ago the way inflation's going crazy today.

I go back through the lobby, elevator, get on it, upstairs, their floor, past the men's room, into their office and the receptionist says and I say "I know, but I" and point to it and the partners come out of the room we were talking in before just as I grab my umbrella and look at me but don't say anything when I say hello but just walk into another room and I say good-bye to the receptionist and she nods at me and starts typing rapidly and I leave the office, elevator, lobby and see it's raining heavily again. Rain coming down like, streets filled with water like, people running out of the rain like, sky like, traffic like, I open the umbrella and walk in the rain totally protected because of my umbrella, long raincoat and boots and think "Well, I at least did one thing right today and that's going back for the umbrella, and maybe one other thing and that's wearing the right rain clothes," when someone ducks under my umbrella, a woman, hair soaked by the rain, and says "Mind if I walk with you as far as the bank on the corner? It closes in a few minutes and I have to put in some money by today."

"Sure," I say and we walk, I hold the umbrella, she her coat together at the collar, and talk, she "Can we walk faster?" I say sure, she asks where I was going, I say to an office building a block past her bank, she asks, I tell her, she says "Well what do you know," because it seems she's a good friend of the very man I want to see most about the same story project I spoke to those partners about, but who I haven't been able to get an appointment with for more than a month. So I suggest, she says "Yes, but let me get done with my bank first," goes in, comes out, we have coffee at a coffee shop across the street, she asks, I tell, starting with the guy who comes in and says and I say and we do and the woman and all we said and did and then the partners, men's room, lobby, sunshine, umbrella, should I? shouldn't I? upstairs, receptionist and partners again, I retrieve, I leave, typing rapidly, raining heavily, everything looking like something else, open the umbrella, woman ducks under, though at first I didn't think it was a woman, I thought it was a mugger, walk, talk, faster, she asks, I say, well what do you know, she knows so and so, I suggest, she says yes, bank, coffee shop and coffees. "So what do you think?" I say. "Your friend will like it or not or am I fooling myself?"

"If he doesn't like it he ought to change professions," she says and borrows a coin from me, makes a phone call, comes back, "He says to hustle right over," we do, elevator, office, receptionist, secretary, big how do you do from her friend who I tell the whole story to from the beginning, he says "Better than I expected even from what Pam told me it would be over the phone. I'll take it" and we shake hands, sign a contract, he writes out a check, we drink champagne to our future success, Pam and I leave, downstairs, lobby, sunny outside. Oh my God, I think, I forgot my umbrella again. "Oh my God," I say, "I left my umbrella upstairs."

"Leave it," she says, "since you now have enough money to buy ten umbrellas. Twenty if you want, though I don't know why you would." "True," I say. "Want to go for another coffee?" "Coffee?" she says. "I think a drink's more what we deserve. I know I sure do after what I just did for you." "True," I say, "and we'll go to the best place possible" and we start walking. Sun goes, clouds come, we walk faster, looking for a classier bar than the three we pass, but not fast enough, as the rain suddenly comes, drenching us before we can find protection from it.

"I knew I should have gone up for my umbrella," I say. "So we're wet," she says. "So what? It'll make the day more memorable for you. In fact, what I'd do if I were you, just to make the day one of the most memorable of your life, is—" but I cut her off and say "I know, I might" and she says "Not you might, you should" and I say "I know, I will" and she smiles, I smile, we take each other's hands, put our arms around each other's waists, "Let's," she says, "Let's," I say, and run out from under the awning into the rain. "Dad, look at those crazy people getting wet," a boy says, protected by his father's umbrella.

"You know what I want most of all now that I've sold my story project?" I say to her, standing in the pouring rain and holding and hugging her and looking over her shoulder at the boy being pulled along by his father because he wants to stay and watch us and she says "What?" and I tell her and she says and I say "And also to eventually walk in the pouring rain with an umbrella over my future wife and me and future daughter or son, but with the child being around that boy's age." "Why an umbrella?" she says and I say and she says "Silly, you don't get colds that way" and I say and she says "No" and I say "Oh." Just then a cab drives by too close to the curb and splashes us up to our waists and I start cursing and shaking my fist at it and she says and I say "You're right, raincoats and all we're already slopping wet" and we laugh and go into a bar a half-block away and order a glass of wine each.

"What are you two so happy about," the bartender says, "besides getting yourselves dripping wet and probably catching your death?" and I say "Really interested?" and he says "Interested" and I say "Then I'll tell you" and do, starting from the time the man came in, woman, partners, office, men's room, lobby, sunny again, umbrella and rain, woman and bank, coffees, what do you know, so and so, deal, champagne, check, no umbrella, mixing the story up a little here and there, sun goes, rain falls, running through it, father and son, my thoughts and wants, bar, drinks, bartender and he says "That story rates a drink on the house if I ever heard one" and pours some more wine into our glasses, we toast and drink, he holds up his glass of soda water, people coming in ask what the celebration's about, I tell them, from beginning to end, leaving a little out now and then. "Very interesting," one of them says and buys us another wine each. By that time the rain's stopped but we're not dry yet and I say to Pam "Let's make it a perfect end to a great day" and she says "No, really, I've had a change of mind, besides my boy friend waiting at home" and goes.

Just then a man comes in and I say "You wouldn't believe—" and he says "Wouldn't believe what? Because if you think you've something to say, listen to my story first" and he tells me about his wife who suddenly left him last week same day his dad got a coronary and his dog ran away and I say "Excuse me, you're right, and I think I better get home before it rains again" and I get off the stool. "Wait," he says, "you haven't heard the worst of it yet," but I'm out the door, rain's started again, I hail a cab, feel in my pockets, no wallet, wave the cab away and walk the two miles to my home. Phone's ringing when I enter the apartment. It's the man who bought my story project. He says "Tear up that check and contract as I just received a cable from overseas that says our company's gone bankrupt." I shout "Liar." He says "Not so." I slam down the receiver, am shivering, sneezing, want to get into a hot tub, but for some reason the water only runs cold.

HARRIET DOERR

Harriet Doerr is the author of a novel, Stones for Ibarra *(Viking Press and Penguin Books, 1984), and of short stories that have appeared in* The New Yorker *and in literary journals. Entering Stanford in the class of 1931, she received her B.A. in 1977 and was a Wallace Stegner Fellow in 1980–81. She received a Transatlantic Review–Henfield Foundation award in 1982, a National Endowment for the Arts grant in 1983, and the American Book Award for First Fiction in 1984.*

"From the moment I began to invent Chuy Santos, before I had any idea he could sing or drive a car by the light of the moon, he had me in thrall. As he took shape on the page, it became increasingly clear that he and I were to have little in common. He finally grew into my opposite, a blithe, amoral, tenor storehouse of all the songs ever written. That must be why I love him."

◆   ◆   ◆

The Red Taxi

From *Stones for Ibarra*

CHUY SANTOS WAS NOT the sort of man who would kill his two best friends in order to own a car. The part in his hair was too straight, his glance was too direct, and his voice was the voice of an archangel.

On Christmas, Ash Wednesday, Good Friday, and his saint's day Chuy attended mass in the parish church of Ibarra, having confessed the previous day to his transgressions of the intervening months. The cura, on his side of the curtained screen, listened absentmindedly to Chuy's accounts of lust and avarice and said to himself, This man is Jesús Santos Larín, who should have been singled out as a boy and guided to the seminary. Such a voice should properly be an instrument of God. At the end of the confession the priest recovered himself and told Chuy to sin no more.

When the idea first came to Jesús Santos that he might establish a taxi service between the village of Ibarra and Concepción, he was the proprietor of a side-street café of four tables and twelve chairs. Here his wife knelt every morning to scrub the floor with a fiber brush while her hair fell over her shoulders into the greasy suds. Then she would cook tripe on a stove in the corner and set out twelve earthenware plates as if they might attract twelve diners.

Chuy did not confide to his wife his ambition to own a taxi. He only said, "This café might as well be situated at the entrance to the graveyard." Or occasionally, "I should have married a beautiful woman or a good cook, one or the other."

But when Chuy made these complaints he had already been to Concepción to visit a certain weedy piece of ground that was partly a used-car lot and partly a junkyard. He had only to walk two minutes along the ruts, stepping around rusty axles and inserting himself between crushed fenders, before he discovered the car that was to be his. It was a twelve-year-old Volkswagen with patched tires and a windshield so splintered that through it the sky and two huisache trees in full yellow flower and all the accumulated wreckage surrounding it appeared as fragments of precious gems. Chuy pulled open a door that hung loose from its hinges, sat behind the steering wheel between two coiling springs, and leaned from left to right. This motion caused the appearance and disappearance before his eyes of emeralds, amethysts, rubies, and a mosaic arch of sapphires over it all.

Chuy put his hands on the wheel and listened to his own arresting voice talking to itself.

"This glass will have to be replaced as a condition of purchase," Chuy heard himself say. "And the engine, of course, must be inspected. Another thing, what about the lights?" As though commanded by his own words he pulled out a knob and a single headlight lit up, as well as a weak bulb over his head.

"I will insist on a review of the entire electrical system," said Chuy, and as it indeed came about, the faulty headlight and one taillight were in time adequately repaired. But the left taillight, through an eccentricity of the wiring, never stopped blinking from the moment it was put in order. Because of the confusion caused by this unintended signaling, the Volkswagen later on became involved in a number of accidents, but none of these resulted in fatalities.

Nor could the bulb in the ceiling be turned off except by unscrewing it. Most of the time Chuy considered this to be more trouble than it was worth, so the light generally shone night and day. Those of Chuy's passengers who traveled after dark became accustomed to the continuous glow in which they sat faintly visible to all the world, like actors on a stage lit by fireflies.

Chuy discussed the purchase of his car with the two men in Ibarra who had been his best friends since childhood. Together they shared these things: the ability to keep a secret, the desire to become rich, and the same godfather. But this godfather had already died in an accident involving foolhardiness, pulque, and knives.

Like Chuy, whom the cura addressed as Jesús Santos Larín, these friends had three names. The first name their parents gave them at birth, then their father's last name, then their mother's family name, which would not succeed them, and, once carved on their gravestones, would be abandoned there. But there was no need to know the names of Chuy's friends. They had never been called anything but El Gallo and El Golondrino, the Rooster and the Swallow. These nicknames suited each man as neatly as a sheath fits a blade.

El Gallo had a big chest, chips of flint for eyes, and a habit of kicking at the ground wherever he stood, whether there were pebbles and clods underfoot or not. Had he actually been a rooster in a barnyard he could have claimed six hens. These were his wife, his second cousin Lili, the two Benítez girls, a woman in Loreto, and a woman in Lagos.

El Golondrino was small-boned and light as a tissue-paper kite on a gusty March morning. He could cross the plaza from one arcade to another and never be seen in passage. The Swallow lived alone in a mud house furnished with packing crates for tables and nail kegs for chairs.

Within three hours of his visit to the used-car lot Chuy Santos outlined his plan to El Gallo and El Golondrino. They met where they could have privacy, in the middle of an old stone bridge on the outskirts of the village. This bridge crossed the arroyo between two mining properties that, once gutted of pure silver, had been abandoned to cave-ins and rising water.

At first Chuy's friends listened in silence. Then they said, "What is the price of this car?"

Chuy looked up the arroyo past the low white house of the North Americans, past the old monastery, to the hoist tower of La Malagueña, the copper mine where El Gallo and El Golondrino worked underground.

"Twenty thousand pesos," said Chuy, "and three years to pay at 40 percent annual interest. Remember this. While we are buying the car we will be living on its profits." Then Chuy looked the other way, toward the bend of the arroyo and the nuns' school where the three men now on this bridge had sat at one desk in the first grade. "The down payment is a third of the total cost."

El Gallo scuffed at a stone block with his right foot.

Chuy went on as if he had studied law at the autonomous national university. "As driver, the car will be registered in my name. As equal investors in the down payment, you will have your money back in one year and double it in the next. But first I will try to borrow the entire amount from don Ricardo, the American. He is a man who acts on impulse." Chuy smoothed his hair with both hands. "An example of this is his presence here in Ibarra. And the presence of the wife he brought with him."

The men leaned silently on the ancient balustrade of the bridge.

"What color is it?" asked Chuy's friends, and first Chuy said, "Like a tomato." Then, "More like fresh *vino tinto*." He thought again. "Exactly the color of a cardinal's cape," and the other two nodded as if the Cardinal of Mexico had celebrated mass in the parochial church of Ibarra yesterday and emerged later on into the sun to prove to the mongrels on the steps the eternal verity of red.

On a cold starry evening Jesús Santos went to the house of the North Americans and stood outside the window of the dining room. Don Ricardo Everton and his wife, doña Sara, were inside, eating *chiles rellenos* and dividing a single bottle of beer between them. This economy seemed odd to Chuy, who knew that in the regular size Dos Equis cost only three pesos and was even less by the case. Wall lamps lit up the room and two unnecessary candles burned in green glass chimneys on the table.

There is no way to understand this señor Everton and his señora, said Chuy to himself. So rich and yet so poor. He tapped on the window and saw don Ricardo stop eating and cross the hall to open the front door.

From her place at the table Sara heard Chuy's voice and sat transfixed, listening, her beer glass raised in her hand. When the door closed behind the visitor she said, "Who is that man with the beautiful voice?"

"Chuy Santos," said Richard. He looked at his wife, who was gazing abstractedly through the window into the dark. "But I have no idea if he can sing." For he had detected behind her eyes an image, a gathering of people in the walled patio under an April moon. There would be paper lanterns strung from trees, and roses and grapes on the vines. Notes of a guitar would scatter like a broken necklace on the tiles. Then the voice of Jesús Santos would pour into the night to astound the gentlemen in hand-tooled boots and the ladies in thin silk slippers.

Richard noticed all this unfolding in his wife's eyes and said, "Chuy wants to borrow twenty thousand pesos. For a taxi. Who knows if he can sing?"

Jesús Santos met again with his two friends on the bridge. "The American will not cooperate," he said.

El Gallo clapped his arms against his side as if he felt a chill. "Then we must acquire the money some other way," he said. He looked down into the arroyo where a few plastic bags and rusty cans had been cast away for the first heavy rains to float off to the valley. "I have an idea in connection with a tunnel at the mine," he said, and met the eyes of El Golondrino.

The Swallow said nothing. He picked up a rock from the bridge and with a single wide swing of his arm let it fly at an Orange Crush bottle twelve meters away, causing the glass to explode into tawny fragments that burned like coals on the sandy bottom.

"What do you propose?" said Chuy to El Gallo.

"I must discuss this matter first with the Swallow here," said the Rooster, and tapped his small friend on the shoulder. "But before we execute my plan, which is dangerous, we must try two other things."

"What things?" said Chuy.

"First you must go to the owner of the car and persuade him to lower the price. Then you must go again to the American and prove to him that the vehicle is now a bargain."

"I may or may not do these things," said Chuy.

♦   ♦   ♦

The next morning he was waiting at the iron gate of the used-car lot when the owner pulled it open. The Volkswagen, looking brighter and more powerful than ever, was still there.

"I would like to try it out," said Chuy.

"Come back in one month," said the owner. "But leave a deposit."

Chuy pulled out a wad of money and from the top peeled off the two five-hundred-peso bills he had borrowed the day before from his father-in-law. These he held casually, as he would have held a losing lottery ticket or a burned-out cigarette. Now the dealer, all at once turned cordial, invited him to enter the detached cab of a truck which he used as an office. Here the two men bargained and at the end of an hour, half of talk and half of silence, the price of the car had dropped from twenty thousand to fifteen thousand pesos, the down payment to only five thousand.

They returned to the red Volkswagen, where Chuy stood a moment in reflection, his hand resting on the hood through which he felt the echoes of the engine's long career. He gave the dealer one of the bills.

"My restaurant business permits me very little time away," said Chuy. "I cannot return here for two months." And he gave the proprietor a second bill. "That is your deposit, to be applied against the down payment. But I must drive this car before I buy it." His palm still lay on the blistered paint. "And it must be in the finest condition." With this, Chuy lifted his hand and walked away.

He returned to the North Americans' house that afternoon and asked to speak to don Ricardo. He made his request of the señora who, bareheaded and wearing workman's pants, was standing on a stone wall three meters high to thin out the olive tree that stretched over it.

Soon she will be climbing the branches, thought Chuy, which, thin as she is, may fail to support her.

"*Buenas tardes,* señora," he said out loud.

Sara, halfway into the tree, her head sprinkled with silver leaves and her face with powdery dust, heard his voice and was struck motionless, holding a branch in her left hand, a pair of clippers in her right. She waited for him to speak again, and when he did not she disengaged herself from the tree and looked down. A web, with the spider curled tight at the center, hung from her shoulder.

"You are Jesús Santos," she said. From the wall she stared at the part in Chuy's hair, so exact it might have been plotted by instruments. "Do you sing?" she asked.

Chuy ignored this question. "Look, señora," he said. "I must speak to your husband."

"What about?" said the woman, making no move to descend from the wall, though a ladder was propped against it.

"A matter that can only be discussed with don Ricardo himself."

"He is working on the drawings of a new head frame for the mine and has asked not to be disturbed."

She is lying, thought Chuy. She wants no one to know that don Ricardo is ill again.

"*Otra vez la gripa?*" he said out loud in tones that seemed to have healing powers of their own. Above him the American señora denied this and set off a small rain of leaves which fell from her head down to his.

Leaves still dotted her hair as she descended the ladder and pulled the cobweb from her sleeve. "Is it about your taxi?" she asked.

"About my taxi, yes," said Chuy. "But the entire situation has changed as of this morning."

"Tell me," she said, and they sat down under an olive tree on a carved wooden bench with a cracked back.

"This car," began Chuy, and went on to describe it as he might describe a racing stallion, the ex-president's yacht, or the Emperor Maximilian's festooned and gilded carriage, three things he had never seen. He noticed that don Ricardo's wife listened attentively to every word he spoke. When he paused briefly in his recital she said nothing and seemed only to be waiting for him to go on.

At last she spoke. "But who will your passengers be? To travel by bicycle or bus is much less costly."

"Señora, you have forgotten those to whom time is a matter of life or death. Those who, if they hope to survive, must travel by car whether they can afford it or not. Those with lungs that bleed and wounds that fester. You are not considering the damage inflicted by knives and guns, and by the maniacs at the wheels of trucks."

Sara remained silent.

"Think of this, señora," Chuy went on. "While the mine's van is delivering an accident victim to the hospital in Concepción, at the same time I, in my taxi, can deposit at the specialist's door the grandmother with the abscessed tooth, the infant with the club foot, the young wife who has been in labor for two days."

"Come back tomorrow afternoon," said doña Sara. "I will speak to my husband before then. But don't count on his support."

It is hard to move the hearts of these Americans, Chuy thought to himself.

Later the same day Chuy met his friends on the arch of the bridge. When they heard his report El Gallo looked toward the hills with eyes the color of lead and El Golondrino produced a slingshot, loaded it with a pebble, and killed a sparrow perched on the branch of a cottonwood.

To stiffen their resolve Chuy said, "Remember. The price is down and the American may yet support us in some way. Unless it is true that he is losing money on the mine."

El Gallo fixed the shards of his slaty glance upon his friend. "He is certain to be losing money. The *conquistadores* themselves could have found no profit in this ore." He kicked at a milkweed that had sprouted from a crack. "But all that is about to change. Eh, Golondrino?" and he poked the little man's ribs.

"Next week we will enter an unwatered tunnel where no one has set foot since the War of the Independence. This tunnel might as well have been excavated by an earthworm making a path through the roots of a cedar tree." El Gallo let forth a strident laugh. "It is so crooked that not a man working there will see the neighbor to his right or to his left." And El Gallo thumped his fellow miner hard upon the back.

"What is there to gain from that?" asked Jesús Santos, the restaurant proprietor.

"Precisely this," said El Gallo. "This tunnel intersects an unexplored deposit of silver. Not mere traces of silver but enough to be separated and weighed."

At these words Chuy heard a motor start up eighty kilometers away. He watched a car that was out of sight, beyond the mountains, split the countryside in two, dividing the landscape as a line of red ink would divide a map. He saw himself at the wheel of this car.

The next afternoon Chuy presented himself at the Evertons' door. To his regret it was doña Sara who opened it.

"Forgive me, Jesús," she said, as if she had committed an infraction of federal

law. "There were so many . . . I had so much . . ." At this point her voice
wandered off and was lost.

Chuy stared at her and said to himself, It is becoming increasingly difficult
to communicate.

Finding a few words at last, she asked him to wait inside. Then she disappeared, closing two doors behind her.

He stood in the hall next to a scarred leather chest which in his opinion would
have been better strapped to the back of a tinsmith's mule. On the chest was
the señora's handbag. Also a wooden religious figure in poor condition, its
painted robe scattered over with chipped roses.

"Who is this personage?" Chuy asked himself, speaking aloud since there
was no one to hear. He gazed for a moment at doña Sara's bag, then back into
the sunken eyes of the figure. "It is not San Juan, San Antonio, or San Francisco.
It might be San Pedro without his keys." Again he considered the señora's
handbag. "She is a reckless woman," he said, "to leave her valuables in open
view, next to the unlocked door." Listening, and hearing two voices at a great
distance, Chuy opened the bag. Then he turned his back to the figure on the
chest, took from the wallet two five-hundred-peso bills, and folded them into
his pocket.

Now footsteps approached from behind the closed doors. Chuy was disappointed for the second time to see the señora appear instead of the señor.

She brought the answer he anticipated. Don Ricardo refused to finance the
Volkswagen and would promise only this, that if neither the mine pickup nor
his own car were available he would depend on Chuy's taxi in the event of an
emergency at the mine.

Then doña Sara said, "With all the warnings to miners and the posting of
signs there should be no accidents. Even the dynamiting of tunnels is under the
supervision of a cautious foreman. Therefore," she went on, "it is hard to believe
an accident could occur." And Chuy saw that she had deposited her faith, all at
one time, not in God but in the common sense, good nature, and predictable
behavior of man.

"I imagine you can borrow the money to cover the down payment from any
bank," said the señora.

What an imagination, thought Chuy. This woman probably notices faces in
clouds, spirits in water, and words in the wind.

On the following Saturday Chuy, making an unscheduled visit to the church,
sat across from the cura in the confessional booth. He had no sooner said, "Pray
for me, father, for I have sinned," than the priest recognized him as Jesús Santos
Larín and began to wonder if he might be taught to sing aves and alleluias.

First Chuy confessed to the ordinary vices, then he allowed a silence to fall,
and finally said, "I came across two five-hundred-peso bills and kept them."

The cura concentrated with an effort. "Did you ask those around you if the
money was theirs?" And when he was told there was no one in sight, the priest
said, "In that case the two bills were yours to claim since the next passerby
would have picked them up if you had not." Chuy was silent again and in order
to listen a little longer the cura asked him how he would spend this money.

At that, Chuy entered into a complicated response, beginning with an analysis of the Volkswagen and ending with an account of the proposed taxi service, but the cura heard only the rich tones that conveyed this torrent of information.

The priest, who had a collection of old Victor records, identified Chuy's voice as tenor and soon found himself becoming fretful once again as to why he had been passed over for elevation to monseñor and eventually to bishop. For the present occupant of the episcopal throne had been a country boy like himself and they had entered the seminary on the same day. There was no more difference between them than between two pinto beans. A simple matter of politics, thought the parish priest as he listened to Chuy's resonant appraisals of pistons and valves.

Had I had the good fortune to be appointed bishop, the priest told himself, I might have attended the ecumenical council in Rome and from there traveled the length of Italy from Naples to Milan. And while Jesús Santos Larín explained one by one the rehabilitations his car would undergo, the cura removed himself from Ibarra, first to a tier of boxes at San Carlo *(Tosca)* and then to a red velvet seat at La Scala *(Bohème)*. When Chuy stopped talking the priest restored himself in a single second to his parish, absolved the penitent, and said, "It would be appropriate for you to make a donation to the church out of your new prosperity." Chuy accordingly, as he approached the warped and massive outer door, pushed ten pesos into the slot of a box marked FOR THE PROPAGATION OF THE FAITH.

From now on events that had merely crept began to surge ahead. El Gallo and El Golondrino put their plan into effect. Every morning after the daily dynamite blast they stationed themselves ahead of the others at the entrance of the tunnel under a sign that read: FOR YOUR SAFETY—LOOK, LISTEN, AND THINK BEFORE YOU ACT. As soon as the foreman gave his signal El Golondrino, guided by the lantern in his helmet, raced in faster than his Chichimeca ancestors could run at the height of their dynasty, located the most promising site, and claimed it until his friend arrived gasping a few paces behind.

Crouched against the dripping walls, their mouths bitter with the taste of explosives and metal, they ate their lunches of rice and *chiles,* drank Pepsi-Cola, and into the henequen bags that had held these things they stuffed all the ore they could take away without suspicion. At the end of eight hours they carried the vividly striped sacks out of the tunnel, into the hoist elevator, and off down the road as if they weighed nothing and it was only pots and bottles that made them bulge.

Each evening they met at the house of El Golondrino and here behind the shuttered window and bolted door transferred the day's accumulation of ore to a thick paper sack labeled CEMENTO AZTECA, S. A. Twice a week Chuy lifted these sacks to the top of the bus, where they traveled among baskets of pottery and trussed pairs of live turkeys to the town of Caballo Muerto. Chuy had a friend in Caballo Muerto who collected the sacks and delivered them to San Luis, where an associate was connected with the smelter. Payment for the silver came back at the end of every week by the same route the ore had taken.

After a month Chuy said to his friends, "We will need twice as much ore, or twice as rich ore, if we are to meet our obligation in thirty days."

El Gallo eyed him from profile. "There is only one way to get more," he said, and El Golondrino nodded.

After that Chuy's friends no longer waited for the signal to enter the tunnel. While the foreman held back the rest of the shift, the Rooster and the Swallow edged behind his back into the choking dust and drifts of rock until they saw silver.

Within three weeks the profits from the smelter doubled. When only seven days remained until the down payment was due, Chuy said, "We are still two thousand pesos short." But in this calculation he did not include the money he had taken from the American woman's purse. "You will have to get into the tunnel sooner in order to have more time to work the vein alone."

"Are you trying to blow us up?" said Chuy's friends.

On the morning of the accident Richard was alone in his office between the carpenter shop and storeroom of the mine. He heard the explosion and felt it under his feet, but the shuddering reverberation of a dynamite blast was as commonplace to him as the striking of a clock or the purring of a cat. When the hoist operator burst in, the owner of the mine looked up from a sheet of drawing paper with a compass still in his hand. The hoist operator might as well have spoken two words instead of a thousand. All Richard heard was, "Both dead."

Standing outside in a crowd of men he issued the necessary orders: "Notify the priest." And someone went. "Advise the state coroner." And another turned to go. "Let the families know and bring them here." But no one moved. "El Golondrino lived alone and the wife of El Gallo is visiting relatives in the state of Veracruz," said the men watching Richard.

These exchanges were only the monotonous accompaniment, as of muffled drums, to the hollow tolling of bells. "Both dead," rang the bells.

"Let me speak to the foreman."

"Sí, señor," answered the crowd.

Tears had streaked the grime on the foreman's face. "But there is no way to explain it," he said. "Two experienced miners."

"You are blameless," said Richard Everton.

Before he left the mine he said, "Who were the closest friends of these men?"

"Chuy Santos," said the chorus around him. "The closest friend of El Gallo and the closest friend of El Golondrino."

"Then ask Chuy Santos to come to my house this evening."

"Sí, señor," replied the chorus.

The foreman spoke as Richard turned away. "Both dead," said the foreman.

The following morning Jesús Santos crossed the market square of Concepción and approached the coffin shop. When he entered La Urna de Oro still humming, the salesman came forward soberly and said, "If you have suffered a bereavement, may I extend my sympathy?"

But Chuy was already walking up and down the row of coffins designed to accommodate adults. Behind him, on the opposite wall, the small white ones intended for infants were stacked to the ceiling with a lid propped open here and there to expose a stitched pink or blue lining.

"Is it for a gentleman or a lady?" said the salesman.

"For a gentleman. That is to say, for two gentlemen," said Chuy.

"You are buying two caskets?"

"Yes, two. Identical in style and price. And in size, too, for that matter, although in one instance it will mean wasted space."

"To what extent will your finances allow you to honor these deceased?" asked the salesman, who had noticed Chuy's frayed cuffs and turned collar the moment he entered.

"It is not my money that will pay for these coffins," said Chuy. "It is the money of the mining company."

At these words the manager of the shop came out of the back room where he had been listening and said, "What mining company?" When Chuy said, "I represent the owner of the Malagueña mine in Ibarra," and showed a note to prove it, the manager sent the salesman on an errand to the upholsterer six blocks beyond the plaza.

"Are the caskets for the victims of yesterday's disaster?" asked the manager, who had read a full report in the morning *Heraldo*.

"Yes, for those two miners," said Chuy, "who might have been buried in the plain pine boxes made by the company carpenter and provided gratis. But in the cases of these men no families were at hand to choose between the pine there and the oak here."

"So the decision has been left to you, to choose and spend as you please."

"Yes, and this is why. The American owner, don Ricardo Everton, has taken the entire responsibility for the accident upon his own conscience, as though he himself had purposely lit a fuse to destroy two men."

"Here is our finest casket," said the manager. "Lined in tufted satin with a cushion for the head. Included is a satin quilt to pull up as you please and a full-length mirror inside the lid."

"A mirror," said Chuy, and he stood silent for a moment, considering the suitability of mirrors for El Gallo and El Golondrino.

"What is the price?" he asked.

"Four thousand pesos each."

"That is a great deal of money to sink into the ground," said Chuy. "And the Malagueña is not Anaconda."

The manager fell silent to meditate. He leaned back against a coffin. "If you will take these two the price will be three thousand each and the difference yours, for patronizing my shop."

Chuy wasted no time considering this offer. "Many thanks," said Chuy.

"The mining company will be billed the regular price of four thousand," said the manager. "Please sign this invoice."

After he left the Urna de Oro, Chuy stopped at the used-car lot and sought out the proprietor. "I will be here on Saturday for my car," he said.

"And you will bring with you the balance of the down payment, four thousand pesos," said the owner of the Volkswagen.

"Do you take me for a man who plays jokes?" said Chuy.

The taxi became a familiar sight to every settlement on the way from Ibarra to Concepción. Men plowing furrows and women baking bread watched as the red car appeared on the level stretches of road between vineyard and farm as suddenly as a drop of blood pricked from a vein. Goats and children fled from Chuy's path and pigs escaped by their native cunning alone.

If he had no other customers Chuy would crowd five men into the Volkswagen and, for two pesos each, drive them from the plaza of Ibarra to their shifts at the mine. Sometimes when he passed the Evertons' gate the two Americans were standing there and waved. Through the suffocating fumes of his exhaust they could see Chuy waving back.

"That car needs a ring job," said Richard.

"Chuy Santos was singing," said his wife.

For indeed it turned out that Chuy could sing. He sang all the Mexican songs ever written. When he proceeded from verse to verse of "Adelita" he transformed himself into Pancho Villa's soldier serenading the camp follower he loved. Chuy sang "Ojos Tapatíos." *"Todas las flores suspiran de amor,"* sang Chuy, and the roadside weeds seemed to languish as he passed. *"Bésame,"* sang Chuy, waiting for his passengers to emerge from the surgery in Concepción. *"Bésame mucho,"* and people on the sidewalk stopped buying newspapers and counting change to listen.

So that before long it was not only the people of Ibarra who recognized Jesús Santos Larín but many in Concepción and on the road between. And recognized the red Volkswagen, too, and even admired it, aware that it traveled on errands of mercy.

But Chuy had postponed the ring job. His exhaust continued to blacken the air and enshroud the two ghosts who trailed behind.

RICHARD ELMAN

Richard Elman has published twenty-one books of fiction, poetry, and journalism. He attended Stanford in 1956–57 and was awarded a creative writing scholarship and was to be the recipient of the Royal Victor Fellowship for graduate studies in English when he turned his hand to journalism. He's fifty-three years old, twice a father, and lives in Stony Brook, N.Y., where he sometimes serves as "utility infielder" for the SUNY English Department, or is an itinerant professor of creative writing at other universities, and mostly hangs about at home and writes a lot. He is married to the writer Alice Neufeld.

"'Béisbol' came about pretty much as I describe it in the story. Some years after that day, between trips to Central America, I recalled that day and it seemed to tell me a lot about a time that was still so actively transpiring, from day to day. It was a muddy and ambiguous time, murderous, and unfeeling, and this moment remained fixed, and lambent for me. It came to kick off the collection I later called *Disco Frito*. So much time has passed; I still remember that day, in my memory, my imagination."

◆　　　◆　　　◆

Béisbol

JUST BELOW BARRIO QUINTA Nina, in some fields bordering Lake Managua, I used to watch the teenage kids playing *béisbol*. They were prodigious athletes: Though their curve balls hung in the wind and they often had to run uphill to reach first base, their energies never flagged. From hovels of cardboard and scrap wood, where lives were poisoned with the chemic greases and ordures of lakeside sewage, they emerged during the late afternoons to disport themselves in club satins and neon-colored pin stripes: caps the hue of papaya flesh or tomatoes; genuine spiked black shoes on the feet of boys who usually went barefooted.

Everybody in the neighborhood took *béisbol* very seriously, and some made it a habit of the spirit, something as Nica to them as all the exotic colors in Ruben Dario's poetry. They had newspaper knowledge of the big leagues in El Norte, were adept at the various major league styles. This one hit like Clemente or one-handed flies like a young Willie Mays. They knew how to simulate Mike Marshall's screwball overhand pitch and took hook slides in those fields of manure paddies and debris. Some even had the looks of future standouts like Denny Martinez. But they used balls as wilted as ragged vegetables from the

Central Market; and their bats pinched hands when they connected with the ball.

The small knots of younger kids who stood by as a cheering section seemed to enjoy the games almost as much as the players. They shouted pet names, jeered all errors. Nearby the women of the barrio washed clothes in concrete troughs; and the grown men drank beer and *agaludiente* and cleaned their weapons (for the *Guardia* might be coming at any time, even in the middle of the night, to look for weapons). The scene looked as tranquil as some mid-American meadow in late July; picnicking *campesinos,* women attending to chores, boys playing ball—except that when the games were over all the boys disappeared. They literally went underground, into an abandoned storm sewer along the lakeshore, where they fabricated contact bombs and mortar pipes. At night, with thoughts of Clemente and Martinez still in their heads, they sneaked out to take part in actions, or to scribble graffiti on municipal walls against the dictatorship and its hated gringo friends.

I can only remember the name of one team from that Little Summer of 1978: *Quenipes.* They were all quite small, wore flashy green uniforms, garish with orange pin stripes as representations of those tart grapelike fruits. Caps shaped like melon ends. All of one month of summer I watched those midget champions cavort and then disappear, perhaps to die. Or they'd arrive without their usual first baseman, with bandaged legs and brows. Once they played a team of grown men from the nearby barrio of Vietnam and were swamped with homers, but every grounder hit to the infield was scooped up and thrown out by agile hands.

It was right about then that the first openly fought battles between the rebels and the Guard took place. I had business elsewhere, saw much that still haunts me. That Sandinista campaign of August–September 1978, though ultimately defeated, brought many of the cities to rubble. When I returned to Quinta Nina in late September, guardsmen in jeeps patrolled every street corner. I was a little reluctant to show my *La Prensa* credentials. The game was still in progress, though: *Quenipes* disporting themselves against a team of Creole mulattoes from the east coast who'd been transplanted to a nearby barrio and were thought to be politically reliable by the functionaries. They all had very large hands and feet and powerful hams, and I noticed their pitcher was easily overpowering *Quenipe* batters with his heavy fastballs.

After some time I also was aware my *Quenipes* team was almost entirely made up of replacements. They wore the same uniforms with the same nicknames sewn across their chests, but these were definitely not the same players, not the same Oscar and Pepi and German I'd watched once before.

Then I also noticed the two plainclothes men from the paramilitaries who were spectating the game, each with an Uzi machine pistol on a sling dangling into his hand. This new game was being staged more for their benefit, I observed, than for the benefit of the players. I stayed around to watch.

Quenipes were behind 5-to-1 by the time I came along. They barely swung their bats at incoming balls. Aside from an occasional walk to their littlest boys, they went down in order.

In the fifth inning, contact bombs exploded down lakeside near the big, white Bank of America building. In the silence between bursts, men and boys stood about wondering what was about to happen next, and then abruptly they fled from one another and left me standing in an almost empty field.

A large pile of old bats had been left behind, along with somebody's spiked shoes. Nearby some women herded pigs. I started toward them but was stopped by the noise of more automatic rifle fire that seemed to trip my feet from under me. Some 50 feet away, two young women were still laying out a wash.

"The cathedral can have our relics," said one.

"The soldiers won't be coming now," the other said. "They have too much to do in Managua."

Night would soon be coming on, so I got up again, despite my fears, and loped toward the center of the barrio. At the first checkpoint I was stopped by a handsome Guard lieutenant who looked a lot like one of the boys who pose for Salem ads in the Latin countries: brown, but clean-cut. He wore U.S.-issue Mickey Mouse boots. When I found my papers and showed them to him, he seemed easily satisfied but asked, just to make talk, what I was doing in Quinta Nina. Lamely I said I'd come to watch a baseball game.

The lieutenant seemed awfully pleased with me. "*Hermano,* you can't see better *béisbol* anywhere in the world," he said. "Not even in Cuba. There are Nicaraguans in the big leagues. But, of course, the best players are in León . . . not here in Managua . . . but in León. . . ."

"I like their spirits," I insisted.

"You gringos always make that mistake," he pointed out, in a kind of Spanglais, for my benefit. "You buy the worst hammocks and you watch the worst *béisbol;* you are always looking for true grit in a greased pig."

When I asked if I could go now he seemed reluctant to dismiss me.

"If you want to see a pitcher," my new guide said, "you should see *Caballo Negro* of Number One León. He's old now, but once he struck out the entire Yankee lineup in order. . . ."

Then it suddenly went dark and the lieutenant told his squad to take cover. He also informed me he would drive me out to the main highway.

Thinking we would talk more *béisbol,* I got into the front seat with him. As soon as we were on the move, the lieutenant assured me he had very little use for the current state of affairs, or old Somoza and his whores. He was learning English "plain as the smile on your face"; and he wanted to go back to school in the States, to study sociology, at UC Berkeley. He wished above all to be a "humane" penologist, or teach penology at a university. He could read Talcott Parsons, but he was just not a Red. He said, "I am a compassionate person."

I told Lt. Martinez that, if I knew his address, when I got back to the States I would send him some college catalogs so he could make intelligent choices. Or I would just send the materials to Lt. Raoul Martinez at the Army Base, Campo de Marzo, Managua.

We'd reached the *carretera.* "I would like the States, I know it," he said, "as I am sure you can tell."

"I'm sure."

"Bird in hand," he said, sticking out his hand. We shook, and then I left him there.

I know he didn't die in the fighting; I've checked the lists. So perhaps he's fighting even now as a contra for the CIA and "humane" penology or is in exile in Miami touting Nicaraguan baseball, telling his *hermanos* how he would someday like to translate Talcott Parsons into Spanish.

As for those Nicaraguan "boys of summer," many died fighting in the streets of Managua, Estelí, and Matagalpa. Some are minor bureaucrats of the new regime. Some married, some went abroad to join the contras or remain uninvolved, draft dodgers in Miami, Houston, or San José, Costa Rica.

Baseball is played as much as ever in Nicaragua.

The warm tropical nights flow through the loins of all of us, even in our sleep, and the next morning we are all just a little older and feebler.

KENNETH FIELDS

Kenneth Fields (b. 1939) received his Ph.D. from Stanford, where he was a Stegner Fellow. He has been a member of the Stanford English Department and Creative Writing Program since 1967. His collections of poems are The Other Walker *(Talisman),* Smoke *(Knife River),* Sunbelly *(Godine),* The Odysseus Manuscripts *(Elpenor), and* Anemographia: A Treatise on the Wind *(Hit and Run). He has three daughters and is married to Nora Cain.*

"These poems come from a collection in progress, *Classic Rough News: A Book of Impromptus.* 'The Rules of the Game' has appeared in *TriQuarterly,* 'La Salamandre' in *Writers' Forum.* 'Opening Line' is a *cento:* It may be true, I have gone here and there, but I am no pickpurse of another's wit."

◆　　◆　　◆

The Rules of the Game

At first it was better than fun—the companionable nights,
the whiskey by the fire, the dark behind us,
the light inside us lifting the old tales
over the ancient woods. But even then
the game was receding from our hearts. By now
it has been years since anybody saw
the great brown bear, now even the squirrels and rabbits
are talking to themselves, and the old forest
has dwindled to this lawn below the porch
where I've sat hunting in my peculiar way,
the lights and liver darkening, the last cloud
no bigger than a man's hand, one of my own.
So whistle up the dogs, and piss on the fire,
this was the last hunt, and it's over now.

◆　　◆　　◆

La Salamandre

For Yves Bonnefoy

"The alcohol of the declining day
will spill out on the stones," and there he is,

burning and cool a moment, and then gone,
product and agent of decomposition,
the solvent of our care. He has gone through hell,
or at least another dim quotidian sun
where formerly there were fires, and heraldry.
He dreams of quick clear water over stones,
which never seems enough, and of pure air,
of transformations in the purple light
into where ever he is. A little alembic,
he would distill an essence in himself,
so lost, so fragile, so much everything
as to be nothing in the afternoon.

♦   ♦   ♦

Opening Line

"Was the universe a quotation?" Burton wondered—
"Thus is man that great Amphibian.
Either someone like us night-foundered here
(this pendant world, in bigness as a star
of smallest magnitude close by the moon)
groping for trouts in a peculiar river,
or in the emptier waste, resembling air,
servile to all the skyey influences.
Rejoice; for I will through the wave, and foam,
and shall in sad lone ways, a lively sprite,
make my dark heavy poem light, and light.
For who can speak of eternity without
a solecism, or think of it without an ecstasy?
For though through many straits, and lands I roam,
I launch at paradise, and I sail towards home.
Love me, that I may die the gentler way,
Tomorrow is just another name for today."

PETER FISH

◆   ◆

Peter Fish was a Mirrielees Fellow in fiction in 1977–78 and received his Stanford M.A. in creative writing in 1980. In 1983 he was a Hoyns Fellow in fiction at the University of Virginia; in 1985 he was awarded the San Francisco Foundation's James Phelan Award. He lives in Palo Alto, works as a magazine editor, and is completing a collection of short stories.

"Since leaving the Jones Room I have spent much of my working life on airplanes, and 'Imperial Beach' began at a window seat of a United 737 departing Lindbergh Field in San Diego. It was mostly written by the time we touched down in San Francisco. That's one of the blessings of the Stanford Creative Writing Program: in granting you a year of ideal circumstances in which to write, it gives you strength to write in circumstances less than ideal later on."

◆   ◆   ◆

Imperial Beach

I WAS BORN IN Tulare. My father ran a hardware store there. I have a snapshot taken of me then, wearing a sunfrock and posed to the immediate right of the cash register. Baby Helen At Two, is the label. A canted stand of doorknobs forms the backdrop, and my mother's large, whitened hand reaches in from nowhere to steady me.

In the summer we would drive Highway 46, on which some summers later James Dean was killed, across the valley ranches and over to the coast. Even during the war and rationing we made the trip—Pismo Beach, Morro Bay, San Simeon. From that last place you could sit on the sand and look up through the curtains of eucalyptus to where Mr. Hearst's house was hung at the crest of an endless mustard hill.

On the drive home, still damp and smelling of seaweed, I'd ignore the familiar miles by planning my own mansion, much larger than the one we'd left behind us. When I was old enough to know what the words for things were, I led imaginary gaggles of guests through its rooms. "We are now standing in the vestibule," I told these people, whom I conjured up as being dressed for some frosty, formal cotillion—the men in tuxedoes and the women in beaded gowns with matching clutch purses. "To the right you can see the salon. To the left is our boudoir. Ahead of us is the drawing room, where we hang our tapestries. All of our rooms have carpets, and all of the carpets are French carpets imported from France just for us. Nobody else has carpets like these. We will be happy if you do not smoke or spit while you are walking on them."

In the winter, school. I met Dick in the tenth grade and we were married two weeks after graduation. We honeymooned in Pismo—it was June, the middle of the foggy season, and so gray that you heard the ocean with more assurance than you saw it—and then he went off to Korea. Even without him I took to being married. It became me, I thought. I enjoyed signing things: Mrs. Richard Boyd, a new person's promising name but one written in my own safe old handwriting. I enjoyed having the other girls from my class ask advice about their weddings. A-line or empire waist gown? Alencon or Venetian point lace? When customers at the hardware store—I started there after my father had the stroke—commended my gold band I told them my husband in Korea was that very second wearing one identical to it.

Dick was mustered out in August of 1953. We spent about a month together in my mother's house—my father had by then died, and she had sold the store—and then made plans to leave Tulare. It was so hot there, and the air was so thick, fertilized. It weighed on you by the end of each day.

We went a little north and tried Fresno and Merced, but they were not much better. Dick was finding it hard to stick at any one job. He had returned from the fighting bristly, not at ease. Nobody could tell him what to do. When he disagreed with someone he had a way of folding his arms solid across his chest, as if to demonstrate that the idiocy being spouted would not have the slightest power to budge him, and after six months at any given employment it was even odds whether he'd quit or be fired. Other women might have found trouble in this, but I didn't. He was not once anything less than good to me.

We worked our way to Sacramento, and then to Redding, where Dick found a job with a lumber mill and I one as the receptionist for a veterinary clinic. Of all the things I've done, that suited me the best. Those animals—it seemed I was made for them. Siamese that had everyone else fearful for cheeks and nylons I'd leave purring. Cockers that scrambled for a place to do a mess I'd have panting happily for their distemper shots. Owners would thank me just for being there.

The mill shut down in October, and we decided that it was again time to leave. Even this far north the summer had been a valley summer, each day dulled and hot, and now winter was arriving well before we were ready for it. When Dick suggested the southern coast, I remembered all my vacations and agreed. We tried Carpenteria, then Port Hueneme, where I was a clerk in a lima bean warehouse, and then traveled to the low end of the state, to San Diego and beyond, to a Navy town called Imperial Beach.

Imperial Beach. I liked the name of it: it carried to mind princesses and monocled consorts, and long chromey cars from which Dick and I would descend, each of us holding a beach towel and a bottle of champagne. It was that period of years when it seemed that people, no matter where in their lives they stood, were making fresh starts of things, and this seemed a good place to do so. The town had slid into a lazy trough between one war and the next. There were still jobs to be had by looking, but the bases had been slowed and half-emptied of their men, and landlords were happy to rent to you. In the used goods stores you could find bargain furniture and even clothing the sailors had left behind. I purchased a shirt someone had brought home from a Pacific tour of duty and then regretted: GUAM, it said on the front in letters orange as a lit jack-o'-lantern, and on the back a flame and black patterned tiger leaped from between my shoulder blades. I still have a color snapshot of me wearing that shirt. I look fine.

Dick found good work as a welder, and we rented the top half of a duplex, whose windows led your eyes out over the flat, scattered-rock roofs of the other duplexes to a bright strip of ocean. I have never been in a place as bright as that place. It was not just that the sea was glazed and hard as something kilned, or that the bits of mica caught in each exterior wall blinked at you as you walked down the street. It was that the light seemed to reach around every corner and into every recess, never scorching—there was a soft, constant breeze from the water—but giving things a vividness that made you think you were seeing them for the first time. I recall it as I might recall a dream.

Dick was earning enough, and our rent was low enough, that I didn't have to work. In letters to my mother I styled myself, "Your Helen, the lady of leisure." I spent much of my days buying things for the duplex. A couch, two Naugahyde chairs, and as decoration a fishing net, woven from strands of hemp almost as thick as my wrist and studded with abalone half-shells whose insides possessed a curdled iridescence I had never seen in anything else. I stretched the net across one knotty pine wall and on another I hung two storm lamps and a mahogany ship's wheel that still turned.

"Ahoy there," Donna would say when she came up to check my progress. "All women on deck." Then she would laugh and say, Helen, you are working wonders, wonders.

Donna lived downstairs with a son she'd had by an ex-husband. She didn't look like anyone who had borne a child: she wore white shorts, and bandanna-tied tops that favored her breasts and bared a tummy whose navel bumped out dark and round as a filbert. It pleased me to have her as a friend. I made them easily, I thought, but in the past they had always been freckled, slow-speaking valley girls much like me. Too much like me: sometimes I would look at one of them and feel I was talking to a mirror. I could never feel that way about Donna.

Donna worked lunch shift at a Mexican restaurant, but she harbored much loftier ambitions. We all did, then. She'd ask me to help make lists of occupations that better suited her gifts.

"Let's see," she would ponder, pencil in hand. "I can sell real estate. What else?"

"You could work in a department store," I'd encourage. "You could demonstrate makeup. You certainly have the features for it."

"That's good. That's very good." Donna set the words down—"demonstrate makeup"—as if they were something on which she might be tested.

"Or else," she said, "I could find a very, very rich husband and be like you and never have to lift a finger for the rest of my life."

"There's the ticket," I'd laugh.

Occasionally I would ask Donna how someone like her had ended up in Imperial Beach without a husband, but she was always coy with me. "I hated his haircut! He called me his sugar pie!" And, one day, "I have this theory about people and colors."

Donna explained this to me. Everyone in the world possessed an individual color, but it had nothing to do with your skin. Donna's colors lay hidden inside you, or perhaps (I was never too certain of these fine details) rayed gauzily around your head like the halo of a Woolworth Jesus. Wherever they were, they managed your life. Whom did you choose to befriend, to love? Only those people whose shades complemented yours. But there was a catch: a person's colors could change. Just like that. No one had any control. And when this change occurred, a person's colors would no longer complement yours but would clash, and to do anything but flee would bring you sorrow.

I sat through this nodding at her, and smiling, and thinking that it was the silliest thing I had ever heard. All I could see was my parents' hardware store and the charts of Sherwin-Williams Paints. I envisioned people walking around with sample chips—No. 47, Dusty Rose; No. 28, Tahoe Turquoise—scotch taped to their foreheads, squinting at the person next to them to ascertain whether his or her chip was of an acceptable tone.

Not that I gave my opinions voice. Donna was my friend. All I asked was, "Well, what color do you think I am?"

She looked me up and down. "I feel," she said at last, "that you are a lovely, delicate apricot."

"Oh good," I told her, anxious to end this. "That's almost orange, and orange is Dick's favorite color."

Because we were all new-arrived in town, the four of us—Dick and I and Donna and Donna's son, Jimmy—played tourist together. On weekends we visited the zoo, took in the bullfights in Tijuana, inspected battleships for Navy Open House Day. Occasionally Dick would bring along someone intended for Donna—other welders, a shortstop or first baseman from his softball team, a cousin who lived in El Cajon—and come bedtime we would lay odds on these fellows' chances. But it was all play-acting. We could see that none of them were for Donna.

Weekdays, when Donna came home from her shift at the restaurant and Dick from his at the machine shop, we would walk to the beach and go swimming. By that late in the afternoon the sun had drifted low across the sea, shedding a patch of itself on each wave it passed and warming the water to such a temperature that it seemed even gentler than the air.

Dick and Donna were always out in the waves first. Dick had spent even less time around oceans than I had, but Donna taught him to bodysurf and he mastered it as easily as if he'd been raised on a reef. The two of them would swim to where the breakers were building, out farther than I thought was safe, hold themselves there as the sea rose around them then all at once Australian crawl to catch the cresting wave and shoot with it violently to shore. Against the foam Dick seemed as beetle brown as Donna. They could have been a cavorting pair of south sea islanders.

"She swims like a dolphin, your mother," I told Jimmy.

"She has a shoebox full of ribbons for it," he said. "She learned when she was one and a half years old."

He was a thin boy, and shorter than most ten-year-olds, with wispy red hair that was not at all like Donna's. When she would talk about him her talk was full of exasperated affection—"Oh, that little rug rat," she'd say, "he's a regular little dynamo"—as if Jimmy were some beloved incorrigible who never gave her a second's peace. But in fact he was timid, and silent more than not, with a habit of blinking slowly at you as if waiting for you to say something you hadn't thought to say. Donna found him a burden, I think, and was happy I could bob with him in the shallows, our noses iced with zinc oxide to spare us from burning, while she and Dick braved the water farther out.

Once he came to trust me Jimmy would perforate his silence with brief, to-the-point statements. His middle name was Charles. His class was studying the ocean. Did I realize the ocean swells we saw might have started hundreds of miles away? But the water that formed the swells did not travel far, he said: each molecule, save those trapped within the breaking surf, moved round in an easy circle as the disturbance passed through it and then returned to its original place.

"Good to hear," I said, not knowing how else to respond.

After our swims the four of us would return home and shower, then go out to dinner. We'd order food I had never seen before. Lobster, swordfish, ceviche, all those dishes that are so expensive now. Later in bed I would lie against Dick and continue to hear the sound of waves stroking sand.

The weeks slid by, sunny, vague, indistinguishable from one another. Dick got a raise and we bought appliances. To my mother I wrote, "It is heaven to put on a clean, warm-as-toast bathing suit every afternoon. Here just six months and already a washer-dryer!" That sounds gloating, but I didn't mean to seem so. It was just that our purchases gave a feeling of success and of permanence to our stay in Imperial Beach that gladdened me: I'd grown tired of leaving places, of watching as my life shrank in the rearview mirror while I sighed, "But I was happy there." I felt like one of those molecules which after brief turbulence had regained its peace.

When Dick received his next raise we even began to talk of new cars. Our old one that had done so well in the valley was rusting in Imperial Beach's salted air. Dick and Donna and Jimmy and I would walk from one bunting-decked showroom to the next, collecting salesmen's cards with monthly payment figures scrawled on them and thumbing through brochures that pictured women preened against taillights and grilles.

"That's what you should do," I told Donna, pointing out a photograph of a model lounged across a Plymouth. "Pose like that. You're prettier than any of these girls."

"What?" Donna held a cupped hand against her ear to mime deafness. The showroom was noisy: all of them were, jammed with people like Donna and Dick and me. It was as if everyone in Imperial Beach, everyone in the country, had received a blank check in the mail and had gone out to buy a car.

"Look at this one," Dick shouted to Donna, and they headed off to view some lithe red thing the dealer had placed on a rotating platform. They were in a silly mood: they giggled over the dream trip we could make in a car such as this car, listing off each stopping point—Hollywood! Vegas! Chicago! Broadway!—as they went. The salesmen, worried that they were never going to cadge a commission from this noisy twosome, pressed their hands together in annoyance, and over by the water cooler the office manager opened his newspaper—*Eisenhower Orders Troops to Beirut*, the shaky headlines read—in front of him with such irritation I thought he would rip it in half. But no one else seemed to mind. A few of the jollier customers even made their own suggestions. "Ensenada," said one, and another "Honolulu," as if that were a place to which any of the arrayed V-8s might deliver him.

Jimmy and I were sitting like bookends in the chairs placed up against the showroom's plateglass window.

"Don't be such wet blankets," Dick shouted to us. "Come on over here and take a look." And I remember thinking then: he truly does want everyone in this room to be happy.

Come summer, Jimmy, released from school, spent afternoons with me while his mother worked. Donna didn't insist on it—he was well-enough behaved to pass entire days alone—but in his quiet way he seemed to like coming upstairs. I made him sandwiches; he helped me load the dryer; we played Go Fish with a deck Donna had brought home from work.

"Look at those eyes," I told Jimmy. I pointed to the fire-toned portrait of a woman decorating the backs of the cards. "Lustrous. That's what they're called. Your mother has lustrous eyes."

Jimmy was pawing the deck for a jack of clubs and didn't answer right away. He was a difficult boy to entertain. Or, rather, he was a difficult boy for me to entertain. He wanted to know things. As I knew very little, this posed certain difficulties. Once I had shared my scraps of vocabulary, magazine words like "lustrous," and the dim examples of savvy I had gained from various jobs— what purposes different grades of sandpaper served, why Dobermans had their ears clipped, how much two tons of lima beans cost—I worried that he would grow bored with me. But he did not: instead he took the opportunity to relieve my ignorance, reading to me from his schoolbooks and displaying newly acquired facts the way more trivial children display toys or small shining objects. Babylonians wrote in triangles. Squids shot ink.

This day it was, after he had found the jack: "Spanish women squeezed orange juice into their eyes to make them bright."

"Well, I don't think your mother does that."

"She'd do anything if it didn't hurt," he said.

I heard the dryer halt itself and went to pull out the whites before they wrinkled. There was something in the smell of all that chaste cleaned cotton, in the rhythm of Jimmy slapping card upon card on the table, in the bit of ocean that hit my eye as I stood by the dryer, which made it seem things were still possible for me. You set out on your life with the most ridiculous dreams, and after a while their very unlikelihood becomes a strain, like the weight of too much costume jewelry, and you learn to trade them in for something lighter. This is commonly known as maturity: I had it in spades. If Dick and Donna had decided to do tricks together for a while, so be it. "I can stand that for a while," I said to myself. "That I can stand."

Jimmy set down his cards. "I'm tired of playing this."

"Here," I said. "I'll tell you your fortune." I gathered up the deck and shuffled it, then dealt a slipshod arrangement of eight cards face down and three cards up. I doubt that Jimmy was fooled; it certainly made no sense to me.

"You know what that signifies?" I asked. I was brandishing some completely omenless card like the two of diamonds. "It signifies that you will have a happy, wonderful life because you are a happy, wonderful person."

Jimmy said, "I have to go home."

"Aren't you coming swimming with me?"

"With you?" he asked. "You mean with all of you. No."

"You're certainly Mr. Pleasing Disposition today," I told him.

Each afternoon when Donna returned from work I would hear her prowling her half of the duplex, shouting "Anybody home?" Then the sandaled footsteps clattered up our stairs; the bell rang, the door jiggled with her knock—insistent, reiterated rat-tat-tats, like a woodpecker stabbing bark—and she called out in the treble voice with which she demonstrated enthusiasm, "Jimmy? Jimmy are you there? Helen, where is my little squirt hiding today?"

While I stood watch Donna poked through the house on her exaggerated search, peeping out windows, flinging open doors. She was a person, I decided, who believed that life consisted of surprise after surprise and if on some days no surprises were at hand happily made them up. Inevitably it turned out that Jimmy had lodged himself in some perfectly predictable locale: in his room, reading, or, at his most adventuresome, playing with a model car on the next-door neighbor's lawn. But Donna was daily baffled. "You're a gremlin," she'd accuse as he stood wordless before her. "You vanish at the drop of a hat. At the drop of my hat, anyway."

After she had ordered Jimmy back to whatever harmless site he had been occupying in the first place, Donna would ask if I had saved any of the morning's coffee, then collapse at the kitchen table.

"He is such a handful," she'd complain. "You only see his good side. I'm sure he hid my mascara yesterday. I know *I'd* never leave it in the living room."

Donna pushed her bangs up off her forehead. She always seemed ragged when she returned from work, and hot, as if by accident she'd been forgotten on the warming counter along with some customer's combination plate.

"I went to the civilian personnel office at the base," she said. "But even with those troops going to Booboo Bayroo the Navy still has a hiring freeze on. What am I going to do about a job? I wish I could be as que sera sera as you are. You never let anything get to you. You just stay placid and peaceful and gentle and sweet."

I repeated that last list of adjectives and asked myself, of what does that description remind me? Yes, I realized, of course: she thinks I am a cow. Holstein or Guernsey, I wanted to ask her, but Donna quite suddenly had begun to cry.

"I will never get anything I want," Donna said. "Never never never." She looked up at me from beneath the frizzled bangs, and I wondered if I was being given some kind of test. If I didn't attempt to soothe her, would she know I saw what she and Dick were up to? I patted the shaking shoulder, and made what seemed to me suitable lowings of comfort. "There, there," I said. "You will. Of course you will."

There was a daydream I indulged in about that time, one which at first encompassed nothing more than Dick pleading repeatedly for absolution ("Yes, Helen, at last I have come to my senses," he'd bleat), but which took on more pleasing convolutions every time I let it play across my mind. I liked to picture Dick sweating on the edge of the sofa. The sofa, however, had been trundled downstairs, for, after being dumped by Dick, Donna had managed to snare a new husband (a retired Chief Petty Officer who was occasionally short-tempered with her, though never with Jimmy) and had moved across town: we in our turn had expanded to take over the entire duplex, fashioning numerous improvements along the way. We now enjoyed a living room with a sunken conversation pit, a rec room for those days when Jimmy visited (by himself, as Donna and Floyd seldom found the time), and a spiral staircase that coursed airily through the middle of it all. Time after time I swept down that staircase like Loretta Young, white chiffon billowing for two or three steps behind me, and when I saw Dick sitting on the sofa, abased, dissipated, I paused. My gloved forefinger tapped the railing. When at last I whispered, "I forgive you," I drawled the words with such languid indulgence he was not at all sure he had heard me correctly, and I added as he stumbled wonderingly up those stairs, "We will put this sordid incident behind us and look forward to the lovely years ahead."

Then, with the incoherent ease things attain only in such dreams, the lovely years had arrived, and Dick and I had ripened to become one of those content elderly couples I sometimes spied strolling the beach. There we were in matched windbreakers, agilely peering in tidepools, stooping to fill our pockets with pretty shells. And all around us were other people strolling and peering and smiling, their faces so similarly etched by life that at a distance it was hard to tell one person from the next.

Towards the end of August a typhoon stalled off the Mexican coast some miles to the south of us. It was something: though the sky remained our Imperial Beach sky, seamlessly blue, the ocean was imported, dangerous, at war with itself and with every other object. When you turned west all you saw was foam and chop and waves of such careless anger they looked to be tugging loose the horizon. Even Jimmy let himself join our afternoon treks to view this spectacle, though neither he nor I ever entered the water. Instead we sat on our towels, drank lemonade from the thermos he had brought, and read—he read, and I listened—from a book on jellyfish.

At one point I glanced up and saw Dick sliding on the shoulders of an enormous tunnel-shaped wave that threw him like a stiff little piece of driftwood straight onto the ocean bottom. I have since read of people who were killed in such ways, or sentenced to lives in beds and wheelchairs, but Dick was lucky: those things at least would never happen to him. When he bumbled up from the foam he was scraped and bruised and bleeding from where he had bit his own lip, but he did little more than catch his breath, tug at his bathing suit—it was filled with sand—and shout, "Hoo-wee, Donna! What a ride! I think I broke the sound barrier! Hoo-wee, Donna! What a ride!"

Jimmy stopped reading. "You're tired," he said.

"I am, a little," I told him.

He reached for the thermos and asked if I wanted some lemonade.

"No thank you."

"Last night she told me we're moving. The week after next. She's sick of it here, she says."

"Oh," I said. I felt I might never again rise from my towel. "Where are you going?"

"Florida. She has a friend there. His name is Hank. I met him once, but she says I'll like him more this time."

"Florida's so far away."

"I know."

"You're a nice boy," I said.

"You're a nice lady."

"Thank you, Jimmy."

Jimmy began again to read, and Dick and Donna continued to play in the surf. Often the only parts of them you could discern were the two sets of thrown-forward arms, one set dark, one set scratched and red, shooting on separate paths through the foam. The waves lifted and roared. Jimmy shut his book and gazed out at them with a look of pleased expectancy that pierced me the moment I saw it for what it was. "You be careful," I was going to say to him, but I didn't. All I did was sit beside him. I faced as he faced, and tried to keep my eyes where his were, steady as I could on that sea.

♦ ELIZABETH FISHEL ♦

*After my training at the Stanford Creative Writing Program, I moved to Berkeley and turned to writing nonfiction. My two books (*Sisters *and* The Men In Our Lives—*both published by William Morrow/Quill), my many articles in Mc-Call's, Parents, Redbook, Newsday, and Ms., among others, and my teaching writing at the University of California, Berkeley Extension, and in the Radcliffe Seminars Program have all grown out of personal experience and my interest in human relations, psychology, and family life. Now the mother of two young sons, I am working on a new book to be published by Houghton Mifflin called "Our Children, Our Parents, Ourselves."*

"The following passage introduces my second book, *The Men In Our Lives: Fathers, Lovers, Husbands, Mentors.* Where my first book, *Sisters: Love and Rivalry Inside the Family and Beyond,* explored a world of women and sisters' influence on each other, *The Men In Our Lives* examines another side of the world—the ways relationships with men affect women's lives. Using my own experience as well as numerous interviews and questionnaires and an overview of the psychological literature, I explored territory that at first, as I explain here, was mysterious and unfamiliar. Now with two young sons, I will some day have to write a postscript."

♦   ♦   ♦

Introduction

From *The Men In Our Lives*

THE WORLD I GREW up in was a world of women—mother, sister, schoolmates, friends. Against this landscape, boys and men stood out both mythic and mysterious. In relation to them, the girls at my New York City girls' school were loving and fearing, yearning and retreating. We daydreamed about phantom princes and used our wiles to please, when the rare opportunity permitted. But more often we hurried back to the haven of comfort and safety provided by the other girls. I saw the world of men refracted through our shared lens, and the distorted image both protected and frightened me. In our world women held sway. We were the rule, men the exception. Women articulated ideas, created art, unearthed discoveries, set the tone, called the shots. In our own world I believed we women were perfectly powerful, and among them I, too, could reach as far as I dared.

But I also sensed that outside the safe boundaries of our school, this power was undependable. In the "real" world—the world of men—our strength did not count for much. To share power with men was to lose it. I marked how vigilantly men were excluded from our school (in my thirteen years there, I remember only three who pierced the barriers: an elevator man, a choral conductor, and one lone math teacher who lasted a year under trial-by-fire of the girls). Perhaps this vigilance masked fear, camouflaged envy, curtailed threat. But being excluded, men became infinitely more dangerous and more desirable. They were intruder and enemy, but to find one, to tame one was to have an entrée into a forbidden and seductive world. They seemed unattainable, but to be without one was to be incomplete. They were undefinable in the terms of our world, but to define one would be to define oneself.

My connections with the women in my world were from the first palpable in body and blood. For I could see how like my mother I was in my hands, my hopes, my habits. (Even now, using Jergen's on my hands every night, as she does, I am linked with her. That faint smell of almonds in the lotion brings her immediately to the room.) I could hear myself even in my younger sister's voice, her laugh, her mannerisms. I could imagine in my teachers images of the women I might become, with their beads and boots and Marimekko dresses and the sureness of their opinions about Woolf and Wordsworth and the world. I could feel my sympathies lighting effortlessly on the shoulders of my girlfriends, as we chattered and cried through childhood, stumbled and spread our wings through adolescence.

But as tangible as this bond with women, so intangible was the bond with men. How the men in my life left their imprint on me was not as definite as the shape of my hands; how they influenced me, what they taught me was not as recognizable as the lessons of mother and sister, nor as accessible as the wisdom of my teachers. The women's voices spoke clearly from faces like my own. The men's were more muffled, as if coming from behind masks or across vast continents.

On the terrain of my childhood the men whom I loved loom larger than life. Their shadows are as tantalizing as their images, their messages as provocative unspoken as spoken. First, I see my grandfathers. One had been a financial wizard, but was already past his heyday when I knew him. Setbacks took their toll on him, and he withdrew into the privacy of his thoughts. My father showed me his father's picture as a younger man, wanting me to remember him that way: dapper and debonair on a boardwalk in Atlantic City, flushed with possibilities for the future. But I knew him only afterward, when the possibilities had not led where he hoped. A child of three, awed and puzzled by his silence, I circled round him and murmured to myself, "Not a word, not a word."

My other grandfather I knew to be a doctor whose specialty was helping women conceive. Women flocked to him from around the world, and I saw them in his waiting room in various stages of expectancy and fulfillment. On his desk was a bronze sculpture of his hands, just his hands, and lining the office walls were photographs of babies, emblems of his patients' gratitude, symbols to me of his omnipotence. When he died, I was still too young to understand death, and for years afterward I would see a shock of white hair, a certain elderly gait and be convinced it was he. From my grandfathers I learned about the grandeur of wishes and the disappointment of loss. Their lives suggested that life was fragile, that it was grand, that it could last forever, that it would have to end.

But in these early years no one stands taller than my father. Hero and protector, he would carry me on his shoulders into the summer ocean, and when the waves rose on the horizon, he would cry, in mock despair, "What *shall* we do?" Then he would sink beneath the water, effortlessly as Neptune, carrying me with him, while the waves crashed over our heads. When we rose—I terrified and delighted, he victorious—the sea was calm as a baby's blanket. This was his role in my childhood: magician, savior from storms, calmer of the sea.

I saw him living in a house of words: buried beneath *The New York Times* at the breakfast table, hunched over his mahogany desk writing ad copy for products he swore the world did not really need but were magical to me (trees that bore lemons and oranges on the same branch, a glass globe over a tiny replica of the White House—shake it, and it filled with snow). And most of all I saw him reading, reading from evening until the still center of the night, reading books and papers and magazines (running his fingers through the pages of *The New Yorker,* he would say, "Feel the paper, it's like silk"). Is it any wonder that when I was old enough I wanted to make my way into that kingdom of words? There was my father, incessantly reading, smoking his cigars, dreaming his dreams. From him I learned how to pursue my own.

His was a tall figure to fill. Looking back over the young men in my life, I realize that for a long time I did not truly wish to replace him. When I looked for love, I had an unerring instinct for picking out the fey, the wild, the dangerous—in short, the inappropriate. I spent my adolescence refining (if not finding) my romantic type, from the whimsy of the Little Prince to the intensity of Dean Moriarty (asked in high school to write about "The Most Attractive Man in English Literature," I chose without hesitation Kerouac's antihero, a character as far beyond the confines of our school as I could find). The first boy I fell in love with knew all the words to "Blonde on Blonde" and carried his treasures in a box lined with black velvet. To me, at sixteen, this was the stuff of poetry. That he loved me gave me the first inkling I was lovable. That he left me, left me wondering.

After him came a succession of long-haired drummers, leather-jacketed revolutionaries, dreamers of dreams. One introduced me to Marx, another to Buddha, another to Antonioni. Some read poetry to me; few read the poems I wrote. There were those who loved me more than I loved them, who courted me as avidly as I courted others—the ones who would not love me back. What separated these two groups was more than chemistry but less than reason. In memory these men exist almost more in the telling, the rehashing, than in reality, in themselves.

I measured myself against them, with them and without them. I gauged their world against the world I might find on my own. I listened to their messages, their pearls of wisdom, delivered always with utter self-seriousness and conviction. And I wondered to myself how their words—then the words of boys, but all too soon to be the words of men, of my father and grandfathers—would ever apply to me. For me, growing up meant moving from the cozy certainty of the world of women to that foreign country, men, whose language I did not speak, whose customs I did not know, whose currency I surely did not own. All

I felt sure of was that everything we women were, men were not. They were brash, we were gentle. They were competitive, we were conciliatory. They thought with their heads, we felt with our hearts. They were indescribably mysterious—opposite and other. Along with most women of my generation, I would be unlearning this particular lesson many times over, as my search to unravel the mystery of men became more and more the search to unravel my own.

My own experience growing up, raised and schooled by women, is by no means typical. But my sense of living in a world apart from men—with different language, habits, customs—is, I believe, shared by many women and leaves many of us wondering, as we approach adulthood, how our worlds can ever overlap, how we can retain our identity while sharing common ground. Much has been written about woman-as-other, about men's love and fear of her mysteries. My intention in this book is to pursue the alternate course: to begin with the mystery that father presents to daughter, the awesome otherness of his presence, which then in various ways is echoed and embellished by other crucial men in her life: grandfathers and brothers, lovers and husbands, teachers and mentors. And from there I want to examine the subtle, complex, and lifelong process by which the daughter comes to understand and define the world of her father, and then the world of men, and gradually decides which of its teachings, its messages and mores to adapt for her own. (Concentrating on the daughter's formative years of development around the issues of love and work, I decided to stop before the daughter becomes a parent herself. At least another book could be written about mothers and sons.)

My exploration of the panorama of men who share a woman's journey began, of course, with questions about her father, that first giant in her life. I was surprised at how haltingly and hazily the initial responses came. When I had interviewed women for my first book, *Sisters,* the memories rushed out, colorful and detailed, stories recounting years of shared times and territory. But this time, the stories were sketchier at first. The figures drawn often seemed more mythic than flesh and blood.

The most striking fact about father was, of course, his absence. (Here I should point out that for the most part the women in my study came from traditional families in which father worked outside the home and was the champion of that province and mother stayed at home with the children and was the linchpin there.) For most daughters father was simply gone all day working; many admitted not knowing, as children, where or at what. One woman in her thirties recalled a father who worked three jobs, gone from eight one morning till one the next morning. Her relationship with him was a nightly phone call at seven. Another woman spoke of how the "family must have seemed like a photo album collection" to her father, so distanced was he from their everyday lives. So the daughter may often seem as much an illusion to her father as he is an enigma to her.

Even at home the fathers of early memory were often absent, hidden behind books or newspapers, not to be disturbed from their important thoughts, their well-earned rest. For one woman in her fifties the image of her father was of a man deep in reverie behind his evening paper. Once able to stand the distance no longer, she threw herself in a rage on his newspaper. "Darling," he said, emerging from that faraway place where daughters were not allowed to tread, "you're everything to me." And as if those words closed the case forever, he retreated once more, leaving his daughter still ruffled and unsoothed, to face a future of tearing down that paper time and time again, as she searched for a man who would finally listen to her, let her into his world.

Writing about the father's role in his daughter's formative years, Simone de Beauvoir underlines his mythic presence:

> The life of the father has a mysterious prestige: the hours he spends at home, the room where he works, the objects he has around him, his pursuits, his hobbies, have a sacred character. He supports the family, and he is the responsible head of the family. As a rule his work takes him outside, and so it is through him that the family communicates with the rest of the world: he incarnates that immense, difficult and marvelous world of adventure; he personifies transcendence; he is God. This is what the child feels physically in the powerful arms that lift her up, in the strength of his frame against which she nestles.

De Beauvoir was of course writing for a generation that recognized only subliminally its status as second sex. But for contemporary women who have begun to articulate their outrage, the struggle against father nevertheless remains an ancient one. For most daughters part of growing up means coming to terms with the mystery that surrounds father, decoding and learning his language, challenging his prestige, confronting his very godliness in a way that may be both terrifying and liberating. In the wake of the Women's Movement many of us have found ourselves at once rebelling against but also coveting our fathers' world. In the earliest throes of feminist anger we may have resisted its patriarchal values with zealous fury. Liberation often translated as emancipation from father. The early stages of struggle necessitated criticism and rage, distancing and separation from father, his male cohorts, and the patriarchy they stood for.

But in more recent years this clear and cleansing, but also tiring anger has been transformed into a more complex and unsettling ambivalence—about fathers whose approval is sought in the midst of turbulent rebellion, about lovers and husbands whose affection is needed in the midst of rage, about teachers and mentors whose counsel is valued in the midst of disdain for the hierarchy they may represent. After the last decades of change many of us have seen the world of our fathers—the world of work, of power, of money— gradually opening up for us, and the possibility is both tantalizing and frightening. Many of us wish to enter this formerly all-male territory, yet fear the stranglehold of its edicts and pressures. Or we would like to share its prizes and adventures, but question our entitlement to them or are all too wary of the risks and pitfalls that accompany them. Or beckoned by the world of our fathers, we feel guilty about deserting our mothers and their world of home and nurturance and family. Still, for many women who for years have defined ourselves in opposition to men, it is oddly disconcerting to find that men's choices may be becoming our own.

So the women I have chosen to study are those for whom personal and social changes have collided in various complicated ways that create conflict but also dazzling leaps of growth. For many of us, coming to adulthood has meant reexamining and renegotiating mother and father's lessons, questioning the old models they presented and beginning to fashion new ones, new images of masculine and feminine and what is appropriate or possible for each. "The central struggle for women of this generation," observed Stanford sociology professor Ann Swidler in an interview, "is to redefine the categories of male and female, father and mother, nurturer and nurtured. Our task is to reorganize the psychic elements of the early years into something more plausible for maturity."

My interviews for this book focus on women immersed in this process of redefinition of male and female, of themselves and the men in their lives. They are women in transition, women on the cusp of change. In all, I spoke with about seventy women in lengthy, detailed and intense personal interviews. They are women primarily in their twenties, thirties, and forties, because I felt that their life decisions were most dramatically altered by the tumultuous changes of the past decades. But I also talked with women at either end of the life cycle who are most certainly feeling the fallout from these changes as well. I also looked for a variety of background and history, of education and occupation, of sexual preference and family style. There are lawyers, secretaries, actresses, students, and mothers. Some of the women are well known for their recent achievements; some are daughters of celebrated fathers. But most are unknown and remain anonymous, except, I hope, in the power and persuasiveness of their stories.

Besides personal interviews, I also sought written autobiographies from women around the country, both through requests after lectures I gave and through ads placed in numerous publications, including *Mother Jones, The New York Review of Books,* the newsletters of Union W.A.G.E. and several other women's networks. This gave me broader access to women of disparate backgrounds whom I could not meet in person.

This excerpt from one of the letters in response to my ad explains the kind of dilemmas that drew women toward my subject:

> I am married, pregnant with my first child, and an architect at a well-known design firm. The pressures were conflicting while I was growing up and are still. Before I became pregnant, my father used to call me out of meetings at work to ask when I was going to have a baby. He would then hang up, call my sister, who had her first child last summer, and ask when she was going to get a job and *do* something with her life!

In all, I heard from some one hundred women from all over the country, who wrote voluminous and passionate autobiographies, about their relationships with men from father forward and the influence of these relationships on their choices in love and work.

MIRIAM FLOCK

Miriam Flock attended the Stanford Creative Writing Program in 1980 and 1981. The sequence excerpted here, "From the Dark Lady," appeared in Georgia Review *and* Chicago Review. *She has work forthcoming in* Shenandoah *and* High Plains Quarterly. *Currently she teaches at Santa Clara University.*

"These two poems are part of a series, 'From The Dark Lady.' The dark lady was born and nursed to maturity in the writing workshops of Ken Fields and W. Simone Di Piero. To them and to my colleagues during those challenging and luxurious years of having nothing to do but write, I remain extremely grateful."

From The Dark Lady

IV.
The argument we had, I should have had
with my last lover. Because you wanted me,
as he had, when I wore this flannel shirt,
I saw him tossing the cloth across the lamp,
and in the green glow, closing over me.
But mostly, I recalled he didn't love
the way my hair held smoke; that once I gripped
his back so hard, the skin striped red and white;
the way I couldn't let things go. Tonight
I couldn't; you were right. I was afraid
to be undone. Some day I'll let you touch
my heart, not just its place beneath the plaid,
or with my own hands, tear the buttons free,
and let that be my argument with him.

VII.
You thought the darkness was some missing thing—
the cleft between or else the space inside.
But I could show you substance to the dark
insides of mouths, a gravity to eyes
so dense they swallow light like chunks of jet.
This darkness has the mass and warmth of hips
beneath an army blanket—hills at dusk

not green, not any color, giving back
the day's heat. Before your iris opens,
the dark you encounter takes these shapes:
my breasts will be brown pears you carry in your palm;
my head, a black cat sleeping on your chest;
my legs, dark swans that bill and glide apart;
my body, darkness that surrounds the dark.

ERNEST GAINES

Ernest J. Gaines was born on River Lake Plantation, Pointe Coupee Parish, January 15, 1933. He can remember working in the fields at the age of eight for fifty cents a day. After attending elementary school in the church on River Lake Plantation for six years, he went to St. Augustine Catholic School in New Roads for three years, before going with his parents to California for further education. Gaines graduated from San Francisco State College in 1957, and a year later he won the coveted creative writing fellowship to Stanford University to study under the guidance of Wallace Stegner and Malcolm Cowley.

When asked how he got into writing, Gaines will tell you that he has been writing all his life. On the plantation where he lived as a child only a few of the old people could read and write, and he was asked at a very early age to read and write their letters. At San Francisco State and Stanford he was taught how to put his earlier experience into the novel and short story form. To date he has written seven books: the novels are Catherine Carmier, Of Love and Dust, The Autobiography of Miss Jane Pittman, In My Father's House, *and* A Gathering of Old Men; *a collection of short stories entitled* Bloodline; *and a children's book entitled* A Long Day In November.

Gaines has won many awards for his writings, including the Louisiana Library Association Award for The Autobiography of Miss Jane Pittman. *He has been honored five times with doctorate degrees from major universities. He is now writer-in-residence at the University of Southwestern Louisiana, Lafayette.*

"'The Hunter' is a chapter from *The Autobiography of Miss Jane Pittman,* and it concerns one of the main themes in my writing, i.e., the search for each other by black father and son. Having been torn from their motherland, Africa, and separated on the auction blocks of slavery, father and son have been searching physically, spiritually, intellectually for each other the past three hundred years. . . ."

◆　　　◆　　　◆

The Hunter

NIGHT CAUGHT US BUT we kept going, traveling by the North Star all the time. I reckoned it had been dark about three hours when we came in a thicket of pine trees, and I smelled food cooking. I stopped quickly and held out my arms so Ned would be quiet. I turned my head and turned my head, but I couldn't see the fire or the smoke. Now, I didn't know what to do—go back, go forward, or move to one side.

Then somebody spoke: "Now, don't this just beat everything."

I turned around so fast I dropped the bundle on the ground. But I felt much better when I saw another black face standing there looking down on us. He had a green stick about the size and link of a bean pole. He had come on us so quietly he could have killed both of us with that stick before we even saw him.

"What the world y'all doing way out here?" he said. "Y'all by y'all self?"

"Just me and this little boy," I said.

"Lord, have mercy," he said. He was one of the fussin'est people I had ever seen. "Y'all come on over here," he said.

I picked up my bundle and me and Ned followed him back to his camp. He had a rabbit cooking on the fire. He nodded for me and Ned to sit down. I saw a bow and arrows leaning against one of the trees. The man squatted by the fire and looked at us.

"Now, where the world y'all think y'all going?" he said.

"Ohio," I said.

"My Lord, my Lord," he said. "I done seen things these last few weeks, but if this don't beat everything, I don't know. Coming and going, coming and going, and they don't bit more know what they doing than that rabbit I got cooking on that fire there. I bet y'all hungry."

"We got something to eat," I said.

"What, potatoes and corn y'all done stole?" he said. "Don't have to tell me, I already know. I done met others just like y'all."

He took the rabbit off the fire and laid it on the leaves he had spread out on the ground. Then he took a knife from his belt and cut the rabbit up in three pieces. When it had cooled off good he handed me and Ned a piece. He had seasoned it down good with wild onions that he had found out there in the swamps.

"You going North?" I asked him.

"No, I'm where I'm going right now," he said. "South."

I quit eating. "You got to be crazy," I said.

"I reckoned you got all the sense, dragging that child through the swamps all time of night," he said. "Good thing I'm a friend, not a enemy. I heard y'all long time before you stopped back there listening. I had been leaning on that pole so long I was fixing to fall asleep."

"We was quiet," I said.

"Quiet for you, not for me," he said. "A dog ain't got nothing on these yers. What you think keeping me going, potatoes and corn?"

I didn't answer him. The rabbit was good, but I didn't want show him how much I liked it. Just nibbling here and there like I was particular.

"Who you know in Ohio?" he asked me.

"Just Mr. Brown," I said.

"Mr. Brown who?"

"Mr. Brown, a Yankee soldier," I said.

"Lord, have mercy," the hunter said, shaking his head. "Now, I done heard everything."

"How come you going back South?" I said.

"What?" he said. He wasn't eating, he was thinking about me looking for

Brown. "I'm looking for my pappy," he said. But looked like he was still thinking about me looking for Brown.

"Your mama dead?" I asked.

"What?" he said. He looked at me. "No, my mama ain't dead." He just looked at me a good while like he was thinking about me looking for Brown. "I know where she at," he said. "I want find him now."

"Y'all used to stay here in Luzana?" I asked.

"What?" he said.

"Your daddy and y'all?"

"When they sold him he was in Mi'sippi," the hunter said. "I don't know where he at now."

"Then how you know where to look for him?" I asked.

He got mad with me now. "I'm go'n do just what you doing with that child," he said. "Look everywhere. But I got little more sense."

"Well, if you was beat all the time you'd be running away, too," I said.

"I was beat," he said. "Don't go round here bragging like you got all the beating."

I ate and sucked on the bone. I didn't want argue with him no more.

"Who was them other people you seen?" I asked him. "Any of them going to Ohio?"

"They was going everywhere," he said. "Some say Ohio, some say Kansas— some say Canada. Some of them even said Luzana and Mi'sippi."

"Luzana and Mi'sippi ain't North," I said.

"That's right, it ain't North," the hunter said. "But they had left out just like you, a few potatoes and another old dress. No map, no guide, no nothing. Like freedom was a place coming to meet them half way. Well, it ain't coming to meet you. And it might not be there when you get there, either."

"We ain't giving up," I said. "We done gone this far."

"How far?" he asked me. "How long you been traveling?"

"Three days," I said.

"And how far you think you done got in three days?" he said. "You ain't even left that plantation yet. I ought to know. I been going and going and I ain't nowhere, yet, myself. Just searching and searching."

When he said this he looked like he wanted to cry, and I didn't look at him, I looked at Ned. Ned had laid down on the ground and gone to sleep. He still had the flint and iron in his hands.

I told the hunter about the Secesh who had killed Ned's mama and the other people. He told me he had seen some of the Secesh handiwork, too. Earlier that same day he had cut a man down and buried him that the Secesh had hung. After hanging him they had gashed out his entrails.

"What they do all that for?" I asked.

"Lesson to other niggers," he said.

We sat there talking and talking. Both of us was glad we had somebody to talk to. I asked him about the bow and arrows. He told me he had made it to shoot rabbits and birds. Sometimes he even got a fish or two. I told him I bet I could use it. He said I didn't have the strength. He said it took a man to pull back on that bow. I asked him what he knowed about my strength. But he kept quiet. After a while he said: "Y'all want me lead y'all back where y'all come from?"

"We didn't come from Ohio," I said.

"You just a pig-headed little old nothing," he told me.

"I didn't ask you for your old rabbit," I said. Now I was full, I got smart. "I don't like no old rabbit nohow," I said.

"How come you ate the bones?" he said.

"I didn't eat no rabbit bones," I said.

"What I ought to do is knock y'all out and take y'all on back," he said.

"I bet you I holler round here and make them Secesh come and kill us, too," I said.

"How can you holler if you knocked out, dried-up nothing?" he said.

I had to think fast.

"I holler when I wake up," I said.

"I don't care about you, but I care about that little fellow there," the hunter said. "Just look at him. He might be dead already."

"He ain't dead, he sleeping," I said. "And I can take care him myself."

"You can't take care you, how can you take care somebody else?" the hunter said. "You can't kill a rabbit, you can't kill a bird. Do you know how to catch a fish?"

"That ain't all you got to eat in this world," I said.

He looked at Ned again.

"If I wasn't looking for my pappy I'd force y'all back," he said. "Or force y'all somewhere so somebody can look after y'all. Two children tramping round in the swamps by themself, I ain't never heard of nothing like this in all my born days."

"We done made it this far, we can make it," I said.

"You ain't go'n make nothing," he said. "Don't you know you ain't go'n make nothing, you little dried-up thing?"

"You should 'a' kept that old rabbit," I said. "I don't like old rabbit meat nohow."

He didn't want argue with me no more.

"Go on to sleep," he said. "I'll stand watch over y'all."

"No, you don't," I said. "You just want take us back."

"Go on to sleep, gnat," he said.

I shook Ned, and he woke up crying. I told him the Secesh was go'n catch him if he kept up that noise. I let him sit there till he had rubbed the sleep out his eyes, then we got up and left. All that time the hunter didn't say a word. We went a little piece, till we couldn't see the camp no more, then we turned around and came on back. I had made up my mind to stay wake all night.

"Well, how was Ohio?" the hunter said.

Ned laid down in the same place and went right back to sleep. I sat beside him watching the hunter. I felt my eyes getting heavy, but I did everything to keep them open. I dugged my heel in the ground, I hummed a song to myself, I poked in the fire with a stick. But nature catch up with you don't care what you do. When I woke up the sun was high in the sky. Something was cooked there for me and Ned—a crow, a hawk, an owl—I don't know what. But there it was, done and cold, and the hunter was gone.

MERRILL JOAN GERBER

Merrill Joan Gerber has published two collections of short stories, Stop Here, My Friend *(Houghton Mifflin, 1965) and* Honeymoon *(University of Illinois Short Fiction Series, 1985), three novels,* An Antique Man *(Houghton Mifflin, 1967),* Now Molly Knows *(Arbor House, 1974),* The Lady With The Moving Parts *(Arbor House, 1978), and eight novels for young adults. Her stories have appeared in* The New Yorker, Redbook *(thirty-eight to date),* McCall's, The Atlantic, The Sewanee Review, The Virginia Quarterly Review, Shenandoah, Prairie Schooner, The American Voice, *and elsewhere. Her story "At The Fence" won the Andrew Lytle Fiction Prize awarded by* The Sewanee Review; *"I Don't Believe This," first published in* The Atlantic, *was included in* Prize Stories: The O. Henry Awards 1986.

"Early during the year of my Stegner Fellowship (1962–63), I was offered my first book contract from a major publishing house. In exultation, I carried the letter to Wallace Stegner; the offer was for an advance of $150, with $75 returnable if the publisher was not pleased with the finished manuscript. Wisely, Mr. Stegner suggested I not act too quickly. I agreed to wait. By the end of the year, I had sold one story I'd written in the workshop to *The New Yorker,* and another to *Redbook.* I had also signed a contract with Houghton Mifflin for a collection of stories (*Stop Here, My Friend*), with the advance, this time, nonreturnable."

◆   ◆   ◆

Hairdos

ON SUNDAY NIGHT THE three of us were having a Chicken Snack in Big Boy Bob's when my mother said, quite loudly and unexpectedly, "Oh, where are my babies?" She was staring at the booth behind me, in which a large noisy family sat. They didn't interest me much; my eye was on our waiter, a boy who looked like Timothy Hutton, tall, thin, and sensitive. He was careening around a corner just then, carrying three Big Boy Combinations on his forearm. My mother looked right at me, accusingly. "Where *are* they?" she demanded. "They used to be right here, one clanging her knife and fork together, one under the table looking for her saltine crackers and *you,*" she said to me, "*you* were banging your rattle on the high chair tray." She looked at my father as if he had hidden them from her. They were gone forever, just as I soon would be. One sister was married, and one in college. In the fall I would be on my merry way. I had already applied to Berkeley, Cal State, and, just for kicks, to Harvard. I was ready! My mother couldn't stand the way I sat shaking like a pneumatic drill all the time; during dinner one night, I had vibrated the salt shaker right off the edge of the table, smashing it to pieces. My muscles were quivering like a runner's—I was poised, waiting for the gunshot.

My mother's eyes were tired looking. Her hair was half white and half dark brown. She had recently taken me into her confidence about this; she was at a crossroads, she said, and didn't know whether to continue dyeing her hair and avoid the truth for another five or ten years, or to face the facts for good. I don't think I had said the right thing, which was, "What's the difference? You're going to die anyway." "Good point," she'd answered. "I've always known that, but wanted to keep it from you kids in order not to worry you. But now that you know, just remember—when I die—that I had a lot of fun and don't feel too bad or miss me too much."

"Did you?" I asked her, ". . . have fun?" I really wanted an honest answer.

"Yes, of course," she said. "I had a wonderful time. I even had one today, driving to the supermarket. The sun was hanging like an egg yolk over the freeway, and there was one blotch of black smoke coming out of a smokestack, and it was very aesthetic." My mother was worried about the aesthetics of having two tones of hair these days. I had never given the color of her hair much thought. It had always been the same color since the day I was born. I hadn't even known she dyed it till she threw open the question to us one night: "I don't think I want to dye my hair anymore. For one thing, it's deceitful. For another, I hate when those fumes get into my eyes and nose. It can't be good for me. It might even cause cancer. It's ruined two bathrobes already, and, not that you've noticed it—but that's not mold on the bathroom wall. Those little brown spots are Youthful Color, and they won't come off the wall unless I take the paint off too." My father had looked dismayed by the discussion; I supposed it reminded him that he was supposed to paint the bathroom.

"On the other hand, though I don't want to give my daughters the message that staying young is everything, neither do I want them to think that I am leaving the sexual arena entirely."

"*Are* you leaving the sexual arena?" I had asked her. All she and my father talked about was how they were going to manage to pay college tuition for everyone. I wondered if *everyone* ended up talking about money all the time.

The waiter was going by now with two bowls of chili on his forearm. He glanced at me, then down at my Chicken Snack. He paused. "Everything all right over here?"

"Fine," I said. "But could I please have another little thing of honey? I love my honey sweet," I said, ". . . I mean my chicken sweet," and smiled.

The waiter put down the bowls of chili at the next booth, and looked back at me, a little dazed.

"Honey," I reminded him.

He saluted, and ran off, tilted at a dangerous angle.

"Where *has* my youth gone?" my mother asked. "Look over there," she added. Across the aisle from us sat an elderly couple, spooning soup into their mouths. The man was frail and had very fine white hair on his head. His wife had hair black as pitch. "Look at her," my mother whispered. "Who does she think she's fooling? Does she think she can pass for thirty-five?"

My father was busily eating his Chicken Snack. We had all ordered Chicken Snacks since that was the special. It came, for some reason, on two pieces of wet greasy toast. It wasn't bad, really. None of us had gotten anything to drink. We didn't usually in a restaurant because it saved us a lot of money. It was one of the conditions my father had set down about our eating out; soft drinks alone could add three dollars to our bill. We always had water. Sometimes I looked longingly at someone else's icy Coke or triple-thick milkshake while I drank my water, which tasted something like diluted chlorine.

"Now look over there," my mother said. I followed her eyes to where a pair of older women sat, also eating in our section. They both had gray hair, closer to blue-white, set in tight little curls, fresh from a beauty parlor.

"I'm still young," my mother moaned. "Do I want to look like that?"

The waiter came back and dropped six little packets of honey beside my plate.

"I didn't need *this* much," I said, pleased.

"No problem," he said. "We have truckloads." His features weren't as fine as Timothy Hutton's, but he had a more relaxed smile. He wore a little leather apron around his hips, with pockets. "Everything fine here?" he asked my parents. "Could I get anyone dessert?"

"I'd like a piece of hot fudge cake with vanilla ice cream," I said, looking at my father. "We could all have some." Sometimes, because we never got anything to drink, he would allow us to get dessert, which we would all share.

"I was thinking," he said, slowly, as if he had given it a lot of thought, ". . . there's that doughnut shop across the street. We could get a whole box of doughnuts for what one dessert costs."

"Oh," I said. "But hot fudge cake tastes better than a doughnut, Daddy."

The waiter was standing on one foot, with his pencil poised. He had already laid the bill on the table. He was balanced there, waiting for the signal to pick it up and add on dessert. I loved how tall and thin he was. I loved his shape, his long loose legs, and his smile. I knew my life was going to be rich and full and wonderful, and it would be a lifetime before my hair would be anything but its shining golden brown wavy glorious self.

"Let her have dessert," my mother said to no one in particular. "Life is short."

◆   ◆   ◆

The baby in the high chair at the next table banged her plastic bottle on the tin top of her tray. "I just don't know where it all went," my mother sighed. I turned around to see where my waiter was; he was behind a mottled glass pane which divided the work area from the eating area. He seemed to be laboring over something. He kept bending down, and moving his shoulder, as if he were digging in a hole.

"I guess I believed my girls would be little babies forever. I didn't notice the sixties at all—they just flew by me as if I were buried in the bag of my vacuum cleaner. All that news—the war, riots, the music—I didn't pay attention to any of it. I was folding diapers."

"There are still diapers in the trunk of the car," my father said. "I wish you'd get them out."

"I always took care to have extras," my mother said. "I like them there now because they remind me of happy days." She leaned over and wiped a crumb from my father's chin with her napkin.

"I guess I could always use them to clear the fog off the windows," he said.

"I'd rather you didn't," my mother said. "I'd like to keep those diapers for a souvenir."

My waiter was now conferring with two waitresses wearing pert little caps. They, like he had been, were digging in the hole which was not in my line of sight. One would dig, then the other, then my waiter would dig. They seemed quite desperate. I wasn't even very hungry for hot fudge cake now. "Maybe I should go punk," my mother said. "If I dyed my hair green or pink, I wouldn't have this problem to deal with, would I?"

My father looked at my mother as if he were seeing her for the first time in years. "If you're asking me, I don't really like gray hair that much. I liked you better with your old color," he said.

"I liked *you* better with *your* old color," she said, quite passionately, almost furiously. "You liked me better young and I liked *you* better young. But I don't see you dyeing your hair to please *me*."

"Why would I dye my hair?" my father said.

"Why would I dye mine?"

"I don't know," he said, baffled. "I never gave it much thought."

"Don't you think I would like to be young?" my mother said, taking a chunk of ice out of her glass and dropping it in the ashtray where it melted almost instantly.

My father looked at his watch. "If we leave in the next five minutes," he said, "we can get home in time to watch 'Sixty Minutes.'"

My waiter caught my eye. He looked pained. One of the waitresses had just handed him a silver bullet-shaped urn to hold. He rested his head against its mirrored side and stared at me sadly.

"I used to like sweets," my mother said suddenly. "And then I stopped liking them. Not that I miss them that much, but what makes me sad is that I miss *wanting* them."

"What are they doing back there? Baking the cake?" my father said.

"I'll go see," I said, and jumped up, ejecting myself into the aisle. I went behind the mottled glass divider and said to my waiter, "Trouble?"

"Trouble," he said, his face still against the silver urn, his arms around it in a hug.

"Like what?"

"The waitresses from the last shift are supposed to put in a new batch of hot fudge when they go off duty, but they didn't, they never do, and we're trying to get enough together for your cake."

The two waitresses, trying to help my waiter, were leaning over a deep vat, their rumps shaking as they dug for fudge.

"Don't worry about it," I said. I could see myself in the silver side of the urn in his arms, a little distorted, but looking really good. My smile was terrific; my hair was golden. My big wool sweater looked soft, a soft but bright blue color. "Don't take it so seriously," I said. "It's only hot fudge." I smiled at him. He smiled at me.

"I think we've got enough," one of the girls said, from deep in the vat.

"We're going to make it," my waiter said to me, still keeping his eyes right on my face, looking right into my eyes.

"You bet we are," I said. I laughed out loud, and so did he. I glanced over at my table, where my father was leaning back with his eyes closed, where my mother sat looking at the delicious desserts on the table of the young family, the streak of white in her hair giving her the look of a small frightened wild animal, a skunk or a chipmunk.

"I'll go sit down now," I said, knowing we had to get back into our proper forms.

"I'll bring it," he said with a grin, a signal that we had made contact outside the forms, and that life was fantastic.

I slid into the booth with my parents. In a minute my waiter came to me with a white napkin over his arm, and bowed gallantly as he set the hot fudge cake before me. He put down a clean fork with a sharp clink and grazed my arm as he moved his away.

My mouth watered. I had a vision before me of brilliant contrasts: the chocolate cake, the ice cream, the fudge, the whipped cream.

"I wish I wanted some of that," my mother said.

I plunged my fork into it.

"Don't eat it!" she cried. "It's unfair! They have no right to charge us for a mess like that!"

I looked down and saw that the fudge was clotted and clumped around the edges of the plate in irregular brown dots, dropped there, piece by piece, scraped from the far reaches of the emptied vat. The whipped cream had gone a little flat and watery, too. The cake looked dry. But still I wanted to eat it.

My mother was waving now to the waiter. Worried-looking, he came rushing over to us.

"Do you think it's fair for us to have to pay for this mish-mosh?"

My father looked embarrassed.

"I think we should at least get a discount," my mother demanded.

The waiter clapped his hands together, thinking. I felt the muscles in my thighs begin to vibrate.

"Would it be okay if I take it off your bill?" the waiter asked nervously, looking over his shoulder.

"But I want it," I said to my mother.

"The fudge is cold. It's got to be cold," she said.

I scooped one of the soft clumps onto my fork, and ate it. "It's delicious," I said.

The waiter was crossing it off the bill. He fixed the addition and put the bill down. He hurried away without looking at me.

I continued to eat the hot fudge cake, in big forkfuls, washing it down with my chlorine-scented water. My mother took the fork from her Chicken Snack and wiped it on a napkin. She slid it across the table to my plate, and whacked off a corner of fudge cake. "I just want a little taste," she said.

My father looked worried. He said, "You don't understand the principle involved here. If you eat it, you should pay for it, and if you want it taken off the bill, you should have the boy take it away."

"*You* don't understand the principle," my mother said. "It's just a little taste, it's not a crime to want a little taste."

I turned my head and saw the waiter leaning against the mottled glass divider, one hand inserted between two buttons of his brown Big Boy vest. He was watching me. Rather, he was admiring me—he smiled to make it clear. My heart swelled.

"Here, Mom," I said, sliding my entire plate her way. "I'm stuffed. You have all the rest."

"Well—I don't know. But okay, only if Daddy will share it with me."

My father opened his mouth to protest, but my mother was already holding the fork to his lips. She pushed some loose chocolate crumbs toward his mouth with her other hand, which she held cupped under his chin. She fed him like a baby and in spite of himself my father laughed—he actually laughed—and gobbled up the sweets.

REGINALD GIBBONS

◆   ◆

Books: poems, Roofs Voices Roads *(1979),* The Ruined Motel *(1981), and* Saints *(1986); volumes of translations from Spanish (Luis Cernuda and Jorge Guillen); edited works,* The Poet's Work, The Writer in Our World; *and others. Editor of* TriQuarterly *magazine and professor of English at Northwestern. Guggenheim and N.E.A. fellowships in poetry, and the short story award of the Texas Institute of Letters.*

"Stanford had a decisive effect on me, and my time there was full of intensities of thinking, friendship, conscience, and writing. As a poet-teacher, Donald Davie was both demanding and generous, and thus immeasurably helpful to my understanding of the vocation of poetry as well as the writing of it. And: the hills, the bay, the coast, the sea. . . ."

◆   ◆   ◆

Eating

As if it's been waiting until he can't have it,
some moment they lived, that he didn't want
when it was his, begins to raise a craving in him—
good dinner that she used to hear him
bring thoughtfully upstairs to where
she was waiting—reading or watching TV.
They'd spend a half-hour eating it,
their familiar life was a comfort, then from
the next room where he'd be brooding
over books or just hoarding himself
he'd listen for her quiet movement,
sometimes laughter as she watched TV or read.
Did she want him to think she was happy?
But he'd sit still and ponder what
was expected of him, or hoped.
Later they'd snack, or one of them would.

Remorse now makes him remember her saying
one time when they were crying in her new
living room filled with familiar things
that were just hers, not his any more,
"I wish I'd stayed to have breakfast with you."

She meant all those mornings she had
hurried away to work, him still in bed
debating with himself whether to get up,
whether to have an egg or skip to lunch.

(Once at a dinner when they were admiring
all the work their hosts had finished together
on floors and walls, but famished, she had
told him how she liked something he had done
and he'd bitten at her, red with his own
unsuspected anger, then sick at her tears.)

It wasn't her fault he'd lain in bed.
His too-wistful asking her to stay those mornings
only showed he thought it would be easier
if she went, though there were days
he'd get up to walk to the diner
with her at that special pace they hit
together, that came to life from them
like a child, but was broken
when after breakfast he watched her go on
alone to work and he walked the other way
full of coffee and bread—

As it would break if they were tired
after those dinners with friends
when they'd eaten too much. And even if
he'd done nothing cruel, walking home
side by side late and out of step,
each could silently take back—
and he often would—what had seemed
affectionately given in the company of others.
A brief safe walk to bed—the distance
sometimes growing, the closer they got to home.

And in bed, whether they did or they didn't;
snugged against each other or not;
with the silence denying all hurts
or tears from either or both;
with him refusing to answer
or her taking a sharp
quick breath to say *yes;*
good food and too much wine
or bad and none—
                    they were hungry
lying awake, and hungry they fell asleep,
and sleeping, all night long, they were hungry.

◆   ◆   ◆

No Matter What Has Happened This May

I love the little row of life along the low rusted garden-wire fence that divides my small city backyard from my neighbor's. The wild unruly rose, I hacked like a weed last spring; then it shot quick running lengths of vine in every direction and shuddered into a thickness of blown blossoms—the kind you can't cut and take in because they fall apart—so I think I should cut it back as if to kill it again. The violets, just beautiful weeds. Then there are yellow-green horseradish leaves, they rose as fast as dandelions in today's rain and sun; and the oregano and mint are coming back, too, you can't discourage them. Last year's dry raspberry canes are leaning, caught in the soft thorns of the new, at the corner. And beyond them, the mostly gone magnolia in the widow's yard, behind ours, the white petals on the ground in a circle like a crocheted bedspread thrown down around the black trunk.

I went out to see what the end of the day was like, away from everything, for a minute, and it was drizzling slowly. I touched the ground, just to feel it wet against my palm; and the side of the house, too. They were there. It was quiet, and I saw two robins bringing weeds and twigs to a nesting place in the new leaves at the stumpy top of a trimmed buckeye limb. How little they need—weeds and some time—to build with.

In a month I may find a new one not yet fully fledged, lost from the nest, and put it on the highest limb I can reach, but not high enough to escape harm's way, I imagine, when the harm is a shock within it, a giving up already; and it will be dead before morning. That's happened before. But these robins were just building, and one came with a full beak and paused a moment on a lower branch and cocked its head and looked upward and shifted as if it were a muscled cat, of all things, about to leap, and then it did leap and disappeared into the clump of leaves, and shook them, as the single drops of rain were gently shaking them one by one, here and there.

I was getting wet but I felt held outside because I could hear, from inside the house, a woman and a child—my wife and my daughter—laughing in the bathtub together, their laughter not meant for me but brought out to me like a gift by the damp still air so I could see that like the rain and the robins and the row of weeds they too were working and building. I'm not going to mention, now, any harm or hurt they have suffered; no winter nor summer government; no green troops nor trimmed limbs of trees; no small figures beaten or fallen. I wiped the dirt off my palms and I picked up again the glass of wine I had carried out with me. I rejoiced. There was no way not to, wet with the sound of that laughter and whispering in the last light of a day we had lived.

IVY GOODMAN

Ivy Goodman was a Mirrielees Fellow at Stanford in 1975–76. Heart Failure, *a collection of short stories, was published by the University of Iowa Press in 1983. Her work has also appeared in* Prize Stories: The O. Henry Awards, The Signet Classic Book of Contemporary American Short Stories, *and other anthologies.*

"Innocently, at the start, I chose to write without thinking how I'd go on if I failed. I was a fool back then, if I thought I wouldn't sometimes fail. Now, more than ten years out of Stanford, I can only repeat the cliché, Writing is a hard life, but I say it with free will and masochistic pleasure."

♦　　♦　　♦

In Twos

WHEN HE'S DEAD, HE imagines he'll still live in the phonebook as Herbert Beeton and Company. Last month he was bought out of his own firm and kept on to fool the eye. But really, he doesn't care. He's made money enough to last till the end. He's not humiliated, though Phillip Haricot has been claiming that he is. Also, he feels tip-top. Haricot, now leaning against Beeton's office door, has been spreading rumors that the older man hasn't long to live.

"Well, Herb," Haricot says, "what's up?"

"Come in, Phillip. It's Lansburgh and Ryder." Beeton has been told by the parent company to fire someone, promote someone else, to sort through papers and the drawers of his desk.

"You're firing Lansburgh?" Haricot asks.

"You'll do the honors, I hope."

"Herb, my pleasure." Haricot smiles with psychopathic eagerness, his hair, skin, and teeth all variations on shades of yellowing bone. Did the devil assemble him in a hurry from materials on hand and then catapult him earthwards to fetch one Herbert Beeton? Is that why he says, why he seems to know, Beeton hasn't long? And yet, of the two, Haricot looks less well. That is, until he moves, quickly, energetically, though slightly bent forward, like a middle-aged former college athlete who has compromised with his posture to soothe old pains. Or, like a petty thief who has adopted the habit of hunching to conceal goods inside his overcoat, a habit maintained for consistency, whether or not the man is wearing his overcoat or concealing bounty.

The man—athlete, thief, rumor-monger, the devil's missionary, a simple working publicist with a wife, a child, and an eastside co-op to support—sits and tamps his cigaret on the wooden arm of Beeton's green leather, brass-studded visitor's chair.

"Phillip, those aren't good for you. A banana instead?" Beeton offers the bunch. Bananas are his own eccentricity, the peasant pottery plate beneath his former wife's idea. "The best source of potassium. On doctor's orders I eat one daily."

"You aren't well?"

"Don't you know? You're the expert."

"Hmm? I'm a little lost." Squinting, Haricot projects his head forward a bit, as though meeting senility halfway. "Come again, Herb?" He speaks in senile parlance as well.

"If I'm too much for you, back to Lansburgh then." Beeton clears his throat and puts a sour elegance in his voice. If he were to say the word *either* now he would pronounce it with a long *i*. "Lansburgh goes. You concur with me on that?"

"Definitely. She's the one." As Haricot talks, he opens his matchbook, and Beeton finds an odd similarity in the revelation and orderly overabundance of Haricot's teeth and matchsticks. "When's it happening, Herb?"

"Soon. You've taken them both to lunch?"

"Last month. I dropped my reports on your desk, but maybe they got lost in all that other mess. Oops . . ." With that, Haricot disguises himself as a friend who's forgotten for a moment and inadvertently brought up his friend Herb's failures. "Sorry."

"No need. By the 'other mess' do you mean the buyout? I don't think of it like that. And I did read your reports. 'Smoked salmon; Lansburgh ate a caper or two.' Very fine. You're first-rate, Phillip." Glass salt and pepper shakers, shiny silverplate and starched white linen, a basket of rolls, pats of butter on cracked ice, hot plates, hot coffee: Beeton knows that Haricot finds himself as equally at home in a restaurant as any of those things. "Yes," Beeton says, "you're the man to watch employees over lunch. Check them out in public before clients deal with them, that's the way."

"Poor Lansburgh. The silver rattled in her hands. Pathetic. There's just no need for that."

"She's beneath contempt?" Beeton asks. "Beneath seduction?"

Haricot chortles and once more flashes his smoker's teeth, fitted together tightly at the gum and fanning out toward the world. "You know I'm happily married, Herb."

"And I'm happily not." Beeton looks now for any betrayal of an ironic or even simple thought on Haricot's face. He might be searching for signs of life in plaster of paris, except there are real dull blue eyes in these sockets and a storehouse of innuendo in the brain behind. "Do you think that's possible, Phillip?"

"If you're the example, I'm sure it is."

But Haricot has been whispering in the halls that Beeton lost his wife as he lost his business, through the childlike bumbling that afflicts old men. He doesn't account for two people's misery, cuckoldry, or philandering. He simplifies for the simplest moral effect. Yes, Beeton chases skirts; yes, he showed Haricot photographs of girls he met on his Rio trip. Yes, and so? Beeton's favorite girl ate plums, breaking them open along the faint cleft that marked two halves, the skin parting from tension, the flesh bursting out the way full women burst out of tight clothes.

"Herb?" Haricot asks.

Beeton starts. Now Haricot has something else. *The old coot drifted off, believe it or not.* But Beeton will get back. "Just thinking. Lansburgh and Ryder. Think Lansburgh knows? Or Ryder? Rumor has it you're a gossip, Phillip."

"What?" The masked man comes alive, blanches, reddens, parts dry lips, blots his forehead with his palm, the contradictory symptoms coming all in a rush, as though he were a living version of time-lapse photography. "Who said that?"

"The real gossip, I guess. Don't worry, Phillip, I knew it wasn't true. Just so you remember that spreading lies is the devil's work."

Haricot reaches toward the ashtray and snickers; he's fine already, better than ever. "Are we working for the fundamentalists?"

"Not I. But I bet you will someday. Here's what," Beeton says, rubbing his hands together. "I don't mean to cut short our talk, but this will appeal to you. Send for Ryder and let her hear you fire Lansburgh over the phone. Make it a one-way conference call, so Ryder and I can listen in. All right? Take my desk. I prefer the sofa." Beeton's chair on wheels rolls back, the rolling echoes, and he stands, cell by cell, until his whole body gets the message. He sees Haricot put out an arm and coolly invite him to use it as a railing. The man's disinterested, Beeton judges. He doesn't want to witness Herb Beeton's collapse and death, though for all he cares Beeton can go ahead and die, certainly, once Haricot's out of the room.

"Phillip, I'm fine," Beeton says, "though I appreciate your concern." He walks alone across the carpet and lowers himself onto the sofa, flanked on either end by brass, green-shaded table lamps that Beeton thinks of whimsically as his accountants. He likes the lamps; he likes the sofa; his smile is genuine. "Make yourself at home, Phillip."

Haricot hesitates and then sits down at Beeton's desk with an air of taking over finally. *This is it!* He lifts the telephone receiver, and Beeton, though blocking out the words, cannot mistake the sound of braggadocio.

"Herb?"

Catching the loud whisper, Beeton turns. Haricot has cupped one hand over the receiver. Is the shape to him, too, reminiscent of a breast? Not the feel, surely—hard, cold, pinpricked. "Do you like my phone, Phillip? It dates from the 1930s."

"Vintage. Want Ryder up here right away?"

"Pronto."

When she arrives, she is out of uniform: the scaled-down female suit, simple blouse, grosgrain tie. Instead she wears a tunic of blue silk that is almost black. Beeton rises to say hello. "What color is your lovely frock?"

"Midnight. How do you do, sir." She extends a hand and reveals that her narrow tunic hides dramatic pleats beneath its arms. Now the sleeves, like wings, seem attached to the body by membrane, the dress itself designed as a tribute to the bat.

"You're being promoted, Miss Ryder, or did you know?"

"Yes, I did. I'm very happy." Her smile suggests a conspiracy of other girlish smiles, girlish whispers, muffled girlish laughter. She has brought all of girlhood upstairs with her.

"Won't you sit?" He gestures toward the sofa.

"Thank you." She bends; she smooths her skirt boldly over her rump and down her thighs, and Beeton sees another identical but invisible pair of hands at work, still smoothing, still titillating. He sees Miss Ryder doubled, twinned, in sapphic relation to herself, at the adolescent, fondling stage of love, continually aroused but not yet consummated. She scoots around, toward Haricot. "Good morning, Phillip." She laughs, perhaps at her daring use of a man's first name, and Beeton hears a second, silent laugh. As though her twin lover has just touched her in a secret place and then pointed at Beeton again, she redirects her arousal. "I had a premonition this morning, Mr. Beeton. I awoke wanting to wear something special." She shakes her head, shakes her double's naughty, teasing fingers out of her tresses. "Something, oh, Asiatic."

At the desk, Haricot spins the old-fashioned dial laboriously. There is a sound in the room of clicking, clicking in different multiples. A vein throbs on Miss Ryder's ivory temple. Her nose and chin, her plump mouth, all her beauty has only just budded forth out of her exquisite skin. Beeton isn't being fair to her. She is so young. She must be smart, and she may prove brilliant. Perhaps he should apologize. "Tell me, Miss Ryder, am I a misogynist?"

"Well, Mr. Beeton . . ." She inclines her right ear toward her shoulder, and Beeton cannot help himself: he sees her mirror image inclining, too, so they can put their heads together over this. They do; they giggle, and the visible woman coyly rights her head. Now he watches for signs of the other one, lighting all the essential wicks with her practiced touch, here and here and here, the other one, the proxy, arousing her for him. "I can't say yet, Mr. Beeton, but I hope to find out."

"Once we start working together, more closely?"

"Why, yes. I suppose."

"You're very desirable. So far, is that your greatest success?"

The real Miss Ryder's mouth quivers, and the secret one steps back, her fingertips suspended. "I'm not sure what you mean. Relative to business." Beeton can tell she is going to be sick, but she will hold it in and wait to be alone with herself. Her twin then will grasp her under the arms and together, piggyback, they will double over. *Sure he promoted you, but he was toying with your mind. How could you go along with that? Aren't you sick of acting cheap?* For now, though, she holds it in and reduces it to a foreshadow, a just perceptible taste in her mouth.

"Would you like some water, Miss Ryder?"

"Oh, no, thank you." She twitches the corners of a smile and then quickly lets it go.

"Herb?"

Saved by that voice, Miss Ryder relaxes, and even before Beeton she looks to Haricot, that large blonde man miming with large gestures—a nod that spans at least twelve inches from hairline to chin until it gradually levels out, a wet open mouth and a hovering tongue inside, together divulging childishly that the man is concentrating on two things at once: the gathering in the room and the voice coming over the phone at which he points one square-tipped forefinger obscenely, as if from behind the other party's back. His eyes move from Beeton and Ryder to the desk and the phone, hopping from level to level of thought.

". . . yes, I know the Balin project, but I'm not calling about that, Miss Lansburgh." Haricot presses a knob on the conference console, and Miss Lansburgh's static whisper spreads like dust across the room: "Oh?"

Haricot explains that hiring and firing are simply matters of personal taste. In so many words, though Miss Lansburgh isn't good enough for this particular firm, of course she will be good enough for someone else. Lansburgh responds with silence, and Haricot embellishes on, pleased with both his self-importance and his gift of gab. He swivels right and left in Beeton's leather desk chair; he taps a pen on Beeton's worn, gray blotter; he stares at the ceiling as though fascinated by the accountant lamps' shadows, funneling out and crossing paths. "Are you still there, Miss Lansburgh?"

The blurred voice comes again over the intercom: "Yes."

Suddenly Miss Ryder stands. Her secret twin waits behind her, and the two shy girls clasp fingers. No, no, they reassure each other, we're not in trouble; it's Miss Lansburgh. A sibling, a schoolmate, a fellow worker, perhaps a friend, someone is being punished, and Miss Ryder stands uncomfortably, marginally on the safe side. She looks at Beeton as if he were the boy who told, who put the process in gear.

". . . your work is excellent," Haricot continues, "in every evaluation, Miss Lansburgh, but as I was saying, in matters like these of taste . . ." He rolls his eyes as one is wont to when explaining the obvious to an idiot. "Yes, quite excellent, and you can be sure that our letter of reference . . ."

"Couldn't you have warned me?" Miss Lansburgh's whisper appeals to the room. "Or pointed out problems right along? What, specifically, is wrong with me?"

Beeton summons his memory of her when she was hired, a tiny young woman, tiny but not pretty, tiny and on closer inspection not all that young. But there was a novelty, a charm in her size, like the charm of those tiny, short-haired nervous dogs that can fit comfortably in teacups. He envisions her today, a tiny woman dressed in the most miniature of scaled-down suits and jabots; she raises her desk chair as high as it goes, twists and coils herself in thought, bends nearer the page, her myopia worsening by the moment, and writes the first drafts of her fine reports in an arabesque, spiraling scroll. She glances up, her mouth gluey. The phone is ringing. With a swallow, she revives her vocal cords. *Yes?* It is only Phillip Haricot, calling to fire her as a friend might call to say hello, while other friends listen on in the room.

"Miss Lansburgh, please," Haricot says, "don't be angry."

"I'm upset," the voice answers. "I'm not angry."

She doesn't get angry—no. She leaves that to whom? Her imaginary other half, suddenly spotted by Beeton and defined. The two of them aren't fondlers and friends, all atwitter like the two Miss Ryders. Certainly not. The Miss Lansburghs know each other too well for that. The weaker one sputters at her desk. Maybe she leans her head on the upholstered partition that separates her from her neighbor's cell.

"Oh, did I mention, Miss Ryder," Beeton says, breaking his trance. "You'll have your own office now. You'll leave the basement hive."

Miss Ryder, too, looks up from a trance. He has offered her a privilege, and though she does not leap to take it, she remembers her manners and tells him, "Thanks."

Meanwhile the static in the room quickens. In the fuzzy distance, something cracks, and Miss Lansburgh, breathing close up, broadcasts a startled, jagged cry.

"What's that? Interference?" Haricot asks.

"A broom fell." Again she sobs. "Someone left a broom in the corner. The maid, I guess, I . . ."

Her double's broom! Of course! Beeton sees that the double has been in the hive all along, cleaning up. Miss Lansburgh's pauses can be explained by the presence of that other one, demanding to know, *Who's that? Who's on the telephone?* Weak and brainy, brawny and dull: they are not true twins but opposites. The double yells to be heard above the clanking furnace. *Who is it?* In anger, she slops the dingy, sudsy contents of her bucket onto the floor. *You aren't crying, are you?* She wipes her hands and streaks her broad skirt with grimy fingerprints. *Who's on the telephone? Answer me!* Her gray hair, rolled back, twisted, and clamped at the neck, is an example to everyone of how she punishes unruliness. Like the worst things one knows about oneself, she looms, she nears. *What! You've been fired! Didn't I warn you!*

"I . . . I . . ."

"Take it easy, Miss Lansburgh, come on." Haricot apes sympathy and confidentiality, the finest of counseling techniques. For his audience in the room, he curls his tongue between his lips and teeth to swell his mouth into a muzzle and like a primate scratches quizzically beneath one arm. He's enjoying himself; he laughs. "Pardon me, something in my throat. Truly, Miss Lansburgh, when I promise . . ."

"Mr. Beeton?" Miss Ryder sways closer, her words immediate, her air perfumed. Fashionable young women—devotees of peculiar clothes—do not look at him usually. This one does. "Was it your idea to fire Rochelle Lansburgh in front of me?"

"Are you asking to be excused? To go to the powder room?" Beeton inquires. "You waited this long to complain because you hadn't caught on till now?"

She jerks away, toward Haricot. "Phillip, did you . . ."

He waves her off and mouths, *Quiet!* "Miss Lansburgh," he concludes aloud, "no one in the business, in New York or Washington or wherever you go, not a soul will hear any negative words from the firm. Be assured."

Miss Lansburgh responds with taps, creaks, the sounds of struggle. Beeton hears the phone being wrested by the other, stronger one. The other's voice, like something rusty dragged in the street, cries out: "No recommendations, nothing, understand? I won't thank you to lie on my behalf, not any of you!"

The line goes dead and silent. Haricot, grinning, suspends the receiver halfway between its cradle and his ear. "Hate to give up your desk, and you know it, don't you, Herb."

Miss Ryder sighs; her sleeves billow. "Could we pretend I just walked in? My timing's awful."

"But you did good work," Beeton says. "Good work all around." As if from afar already, he watches them in his office, among the furniture and memorabilia he will not take with him when he leaves. He shuts his eyes, a stale air presses in on him, and he feels himself transported, trapped downstairs between the two Miss Lansburghs who embrace each other as they always have in bad times.

HANNAH GREEN

Hannah Green was at Stanford and in Wallace Stegner's and Richard Scowcroft's writing workshops in the early fifties. She is the author of The Dead of the House, *of "Mister Nabokov" and other stories published in* The New Yorker, *of "A Journal in Praise of the Art of John Wesley" (her husband), of a little book for children,* In the City of Paris, *and of* Golden Spark, Little Saint: A Voyage Through Conques, *which Random House will publish. She has taught at Columbia in the School of the Arts (1970–80), at New York University, and at Bennington in the Summer Writing Program. She has been a Fellow at the Bunting Institute at Radcliffe College (1978–79) and a recipient of grants from the N.E.A. and from the Ingram Merrill Foundation.*

"I began what was to become *The Dead of the House* while I was still at Stanford. I was finished with the writing workshops then and teaching, but I remember rushing to show Mr. Stegner, my mentor, the first thirty or so pages of what, after many false tries, would really be the book. He liked it and that gave me great courage. Later, though, I ran into trouble because something turned out to be wrong with the structure of the book. I kept working on it but something was wrong and it slowed me down. After a long time I decided that I must, for the sake of my ego, publish some sections of the still not finished book. The trouble was I had sections of the book, but no whole stories as such. Then one night suddenly I got the first sentence of 'The Sphinx and the Pyramid' and I saw the parts I could put together in it, and since it was almost all written, it took me only three days to put it together and send it off to *The New Yorker*. They bought it. Shaping the rest of the material into stories solved the problem of the structure of the book. A lot of what I had written had to be left out; and 'The Sphinx and the Pyramid' was woven eventually into the long central section of the book and, to my sorrow, ceased to exist as a separate story."

◆　　◆　　◆

The Sphinx and the Pyramid

MANY YEARS AGO, ON the Fourth of July, 1876, a balloonist made an ascension from the Cincinnati Zoo and took along a baby lion as an added attraction. On that sunny Fourth, my Grandfather Nye, who was a boy then, was swimming with his friends at the Dayton sandbar on the Kentucky side of the Ohio.

"We were swimming naked, of course," my grandfather said once, when we went, as we often did, to his house in town for dinner. "We looked up and saw a huge silver balloon, with ribbons floating around the basket, drifting downward and about to fall in the river. It landed in a foot or two of water at the edge of the bar, and we boys rushed to grab the basket. The aeronaut was half frightened to death and pale as a sheet. The lion jumped out. It was about the size of a large police dog, and as the poor thing started to trot off across the sand I ran after it and caught it. I picked it up and petted it to soothe it. It was quite tame and seemed to enjoy being held in my arms. And that," my grandfather concluded, "is the only time I ever held a lion in my arms."

But years later, in France, he did go up in a balloon. He was preparing "A Bird's-Eye View of France" for the series of lectures he gave all over the Midwest and parts of the South in 1891 and 1892, with "Magnificent Dissolving Stereopticon Views." When his balloon passed over the château of a famous duke, the duke came out on the terrace and called up, "Come down, come down for lunch!" But Grandpa Nye just doffed his hat and sailed on through the wonderful upper regions of the atmosphere.

And years after that, hearing the story, I imagined him up there in the balloon's basket, floating by in his high silk hat and his Prince Albert coat, with a smile on his face and a debonair tilt to his head, looking just as he did in the picture of him taken in 1915 when he was handing the trowel to William Howard Taft to lay the cornerstone of the new Hamilton County Courthouse. The old courthouse had been gutted by fire during the riot of 1884, and Grandpa Nye, who was known in Cincinnati for his devotion to civic causes, had, in 1914, been appointed head of the commission to build the new courthouse. He was in those days the president of the Morgan Burke Company, which bought and sold pig iron and coal and owned a great foundry down the river, as well as mines and little blast furnaces with names like the Princess, the Bessie, all over the South. Taft, who had finished his term as the twenty-seventh President and hadn't yet been appointed to his seat as Chief Justice, wore a bowler and had a genial expression, with his white walrus mustache and a rose in his buttonhole; he was very wide—he took up two-thirds of the picture, and Grandpa Nye, who was tall and thin, stood sidewise.

In that picture, which hung among many other old photographs in the upstairs hall of my grandfather's house, my grandfather looked so much like my father I would have thought it was my father in the picture except that he wasn't wearing my father's silver-rimmed glasses.

When I remarked the uncanny resemblance, my mother said, "It's the charm. The Nyes—they all have it."

She touched my father's back and he, pleased, recalled the time when he was little and Taft was President and the President came to dinner. "Papa said to me, 'Morgan, will you speak to the President?' I spoke to the President," my father said. "He ate voluminously, but very neatly."

Next to the picture of Grandpa Nye and William Howard Taft hung the picture that puzzled me. For years I stared at it absently, wondering who the people were. Five women and one man and a boy were all on camelback in the desert. Behind them loomed a sphinx and a pyramid. The women were sitting sidesaddle in their long skirts and their huge puffed sleeves; their shoes were just peeking out from under their skirts. The boy was twelve or thirteen and he had large eyes. The man wore a big, dark, old-fashioned mustache and a very big white desert hat.

One evening, my father came upon me looking at that picture and he told me it was taken on the famous trip when Uncle George, my father's great-uncle George DeGolyer, went around the world with the five DeGolyer sisters—my father's grandmother and his great-aunts Eda, Belle, Kate, and Jenny—and Uncle Andrew. "That was in 1892 and '93, the year after your Great-Grandfather Joab Nye's death," my father said. "Your great-grandmother, Vanessa DeGolyer, had been left a widow, and then that same summer their house on College Hill was struck by lightning and burned to the ground."

I always knew how my great-grandfather had died—but only later did I read what Grandpa Nye wrote of him in the Nye Family Record: "Though my father became a successful man of business, he retained his scholarly quiet ways. He read Latin and Greek at sight and he spoke French fluently. He graduated from McGill in the year 1861, the valedictorian of his class, and after he and Mother were married he taught Latin at McGill. He was a fine teacher. In May of 1872, we removed to Cincinnati, and Father joined the firm of Queen City Carriages, of which he was treasurer at the time of his death. We lived in College Hill and Father rode to and from the city on the old narrow-gauge railway. He always carried a book, for he was an omnivorous reader. On the second of July, 1892, he had with him Hardy's *Tess of the D'Urbervilles*. He was down at the Gest Street Station of the old C. H. & D., waiting for the train on which he was accustomed to ride home in the evening, and, absorbed in reading *Tess,* he started across the tracks, as was his wont. He did not hear the switch engine that bore down on him, though they said they rang and rang the bell. He died without regaining consciousness two hours later at the Cincinnati Hospital, where the ambulance had taken him.

"His death came to us not only as a shock but as a profound sorrow. He was a lovable man, devoted to my mother and to his children, and we all grieved for him. To this day, I mourn him and feel that his death, in his fifty-fifth year, was a calamity. Life for him was so full and he enjoyed it so much that I could never dismiss the feeling that in some way he had missed the years that would have been the sweetest to him. As I write this, I am many years older than he was when he died, yet I always think of him as much older than I am or older than I could be; that is, years have not changed the relation of parent and child.

"After my father's death, the commodious new residence he had built was struck by lightning, which set fire to the roof, and the whole house was destroyed. All the furniture, the books, and the bric-a-brac were consumed. There were the accumulations of many years, and the clothing, too, was destroyed, so my mother was left with only the clothes on her back. After Father's death, Uncle George and Aunt Jenny had taken over the house, and Mother lived with them. The destruction of the house made them all so unhappy that they determined not to attempt to rebuild or to keep house again. They took a trip around the world, and were gone for more than a year."

"Yes," my father said, coming closer to scrutinize the picture, "this was probably taken early in the year 1893 on that famous trip." Then he tried to figure out for me which of his great-aunts was which. He mumbled. "No, no, this one must be Eda," he said, pointing. "She was the one who always smelled of perfumes and powders. She was John Randall's grandmother." He mumbled again. "No, *this* is Belle," he said. "She was the one with the thick ankles." (I couldn't see her ankles in the picture.) "This one is Kate. I despised her. De*spised* her. She was an artist, you know. She had a studio in the old Chelsea building in New York. She didn't like people. She had a harsh female voice. And she married *no one*. I refused to go to her funeral."

He paused, and then he said, smiling, "Now, this is Aunt Jenny. She and Uncle George were husband and wife, and they were also first cousins, you know. When they were children, they always said they were going to get married. I suppose everyone just thought it was charming. Certainly no one took it seriously. Then one day when they were sixteen they went off together down the road until they came to a justice of the peace. It was much easier to get married in those days. They came back home for supper and announced that they were married, and that was that. In later years . . ."

"What?" I asked.

"In later years, Uncle George had a . . . a sweetheart, and Aunt Jenny was exceedingly jealous. Ex*ceed*ingly jealous," my father said, smiling to himself. "Now, this is my grandmother, Vanessa. She was a wonderful woman, wonderful. She loved people. She fought for women's rights in the days when women didn't do such things. She corresponded with Lucy Stone. She was responsible, you know, for having the 'NO SPITTING' signs installed in the streetcars of Cincinnati. Once, she was ridiculed in the papers for appearing before the City Council to demand playgrounds for the city's children. The headlines said she said, 'SANDPILES CURE BOWLEGS.' And this," my father said gently, pointing to the boy, "is Uncle Andrew. Do you remember him?"

"Oh, Daddy, of course. I loved him so much," I said.

"Uncle Andrew was nearly twenty years younger than his oldest brother, Grandpa Nye, and he always seemed to be one of the children with us. One time, I sat next to him at dinner at Grandpa Nye's and I told him something disgusting to try to make him unable to eat. And he told me back something five times as disgusting, about a cow he ate in Arizona, that I've never been able to forget."

Uncle Andrew had a big square face and was pale, and he had very big, very pale-blue eyes that looked innocent and startled, and a high wide bumpy forehead, and very curly brown hair cut short and brushed back. His voice was hoarse and it had sadness in it, because, I thought, his wife whom he loved so much had died. Her name was Francie. She was a Floradora girl when he met her in New York. He was studying mining engineering at Columbia. He was on the football team in 1902. After they were married he brought her home to Grandpa Nye's. The family disapproved because she was a dancing girl. Daddy said all the family gathered in the library to meet her, and once he looked over and saw her standing alone near a window. As he watched, a tear rolled down her cheek. Daddy hated the family for making Aunt Francie feel that way. She was the most delicate, the most beautiful creature in all the world—so frail and so lovely—and she went with Uncle Andrew in a dugout through the jungles of Guatemala, when he was working for the U.S. Coast and Geodetic Survey, looking for gold. And later she went with him to India. His job was to set up a great pig-iron blast furnace whose dismantling he had overseen in Batelle,

Alabama, where it had been built but never used. Uncle Andrew marked and plotted the bricks and the steel, blueprinted the furnace piece by piece, and shipped it on a huge freighter to the Tata Iron Works, near Calcutta, and there he rebuilt it.

But in India Aunt Francie died. She was only thirty-one. Uncle Andrew wandered grieving through Tibet and China, and when, after many years, he came home, he put his hand in his pocket and pulled out a small object, which he held in his palm. "Morgan," he said to my father, "look at this!" It was a soybean. Uncle Andrew explained its significance. "That would have been about 1924," my father told me, "and the soybean was relatively unknown here, though it had been grown in China since before written history and was one of the five sacred grains considered essential to the existence of Chinese civilization."

Later, Uncle Andrew married again, but he never stopped grieving for his beautiful Francie who died when she was still so young. He practiced yoga in his back yard in College Hill. And then one morning in 1937 he woke up and put his feet out of bed and died. "Like that!" my father said, snapping his finger and thumb.

"He was the replica of his father," my father said. "Your Great-Grandfather Joab Nye, who was killed, you know, while he was reading *Tess of the D'Urbervilles*." Suddenly my father was trembling with anger. "Don't let anyone ever tell you it was not . . ."

"Not what?" I said.

"Not an accident," he said. His lips were twitching with fury.

Often in my mind, I saw him, my great-grandfather, Joab Nye, tall and gentle and lovable, reading, his blue eyes far off and deep in *Tess of the D'Urbervilles*, walking the Yorkshire hills he'd left when he was three, as he crossed the tracks amid the heat and city sounds of a July evening in the Queen City of the West and looked up (his blue eyes Uncle Andrew's eyes), startled, in the moment he was taken from his book and killed.

CHARLES GULLANS

Charles Gullans is the publisher of The Symposium Press, which has issued books by Edgar Bowers, Turner Cassity, J. V. Cunningham, Janet Lewis, Timothy Steele, and others. His most recent publications are Many Houses, Under Red Skies, Local Winds, A Diatribe to Dr. Steele, *and* The Wrong Side of the Rug. *Three of them are published by R. L. Barth.*

"I write metrically because I believe that meter gives the most complete potential control over one's material of any method of rhythmical organization as yet invented for words alone. Music offers other opportunities, but I do not write music. I aim at idiomatic expression, clarity, brevity, and hope to achieve distinction of diction, as well as a congruence with my subject matter."

The Wall

Here and no farther. On the other side
The tides of fortune roll in violence:
Men fall in battle and their flags fall, too,
Each in his agony. I draw a line.
Here for a little while, you plant your trees
And train their branches out against my stone,
Which stores the sunlight up and gives them back
Sheltering warmth by night. The trees will grow
And bear sweet fruit, which you will eat, and men
Will walk here and will speak in measured words
Of Time and of the Fortune no man knows.
Landslip and storm and malice rage outside,
But my stone and my mortar both are firm
On firm foundations, set to their true plumb,
And level with the pillars of the earth.
Books line the rooms that I enclose. And men
Read the true words upon the page, and add
Their glosses in the margins, script on script,
And text upon old text. And they are slow,
Because their thought is slow before the rush
Of kings that fall and crowns and dynasties,
Before the haste of their own vanishing
In the long night, like those who wrote the words

That they are reading on the vellum pages.
Perhaps they think of men to follow them,
Whose hands could till the fruit trees, edge the walks,
And prune the roses year by patient year,
Until another mind might come to birth
Whose thought could add another perfect page.

◆   ◆   ◆

The Aglaonema

For Randie and Michael

The *aglaonema,* Chinese Evergreen,
High on its bamboo stand, thrusts in between
Me and my favorite picture on the wall,
A cliff near Morro Bay in early fall.
And here in early fall and afternoon,
The strong, clear light expands my living room
With its late splendor. Nape and back are warm.
There is no hint of the chill, later form
The year will take when, looking to the north,
We see black storm clouds mass against the drought
Of a long summer. Seasons on their way
Tell me exactly what I want to say.
No, not another ode to loneliness;
But bright, cut flowers in the yellow vase,
Which I have changed a hundred times this year;
The Queensland rain plant here in miniature;
The sedual wood, the walnut, oak, and teak
That make my chairs and tables; and the bleak,
White walls ablaze with landscapes—these are friends
In the long seeking for the proper ends
Of our intelligence and our concerns.
And equally, now that the season turns,
They are companions through the lucid fall,
Though less demanding than the animal
Through whom I live my life in sun and air.
There is a world in here, a world out there,
That interpenetrate and they will stay.
They are the real we live with every day,
They are the true. The green and living tree,
The legacy of nature, comforts me.
The artifacts of table, picture, vase,
Each shaped by human hands, take their right place
As legacies from others in my life—
The gift of other minds. And like a wife,

They open doors and welcome out to in.
They are the causeways back and forth for men
From the imprisonment of self-concern.
These are the early maps we have to learn.

THOM GUNN

I was born in 1929 in Gravesend, England, and raised in London. In 1954, I came to Stanford on a creative writing fellowship, in Yvor Winters's time (I have written about that in an essay called "On a Drying Hill"); since then I have lived in northern California and think of myself as an Anglo-American poet. I live in San Francisco, teach spring semesters at Berkeley, and have published seven books of poetry.

"These are two poems I wrote in 1987, a year bad for experience and good for poetry. Would it had been the opposite. The poems are about the deaths of two friends. What I didn't realize until this moment is that each poem contains a dream and a questioning of it. Since I only just noticed the resemblance, I don't know what to make of it."

•   •   •

The Reassurance

About ten days or so
After we saw you dead
You came back in a dream.
I'm all right now you said,

And it *was* you, although
You were fleshed out again:
You hugged us all round then,
And gave your welcoming beam.

How like you to be kind,
Seeking to reassure.
And, yes, how like my mind
To make itself secure.

•   •   •

Sacred Heart

For one who watches with too little rest
A body rousing fitfully to its pain
—The nerves like dull burns where the sheet has pressed—

Subsiding to dementia yet again;
For one who snatches what repose he can,
Exhausted by the fretful reflexes
Jerked from the torpor of a dying man,
Sleep is a fear, invaded as it is
By coil on coil of ominous narrative
In which specific isolated streaks,
Bright as tattoos, of inks that seem to live,
Shift through elusive patterns. Once in those weeks
You dreamt your dying friend hung crucified
In his front room, against the mantelpiece;
Yet it was Christmas, when you went outside
The shoppers bustled, bells rang without cease,
You smelt a sharp excitement on the air,
Crude itch of evergreen. But you returned
To find him still nailed up, mute sufferer
Lost in a trance of pain, toward whom you yearned.
When you woke up, you could not reconcile
The two conflicting scenes, indoors and out.
But it was Christmas. And parochial school
Accounted for the Dying God no doubt.

Now since his death you've lost the wish for sleep,
In which you might mislay the wound of feeling:
Drugged you drag grief from room to room and weep,
Preserving it from closure, from a healing
Into the novelty of glazed pink flesh.
We hear you stumble vision-ward above,
Keeping the edges open, bloody, fresh.

Wound, no—the heart, His Heart, broken with love.

An unfamiliar ticking makes you look
Down your left side where, suddenly apparent
Like a bright plate from an anatomy book
—In its snug housing, under the transparent
Planes of swept muscle and the barrelled bone—
The heart glows, and you feel the holy heat:
The heart of hearts transplanted to your own
Losing rich purple drops with every beat.
Yet even as it does your vision alters,
The hallucination lighted through the skin
Begins to deaden (though still bleeding), falters,
And hardens to its evident origin
—A red heart from a cheap religious card,
Too smooth, too glossy, too securely cased!

Stopped in a crouch, you wearily regard
Each drop dilute into the waiting waste.

ALLAN GURGANUS

Allan Gurganus has been asked to write his autobiography in five sentences and, having stated this, he has already used up one of those, darnit. (2) Born of hardworking stock in Rocky Mount, N.C., educated as an easel painter in Philadelphia at the U. of Penn and the Penn Academy of Fine Arts, he then ran afoul of the U.S. military during the war in Vietnam; (3) after living four years on an aircraft carrier, transformed into a writer by journal-keeping, serious daily reading, and the ship's unwillingness to allow easels onboard, he re-paired—after a stint as hotel nightclerk—to study with Grace Paley at Sarah Lawrence, then John Cheever and Stanley Elkin at Iowa, and finally with John L'Heureux, Dick Scowcroft, and Albert Guerard during his Stanford Stegner year (their highest praise usually ran: J.L.: "It's positively wick-ed." D.S.: "Clearly the thing is exceptionally well put-together." A.G.: "Such delicatesse. It's almost . . . French."). (4) Made comfortable by Dolly Kringle, then the so-called Department Secretary but actually a beautiful charming woman the near-equal of Madame de Staël and who deserves mention in any history of the Stanford Program, Gurganus changed that year from being a student—writing for others' approval—to being a writer—rising at six and working till two-thirty P.M.—for oneself and strangers and for the joy of the work itself; semi-colons allow related topics to trail along—this one being, pro-forma, publica-tions in The Atlantic, The New Yorker, Harper's, Paris Review, *and the forth-coming, long and long-awaited (by him especially) novel from Knopf,* Oldest Living Confederate Widow Tells All *(1989). (5) In this last sentence, a sunset might be described—its horizontal bars the shade of caramel and higher, back lit, spokes of gold fanning forth, each beam narrow at bottom but widening at top, bespeaking new possibilities and another century for a Stanford Writing Program that has done so much for American expression, for its earnest practitioners, and for writing: our beloved manual labor.*

"This story was commissioned by the composer Bruce Saylor. He wanted a very short tale to set for mezzo and piano. The piece had its premiere in Rome, April of '85, and was sung by Constance Beavon. 'It Had Wings' subsequently appeared in *The Paris Review,* and *Harper's* reprinted it. The story was inspired by a literal dream involving most of its present elements.

"P.S.: My own most vivid Stanford memory remains the generosity and brilliance of my classmates and fellow Fellows: Tobias Wolff, Nahid Rachlin, Stephen Tracy, and Ivy Goodman, plus Dean Crawford, Brett Singer, Joanne Meschery. We wrote alone in low-rent bungalows; we walked or rode our bikes or cars to a mutually-agreed-upon oblong table and, once there, really *heard* each other. How it helped!"

♦   ♦   ♦

It Had Wings

FIND A LITTLE YELLOW side-street house. Put an older woman in it. Dress her in that tatty favorite robe, pull her slippers up before the sink, have her doing dishes, gazing nowhere—at her own backyard. Gazing everywhere. Something falls outside, loud. One damp thwunk into new grass. A meteor? She herself (retired from selling formal clothes at Wanamaker's, she herself—a widow and the mother of three scattered sons, she herself alone at home a lot these days) goes onto tiptoe, leans across a sinkful of suds, sees—out near her picnic table, something nude, white, overly-long. It keeps shivering. Both wings seem damaged.

"No way," she says. It appears human. Yes, it is a male one. It's face up and, you can tell, it is extremely male (uncircumcised). This old woman, pushing eighty, a history of aches, uses, fun—now presses one damp hand across her eyes. Blaming strain, the lustre of new cataracts, she looks again. Still, it rests there on a bright air mattress of its own wings. Outer feathers are tough quills, broad at bottom as rowboat oars. The whole left wing bends too far under. It looks hurt.

The widow, sighing, takes up her mug of heated milk. Shaking her head, muttering, she carries the blue willow cup out back. She moves so slow because: arthritis. It criticizes every step. It asks—about the mug she holds, Do you really need this?

She stoops, creaky, beside what can only be a young angel, unconscious. Quick, she checks overhead, ready for what?—some T.V. news crew in a helicopter? She sees only a sky of the usual size, a Tuesday sky stretched between weekends. She allows herself to touch this thing's white forehead. She gets a mild electric shock. Then, odd, her tickled finger-joints stop aching. They've hurt so long. A practical person, she quick cures her other hand. The angel grunts but sounds pleased. His temperature's a hundred and fifty, easy—but, for him this seems somehow normal. "Poor thing," she says and—careful—pulls his heavy curly head into her lap. The head hums like a phone knocked off its cradle. She scans for neighbors—hoping they'll come out, wishing they wouldn't, both.

"Look, will warm milk help?" She pours some down him. Her wrist brushes angel-skin. Which sticks the way an ice tray begs whatever touches it. A thirty-year pain leaves her, enters him. Even her liver spots are lightening. He grunts with pleasure, soaking it all in. Bold, she presses her worst hip deep into crackling feathers. The hip has been half-numb since a silly fall last February. All stiffness leaves her. He goes, "Unhh." Her griefs seem to fatten him like vitamins. So, she whispers private woes: the Medicare cuts, the sons too casual by half, the daughters-in-law not bad but not so great. These woes seem ended. "Nobody'll believe. Still, tell me some of it," she tilts nearer. Both his eyes stay shut but his voice—like clicks from a million crickets pooled—goes, "We're just another army. We all look alike—we didn't, before. It's not what you expect.

We miss this other. —Don't count on the next. Notice things here more. We wish *we* had."

"Oh," she says.

Nodding, she feels limber now, sure as any girl of twenty. Admiring her unspeckled hands, she helps him rise. Wings serve as handles. Kneeling on damp ground, she watches him go staggering toward her barbecue pit. Awkward for an athlete, really awkward for an angel, the poor thing climbs up there, wobbly. Standing, he is handsome, but as a vase is handsome. When he turns this way, she sees his eyes. They're silver, each reflects her: a speck, pink, on green green grass.

She now fears he plans to take her up, as thanks. She presses both palms flat to dirt, says, "The house is finally paid off. Not just yet," and smiles.

—Suddenly he's infinitely infinitely more so. Silvery. Raw. Gleaming like a sunny monument, a clock. Each wing puffs, independent. Feathers sort and shuffle like three hundred packs of playing cards. Out flings either arm; knees dip low. Then up and off he shoves—one solemn grunt. Machete-swipes cross her backyard, breezes cool her upturned face. Six feet overhead, he falters, whips in makeshift circles, manages to hold aloft then go shrub-high, get gutter-high. He avoids a messy tangle of phonelines now rocking from the wind of him. "Go, go," the widow, grinning, points up, "Do. Yeah, good." He signals back at her—open-mouthed and left down here. First—a glinting man-shaped kite, next an oblong of aluminum in sun. Now a new moon shrunk to decent star, one fleck, fleck's memory: usual Tuesday sky.

She kneels, panting, happier and frisky. She is hungry but must first rush over and tell Lydia next door. Then she pictures Lydia's worry-lines bunching. Lydia will maybe phone the missing sons, "Come right home. Your Mom's inventing . . . company."

—Maybe other angels have dropped into other Elm Street backyards? Behind fences, did neighbors help earlier hurt ones? Folks keep so much of the best stuff quiet.

Palms on knees, she stands, wirier. This retired saleswoman was the formal-gowns advisor to ten mayors' wives. She spent sixty years of nine-to-five on her feet. Scuffing indoors, now staring down at terry slippers, she decides, "Got to wash these next week." Can a person who's just sighted her first angel already be mulling about laundry? Yes. The world is like that.

From her sink, looking out again, she sees her own blue-willow mug in the grass. It rests in muddy ruts where the falling body struck so hard. A neighbor's collie keeps barking. (It saw!) Okay. This happened. "So," she says.

And plunges hands into dishwater, still warm. Heat usually helps her achy joints feel agile. Fingers don't even hurt now. The bad hip doesn't pinch one bit. And yet, sad, they will. By suppertime, they will again remind her what usual suffering means. To her nimble underwater hands, the widow—staring straight ahead—announces, "I helped. He flew off stronger. I really egged him on. Like *any*body would've, really. —Still, it was me. I'm not just somebody in a house. I'm not just somebody alone in a house. I'm not just somebody else alone in a house."

Feeling more herself, she finishes the breakfast dishes. In time for lunch. This old woman should be famous for all she has been through—today's angel, her years in sales, the sons and friends—she should be famous for her life. She knows things, she has seen so much. She's not famous.

Still, the lady keeps gazing past her kitchen café curtains, she keeps studying her own small, tidy yard. A fence, the picnic table, a barbecue pit, new Bermuda grass. Hands braced on her sink's cool edge, she tips nearer a bright window.

She seems to be expecting something, expecting something decent. Her kitchen clock is ticking. That dog still barks to calm itself. She keeps gazing out: nowhere, everywhere. Spots on her hands are darkening again. And yet, she whispers to whatever's next: "I'm right here, ready. Ready for more."

Can you guess why this woman's chin is lifted? Why does she breathe as if to show exactly how it's done? Why should both her shoulders, usually quite bent, be braced so square just now?

She is guarding the world.
Only, nobody knows.

DONALD HALL

Donald Hall, a fellow in creative writing at Stanford 1953–54, lives in New Hampshire and supports himself as a free-lancer, writing poems, magazine articles, juveniles, textbooks, biography, plays, and short stories. In 1988, Ticknor & Fields published his ninth book of poetry, The One Day.

"The second of these poems was written in Menlo Park after my son Andrew was born at the Stanford Hospital on April 15, 1954. I believe that Yvor Winters found it acceptable. My recollections of the workshop with Winters, his literature classes, and our conversations outside the classroom increase in intensity as I grow older."

◆　　　◆　　　◆

Ox Cart Man

In October of the year,
he counts potatoes dug from the brown field,
counting the seed, counting
the cellar's portion out,
and bags the rest on the cart's floor.

He packs wool sheared in April, honey
in combs, linen, leather
tanned from deerhide,
and vinegar in a barrel
hooped by hand at the forge's fire.

He walks by his ox's head, ten days
to Portsmouth Market, and sells potatoes,
and the bag that carried potatoes,
flaxseed, birch brooms, maple sugar, goose
feathers, yarn.

When the cart is empty he sells the cart.
When the cart is sold he sells the ox,
harness and yoke, and walks
home, his pockets heavy
with the year's coin for salt and taxes,

and at home by fire's light in November cold
stitches new harness
for next year's ox in the barn,
and carves the yoke, and saws planks
building the cart again.

◆　　　◆　　　◆

My Son My Executioner

My son, my executioner,
　I take you in my arms,
Quiet and small and just astir,
　And whom my body warms.

Sweet death, small son, our instrument
　Of immortality,
Your cries and hungers document
　Our bodily decay.

We twenty-five and twenty-two,
　Who seemed to live forever,
Observe enduring life in you
　And start to die together.

James Baker Hall

While teaching poetry and fiction writing at the University of Kentucky, I live, with my wife, the writer Mary Ann Taylor-Hall, at some distance from Lexington, out in the boonies, beautiful ridge country at the edge of the Bluegrass. In addition to my writing, I continue my life-long passion for making pictures, films now as well as stills.

"This occasion summons my life's fondest roll call: greetings that become more intense as the years pass to Chris, Judith, Larry, Randy, Peter, Joanna, Robin, Jim, Arvin, Ken, and Gurney. And to Misters Cowley, O'Connor, and Stegner. And especially to dear, courageous Dick Scowcroft. And the sine qua non, Dolly."

◆　　　◆　　　◆

Organdy Curtains, Window, South Bank of the Ohio

I lived the whole time with my hands cupped to the open eye,
the light advancing like a flock of turkeys.
If the shadow of the catalpa touched

the sun wall of the house at 3:30
I waited several minutes
and entered behind it,
branching out slowly,

respectful of such a broad expanse of white, of silence,
the one small window, a mother's hand, that once,
at the curtain. I knew when to look head on,
when to squint. Things happened, beginning with her,

on a clothesline, flashes of this or that against the sky,
colors, faces, lips moving, snatches of faces—

Then suddenly no wind at all. Light hangs in the organdy,
south bank of the Ohio, I don't remember the year.
I can tell by the way my protective hands move
which eye is open, how vast the orphanage

of silence, how still
each blade of tall grass.
Once inside I am alone

briefly, hanging there,
in the light.

◆   ◆   ◆

Sitting Between Two Mirrors

What I like best
is making lists of what I like
best. The good days

are inventories, near and far. I seldom leave
without a book. Where would I go without a book?
You would say my life is a lottery—
that I am the only one

without a ticket. You would say
your life is better—you say it over and over,
you do. What do I do? I put things in boxes.

I move boxes around. I have many things,
some of them mine. I care for them.
That is what I do. I do simple things.
I move them around clearing places
to move them around. I tell you
I do things, over and over.
Now you tell me

something. Talk is what you do. It comforts
me to hear you talk. You would say that you are
mine too, my not-simple thing. Say it
again, today, I want to hear you say
something, today. I wash your clothes.
I buy you fresh bread.
I get the paper

to see what day it is. I laugh. I act
as though I know what day it is. I laugh
again—it comforts me to hear you
laugh. I talk

on the phone. I water the plants while I talk
on the phone. I make coffee while I talk
on the phone. I am a person

like anyone else. I act
like a person. A person

calls and says whatever it is
a person says. Says
today. A person says today.
I say today

over and over, getting it straight. Getting it
straight is what I do, I want to get it
straight. I say

What did you say?
Tell me something again,
comfort me.
Today? Yes, today.
Is that it?
And when is that?

RON HANSEN

Ron Hansen was a Wallace Stegner Fellow and a Jones Lecturer in creative writing at Stanford from 1977 to 1981. He has published two novels, Desperadoes *and* The Assassination of Jesse James by the Coward Robert Ford, *a children's book,* The Shadowmaker, *and a collection of stories,* Nebraska.

"'Nebraska' was written as a prologue to a commemorative issue of *Prairie Schooner* that celebrated the hard and ill-known region I had grown up in. I began the piece with the hope of producing a short story that would simply have its setting in the Great Plains, but I was soon overwhelmed by hundreds of scenes and impressions that finally seemed to say more about Nebraska than a conventional narrative could. Although I still call 'Nebraska' a story, the pages that follow may be better described as a prose poem about a place."

◆　　　◆　　　◆

Nebraska

THE TOWN IS AMERICUS, Covenant, Denmark, Grange, Hooray, Jerusalem, Sweetwater—one of the lesser-known moons of the Platte, conceived in sickness and misery by European pioneers who took the path of least resistance and put down roots in an emptiness like the one they kept secret in their youth. In Swedish and Danish and German and Polish, in anxiety and fury and God's providence, they chopped at the Great Plains with spades, creating green sodhouses that crumbled and collapsed in the rain and disappeared in the first persuasive snow and were so low the grown-ups stooped to go inside; and yet were places of ownership and a hard kind of happiness, the places their occupants gravely stood before on those plenary occasions when photographs were taken.

And then the Union Pacific stopped by, just a camp of white campaign tents and a boy playing his Harpoon at night, and then a supply store, a depot, a pine water tank, stockyards, and the mean prosperity of the twentieth century. The trains strolling into town to shed a boxcar in the depot side yard, or crying past at sixty miles per hour, possibly interrupting a girl in her high wire act, her arms looping up when she tips to one side, the railtop as slippery as a silver spoon. And then the yellow and red locomotive rises up from the heat shimmer over a mile away, the August noonday warping the sight of it, but cinders tapping away from the spikes and the iron rails already vibrating up inside the girl's shoes. She steps down to the roadbed and then into high weeds as the Union Pacific pulls Wyoming coal and Georgia-Pacific lumber and snowplow blades and aslant Japanese pickup trucks through the green, open countryside and onto Omaha. And when it passes by, a worker she knows is opposite her, like a pedestrian at a stoplight, the sun not letting up, the plainsong of grasshoppers going on and on between them until the worker says, "Hot."

Twice the Union Pacific tracks cross over the sidewinding Democrat, the water slow as an ox cart, green as silage, croplands to the east, yards and houses to the west, a green ceiling of leaves in some places, whirlpools showing up in it like spinning plates that lose speed and disappear. In winter and a week or more of just above zero, high school couples walk the gray ice, kicking up snow as quiet words are passed between them, opinions are mildly compromised, sorrows are apportioned. And Emil Jedlicka unslings his blue-stocked .22 and slogs through high brown weeds and snow, hunting ring-necked pheasant, sidelong rabbits, and—always suddenly—quail, as his little brother Orin sprints across the Democrat in order to slide like an otter.

July in town is a gray highway and a Ford hay truck spraying by, the hay sailing like a yellow ribbon caught in the mouth of a prancing dog, and Billy Awalt up there on the camel's hump, eighteen years old and sweaty and dirty, peppered and dappled with hay dust, a lump of chew like an extra thumb under his lower lip, his blue eyes happening on a Dairy Queen and a pretty girl licking a pale trickle of ice cream from the cone. And Billy slaps his heart and cries, "O! I am pierced!"

And late October is orange on the ground and blue overhead and grain silos stacked up like white poker chips, and a high silver water tower belittled one night by the sloppy tattoo of one year's class at George W. Norris High. And below the silos and water tower are stripped treetops, their gray limbs still lifted up in alleluia, their yellow leaves crowding along yard fences and sheeping along the sidewalks and alleys under the shepherding wind.

Or January and a heavy snow partitioning the landscape, whiting out the highways and woods and cattle lots until there are only open spaces and steamed-up windowpanes, and a Nordstrom boy limping pitifully in the hard plaster of his clothes, in a snow parka meant to be green and a snow cap meant to be purple, the snow as deep as his hips when the boy tips over and cannot get up until a little Schumacher girl sitting by the stoop window, a spoon in her mouth, a bowl of Cheerios in her lap, says in plain voice, "There's a boy," and her mother looks out to the sidewalk.

Houses are big and white and two stories high, each a cousin to the next, with pigeon roosts in the attic gables, green storm windows on the upper floor, and a green screened porch, some as pillowed and couched as parlors or made into sleeping rooms for the boy whose next step will be the Navy and days spent on a ship with his hometown's own population, on gray water that rises up and is allayed like a geography of cornfields, sugar beets, soybeans, wheat, that stays there and says, in its own way, "Stay." Houses are turned away from the land and toward whatever is not always, sitting across from each other like dressed-up children at a party in daylight, their parents looking on with hopes and fond expectations. Overgrown elm and sycamore trees poach the sunlight from the lawns and keep petticoats of snow around them into April. In the deep lots out back are wire clotheslines with flapping white sheets pinned to them, property lines are hedged with sour green and purple grapes, or with rabbit wire and gardens of peonies, roses, gladiolus, irises, marigolds, pansies. Fruit trees are so closely planted that they cannot sway without knitting. The apples and cherries drop and sweetly decompose until they're only slight brown bumps in the yards, but the pears stay up in the wind, drooping under the pecks of birds, withering down like peppers until their sorrow is justly noticed and they one day disappear.

Aligned against an alley of blue shale rock is a garage whose doors slash weeds and scrape up pebbles as an old man pokily swings them open, teetering with his last weak push. And then Victor Johnson rummages inside, being cautious about his gray sweater and high-topped shoes, looking over paint cans, junked electric motors, grass rakes and garden rakes and a pitchfork and sickles, gray doors and ladders piled overhead in the rafters, and an old wind-up Victrola and heavy platter records from the twenties, on one of them a soprano singing, "I'm a Lonesome Melody." Under a green tarpaulin is a wooden movie projector he painted silver and big cans of tan celluloid, much of it orange and green with age, but one strip of it preserved: of an Army pilot in jodhpurs hopping from one biplane and onto another's upper wing. Country people who'd paid to see the movie had been spellbound by the slight dip of the wings at the pilot's jump, the slap of his leather jacket, and how his hair strayed wild and was promptly sleeked back by the wind, but looking at the strip now, pulling a ribbon of it up to a windowpane and letting it unspool to the ground, Victor can make out only twenty frames of the leap and then snapshot after snapshot of an Army pilot clinging to the biplane's wing. And yet Victor stays with it, as though that scene of one man staying alive was what he'd paid his nickel for.

Main Street is just a block away. Pickup trucks stop in it so their drivers can angle out over their brown left arms and speak about crops or praise the weather or make up sentences whose only real point is their lack of complication. And then a cattle truck comes up and they mosey along with a touch of their cap bills or a slap of the door metal. High school girls in skintight jeans stay in one place on weekends and jacked-up cars cruise past, rowdy farmboys overlapping inside, pulling over now and then in order to give the girls cigarettes and sips of pop and grief about their lipstick. And when the cars peel out the girls say how a particular boy measured up or they swap gossip about Donna Moriarity and the scope she permitted Randy when he came back from bootcamp.

Everyone is famous in this town. And everyone is necessary. Townspeople go to the Vaughn grocery store for the daily news, and to the Home restaurant for history class, especially at evensong when the old people eat gravied pot roast and lemon meringue pies and calmly sip coffee from cups they tip to their mouths with both hands. The Kiwanis Club meets here on Tuesday nights, and hopes are made public, petty sins are tidily dispatched, the proceeds from the gumball machines are tallied up and poured into the upkeep of a playground. Yutesler's Hardware store has picnic items and kitchen appliances in its one window, in the manner of those prosperous men who would prefer to be known for their hobbies. And there is one crisp, white, Protestant church with a steeple, of the sort pictured on calendars; and the Immaculate Conception Catholic church, grayly holding the town at bay like a Gothic wolfhound. And there is an insurance agency, a county coroner and justice of the peace, a secondhand shop, a handsome chiropractor named Koch who coaches the Pony League baseball team, a post office approached on unpainted wood steps outside of a cheap mobile home, the Nighthawk tavern where there's Falstaff tap beer, a green pool table, a poster recording the Cornhuskers' scores, a crazy man patiently tolerated, a gray-haired woman with an unmoored eye, a boy in spectacles thick as paperweights, a carpenter missing one index finger, a plump waitress whose day job is in a basement beauty shop, an old woman who creeps up to the side door at eight in order to purchase one shotglass of whiskey.

And yet passing by, and paying attention, an outsider is only aware of what isn't, that there's no bookshop, no picture show, no pharmacy or dry cleaners, no cocktail parties, extreme opinions, jewelry or piano stores, motels, hotels, hospital, political headquarters, travel agencies, art galleries, European fashions, philosophical theories about Being and the soul.

High importance is only attached to practicalities, and so there is the Batchelor Funeral Home, where a proud old gentleman is on display in a dark brown suit, his yellow fingernails finally clean, his smeared eyeglasses in his coat pocket, a grandchild on tiptoes by the casket, peering at the lips that will not move, the sparrow chest that will not rise. And there's Tommy Seymour's for Sinclair gasoline and mechanical repairs, a green balloon dinosaur bobbing from a string over the cash register, old tires piled beneath the cottonwood, For Sale in the side yard a Case tractor, a John Deere reaper, a hay mower, a red manure spreader, and a rusty grain conveyor, green weeds overcoming them, standing up inside them, trying slyly and little-by-little to inherit machinery for the earth.

And beyond that are woods, a slope of pasture, six empty cattle pens, a driveway made of limestone pebbles, and the house where Alice Sorensen pages through a child's World Book encyclopedia, stopping at the descriptions of California, Capetown, Ceylon, Colorado, Copenhagen, Corpus Christi, Costa Rica, Cyprus.

Widow Dworak has been watering the lawn in an open raincoat and apron, but at nine she walks the green hose around to the spigot and screws down the nozzle so that the spray is a misty crystal bowl softly baptizing the ivy. She says, "How about some camomile tea?" And she says, "Yum. Oh boy. That hits the spot." And bends to shut the water off.

The Union Pacific night train rolls through town just after ten o'clock when a sixty-year-old man named Adolf Schooley is a boy again in bed, and when the huge weight of forty or fifty cars jostles his upstairs room like a motor he'd put a quarter in. And over the sighing industry of the train, he can hear the train saying Nebraska, Nebraska, Nebraska, Nebraska. And he cannot sleep.

Mrs. Antoinette Heft is at the Home restaurant, placing frozen meat patties on waxed paper, pausing at times to clamp her fingers under her arms and press the sting from them. She stops when the Union Pacific passes, then picks a cigarette out of a pack of Kools and smokes it on the back porch, smelling air as crisp as Oxydol, looking up at stars the Pawnee Indians looked at, hearing the low harmonica of big rigs on the highway, in the town she knows like the palm of her hand, in the country she knows by heart.

WILLIAM J. HARRIS

William J. Harris is an associate professor of English at SUNY, Stony Brook. He has published two books of poetry, Hey Fella Would You Mind Holding This Piano A Moment *and* In My Own Dark Way, *and a critical study of Amiri Baraka,* The Poetry and Poetics of Amiri Baraka. *Currently he is at work on a critical study of the novels of Ishmael Reed.*

"The poems I have chosen from my work, 'Hey Fella' and 'Modern Romance,' are two of my favorites, and I hope that they contribute to the comic tradition of such unconventional poets as Edward Field and Ronald Koertge. 'Hey Fella,' written at Stanford while I was a graduate student, is a youthful fantasy about hidden genius, and 'Modern Romance,' written at Cornell University during my first teaching job, is about a science fiction love triangle cast in a set of dramatic monologues in which I try to create a narrative, tell a story."

Modern Romance

One: The Wife

The reason
we got rid
of the robot
was
she was an
absolute slut.
You must
understand,
my Mortimor
is a strong
man
but how long
can even a good
man resist
temptation?
The way
she used to
look at him
and rub

against
him
every chance
she got. She
was a tramp,
that fancy
vacuum cleaner
with tits.

Two: The Husband

My wife never understood Doris.
I mean, the domestic robot.
She was a delight.
Intelligent yet submissive.
Sexy but didn't mind housework.
And she knew her place.
The perfect woman.
Must have been designed by a man.

Of course, a flesh and blood woman
is preferable to a machine
no
matter how perfect
and beautiful
and understanding
and responsive.

Poor Annie was so upset
by this whole mess.
I think a vacation would do her
a world of good.
The Grand Canyon? That's the place . . .

Three: The Robot

Imagine me, marrying
a man like Mortimor.
Why this is the
happiest day of
my life & a true
advancement for
my people. I am
the first robot
in history
to marry a man
of Mortimor's stature.
Oh, he's so

brave to withstand
public opinion
and so strong
to
overcome that
tragedy
of last weekend
when his wife accidentally
fell to her death
from a great height
in Arizona.

◆　　　◆　　　◆

Hey Fella Would You Mind Holding This Piano A Moment

For Reg & Susie

As you are walking
down the street
this guy asks you
to hold his violin.
It's a Stradivarius.
Soon as it falls
into your hands
you start playing like crazy.
The violin
almost plays itself.
Your powerful hands
nearly break the instrument
but the music is gentle and sweet.
You sweep your long artistic hair
out of your face.
Everybody
in the room,
in the bull ring, in the
audience, in the Coliseum
starts clapping
and shouting "Encore & Wow."
Everybody whoever
thot you were
dumb & untalented
goes apeshit
over your hidden genius.
"Gee, I never knew you
played," says your astonished high school
principal.

◆ JEFFREY HARRISON ◆

Jeffrey Harrison grew up outside of Cincinnati, Ohio, and was educated at Columbia, the University of Iowa, and Stanford, where he had a Stegner Fellowship in 1985–86. His first book, The Singing Underneath, *was selected by James Merrill for the National Poetry Series and published by E. P. Dutton in 1988.*

"Canoeing with my wife before she was my wife, in a much-loved chain of Adirondack lakes—that's the first poem. (Sticklers for natural detail: the water hyacinth is really pickerel weed, but we've always called it water hyacinth, and 'pickerel weed' didn't fit the meter.) The other poem (the otter poem) is set in Washington, D.C., but I wrote it at Stanford, and the memory may have been triggered by those other otters in the Monterey Aquarium. Both are love poems, in a sense."

◆　　　◆　　　◆

The One That Got Away

For Julie

We paddled through the winding waterway,
past lily pads and water hyacinths,
into the other lake: perfectly calm
and of a blue much deeper than usual.
It was that time of day when late sunlight
intensifies the beauty of everything,
transforming the trees into a green fire.
They leaned over us as we paddled by
as if with the desire to be draped
in undulating nets of yellow light
projected by the waves from our canoe—
waves in which those very trees were mirrored,
stretched and wavering. We drifted in silence.
The paddle that I held across my lap
dripped, as if to count the passing moments—
getting slower, but we knew they wouldn't stop.
And we knew those nets of light, unraveling
all the while, wouldn't catch the afternoon

for us to keep—though you turned to me and said
that this was all you wanted in the world.

◆   ◆   ◆

The Otter in the Washington Zoo

is in love with a little girl.
Maybe it's because he's been
alone too long—or is it just
her red shirt he's attracted to?

She runs from one end to the other
of his window, and he follows,
swimming undulously, bubbles
trailing along his slick body.

She stops in the middle, and he
swerves to a halt, floating upright
with only his head above the water.
They are about the same size.

They stare into each other's eyes.
Then she ducks down, and he
dives to the bottom of the pool.
She is laughing and he is laughing bubbles.

The glass becomes a kind of mirror:
he returns her every movement with
a replica more graceful and alluring
to make her stay—leading her on

by following her lead. But now
her mother says it's time to go,
and she leaves him looking after her,
pawing lightly at the wall of glass.

ROBERT HASS

Robert Hass grew up in the San Francisco Bay Area and attended St. Mary's College. He did graduate work in English at Stanford from 1963 to 1967. He is the author of three volumes of poetry, Field Guide, Praise, *and* Human Wishes, *and a collection of essays,* Twentieth Century Pleasures: Prose on Poetry; *he is co-translator of several volumes of verse by the Polish poet Czeslaw Milosz. He received the Yale Younger Poets Award, has been a Guggenheim and a MacArthur fellow, a medalist of the American Academy and Institute of Arts and Letters, and received the National Book Critics Circle Award in criticism in 1984. At Stanford in the early sixties, he was not a member of the poetry workshop, though he was active in the group of writers that included John Matthias, Robert Pinsky, James McMichael, and John Peck. He studied with Donald Davie and profited from the presence of Mitchell Goodman and the Wordsworth seminar of Albert Guerard.*

"Stanford in 1963: I remember Yvor Winters in a baggy, pigeon-colored suit and a black armband for the girls killed that summer in the bombing of a Mississippi church, lecturing on renaissance poets, my first sense of what absolute intellectual passion would be like. And Donald Davie in a seminar, trying to keep his pipe lit, going over the experimental work of the younger American poets, his generous sense of curiosity about his art. Seems in retrospect a good place to begin to write poems."

Palo Alto: The Marshes

For Mariana Richardson (1830–1891)

1.
She dreamed along the beaches of this coast.
Here where the tide rides in to desolate
the sluggish margins of the bay,
sea grass sheens copper into distances.
Walking, I recite the hard
explosive names of birds:
egret, killdeer, bittern, tern.
Dull in the wind and early morning light,
the striped shadows of the cattails
twitch like nerves.

2.
Mud, roots, old cartridges, and blood.
High overhead, the long silence of the geese.

3.
'We take no prisoners,' John Fremont said
and took California for President Polk.
That was the Bear Flag War.
She watched it from the Mission San Rafael,
named for the archangel (the terrible one)
who gently laid a fish across the eyes
of saintly, miserable Tobias
that he might see.
The eyes of fish. The land
shimmers fearfully.
No archangels here, no ghosts,
and terns rise like seafoam
from the breaking surf.

4.
Kit Carson's antique .45, blue,
new as grease. The roar
flings up echoes,
row on row of shrieking avocets.
The blood of Francisco de Haro,
Ramon de Haro, José de los Reyes Berryessa
runs darkly to the old ooze.

5.
The star thistle: erect, surprised,

6.
and blooming
violet caterpillar hairs. One
of the de Haros was her lover,
the books don't say which.
They were twins.

7.
In California in the early spring
there are pale yellow mornings
when the mist burns slowly into day.
The air stings
like autumn, clarifies
like pain.

8.

Well I have dreamed this coast myself.
Dreamed Mariana, since her father owned the land
where I grew up. I saw her picture once:
a wraith encased in a high-necked black silk
dress so taut about the bones there were hardly ripples
for the light to play in. I knew her eyes
had watched the hills seep blue with lupine after rain,
seen the young peppers, heavy and intent,
first rosy drupes and then the acrid fruit,
the ache of spring. Black as her hair
the unreflecting venom of those eyes
is an aftermath I know, like these brackish,
russet pools a strange life feeds in
or the old fury of land-grants, maps,
and deeds of trust. A furious dun-
colored mallard knows my kind
and skims across the edges of the marsh
where the dead bass surface
and their flaccid bellies bob.

9.

A chill tightens the skin
around my bones. The other California
and its bitter absent ghosts
dance to a stillness in the air:
the Klamath tribe was routed and they disappeared.
Even the dust seemed stunned,
tools on the ground, fishnets.
Fires crackled, smouldering.
No movement but the slow turning
of the smoke, no sound but jays
shrill in the distance and flying further off.
The flicker of lizards, dragonflies.
And beyond the dry flag-woven lodges
a faint persistent slapping.
Carson found ten wagonloads
of fresh-caught salmon, silver
in the sun. The flat eyes stared.
Gills sucked the thin annulling air.
They flopped and shivered,
ten wagonloads. Kit Carson
burned the village to the ground.
They rode some twenty miles that day
and still they saw the black smoke
smear the sky above the pines.

10.
Here everything seems clear,
firmly etched against the pale
smoky sky: sedge, flag, owl's clover,
rotting wharves. A tanker lugs silver
bomb-shaped napalm tins toward
port at Redwood City. Again,
my eye performs
the lobotomy of description.
Again, almost with yearning,
I see the malice of her ancient eyes.
The mud flats hiss as the tide turns.
They say she died in Redwood City,
cursing 'the goddamned Anglo-Yankee yoke.'

11.
The otters are gone from the bay
and I have seen five horses
easy in the grassy marsh
beside three snowy egrets.

Bird cries and the unembittered sun,
wings and the white bodies of the birds,
it is morning. Citizens are rising
to murder in their moral dreams.

◆   ◆   ◆

Meditation at Lagunitas

All the new thinking is about loss.
In this it resembles all the old thinking.
The idea, for example, that each particular erases
the luminous clarity of a general idea. That the clown-
faced woodpecker probing the dead sculpted trunk
of that black birch is, by his presence,
some tragic falling off from a first world
of undivided light. Or the other notion that,
because there is in this world no one thing
to which the bramble of *blackberry* corresponds,
a word is elegy to what it signifies.
We talked about it late last night and in the voice
of my friend, there was a thin wire of grief, a tone
almost querulous. After a while I understood that,
talking this way, everything dissolves: *justice,
pine, hair, woman, you* and *I.* There was a woman
I made love to and I remembered how, holding
her small shoulders in my hands sometimes,

     I felt a violent wonder at her presence
like a thirst for salt, for my childhood river
with its island willows, silly music from the pleasure boat,
muddy places where we caught the little orange-silver fish
called *pumpkinseed*. It hardly had to do with her.
Longing, we say, because desire is full
of endless distances. I must have been the same to her.
But I remember so much, the way her hands dismantled bread,
the thing her father said that hurt her, what
she dreamed. There are moments when the body is as numinous
as words, days that are the good flesh continuing.
Such tenderness, those afternoons and evenings,
saying *blackberry, blackberry, blackberry.*

EHUD HAVAZELET

Ehud Havazelet was born in Jerusalem and raised in New York City, where he attended Columbia University and the World Series game where Reggie Jackson hit three home runs. He came to Stanford in 1984 as a Stegner Fellow, and is currently a Jones Lecturer in the Stanford Creative Writing Program. "Solace" is from his collection, What Is It Then Between Us?, *published by Scribner's in 1988.*

"I saw the black man at the story's center in the early seventies, while working at Goldwater Hospital, a chronic care facility in New York City. He was young, muscular, clearly an athlete, and so weak he had to put his face on his tray and feed himself by pushing food into his mouth. I wasn't writing then, didn't know much about it, but several years later, when I was trying to write, I thought about this man and how I felt watching him, and this story had a beginning."

Solace

SUNDAY MORNINGS IN WINTER, the boy waited for his father to awaken. Lying in bed, with the room chilled around him, he listened for the faint rumble of the water heater and then his father's slippers on the hardwood floor. Outside his window, the night shone blue as if cold reflected itself, and stars turned over like falling ice.

He hurried into the bathroom when his father was done, while the tiles still held warmth from the shower. The heater was good for only one shower at a time, and the boy took his in the evenings before the house cooled down. He pulled his clothes on in the corner, his black tie, already knotted, already in the collar of his white shirt. He brushed his teeth, splashed his face, and pulled the tie close to hide a missing button. When he opened the bathroom door, the smells from the kitchen were in the hall: cocoa, cinnamon rolls, strong coffee. The boy made his feet loud on the stairs so his father would hear him coming, in case he had not yet mixed whiskey with the coffee in his thermos. His father would be angry then.

He pushed the swinging door to the kitchen. His father sat at the table, straighter than any man he had ever seen, straw hat and newspaper before him on the immaculate white cloth. He had not heard. He held the big Stanley thermos in one hand, a bottle of Dewar's over the top with the other.

He said the boy's name: "Stuart."

The boy took a step back and watched the wooden door swing to a stop.

To reach the hospital after the patients' breakfast, they had to leave before dawn. The car door handle stung to the touch, and the vinyl seats radiated cold. While his father drove, Stuart pulled his jacket up and closed his eyes, the motion jarring him to full wakefulness.

Paterson's predawn streets had once held out to him an excitement he could almost taste. The men in their long coats were spies; the barreling trucks, filled with machine guns and jewels; the cars that sped by without lights, fleeing gutted and smoking bank vaults on the other side of town. But his father and he had been making these weekly trips into New York for three years. Stuart pulled his jacket around him, closed his eyes, and moved toward his side of the seat, into the air heater's intermittent blast. His father sipped coffee and hummed show tunes, spirituals, tunneling after the headlights into the thinning dark.

They timed it right; they reached the George Washington Bridge for sunrise. Mists came off the river and Washington Heights was outlined in brightness. The suspension cables flickered by, singing, and the main support, just tingeing silver, sloped upward out of sight. His father said, "Take a look at that, would you? My God, just take a look at that."

Stuart opened his eyes, took in the view, then turned toward his father. His father had had several cups of his mixture; he was leaning forward as though about to stand. Pushing over the steering wheel so he could see it all, his father lifted his face to the light from the east.

The hospital Stuart's mother had died in was on Roosevelt Island, in the East River. Stuart was six when she died, and she had been ill all of his lifetime. There was a question of contagion, and not being a robust child, he was not allowed to see her often. That, at least, was the way he remembered it.

The first time was soon after she entered the hospital. Stuart remembered coming into the long ward and somehow, knowing which bed was hers, running directly to it. He remembered she looked very pretty and sad in her white gown, and that they had to leave because she was tired.

The other time was just before she died. Her skin was puffy like a baby's and there were wide bruises around her eyes as if she'd been hit. Tubes were running into her and she couldn't have moved her arms if she'd wanted. She opened her eyes at one point and looked directly at Stuart, but he didn't know what she saw. When they took him away from the bed, he didn't want to see her anymore.

The hospital walls were green, the color of shallow water. Stuart's father assumed he would keep up. He walked ahead, pants floppy on his thin legs, briefcase swinging. The Volunteer office did not open until 10 A.M., and they no longer bothered with it.

Men were lined up in the hallway, some in chairs, some prone on white-sheeted carts. The men were naked under their loose hospital gowns and some did not cover their thighs as Stuart and his father passed. His father nodded to a black man by the window who followed them with eyes and a face completely without expression.

They entered the ward, a long room with thirty beds on a side. Tables were arranged in the center aisle, and two men played checkers while a third leaned over the board. Music from a transistor radio echoed flatly along high walls which curved overhead into a wide archway, painted blue. Stuart's father stood by the entrance; he was handsome, with the strained, eager look of a man searching a gangplank for relatives. His eyes were active, his face worked elaborately around a smile. The hand holding the thermos shot into the air and Stuart followed his father to a bed on the far right.

Mr. Dobkin sat erect, white hair combed to a gentle crest across his scalp. His mild blue eyes caught light, and his expression was of small, perpetual surprise. A hollow tube projected from the middle of his throat, and through this, he breathed. He tried not to move his head.

"Mr. Dobkin," Stuart's father said. "You look wonderful."

Mr. Dobkin smiled. The bed was neatly made around him, his feet, two slopes halfway down the mattress. There were two chairs, one covered with clothing. On the cluttered nighttable was a black-and-white photograph of a young woman whose lips had been retouched bright red. Her lips made her look like she was waiting to be kissed. Stuart's father poured coffee into the thermos top.

"We came to see you first of all, Mr. Dobkin." His father spoke loudly, animatedly, and around the room, heads looked up. Some of them smiled. "In the car on the way over, Stuart said, he said, 'Daddy, why don't we go see Mr. Dobkin as soon as we arrive?' I believe you must be his favorite."

The boy looked at his father, then back at the man in the bed.

Mr. Dobkin raised a tissue to his throat. His voice was like a hull scraping rocks and came from somewhere in his chest. The boy could not understand what he said. His father laughed.

"Stuart? Of course. What did you think? Stuart, come say good morning to Mr. Dobkin."

Stuart tried to watch the blue eyes as he approached. On the blankets, a thin green tube coiled toward a machine behind the bed. The old man smiled. His hands felt smooth on the boy's skin, dry and fine like worked wood. They moved up the boy's arms until the elbows, where they gripped and gave him a little shake. His father laughed again. Mr. Dobkin turned his head carefully a few degrees and groped around the night table. He brought back a round tin with a painting of a girl sitting among sheep on its cover. With delicate fingers, he twisted the lid off and held the tin out to the boy. Small crescent-shaped candies lay in a dust of sugar powder. Stuart took a candy and felt its weight on his tongue.

"You spoil the boy, Mr. Dobkin." His father's voice was rich with pleasure. "You'll spoil him silly." He raised the briefcase onto the bed and sprang the snaps. "Well. What will we have today? Epic? Romance? Milton?" His bright eyes ranged the wall above the bed. "Or more from Lord Alfred, yes, Mr. Dobkin?

> Now folds the lily all her sweetness up
> And slips into the bosom of the lake
> So fold thyself, my dearest, thou, and slip
> Into my bosom and be lost in me."

Stuart sat in the chair which was draped with the old man's clothing. He held the book on his knees and read the poetry with his eyes to the page, and he did not stop, even when Mr. Dobkin pulled the green tube to his throat and the suction machine clattered to life.

They stopped at most of the beds in the ward, then at many in the identical ward on the floor above. Stuart's father had something for every patient. He knew which ones to soothe, which to joke with. He remembered that Mrs. Dorsey's grandson was a running back on his high school team, and that Mr. Feld was inconsolable over the loss of a set of dental plates. He sat by the beds and talked about whatever they wanted. He sipped his coffee and nodded his head, and when a man with pneumonia asked to have some letters mailed, he sent Stuart to the mailbox in the lobby immediately, so they would be in the early morning pickup.

When Stuart returned, his father was sitting by the bed of a man with a beard who was wiping his eyes. "This is my boy, my son, Stuart. Wordsworth is his favorite poet, too," his father said.

Stuart held the worn poetry book, the texture of the leather coming through to his fingers. He read "My Heart Leaps Up" and a section of *The Prelude* his father chose. When he had finished reading, he waited. The two men looked into the air in front of them.

In the cafeteria, a young black man with an athlete's body lay his head on the table and pushed food into his mouth with a hand. When he lifted his head, there was food on his face and his eyes were closed.

Stuart's father did not eat. He bought coffee and joked with the people behind the counter. They all knew him. The woman at the cash register gave him an apple and waved at Stuart. His father took his thermos and briefcase and left the room for a minute, and when he returned, added from the thermos to the coffee in his cup.

"How's the burger?"

"Okay."

"When I was your age, I could eat a ton of burgers. Six, seven, ten burgers. They had to pull me away from the table."

Stuart took a bite to indicate he could eat another hamburger if he had to. His father held out the apple.

"Mrs. Wilson said this is for you if you've been good."

Stuart took the apple. His father leaned forward and jabbed the air over his plate with a forefinger.

"I said, Mrs. Wilson, that boy's not just good. He's lucky. And I don't mean sweepstakes lucky, I don't believe in sweepstakes luck. Luck is just rewards, I said. Rewards to the deserving. That boy, I said, is a laborer. That boy knows about pain."

He brought his hand down to the coffee and raised the cup over his face. He nodded while he drank, sloshing coffee onto the lapel of his suit. He did not wipe it off.

"Look around this room, Stuart. There's your luck. These people need what we have to give. They *need* it. You know what's out there?" Without turning, he gestured at the window. "You know? Nothing. Cold, unforgiving nothing. You be glad we're in here, with work to do. You be glad."

A man in a wheelchair was having trouble maneuvering between the tables. Stuart's father took a quick swallow from his cup and jumped up to assist. Leaning over, with his mouth to the man's ear so they could talk, he pushed the wheelchair out the door toward the elevators.

Stuart put the apple down. Mrs. Wilson smiled at him and he looked away. Outside the window, asphalt stretched down to the river wall. A boy in a denim cap was throwing rocks at beer bottles he had lined up on the wall. When he shattered one, he performed a little dance of congratulation, patting himself on the back and waving his arms in the air. Beyond him, the muscular river coiled in the light. Stuart's father returned and sat heavily in his chair.

"Ezra Williams," he said. "Cancer. Five East. Remember cowboy books, Stuart. Zane Grey."

He looked at the floor and did not speak. Stuart looked out the window, pleased to see the boy had broken his last bottle. Throwing his remaining stones randomly into the water, he skipped onto the river wall and ran out of sight.

"Will we be leaving after lunch, Dad?"

"No. Too much to do. There's Lyle Johnson on three and that Russian woman in the thoracic unit. And Mrs. Holbrook. We've missed her two weeks now."

He began rummaging inside his briefcase. Stuart's face had grown hot and he could hear the river. He dropped the hamburger on the plate and pushed it away.

"What's the matter?" his father said.

"I don't want it."

"You have to eat, Stuart. A sound body is—"

"You didn't."

His father looked up from his briefcase, his mouth turned into a smile. "You don't want it?" His voice was very soft. "You don't? Then don't eat it, Stuart. Don't touch it."

"I had enough," the boy said, looking away.

"You had enough."

Stuart left the trays on the aluminum cart in the corner and followed his father into the bathroom. His father turned on the faucet, straightened the boy's tie, and ran a wet comb through his hair. Stuart felt the water collect in his shirt.

♦   ♦   ♦

Mrs. Holbrook's bed was high off the ground and she lay beneath the blankets, massive and rising into the air. Something in her disease made her swell, and Stuart had seen four orderlies move her, each lifting a part, and once a tube had snapped, trailing liquid across the sheets. He stood by the foot of the bed and felt his breath escape in tiny spurts. He could hear the river, and he looked at the corners of the room and at the wide automatic doors leading out to the hall.

His father held her hands. Her fingers were gray and pliant, and the boy watched his father caress them. He patted and soothed; his hands said he would stay with her, he would not leave, and they did not stop, even when no words were being spoken.

"Mrs. Holbrook," he said. "We can't have that. We mustn't give in to despair. Sometimes I think despair is the only death, Mrs. Holbrook."

"My Anna stopped coming. I ain't seen the babies in weeks, now. One of them had a birthday in April."

"Anna must have her reasons. You know she must have good reasons."

"She don't come at all, now. I think the doctors told her she can get something from me and give it to the babies. She's afraid to come."

She was crying. She brought her eyes around; they were wild and white and her skin was gray. When the eyes passed over Stuart, his scalp tightened and the wind flew out of him. He inhaled deeply. The smell rising off the bed hit him with every breath, and every breath was a crashing in his ears.

"Anna loves you, Mrs. Holbrook," his father said. "This is hard for her, too."

The woman in the bed nodded and tried to smile. She looked again at Stuart.

"Would you like to say hello to Stuart, now? He's been anxious to see you all day. Would you like to say hello?"

Stuart walked to the side of the bed. The woman reached out and he leaned at the shoulders. Her hands touched his arms, his neck. She pulled him gently to her broad thawing chest and held him, stroking his hair. The boy was rigid, trying to be soft. In the chair, his father smiled.

When the coughs came, Stuart closed his eyes and tried not to hear. The coughs were deep and luxuriant and tore easily through something in the woman's body. They came up in her chest to where the boy lay pressed, but her hand on his face continued, soothing, calm. He told himself to wait.

Stuart waited in the car, his father's thermos on his knees. The thermos was a cool blue metal that felt good to hold. It was a deluxe two-quart model, ordered directly from the company in Nashville, Tennessee. Stuart remembered the day it had come in the mail. His father had pulled it out of the newspaper wrapping and showed him the inside, the dark glass reflecting. More money than he could easily justify, his father had said with a smile.

Stuart slid off the front seat. Kneeling under the dashboard, he took the thermos in both hands and brought it down hard on the floor, over and over, until he felt something give way inside it. He leaned it against his father's door and sat back on the seat.

His father came across the lot to the car, briefcase swinging before him at every stride. When he opened the car door, the thermos fell to the ground and rolled, making a noise. His father put the briefcase down and gave Stuart a quick glance. The boy couldn't tell what was on his face. His father picked up the thermos, unscrewed the top, and poured. Through the brown liquid, shards glinted like bits of ice in his hand.

KATHRYN HELLERSTEIN

Kathryn Hellerstein's two books are translated editions of Yiddish poems by Moyshe-Leyb Halpern, In New York: A Selection *(JPS, 1982), and Kadya Molodowsky,* Nights of Heshvan and Selected Poems *(JPS, forthcoming). She translated a selection of poems by Malka Heifetz Tussman, Halpern, Yankev Glatshteyn, and Berish Vaynshteyn in* American Yiddish Poetry: An Anthology *(University of California, 1986). Individual translations have appeared in* The Kenyon Review, Partisan Review, *and* Tikkun. *Her poems have appeared in* Poetry, Tikkun, Imagine, The Atavist, *and anthologies. Grants from N.E.A. and N.E.H. have supported her translations of and scholarship on Yiddish poetry. Currently she lives in Philadelphia with her husband and is writing a book on women Yiddish poets.*

"Writing and translating poems go hand in hand for me. I started 'A Universal Language' in Donald Davie's poetry workshop and finished it eleven years later. The summer before that workshop, I had begun to translate from the Yiddish. I took to heart Ezra Pound's early dictum, 'Young poet, translate!' but felt compelled to reinterpret his tradition in a way that included mine. Whenever Malka Heifetz Tussman (z"l) scolded me for writing in closed forms, I would translate another of the Yiddish poems from her seven books, including 'My Great Poem.'"

◆   ◆   ◆

A Universal Language

Orange bulbs code the take-off. We expect
Some turbulence in the midwest. Before me
In the air line magazine, is Margaret Mead's
"A Universal Language for the World!"
The runway lights make pictures like the stars'
Old points of reference, forms recognized.

"A universal language would bring out
The commonality of all mankind."
Fishwives and kings could gossip naturally.
A universal language would permit
The ministers of governments at war
To chat with ease about their hostages.
Abstract beyond particulars of place,

Time, culture, class, or sex—translation's Ur—
A universal language is the Word.

All alphabets take form in human mouths:
The Hebrew and Phoenician "A" is not
Vowel, but breathing. English sounds twelve "A"s
As tongues in damp warmth settle front or round.
Land-locked, alphabets were written first
As hieroglyphs in caves and cuneiform
Pressed into clay. Some Neolithic scratched
Symbols on bones. The Greeks fired letters on
Amphora, kylix, krater, lekythos,
And molded words on bronze, much-fingered coins.

From callused palm to palm, this currency
Traversed the criss-crossed, narrowing blue sea.
But throat and tongue cannot transform the sea:
"The water never formed to mind or voice,"
Though scooped up glistening by a mute jug
And poured still shining down an open throat,
Though wavelets like an alphabet with gulls'
Accents against an aging blue, would spell
The changing and the constant distances.
We have in common only distant shores.

"Chinese written characters are ideographs,
Depicting things in action as ideas."
E. Fenollosa comments from the West
Upon the East (its image: sun behind bare trees).
Enchanted by these new discoveries,
The earnest ear goes deaf as speakers yell,
Whisper and sing, and rising sun-shafts gild
And flicker on bare branches swelled with buds.

A budding student, confident with text
And tape, when listening, seeks a cognate root
And thinks he understands a poem droned
By natives, while he's making up his own.

A Russian boy hears puns of "list" and "lust"
In Thomas Wyatt's "Whoso list to hunt,"
And argues with a nice American girl
He's parked with in a sidestreet summer storm
That puns are signs for action: "Let's make sex."
He makes no sense. His hands stroke breast and thigh.
"Let's make it." Thunder crackles overhead.
Sheet-lightning, flashing by, makes spectacle
Of rooftops in relief against wild trees.
A gust. Spread knees. The rain encloses rain.

Learning a language, one learns more than words.
To a young translator, the old man said,
"You study Yiddish hard, all day, all night,
But you must learn the spirit," stared at her,
"You have a *shikse's* nose." A language is
Composed of grammar, spirit, shapes of a nose.

The family nose, a heritage of bones
In the hollow architecture of our race,
Passes from branch to branch of the flowering tree,
Yet peoples speaking in proximity
Their sibling languages are enemies,
Hiss sibilants in common face-to-face,
And crush bones in their murderous embrace.

A universal language, beacon source,
Blazes across the molded metal seams
Of engines jetting our craft through the storms.
Unlike the gibberish of towns and stars
(Dark space between) it is a flash that stills
The roiling clouds for miles till dark resumes.
The pulse reveals its presence to airplanes,
Strange beings, night-birds flying, sleepless men
At windows, lovers making love in cars.

♦   ♦   ♦

My Great Poem

By Malka Heifetz Tussman (1893–1987)
Translated from the Yiddish

Throughout the night
I wrote,
Without pen and ink
I wrote,
Without pen and ink, throughout the night
I wrote
My
Great
Poem.

At the break of day
I wrote down,
With pen and ink
I wrote down
At the break of day,

Black on white, with pen and ink
I wrote down:
Sweet One!
I have worshipped in a temple that
Has no windows
To heaven.

ALICE HOFFMAN

Born in New York City and raised on Long Island, Alice Hoffman was a Mirrielees Fellow at Stanford in 1974. Since that time, Hoffman has published seven novels: Property Of, The Drowning Season, Angel Landing, White Horses, Fortune's Daughter, Illumination Night, *and* At Risk. *She currently lives with her family in Boston.*

"I believe in writing programs, because the Stanford University Writing Program changed my life. The program allowed me to believe I could be a writer; it introduced me to other serious, young writers of fiction; and, perhaps most importantly, afforded me the great pleasure and opportunity of studying with Albert Guerard, a truly inspiring teacher."

The Giant of Chilmark

From *Illumination Night*

THE GIANT OF CHILMARK sells zinnias and eggs in the summer, pumpkins and chrysanthemums in autumn. None of his customers ever sees him. They buy his goods from a roadside stand made out of rough planks of pine. They comment on the difference between country and city life as they slide their money through a slit in the top of a coffee can. Cowed by good faith, people are usually honest, paying for their squash or bunches of flowers, making their own change. A few times a year, teenagers pocket the money they find in the coffee can. Local children occasionally steal eggs with which they gleefully pelt each other. The Giant sees the remains, bits of cracked brown shell and streaks of deep yellow, along the center of the road. When it grows dark he carries a bucket of water up from his house and washes away as much of the dried eggs as he can. Crows will take care of whatever is left.

Contrary to the reports of the delivery boy who brings groceries and chicken feed, the Giant is not an old man. He is not eight feet tall, although he has to crouch at certain points in his house so that his head won't graze the ceiling. His is an old house, built for a shorter man, the Giant's grandfather, Edward Tanner, who was five foot six. The Giant, who drinks coffee every morning from a blue-and-white Staffordshire cup his grandfather brought with him from England, is twenty-four years old. Most people in Chilmark haven't seen him in so long they've forgotten he ever existed. A few old women remember his grandfather Edward Tanner well; they were kissed by him on summer evenings.

The Giant arrived in October. It was a rainy, wood-scented night and his grandfather was drinking beer and polishing his boots. When there was a pounding on the door, the Giant's grandfather had the urge to jump into bed and pull the quilt up. Something told him not to open the door. He'd had quite a few angry husbands come looking for him, and although he was old for that now, there were other scores unsettled. He owed a little money and he had never believed in taxes. He had the feeling it was someone official because of that sturdy knock.

The Giant was out there, swallowing rain. He was ten years old and already six feet tall. When Edward Tanner opened the door all he saw was a tall man in a black overcoat.

"Don't come looking for me unless you're looking for trouble," Edward Tanner said. He held his boot up, menacingly.

The chickens in the henhouses were clucking like mad. It was raining so hard all the sweet potatoes in the garden were unearthed and washed away.

"Grandpa?" the Giant said in a high tentative whisper. It was as though a hidden ventriloquist were throwing a child's voice into this man's shape.

"Don't kid a kidder!" Edward Tanner said. He could not have been more afraid if a ghost had appeared at his door.

"It's me, Eddie," the Giant said in his sweet boy's voice, and Edward Tanner the elder fell on the floor in a dead faint.

There is such a thing as rotten parents, and the Giant's parents were as rotten as they come. They might have had problems even if their son hadn't been a giant, but Eddie's height put an end to their marriage. The Giant's father was nearly forty when Edward Tanner's nineteen-year-old daughter, Sharon, who was easily persuaded, followed him off the Island. In fact, their marriage lasted longer than Edward Tanner had predicted. The Giant's parents were together for eight years before the Giant and his mother were deserted in southern New Jersey.

Sharon set out to find another man and dragged her son around four states before she found what she wanted at a naval base in Rhode Island. She figured Eddie was her punishment, and she preferred him to stay well out of sight. When her boyfriends came over he hid in the hall closet and prayed that night's sailor hadn't worn a coat. Finding a giant in the closet when you're merely reaching for a hanger is enough to give even a strong man a heart attack. The Giant knew what he was from the time he was two. He had seen pictures of himself in books. He was the creature beneath the bridge who devoured goats. He was the owner of the harp who fell asleep at his own dinner table. One morning he would wake and find his head through the roof, his arms and legs akimbo out the windows. Vines would grow over him. Birds would perch in the crook of his elbows.

The Giant went to school until the fourth grade, but when they moved to Rhode Island he didn't bother with it anymore. He couldn't take the merciless teasing and there was no one to check up on him. Sharon was gone more than she was home. To fill up his days, the Giant began to make pictures, at first using pencils and tubes of lipstick and eye shadow stolen from his mother's purse, later saving enough money for cheap watercolors and brushes. Because he wanted to keep his painting from his mother, who'd only laugh at him, and because paper was scarce, the Giant worked at miniatures. A whole year's worth of his paintings could fit in a rubber boot. An entire state, New Jersey for instance, could be reduced to the size of a strawberry. Painting one perfect, tiny face or a tree filled with flowers might take him an hour. If he was lucky, he would not finish before he went to bed and would then have a reason to wake up in the morning.

The Giant often caught Sharon staring at him, as though she were disgusted by him or, worse, afraid. She may have kept him just to spite her father, whom she alternately adored and despised. She urged her boyfriends to use the one photograph she had of Edward Tanner as a dart board. But sometimes she took the thumbtacks out and brought the photograph down to show the Giant. The Giant's grandfather was sitting on a chair in his living room. He looked directly into the camera and he seemed annoyed. When she had lived with him Sharon had dreamed of burning down the house and escaping to New York. Now she described each room lovingly. She had, after all, named the Giant after her father. And, the Giant knew, she was capable of changing her mind with startling quickness, for no apparent reason. When she was kind, offering him a chocolate or cooking him dinner, he never trusted her. When she was awful, he knew it wouldn't last. He had learned, early on, that he must be careful. He couldn't afford to have fits of temper. Not with Sharon. Once she had borrowed a car from one of her boyfriends and had taken the Giant with her on a picnic. The Giant was nine years old, and because Sharon was being so nice to him, he felt a little too comfortable. On the way home they drove along 95. The Giant was in the passenger seat holding a paper bag in which there were still some sandwiches and cupcakes. He had saved the best for last, a chocolate cupcake with rainbow-colored sprinkles. He reached into the bag, but when he pulled it out the cupcake broke into pieces. All he could think about was how much he wanted that cupcake. He forgot himself. He forgot who he was with. He let out a wail and kicked the dashboard.

"Oh, for God's sake," Sharon said to him. "Don't be such a baby. Take another one."

"I don't want another one," the Giant had said.

"Take another one," his mother told him.

"No," the Giant said. "I won't."

When he kicked the dashboard, Sharon reached over and grabbed his leg. The car swerved out of its lane.

"Are you a moron?" Sharon shouted. "Do you want to ruin this car and get me in trouble? Take another cupcake. Now."

The Giant looked at the sprinkles sifting over the car seat and started to cry.

"I won't," he said.

Sharon pulled the car over onto the shoulder of the road. It was nearly rush hour and crowded.

"Get the fuck out," she said.

The Giant stared at her.

Sharon leaned over him and threw open the door. She gave him a shove.

"You heard me!" she said.

When the Giant put his hands on the seat to steady himself he left streaks of chocolate frosting on the upholstery.

"Do it!" Sharon said, and she pushed him halfway out of the car. He wouldn't let go of the door, so she slapped his hands, and as soon as the Giant loosened his grip, she pulled the door closed.

She stepped down hard on the gas. Without bothering to look at oncoming traffic, she pulled into the highway, cut off a station wagon, and kept right on going. The Giant followed her, running along the side of the road. He kept right on running, even when he didn't see the car anymore. His eyes and throat were filled with tears. He was screaming "Mommy" over and over again until it wasn't even a word. Up ahead, a car was pulled over on the shoulder, black exhaust rising from the tailpipe as it idled. The Giant wasn't certain it was the right car until he got up beside it and saw Sharon inside, crying.

The Giant stood on the side of the road and wiped his face with his shirtsleeve. He was so hot that his hair was soaking wet. Sharon got out of the car and walked around to him. Every time a truck went by the earth shook. Sharon kept crying and didn't even try to hide it.

"Look, I don't want you," Sharon said.

There was goldenrod along the side of the road, and a flat tire someone had left behind.

"Can you understand?" Sharon said.

The Giant had a stitch in his side from running so fast. Every time he breathed he could feel the stitch tighten.

"I'm a person, too," Sharon said. "You know?"

The Giant was so grateful to her for not driving on without him that he almost started crying again. He didn't care what she said to him. He didn't care what she thought of him. What he wanted more than anything was for his mother to hug him but he knew it was too much to ask.

"Get in the car," Sharon said to him. "Just get those goddamn sprinkles off you before you sit down and ruin everything."

Sharon started staying out more often after that, and the Giant never asked where she was going or when she was coming back. He learned to cook, he set his own bedtime, he washed his clothes in the bathroom sink. He was so used to being alone that when Sharon disappeared for good, it took a week before the Giant realized she wasn't coming back. He wasn't really surprised, he didn't feel much of anything, but he couldn't sleep. He kept checking the light bulbs in the apartment to make sure they wouldn't burn out and leave him in the dark. He slept during the day, in a chair by the window, and when he ran out of food, he put on an old black overcoat that used to belong to his father and went out to buy groceries at a local market. He knew his voice would betray him, so he pointed to what he wanted. Hot dogs and rolls, a carton of milk, mustard, M&Ms. He found his grandfather's address in a drawer beneath a black nylon slip. He still wonders if his mother left thirty dollars in the sugar bowl on purpose or if, in her hurry to cut her losses, she simply hadn't bothered with it.

The Giant, who has lived on his own since his grandfather's death five years ago, sometimes forgets the sound of his own voice. The chickens he raises for eggs are great-great-grandchildren of his grandfather's stock. He has continued to paint and some of his miniatures are so small he needs to use a magnifying glass for the more detailed work. He mail-orders paints and the heavy cream-colored paper he prefers. The farmstand and the inheritance of his grandfather's life savings—eight thousand dollars kept in a metal strongbox in the chicken coop—allow the Giant the luxury of avoiding other people. He knows he has missed out on many things: owning a car, friendship. Mysterious things like movie theaters and hardware stores. He has never been to Lucy Vincent Beach, which is less than a mile from his house. He can live with these small losses. He despairs only when he considers his chances for ever falling in love.

Jody hears about him again from one of the boys who used to steal eggs. It is Jody's senior year. She has managed to persuade her parents to let her stay on until graduation. The idea of going back to Connecticut, even for a weekend, makes her sick. She is thinner than last year and much more careful. She has not made love with anyone since Andre, but high-school boys still vie for her even though she barely talks when she dates them. She is now included in a group of boys and girls whose common interests are fast cars and cutting classes. She often drags her friend Garland along, not because she feels sorry for Garland, who has fewer dates, but because she wants a chaperon. She has decided to remain true to Andre, even though he has deserted her. Whenever she calls and offers to babysit for Simon, Vonny says she's much too busy with her pottery to go out. Jody is certain this is a lie. Andre is the one who doesn't want her around, not that Jody intends to let that stop her. She can wait, she has time. And if a boy wants to help her pass that time, fine, but when he takes Jody out, he gets Garland, too.

They're on their way to Edgartown, and Garland is forced to sit in the backseat next to Rosellen and Carl, a couple who can't keep their hands off each other. When Greg, the boy driving, starts talking about the Giant, Jody doesn't believe him. She flips down the sun visor, looks at Garland in the small mirror, and rolls her eyes.

"You people think off-Islanders will fall for anything," Jody says.

"It's the truth," Greg says. "There were two nights when he tried to get me and I outran him both times. He's almost nine feet tall, you know."

"Creepy," Rosellen says. She makes herself shiver.

Greg glances over at Jody to see if she's impressed by his battle with the Giant. She takes out a comb and fixes her hair. As they pass by the farmstand she can see coffee cans filled with yellow chrysanthemums.

Carl untangles himself from Rosellen so he can lean forward. "Manute Bol of the Washington Bullets is seven foot six," he says to Greg. "You want me to believe this guy's a foot taller?"

"Are you calling me a liar?" Greg asks him.

"Hell, no," Carl says. "A bullshitter."

"Oh, yeah?" Greg says. He makes a quick U-turn, tires screeching. He's still trying to impress Jody, and it's still not working. When they're parallel to the farmstand, Greg makes an even sharper U-turn that throws Jody up against the car door. Then he pulls right up to the farmstand. The motor idles loudly. The Giant's house is set in a hollow behind a grove of locust trees, and all they can see of it is a slightly tipped chimney. Already the boy in the back seat is losing his nerve.

"We're never going to get to Edgartown this way," he says.

"Got the guts to take something?" Greg goads his friend.

"Come on," Carl says. "What do I want with flowers?"

"Get the eggs," Greg says. "We'll attack the farmstand, then the Giant will have to come out."

"They're ridiculous," Garland says to Jody. "Grow up," she tells the boys.

"Well?" Greg says when his friend hesitates. Greg grins, then leans over the seat and pushes down on the door handle so that the back door swings open. Rosellen screams. Carl quickly grabs the door and slams it shut.

"Not me," he says. "You won't catch me out there."

"Then you believe me," Greg says. "Right?"

Greg is hoping he won't have to get out of the car to impress Jody. The truth is, he's shaking, just as he did when he was twelve and the Giant and some old man called out to him as he stole some eggs and an already decaying pumpkin. At least this time he has not peed in his pants. But of course, he has not seen the Giant yet.

"Let's get out of here," Garland says.

The sky is no longer quite so blue. The locust grove throws shadows on the already dark moss. They have all begun to whisper. As Jody places her pocket-book on the floor near her feet she is making a bargain with herself. If she doesn't see the Giant, she'll keep her mouth shut. If she sees him, and survives, she'll tell Vonny everything. Andre will hate her at first, but he'll get over it.

Jody snaps her door open.

"Hey!" Greg says. He tries to grab her arm, but Jody is already out of the car.

"Get back here!" Garland calls.

The weather has turned chilly. When a car passes wind rises up. The earth is dark and rocky, but a path has been worn from the side of the road to the farmstand. Jody keeps her eyes on the path in front of her. As she gets closer to the farmstand she can smell the rough pine boards and the slightly sweet odor of rotting vegetables. Jody would rather face a giant than Vonny, but she will go to Vonny if she has to. She never breaks the bargains she makes with herself.

Greg is probably a liar, although he's honking the horn like a madman to get her attention. If there is a giant he certainly won't be caught sleeping with that horn honking. Greg doesn't let up on the horn until Jody reaches the farmstand. And although he gets out of his car and watches her, he doesn't have the courage to go after her.

Now Jody sees that the bunches of flowers are different shades of yellow, from gold to pale ivory. The stand fronts a dark, cool shed in which there are melons and squash. Jody reaches past the tin of money for a basket of brown eggs. Either she is so nervous her hands are hot or the eggs are still warm. Would she really break up a family? Maybe it would be a relief to everyone involved. Maybe Vonny wishes she were back in Boston. A confession might be an act of mercy. Jody follows the path down into the hollow. In the basket, the eggs hit against each other. She can no longer hear the idling motor of Greg's car or traffic up on the road. The grass here is oddly soft and pale; it has never been mowed. She can see the house and it's much too small for an alleged giant. All she has to do is get a glimpse of him and she can tell Vonny everything. She walks down to the house, which has a fresh coat of gray paint. The foundation is made of brown and red stones. The door, at which visitors never knock, is the color of blood. Jody peeks in the front window. Her breath is coming hard and it's difficult to see; the window is old glass, the kind that distorts. She thinks she sees a stone fireplace, a blue couch, an old wooden table. She can hear the chickens now, and she follows their clucking behind the house. There is a sunny fenced-in area with several chicken coops. The chickens whose eggs Jody has stolen are red bantams. Their feathers shine in the sun. When a rooster crows the sound raises bumps along Jody's arms and legs. She looks to the side of the henhouses and sees him. He has been frozen, unable to move or even breathe since she walked down from the house. He sits in a metal chair, a cup of coffee in one hand, a newspaper on his lap. He wears beige slacks and a white shirt. His hair, which he washed in the kitchen sink, is still wet and combed back, drying in the sun. The sleeves of his white shirt are rolled up. From where Jody stands it is impossible to gauge how tall he is, but the old workboots he wears are huge. He is, by far, the most beautiful person Jody has ever seen. He makes everyone else seem deformed. Unsteadily, Jody bends down and, still looking at him, she places the basket of stolen eggs on the ground. Then she turns and runs. She nearly loses her balance climbing back up the hollow. The Giant wishes he could help her, but he dares not stand up and let her see him for what he is. So he watches helplessly. A teenage boy comes to the top of the hollow and throws two sharp rocks at him, but the Giant remains where he is. At last she makes it up the slope. When she is gone, the Giant gets up and slowly gathers the eggs.

JAMES D. HOUSTON

James D. Houston is the author of five novels, including Love Life *(1985),* Continental Drift *(1978), and* Gig, *which won a Joseph Henry Jackson Award while he was a Stegner Fellow at Stanford in 1967. Among his nonfiction works are* Farewell to Manzanar *(1973), co-authored with his wife, Jeanne Wakatsuki Houston, and* The Men in My Life *(1987). He lives in Santa Cruz.*

"*Love Life* is the second of three novels dealing with members of the Doyle family. The first was *Continental Drift* (1978), also set in the Coast Range of northern California. The third is now in progress. *Love Life* is the story of Holly Doyle, nine years married, with two young children. On her thirty-second birthday, after discovering her husband is entangled with a younger woman, Holly finds herself at 'The Last Roundup,' a country-western club where her friend, Maureen, tends bar."

The Last Roundup

WE DRANK UNTIL ALMOST seven, when Maureen had to report to work. During that time she had twice called the shop and been told her car still wasn't ready. I offered to drop her at the club. That was my intention, just to drop her off. By the time we got there I saw that I was not ready to go home, nor was I ready to be alone. I parked and walked in with her. I was taking one thing at a time.

The band started at eight on Saturday nights. They were already setting up. I knew a couple of the musicians, the drummer and the pedal-steel player, Eddie McQuaid. I was glad to see Eddie. It meant the music would be good. He and Grover had worked a few jobs together over the years. He was known to play the sweetest pedal steel in the county.

When the mike levels were adjusted and all the instruments plugged in, he came back to the bar. He was wearing faded jeans and a custom-made white satin rodeo shirt with mother-of-pearl snap buttons. From a distance he had a lean and rugged look. Up close you could see how delicate his fingers were, how delicate his mouth behind the close-trimmed beard. I hadn't seen him in months. I stood up and gave him a big hug, let my hands linger on the white satin, the way it stretched across his back. This probably conveyed more than I meant it to convey. He sat down and asked me what I was drinking.

"Firewater," I said.

He signaled to Maureen. "We'll have two more of whatever Holly's drinking. I like what it's doing to her."

"Is this a new group, Eddie? Some of these guys I haven't seen before."

"We've been working out together for a couple of months."

"You feel good about the music?"

"Tonight'll be the test. I'm glad you're here. You can tell us how it sounds."

"You know I love to listen."

"Too bad Grover's not around. He might like to sit in later on. Where the hell is he, anyway? He meeting you here?"

"Nope. Grover is . . . occupied. It's ladies' night out."

I could see his mind working as I said this. I guess I wanted him to read it the way I knew he would. How can I describe the relationship I had with Eddie? A precarious friendship? For years we had flirted back and forth, before and after gigs, with innuendoes and glancing body contact, dancing up close to the brink of seduction, backing off. Somehow we had always agreed that was the way it had to be. Sometimes I told myself we were afraid to risk damaging the mutual pleasures that came with the music itself.

The drinks appeared, Wild Turkey over ice. When we had toasted our little reunion, Eddie held the glass to his nose and inhaled a snootful, for the aroma. With a fake Irish accent he said, as if this might be a gag line, "There's a sadness in you, Holl."

I tried to match it. "And what might you mean by that, Mr. McQuaid?"

"Is it because this Grover fella lets a handsome colleen like yerself run about loose on a Saturday night?"

"This Grover fella you mention is the one who seems to be doin' most of the runnin' about," I said and instantly regretted saying too much.

Eddie waited a few moments. He dropped the accent. "You want to talk about it?"

"Well . . . I do, and I don't."

"None of my business one way or the other."

His tone was brotherly and his eyes were sincere and my tongue was loose and my heart was full. "I've just found out he has something going with another woman. Basic stuff. It's a little hard to take, that's all."

"I'm sorry to hear that, Holly, I really am."

"Not as sorry as I am."

"You aren't splitting up, are you? I mean, it hasn't gone that far."

"I don't know how far it's gone, Eddie."

Onstage the rhythm guitar player was chunking chords into the mike. Eddie stood up.

"I hope you're not going anywhere between now and the time we finish the first set."

"I told you I love to listen to your music."

"Maybe you'll come up and sing one for us. You in the mood?"

"I could be, Eddie. I could be talked into it, depending on how good you guys are."

I watched him walk back to the bandstand and slide behind his three-tiered bank of metal strings and carefully slide the picks onto his slender fingers. I liked Eddie. I liked looking at him. I had known him for years, and he was still exotic to me. I think it was because he worked at night. Night people run on a different frequency from day people. With a row of buttons next to his right foot he could control the stage lights. They were white when he sat down. Now they went blue. The thick blue light flooding the band made me think of those deepwater fish they say have special radar for navigating through sunless waters.

The lights became bordello-red, and the band started the first tune, without any introduction, just to warm up the room. It was an old Jimmie Rodgers number called "No Hard Times Blues." As soon as I heard the first chorus I knew I could sing with this band. By the end of the second tune I was aching to sing with them, aching for Eddie to call me up there. I looked at my clothes. I had not thought of my clothes since I'd left the house. I was wearing the jeans that fit me best and a high-waisted buckskin jacket and underneath that a long-sleeve shirt with a collar. They would do. Maybe, for effect, I could take off the jacket as I started to sing. I had seen Emmylou Harris do it once at the start of a concert. In my unvoiced fantasy she was the singer I most hoped to resemble—long-legged and long-haired and sexy and earthy and elegant. If I ever got all the parts of my life and body in perfect running order, that is how I would look when I took the stage to sing a song.

I had already picked out the tune, running the words through my mind to make sure I could keep the verses straight. It was one of my own, called "Love Life." Thinking the words took me back to the last time I had sung it, at a country-music jamboree and benefit for all the Democratic candidates in the county. Eddie was playing that day too. A wave of remorse went cascading through me as I realized an entire year had passed. Where had it gone? I used to do this all the time. On and off through college I had sung with pickup bands, at parties, and with the various groups Grover had put together or played with in the years since then. It was not my profession, but it was part of my life, the part I often told myself would have the chance to blossom and bloom once the kids were older and the UFO stage had passed. I had not given it up. I had my piano. I was still writing songs, at least writing down lines when they came to me. But how had a year slipped past? I fell into a reverie of befuddled nostalgia, which was interrupted some time later by the sound of my name.

Eddie was leaning toward the mike above his steel. "I know you'll recognize the voice as soon as you hear it. She used to sing with the Bear Flag Republic band and after that with the Land and Title Company. She happens to be passing through the club tonight. We asked her to come up and help us with our debut. Holly—you ready to do it?"

There was a sprinkling of applause as I moved toward the stage. I stopped to confer with Eddie about the key, then stepped up to stand between the rhythm guitar and the fiddler.

It was a big room, about half full. The white lights were on, between numbers. As I gazed into the crowd, as I took my jacket off, I relived all the performances of my life. In the next instant I was reliving all the things I did not do, moves I had not made. Like this year that had just slipped through my fingers, they were the lost opportunities, the times I could have gone to bed with Eddie, and didn't, the time I almost took off with another man, and didn't, choosing Grover once again, the time I could have taken a full-time singing job with a traveling band, and didn't, because we both agreed, Grover and I (always Grover), that, as Willie Nelson says, "the night life ain't no good life"—better, we agreed, to maintain the amateur status and spend your days and years on something wiser, more substantial, less precarious. Did I let him talk me into that? Could I now be standing where Emmylou Harris stands, instead of here, a walk-on, in this half-filled saloon on a rainy Saturday night?

These memories came tumbling in the seconds before Eddie kicked the floor button, drenching the stage in red. He had worked out an intro that could make your eyes water and your nose run, it was so poignant and heart-wrenching. The sound of it pushed me right over the edge. All the rage and hurt and jealousy building these past ten hours or so were channeled into the song. I could not see the crowd, but I knew I had them, the moment I opened my mouth.

It is a song about a woman who has given all her love to one man and she has just found out he has betrayed her. She is sitting in a bar, which is where you have to be sitting in a country-and-western song when it is time to think about your love life. She is listening to other lonesome songs on the subject coming from the jukebox, and she is bitter because she has loved so many other men along the way, or could have. She is feeling the loss of all the love that could have been expressed and wasn't, when into this same bar comes the guy himself. Before you know it, he is begging for forgiveness. By the end of the song you know that underneath the hate and the bitterness she still loves him and that she will be able to forgive him because there is something that runs deeper than the misfortunes of her love life, and that is her love of life itself.

I am not going to write out the lyrics, even though of all the songs I have composed, it is still my favorite. Country-and-western lyrics hardly ever stand up by themselves. You have to feel the tempo, fast or slow, and the mood, whether raucous or mournful. And you have to hear the instrumentation at every crucial moment in the story, what the strings are doing to underscore the feeling. I wish you could have heard what Eddie did that night when he took the middle chorus. Something happened between him and the fiddler. It was angelic. It was as good as a Mozart violin sonata with harpsichord, but with the added flavor of a roadside saloon and a brokenhearted woman. Later, when I finally stepped off the stand, Eddie told me it was the best this band had sounded and that it was due to something in my voice, the power of my voice. I told him it was because I was so pissed off at Grover, and he said, "Well, purely in the interests of country music I would encourage you to keep that battle alive."

The crowd got so much more than they had expected they went wild when "Love Life" was over. They were banging on the tables and calling out for more. I confess it did me some good. At that point I needed any encouragement I could get. We did another one of my tunes. Then I sang "Crazy" for Maureen. When I dedicated it to her, the crowd burst into spontaneous applause. When it was over, a line of funlovers at the bar began chanting, "Maureen, Maureen, Maureen." As far as they were concerned I could have kept singing all night. But three was enough. I was content with that.

Back at the bar another shot of Wild Turkey waited for me, a gift from Maureen, I thought at first, for singing her song. But she said, "No, it is an offering, from an admirer who shall remain forever nameless. I hope."

Nameless admirers seldom stay nameless for long, of course. This one turned out to be a fat guy in a cowboy hat who said he had heard me sing once at another club in another town. I told him I had never set foot inside that club. I had to tell him twice. He backed off about two feet and said, "Well, hell! I just wasted two dollars on the wrong soprano!"

"Alto," I said, which got a good laugh up and down the bar.

I drank his drink anyhow, the way you can down your fourth or fifth or sixth or seventh. Too fast. I began to lose track of details. Little moments disappeared completely, while others seemed rich with meaning. I remember some guy leaning across the bar to tell Maureen a joke. "Did you hear about the Texas wino?" he said. "I have known a lot of Texas winos," she replied. And he said, "Well, somebody asked this particular Texas wino how much he drank every day. A fifth? A quart? And the Texas wino grinned and said, 'Shee-it—I *spill* that much!'"

The next thing I knew Eddie was sitting there asking if I wanted to move to a table where we could talk. He had something to show me.

"It was great to hear you, Holly," he said as we sat down. "Your singing always knocks me out."

"You're a sweetheart to say that. It's been a long time."

"Whenever you want to sit in, just let me know."

"I may take you up on that. Sure feels good."

I didn't know who provided them, but more drinks appeared from somewhere. Eddie raised one glass and pushed one toward me for another toast. Far far in the back of my mind a voice was saying, "This is the one that will do you in." A very soft voice. And quickly forgotten. As we sipped, he unrolled some notation charts and spread them out on the table.

"I started tinkering with this right after we worked together the last time," he said. "Been carrying it around in my car ever since."

It was an arrangement for "Honky Tonk Angels," featuring female voice and pedal steel. Eddie knew I liked that song. The fact is, it described the way I was starting to feel that night, killing time in the half-dark of The Last Roundup, with my face turning numb. I remember that the music in the room, on the between-sets tape loop, was Emmylou singing "Queen of the Silver Dollar." I remember that, but I don't remember what I said about Eddie's arrangement. I couldn't concentrate on it. The table's candle lamp was tinted such a deep orange I couldn't see the charts. We talked awhile, then I heard him asking if I thought tonight might be a good night to start working on it.

"You mean without rehearsing?"

"I was thinking maybe over at my place. Just working with acoustic guitar and voice. We could work through some of the changes."

I think I smiled. I have to admit it was flattering to be propositioned that way. It gave me a lift. But I was disappointed too, disappointed that he did not have . . . more tact, more patience.

I leaned forward and looked into his eyes. "I thought you considered yourself Grover's friend."

"I do. I love Grover. We have had a lot of fine times."

"Do you think you ought to be hitting on his wife her first night out of the house?"

"Hey, Holly. I'm not hitting on you. I mean, I am not just another guy who saw you across the dance floor. We go back a ways, don't we? You want to know the gospel truth, I have admired you for a long long time. As a woman.

For a long long long time. And don't act like you didn't know it either, because a lot has passed between us. I have seen you looking at me in a certain way."

That made me giggle. "What certain way was that, Eddie?"

"The way a woman looks when she's interested."

"I am interested in a lot of people. As people. You know what I mean? What makes you think I'd want to single you out of all the people I am interested in?"

"Because I am right here. And tonight is tonight. And because I appreciate you for who you are. You know, you are a lot better-looking now than you were five years ago. You are more worldly now. And, well . . . you know damn well I am crazy about you and been crazy about you. That song you just sang, you were singing what I was feeling, 'crazy for trying, crazy for crying . . .'"

"Ah, Eddie, that's sweet. But don't overdo it."

He was moving toward me. I knew I should have moved away, or turned my head. I delayed, and his face was next to mine, his Wild Turkey breath, his lips touching mine, brushing. I was not kissing back. Neither was I refusing to kiss. He could kindle desire in me. He had done it before, though I would never have told him so, at least not that night, not stroke him with the confession that the pedal steel itself, the plaintive rise and quiver he could send through the notes, had worked on me many times. Soft on musicians all my life. But in my muddled way I was thinking that if we were going to do something, this was a pisspoor time to start necking, since he had two more sets to play. His timing was bad. It was just too soon, too fast. There was too much else pulling at me, in spite of the whiskey. I pulled back and looked away.

He said, "What's the matter, baby?"

"You're a good-looking man, Eddie, and a good guitar player. Maybe even a great guitar player. But there is too much hustler in you, did you know that? You're rushing me. I don't like to be rushed."

"Sometimes," he said—and he was suddenly desperate, I could tell—"sometimes it's a way to ease the pain."

"Oh shit, Eddie. You've been listening to country music too long. Why'd you have to say a thing like that?"

This defused him. His eyes pinched up. "You sure know how to make a guy feel wanted."

I took his hand. I was drunk. He was getting there. But something had just cut a wide hole through the drunkenness, a tunnel of clarity through the great cloud of whiskey vision. I said, "I guess I just don't want everything to change on me all at once."

It was a one-way tunnel. Eddie's end was closed off. I could see him down there. I knew he did not know what I was talking about. He was looking at me, but he was peering into fog. I didn't mind. It was not a moment for sharing. It was a moment for *seeing*. I could see every pore in his face, every hair follicle. I could see every black hair in his beard and across the top of his forehead where he combed it back, the hairs close together yet separate, as if I were gazing into a forest. His face was not a mask, it was a perfect replica of a human face, which I had this rare opportunity to study at close range. I had never before observed anything in such detail. I was putting my full concentration on it, and suddenly Eddie's face rose up. I was gazing at the mother-of-pearl buttons on his rodeo shirt.

I heard Grover's voice saying something like "Get your goddam hands off my wife!"

I did not know how long he had been in the club or how much of this scene he had witnessed. But there he was. Later I learned he had been driving all over town and this was his final stop. He was boiling with frustration, in the mood to hurt somebody, and poor Eddie McQuaid, his favorite guitar player, was the first to get in his way.

Grover had him by the shoulders, literally lifted him out of the chair and spun him around with a fury that was new to me. He could carry a lot of anger, but most of it went unexpressed. Later I would come to appreciate what happened that night. Joking, I would be able to say, "If it weren't for Sarah teaching you how to express your deepest feelings, I would never have known how beautiful you are when you're angry."

That night, of course, I wasn't seeing it that way. They say Wild Turkey does things to you like no other brand of whiskey. I believe it. Grover decked Eddie there in The Last Roundup, just laid him out cold. Then he came for me, and I did something that took us both by surprise. I swung on him. In my paranoia I saw him as The Enemy Incarnate. I caught him on the jaw. It stunned him. He dropped back and fell into a chair at the next table.

He wouldn't look at me. I began to cry. Maureen came out from behind the bar carrying a white rag, just like the bartenders do in bad westerns after the fight is over. The next day I told her we were all acting like those people you hear about on the jukebox. No matter how hard you try, sooner or later you end up somewhere inside a country-and-western song.

ANDREW HUDGINS

Currently I teach at the University of Cincinnati. Before coming to Stanford, I was educated at, in reverse order, Iowa, Syracuse, Alabama, and Huntingdon College. I've published two books: Saints and Strangers *(Houghton Mifflin, 1985) and* After the Lost War: A Narrative *(Houghton Mifflin, 1988).* Saints and Strangers *received awards from the Society of Midland Authors, the Great Lakes College Association, and the Texas Institute of Letters; it was also one of three finalists for the Pulitzer Prize in poetry.*

"Both of these poems were written while I was a Stegner Fellow at Stanford— a year that meant a great deal to me, both for the time to write and for the teachers I was fortunate to meet and study with. 'From Commerce to the Capitol' is a poem I couldn't have written without being away from the South, but 'Compost: An Ode' grew very much out of my experiences at Stanford. To supplement my income as a Stegner Fellow, I found a job working as a yard boy for a family living in the Portola Valley. I received room and board in exchange for mowing, raking, sweeping, and cleaning the pool, as well as for such occasional jobs as repairing the roof, cleaning out drains, digging up the septic tank, and burying the family dog when he was struck by a car. One of my regular duties was to put the family's table scraps in the compost heap—a job everyone else wrinkled his or her nose at, but which I enjoyed because I became fascinated by all the life—bugs, worms, heat—thriving in the place of decay."

◆ ◆ ◆

From Commerce to the Capitol: Montgomery, Alabama

Despite the heat that stammers in the street,
each day at noon I leave my desk and walk
the route the marchers took. I windowshop,
waste time, and use my whole lunch-hour to stroll
this via dolorosa in the heat-drugged noon—
the kind of heat that might make you recall
Nat Turner skinned and rendered into grease
if you shared my cheap liberal guilt for sins
before your time. I hold it dear. I know
if I had lived in 1861

I would have fought in butternut, not blue,
and never known I'd sinned: Nat Turner skinned
for doing what I like to think I'd do
if I were him. The fierce blast furnace heat
of summer loosens my tight neck, grown stiff
from air-conditioning.
                              Outside the door,
an old black man, weight forward on his cane,
taps down the steaming asphalt. Before the war
half-naked coffles were paraded to
Court Square, where Mary Chestnut gasped—"seasick"—
to see a bright mulatto sold.
I'm sure the poor thing knew who'd purchase her,
said Mrs. Chestnut, who plopped on a stool
to discipline her thoughts. Today I saw,
in that same square, three black girls toe loose tar,
then throw it at each other's bright new dresses
to see if it would stick. I'll bet those girls
caught hell when they got home, their dresses smudged
with tar. I can't recall: Was it three girls,
or four, blown up in church in Birmingham?

The legendary buses rumble down the street
and past the Dexter Baptist Church,
where Reverend King preached when he lived in town—
a town somehow more his than mine, despite
my memory of standing outside Belk's
and watching, fascinated, a black man cook
six eggs on his Dodge Dart. Because I'd watched,
he gave me one with flecks of dark blue paint
stuck on the yolk. My mother slapped my hand.
I dropped the egg. Then, when I tried to say
I'm sorry, Mother grabbed my wrist and marched
me to the car.
                    The uphill walk past banks
and courts, past shops, and past the Feed and Seed
gets sweat to running down my back. My wet
shirt clings like mustard plaster to my back.
Before I reach Goat Hill, I'm drenched. My neck
loosens. Atop its pole, the stars-and-bars,
too heavy for the breeze, hangs listlessly.

Once, standing where Jeff Davis took his oath,
I saw the crippled governor wheeled into
the Capitol. He shrank into his chair,
so flaccid with paralysis he looked
like melting flesh—face white as schoolroom paste,
hair black as just-paved road. He's fatter now.

He courts black votes, and life is calmer than
when Muslims shot whites on this street, and calmer
than when the Klan blew up Judge Johnson's house,
or Martin Luther King's. It could be worse.
It could be Birmingham. It could be Selma.
It could be Philadelphia, Mississippi.

Two months before she died my grandmother
remembered when I'd sassed her as a child,
and at the dinner table in mid-bite,
leaned over, struck the grown man on the mouth,
and if I hadn't said *I'm sorry*—fast!—
she would have gone for me again. My aunt,
from laughing, choked on a piece of cherry pie.
But I'm not sure. I'm just Christian enough
to think each sin taints every one of us,
a harsh philosophy that doesn't seem
to get me very far—just to the Capitol
each day at lunch, walking the heat-stunned street.
On my way back, I buy a large cheeseburger
and eat it at my desk on company time.
Slowly unsticking from my skin, the shirt
peels loose and dries. Outside, on Commerce Street,
heat builds to four or five, then breaks, some days,
in thunderclouds that pound across the river—
bruise-colored clouds unburdening themselves
of rain that's almost body temperature.
I work late. Till it stops. When I drive home,
the tempered heat feels cool. The streets are hushed.
The sky's as blue as Billie Holiday.

♦   ♦   ♦

Compost: An Ode

Who can bring a clean thing out of an unclean?
                                        JOB 14:4

The beauty of the compost heap is not
the eye's delight.
                    Eyes see too much.
                                        They see
blood-colored worms and bugs
                              so white they seem
to feed off
            ghosts. Eyes do not see the heat
that simmers in the moist
                          heart of decay—

in its unmaking making fire—
                              just hot
enough to burn
                    itself. In summer, it
burns like a stove.
                    It can—almost—hurt you.
I hold my hand inside the heap and count
one, two, three,
              four.
                    I cannot hold it there.
Give it to me, the heat insists. *It's mine.*
I yank it back and wipe it
                        on my jeans,
      as if
          I'd really heard the words.
                                    And eyes
cannot appreciate sweet vegetable rot,
how good it smells
                    as everything dissolves,
dispersing
          back from thing
                        into idea.
From our own table we are feeding it
what we don't eat. Orange rind and apple core,
corn husks,
          and odds and ends the children smear
across their plates
                    are fed into the slow
damp furnace
              of decay. Leaves curl at edges,
buckle,
        collapsing down into their centers,
as everything
                turns loose its living shape
and blackens, gives up
                        what it once was
to become pure dirt. The table scraps
and leafage join,
                indistinguishable,
the way that death insists
                          it's all the same,
while life
          must do a million things at once.
The compost heap is both—life, death—a slow
simmer,
        a leisurely collapsing of
the thing
          into its possibilities—

hollyhock and cucumber,
                          bean and marigold—
potato, zinnia, squash:
the opulence
                of everything that rots.

DAN JACOBSON

Dan Jacobson was born in Johannesburg, South Africa, in 1929. He was a Fellow in the Stanford Writing Program in 1956–57. He is the author of several novels, collections of stories, and critical works. He is a professor of English literature at University College, London.

"This story is one of the many written in the first person and based on childhood experience in the small South African town to which I have given the name 'Lyndhurst.'"

Another Day

I WAS LYING IN the shade of a peach tree that grew to the side of the lawn. Behind me sprawled our house, with its broad red stoep, its white pillars and white wooden shutters. Overhead, above the thin, tapering leaves of the peach tree, was the clear sky. It was a Sunday morning: one of the vacant, interminable, never-changing Sunday mornings of childhood. My parents were out of the house, but I could hear the African servants talking idly to one another in the backyard. The air was warm; a contrasting coolness rose from the grass underneath me; in my nostrils was the faint, bitter, almond-like scent of peach leaves. Every sensation I was conscious of seemed to contribute to the wide, full stillness of the day; each was part of its calm. I held a book in my hands, but I wasn't reading it.

I was roused by a strange rumbling noise coming from the road. The noise grew louder; within the rumble I could hear the squeak of metal, the crunch of sand or gravel against the tar of the road. Drawn by curiosity, I went to the fence and looked outside.

I was shocked to see what had broken into the morning's suburban silence. The noise I had heard was that of a funeral procession. But what a funeral procession! What a cortège of mourners! What a hearse! On a flat, wooden two-wheeled barrow of the kind used to carry vegetables and coops of chickens in the market square, a metal frame had been erected, from which there hung a canopy of a few black strips of cloth. Beneath this wretched canopy, naked on the planks of the barrow, rested a small coffin. As the wheels turned, metal rims grating on the tar, the barrow shook at every joint; and the coffin on it shook too.

The coffin was a child's. It was a plain wooden box without handles or ornament of any kind. At its corners, roughly sawn, the heads of a few nails shone brightly. The child in the coffin must have been even younger than I was at the time: the box wasn't more than three feet long. Next to it, on the planks, there lay a spade.

The barrow was level with me; then it had gone by. None of the three people following it had noticed me. The man pushing the barrow was a young, strongly built African dressed in a pair of shorts and striped cotton shirt. His head was bare, and so were his feet. The calf-muscles of each leg bunched as he took his strides off the balls of his feet, leaning forward slightly against the barrow. His head was lowered, and from his mouth there came a wordless, tuneless chant. Behind him walked two African women, long dresses trailing around their ankles, and fringed shawls about their shoulders and over their heads. They both clutched their shawls together with their hands in front of their mouths, so that their faces were veiled, hidden.

No one else was in the street; no one else seemed to be standing in any of the gardens to watch the procession go by. I went to the gate and began to follow them.

Groaning and rumbling, the barrow went down the road. We covered the distance of one block, a second, a third. Here and there someone working in his garden paused for a moment to stare, or an African walking up the road stopped, shook his head, and went on. No one seemed to associate me with the group. I followed under a compulsion I did not understand but could not disobey, unable to take my eyes off the powerful legs of the man pushing the barrow, the bowed heads of the women, and the light, shaking box that contained the corpse of a child younger than myself.

We passed a police station and some small shops. The road descended into a subway and passed under the railway lines. Beyond the railway the road was no longer tarred; the area was an outright slum, inhabited by poor whites and Cape coloureds, bordered by acres upon acres of the mine-dumps which lay all around the outskirts of our town. The dumps were enclosed within a fierce barbed-wire fence, twelve feet high. The group with the barrow turned and followed a dusty, pitted road that ran parallel to the railway lines. Soon there were no houses around us at all. On one side were the railway lines, on the other the barbed-wire and the mine-dumps.

I thought I knew where we were going. About a mile farther down the road there was an African 'location,' thrust down on a flat stretch of ground, where the mining company's wire curved away from the railway. However, when the group came to a fork in the road, only the two women went straight on to the location; the man pushed the barrow some way down the road to the left before halting and throwing himself down in the shade of a little camel-thorn tree that grew to the side of the road. He left the barrow with the coffin on it standing in the sun. The women were soon lost to sight in the confusion of rust-coloured, dust-coloured shacks that stretched away indistinguishably across the bare, level earth. In the strong sunlight the location looked vast but insubstantial.

Hesitantly, hearing the sound of my own footsteps on the road and watching my own shadow in front of me, I approached the man. Only when I was within a few feet of him did I look up. He had drawn himself up at my approach; he was sitting with his knees raised in front of his chest and his arms behind him, propping up his body. He smiled cheerfully at me. His teeth were white, his skin smooth, his face broad. Over each eye there was a protuberance of bone which might have given his face an angry, lowering aspect if his expression had not been so amused. His eyes seemed to peep slyly at me under his heavy brows.

'What are you looking for?' he asked me, in Afrikaans. His voice was deep, and had an idle, teasing note to it.

I could not answer him. Yet it seemed that he knew what I wanted, and was ready to tell me all he could. He turned his head away from me and looked at the coffin, wrinkling his brow against the brightness of the sunlight beyond the shadow in which he lay.

'The little boy in there—he had a sickness in his chest. They fetch his *ouma*, the grandmother, now. Then we go to the graveyard.'

He held up a single dust-stained finger. 'I do all the work for a pound. Just one pound, and I make the coffin, and I take it where they want me to, and I dig the hole also.'

He fell silent, still regarding me from under his brows, half-threatening, half-quizzical. Then he said: 'You want to look inside? Come!' And he rose swiftly on the word.

I turned and ran. Behind me I heard the man laughing; then a scurry of footsteps in the sand. He was coming after me. Sickeningly, the earth seemed to turn across all its width, like a great, flat, pallid wheel; I could not keep my balance on it. I fell, and looked up. His smiling face was over me.

'Don't run away,' he said. His hands grasped me gently. I was sure he would never let me go. Death itself stood over me, determined to punish my curiosity by satisfying it utterly. What had happened to that other child was going to happen to me. I was going to learn all that he had learned.

I don't remember the man letting go of me, or hearing his footsteps retreating. All I knew when I opened my eyes was that the man's face was no longer between me and the sky. I did not look where he had gone. I got to my feet and took a few paces, but felt too weak and unsteady to go on. There was a ditch to the side of the road, and I crept into it. How long I lay there, with my head on my arms and my eyes closed, I do not know. When at last I stood up, I found that the man and his barrow were gone. I also found, without surprise, that having come so far I felt I must go on.

I could see the wheel tracks that the barrow had left in the sand and I began to follow them. A car passed me, with a swirl of dust at its tyres, and I saw the people in it looking at me curiously. I went on walking. To the left, the barbed-wire fence ran straight, the dumps of earth lying empty behind it. On the right, almost as bare of vegetation as the dumps, was a stretch of veld where a few piccanins were playing with a ball. The spaces around them made their figures look tiny. Then I saw the location's cemetery.

It looked much like the veld where the piccanins were playing, only its surface was more irregular, broken by innumerable little mounds of earth. There was no fence around it. From hundreds of the mounds there gleamed little points of light: reflections from the jam tins which were used to hold the flowers brought by mourners. There were only a few formal tombstones to be seen; there were more wooden crosses, some of them tilted at angles; there were many strips of corrugated iron thrust upright into the ground, with names painted on them.

Some of the graves had their borders carefully marked out by small boulders laid in rows on the ground. But most of them were quite without adornment, identification, or demarcation of any kind. It was impossible to tell where each ended or began. There was not a tree, not even a bush, anywhere. Among all the low mounds and humps of earth, the people I was looking for stood out distinctly. There were three women, and the man working with a spade.

The women stood aside from the man, next to the barrow with the coffin on it. They did not seem to be weeping; merely watching and waiting. When the hole was a few feet deep—the rim of it came to the man's waist when he stood in it—he clambered out, wiped his brow, and simply picked up the coffin and carried it in his arms to the grave, holding it in front of his chest. The women cried out briefly, then were silent. The man slid the coffin, end foremost, into the grave and climbed in after it to lay it flat. A moment later he had climbed out again and had set about shovelling the earth inside the hole, working very fast.

The women waited until he had done. Then they turned and began walking towards the location, taking a short cut across the veld. The man, alone once more, pushed the empty barrow to the road, where I was standing. The going was difficult for him, among the graves, and it took him some time to draw near.

Eventually he reached the road. He blew out his breath noisily and smiled. In his deep, mocking voice he said, 'Another time.' He pointed a finger at me and shook it. 'Another day.'

I began walking home, ahead of him. All the way home I heard the rumble of the barrow behind me. At the gate of the house I stood and watched the man go past; I knew he was conscious of me, but he did not look in my direction. He did not need to. His head was lowered, from his lips came that tuneless, wordless chant I had heard before. The muscles of his legs quivered with every long stride he took.

DONALD JUSTICE

Born in Miami, Florida, in 1925, Donald Justice did graduate work at Stanford in 1948–49, where the money won as a fiction prize paid his train fare home. He teaches now at the University of Florida. In 1980, his Selected Poems *received the Pulitzer Prize. Latest book:* The Sunset Maker *(Atheneum, 1987).*

"This is a companion piece to several pieces in *The Sunset Maker* dealing with early piano lessons and teachers. Mr. Winters would hardly have gone along with the run of extra syllables here, but without what he gave—a strong, clear sense of the underlying iambic—I could never have undertaken my jazzier 'improvisations.'"

Dance Lessons of the Thirties

Wafts of old incense mixed with Cuban coffee
Hung on the air; a fan turned; it was summer.
And (of the buried life) some last aroma
Still clung to the tumbled cushions of the sofa.

At lesson time, pushed back, it used to be
The thing we managed always just to miss
With our last-second dips and twirls—all this
While the Victrola wound down gradually.

And this was their exile, those brave ladies who taught us
So much of art, and stepped off to their doom
Demonstrating the foxtrot with their daughters
Endlessly around a sad and makeshift ballroom—

O little lost Bohemias of the suburbs!

KEN KESEY

Ken Kesey, the original "Merry Prankster," lives in Oregon with his wife, Faye. While a graduate student at Stanford in the late 1950s, Kesey became a paid volunteer for government experiments with psilocybin and LSD. His novels One Flew Over the Cuckoo's Nest *and* Sometimes A Great Notion *are worldwide best-sellers.*

"The evil 'combine' which serves as the setting for *One Flew Over the Cuckoo's Nest* is based on the psychiatric ward of the Palo Alto Veterans Administration Hospital, where Kesey worked during his Stanford days. The job provided him with one of the enduring themes of his work: the oppression of consciousness. For Kesey, 'the energy of madness can, and must, live on.'"

◆   ◆   ◆

From *One Flew Over the Cuckoo's Nest*

I KNOW HOW THEY work it, the fog machine. We had a whole platoon used to operate fog machines around airfields overseas. Whenever intelligence figured there might be a bombing attack, or if the generals had something secret they wanted to pull—out of sight, hid so good that even the spies on the base couldn't see what went on—they fogged the field.

It's a simple rig: you got an ordinary compressor sucks water out of one tank and a special oil out of another tank, and compresses them together, and from the black stem at the end of the machine blooms a white cloud of fog that can cover a whole airfield in ninety seconds. The first thing I saw when I landed in Europe was the fog those machines make. There were some interceptors close after our transport, and soon as it hit ground the fog crew started up the machines. We could look out the transport's round, scratched windows and watch the jeeps draw the machines up close to the plane and watch the fog boil out till it rolled across the field and stuck against the windows like wet cotton.

You found your way off the plane by following a little referee's horn the lieutenant kept blowing, sounded like a goose honking. Soon as you were out of the hatch you couldn't see no more than maybe three feet in any direction. You felt like you were out on that airfield all by yourself. You were safe from the enemy, but you were awfully alone. Sounds died and dissolved after a few yards, and you couldn't hear any of the rest of your crew, nothing but that little horn squeaking and honking out of a soft furry whiteness so thick that your body just faded into white below the belt; other than that brown shirt and brass buckle, you couldn't see nothing but white, like from the waist down you were being dissolved by the fog too.

And then some guy wandering as lost as you would all of a sudden be right before your eyes, his face bigger and clearer than you ever saw a man's face before in your life. Your eyes were working so hard to see in that fog that when something did come in sight every detail was ten times as clear as usual, so clear both of you had to look away. When a man showed up you didn't want to look at his face and he didn't want to look at yours, because it's painful to see somebody so clear that it's like looking inside him, but then neither did you want to look away and lose him completely. You had a choice: you could either strain and look at things that appeared in front of you in the fog, painful as it might be, or you could relax and lose yourself.

When they first used that fog machine on the ward, one they bought from Army Surplus and hid in the vents in the new place before we moved in, I kept looking at anything that appeared out of the fog as long and hard as I could, to keep track of it, just like I used to do when they fogged the airfields in Europe. Nobody'd be blowing a horn to show the way, there was no rope to hold to, so fixing my eyes on something was the only way I kept from getting lost. Sometimes I got lost in it anyway, got in too deep, trying to hide, and every time I did, it seemed like I always turned up at that same place, at that same metal door with the row of rivets like eyes and no number, just like the room behind that door drew me to it, no matter how hard I tried to stay away, just like the current generated by the fiends in that room was conducted in a beam along the fog and pulled me back along it like a robot. I'd wander for days in the fog, scared I'd never see another thing, then there'd be that door, opening to show me the mattress padding on the other side to stop out the sounds, the men standing in a line like zombies among shiny copper wires and tubes pulsing light, and the bright scrape of arcing electricity. I'd take my place in the line and wait my turn at the table. The table shaped like a cross, with shadows of a thousand murdered men printed on it, silhouette wrists and ankles running under leather straps sweated green with use, a silhouette neck and head running up to a silver band goes across the forehead. And a technician at the controls beside the table looking up from his dials and down the line and pointing at me with a rubber glove. "Wait, I *know* that big bastard there—better rabbit-punch him or call for some more help or something. He's an awful case for thrashing around."

So I used to try not to get in too deep, for fear I'd get lost and turn up at the Shock Shop door. I looked hard at anything that came into sight and hung on like a man in a blizzard hangs on a fence rail. But they kept making the fog thicker and thicker, and it seemed to me that, no matter how hard I tried, two or three times a month, I found myself with that door opening in front of me to the acid smell of sparks and ozone. In spite of all I could do, it was getting tough to keep from getting lost.

Then I discovered something: I don't have to end up at that door if I stay still when the fog comes over me and just keep quiet. The trouble was I'd been finding that door my own self because I got scared of being lost so long and went to hollering so they could track me. In a way, I was hollering for them *to* track me; I had figured that anything was better'n being lost for good, even the Shock Shop. Now, I don't know. Being lost isn't so bad.

All this morning I been waiting for them to fog us in again. The last few days they been doing it more and more. It's my idea they're doing it on account of McMurphy. They haven't got him fixed with controls yet, and they're trying to catch him off guard. They can see he's due to be a problem; a half a dozen times already he's roused Cheswick and Harding and some of the others to where it looked like they might actually stand up to one of the black boys—but always, just the time it looked like the patient might be helped, the fog would start, like it's starting now.

I heard the compressor start pumping in the grill a few minutes back, just as the guys went to moving tables out of the day room for the therapeutic meeting, and already the mist is oozing across the floor so thick my pants legs are wet. I'm cleaning the windows in the door of the glass station, and I hear the Big Nurse pick up the phone and call the doctor to tell him we're just about ready for the meeting, and tell him perhaps he'd best keep an hour free this afternoon for a staff meeting. "The reason being," she tells him, "I think it is past time to have a discussion of the subject of Patient Randle McMurphy and whether he should be on this ward or not." She listens a minute, then tells him, "I don't think it's wise to let him go on upsetting the patients the way he has the last few days."

That's why she's fogging the ward for the meeting. She don't usually do that. But now she's going to do something with McMurphy today, probably ship him to Disturbed. I put down my window rag and go to my chair at the end of the line of Chronics, barely able to see the guys getting into their chairs and the doctor coming through the door wiping his glasses like he thinks the blurred look comes from his steamed lenses instead of the fog.

It's rolling in thicker than I ever seen it before.

I can hear them out there, trying to go on with the meeting, talking some nonsense about Billy Bibbit's stutter and how it came about. The words come to me like through water, it's so thick. In fact it's so much like water it floats me right up out of my chair and I don't know which end is up for a while. Floating makes me a little sick to the stomach at first. I can't see a thing. I never had it so thick it floated me like this.

The words get dim and loud, off and on, as I float around, but as loud as they get, loud enough sometimes I know I'm right next to the guy that's talking, I still can't see a thing.

I recognize Billy's voice, stuttering worse than ever because he's nervous. ". . . fuh-fuh-flunked out of college be-be-cause I quit ROTC. I c-c-couldn't take it. Wh-wh-wh-whenever the officer in charge of class would call roll, call 'Bibbit,' I couldn't answer. You were s-s-supposed to say heh—heh—heh . . ." He's choking on the word, like it's a bone in his throat. I hear him swallow and start again. "You were supposed to say, 'Here sir,' and I never c-c-could get it out."

His voice gets dim; then the Big Nurse's voice comes cutting from the left. "Can you recall, Billy, when you first had speech trouble? When did you first stutter, do you remember?"

I can't tell is he laughing or what. "Fir-first stutter? First stutter? The first word I said I st-stut-tered: m-m-m-m-mamma."

Then the talking fades out altogether; I never knew that to happen before. Maybe Billy's hid himself in the fog too. Maybe all the guys finally and forever crowded back into the fog.

A chair and me float past each other. It's the first thing I've seen. It comes sifting out of the fog off to my right, and for a few seconds it's right beside my face, just out of my reach. I been accustomed of late to just let things alone when they appear in the fog, sit still and not try to hang on. But this time I'm scared, the way I used to be scared. I try with all I got to pull myself over to the chair and get hold of it, but there's nothing to brace against and all I can do is thrash the air, all I can do is watch the chair come clear, clearer than ever before to where I can even make out the fingerprint where a worker touched the varnish before it was dry, looming out for a few seconds, then fading on off again. I never seen it where things floated around this way. I never seen it this thick before, thick to where I can't get down to the floor and get on my feet if I wanted to and walk around. That's why I'm so scared; I feel I'm going to float off someplace for good this time.

I see a Chronic float into sight a little below me. It's old Colonel Matterson, reading from the wrinkled scripture of that long yellow hand. I look close at him because I figure it's the last time I'll ever see him. His face is enormous, almost more than I can bear. Every hair and wrinkle of him is big, as though I was looking at him with one of those microscopes. I see him so clear I see his whole life. The face is sixty years of southwest Army camps, rutted by iron-rimmed caisson wheels, worn to the bone by thousands of feet on two-day marches.

He holds out that long hand and brings it up in front of his eyes and squints into it, brings up his other hand and underlines the words with a finger wooden and varnished the color of a gunstock by nicotine. His voice as deep and slow and patient, and I see the words come out dark and heavy over his brittle lips when he reads.

"Now . . . The flag is . . . Ah-mer-ica. America is . . . the plum. The peach. The wah-ter-mel-on. America is . . . the gumdrop. The pump-kin seed. America is . . . tell-ah-vision."

It's true. It's all wrote down on that yellow hand. I can read it along with him myself.

"Now . . . The cross is . . . Mex-i-co." He looks up to see if I'm paying attention, and when he sees I am he smiles at me and goes on. "Mexico is . . . the wal-nut. The hazelnut. The ay-corn. Mexico is . . . the rain-bow. The rain-bow is . . . wooden. Mexico is . . . woo-den."

I can see what he's driving at. He's been saying this sort of thing for the whole six years he's been here, but I never paid him any mind, figured he was no more than a talking statue, a thing made out of bone and arthritis, rambling on and on with these goofy definitions of his that didn't make a lick of sense. Now, at last, I see what he's saying. I'm trying to hold him for one last look to remember him, and that's what makes me look hard enough to understand. He pauses and peers up at me again to make sure I'm getting it, and I want to yell out to him Yes, I see: Mexico *is* like the walnut; it's brown and hard and you feel it with your eye and it *feels* like the walnut! You're making sense, old man, a sense of your own. You're not crazy the way they think. Yes . . . I see . . .

But the fog's clogged my throat to where I can't make a sound. As he sifts away I see him bend back over that hand.

"Now . . . The green sheep is . . . Can-a-da. Canada is . . . the fir tree. The wheat field. The cal-en-dar . . ."

I strain to see him drifting away. I strain so hard my eyes ache and I have to close them, and when I open them again the colonel is gone. I'm floating by myself again, more lost than ever.

This is the time, I tell myself. I'm going for good.

There's old Pete, face like a searchlight. He's fifty yards off to my left, but I can see him plain as though there wasn't any fog at all. Or maybe he's up right close and real small, I can't be sure. He tells me once about how tired he is, and just his saying it makes me see his whole life on the railroad, see him working to figure out how to read a watch, breaking a sweat while he tries to get the right button in the right hole of his railroad overalls, doing his absolute damnedest to keep up with a job that comes so easy to the others they can sit back in a chair padded with cardboard and read mystery stories and girlie books. Not that he ever really figured to keep up—he knew from the start he couldn't do that—but he had to try to keep up, just to keep them in sight. So for forty years he was able to live, if not right in the world of men, at least on the edge of it.

I can see all that, and be hurt by it, the way I was hurt by seeing things in the Army, in the war. The way I was hurt by seeing what happened to Papa and the tribe. I thought I'd got over seeing those things and fretting over them. There's no sense in it. There's nothing to be done.

"I'm tired," is what he says.

"I know you're tired, Pete, but I can't do you no good fretting about it. You know I can't."

Pete floats on the way of the old colonel.

Here comes Billy Bibbit, the way Pete come by. They're all filing by for a last look. I know Billy can't be more'n a few feet away, but he's so tiny he looks like he's a mile off. His face is out to me like the face of a beggar, needing so much more'n anybody can give. His mouth works like a little doll's mouth.

"And even when I pr-proposed, I flubbed it. I said 'Huh-honey, will you muh-muh-muh-muh-muh . . . till the girl broke out l-laughing."

Nurse's voice, I can't see where it comes from: "Your mother has spoken to me about this girl, Billy. Apparently she was quite a bit beneath you. What would you speculate it was about her that frightened you so, Billy?"

"I was in luh-love with her."

I can't do nothing for you either, Billy. You know that. None of us can. You got to understand that as soon as a man goes to help somebody, he leaves himself wide open. He *has* to be cagey, Billy, you should know that as well as anyone. What could I do? I can't fix your stuttering. I can't wipe the razor-blade scars off your wrists or the cigarette burns off the back of your hands. I can't give you a new mother. And as far as the nurse riding you like this, rubbing your nose in your weakness till what little dignity you got left is gone and you shrink up to nothing from humiliation, I can't do anything about that, either.

At Anzio, I saw a buddy of mine tied to a tree fifty yards from me, screaming for water, his face blistered in the sun. They wanted me to try to go out and help him. They'd of cut me in half from that farmhouse over there.

Put your face away, Billy.

They keep filing past.

It's like each face was a sign like one of those "I'm Blind" signs the dago accordion players in Portland hung around their necks, only these signs say "I'm tired" or "I'm scared" or "I'm dying of a bum liver" or "I'm all bound up with machinery and people *pushing* me alla time." I can read all the signs, it don't make any difference how little the print gets. Some of the faces are looking around at one another and could read the other fellow's if they would, but what's the sense? The faces blow past in the fog like confetti.

I'm further off than I've ever been. This is what it's like to be dead. I guess this is what it's like to be a Vegetable; you lose yourself in the fog. You don't move. They feed your body till it finally stops eating; then they burn it. It's not so bad. There's no pain. I don't feel much of anything other than a touch of chill I figure will pass in time.

I see my commanding officer pinning notices on the bulletin board, what we're to wear today. I see the US Department of Interior bearing down on our little tribe with a gravel-crushing machine.

I see Papa come loping out of a draw and slow up to try and take aim at a big six-point buck springing off through the cedars. Shot after shot puffs out of the barrel, knocking dust all around the buck. I come out of the draw behind Papa and bring the buck down with my second shot just as it starts climbing the rimrock. I grin at Papa.

I never knew you to miss a shot like that before, Papa.

Eye's gone, boy. Can't hold a bead. Sights on my gun just now was shakin' like a dog shittin' peach pits.

Papa, I'm telling you: that cactus moon of Sid's is gonna make you old before your time.

A man drinks that cactus moon of Sid's, boy, he's already old before his time. Let's go gut that animal out before the flies blow him.

That's not even happening now. You see? There's nothing you can do about a happening out of the past like that.

Look there, my man . . .

I hear whispers, black boys.

Look there that old fool Broom, slipped off to sleep.

Tha's right, Chief Broom, tha's right. You sleep an' keep outta trouble. Yasss.

I'm not cold any more. I think I've about made it. I'm off to where the cold can't reach me. I can stay off here for good. I'm not scared any more. They can't reach me. Just the words reach me, and those're fading.

Well . . . in as much as Billy has decided to walk out on the discussion, does anyone else have a problem to bring before the group?

As a matter of fact, ma'am, there does happen to be something . . .

That's that McMurphy. He's far away. He's still trying to pull people out of the fog. Why don't he leave me be?

". . . remember that vote we had a day or so back—about the TV time? Well, today's Friday and I thought I might just bring it up again, just to see if anybody else has picked up a little guts."

"Mr. McMurphy, the purpose of this meeting is therapy, group therapy, and I'm not certain these petty grievances—"

"Yeah, yeah, the hell with that, we've heard it before. Me and some of the rest of the guys decided—"

"One moment, Mr. McMurphy, let me pose a question to the group: do any of you feel that Mr. McMurphy is perhaps imposing his personal desires on some of you too much? I've been thinking you might be happier if he were moved to a different ward."

Nobody says anything for a minute. Then someone says, "Let him vote, why dontcha? Why ya want to ship him to Disturbed just for bringing up a vote? What's so wrong with changing time?"

"Why, Mr. Scanlon, as I recall, you refused to eat for three days until we allowed you turn the set on at six instead of six-thirty."

"A man needs to see the world news, don't he? God, they coulda bombed Washington and it'd been a week before we'd of heard."

"Yes? And how do you feel about relinquishing your world news to watch a bunch of men play baseball?"

"We can't have both, huh? No, I suppose not. Well, what the dickens—I don't guess they'll bomb us this week."

"Let's let him have the vote, Miss Ratched."

"Very well. But I think this is ample evidence of how much he is upsetting some of you patients. What is it you are proposing Mr. McMurphy?"

"I'm proposing a revote on watching the TV in the afternoon."

"You're certain one more vote will satisfy you? We have more important things—"

"It'll satisfy me. I just'd kind of like to see which of these birds has any guts and which doesn't."

"It's that kind of talk, Doctor Spivey, that makes me wonder if the patients wouldn't be more content if Mr. McMurphy were moved."

"Let him call the vote, why dontcha?"

"Certainly, Mr. Cheswick. A vote is now before the group. Will a show of hands be adequate, Mr. McMurphy, or are you going to insist on a secret ballot?"

"I want to see the hands. I want to see the hands that don't go up, too."

"Everyone in favor of changing the television time to the afternoon, raise his hand."

The first hand that comes up, I can tell, is McMurphy's, because of the bandage where that control panel cut into him when he tried to lift it. And then off down the slope I see them, other hands coming up out of the fog. It's like . . . that big red hand of McMurphy's is reaching into the fog and dropping down and dragging the men up by their hands, dragging them blinking into the open. First one, then another, then the next. Right on down the line of Acutes, dragging them out of the fog till there they stand, all twenty of them, raising not just for watching TV, but against the Big Nurse, against her trying to send McMurphy to Disturbed, against the way she's talked and acted and beat them down for years.

Nobody says anything. I can feel how stunned everybody is, the patients as well as the staff. The nurse can't figure what happened; yesterday, before he tried lifting that panel, there wasn't but four or five men might of voted. But when she talks she don't let it show in her voice how surprised she is.

"I count only twenty, Mr. McMurphy."

"Twenty? Well, why not? Twenty is all of us there—" His voice hangs as he realizes what she means. "Now hold on just a goddamned minute, lady—"

"I'm afraid the vote is defeated."

"Hold on just one goddamned *minute!*"

"There are forty patients on the ward, Mr. McMurphy. Forty patients, and only twenty voted. You must have a majority to change the ward policy. I'm afraid the vote is closed."

The hands are coming down across the room. The guys know they're whipped, are trying to slip back into the safety of the fog. McMurphy is on his feet.

"Well, I'll be a sonofabitch. You mean to tell me that's how you're gonna pull it? Count the votes of those old birds over there too?"

"Didn't you explain the voting procedure to him, Doctor?"

"I'm afraid—a majority *is* called for, McMurphy. She's right, she's right."

"A majority, Mr. McMurphy; it's in the ward constitution."

"And I suppose the way to change the damned constitution is with a majority vote. Sure. Of all the chicken-shit things I've ever seen, this by God takes the *cake!*"

"I'm sorry, Mr. McMurphy, but you'll find it written in the policy if you'd care for me to—"

"So this's how you work this democratic bullshit—hell's bells!"

"You seem upset, Mr. McMurphy. Doesn't he seem upset, Doctor? I want you to note this."

"Don't give me that noise, lady. When a guy's getting screwed he's got a right to holler. And we've been damn well screwed."

"Perhaps, Doctor, in view of the patient's condition, we should bring this meeting to a close early today—"

"Wait! Wait a minute, let me talk to some of those old guys."

"The vote is closed, Mr. McMurphy."

"Let me talk to 'em."

He's coming across the day room at us. He gets bigger and bigger, and he's burning red in the face. He reaches into the fog and tries to drag Ruckly to the surface because Ruckly's the youngest.

"What about you, buddy? You want to watch the World Series? Baseball? Baseball games? Just raise that hand up there—"

"Fffffffuck da wife."

"All right, forget it. You, partner, how about you? What was your name— Ellis? What do you say, Ellis, to watching a ball game on TV? Just raise your hand . . ."

Ellis's hands are nailed to the wall, can't be counted as a vote.

"I said the voting is closed, Mr. McMurphy. You're just making a spectacle of yourself."

He don't pay any attention to her. He comes on down the line of Chronics.

"C'mon, c'mon, just one vote from you birds, just raise a hand. Show her you can still do it."

"I'm tired," says Pete and wags his head.

"The night is . . . the Pacific Ocean." The Colonel is reading off his hand, can't be bothered with voting.

"*One* of you guys, for cryin' out loud! This is where you get the edge, don't you see that? We have to do this—or we're *whipped!* Don't a one of you clucks know what I'm talking about enough to give us a hand? You, Gabriel? George? No? You, Chief, what about you?"

He's standing over me in the mist. Why won't he leave me be?

"Chief, you're our last bet."

The Big Nurse is folding her papers; the other nurses are standing up around her. She finally gets to her feet.

"The meeting is adjourned, then," I hear her say. "And I'd like to see the staff down in the staff room in about an hour. So, if there is nothing el—"

It's too late to stop it now. McMurphy did something to it that first day, put some kind of hex on it with his hand so it won't act like I order it. There's no sense in it, any fool can see; I wouldn't do it on my own. Just by the way the nurse is staring at me with her mouth empty of words I can see I'm in for trouble, but I can't stop it. McMurphy's got hidden wires hooked to it, lifting it slow just to get me out of the fog and into the open where I'm fair game. He's doing it, wires . . .

No. That's not the truth. I lifted it myself.

McMurphy whoops and drags me standing, pounding my back.

"Twenty-one! The Chief's vote makes it twenty-one! And by God if that ain't a majority I'll eat my hat!"

"Yippee," Cheswick yells. The other Acutes are coming across toward me.

"The meeting was closed," she says. Her smile is still there, but the back of her neck as she walks out of the day room and into the Nurses' Station, is red and swelling like she'll blow apart any second.

But she don't blow up, not right off, not until about an hour later. Behind the glass her smile is twisted and queer, like we've never seen before. She just sits. I can see her shoulders rise and fall as she breathes.

McMurphy looks up at the clock and he says it's time for the game. He's over by the drinking fountain with some of the other Acutes, down on his knees scouring off the baseboard. I'm sweeping out the broom closet for the tenth time that day. Scanlon and Harding, they got the buffer going up and down the hall, polishing the new wax into shining figure eights. McMurphy says again that he guesses it must be game time and he stands up, leaves the scouring rag where it lies. Nobody else stops work. McMurphy walks past the window where she's glaring out at him and grins at her like he knows he's got her whipped now. When he tips his head back and winks at her she gives that little sideways jerk of her head.

Everybody keeps on at what he's doing, but they all watch out of the corners of their eyes while he drags his armchair out to in front of the TV set, then switches on the set and sits down. A picture swirls onto the screen of a parrot out on the baseball field singing razor-blade songs. McMurphy gets up and turns up the sound to drown out the music coming down from the speaker in the ceiling, and he drags another chair in front of him and sits down and crosses his feet on the chair and leans back and lights a cigarette. He scratches his belly and yawns.

"Hoo-*weee!* Man, all I need me now is a can of beer and a red-hot."

We can see the nurse's face get red and her mouth work as she stares at him. She looks around for a second and sees everybody's watching what she's going to do—even the black boys and the little nurses sneaking looks at her, and the residents beginning to drift in for the staff meeting, they're watching. Her mouth clamps shut. She looks back at McMurphy and waits till the razor-blade song is finished; then she gets up and goes to the steel door where the controls are, and she flips a switch and the TV picture swirls back into the gray. Nothing is left on the screen but a little eye of light beading right down on McMurphy sitting there.

That eye don't faze him a bit. To tell the truth, he don't even let on he knows the picture is turned off; he puts his cigarette between his teeth and pushes his cap forward in his red hair till he has to lean back to see out from under the brim.

And sits that way, with his hands crossed behind his head and his feet stuck out in a chair, a smoking cigarette sticking out from under his hatbrim—watching the TV screen.

The nurse stands this as long as she can; then she comes to the door of the Nurses' Station and calls across to him he'd better help the men with the housework. He ignores her.

"I said, Mr. McMurphy, that you are supposed to be working during these hours." Her voice has a tight whine like an electric saw ripping through pine. "Mr. McMurphy, I'm *warning* you!"

Everybody's stopped what he was doing. She looks around her, then takes a step out of the Nurses' Station toward McMurphy.

"You're committed, you realize. You are . . . under the *jurisdiction* of me . . . the staff." She's holding up a fist, all those red-orange fingernails burning into her palm. "Under jurisdiction and *control—*"

Harding shuts off the buffer, and leaves it in the hall, and goes pulls him a chair up alongside McMurphy and sits down and lights him a cigarette too.

"Mr. Harding! You return to your scheduled duties!"

I think how her voice sounds like it hit a nail, and this strikes me so funny I almost laugh.

"Mr. Har-*ding!*"

Then Cheswick goes and gets him a chair, and then Billy Bibbit goes, and then Scanlon and then Fredrickson and Sefelt, and then we all put down our mops and brooms and scouring rags and we all go pull us chairs up.

"You *men*—Stop this. *Stop!*"

And we're all sitting there lined up in front of that blanked-out TV set, watching the gray screen just like we could see the baseball game clear as day, and she's ranting and screaming behind us.

If somebody'd of come in and took a look, men watching a blank TV, a fifty-year-old woman hollering and squealing at the back of their heads about discipline and order and recriminations, they'd of thought the whole bunch was crazy as loons.

WILLIAM KITTREDGE

William Kittredge grew up on the MC ranch in southeastern Oregon, stayed home with the farming until he was thirty-five, studied in the Writers Workshop at the University of Iowa, and is at present a professor of English at the University of Montana. He held a Stegner Fellowship at Stanford University, received two creative writing fellowships from the National Endowment for the Arts, two Pacific Northwest Bookseller's Awards for Excellence, and the Montana Governor's Award for the Arts. Kittredge has published stories and essays in The Atlantic, Harper's, TriQuarterly, Outside, Rolling Stone, *and* The Paris Review. *His most recent books are a collection of short fiction,* We Are Not In This Together *(Graywolf Press, 1984), and a collection of essays,* Owning It All *(Graywolf Press, 1987). He was also co-winner of the Neil Simon Award from American Playhouse for his work on the script for the film* Heartland.

"It was the winter of 1976, I think, anyway my brother was in Missoula at the time. I got a note from one of my old teachers at Iowa, Bob Coover, asking if I could write a 'mythological' story for an issue of the *Iowa Review*. So I thought, ever ambitious, *hell* yes, I'd write a story about the Lone Ranger. Should be a lay in. All winter I had been teaching a course in Western movies, and I had a lock on gun-slinger mythologies. But the first problem was finding time, and then my typewriter broke down. So I ended up writing the first drafts of 'Phantom Silver' over a long weekend at my brother's kitchen table. He wouldn't trust me to take his typewriter to my place. At the same time we were both reading a great book, *Goodbye to a River*, by John Graves (the yellow bloom of cottonwood in the fall is a direct steal from Graves; no doubt there are many more). So I would type, hoping to make a few pages I liked, and I did like this story, right from the start, we would go uptown for nights of fun, get organic in the morning, and I would write some more, in my brother's place with John Graves ringing around me in the hungover air. It is a time I recall with great idiot fondness; we are most of us too old for the biochemical consequences any more."

◆　　　◆　　　◆

Phantom Silver

THE GREAT WHITE HORSE rears above the rolling horizon, which is golden and simple in the sunset, and those sparkling hooves strike out into the green light under dark midsummer thunderclouds. Far away there is rain, and barn swallows drop like thrown stones through clouds of mosquitoes near the creek. A single planet and then stars grow luminous against the night, and the great horse is gone. Moths bat against the screen around the veranda porch, and we are left in that dreamed yesteryear where the masked man rides away. The light is cold in the early morning, and the silver bullet rests on the mantle like a trophy. Only in the morning is it possible to think of that masked man as old and fat and slow and happy.

That crew of clean-shaven Texas Rangers was all brave and unmasked in the beginning, before the Cavendish gang did them in, leaving him for dead and alone, his comrades sprawled around him and killed. They had ridden into a box canyon, and rifle fire crackled from the surrounding rims. They were ambushed; horses reared and screamed; the good men fell, and in only a few beats of a heart it was over. The Cavendish boys walked the stony ground amid the bodies and smiled as if they would live forever.

But he was not dead, only scarred. Revenge became his great obsession, revenge and justice, notions which served him like two sides of a coin, and he changed like a stone into gold. He rode that white stallion named Silver, he disguised himself behind that mask, he traveled with his dark companion, and they began their endless conquest of wrong-doing.

There was ranch after ranch saved from eastern bankers and monied second sons from Baltimore. Always another gold shipment to be rescued. Another sod-buster and his family to be protected. Another evil law-man to be confounded. Another wagon train saved from the clutches of circling savages. How many homesteaders' wives stood in the doorway of plain unpainted cabins with that silver bullet still warm in their hands while they wondered aloud who that masked man could have been, and the great stallion reared?

The real beginning was a mortal family, a strong handed father and a mother who split their wood, and two children, a brother and a sister, all of them having come west to Texas after the Civil War. They had been living as they were supposed to live in a juniper log cabin alongside the Brazos River before that summer morning when Comanche came down like slaughtering, screaming rain.

They thought they were safe. The Comanche had been corralled for seven years on the Oklahoma Territory, eating mainly on dole meat, and the father was a slow-spoken German other white men did not deal with easily, and so left mostly alone. But there on that bright morning was the truth, Comanche out of season.

Down in the bulrushes near the water of the Brazos there was another morning sort of time and the dumb blankness of eyes rolled back to their extreme station, the hardness of lean hipbones under the flesh, handholds as this brother mounts his sister from behind, the younger brother, the older sister, her skirt tossed up where they were down there on the matted grass, hidden from the house by tules and nodding downy cattails, the sister on her knees and elbows and the brother behind, going weak and dizzy that morning with her and afraid the screaming he heard so distantly might be her or even himself, but that was foolish, they were practiced and wouldn't. He stopped, crouched over her, listening, and she thrust herself back against him.

"Don't you quit now," she said.

But he did. He had. The screaming he heard was not really screaming, not fearfulness, that came later, but high-pitched joyous whooping, and now he could hear the horses, the hooves beating down the hard-packed wagon road. There were lots of them, and riding hard.

"Don't you stop," she said, but it was too late for that, already he had fallen back away from her, turning, knowing there was no way to see anything from where they were, that was why they were safe there on those hidden mornings down near the river. Already he was frightened, and later he would sense she had always been stronger, had always cared more than he did about what was going on right at the time; later he would understand it was an undivided mind that gave her what proved in time to be the strength of her indifference.

"Dammit," she said. "Then get yourself together."

What she meant was for him to pull up his pants and tuck in his shirttail, and to do it quietly. It was her that kept him quiet and crouching there those next hours as the smoke from the burning cabin and the barns rose thin and white into the clear sky, after the first bellowing from their father and their mother's frantic shrieking, after the horses had gone away, as the smoke dwindled and twilight came and the frogs called to one another in the quiet. It was her that kept him crouching and hidden there until the next day; they were saved at least in the sense that they could walk away, they were not killed and not captured, not bloody and hairless like the bodies of their father and mother.

She was sixteen that summer of 1867, and he was two years younger, and for a few months, after they had walked those miles upstream to the nearest homestead on the Brazos, toward the Palo Pinto, they were pitied and fed. Then October began to settle into fall, and in November the green-headed mallards and the Canada geese and the Sandhill Crane began coming south, circling and calling as they settled toward the river. The clump of pink-blooming roses on the south wall of the cabin froze, the tamarack hung dark red against the gray hillslopes, and the big cottonwood flared yellow one morning in the sun, but the real cold came all in one day the week before Thanksgiving, weather a line of shadow on the morning horizon, the air greasy and hushed all that day and at twilight a hard northern wind and driven sleety rain. But they didn't leave until after the Thanksgiving goose and all the fixings. It was her that decided.

"We are going," she said.

By Christmas they had hooked wagon rides south to San Antonio, and she would no longer let him touch her. "If we had been going to stay there we would have stayed forever," she said, and after the beginning of the new year she took to leaving him alone for days while she went around to the taverns on the banks of the San Antonio River, and she came home with money. She had her blankets in the room they shared, but she would not let him come under them with her.

"You have done me what damage you could," she said. It was not that she did not love him, she explained, it was simply that the damage was done. He took to breaking horses for a livery stable. He had always been good with horses. He could not remember his parents, they had gone away into those scalped bodies the Comanche left behind, he could not think about them at all, and the thing he hated most was the notion of horses he loved being driven north toward the territories by those savages.

Three summers later when he was seventeen she left him behind altogether. "You are man enough," she said. "You take care of yourself like I am going to take care of myself." She was loading just a few things into saddle bags, rich-looking carved-leather bags provided by the tubercular-looking white-haired man she was with, a man who wore one quick gun and claimed to be a medical doctor, although no one had ever known him to cure anything.

"We are going to settle north," she said, talking about her reasons for traveling, as though the white-haired man meant nothing. "He is going to do some work," she said, talking about the eastern Wyoming Territory around Laramie. "Things are cleaner in the north," she said, before she rode off alongside her man. "But you stay around here. You can be what you want to be around here."

By the next summer he was riding with the Texas Rangers and thinking about the man she had ridden away with, going north to some trouble centering around the long-horned cattle being driven that way out of Texas in the great herds, thinking about how he was going to learn this law business clean, getting set for another one-day meeting with that white-haired medical doctor. He could not stop thinking about her with that man, in his bed, on her knees and her elbows as she had been when the Comanche struck. He knew she was that way with the white-haired man, and he watched them in the darkness and kept his hands off himself, getting ready.

Then in the spring of 1876 the Cavendish gang left him there shot in the face, thinking him dead on the rocky dry riverbed, and there came along the single man without a tribe on his paint horse, the good dark man who found him and nursed him, and he recalled that long-ago morning the Comanche struck and knew this was a different life. As he recovered, he knew childishness was left behind, that somewhere in the kindness of this new companion there was a force he would hold always steady against what, until now, he had thought he loved: her white flesh in the sunlight that morning while she crouched with her skirt thrown forward.

For a long while things were so easily clear, there was this new friend and there was the great white horse, and both sides of what was right, like the Indian and buffalo on the United States nickel. The mask and silver bullets were emblems of the need to be distant if you were to be great and correct. Emblems were only ways of getting the work done, he understood that, even though the mask covered that dark purple scar, the twisted hole that had been his nostrils before the Cavendish gang shot him down and rode away, thinking he was dead, seeing as he looked drowned in blood.

What luck that he could shoot so perfectly without any sense of aiming, the silver bullets were after all part of the way he thought, the shooting more a business of balance and intent than anything he understood, the bullets just going where he saw they would, as though he could see a pistol in the hand of some craven man and shoot it away with only a thought.

Those were the legendary wandering years when he did not think about his sister. There was plenty of time; time was a trapeze that only swung you back and forth. Those were the years our union advanced in its skip-step way toward the Pacific and the meeting of fresh water with salt tides in the Golden Gate, the years our passenger pigeons were clubbed out of trees and Indian children were clubbed out of bushes as the nation made ready for the clubbing of Cuba and the Philippines and China. The Pony Express riders mounted their quickly saddled horses at a run while savages burned the way stations behind them; all but the impounded remnants of our sixty-odd million buffalo were slaughtered for their tongues and humps and hides and bones; the long-horned cows wore their way north to the grassy plains of Montana and Wyoming, surviving stampede while the lightning flashed, surviving quicksand on the Platte, only to perish in the snowy blizzard of 1885. The horse-drawn stages scattered dust between towns like Helena and Butte, Goldfield and Tonapah, carrying treasure in their strongboxes and enticing weak black-hatted men into banditry; the railroads came, building their graded roadbeds inexorably up through the passes, over Donner Summit and through the Marias in the northern Rockies; the nester fought the cattle barons; the cattle men fought the sheep and the rich fought the poor; the barbed wire fought the wind; the sod-grass was plowed under; the streets of Carson City were paved with brick that had served as ballast on sailing ships from China; Joseph and Looking Glass fought off tourists in Yellowstone, which was already a National Park, before losing everything they had suffered for in the Bear Paw Mountains. Somewhere far away the last visionary chiefs were dying. Crazy Horse was dead, and what there was to defend was somehow over as the first popping of the internal combustion engine began to be heard. There was nothing right left to do most of the time, nothing at all to do, and our man who began down on the Brazos was not yet fifty years of age, still quick-handed as he had ever been, and bored.

In 1912 Tonto found a woman and stayed in Grants Pass amid blossoming spring apple and cherry trees and what the masked man called wine-berries. The woman had come west as a child from the plains after her toes were frozen off in the aftermath of the great Ghost Dance massacre on the Pine Ridge Reservation of South Dakota in December of 1891. "We were like animals," the woman said, "so they let us run."

The earth shook San Francisco where he knew she was, where she had to be, that most sin-filled and elegant city, with water all around. The trench warfare began in Europe, and he was too old. Over there they fought each other from craft in the air, he would have liked that, it seemed right, and he was too old. Then the war was over and he started toward the coast, rode the white horse through the mountains of northern New Mexico, along the old trails that had been graded into roadways, wintered alongside a lake in the Sierras, and in spring drifted down to the valley towns of California, wondering what next, trying to stay furtive, hiding out, taking his time on his way to San Francisco, perfecting disguises.

He was old and alone with the white horse, thinking of her hair, the dark marks of age on her hands, which would be like his. The man she left San Antonio with was no doubt dead, but she would have another in San Francisco. In some elegant house on one of those hills she would be pouring tea from a silver service, pouring steadily, her hands not shaking at all. He would lift the delicate cup made of fragile English porcelain, and she would smile.

The summer day was cool that close to the ocean as he came up the old El Camino into the Mission District. Off west the Twin Peaks were green with forest and above them the gray fog stood like an arrested wave. The Pacific was over there and he had never seen an ocean, real waves coming from Asia. The solid ground felt precarious, like it might tip and slip away without the strength of the continent spread around. He smiled at himself, knowing he should have come here when he would have liked this walking on eggs, this vast uneasiness was so much more important to confront than some fool with a model 1873 Colt revolver. So he stabled the white horse in a barn on the swampy ground of the upper Mission, and he rode an electrified trolley car out toward the ocean, to see what it was.

It was like he was invisible, disguised as an old man with a shot-off nose that was impossibly ugly to look at. The black man at the livery stable had treated him like a customer, and the people crowding around him on the trolley car talked and laughed like this was what they did all the time—as though his wound were only a matter of accident. Four seats down there was an old woman with an enormous goiter on the side of her neck, and no one looked at her either. Except for him, he watched her, and once she looked up and caught him and smiled.

They passed beyond the Twin Peaks, beneath the fog and out onto the grassy dune-land that descended toward the sea. The trolley line ended, and a board-walk went on. He felt he was coming toward the edge of what he had always been. But it wasn't. The air was heavy with dampness, the fog thick around him, the waves gray and white the little way out he could see, but it wasn't like the edge of anything. He took off his boots and left them in the sand, walked down until the cold water lapped on his blue-white feet, and rolled himself a cigarette. He fired one shot out into the very center of that gray circle of oncoming water and fog and smiled at himself because there was nothing there to disarm.

Of course she wasn't up there on those hills in some rich man's house. He knew that. She would not have gone that way. Down on Market Street, the next day after he slept in the stable beside the white horse, that was where she would be. She would be in the right place, down with the injured where arrogance was equal to foolishness. Over the years she would have figured it out. She would have left the white-haired man before he died, she would have gone right and poor.

But she was not there. This day he went without his guns again, without his mask and the gun-belt stocked with silver bullets. The white horse munched oats calmly as if this were not a new world, and he walked the barrooms, expecting to see her laughing and quarreling, maybe selling flowers on a street corner. That night he stayed in a room which smelled of urine and ammonia and the old nervous sweat, not really sleeping, just resting there and dreaming she was nearby. But she was not. He walked the muddy streets toward the outskirts of the city as a common man, and she was not there.

At least he had not recognized her.

So it was her turn.

He went back to the only things there were: his mask, his silence, those guns, the great white horse. No matter what the comforts of nearby water, he would not be a common man.

Trussed out in his black leather gun-belt so she would see, he would be what he had always been, so prepared for whatever happened he had always been able to see the moment of his own death: the lurking coward, the high-power rifle and the shot from behind, the loud after-crack echoing where the Staked Plains fall off the Cap Rock in west Texas, swallows flushing and turning through the afternoon, deer in thickets by the Brazos lifting their heads after the impact, as the darkness closed and the far away silence began. These last gunless days of searching in this city where even the sound of the last rifle shot would be lost amid the cobbled streets, as he went aimlessly where she might be, that moment of dying seemed closer.

But he would not die dumb and amiable. So he made inquiries. Who was the most evil and wretched man in this town? She would see, he thought, as the great horse cantered on the bricks. He would not be a common man.

There was no worst man, but there was the man rumored to own the worst men. From far above we see the city on the hills in the sunlight of that morning, the water gleaming around the ferry boats, the sidewalk crowds along Market Street and the trolley cars clanging, the square black automobiles and the masked man on his white horse cantering proudly between the stone buildings, up from the Mission and then down Market toward the building where the ferry boats were docking.

The white horse prances and his mane blows in the sea breeze. The masked man stops before a tavern. In through the gleaming clean windows he can see old men and old women lost in the great interior depths. In his steady voice he calls out the worst man in San Francisco, an old Chinese gentleman with a white thin beard and so the story went, hordes of killer functionaries, both white and oriental, some brutal, some cunning. The masked man sits his horse with his hands poised at his guns. At least his old magic will bring down one or two before he goes, even though the deer along the Brazos will never hear of it. But the aged Chinese gentleman comes out alone, wearing a long brocade gown decorated with silver and gold thread, and he holds his hands together before him, as though praying.

"You come in," he says in his quavering voice, gesturing at the masked man.

"You come in with us," he says.

"You shake your hands at your sides," he says, "and you feel the sun on your back, and the great knot will untie itself."

"Feel the warmth," he says, "move your fingers."

"Twist your head on your neck, and feel the cracking as things come loose. Feel the movement of each finger, the warmth of the sun and the coolness of the sea." The Chinese gentleman begins moving his hands up and down at his sides in motions like those of newborn birds, the deep sleeves on his embroidered gown flapping as if he might at any moment fly.

As if his body might at last be doing what it wants with him, the masked man finds his fingers flexing and unlocking and his head slowly turning from one side to the other, lifting and falling as the old small bones begin to crack apart from one another. "Feel the aching in your joints," the Chinese gentleman says.

Like a child out on that street astride his great white horse the masked man knows something has begun. It is important in this old age to risk foolishness. The heavy revolvers at his sides will never again be part of what he is; he feels encumbered by these trappings of greatness, the guns and heavy silver bullets in the stiff leather belt.

"Step down," the Chinese gentleman says, "and accept this present from an old man." From the folds in his gown the Chinese gentleman produces an orange, which he holds as a gift toward the masked man.

"They are the sweetest in all the world," the Chinese gentleman says. "In the south of China they are like fire amid the emerald leaves."

Thus the masked man comes to stand in the cool and cavernous darkness of the tavern with his fingers feeling like feathers, a China Orange before him on the hardwood surface of the bar. The people around him are old and talking as old people will, sometimes gesturing angrily, but talking. A fat old woman with bright red lipstick and a pink flowered dress, who could never have been his sister, rubs at his neck, digging her thumbs between the blades of his shoulders, and there as the masked man listens to the cracking of bones loosening themselves from one another he knows the knot is coming undone, unstringing him from what he has always been, and the guns at his side are a heavy and foolish weight.

"You stay here with us," the Chinese gentleman says.

The masked man lifts his guns from their holsters and places them carefully on the worn mahogany surface of the bar. Alongside them he places a silver bullet, and he orders a drink, a round for the house, for what he calls his friends, and an Irish bartender in a stiff collar sets him up a bottle of whiskey and accepts the silver bullet as payment. The masked man peels off his mask and stands barefaced beside the aged Chinese gentleman and does not feel mutilated as he sips his drink and listens to this society he has joined, the old Finns and the French and Britishers around him talking, the crackling of old men, old women telling of childbirth after raising the drinks he has bought to toast him silently.

"There was a morning . . . " The masked man begins to speak, but no one is paying any special attention, so he peels the soft glowing China Orange, stripping the peel away in a long spool and then separating the sections and aligning them before him on the bar before eating the first one. For him it is over. He will be ancient when the great fires blossom over.Dresden and Japan, after the millions die, and he will not know he should care. Salmon die in turbines and he does not know at all.

But there was a moment when great silence descended. Beyond the Staked Plains and the Cap Rock of west Texas the swallows flushed and turned through the afternoon. Deer in thickets by the Brazos lifted their heads. In our silence amid bulrushes by the river, a girl crouches on her knees with her skirt thrown forward, her flesh so perfectly white under the fresh morning sun. "Don't you stop," she says, and that great white horse rears above the rolling horizon, which is golden and simple in the sunset, sparkling hooves striking out into the green light under dark midsummer thunderclouds, and far away there is rain as the stars grow luminous.

MICHAEL KOCH

*Michael Koch was raised in Philadelphia, Pennsylvania, and educated at LaSalle
University, Wichita State University, and Stanford. He teaches in the Creative
Writing Program at Cornell University.*

"I wrote the first draft of this story in the year before I came to Stanford, and I
put up what was the next-to-last draft in Albert Guerard's workshop during my
Stegner year. At that time I was fascinated (in a way which I now think of as
stupid and wrongheaded) with self-reflective fiction, so reading this, these years
later, I am troubled by the form of the story. But at the risk of being wrong, as
dead wrong as writers often are in discussing their own work, I think something
true abides in the story, something which transcends the form. A cry?"

♦   ♦   ♦

Abyssinia, Abyssinia

THE STORY WHICH IS not here begins with me and a 1955 Royal Portable
typewriter and my grandfather who as a young man half crazy for a Byronic
death once met a lunatic dervish in Abyssinia on the road to Addis Abbaba.
One will not be there without the other: the story, my grandfather, the lunatic,
me. Of course the typewriter is a matter of circumstance, the fixed center of
vortex in which whirl things I know and cannot possibly know, things I suspect
and fear, imagined light, my dead wife, an awful pearl, my daughter, death, the
riot of seasons. These things will have at once everything and nothing to do
with my grandfather's story. Everything and nothing: the distance from Abyssinia in the past to the typewriter in the present, a gossamer of space in time;
the distance from me to you, a perfect lie which is no less the truth.

Listen.

I lean a small square mirror against the desk lamp and a photograph of my
grandfather against the mirror. I want to see around him, look over his shoulder,
see past the facts. I want him to live beyond these black and white shadows, to
take on another life which is also, in a sense, black and white. I watch myself
watching over my grandfather's shoulder.

In a garden in Philadelphia on the edge of the city, I took this photograph.
My grandfather is sitting under a pear tree, before a nondescript audience,
winking at the camera with his right palm outstretched. I peer into his eye and
try to remember what he is saying. I know he is telling the story of the lunatic
for it was this photograph which prompted me to write my grandfather's story.
But what is he saying?

I remember this: In the summer of 1932, deep in the glare and dust of Abyssinia, my grandfather met a lunatic on the road to Addis Abbaba. My grandfather was riding a horse which was either white, black, brown, or gold, depending on whom you believe—my mother, my grandmother, or my father, who cannot decide between the last two colors. To my knowledge, my grandfather never specified the color. He would say only that he was on horseback and the dervish came trotting through the dust. "You could tell the man was a lunatic straightaway," grandfather would recall, and befuddling his listeners (for we are a family of storytellers), he would leave it at that. Leave it at that and then produce the pearl from his vest pocket.

The pearl, a grainy mongoloid, he rolls marble-big between his thumb and index finger, revealing in panes of breathless violet, aquamarine, and lumpy rose, the thing, a platonic nightmare, ". . . stuck," he tells this drooling, itching crowd, eager to get hands on the freak, "in my right nostril as I bent down to listen to the damned idiot's story." Mesmerized by the promise of a story, of queer revelations on the thick breath of insanity, they watch as he rolls the awful pearl into his palm, works it about and out onto his thumbnail, flicks it into the air where it turns, rolls up-air, coruscate with sweat to, just, kiss the milky puckered blossoms of the pear tree.

Across the wave of upturned faces, my grandfather's hazel eyes glisten. He winks at me, for I do not follow the tumbling pearl, am on to the old magician, the sleight of hand, the distractions. He winks. I snap the picture and in the instant whorl of the shutter his eye becomes

the eye of my dead wife looking back at me from a mirror, the eye which only recently I've come to see is not hazel but green and darting with drug madness. "I've decided," she says, "that I can fly." I am not surprised to hear this because we are living in California and it is 1968 and endlessly here, it seems, people attempt flight. But I believe she is only jabbering, drugs and jabber. Now, beaded fresh from the shower, my wife rolls a rough lilac towel about her breasts. On one the tattoo of a splayed, yellow butterfly is alight on the wine-ruddy circle of a pearl-white tipped nipple. Miniature, perfect in memory, in fact until the sag of flesh, till a certain drug-charged, electric, gay tumble from a rooftop, the insect hovers over that sweet bud, strange honeyed flower forever as my grandfather's pearl endlessly kisses the buds of a pear tree in a garden in Philadelphia.

You see, I have known lunatics too. But I am wandering. What else can I tell you?

This desk is set under a window in my grandfather's study. From where I sit, I can see the pear tree in the garden, nude now in winter, like the skeleton of a monstrous crystal flower—yesterday we had an ice storm. The branches clack and tinkle on driving wind. The sun is at the ice and a thousand, thousand lights wink rose and violet, white hot, lavender and gold: a tree of light. Good. For I must have light for my grandfather's story. I must think of the strange and wonderful light of Abyssinia in 1932.

I have read *Waugh in Abyssinia*. I have looked at photographs and picture books. I have committed to memory the names and descriptions of twenty-five trees and shrubs native to the country. I know the animals of Abyssinia and how they slouch in summer. I have read cruel tales and legends and know the figures of Abyssinian myth. I know of the Abyssinian religions and how a man might lose his soul. These things sigh in my mind like wind in the lion grass. But I will not tell you about them now. That is for the story which is not here.

So what can I tell you?

Behind me on the wall is another photograph, black and white, in a black frame. Perhaps it's the yellowing of the snapshot, a color of grease, or the clothing, antique and for a world I've never known; perhaps it's the young face of my grandfather, lit with the hope and toothy confidence and swagger of a white man in a black country in 1932; perhaps it's the memory of the fights this photograph has caused—the terrible screeching fights of lovers, my grandparents, the liquor fights which galloped, nightmares, through my childhood dreams; perhaps it's the weight this photograph assumes: the innuendo, the sad puzzle, the sum of sullen ruin, the blank years in another country (for this is the only surviving photograph of my grandfather's youth, he having chosen to burn them all and create a past of words, of stories); perhaps it's the knowledge that my story will spread feathery spider roots deep into this photograph so that its texture will change for me, and so I find this photograph hard to contemplate for I'll destroy a kind of life creating my grandfather's story. I'll destroy that mystery which my grandfather so carefully made.

You ask, what could this photograph be? I will tell you for I can see it clearly in this mirror. The photograph is on the wall behind me, so looking over my grandfather's head in the garden in Philadelphia, looking over my own left shoulder, I can see my young grandfather, hale, smiling, in the peach light of Abyssinia. You say, but the photograph is black and white. Trust me. I know this light. I am telling you the truth. But I will tell you only this (the rest is for the other story): he is holding the hand of an Abyssinian princess. They are garlanded with flowers of a Rembrandt gold which are wilting in the heat so that the petals, clinging to their damp bodies, leave a dust of gold. Later they will retire to an alabaster room and in the cool evening, while monkeys scamp and chatter on the balcony, press this golden dust into each other, my grandfather pressing deep into the walnut skin of his princess, her hyacinth robes in a heap, her diamonds scattered like the tears of one of her gods about the marble floor. But that is later. Now her chin is raised, and the sun glints on her golden jewelry, cupping her face in a soft yellow corona. Her mouth parts and the tip of her tongue worries the edge of her teeth as a dove splashes in air at the end of her outstretched fingers, and she blinks just as the camera clicks. It is as if, having lived this moment, she could not bear to look back this way at my grandfather, old, spinning tales in a garden in Philadelphia, my grandfather waiting for a pearl to drop from a pear tree.

Is that all? No. There is one more thing I must tell you. I have been hesitant until now. No. I have avoided it on purpose, refused to face it, but now I must. I can't begin my grandfather's story until I do. It is horrible and concerns my daughter. No. It really concerns me.

As I sit staring into this mirror, over the shoulder of my old grandfather at my young grandfather and his princess who stare back at me and out this window before me, I see reflected in the glass covering the photograph on the wall, shimmering in the white light which dances to the beat of the wind on the window, I see my daughter stomping across the garden, carrying a cat like a sack, to stand under the pear tree. This is a fairy world she moves in: scudding light on glass, a spume of what is real. I can with the subtlest slip of focus see past her into Abyssinia, into this same garden in spring, into my grandfather's eyes, into the day he died, my grandfather, stock and still as a stump, a cat glossing his corduroy trousers, he nods and sputters and slumps, and his toes take root, his hair goes wild to weeds, a vine turns up his arm, a bluejay nests in his hat, a bee drunk on rotten pears lodges in his ear, snapdragons and marigolds take seed in his pores, his heart explodes in a shower of dew, his lap is a birdbath, his teeth roses, his ears butterflies

butterflies

But I am wandering because I don't want to face the problem of my daughter. She is in the garden, singing. I can't hear her, but I can see in these reflections her mouth moving as she rocks her cat. Soon she will turn this way and I will strain in these mirrors to find in her eyes something of the madness she might have suckled at her mother's breast. For years I have been avoiding this, since that night in California my poor crazy wife pitched into space from a rooftop. But I can no longer avoid it; my grandfather's story has forced me against it.

I swear I could not live if I saw madness in the eyes of my daughter, but I must tell you—and you are the only one I will ever tell—if I saw it there, despite my fury and horror, there is a part of me that would record it. I can't help myself. I know you think me a monster, but I am not. Believe me. If I saw madness in the eyes of my daughter, my world would wheel in rage. I would smash these mirrors and slash my skin. I would howl in a way that would send your soul weeping from your body.

But listen. All the while there is a part of me that would make note of the temper of her eyes, the crazy color, the flaming, aqueous eyes straining in her sweet face; and then a pearl would drop from a pear tree into the hand of my dead grandfather; my crazy wife would take to air; a dove would alight on the hand of a princess of Abyssinia; and a part of me would begin to compose, to fall back forty-seven years into a summer day in Abyssinia, to shape words, to tell you exactly what it is my grandfather sees in the eyes of a dervish who comes trotting through the dust of the story which is not here.

PAUL LAKE

I'm a native of Maryland, born in 1951 in Baltimore, and I came to Stanford on a Mirrielees Fellowship in 1977. After completing my master's degree, I taught for two years as an adjunct lecturer at the University of Santa Clara, and I am currently an associate professor at Arkansas Tech University. The University of Chicago Press published my first full-length poetry collection, Another Kind of Travel, *in 1988.*

"The time I spent at Stanford had an important, perhaps a decisive, impact on the way I write poems. The seriousness with which our writing was treated and the strong tradition of poetry writing there could not but improve us as poets. I always wanted to thank the University and the fine teachers I had for the fellowship that enabled me to get my master's degree. Now seems as good a time as any. Thanks."

Introduction to Poetry

She comes in late, then settles like a sigh
On the first day, returning every week
Promptly at ten, each Monday Wednesday Friday,
To study Shakespeare, Jonson, Donne, and Blake;

Enters the room to an approving murmur,
Straightens her dress, then, brushing back her hair,
Arches her body with the slightest tremor,
And sits, while the room grows breathless, in her chair;

Sits for an hour, while busy sophomores worry
Each turgid line, a Botticellian smile
On her rapt face, who's learned how little study
Love involves; who, walking down the aisle,

Knows in her bones how little poetry
Words breathe, and how—on turning to go home—
All eyes will watch her rise above her "C"
And walk off, like a goddess on the foam.

◆   ◆   ◆

The Boat

Sit down a minute. The roast is in the oven
And it will be an hour before the men
Come clattering and banging up the driveway
Loud with their talk of this year's ten-point buck
That tiptoed past their stands, just out of range.
You've done your best. . . . I guess you've been too patient. . . .
I'll do the talking now to hurry things—
Though what it is I hardly dare tell you,
Much less my Bill, who thinks my life began
When our two met, and runs beside his now,
Like tractor tires, that's how he'd likely say.
Best to begin by saying it right out:
My recent "troubles," as some would have them called,
They're . . .
        nothing I can name. . . .
                        I want to say
"A man I used to love," but when I hear it,
I only think that, if I met him now,
He'd seem a boy, about my Cindy's age
Or older—tanned, with short brown hair combed back
Under his hat—a wide-brimmed Panama
With a red band, that made me laugh so hard
When I saw it that he had to laugh himself—
A quiet, shy, intellectual Yankee boy
From Harvard, no less, here in Arkansas!
You look at me now and find it hard to imagine,
But I was younger then, and not so shy
That when we asked to use my Daddy's boat
He cocked his eye and thought before answering.
(It had a cabin small as a doll's house
And a child-sized bunk. . . . But we were children then.)
I wish now, when I wish for anything,
To have spent that day, instead, without the sailing.
But there are no insteads. I've learned that much
From piling one instead on top another,
Thinking how that day might have turned out different
If Jack, at our first thought of turning back,
Hadn't brushed his hand so lightly against my thigh
And left it there. . . .
                Or when the boat blew over
And righted again, not fifty yards from shore,
We'd swum the distance home and then gone back
With an outboard and a rope.

                    Instead, we giggled.
I kicked my shoes off. Jack just smiled and smiled
And treaded water. Then I stripped my pants
And laughed, "Come on, you Yankee Puritan,
Get those clothes off. . . . You can keep the hat,"
And teased him till he got behind the mast
And flutter-kicked while I tugged from a rope
On the bowsprit. We pulled and kicked and pulled—
You could see the boat's deck three feet under water—
And paddled slowly toward the nearest shore,
Which seemed so close, at first, then seemed so distant.
We heard the people talking on the sand,
But refused their help, urging each other on
With jokes until our breath grew short. Then Jack,
Seeing a block of wood bob to the surface
From down below, reached out to haul it in
And let go of the mast.

                    The boat kept moving
Faster than I'd have guessed. When I looked back,
Jack smiled at me that tight-lipped Yankee smile—
Too nervous or shy or tired to ask for help—
And disappeared. I called, "Stop teasing, Jack,"
Smiling myself—then growing desperate,
Swam to where he went down and tried to dive. . . .

He'd left his wet clothes on. I've tried to think
How he could smile, feeling himself go under—
But what can thinking mend? He's drowned. I'm here.
And there, our husbands clattering down the road
With the tailgate down and hungry for their supper
Will expect loud talk and smiles on their return;
Our children, like a barefoot, screaming tribe,
Will run to greet the truck, and everyone,
Not knowing by what misses we're brought here
Instead of somewhere else, or not at all,
Won't sense the lives they've missed, while I feel mine
Always below me, like a sunken deck,
Hauling its nightmare tonnage of dark water.

DEBORAH LARSEN

*Deborah Larsen taught at the university level for several years before holding the Stegner Fellowship in poetry at Stanford in 1987–88. In May of 1988, she won the New York "Discovery"/*The Nation *award. Her work has appeared in such places as* Western Humanities Review, Oxford Magazine, The Gettysburg Review, *and* The Nation. *She has recorded poetry for BBC Radio 3, London.*

"The year of the Fellowship, 1987–88, I continue writing poems based on Matteo Ricci's record of his entrance into sixteenth-century China. My original hope was that this narrative of the meeting of eastern and western scientific, artistic, and religious traditions would reveal the beginnings of the mystics (I echo Edward Schillebeeckx but use his terms more loosely), becoming more prophetic and the critic-prophets becoming more mystical. But then, here in the program, I am reminded by grave and kind persons that I am still on the road. What really might have gone on, in quiet, there? Or here."

Stitching Porcelain

You yield every species of grain—barley,
millet, winter wheat. You yield rice, figs,
oil of sesame, beef, lamb, goat meat,
hens, ducks, and geese. You do not yield olives
nor almonds: I do not wish for almonds
nor olives. You yield countless horses,
unshod, and no match for the Tartars':
my desire was never to fight the Tartars.
The Yangzi and Yellow Rivers are dense
with your fishes: I lie shuddering with them
at night, dark gill to gill. Though you yield
no lions nor elephants, I once caught sight
in a court in Beijing, of an elephant you had imported.
Your porcelain is so fine, so thin,
a brass wire can repair it
to hold liquids without any leakage.
Once I saw you beneath the bamboo
of a thousand facets—slim sticks,
nodes, and joints—bent back
from the world, stitching porcelain.

I write you a letter of praise
on your own fine cotton paper. I inscribe
all its fibers. My pleasure is in your tea,
your rhubarb, your lacquer, your ginger; I lie
down at the base of your cedar, your tree of mourning.
Here is a candle, rare wax, from the worms you breed
in these trees: its light falls
on hooves that never knew iron,
on no olives nor almonds,
on no indigenous elephants.

◆   ◆   ◆

A Captain in His Pride: 1578

When I was titled Captain and went down to the sea,
to the port of Lisbon to muster my fine sailors,
those of our Portuguese navy, the finest on the waters,
the bells of the Church of the Wounds of Christ
began to toll, there was a parade in my name,
there were jugglers, long silk flags, flotillas
glittering for my pleasure in the sun.
        And when I drew close to that same sea,
so close I saw the ropes bundling firm the planks
of my carrack's stern, my fine sailors
proved tailors, cobblers, lackeys, ploughmen,
new recruits from the countryside, and I in my
pride, then, had to teach them
port from starboard by tying great heads of garlic
on one side of the *Jesus* and long strings of onion on the other.
                And after I put out to that same sea,
it was then I was blown backward two days' running
off the Cape of Storms, it was then the green timbers
gave up their nails, then that the keel wood
split and the astrolabes stuck, then that all our bile
turned the shadowed decks slick and shining and I became captain.

PHILIP LEVINE

Born 1928, Detroit. Began writing poetry at fourteen but gave it up at sixteen. Discovered the moderns at Wayne University and began again with more determination and less fun. Still at it. Have published thirteen books of poetry, including Selected Poems *(Atheneum, 1981) and most recently* A Walk With Tom Jefferson *(Knopf, 1988). National Book Critics Award for* Ashes *and* 7 Years From Somewhere, *American Book Award for* Ashes, Lenore Marshall Award for* The Names of the Lost. *In 1987 received the Ruth Lilly Award from* Poetry *and the American Council for the Arts "in recognition of outstanding poetic achievement."*

"My coming to Stanford was my coming west for the first time, and it had its elements of magic and pain, some of which I've tried to capture in the poem '28,' which I wrote when it suddenly occurred to me that I was the same age Yvor Winters was when he was my teacher. I will forever be indebted to Arthur and Janet for their kindnesses to me and my family during poor times and for introducing us to the most amazing woman we ever met, Marie Louise Koenig."

◆   ◆   ◆

28

At 28 I was still faithless.
I had crossed the country in a green Ford,
sleeping one night almost 14 hours in a motel
above Salt Lake City. I discovered
I'd had a fever all that day and thus the animals
that dotted the road, the small black spots
that formed and unformed crows, the flying pieces
of slate that threatened to break through
the windshield . . . were whatever they were.
I took two aspirins and an allergy pill—that was all
I had—and got into bed although it was light out.
That was 28 years ago. Since then I have died
only twice, once in slow motion against
the steel blue driver's side of a Plymouth
station wagon. One moment before impact I said
to myself, seriously, "This is going to hurt."
The kids in the Plymouth's back seat gaped
wildly, shouted, leaped, and the father held firm

to the steering wheel as I slipped through the space
that was theirs, untouched, skidding first
on the black field of asphalt and broken glass
that is California 168, Tollhouse Road, and over
the edge of the mountain, the motorcycle
tumbling off on its own through nettles and grass
to come to a broken rest as all bodies must.
Often when I shave before a late dinner, especially
on summer evenings, I notice the white lines
on my right shoulder like the smeared imprint
of a leaf on silk or the delicate tracings
on a whale's fins that the smaller sea animals carve
to test his virtue, and I reenter the wide blue eyes
of that family of five that passed on their way
up the mountain.
                    But at 28 I was still faithless.
I could rise before dawn from a bed drenched
with my own sweat, repack the green Ford
in the dark, my own breath steaming
in the high, clear air, and head for California.
I could spend the next night in Squaw Valley
writing a letter to my wife and kids asleep hours
behind me in Colorado, I could listen to Rexroth
reminiscing on a Berkeley FM station in the voice
God uses to lecture Jesus Christ and still believe
two aspirins, an allergy pill, and proper rest were proof
against the cold that leaps in one blind moment
from the heart to the farthest shore to shudder
through the small sea creatures I never knew existed.

It seems the sun passing back and forth behind clouds
this morning threatens to withdraw its affections
and the sky is as distant and pale as a bored child
in the wrong classroom or a man of 28
drilled so often on the names of fruit-bearing trees
that he forgets even the date palm. Here in New England,
no longer new or English, the first frost
has stained the elms and maples outside my window,
and the kids on their way hunch their shoulders
against the cold. One boy drops his lunch box
with a clatter and mysteriously leaves it there
on the pavement as a subtle rebuke
to his mother, to a father holding tight to a wheel,
to a blue Plymouth that long ago entered the heaven
brooding above Detroit. If only they had stopped
all those years ago and become a family of five
descending one after the other the stone ledges
of Sweet Potato Mountain and found me face down

among the thistles and shale and lifted me to my feet.
I weighed no more than feathers do or the wish
to become pure spirit. If I had not broken my glasses
I could have gone on my way with a thank you,
with a gap-toothed smile.
                              28 years ago, faithless, I
found the great bay of San Francisco where the map
said it would be and crossed the bridge from Oakland
singing, "I Cover the Waterfront" into the cold winds
and the dense odor of coffee. Before I settled
in East Palo Alto among divorcees and appliance salesmen,
fifty yards from the Union Pacific tracks, I spent a long weekend
with Arthur, my mentor to be. In a voice ruined, he said,
by all-night draughts of whiskey and coffee, he praised
the nobility of his lemon and orange trees, the tang
of his loquats, the archaic power of his figs.
In a gambler's green visor and stiff Levis, he bowed
to his wounded tomatoes swelling into late summer.
Kneeling in the parched loam by the high fence
he bared the elusive strawberries, his blunt fingers
working the stiff leaves over and over. It was August.
He was almost happy.
                              Faithless, I had not found
the olive trees bursting on the hillsides west
of US 99. I knew only the bitter black fruit
that clings with all its life to the hard seed.
I had not wakened to mockers wrangling in my yard
at dawn in a riot of sexual splendor or heard
the sea roar at Bondy Bay, the long fingers
of ocean running underneath the house all night
to rinse off the pain of nightmare. I had not
seen my final child, though he was on the way.
I had not become a family of five nor opened
my arms to receive the black gifts of a mountain road,
of ground cinders, pebbles, rough grass.
                              At twice my age
Arthur, too, was faithless, or so he insisted
through the long sober evenings in Los Altos, once
crowded with the cries of coyotes. His face
darkened and his fists shook when he spoke
of Nothing, what he would become in that waiting blaze
of final cold, a whiteness like no other.
At 56, more scared of me than I of him,
his right forefinger raised to keep the beat,
he gravelled out his two great gifts of truth:
"I'd rather die than reread the last novels
of Henry James," and, "Philip, we must never lie
or we shall lose our souls." All one winter afternoon

he chanted in Breton French the coarse poems of Tristan Corbière,
his voice reaching into unforeseen sweetness, both hands
rising toward the ceiling, the tears held back so long
still held back, for he was dying and he was ready.

By April I had crossed the Pacheco Pass and found
roosting in the dark branches of the Joshua tree
the fabled magpie—"Had a long tongue and a long tail;
He could both talk and do—"—. This is a holy land,
I thought. At a Sonoco station the attendant,
wiry and dour, said in perfect Okie, "Be careful, son,
a whole family was wiped out right here
just yesterday." At Berenda the fields flooded
for miles in every direction. Arthur's blank sky
stared down at an unruffled inland sea and threatened
to let go. On the way home I cut lilacs
from the divider strip of El Camino Real.
My wife was pregnant. All night we hugged
each other in our narrow bed as the rain
came on in sheets. A family of five, and all
of us were out of work. The dawn was silent.
The black roses, battered, unclenched, the burned petals
floated on the pond beside the playhouse.
Beneath the surface the tiny stunned pike circled
no prey we could see. That was not another life.
I was 29 now and faithless, not the father of the man
I am but the same man who all this day
sat in a still house watching the low clouds massing
in the west, the new winds coming on.
By late afternoon the kids are home from school,
clambering on my front porch, though day
after day I beg them not to. When I go
to the window they race off in mock horror,
daring me to follow. The huge crows that wake
me every morning settle back on the rain spout
next door to caw to the season. I could put them
all in a poem, title it "The Basket of Memory"
as though each image were an Easter egg waiting to hatch,
as though I understood the present and the past
or even why the 8 year old with a cap of blond hair
falling to her shoulders waves to me as she darts
between parked cars and cartwheels into the early dusk.

RALPH LOMBREGLIA

Ralph Lombreglia was a Wallace Stegner Fellow at Stanford in 1982–83. Several of his recent short stories have appeared in The Atlantic *and in* The Best American Short Stories *for 1987 and 1988. The recipient of writing fellowships from the National Endowment for the Arts and the New York Foundation for the Arts, he recently finished a first novel and is now completing a collection of stories.*

"Every former Stegner Fellow yearns to return to Palo Alto and do it again, and I'm no exception. It was an exhilarating experience, a pivotal year in my life. John L'Heureux and the other fine faculty created a perfect environment for making the passage from apprentice to journeyman writer. And I met some wonderful people who remain dear friends. There's no writing program on earth like the one at Stanford University; may it always flourish."

◆   ◆   ◆

Citizens

HALFWAY UP THE HILL, Jesse sat down in the mud and started to cry. Mark picked him up and pointed him toward the top, where the green crest of the hill met the open blue sky. Jesse had been willing to climb up there before, but now he wasn't. He kept letting his legs buckle beneath him, forcing Mark to hold him up by his underarms. They were standing on the slope this way when Mark felt a tremor run through the ground and the air. Before he could realize what it was, one of the Army helicopters bounced up into the sky from behind the other side of the hill. The sudden huge appearance of it frightened him—he could feel his heart chopping just like the aircraft. He expected Jesse to become hysterical as the thing went roaring over their heads, but the spectacle of the helicopter and the pulsing concussion of its sound seemed to erase everything in Jesse's mind—he gaped blankly at the flying machine, tracking it with his eyes as it whizzed away. Mark was sure the men up there were taking pictures of them with telephoto lenses. He considered giving them the finger, then he thought better of it. He put Jesse over his shoulder and struggled up the wet, grassy slope. Jesse was five years old now, and he wasn't light.

At the top, Mark spread out their blanket and sat Jesse down on it. Then he strolled along the ridge, looking out over the land that couldn't be seen from the park below—the colorful geometry of farms and vineyards to the west, and to the east the vast, uniform tract of the Army depot. It was beautiful country, and on that account he was sorry to be leaving it. But then again these fine vistas weren't part of life down where he lived, somewhere out there to the north. Jesse started to cry again; his diaper needed changing. Mark slipped out of his backpack and rummaged in it for one of the extra Pampers. Then he had the amusing thought of a surveillance photograph of his son's dirty diaper, and he decided to wait for one of the choppers to come around again.

He sat on the blanket next to Jesse and looked into the grassy valley where they'd been, a natural amphitheater defined by a range of hills and a lake. An enormous mass of people covered the floor of the valley in front of a large stage erected at the foot of one of the hills. Earlier, Mark had listened to the news on Linda's headphone radio; the Army estimated the crowd at ten thousand. From up on the hill it was obvious that at least twice that many people were actually there. Mark could hear the thin, distant sound of the rock band that was performing onstage at the moment.

Linda was still down there somewhere. She'd wanted to wander around in the crowd awhile before meeting up for lunch. Mark got his binoculars from the backpack and began to look along the lines of media vehicles and propaganda tables near the access roads to the park. People were selling food and drink at some of the tables, and T-shirts printed with stop-the-missiles slogans and designs. The Hare Krishnas were on hand, wending their way single-file through the protestors, chanting and praying. They were easy to spot in their saffron robes. Mark was too far away to make out the features of faces, but he soon recognized Linda—not so much by her white pants and pink sweatshirt, he realized, as by the way she carried herself. Something about Linda's presence made her leap out of a crowd for him, even at this distance. But that had more to do with familiarity, Mark thought, than with some unusual attraction; it wasn't necessarily a sign that they were meant for each other. Linda was talking to a bearded man behind a socialist literature table, gesturing with her hands the way she did when she was trying to express her most heartfelt idea about something. Her American flag was fluttering on its stick from the pocket of her painter's pants.

Mark had one of the flags, too, planted in the ground next to the blanket; more than half the people down there had them. They'd been given out free at the entrance to the park, each one with a slip of paper stapled to the wooden dowel that read, *Let's take back the flag!* Tonight's television coverage of the rally would show an ocean of nuclear protestors waving American flags. When Mark first took part in events like this—the anti-war demonstrations that were going full blast when he got out of the Army and went back to school—the organizers weren't so sophisticated. Something about the new sophistication saddened Mark, but he understood the strength and smartness of it, the necessity to think strategically if you wanted to survive.

He was glad he'd brought Jesse along. When the maniacs destroyed the world, it would have the same effect on Jesse as on everyone else. Jesse would never know that, but that was another good reason for his being here—in his frailty and obliviousness Jesse was just like most citizens of his country, as much like them as he'd ever be. Mark knew that some people would see a boy like Jesse on the TV news tonight and think of him only as further proof that something was wrong with the protestors. But other people might see him and understand.

Mark put down the binoculars. Jesse had crawled off the blanket and was eating a handful of mud and grass. He looked up and laughed when he heard his father call his name. Then he threw the mud and grass onto the blanket and clapped his hands. Mark shook the blanket clean and put Jesse back on it. He wiped out Jesse's mouth with a paper towel. Then he noticed two Army helicopters vectoring his way from different directions, and he smiled and began unbuttoning Jesse's pants.

Linda sat down on the blanket and stuck her American flag in the ground next to Mark's. She called Jesse's name and shook one of his feet. He liked that, and waved his arms at her. Mark was sitting with his back to Linda, one of his legs thrown over Jesse's middle to keep him from running away. He was using the binoculars to look at the Army depot across the highway where the latest missiles were supposed to be stored, the ones that could practically turn a corner on a city street or fly into a living room window.

"I'm back," Linda said.

"I saw you coming," Mark said.

"Can you see anything over there?" Linda asked. "Can you see any of the rockets?"

Mark looked at her over his shoulder. Then he went back to the binoculars. "You must be kidding," he said. "Do you really think they just leave them lying around in plain view like Tinker Toys or something?"

"I thought maybe with the binoculars you could see them," Linda said. "Some people down there are saying that they're not really keeping them here, that the Army just wants us to think they're here."

"They're here," Mark said.

"Well, if you can't see them, what are you looking at?"

"I'm looking at a guard in a watchtower. I think he's looking at me. Be a good soldier, boy. Pace back and forth real nice like they taught you."

"I got you a Nuclear Freeze button," Linda said.

"Great," Mark said.

"I brought back some pamphlets, too. There's one put out by the vets. It has some stuff in it about Agent Orange."

"Terrific," Mark said.

Linda said, "After you left I thought I saw Sarah and Phil. But it turned out to be somebody else."

Mark dropped the binoculars and let them swing from the strap around his neck. Then he twisted himself around until he was facing her. Sarah was Jesse's mother.

"Linda," he said, "why do you have to invent things just to have something to say? You know they're not here. You know they wouldn't come to something like this."

"I'm not inventing anything," Linda said. "For a minute I thought I saw them, that's all. When I thought it was them, I thought how funny it would be if they were here."

"It wouldn't be funny," Mark said.

"O.K., Mark," Linda said.

Jesse lived with Sarah and her second husband, Phil. For a long time after his divorce, Mark didn't see his son. Then when he and Linda moved in together about a year ago, they started keeping Jesse every other weekend. This wasn't one of their regular weekends, but Mark wanted to spend an extra day with him. When he called Sarah to arrange it, she'd made passing mention of the big anti-missiles demonstration and then waited to see what Mark would say. Since she wasn't honest enough to come right out and ask him if he planned to go, Mark pretended not to be interested in the rally. Sarah would have objected to his bringing Jesse.

In two weeks, Sarah was putting Jesse into a home. A week after that, Mark was moving away. He'd sworn never to let his son go into one of those places, and he tried to take custody when Sarah said she couldn't care for Jesse at home anymore. At the custody hearing, the woman from the state agency flustered Mark with harsh questions and statements about Jesse and himself. The woman had had plenty of poison poured in her ears, and she made Mark's declarations of love and duty seem petty and dishonest. The woman said that Mark was still trying to blame Sarah for the way Jesse was, that he was trying to punish her by fighting for the baby, that he really wasn't the kind of man prepared to sacrifice his life to a boy like Jesse. Mark turned to his ex-wife and denied these things to her face, but Sarah only looked away. Then the woman from the state went down her list of hard facts—that Mark wasn't married to the girl he was living with, that there was no evidence of regular advancement in his job, that he frequented bars, that last year he'd been stopped once for drunk driving.

When the hearing was over, Mark felt as though he'd had his insides stolen out of him. Driving home, he saw the whole town as a sad cartoon, a place people only imagined themselves to be living. He hadn't really been alive here all these years. He pulled up in front of his apartment building and it looked like something from a movie set.

He had a friend from Army electronics school who worked for Motorola in Phoenix. Ever since the service, the friend had been raving to Mark about the sun belt, about the wonderfully different life people lived down there. The friend had always said that Mark could walk right into something good at Motorola. By the time Mark climbed the stairs to his apartment that day, he'd moved to Arizona in his mind.

Linda was going to Phoenix with him. They'd both simply assumed she would go, and it had been a great relief to have something not be a struggle. Their simple assumption had felt like cool water percolating up through jagged rocks, clear evidence of hope and goodness. But now—sitting on top of a hill where he could see for miles in any direction, twenty thousand people below him trying to change history and his son next to him on a blanket not knowing who he was—Mark saw that assumptions were evidence only of weakness and fear. He felt encrusted with them. He wasn't sure anymore that Linda should go to Phoenix with him, that he had any business walking into the future with this particular woman. He could almost feel all the assumptions he'd ever made clinging inside him like deposits inside arteries and veins. They were the bad residue of the past, the thing that killed you. He wanted to scrape all the assumptions out of his life.

He turned to Linda and began to speak to her about it. He wanted to express himself carefully, but he ended up blurting it all out in a few sentences that sounded bad. When he finished, Linda just sat there on the blanket a while without saying anything. Then she unpacked their lunch from Mark's backpack and gave Jesse a peanut butter and jelly sandwich. He chortled and ripped the sandwich to pieces and then began squishing one of the pieces between his hands.

"As if I didn't have plenty of doubts myself," Linda said finally.

"I didn't know that," Mark said.

"Well now you know," she said. "It all scares me just as much as it scares you. It just doesn't scare me as much as that." She pointed in the direction of the Army depot. "Perspective," she said bitterly, and then she began to cry.

"Perspective," Mark said, nodding his head.

Linda pulled the lid off a yogurt container. "If you want to back out," she said, "you can back out."

"Some kind of mood has settled on me," Mark said. "I can't think until I shake it off."

"Oh, well you just take your time," Linda said. "But do you think you'll be able to shake it off before we load the U-Haul and drive away? Do you think you could make up your mind before then? Just as a courtesy?"

"That's not fair," Mark said. "You're not trying to understand."

"I'm not?" Linda said. "I've given my notice at work, I've packed all my books and half my clothes. Five minutes ago I was moving to Phoenix. I've never even been to Phoenix." She dropped the open yogurt container on the blanket and put her face in her hands. "Jesus Christ," she said.

"I'm sorry," Mark said. "I need to get out from under this mood."

"You just let me know when you do, Mark," Linda said.

Mark scooted across the blanket and put his arm around Linda's shoulders. He kissed her and then he put the side of his head next to hers, the way people do in wedding portraits or Calypso dance routines. He turned the binoculars around backwards and put one big lens to Linda's eye, one to his. At the end of a long dark tunnel, Mark could see his tiny son. Jesse had Linda's yogurt in his hands. He was scooping the plain white yogurt out of the container and dropping it onto the blanket. When all the yogurt was out, he started eating the blueberry preserves from the bottom.

"See that?" Mark said. "See what he's doing? He knows the good stuff's at the bottom."

"He's always known that," Linda said. "That's not new. Blueberry's his favorite. Hey, blueberry boy," she called out to him as if across a mountain pass, but Jesse didn't pay any attention.

Down in the park, the music had stopped and now a man was at the microphone speaking out against nuclear war. Mark and Linda could hear something like the ghosts of his words, but most of what he actually said was lost in the big open sky. They took their heads away from the binoculars and listened to the man anyway.

"Rhetoric," Mark said after some time. "All completely true, all necessary to say again and again. But hey, mister, tell me something I don't already know."

Linda got up and cleaned the yogurt off the blanket.

"I'm tired," she said. "I feel sick, too. I'm going to take a nap."

"We never had lunch," Mark said. "You'll feel better if you have lunch."

"I'm not hungry. You go ahead and eat. Just wake me up when the bands start playing again."

"Maybe we should just go home," Mark said. "I feel like going home."

"Not me," Linda said. "I like it here. I want to listen to the music and dance for peace with my fellow citizens. That's what I came here to do. That's how Jesse and me are going to save the world. Right, Jesse?"

Jesse was lying on his side on the blanket with one of his arms thrown over his head.

"I'm taking him home," Mark said.

"He's happy here," Linda said. "He wants to stay right here with me."

"That's ridiculous, Linda. He doesn't know where he is. He doesn't even know who you are."

"He knows more than you think," Linda said. "You treat him like he doesn't know anything, but he knows plenty. He knows what we're talking about right now. You've been treating him wrong."

"Don't you ever say that," Mark said. "That's a lie."

"It's true," Linda said. "Isn't it, Jesse?" She stretched out on the blanket next to Jesse and took him in her arms. "Let's snuggle up for a nap, baby boy," she said, "and then we can go dancing later."

Mark got up onto his hands and knees. "You'd actually turn my own son against me," he said. "Well, I'm not letting you do that. Jesse, listen to me. This is your father speaking. Maybe I've been wrong. Maybe I should have tried to explain some things to you before this. I didn't want things to be this way. There's another whole side to this story. I want you to listen to me now."

He pulled Jesse from Linda's arms and rolled him on his back to get his full attention. But Jesse had already fallen sound asleep on his own—blueberry preserves smeared all over his face, his hand stuck inside the yogurt container as though muffling the clapper of a bell.

D. R. MACDONALD

D. R. MacDonald was born on Boularderie Island, Cape Breton, Nova Scotia. He lived most of his youth in Ohio. His fiction has appeared in such magazines as The Sewanee Review, Epoch, *and* TriQuarterly. *He has received an award from the National Endowment for the Arts and The Editors' Book Award from Pushcart Press, which published his collection of stories,* Eyestone, *in 1988.*

"One concern of my stories is often that tie to what we come out of, to what shapes so much of us—family and place. If the place is definite and your family has a definite place in it, the tie, slender though it might become, is affixed to your heart and can extend great distances."

◆　　◆　　◆

Sailing

I TELL MY FATHER to watch his step. He is ascending the small deck that leads to the wooden tub of hot water. He is nearly eighty and it is dark here under the long redwood branches. "If I can't climb this, I'd better turn in my ticket," he says. He was a seaman on the Great Lakes for forty-one years, as long as I have been living. His ticket is his masters papers. A wet February wind gusts through the limbs above us and I think of all the weather he has had in his face, the storms and the ice.

He hisses at the heat, but with a deep sigh settles slowly into the water where I am sitting. He knows he will die soon. It's the soonness I wonder about, what that knowledge does to his mind. His future is waking one morning at a time. I want to ask him about this but we have no tradition of such asking. He knows that somewhere a cold, dark wave has been rising and that it will arrive probably by night and sweep him away.

"More rain coming," he says. "It won't last." He reads the weather easily. We had a storm recently that broke up a string of days he considered weatherless, a picture book of sun and blue sky. He believes, I think, there is a connection between such days and the way I live, with no course, no destination. He was amused at how people on the street looked harried, as if the storm were not a natural occurrence. By nightfall there was heavy wind and rain. Great wooshes rose up through the trees and some came down, their roots not used to such buffeting. My father paced the living room. "Look at that!" he'd say, his grin lit by lightning. The power went out. We played pinochle with two ten-cent candles burning between us while a half-cooked chicken sweated grease in the oven. "People around here never think about disaster," he said, not smugly, but just to let me know he knew the truth.

I too sailed on the Lakes. That was the closest my father and I have ever been, those years I worked my way through college decking and coalpassing on the big ore freighters. We were not such strangers then. I was moving away from him and closer to him at the same time. Because I had gone sailing we had, in the winter, things to talk about. But I left and came to live differently over the years. For him, routine is still the framework of life, a seaman's sense of work and hours. My employment is sporadic and I wake late. He rises at six-thirty and could sleep no longer unless drugged—as unlikely for him as it is likely for me. What kind of dreams does he wake from? Does he always know they are dreams or does he sometimes, for a moment, feel he has sailed over the edge of the world?

Over the Pacific in the west faint lightning trembles. I suggest we go back into the apartment but my father says no, nothing to fear from lightning like that. A soft drizzle works down through the redwood's needles and cools our faces. The air is brighter now with reflected light, like that of an overcast winter afternoon. Ivy glistens through the warm mist. My body feels torpid, weightless. I can see trees towering nearly leafless above the house like bare hedges against the sky. Trees of Heaven. Here autumn and winter merge. A few leaves still cling like snared birds. "I read somewhere people have died in these things," my father says. I assure him we are far from danger. He shrugs, rubbing water over his shoulders like liniment. He would not want to die here, unclothed like a child in a bath.

One evening we happened upon some Cape Breton fiddle music on a small FM station. My father, who was a grown man before he left that Nova Scotia island, got out of his chair and did a few soft steps, heel and toe. "Oh I used to step out with the best of them," he said. He sat down and we listened to the host of this Celtic program—a woman with Irish affections and a mind full of political mist—interview a young man who was, apparently, versed in Cape Breton folk music. But, strangled either by ignorance or stage fright, he could not locate Cape Breton very precisely. "It's west of Ireland, isn't it?" the woman said helpfully. "And east of Quebec?" After a long delay, the man said, "yes," which was true but not useful, and there Cape Breton remained. But my father enjoyed "Donald MacLean's Farewell to Oban" and "Miss Lyle's Reel." He told me suddenly about having pneumonia when he was three years old, an illness often fatal in those days, especially in the country, and how his dad made him a small wooden mallet so he could rap the headboard when he needed anything or was afraid. For the rest of the evening he was quiet.

I do things for him my mother once did, when he was home for the winter. I mix him a whisky in the afternoon and again in the evening when we talk. I bake Bisquick biscuits, cut cheese, cook, ask him if he's comfortable. I do this because he can take care of himself, not because he cannot. Around the corner from us there is a convalescent home and his first day here my father saw a frail old man babystepping by our window on a walker. I had to smile when he said, with real sympathy, "Poor old fella," as if there were years between them. Last night, halfway through his second whisky and feeling good, he remembered a country party ("Long before *I* was married"), a wedding reception back in

Cape Breton. A lot of people came to this cold house on Cape Dauphin, stamping snow at the door, December be damned, and there was dancing and boozing, horses packed flank to flank in the barn. A pal of his got sick from drink, but before going upstairs to find a bed he searched around the yard in the dark, finally yanking out of the snow an enamel creamer to set by his bedside. Not until morning, after he'd thrown up in it twice, did he discover the bottom of the creamer was rusted out completely. My father likes reminiscences like this and laughs easily, shaking his head at how vivid they remain. But after the funny part he said, almost casually, "Your mother was there," and the timbre of his voice changed, just slightly, just enough to notice.

I remember one December when I waited with my mother at a Cleveland dock during a bleary hour of the morning and watched his ship ease like an iceberg into her moorings. Freighted with tons of ice, she had gone down dangerously on her marks because of the added burden. My mother knew about the storm and had been worried. My father, bundled up like an arctic explorer, waved to her from the Texas deck and she gave him the okay sign. Later that winter, at home, my father and I walked along the shore of Lake Erie, our eyes and mouth drawn tight against a wind so cold it pained. We squinted across a jagged icescape which, rough as rockslides and fluted with windrows of snow, had been repeatedly broken up by storms, freezing again and again into new shapes. Beyond it the water seemed calm and green in the distance. We passed a shed built along the lines of a little house and layered with several inches of translucent ice. Beside it a tree crackled, wind-driven spray having turned it as bright and brittle as crystal. Too chilled to bring a hand out of his pocket, my father nodded toward the shed. "Somebody forgot to keep the home fires burning, eh?" he said. He and my mother argued sometimes during the long winter months. She accumulated grievances in her loneliness and sometimes shut herself away in her room after he left. What they quarrelled about I cannot recall. Little things which, I suppose, the strains of separation made larger. It no longer matters, not to him, not to anything. Soon his voice will stop and there will be nothing more he can add to what I know of him. We walked in the wind that day until we could barely speak.

"In a ship," he says, "out there at night . . . it's sometimes like you're at dead center of everything, the works." There are breaks in the overcast now. Clouds tear slowly into pieces and drift off like floes in the dark sky. My father watches them, then points. "The brightest star, there. Sirius. And there, Eye of Taurus." Wherever I am, he has told me, I like to get a bearing. All I know about him are bits and pieces like this. He never talks about himself directly, never did. He prefers stories that entertain—anecdotes, mimicry. Some stories I have heard before, like familiar waters we sail over. I wish we could descend beneath them, that he could reveal things under the surface before it is too late. When he is feeling down he is merely politely silent. Yet I admire his reticence: it seems dignified in a land of public blubbering where people yearn to be heard. At my mother's sudden death a year ago he was, as I expected, stoic, although the shock of her absence had tightened his face. She died next to him in bed, on a normal morning when he rose early and waited for her to come down to breakfast. When he looked at the clock later on, an ordinary day turned into something vaguely expected but never prepared for. "I climbed those stairs like

I weighed a ton," he told me. She was already blue and cold. It troubles him that he did not become alarmed sooner, that he might have reached her in time.

The first night he arrived I passed his room and was struck to see him down on one knee beside his bed, whispering prayer. I had forgotten he prayed that way and I was briefly embarrassed, as if this was senility. No. Like other things about him, it is simple and private, as sincere as a Jew at the wailing wall or a Moslem on his mat. I wondered if he had prayed beside his bunk when he was a deckhand, how he found the chance or if he feared the jibes of his shipmates. What now does he ask for? What does he expect from God?

He has marvelled at the flowers in February. He left the sidewalk one morning to stand among the branches of a tulip tree and touch the pale lavender cups of its blossoms. "You live in a garden," he said. At home he took over my mother's roses and put in peonies of his own, and marigolds. A sudden show of flowers makes him smile, almost shyly. He missed so many summers at sea, and they seem to strike at the heart of his youth when he knew them in the country.

Yesterday we were hit with an earthquake. Still in bed, I woke certain that this was the Big One and I did not want to meet it hungover and naked. I stumbled to the doorway of the living room where a hanging fern swung like a pendulum. My father, half-crouched in front of his chair, had spread his arms like a wrestler—a reflex from years of steadying himself on pitching decks. We stayed as we were, our eyes fixed on each other, until the rolling passed and the house stopped shaking. At the front window my father looked down at the street, his face close to the glass as if he were back in a wheelhouse. "Not the same as a ship," he said. "It's like being thrown off the earth." Then he smiled and raised his voice like a preacher's: "'If I take up the wings of the morning, and dwell in the uttermost part of the sea. . . .'" He lowered his voice to a murmur, "'. . . even there. . . .'"

The moon appears in the southwest. Its light turns the water darkly clear, the way it might be on Lake Superior streaming out a deep green against a wake white and crisp. We can see the pallor of our skin. My father sighs, a habit of his now, though usually no words ever follow. The last months his wife was living she would not enter a dark room. At the threshold she would step back and wait while he went ahead of her and put on a light. At the funeral he looked at her in that casket for a long while, and finally he said, to no one: "Where is she *now?*" I was of no use to him in this matter. I do not know how we move after death, or where.

In our old neighborhood back home five widows have been good to him. They observed his birthday, they bring him meals, invite him to their houses for cards. One has taken to calling him dear, a familiarity he does not encourage. He has named her The Star Widow, but when she calls him darling, he says, he will have to cool her off. "I have old feelings to think about. I don't need any new ones." After my mother died, he burned her letters. My anger puzzled him. "Letters are for the living," he said.

In the Twenties my father wheeled on a small Canadian freighter whose captain, a reckless alcoholic, took her foolishly into a Lake Michigan storm. Her wooden hatches, weakened by boarding seas, were carried away and she soon foundered. He and three other men made it to the wooden raft lashed atop the wheelhouse. All night in the darkness they were swept from it time after time, clawing their way back aboard where they huddled like lovers in the cold. It was November and the water was not much above freezing. A man would stop talking for a while and then he wasn't there, having slipped quietly into the sea. By dawn when the wind had abated, only my father remained, half-conscious and hallucinating. A bearded man kept appearing on the edge of the raft warning him not to eat the ice he'd been nibbling from the lapels of his coat. He heard his dead shipmates calling to him from shore offering him sandwiches. "Go easy, I'm not dead," he said to the Coast Guardsman who'd lifted him like a corpse. He lost two toes and the tip of a finger. "I survived," he told me, "because I was young."

Vapor rises faintly through the moonlight, climbing into the boughs above us whose shadows flash in the steam. I see my father's spare gestures, his pale form. And the occasional spark of his gold tooth, quick as an atom, so contained it seems all I know of him, that tiny glint. He bought that tooth in his bold and single days, just after lay-up, a bonus in his pocket and an aching bicuspid cracked in a fight with a redneck oiler. It always embarrassed my mother, fearful he would grin in church or pick it in a good restaurant. But I like it because it reminds me of his youth about which I know little. In Gaelic, a language his parents spoke, his name means sailor or mariner. As he grew up, I guess he merely eased into what he'd been christened, and that was his life.

We have been up to San Francisco once during his visit. He likes to call it Frisco, a city he has always wanted to see. Indifferent to cities, I take us on a sketchy itinerary of sights. I look for a Scottish bar I've heard about but we soon end up, by mutual consent, in a dark Irish pub where we talk quietly in the cool malty dusk of our Guinness. Outside, people hurry past in the sun. We swap stories about the Lakes, boats we both knew, men we'd worked with, as if we're ashore for a few hours while our ships unload. Later, reluctantly, we stumble out into the glare of the afternoon in time to board the ships docked at the Maritime Museum. We clamber around an old steam schooner, the sort of working ship my father understands immediately. In the fo'c'sle he sniffs a tarry smell. "Oakum," he says, grinning back to that tooth that can still surprise me. We inspect every accessible compartment and only the wheelhouse remains. It is perched high and solitary like the wheelhouses on the old Lake freighters that are no doubt gone by now. We climb to it but the door is locked. No public permitted. My father peers through the glass for a while, hooding his eyes and cataloguing the equipment inside. Then he turns and I snap a picture of him looking older in the cold wind. We hang around the piers. I know he doesn't want to leave. He sees a sloop plunging through the choppy currents off Alcatraz Island and tells me about a skiff he had as a boy, how he rigged a little sail and put rocks in the bottom for ballast. As we drive home, the Guinness seeps ruthlessly from our spirits and I recall how harshly the sun struck us when we stepped into it. We are silent all down the Bayshore where nothing generates talk. I turn on the radio. On our little FM station Pete Seeger is singing . . . "Sailing down my golden river, and I was not far from home. . . ." I look over at my father. He seems dozy. Perhaps his thoughts are somewhere on water, on the cold dark sea of Lake Superior.

He makes swimming motions with his hands. The water ripples and whitens behind him. I remember only one summer when he swam. His boat laid up because of a steel strike and in the afternoons we would catch a bus down to the lake. He would swim out a long way by himself, slowly and carefully, where there were no other swimmers and float for minutes on end, his face a mask on the water. I was too young to follow him, but I knew, anyway, he wanted to be alone. Summer at home was a strange time for him.

He knows that I am still drifting. "A man needs some place to tie up to," he said in the Irish pub. It troubles him that I have lived in so many places, that next year I may have another address. Quite likely it will not have this warm bubbling sea in the backyard. I work on and off as a construction laborer. I dig, fetch, bang nails out of boards, clean up after insolent young carpenters who have seen themselves in too many beer commercials. I don't know where this will lead. In the spring my father was always gone as soon as the ice broke. A different ship but the same places. "Never mind," he told me, wiping Guinness froth from his moustache. "The company gave boats to younger mates and put me mate with them so they wouldn't screw up. I never got my own ship. You had to kiss their ass for that." He looked across the bar at a woman in a slit skirt. "I was into my middle years when you came along, Danny." He kept looking at the woman and nodding his head as if considering what my coming along had meant. Finally he said, "Just don't have anything to do with business. It's not in our blood." We touched glasses and finished our Guinness.

Once a bunkmate and I devised a game. Running up Lake Superior in hard weather, we opened the porthole in our cramped, below-decks cabin and climbed into our bunks. We lay there naked and uncovered, rigid as mummies, listening to the bow smash and split the heavy seas. Which of us would feel the first fiery lash of water so cold it could kill you in minutes? We heard the seas break along the shipside, rise to the porthole's rim, splattering the top of our metal dresser, and we knew that inevitably a good wave would collide with the bow and swell upward. We tensed, our jaws clamped tight. Soon there was the sound—a growing hiss, a roaring whisper—and then a thump of spray shot through the darkness, striking one or both of us with a chill that jerked the body like an electric shock. Whoever yelled first lost. We played until wet bedclothes threatened our sleep. I thought of my father on that raft, that I was he. But I did not think of death: death was too distant, like the bottom of that dark sea two hundred fathoms beneath us, so cold it never gave up the drowned men who drifted there. As I closed the porthole, I was sure I would live forever.

"Too hot," my father says. He rises, emerges from the water. I reach out a steadying hand he does not need. He towels himself slowly, in that careful way of old men, as if briskness would be unseemly. He was never a big man but now he has diminished into age. I think of the only time I saw him in the act of his work. Our ships had tied up at adjacent docks in Toledo and I could see him stepping smartly along the main deck over hatch cables and dock wallopers' shovels to chew out a crewman for fouling a winch. I was surprised: he seemed such a different man, one a gold tooth might well belong to. I envied him. No one on that ship would question anything he said, and I hoped that one day I could gain that kind of respect. But I will always somehow remain an amateur. I have been an amateur in nearly everything of my life, and I am one now. Everything in my mind and in my hands seems uncertain, half-formed. But my father was a professional, skilled in those countless ways that make good seamen, and bring them other good seamen's respect. That part of him was not passed on to me, that ability to find your way, deeply, into what you are good at. When I first went sailing, I knew the ore freighters, having as a boy roamed their cold iron darkness during winter lay-up, but I did not know their work. I felt homesick and inept. But for my father, I tried at least to be a reliable deckhand, for that would get back to him. What didn't get back was the hot summer night I got thoroughly and limply drunk on cognac, me and the other two deckhands, cleaning up ore leavings deep in the cargo holds. Between alcoholic fits of energy, we leaned on our shovels and sang. We dodged the backing bulldozer and the first mate's glances from the hatches above, we flirted with the Hewlett's big iron teeth as its shadow descended over us. When the heat and the cognac struck home around two A.M., I crawled along the sidetanks all the way to my bunk and passed out. As penance, the mate put me to work at sunrise hauling up five-gallon buckets of heavy red mud and dumping them overboard. I felt sick enough to die. I hated every motion of the ship and the dull line of the horizon. I wanted to jump at the next port. But I endured it and said nothing because of the watchman. His name was Gunderson, an ex-gunner's mate with bleeding ulcers, huge hands, a frightening set of false teeth, and identical square-riggers tattooed on both wrists. He came up to me while I was waiting for my bucket to be filled in the hold below. I must have looked grey as the sea, my jaws tight with nausea. "You know," he said, "I been with some sons of bitches, but your old man is a fine mate. He was a deckhand once too." I could have told him, no, he wasn't, they made him a wheelsman right off when he said he'd been a seaman in Nova Scotia, he never had to do this. But I was grateful to Anders Gunderson. I knew then that to feel homesick was foolish, that I was not in a strange place.

I will never forget a photograph my father gave me when I was young. He proffered it without comment one evening after I had pressed him for details about his shipwreck. I took the old clipping to my room where I pored over it more keenly than the pornographic cards we passed around at school. Something in its atmosphere I could not understand, cannot yet. The corpses of nine seamen are laid out in a morgue, the undertaker in his galluses posing at one end of them, his assistant at the other. A railroad ferry had sunk in December during one of Lake Erie's fearsome gales, and these men, the only crewmen ever found, had frozen solid as stone in a battered lifeboat. Their faces, grotesquely calm, skin like putty in the incandescent glare of floodlamps, have been shaped by the mortician into the contours of troubled sleep. For the benefit of cameras they lie in a parallel row, heads slightly raised on makeshift pillows, sheets pulled snug to their chins. You can see the outlines of their arms folded across their waists. But something disturbs the almost Victorian dignity of their arrangement: there is one man, Smith the cook, whose belly is so swollen its girth has lifted the hem of the sheet, exposing the deadwhite flesh of his buttock. It is clear that all of these men are naked. A copy editor has crudely penned on each sheet the surname of each man. My eyes went slowly up and down that row so many times the order of their names became a kind of poetry. Steele. Shank. Allen. Smith. Ray. Hart. Thomas. Hines. Squars. What my father wanted me to learn from this stark picture I do not know. If he wanted me only to remember it, I have.

My father has dried himself and wrapped a big white towel around him toga-like. "At home there's ice now," he says. "Clear across to Canada." He waves. I hear his feet on the wooden steps. He disappears behind the trellis of ivy.

The wind is gone. The moon, its crescent snagged on strands of cloud, filters down through a tracery of branches. Ivy, which has climbed above the fence and found nothing to grab but air, turns back into itself, forming a pitchblack whorl that seems depthless. I do not understand the heavens or their arrangement as they move through the seasons of the skies. Put my father on a dark and empty sea and still he will not be lost. I think he has never been lost. I must memorize the constellations, learn to guide myself through these winter nights. I stare into the vortex the ivy makes and imagine that black hole my father will wither into, gone beyond the skies that helped him, hindered him. All I know, for certain, is that we are sailing.

ED MCCLANAHAN

Ed McClanahan ("The Big Honker") is the author of The Natural Man *(1983)
and* Famous People I Have Known *(1985), both published by Farrar, Straus &
Giroux and Viking Penguin. He was a Stegner Fellow in 1962–63, and a Jones
Lecturer in the Stanford Creative Writing Program, 1963–70. He now lives
with his wife, Cia, and their two children in Port Royal, Kentucky.*

"'The Big Honker' is a chapter from my novel, *The Natural Man,* which
concerns the coming of age of a small-town Kentucky boy named Harry Eastep,
as accomplished under the watchful eye of his worldly friend and mentor Monk
McHorning. An early version of this novel won me a Stegner Fellowship in
1962."

◆　　　◆　　　◆

The Big Honker

ALL WAS NOT AS well as it might have been those days at the New Artistic
Motion Picture Theatre, where attendance had been on the wane since early
summer. At first, Mr. Ockerman had attributed the decline to the usual hot-
weather doldrums, but by September, when the weather turned cool and the
crowds grew smaller still, he'd made a positive identification of the culprit:
television.

Hunsicker's Hardware had sold dozens of the infernal devices in the past few
months, with back orders for dozens more. Antennas were springing up around
the countryside like some giant new noxious weed. Mr. Hunsicker had installed,
as an inducement to trade and for the edification of the poorer classes, an
immense Sylvania in his display window, with an automatic timer that shut it
off at night at a whimsically predetermined hour. The Sylvania towered like a
mahogany outhouse, but the picture was scarcely larger than a knothole, and
the knothole was always out of adjustment; and of course the sound couldn't
begin to penetrate the plate-glass window. Yet every evening after supper, fair
weather or foul, a handful of impecunious dreamers would assemble on Hunsicker's sidewalk in a kind of cataleptic rapture until, perhaps with his lips
moving as if in a tiny scream of protest, an elfin Milton Berle or Herb Shriner
or Chief Don Eagle would be abruptly sucked into a brilliant pinprick of white
light at the center of the screen, the little dumb show gone like quicksilver down
the drain. An instant later the pinprick would swallow itself as well, and then
at last the communicants on the sidewalk would turn to one another—to people
they'd known all their lives!—blinking their amazement, as though the Sylvania

had just gulped down their dearest, most intimate friend, leaving them abandoned among total strangers.

Meanwhile, households that didn't have television yet were discovering a wonderful affinity with nearby households that did; inexorably drawn through the dusky late-summer evenings to the glowing tube, neighbors gathered in the sitting rooms of homes marked by the Sign of the Antenna, to contemplate the Finite. Later, as they stumped home in the dark, they vowed: *I'm gonna have me one of those!* And on the largest silver screen in South-Central Northeastern Kentucky, the great stars played to empty seats.

"But shithouse mouse," sighed Mr. Ockerman, counting his dwindling receipts, "that's show business, Harry."

On the first Saturday afternoon of October, less than a week before his sixteenth birthday, Harry was at the theater just finishing his last popper of popcorn when Mr. O. rushed into the lobby fairly trembling with excitement. "Lookahere, Harry, lookahere!" he called breathlessly, waving a long white envelope. "Some bunch is a-wanting us to put on a show!"

In the envelope was a handbill advertising a movie, produced and directed by one Philander C. Rexroat, entitled *Dads and Mothers* ("Screenplay by Philander C. Rexroat!"), purporting to be "The World's Greatest Sex Hygiene Attraction," narrated by Philander C. Rexroat, and accompanied by a lecture ("On Stage! In Person!") by Philander C. Rexroat, eminent scientist, author, lecturer, scholar, theologian, world traveler, sexologist.

SEE THE BIRTH OF SWEDISH TRIPLETS BEFORE YOUR VERY EYES! the handbill shrieked. SEE THE HORRORS OF VENEREAL DISEASE! SEE THE MIRACLE OF THE HUMAN REPRODUCTIVE SYSTEM! NO ONE UNDER HIGH SCHOOL AGE ADMITTED! SEPARATE SHOWINGS FOR GENTS AND LADIES! IT MAY SHOCK YOU BUT IT WILL MAKE YOU THINK! SO SHOCKING A REGISTERED NURSE MUST BE IN ATTENDANCE AT ALL PERFORMANCES! A PHILANDER C. REXROAT PRODUCTION!

This text was illuminated by a stiff little drawing of a fully clothed couple— indeed, they were in evening dress—in a violent yet abstracted-looking embrace. The woman bore a vampish resemblance to the one in Monk McHorning's tattoo; the gentleman sported a lounge lizard's slicked-down hair and mustache. At the bottom were blank spaces where the name of the theater and the dates, times, and price of admission could be written in. There was also a letter, beginning "Dear Mr. Theater Operator," which announced that the illustrious Dr. Philander C. Rexroat, "the Cecil B. deMille of Sex Hygiene Entertainment," was presently on tour with his famous film, and that although "this colossal educational attraction" had been playing to packed houses throughout the South, there were still a few bookings available if they acted quickly, Dr. Rexroat to provide the Registered Nurse as well as 200 copies of the handbill, he and Mr. Theater Operator to split the gate seventy-thirty, the lion's share to go to the Doctor, for the furtherance of his great educational work. The letter advised interested parties to call a certain Cincinnati phone number for information, then concluded: "Reminding you that 'tis better to light one candle than to curse the darkness, I remain, Yours for Better Sex Hygiene Entertainment, Philander C. Rexroat, Sex.D."

"Ain't that us to a tee-total, Harry?" Mr. O. exulted. "I mean about cursing in the dark and what-not? If that ain't this old town made over!"

Harry didn't respond. He was thinking he might give up his future in sportswriting, and go in for sexology instead. He hadn't realized you could make a career out of it.

"Harry, daggone it, I'm goin' up to the house and give the fella a jingle! Shoot, this'd be just the trick to wake this old place up! Why, shithouse mouse, boy, this here's the Twentieth Sentry!" Mr. Ockerman's enthusiasm had propelled him halfway back out the door when an afterthought drew him up short. "Say, Harry," he said, suddenly apprehensive, "you don't reckon it'd be . . . nasty or anything, do you?"

"Well," Harry reminded him, "he's a doctor and all. They'd get his license, wouldn't they?"

"You bet they would!" Mr. Ockerman beamed. "They'd get his daggone doctoring license! I expect he's one of these doctors of this old vernal disease. If it was nasty, he wouldn't be hooked up with it, would he? I mean, shoot"— he said this on his way out the door again—"I mean, I'd send my own daughter to a show like that!"

Aha! quoth Harry inside his head, as inspiration lit him like a light bulb. If the Cecil B. deMille of Sex Hygiene Entertainment couldn't get Oodles Ockerman hot and bothered for him, then she was stone cold fridgit sure enough! ("I *like* a big honker, myself," Monk McHorning had once confided to a raptly attentive Harry. "They don't give you no tonker-bone trouble, your big honkers don't.") And if there was an unfortunate irony in Mr. Ockerman's being enlisted as the unwitting agent of his own daughter's undoing—well, who was Harry to question Providence? Bring on Cecil B. deMille, the Swedish triplets, the Registered Nurse! Bring on the Horrors of the Human Reproductive System, the Miracle of Vernal Disease!

Bring on . . . the Big Honker!

DENNIS MCFARLAND

♦   ♦

Dennis McFarland's stories have appeared in The New Yorker, Mademoiselle, *and in literary journals. He is the recipient of a Transatlantic Review Award from the Henfield Foundation and of a Stegner Fellowship from Stanford. He also served as a Jones Lecturer at Stanford. He currently lives in Boston with his wife, Michelle Blake Simons, and daughter, Katharine.*

"The seed of this story from real life is the fortune telling. A young woman began reading my palm at a party in New York; we were standing under a very bright light as I recall. She told me I wouldn't win any Nobel Prizes, I'd never have any money to speak of, and never any children. I cut the reading short due to sudden illness. The part about the Nobel Prize and the money has held true. The part about the children has not."

♦   ♦   ♦

Distant Child

MY BROTHER'S LATEST GIRLFRIEND has written a book for children, and I've taken the job of doing drawings for it. I spend each morning at work on the drawings and I've been having trouble. Grateful as I am to Roger—my brother—for getting me the work, he makes things harder for me by telephoning almost daily to "see how the pictures are going." Roger is a lawyer, analytical but not introspective, and the most trivial of his conversations has the flavor of cross-examination. He regards me the way he would a tattoo artist he might come across in a sideshow at a circus. When he visits me, he sits on the edges of things, or doesn't sit at all—as if allowing himself a moment of comfort in my apartment would mean burning his clothes afterward. Each time he telephones, his secretary puts through the calls, and after asking for me by my first name, she says, "Will you please hold for Mr. Grady?"

When Roger's secretary calls today, I say, "No I won't hold for Mr. Grady," and hang up.

Roger telephones after a few minutes. "What's wrong with you?" he says. "My secretary told me you were very rude to her just now. Aren't the pictures going well?"

"The illustrations would be going a lot better, Roger, if you'd stop badgering me about them every morning," I say.

"I'm not badgering you. I just hope you realize that I've an investment here, too. Elizabeth tells me you're ten days behind your first deadline, she hasn't seen the first picture yet, and I'm naturally concerned."

"Your natural concern," I say, "is giving me a great pain."

This silences him for a moment, after which he says, "Gratitude was never your strong point. Elizabeth asked me to drop by your place and see how things are going, and I said I would. How's about five-thirty?"

Elizabeth is the girlfriend, the writer, and I've spoken to her only once, by telephone, right after first reading her book. I liked her book, and she seemed personable and modest. I was sure she was pretty, too; Roger wouldn't have an unpretty girlfriend. A few months ago, while I was still living with Susan, a woman with whom I lived for four-and-a-half years, Roger said to me that I should give Susan more money, so she could buy some decent clothes. This was at a party at his penthouse apartment; the decent clothes he referred to were the snappy-looking red silk dress and expensive shoes his current girlfriend was wearing. I told him that in the first place I didn't give Susan money, she had her own money, and even if I did give her money, she probably wouldn't spend much on clothes, and if he had any further comments about her appearance he felt compelled to make, I wished he would direct them to her and not to me. It was snotty of me, but this sort of conversation has always made me nervous, and I felt sorry for any woman who ended up with Roger; he would constantly hound her to change this and that about herself—the way manufacturers tinker with their products in order to slap a "New!" or "Improved!" on their labels. Roger's women rarely improve to suit him, which is why they're so often new.

I'm certain that Roger's meddling with the drawings for Elizabeth's book is his idea and not hers. I say to him, "Why can't Elizabeth come herself if she's worried?"

"Because she's busy," he says, emphasizing "she's" just enough to let me know what he's thinking: I am an idler, and being one, I don't deserve to know what busy people are busy at. "Is five-thirty okay?" he asks.

"No," I say. "Five-thirty is not okay. I don't appreciate these inspections any more in-person than I do by telephone every day."

"If you can't be more cooperative than this," he says in his starchiest tone, "I'm afraid we might have to give the work to someone else."

I have never been good at responding to threats: I lose perspective and tend to dive in head first. Once, on Forty-second Street, a very tall Oriental man, with a bony face and sharp, black eyes, sidled along next to me and told me to turn left at the next corner or he would blow my pretty white head off. It was funny, the way he said "pretty white"; it came out "putty-white." I also hadn't been called pretty since I was a very young child, and of all the strange times to think it, I thought I should grow a beard. I looked down and saw the pointed protrusion in his jacket pocket—which could have been a gun, could have been his finger, could have been a fountain pen. When we reached the corner, I stepped off the curb, turned to him, said "You will fry in the electric chair," and crossed the avenue. At the next curb, I turned and saw him on the other side, shrugging his shoulders.

"Then give the goddam work to somebody else," I say to Roger and slam down the receiver.

This is the problem I'm having: Elizabeth's book is called *Big and Little*. A touching relationship develops between a big, burly truck driver, sweet and child-like, who has a sickly parakeet as a pet—and an old woman, small and withered, but hard as nails, who has a bull mastiff as a pet. The parakeet, partly out of affection and partly out of affliction, rides on the trucker's shoulder; the foursome meet at a zoo, where they befriend a llama. Ideas have been easy, but once I've begun an illustration, I become interested in the thing for its own sake, and I'm having trouble confining myself to what's applicable to the story. The drawing I was doing today is of the llama. I'm especially proud of the serenity I've got into her face—a kind of self-satisfied expression the "Mona Lisa" seems to have. But somehow, the llama has ended up with my Indian bedspread draped over her back. It's a perfectly good drawing, but there's no bedspread in Elizabeth's story. In other drawings, I've put the parakeet on tiny crutches, which is gorgeous in a number of ways—angelic and pathetic at once; but in the story, the bird suffers from an injured wing, not a broken leg. That's why I haven't yet sent any of the illustrations to Elizabeth's publisher: I know they aren't right, but they are undeniably good—and something which is good and not right at the same time depresses me.

Roger's telephoning depresses me even more. And something about this whole business reminds me of when Susan moved out. She'd decided that despite our knowing each other very well (undeniably good), she was no longer *stirred* by us (not right). I go to my drawing table and look at the llama. I take a pen and darken her eyelashes: serene and sexy. I think I'm falling in love. The llama with the bedspread over her back—as if it were something loose and colorful she's just thrown around her shoulders to greet visitors—is the only thing I can lay my eyes on that lifts my spirits. My apartment is a mess; clothes I wore weeks before lie at the bottom of an evergrowing pile in a chair by my unmade bed; an avocado pit, half submerged in a pot of dirt on the window sill, has grown more wrinkled and brown, refusing to put forth a sprout from the four-month-old crack through its middle; a large photograph of Susan, thumbtacked to my bulletin board, has yellowed and crimped in at the top corners, making her look gloomily pinheaded.

Out the window, I see some black girls listening to a radio on the stoop of the building across the street. A man comes along whom I recognize as the man living in the apartment below mine; his name is Bob, and I think he's gay. One night, when I'd been out quite late and was returning home, I saw him kissing another man in his doorway. Though the man was old enough to be his father, and what I'd seen really could have been a father's kiss, Bob had his hands locked behind the older man's waist. Neither of them seemed the least embarrassed, and Bob even smiled and nodded to me over the man's shoulder as I passed. Out the window, I see Bob take one of the girls by the hand. She leaps from the stoop, and they dance a few steps on the sidewalk; they whirl, the girl squealing, Bob releases her, waves, and crosses the street toward our building.

I look again at the drawings and realize my failure is not that of an artist, but that of a druggist—having improperly filled a prescription. In one of the drawings, the old woman's face looks alarmingly like Roger's. I see the clock on the night table next to my bed; Roger will arrive in a few hours. At the age of thirty-three, Roger is only two years older than me, but I think he looks a good five years younger. He will be dressed in a three-piece business suit when he arrives; perhaps he will have loosened his tie just enough to undo the top button of his shirt. He will pull his blackrimmed glasses down his nose before he puts his hands in his pockets and stands in the middle of the room; he might rise up on his toes a couple of times, bouncing in place. Briefly, I'll think him handsome, and I'll see a semblance of my own face in his; the word "brother" will enter my mind, then Roger will open his mouth to speak, I'll wish him dead, and feel guilty for having wished it.

I decide to take a short walk, get out for some air. On the way down the first flight of stairs, I hear some hammering coming from the landing below. Bob is hanging a poster on the wall of the hallway outside his apartment door. He is wearing jeans and a pale green, ribbed undershirt; he is about my own age and has longish blond hair. Though we don't know each other, we've introduced ourselves once and said hello a few times in the hall. The poster he is tacking up is colorful—some white-faced clowns in blue and yellow costumes, marching in a parade—and looks cheerful in the otherwise plain, dark hallway. When he hears me on the stairs, he turns, smiles, and says, "Have I got this crooked?"

He does, and I go to the poster, lift the untacked corner a half-inch up the wall, and hold it while he hammers in a second tack. I notice him looking at my hands, and as soon as the tack is in, he balances the hammer on the nearby newel, and says, "Let me see your hands."

I hold them out, palms up, as if to say, "I'm innocent . . ." He bends back my thumbs, one thumb in each of his hands, and says, "Why are you such a victim?"

This question is not so much directed to me as it is to my right palm, and I'm shocked, but before I can say anything, he's leading me by the thumbs toward the open door of his apartment. He says: "You're in trouble. Come in here to the light." For an instant, I think he means, "Come in here to THE LIGHT," and I have a brief premonition of a room full of icons and candle-lit religious statuary. Instead, the next moment, we are standing by a window in an attractive room with white, modern furniture and a bright red carpet covering most of the floor. I am astonished that such elegance could be achieved in a shape and space identical to mine, just above his ceiling. He has guided me in, across the floor, to the window, without once taking his eyes off my hands. "I see you're an artist," he says, which I think is less than super-mystical, since my fingers are spotted with three different colors of ink.

"You're sensitive and emotional, not *deeply* emotional, but sensitive in a way that makes you vulnerable to being dumped on." He drops my left hand and begins touching various spots on my right palm. "Fidelity certainly isn't your forte. Your love line looks like a macrame plant hanger. You might find yourself in one longlasting relationship—not necessarily marriage—but it'll be more comfortable than deep or passionate. Fate will be generally good to you—there aren't any real disasters here, but you'll often find yourself drawn in more than one direction. You aren't going to win any Nobel Prizes." He bends my hand down at the wrist. "No money here. Not your own and not anybody else's. No children either . . . or . . . maybe one . . . but it's a distant child. Maybe an adopted Korean refugee or something . . . or—if you are the biological father— the child is severely handicapped."

He drops my hand and starts for the back of the room. "Sit down," he says. "Have a glass of wine. Or were you on your way somewhere?"

"I was just going for a walk," I say, "but I think I need a glass of wine after that. I'm glad you don't see any real disasters."

"Take everything I say with a grain of salt," he says. "According to my life line, I died at the age of sixteen."

We sit on his comfortable couch and drink large goblets of red wine. We remind each other of our names, and I immediately begin telling him about the problem I'm having with the illustrations. I tell him about the llama; I tell him about Roger, about Susan, I even tell him about my avocado pit. I'm completely self-absorbed and probably boring, but he doesn't seem to mind. He keeps refilling my wine glass and nods a lot, as if everything I'm saying is somehow pertinent to what he's already seen in my palm.

I soon feel more relaxed. I notice something hanging on a hook on the back of his door; it looks like a great cream-colored bird, but I squint and see that it's a hat.

"That's a wonderful hat," I say, and Bob rises from the couch, takes the hat from the hook, and puts his hands inside it. "I made it myself," he says. "For a costume party."

The hat is a knitted sock cap with knots of white, puffy cotton around its edges; beige and gray feathers come out of the sides and top; it looks as if it's on fire. "You can have it if you like it," he says.

I laugh and say, "I can't see myself wearing it, but it's beautiful all the same."

"You don't have to wear it," he says. "You like it. Take it."

He hands me the hat, I stroke the feathers as I would a pigeon's back, and we have yet more wine.

Roger stands at my drawing table, looking at the illustrations. I've wondered if the problem with the drawings will be, for Roger, a gradual dawning—which would assume a starting-point of his wanting to like them. I lie on my bed, drunk and filled with pride, my hands behind my head. Roger's first comment is: "I never pictured the truck driver bald. There's nothing in the story about him being bald." And I know he wants entirely not to like the drawings.

I am looking at his back when he turns and looks, not at me, but to one side of me. He turns back to the table. "Isn't this your bedspread on the llama?" he says.

"A facsimile," I say.

"But what's it doing here—on the llama?"

"I don't know," I say and close my eyes.

"And this bird. It's on crutches—"

"Look at the way the wings spread, Roger," I say. "See how the crutches make the wings stand out?"

He shakes his head. "There aren't any crutches—" he starts to say.

"It wouldn't hurt the story any," I say.

He shakes his head again. When he turns to face me, he is still shaking his head. "I don't think these will do," he says. "I wonder what you think you're up to. What am I supposed to do—take these to Elizabeth and tell her to change her story?"

I am silent and close my eyes again; I can't stand the bewildered look on his face.

"I've tried to help you and you don't even make an effort," he says. "And I've taken a risk here. I don't think you understand that this is a woman I might very possibly marry."

Though my eyes are still closed, I can tell from his voice that he has moved nearer the bed, is standing over me, looking down at me, and I'm suddenly afraid he'll plead with me. I open my eyes and see from his face, however, that he is not about to plead. I say, "And I'm your brother. It wouldn't hurt the story any."

"That's what makes this all the worse," he says. "My own brother is hired to do a job that's easy enough to do, God knows, and instead of just doing it, you go sticking in these silly bedspreads and crutches just to be belligerent. That's what it is, you know. You're belligerent. You've always been belligerent. You're belligerent and a slob. Look at this place. It's no wonder Susan couldn't put up with you. Are you going to just lie there like some reclining Buddha with your hands behind your head? You've disappointed every single person who ever tried to help you."

There is a knock at the door, which is slightly ajar, and Bob steps in wearing a long flowing caftan with wide purple and orange stripes. "Sorry to interrupt," he says. "You forgot your hat."

I rise from the bed and feel as if I'm gliding across the floor to take the hat and thank him. Bob gives Roger a big, toothy smile, says, "Hello," and leaves.

Roger sits down on the edge of my bed—just barely on the edge. "What was *that?*" he says, looking at the door.

"*That,*" I say, "was a palmist."

He hangs his head, placing his elbows on his knees. I go to the bed, sit next to him, and feeling perhaps meaner than I have felt in my life, I put on the hat.

Roger looks at me, and I smile. I think I hear music somewhere.

"What is your life coming to?" he asks. "I wish you could see yourself."

And I wish I could, too. I wish I could see both of us, just as we are, in the slanted, pinkish light from the lamp on the drawing table—I in my bird hat, Roger in his black suit—sitting close, framed by the dark wall behind us.

THOMAS McGUANE

I was born and raised in Michigan. But because my parents were from Massa-chusetts and my aunts, uncles, cousins, and grandparents still lived there, I always felt a little ambiguous, as did the rest of our family, as to where home was exactly. This must have been rather mild when compared to the sense of uprooting of my Irish forebears who exchanged the wilds of the West of Ireland for the slums of South Boston. In a handful of generations we went from Ireland to Massachusetts to Michigan to Montana; and my son was born while I was a Stegner Fellow at Stanford in Palo Alto. It's the Celtic diaspora! I live on a ranch near the very small town of McLeod, Montana, and have written for a living since I left school.

"I wrote this story out of the feeling that I didn't know much about death. It was a story which I found almost impossible to write. It hung fire for a year and I gave up on it more than once. I love this story because in place of a rendition of the actual deaths I had known, my own dead as well as the observed public dead, I had found a personal way of suggesting death that rang true for me. At the same time, I learned a way of talking about certain places on earth and about human ceremony as standing for all things which do not die."

♦   ♦   ♦

Flight

DURING BIRD SEASON, DOGS circle each other in my kitchen, shell vests are piled in the mudroom, all drains are clogged with feathers, and hunters work up hangover remedies at the icebox. As a diurnal man, I gloat at these presences, estimating who will and who will not shoot well.

This year was slightly different in that Dan Ashaway arrived seriously ill. Yet this morning, he was nearly the only clear-eyed man in the kitchen. He helped make the vast breakfast of grouse hash, eggs, juice, and coffee. Bill Upton and his brother, Jerry, who were miserable, loaded dogs and made a penitentially early start. I pushed away some dishes and lit a breakfast cigar. Dan refilled our coffee and sat down. We've hunted birds together for years. I live here and Dan flies in from Philadelphia. Anyway, this seemed like the moment.

"How bad off are you?" I asked.

"I'm afraid I'm not going to get well," said Dan directly, shrugging and dropping his hands to the arms of his chair. That was that. "Let's get started."

We took Dan's dogs at his insistence. They jumped into the aluminum boxes on the back of the truck when he said "Load": Betty, a liver-and-white female,

and Sally, a small bitch with a banded face. These were—I should say *are*—
two dead-broke pointers who found birds and retrieved without much handling.
Dan didn't even own a whistle.

As we drove toward Roundup, the entire pressure of my thoughts was of how
remarkable it was to be alive. It seemed a strange and merry realization.

The dogs rode so quietly I had occasion to remember when Betty was a pup
and yodeled in her box, drawing stares in all the towns. Since then she had
quieted down and grown solid at her job. She and Sally had hunted everywhere
from Albany, Georgia, to Wilsall, Montana. Sally was born broke but Betty had
the better nose.

We drove between two ranges of desertic mountains, low ranges without
snow or evergreens. Section fences climbed infrequently and disappeared over
the top or into blue sky. There was one little band of cattle trailed by a cowboy
and a dog, the only signs of life. Dan was pressing sixteen-gauge shells into the
elastic loops of his cartridge belt. He was wearing blue policeman's suspenders
and a brown felt hat, a businessman's worn-out Dobbs.

We watched a harrier course the ground under a bluff, sharptail grouse
jumping in his wake. The harrier missed a half dozen, wheeled on one wingtip,
and nailed a bird in a pop of down and feathers. As we resumed driving, the
hawk was hooded over its prey, stripping meat from the breast.

Every time the dirt road climbed to a new vantage point, the country changed.
For a long time, a green creek in a tunnel of willows was alongside us; then it
went off under a bridge, and we climbed away to the north. When we came out
of the low ground, there seemed no end to the country before us: a great wide
prairie with contours as unquestionable as the sea. There were buttes pried up
from its surface and yawning coulees with streaks of brush where the springs
were. We had to abandon logic to stop and leave the truck behind. Dan beamed
and said, "Here's the spot for a big nap." The remark frightened me.

"Have we crossed the stagecoach road?" Dan asked.

"Couple miles back."

"Where did we jump all those sage hens in 1965?"

"Right where the stagecoach road passed the old hotel."

Dan had awarded himself a little English sixteen-gauge for graduating from
the Wharton School of Finance that year. It was in the gun rack behind our
heads now, the bluing gone and its hinge pin shot loose.

"It's a wonder we found anything," said Dan from afar, "with the kind of
run-off dog we had. Senor Jack. You had to preach religion to Señor Jack every
hundred yards or he'd leave us. Remember? It's a wonder we fed that common
bastard." Señor Jack was a dog with no talent, loyalty, or affection, a dog we
swore would drive us to racquet sports. Dan gave him away in Georgia.

"He found the sage hens."

"But when we got on the back side of the Little Snowies, remember? He went
right through all those sharptails like a train. We should have had deer rifles. A
real wonder dog. I wonder where he is. I wonder what he's doing. Well, it's all
an illusion, a very beautiful illusion, a miracle which is taking place before our
very eyes. 1965. I'll be damned."

The stagecoach road came in around from the east again, and we stopped:
two modest ruts heading into the hills. We released the dogs and followed the

road around for half an hour. It took us past an old buffalo wallow filled with water. Some teal got up into the wind and wheeled off over the prairie.

About a mile later the dogs went on point. It was hard to say who struck game and who backed. Sally catwalked a little, relocated, and stopped; then Betty honored her point. So we knew we had moving birds and got up on them fast. The dogs stayed staunch, and the long covey rise went off like something tearing. I killed a going-away and Dan made a clean left and right. It was nice to be reminded of his strong heads-up shooting. I always crawled all over my gun and lost some quickness. It came of too much waterfowling when I was young. Dan had never really been out of the uplands and had speed to show for it.

Betty and Sally picked up the birds; they came back with eyes crinkled, grouse in their mouths. They dropped the birds and Dan caught Sally with a finger through her collar. Betty shot back for the last bird. She was the better marking dog.

We shot another brace in a ravine. The dogs pointed shoulder to shoulder and the birds towered. We retrieved those, walked up a single, and headed for a hillside spring with a bar of bright buckbrush, where we nooned up with the dogs. The pretty bitches put their noses in the cold water and lifted their heads to smile when they got out of breath drinking. Then they pitched down for a rest. We broke the guns open and set them out of the way. I laid a piece of paper down and arranged some sandwiches and tangy apples from my own tree. We stretched out on one elbow, ate with a free hand, and looked off over the prairie, to me the most beautiful thing in the world. I wish I could see all the grasslands, while we still have them.

Then I couldn't stand it. "What do you mean you're not going to get better?"

"It's true, old pal. It's quite final. But listen, today I'm not thinking about it. So let's not start."

I was a little sore at myself. We've all got to go, I thought. It's like waiting for an alarm to go off, when it's too dark to read the dial. Looking at Dan's great chest straining his policeman's suspenders, it was fairly unimaginable that anything predictable could turn him to dust. I was quite wrong about that too.

A solitary antelope buck stopped to look at us from a great distance. Dan put his hat on the barrels of his gun and decoyed the foolish animal to thirty yards before it snorted and ran off. We had sometimes found antelope blinds the Indians had built, usually not far from the eagle traps, clever things made by vital hands. There were old cartridge cases next to the spring, lying in the dirt, 45–70s; maybe a fight, maybe an old rancher hunting antelope with a cavalry rifle. Who knows. A trembling mirage appeared to the south, blue and banded with hills and distance. All around us the prairie creaked with life. I tried to picture the Indians, the soldiers. I kind of could. Were they gone or were they not?

"I don't know if I want to shoot a limit."

"Let's find them first," I said. I would have plenty of time to think about that remark later.

Dan thought and then said, "That's interesting. We'll find them and decide if we want to limit out or let it stand." The pointers got up, stretched their backs, glanced at us, wagged once, and lay down again next to the spring. I had gotten a queer feeling. Dan went quiet. He stared off. After a minute, a smile shot over his face. The dogs had been watching for that, and we were all on our feet and moving.

"This is it," Dan said, to the dogs or to me; I was never sure which. Betty and Sally cracked off, casting into the wind, Betty making the bigger race, Sally filling in with meticulous groundwork. I could sense Dan's pleasure in these fast and beautiful bracemates.

"When you hunt these girls," he said, "you've got to step up their rations with hamburger, eggs, bacon drippings—you know, mixed in with that kibble. On real hot days, you put electrolytes in their drinking water. Betty comes into heat in April and October; Sally, March and September. Sally runs a little fever with her heat and shouldn't be hunted in hot weather for the first week and a half. I always let them stay in the house. I put them in a roading harness by August first to get them in shape. They've both been roaded horseback."

I began to feel dazed and heavy. Maybe life wasn't something you lost at the end of a long fight. But I let myself off and thought, These things can go on and on.

Sally pitched over the top of a coulee. Betty went in and up the other side. There was a shadow that crossed the deep grass at the head of the draw. Sally locked up on point just at the rim, and Dan waved Betty in. She came in from the other side, hit the scent, sank into a running slink, and pointed.

Dan smiled at me and said, "Wish me luck." He closed his gun, walked over the rim, and sank from sight. I sat on the ground until I heard the report. After a bit the covey started to get up, eight dusky birds that went off on a climbing course. I whistled the dogs in and started for my truck.

Neil McMahon

◆   ◆

Neil McMahon received his A.B. from Stanford in 1970 and his M.F.A. from the University of Montana in 1979. He was a Stegner Fellow at Stanford in 1981–82. His fiction has appeared in The Atlantic, Epoch, *and others.*

"I consider 'Heart' to be a gift story, one that probably could not have been written without the conjunction of a peculiar and rare—for me, at least—set of conditions. These included an intense concern for the subject but enough distance to allow control, a level of ability not great enough to overstep itself, and above all, luck."

◆   ◆   ◆

From "Heart"

AFTER THE FIGHT I coughed for a long time, hunched over on a chair beside the ring while Charlie cut my hand wraps off. When he finished he stared at me with his fists on his hips. "For Christ's sake," he said. "You sound like you got tuberculosis." He tossed the soggy wads of gauze on the floor and came back with a plastic cup of water. It helped some.

A black fighter carrying an athletic bag stenciled "Anaconda Job Corps" nodded to me as he walked by. Earlier, I had watched him knock out one of the toughest of the prison middleweights and make it seem easy. "You look real good out there," he said. He was wearing a wide-brim hat with a plume, patent leather boots that laced to the knee, and a crimson satin shirt. Underneath the shirt, I knew, were hand-sized patches of pink skin. They made me think of a drowned man I had seen once in Chicago. The drowned man had been in the water three days, and his outer layer of skin had peeled like chocolate latex paint, leaving spots the color of old milk. When the black fighter bent close I could smell his sweat.

"You move real good," he said. His long thin hands hung loose at his waist. "You *slim*. You stay away from them big fat boys you be all right." He flipped up his palms and offered them. I slid my own across them. He grinned again, a flash of white on his unmarked face.

"You do all right tomorrow," he said. "You jus keep movin." He turned and sauntered back across the stage, jerking slightly with each step.

"A plume," Charlie said. "Now that's what I call a fancy nigger. Get dressed, let's get the fuck out of this place." He walked to the ring, spread his hands on the ropes, tested them for tautness: remembering.

My fight had been the last of the day. The stage in the prison auditorium was almost empty now. The convicts were mingling with the audience, mainly friends and relatives who had come to see the tournament. All were men; women were not allowed past the visiting room. The boxers who had come from outside were gathering near the doors. I was bracing myself to rise when a hand clamped on my shoulder. It was the man I had just beaten, a three-time loser named Grosniak.

Before the fight, he had taken me aside and recited his record meaningfully: "Armed robbery, grand larceny, and assault with a deadly weapon." He had only been out a week on his second parole when he and a friend got drunk and took a Midi-Mart in Butte. The police were waiting when he drove up to his house. "Eight years this time," he said, with what seemed like satisfaction. "There was bullets in the gun."

Grosniak's hair was bristly and unevenly cut, and he had a wandering eye that I had kept trying to circle around. The roll of flesh above his trunks was still red from punches. He was standing so close his hip almost touched me.

"I got to admit, you beat me fair and square," he said. "I dint think you could, but you did."

"Thanks," I said. Sweat was still running down the pale loose skin of his chest and belly, collecting in little drops on the sparse hair around his navel.

"You got a hell of a left hand," he said. "Your arms are too long for me. I couten figure out how to get inside you. But I'm gonna work on it. Maybe I'll get another shot at you sometime."

"Maybe so," I said.

"I knew you couten knock me out, though. I told you that before. You can pound on me all day, but you can't knock me out. Nobody's ever knocked me out." Dried blood and snot were still streaked across his chin, and dark red bubbles sucked in and out of his nose as he breathed. He was clenching and unclenching his fists.

"You couten take me on the street, neither," he said.

Earlier in the day, it had seemed I could not take a step without a guard eyeing me. Now there was none to be seen. But Charlie was walking back from the ring, thumbs hooked in his pockets, head lowered.

"Let's go," he said to me.

Grosniak's hand stayed on my shoulder. "That's gonna be a real show tomorrow," he said. "Heavy Runner hasn't lost a fight in five years."

Charlie ignored him as if he was invisible. "Build a fire under it," he said.

"Two hundred fights," Grosniak said. "He's won them all by knockouts."

I stood, shaking off his hand, and started toward the locker room. From the corner of my eye I saw him take a step after me, but before I could turn back, Charlie had shouldered him out of the way and was facing him, hands quiet at his sides. Grosniak's feet shifted in an impatient little dance, his walleye squeezing open and shut so it looked like he was winking.

"Too bad you're not in the tournament," he finally said.

"Real too bad," said Charlie. "I love to watch fat boys go down, they make such a nice splat when they hit."

Grosniak stepped back, and Charlie wheeled and walked after me.

"Maybe I'll get a shot at you sometime," Grosniak called.

I fell into step beside Charlie.

"I'll get you both on the street!"

We passed through the door into the locker room, and Charlie turned so fast I ran into him. "Why *ever*," he said, "didn't you take him down?"

"No need," I said. "I knew I had him."

"I god damn well guess you had him. One shot with your right would have done it. You remember what your right is?" He slapped my forearm hard.

"I didn't want to hurt him," I said, already hearing the words sound wrong.

"*Hurt* him? He's been convicted of armed robbery and aggravated assault."

I turned away, but he gripped my bicep and jerked me around, veins standing out on the back of a hand hard from years of working red iron. "Boy," he said, "you think that Indian's going to give you a break when he gets you on the ropes tomorrow?"

His face was tilted back and cocked to one side above his stocky body: tight-clamped jaw, bristly Fu Manchu worn in honor of Hurricane Carter, and a nose that had been redone in rings and bars all over the West. You could tell from his eyes that he wanted to be kind, but he understood when kindness would not do. I had not knocked Grosniak out because I could not stand the smack of my glove against his rubbery flesh, and the sudden fear in his eyes when my left came for his nose again, too quick for him to stop. In the last round, when he lumbered out with his fists drooping, trying to get enough air into his heavy body, I had hit him only to keep him away.

Charlie let go of my arm, looking suddenly tired. "I'll be in the lobby."

"I'll hurry," I said. "I just need a quick shower."

He stopped in the doorway, face gone wry. "You looking to get gang-raped?"

I shook my head.

"Just get dressed," he said. "I can put up with the smell of you for the drive home."

I stripped off trunks and cup and took my clothes from my bag. But I hated the evil-smelling sweat of fighting, and there was no one else around. I went quickly to the sink. The porcelain was covered with greenish scum, and the hot water tap would not turn. I rinsed handfuls of cold under my arms and down my chest and groin. There was no sting when the water touched my face; if one of Grosniak's wild flurries in the first round had scored, I could not yet feel it. When I finished I was shivering. I turned to see a shape, blurred from the water in my eyes, leaning against the doorjamb. I thought Charlie had come back, and said, "Toss me my towel, hey?"

The shape did not move. I blinked my eyes clear, and with a jolt, recognized the man: Louis Heavy Runner, the prison heavyweight champion.

He was not much over six feet tall, two or three inches shorter than me, but his tremendous chest and shoulders filled the doorway. Gleaming black hair hung in a ponytail to his waist. His forehead was high and broad, his jaw narrow, making him look Oriental. He seemed to be staring slightly to the side of me, and I could not tell if he missed my nod or ignored it. Because of a quirk in the seeding, he had fought twice that afternoon. Both times he had ended the bouts in the first round, leaping in with left hooks so fast I had not quite seen them, so savage they knocked 200-pound men clear off their feet. The first got up to take the eight-count. Heavy Runner clubbed him back to the mat in seconds. The other man went down a half-minute into the fight and stayed there.

I started looking in my bag for a towel and realized I had forgotten to bring one, but I rummaged until Heavy Runner pushed off the doorjamb with his shoulder and went back outside. Then I dried off quickly with my jeans. The auditorium was empty when I came out except for a bored looking guard near the entrance. I went to the ring and lined up even with the ropes. It took me just over four full strides to reach the other side.

I had thought so.

The lobby was crowded with visitors and boxers, standing around sipping cokes from the concession stand the convicts had set up. Everybody's eyes looked watchful over the brims of their cups. Charlie was leaning against a wall with his arms folded. He pointed with his chin at the coach of the Great Falls club, a 300-pounder named Fletcher, who was joking with a group of the inmates. We saw him at most of the tournaments, and he sometimes seconded for me in the corner.

"Looks like the big man's renewing old acquaintance," Charlie said.

It had never occurred to me to wonder what Fletcher did for a living. "Is he a cop?"

"He did three years here. I thought you knew that."

I shook my head.

"Blew his old lady away," Charlie said. "I remember it, I was in high school. That was back when they used to say, 'If you can't divorce your wife in Nevada, bring her to Montana and kill her.'"

Fletcher saw us, waved, and started toward us. The convicts and boxers stepped quickly out of his way.

"Shot her fucking *down* in the kitchen," Charlie said softly.

Fletcher slapped me on the back. I started coughing again. "You looked terrific out there," he said. "That Joe Grosniak's a pretty tough old boy."

"He's a meat," Charlie said.

"Well, he's no Louis Heavy Runner," Fletcher admitted. His thumb and forefinger squeezed the muscle above my shoulder as if he was testing me for the oven. "I'll be straight with you, I don't think you have a chance tomorrow." He sounded cheerful. "He's the toughest fighter in the joint, probably in the whole state. But he hasn't had a fight go past the first round in so long, you might be able to wear him out if you can stay away from him. Whatever you do, don't let him tag you with that hook. He killed a guy with it, you know, in a bar fight. That's why he's in here." He looked directly at me, and for the first time, I realized his inky hair and dark skin were those of a half-breed. He slapped me on the back again and said, "I'll be in your corner tomorrow. Sleep tight."

After a long time, two guards separated from the crowd and stood in front of the doors. "Everybody here?" one called. He had small shoulders and wide fleshy hips, and his nightstick and radio seemed too big for him. The other guard yelled into the auditorium that this was the last call for visitors to leave. "Anybody still here's gonna spend the night," the first guard said. The inmates laughed and whistled.

The guards separated the convicts back into the auditorium and counted us twice, then led us across the exercise yard through the raw windy March twilight. Dead grass sprouted through cracks in the concrete where the snow had blown off. Scraps of rusty chain nets hung from basketball hoops, clinking in the wind. The fence around the yard was chain-link topped with barbed wire, eighteen or twenty feet tall, and I could see the guard towers at all four corners of the old stone building, a silhouette in the window of each.

The corridors were wide and brightly lit, with lines painted down the centers of the floor. Metal doors with grilles were set into the walls at intervals that looked too close. Some were open, showing empty cells with bunks and seatless toilets; at others, a man's face would appear, silently watching us pass. At the end of every corridor, a grate of iron bars spanned wall to wall, floor to ceiling, with an armed guard sitting in a barred alcove. He would look us over, exchange words with the guards who led us, then throw the switch that slid the grate aside. Nobody pushed to get through, but nobody lagged behind.

At the last checkpoint, a booth in the main lobby, each of us had to push our hand through another grille and be examined for the invisible fluorescent stamp we had gotten when we entered. I did not think such a stamp would wash off with soap and water, but I was glad I had not showered.

◆　　　　◆　　　　◆

It was almost dark by the time we reached the outskirts of Deer Lodge and passed the last of the signs that read: WARNING: STATE PENITENTIARY AND MENTAL HEALTH FACILITY ARE LOCATED IN THIS AREA. DO NOT PICK UP HITCHHIKERS. From there it was a dozen flat miles through soggy hayfields to the Highway 12 turnoff at Garrison. Charlie lit a Camel, but the smoke tickled my cough. Irritably, he stubbed it out.

"Maybe I should just drop you off at the state hospital," he said. The truck veered as he leaned down to rummage beneath the seat. He came up with a pint of Jim Beam that always looked the same, about half full.

"Shelley's got some codeine," I said.

He swiveled to stare at me, the pint in his fist. "*Shelley*. The night before a fight?"

"I told her I'd come by."

He grunted and sank lower in the seat, chin almost to his chest.

Abruptly there was a dark shape on the roadside ahead to the right, too close to the speeding truck. I jerked up straight, my hands gripping the dash. Charlie swerved, and the shape turned as we roared by: an old Indian woman, coat blown open by our passing, thin hands clutching a bundle. Her black eyes looked like the hollows of a skull.

"You can take that son of a bitch if you just stay away from him," Charlie said. "Don't listen to Fletcher's bullshit. He's trying to set you up."

I craned around. The old lady had already faded into the dark of the Warm Springs Valley.

"You hearing me?" Charlie said.

I turned back. "That ring's three feet short of regulation," I said. "I paced it off."

He shrugged. "I've told you a thousand times, you're an outside fighter. You go in and mix it up with a guy like Heavy Runner, sure you're going to get hurt. But you've got a good three inches reach and you're in top shape."

"And he's got thirty pounds on me and he's twice as fast. Did you see him with those other guys? It was like they were in a cage with a gorilla."

Charlie drank from the pint, then offered it to me. "Just a sip. Clear your throat."

I shook my head.

We topped a rise to see the lights of Garrison, and a minute later we drove through. It consisted of a truck stop, a mill of some kind, and a string of run-down houses along a railroad siding. Only the big diesel rigs idling in front of Welch's Cafe kept the place from looking deserted. Then we accelerated again onto the highway east.

"You want to go in there already whipped, it's okay with me," Charlie said. "It's your ass either way."

I closed my eyes and willed sleep.

◆   ◆   ◆

In those days Shelley lived in the part of town called Moccasin Flats. The streets were mostly dirt, and what was left of her fence was always plastered with windblown paper. A cat's eyes glowed in the headlights as we pulled up, then disappeared into the abandoned chicken house across the street.

"About ten tomorrow," Charlie said.

I gripped my bag and stepped out. He leaned suddenly across the seat, his eyes hard in the argon light. "You let that woman suck all the juice out of you, you ain't gonna be worth a rat's ass." Then the truck's tires crunched on frozen snow, and I was alone.

The faint smell of marijuana smoke hit me when I pushed open the door, old, like it had soaked into the curtains and furniture. "Don't move," she said. I turned slowly to where she was sitting cross-legged in a corner, with a sketch pad across her knees. She was wearing a long peasant skirt and a blouse I had bought her, Central American, with wide bands of deep red and blue. Her pupils were dilated, and her face had a look of almost childish concentration. "The conquering hero returns," she said, and the pencil began to move across the pad.

I tossed my bag on the couch and pulled off my jacket.

"Hey," she said. "Hold still."

"Later."

"But I've got to catch you in your moment of glory." Her voice had an edge that was not quite teasing.

"I'm not in the mood for fucking around, Shelley," I said, and walked into the kitchen.

She came in and stood with her hands clasped in front of her. "Sorry," she said. "Your face isn't beat up, so I thought maybe you won."

"I did," I said. I was tired but did not want to stop moving. "You got any beer?"

She put her hands on my cheeks and turned my face both ways, examining it. "Okay, the sketch can wait," she said, then kissed me. I tasted smoke on her breath. "Tough fight?"

"No," I said. We kissed again, longer this time, then she pulled away and went to the refrigerator. She set a six-pack of San Miguel and two fat New York steaks on the counter.

"Celebrate," she said. "Victory in your last fight. If you lost, you would have gotten Hamm's and tuna fish."

"Shelley, what are you doing spending money on stuff like this?" I said, trying to sound angry. She worked part-time in an art supplies store and could hardly pay the rent.

Her eyes widened mockingly. "I keep telling you, I found a sugar daddy."

I snorted, but I thought of all my out of town construction jobs.

She opened two bottles of beer, and when we raised them, touched hers to mine. "To heroes," she said, with the edge back in her voice. She had never once come to watch me fight. I took a long drink. It was so cold it made my teeth hurt, sharp at first but then soothing to my raw throat.

"It wasn't the last fight," I said.

"Oh, don't tell me," she said, setting her bottle down hard. "You let Charlie talk you into that stupid Golden Gloves thing."

"Tomorrow," I said.

"Tomorrow?"

"This was just eliminations. I've got to go back for the finals."

"I thought you were going to take me to Boulder Hot Springs."

"That was if I didn't win."

"You sort of forgot to tell me that," she said. She walked to the small window above the sink and stood there, gazing out. When I met her eyes, reflected in the glass, she was looking at me from a long way away. "So how do you want your steak?"

I circled her with my arms, her body tight and resisting. "I'm sorry," I said. "I didn't know what my chances were. I'd a lot rather go to the hot springs with you."

"Then why don't you?"

"I have to go back. I won."

She shook her head impatiently. Her hair smelled of lemon and tickled my nose. "Who's going to care if you don't? A bunch of fucking jerks who can't get off on anything but pounding each other's brains out. I could even see it if you got paid."

"That's not the point."

"What *is* the point?" After a moment she leaned back against me and covered my hands with hers. "You hate it, don't you," she said quietly.

I watched the old school clock on the wall, twelve minutes after seven on a Saturday night.

"If you're trying to prove something, lover, I can think of better ways," Shelley said. She twisted around and ran the tip of her tongue along my neck. "Now how about that steak?"

"Rare," I said.

♦   ♦   ♦

After dinner I took a long shower and stretched out on the bed. It was too short for me, so I always ended up sticking my feet through the iron posts at the end. The walls were hung with her sketches and paintings. Many were nudes, and some of couples, mating. The figures were exaggerated, the females with voluptuous breasts and thighs, the men large-boned and heavily muscled, and they grappled and strained like giants. But beneath the sexual quality there was an honesty, a need to get to the heart of whatever it was that made men and women behave in such an outwardly absurd way. Her work had just begun to sell, a few landscapes and wildlife sketches at a gallery in Helena. The nudes remained private. Several were new, and I tried to be interested, but the phlegm rose in my throat and I started coughing again. The stereo was playing quietly in the next room, the dark rhythmic chords and lonesome harmonica of *Blonde On Blonde*. I knew that when she finished the dishes, she would sit for a few minutes with her water pipe.

After a while she came in and lit a candle on the dresser. I watched her take her earrings off, burnished copper teardrops that glowed dully in the flame light. Another night, I might have asked her to leave them on. She undressed, her small breasts stretching flat as she reached into the closet for her robe. I could not stop the coughing, and when she turned back, she said, "You sound just awful."

"Have you got any more of that codeine?"

"I think so." She went down the hall and came back with a small brown bottle and a spoon, then said, "I have to brush my teeth," and left again. I drank the cough syrup straight from the bottle. It was cherry flavored, but you could tell there was something under the sweetness. Across the room, a small dark shape moved patiently, in silhouette, down the wall, fluttering toward the candle.

An instant cold ache would still touch the base of my nose whenever I thought of the Samoan at the Golden Gloves the year before. He was the Northwestern United States light-heavyweight champion; I had not yet had a dozen fights in a ring. Early in the first round, he had stepped in under one of my jabs and hooked me to the ribs. I remembered the blows like jolts of painless electricity, sparking inside my skull, and then blackness caving in the edges of my vision. When I opened my eyes, the referee was on three.

I remembered the glare of the overhead lights, the crouched referee's finger stabbing the air in front of my face with every number he shouted; remembered seeing for the first time the rust-colored stains on the canvas as my head rolled to the side; remembered thinking that the roar of the crowd was just as it is always described. I got up, and then got up again, trying to follow that grinning kinky blueblack head, trying to lash out and destroy it. But as in the dream I had when I was younger, I could not make my arms obey me. There comes a moment when you realize you are not what you have thought. I went home that night with three broken ribs and a nearly dislocated jaw.

You can drive in cars all your life and never think a thing about it, until one night a drunk doing sixty comes across the center line and you wake up wrapped in plaster, sucking liquid through glass tubes. After that, getting in a car is not the same. Being knocked out was a little like that, only it was not the pain. It was just something I never wanted to happen to me again.

When Shelley came back she was fragrant with soap, toothpaste, and a trace of perfume. She slipped off her robe and shook free her hair, a dark mane that came halfway down her back. Then she turned to me, slender and ivory, and commanded, "Lie on your stomach." She straddled me, her hands cool, then warm, on my back, surprisingly strong, kneading out the hours of tension. After a while she told me to turn over. Her face was dreamy, absorbed in the movement of her own hands. As she swayed, her hair would brush my skin. Then her lips began to follow her fingers, moving down my chest and belly. I pressed my palms to her face and pulled her up beside me.

"What's the matter?" she whispered.

I stroked her head, rounding the curve of her skull with my fingers. Finally I said, "That Indian's going to beat the piss out of me tomorrow."

She reared up and put her hands on my shoulders. "My God, are you crazy? You *know* you're going to get hammered, but you're going to go anyway?"

"He's knocked out everybody in the state," I said.

She pressed me back into the bed, leaning forward until her face was only inches from mine. The scent of her perfume pulsed from the soft place where her jaw met her neck. "Stay here with me. You're sick. We'll lie in bed all day. I'll do anything you want."

"It's already set," I said. "Charlie's coming by at ten."

"The hell with Charlie! You think he's your friend, but he's just using you, pushing you to do it because he can't any more. Call him and tell him you can hardly breathe." Her eyes were fiercer than I had ever seen them. "Call him."

"I can't do that."

"Well, *I* can." She slid off me, her feet thumping on the wooden floor. I hooked my arm around her waist to pull her back. "Let me *go*, god damn you," she panted, and twisted my fingers until she broke free.

When she got to the door I said, "Wait. If I'm still coughing in the morning, I won't go."

"Promise?"

I hesitated. She jerked open the door.

"I promise," I said.

Back in bed, she stretched herself over me like a blanket, spreading arms and legs to cover mine. "Sweetie, when are you gonna understand, you're not like Charlie and those others. It's okay. You don't have to be." Her fingers moved to my groin, but I caught her hand. She rose up on an elbow and looked into my face. Then she said, "Okay. See you in the morning." She turned so her back was against me and pulled my arm across her breasts. After a while, her breathing evened.

For a long time I lay there, listening to the ticking of the bedside clock, like a tiny mechanical heart: thinking about what Charlie had said on the drive to the prison. "Most of those poor bastards in for their second or third time, it's because things are too complicated out in the world. So they pull shit until they get caught, and once they're in, somebody tells them what to do every minute and feeds them breakfast. After a while it don't make any difference whether it's a man or a woman they're fucking, and that's it. They're home."

Grosniak, yes. He wore it like a uniform, and so did most of the others I had seen. But a man like Louis Heavy Runner—he was there because there was no place else to put him. A hundred years ago, he would have been riding with Sitting Bull or Joseph, a hero instead of a criminal. That he had broken the law seriously, that he was dangerous, there was no doubt. But what were you supposed to do with a man like that: Give him a job in a tire shop? Hope he stayed on the reservation and drank himself to an early death?

Climb into a tiny arena with him, and for a few desperate minutes, give him a chance to somehow get even?

I did my best to explain to Heavy Runner and all the other convicts who slept alone in cell bunks year after year why I could not make love to the woman beside me tonight. Then I turned onto my other side and stepped into the ring in my imagination, waiting for the bell.

JAMES MCMICHAEL

James McMichael's three books of poems are Against the Falling Evil *(1971),*
The Lover's Familiar *(1978), and* Four Good Things *(1980). He has recently
completed a book of prose entitled* Stephen, Jamesy, James Joyce.

"These poems are part of a book-length sequence about two characters who
sustain a clandestine romance for three years and then marry. The interests of
the sequence as a whole are retrospection, failure, and desire."

◆   ◆   ◆

Two Poems

She likes to be out. Because he keeps us
in more, I help with the baby. She goes out
but wants me to go with her. Though I
go sometimes and like it, I'm sure that she's
insatiable, she's sure that I'm not liking it enough,
and it stays that way. The rest of the time is
mine, the time my writing takes becoming
proper to me, another of my properties, like my
cold hands. I remind her that my work's no fun.
She hadn't forgotten, she says, and neither am I.
It isn't a writer's line, but I say it.
   "You want me to be someone I'm not."
   "You want *me* to be someone I'm not and I'm
being that person."

◆   ◆   ◆

Three years not so much of squabbles as of
routine. Her days in the library, mine at
school and at home. Owen is four. We see friends for
dinner sometimes, talk on the phone to other friends
too far away. We go to Idaho in the summer.
I feel my life is safe because she loves me.
We'd been asleep, twelve years ago, when the
call came about my father. I went downstairs to
answer it, came back, her face asking me who
was it and I told her what. Then her

"No,"
her arms held out to me from the sheet, her body,
the fathomless spare nurturing
"O Jimmie"
which I still hear in anything she says.

LARRY McMURTRY

A descendant of ranchers and cowboys, Larry McMurtry was a Stegner Fellow at Stanford in 1960. He has published eleven novels and a collection of essays about his native Texas. His tenth novel, Lonesome Dove, *was awarded the Pulitzer Prize for fiction.*

"*Lonesome Dove,* from which the following passage was taken, is about a cattle drive that begins in southern Texas and ends in northern Montana during the 1870s. McMurtry speaks thus of his own work: 'In my own practice, writing fiction has always seemed a semiconscious activity. I concentrate so hard on visualizing my characters that my actual surroundings blur. My characters seem to be speeding through their lives—I have to type unflaggingly in order to keep them in sight.'"

From *Lonesome Dove*

SO CAPTAIN CALL TURNED back down the rivers, cut by the quirt of Clara's contempt and seared with the burn of his own regret. For a week, down from the Platte and across the Republican, he could not forget what she said: that he had never done right, that he and Gus had ruined one another, that he was a coward, that she would take a letter to the boy. He had gone through life feeling that he had known what should be done, and now a woman flung it at him that he hadn't. He found that he could not easily forget a word Clara said. He could only trail the buggy down the lonely plains, her words stinging in his heart and head.

Before he reached Kansas, word had filtered ahead of him that a man was carrying a body home to Texas. The plain was filled with herds, for it was full summer. Cowboys spread the word, soldiers spread it. Several times he met trappers, coming east from the Rockies, or buffalo hunters who were finding no buffalo. The Indians heard—Pawnee and Arapahoe and Ogallala Sioux. Sometimes he would ride past parties of braves, their horses fat on spring grass, come to watch his journey. Some were curious enough to approach him, even to question him. Why did he not bury the *compañero?* Was he a holy man whose spirit must have a special place?

No, Call answered. Not a holy man. Beyond that he couldn't explain. He had come to feel that Augustus had probably been out of his mind at the end, though he hadn't looked it, and that *he* had been out of his mind to make the promise he had.

In one week in Kansas he ran into eight cattle herds—he would no sooner pass one than he encountered another. The only advantage to him was that the trail bosses were generous with wire and pliers. The Miles City buggy had been patched so many times that it was mostly wire by then, Call felt. He knew it would never make Texas, but he determined to keep going as long as he could— what he would do when it finally fell apart he didn't know.

Finally he was asked about Augustus and the purpose of his journey so many times that he couldn't tolerate it. He turned west into Colorado, meaning to skirt the main cattle trails. He was tired of meeting people. His only moments of peace came late in the day when he was too tired to think and was just bouncing along with Gus.

He rode through Denver, remembering that he had never sent Wilbarger's brother the telegram he had promised, notifying him of Wilbarger's death. It had been a year and he felt he owed Wilbarger that consideration, though he soon regretted coming into the town, a noisy place filled with miners and cattlemen. The sight of the buggy with the coffin excited such general curiosity that by the time he was out of the telegraph office a crowd had gathered. Call had scarcely walked out the door when an undertaker in a black hat and a blue bow tie approached him.

"Mister, you ain't nowhere near the graveyard," the man said. He had even waxed his mustache and was altogether too shiny for Call's taste.

"I wasn't looking for it," Call said, mounting. People were touching the coffin as if they had the right.

"We give a nice ten-dollar funeral," the undertaker said. "You could just leave the fellow with me and come pick out the gravestone at your leisure. Of course the gravestone's extra."

"Not in the market," Call said.

"Who is it, mister?" a boy asked.

"His name was McCrae," Call said.

He was glad to put the town behind him, and thereafter took to driving at night to avoid people, though it was harder on the buggy, for he couldn't always see the bumps.

One night he felt the country was too rough for evening travel so he camped by the Purgatoire River, or Picketwire, as the cowboys called it. He heard the sound of an approaching horse and wearily picked up his rifle. It was only one horse. Dusk had not quite settled into night, and he could see the rider coming— a big man. The horse turned out to be a red mule and the big man Charles Goodnight. Call had known the famous cattleman since the Fifties, and they had ridden together a few times in the Frontier Regiment, before he and Gus were sent to the border. Call had never taken to the man—Goodnight was indifferent to authority, or at least unlikely to put any above his own—but he could not deny that the man had uncommon ability. Goodnight rode up to the campfire but did not dismount.

"I like to keep up with who's traveling the country," he said. "I admit I did not expect it to be you."

"You're welcome to coffee," Call said.

"I don't take much else at night," he added.

"Hell, if I didn't take some grub in at night I'd starve," Goodnight said. "Usually too busy to eat breakfast."

"You're welcome to get down then," Call said.

"No, I'm too busy to do that either," Goodnight said. "I've got interests in Pueblo. Besides, I was never a man to sit around and gossip.

"I reckon that's McCrae," he said, glancing at the coffin on the buggy.

"That's him," Call said, dreading the questions that seemed to be inevitable.

"I owe him a debt for cleaning out that mangy bunch on the Canadian," Goodnight said. "I'd have soon had to do it myself, if he hadn't."

"Well, he's past collecting debts," Call said. "Anyway he let that dern killer get away."

"No shame to McCrae," Goodnight said. "I let the son of a bitch get away myself, and more than once, but a luckier man caught him. He butchered two families in the Bosque Redondo, and as he was leaving a deputy sheriff made a lucky shot and crippled his horse. They ran him down and mean to hang him in Santa Rosa next week. If you spur up you can see it."

"Well, I swear," Call said. "You going?"

"No," Goodnight said. "I don't attend hangings, although I've presided over some, of the homegrown sort. This is the longest conversation I've had in ten years. Goodbye."

Call took the buggy over Raton Pass and edged down into the great New Mexican plain. Though he had seen nothing but plains for a year, he was still struck by the immense reach of land that lay before him. To the north, there was still snow on the peaks of the Sangre de Cristo. He hurried to Santa Rosa, risking further damage to the wagon, only to discover that the hanging had been put back a week.

Everyone in the Territory wanted to see Blue Duck hanged, it seemed. The little town was full of cowhands, with women and children sleeping in wagons. There was much argument, most of it in favor of hanging Blue Duck instantly lest he escape. Parties were constantly forming to present petitions to the sheriff, or else storm the jail, but the latter were unenthusiastic. Blue Duck had ranged the *llano* for so long, and butchered and raped and stolen so often, that superstitions had formed around him. Some, particularly women, felt he couldn't die, and that their lives would never be safe.

Call took the opportunity to have a blacksmith completely rebuild the buggy. The blacksmith had lots of wagons to work on and took three days to get around to the buggy, but he let Call store the coffin in his back room, since it was attracting attention.

The only thing to do in town besides drink was to admire the new courthouse, three stories high and with a gallows at the top, from which Blue Duck would be hung. The courthouse had fine glass windows and polished floors.

Two days before the hanging was to take place, Call decided to go see the prisoner. He had already met the deputy who had crippled Blue Duck's horse. The man, whose name was Decker, was fat and stone drunk, leading Call to suspect that Goodnight had been right—the shot had been lucky. But every man in the Territory had insisted on buying the deputy a drink since then; perhaps he had been capable of sobriety before he became a hero. He was easily moved to sobs at the memory of his exploit, which he had recounted so many times that he was hoarse.

The sheriff, a balding man named Owensby, had of course heard of Call and was eager to show him the prisoner. The jail had only three cells, and Blue Duck was in the middle one, which had no window. The others had been cleared, minor culprits having simply been turned loose in order to lessen the chances that Blue Duck might somehow contrive an escape.

The minute Call saw the man he knew it was unlikely. Blue Duck had been shot in the shoulder and leg, and had a greasy rag wound around his forehead, covering another wound. Call had never seen a man so draped in chains. He was handcuffed; each leg was heavily chained; and the chains draped around his torso were bolted to the wall. Two deputies with Winchesters kept constant watch. Despite the chains and bars, Call judged that both were scared to death.

Blue Duck himself seemed indifferent to the furor outside. He was leaning back against the wall, his eyes half closed, when Call came in.

"What's he doing?" Sheriff Owensby asked. Despite all the precautions, he was so nervous that he had not been able to keep food down since the prisoner was brought in.

"Ain't doin' much," one deputy said. "What can he do?"

"Well, it's been said he can escape from any jail," the sheriff reminded them. "We got to watch him close."

"Only way to watch him closer is to go in with him, and I'll quit before I'll do that," the other deputy said.

Blue Duck opened his slumbrous eyes a fraction wider and looked at Call.

"I hear you brought your stinkin' old friend to my hanging," Blue Duck said, his low, heavy voice startling the deputies and the sheriff too.

"Just luck," Call said.

"I should have caught him and cooked him when I had the chance," Blue Duck said.

"He would have killed you," Call said, annoyed by the man's insolent tone. "Or I would have, if need be."

Blue Duck smiled. "I raped women and stole children and burned houses and shot men and run off horses and killed cattle and robbed who I pleased, all over your territory, ever since you been a law," he said. "And you never even had a good look at me until today. I don't reckon you would have killed me."

Sheriff Owensby reddened, embarrassed that the man would insult a famous Ranger, but there was little he could do about it. Call knew there was truth in what Blue Duck said, and merely stood looking at the man, who was larger than he had supposed. His head was huge and his eyes cold as snake's eyes.

"I despise all you fine-haired sons of bitches," Blue Duck said. "You Rangers. I expect I'll kill a passel of you yet."

"I doubt it," Call said. "Not unless you can fly."

Blue Duck smiled a cold smile. "I *can* fly," he said. "An old woman taught me. And if you care to wait, you'll see me."

"I'll wait," Call said.

On the day of the hanging the square in front of the courthouse was packed with spectators. Call had to tie his animals over a hundred yards away—he wanted to get started as soon as the hanging was over. He worked his way to the front of the crowd and watched as Blue Duck was moved from the jail to the courthouse in a small wagon under heavy escort. Call thought it likely somebody would be killed accidentally before it was over, since all the deputies were so scared they had their rifles on cock. Blue Duck was as heavily chained as ever and still had the greasy rag tied around his head wound. He was led into the courthouse and up the stairs. The hangman was making last-minute improvements on the hangrope and Call was looking off, thinking he saw a man who had once served under him in the crowd, when he heard a scream and a sudden shattering of glass. He looked up and the hair on his neck rose, for Blue Duck was flying through the air in his chains. It seemed to Call the man's cold smile was fixed on him as he fell: he had managed to dive through one of the long glass windows on the third floor—and not alone, either. He had grabbed Deputy Decker with his handcuffed hands and pulled him out too. Both fell to the stony ground right in front of the courthouse. Blue Duck hit right on his head, while the deputy had fallen backwards, like a man pushed out of a hayloft. Blue Duck didn't move after he hit, but the deputy squirmed and cried. Tinkling glass fell about the two men.

The crowd was too stunned to move. Sheriff Owensby stood high above them, looking out the window, mortified that he had allowed hundreds of people to be cheated of a hanging.

Call walked out alone and knelt by the two men. Finally a few others joined him. Blue Duck was stone dead, his eyes wide open, the cruel smile still on his lips. Decker was broken to bits and spitting blood already—he wouldn't last long.

"I guess that old woman didn't teach you well enough," Call said to the outlaw.

Owensby ran down the stairs and insisted that they carry Blue Duck up and string him from the gallows. "By God, I said he'd hang, and he'll hang," he said. Many of the spectators were so afraid of the outlaw that they wouldn't touch him, even dead. Six men who were too drunk to be spooked finally carried him up and left him dangling above the crowd.

Call thought it a silly waste of work, though he supposed the sheriff had politics to think of.

He himself could not forget that Blue Duck had smiled at him in the moment that he flew. As he walked through the crowd he heard a woman say she had seen Blue Duck's eyes move as he lay on the ground. Even with the man hanging from a gallows, the people were priming themselves to believe he hadn't died. Probably half the crimes committed on the *llano* in the next ten years would be laid to Blue Duck.

As Call was getting into his wagon, a newspaperman ran up, a red-headed boy scarcely twenty years old, white with excitement at what he had just seen.

"Captain Call?" he asked. "I write for the Denver paper. They pointed you out to me. Can I speak to you for a minute?"

Call mounted the dun and caught the mule's lead rope. "I have to ride," he said. "It's still a ways to Texas."

He started to go, but the boy would not give up. He strode beside the dun, talking, much as Clara had, except that the boy was merely excited. Call thought it strange that two people on one trip would follow him off.

"But, Captain," the boy said. "They say you were the most famous Ranger. They say you've carried Captain McCrae three thousand miles just to bury him. They say you started the first ranch in Montana. My boss will fire me if I don't talk to you. They say you're a man of vision."

"Yes, a hell of a vision," Call said. He was forced to put spurs to the dun to get away from the boy, who stood scribbling on a pad.

Tom McNeal

Since his Stegner year at Stanford, McNeal has divided his time between a family construction business and his own short fiction, most of which is set in either the San Bernardino Mountains or the Nebraska panhandle. His most recent stories have appeared in Epoch, Playboy, Redbook, *and* Quarterly West.

"The original draft of this story came easily, too easily, and began stretching out over the pages. I remember reading it aloud to the workshop in the Jones Room late one autumn afternoon. I read and read and read. When at last I was done, no one said a word. Absolute silence. Finally John L'Heureux cleared his throat. 'Well, Tom, this is quite wonderful as thirty-six-page stories go,' he said, which was his own sly way of calling for suggestions to cut, and in the next instant every galoot at the table was clamoring to speak."

◆   ◆   ◆

True

LOUD MEN ALWAYS MADE me edgy, except when I was a little girl, and then it was loud boys. So on this particular night, the new guys in the cabin next door were definitely making me edgy. They were whooping it up big, just the two of them, yelling and throwing empties and generally carrying on in the way youth will.

The fracas had been going on a while, since before *People's Court*, according to Letty, and that began at 7:30. Letty was watching the set, holding Mr. Finny in her lap, doing her best to conduct business as usual. I was sitting in the kitchen watching the TV with one eye and the cabin next door with the other. A personality was doing the 11 o'clock news when one of them came out back of their cabin with a rifle bigger than I knew existed, pointed it carefully at the moon and let fly twice, *Ka-blam! Ka-blam!* Rattled our pans each time, was how big it was.

Letty without looking up from the set said, "Those two're dangerous."

All the one with the rifle was wearing were these black briefs and he was singing a song I didn't know. I'll say this. His voice was not bad, and he himself was not ugly. Letty, on her way to visit the refrigerator, peered over my shoulder for a second, then, after she'd been back at the set for a while, said very casually, "Why you watching those goons anyhow?"

I didn't know, so I said, "What kinda gun is that, Letty?"

"Sharps, I think." Letty knows guns, I never knew from where.

The one on the porch had started in on *Blue Moon*, a little softer, almost crooning it, then all of a sudden stopped, reloaded, and fired off another one over the pines. *Ka-blam!*

The phone rang. It was Earl in the cabin on the other side. He was talking loud about the new neighbors. Earl's not normally excitable but he was in a definite state. I held the receiver a couple of inches from my ear and listened to him calling them shiftless, malicious, and impolite. The impolite part made me laugh and Earl stopped short and said, "This Letty or Lois?"

"Lois," I said and was remarking on the niceness of the crooning goon's voice when another shot went off next door and Letty grabbed the phone from me. In one breath Letty said to Earl that she hadn't called the police but thought somebody ought to because besides everything else she'd heard a little rumor about there being a body in the goons's freezer though she wasn't at liberty to say anything more about it.

"What body would that be?" I inquired when she was done lighting a fire under Earl.

Letty, to compose herself, began feeding Hershey's Kisses to Mr. Finny one at a time. Mr. Finny was short, plump, and more her dog than mine. Finally Letty said, "There was a girl with them when they moved in. That was three days ago. You seen any live girls over there in the last three days?"

"There was a girl moved in?" I said. It was news to me.

"She looked maybe twenty," Letty said. "Hard to tell because it was dark, but she looked out cold. They had to carry her in. Took her straight toward the back bedroom."

Mr. Finny let a half-eaten Kiss roll out of his mouth and waddled off to his water bowl.

"Thirsty," Letty said for him, and picked up the moist Kiss and resealed it in its foil wrapper with a smoothness worth watching. "Course if I was sheriff," she went on almost to herself, "I'd check the freezer. They got a freezer over there big enough to stash three or four girls her size in."

Letty had a way of believing anything that knitted into her feelings about someone. She didn't care for the two goons so she had no problem at all believing there was a corpse in their cooler. Same with our neighbor Sally Ann Newville. At first we liked Sally Ann—she brought over a casserole the day we moved in—but then Sally Ann's viewpoint changed and she began leaning back from us as we talked to her in the street, like there was a smell to us or something, so one time, after reading a story in the newspaper called, "Is Your Neighbor a Space Alien?" Letty decided Sally Ann *was* one. She sent her a letter that went, *Your neighbors in Big Bear know you're a space alien and have notified the appropriate local, state, and federal authorities.* "All it did was make her meaner," I heard Letty telling Earl later, like this was a big surprise.

It was during Johnny Carson's monologue that the sheriff's car pulled up next door. The goons's cabin didn't have any curtains so with all the lights blazing you could watch the goings-on on this side of the house like it was a play on a stage. I saw the ugly goon peek out the front window and yell something over his shoulder to the not-ugly one, who quick pulled on his pants and stashed his buffalo gun in the big freezer.

There was just the one deputy, knocking the first time and pounding the second. Eventually, the crooning goon answered the door and they all stood in the front room. The deputy was doing all the talking for a while, then the goons looked funny at each other and led him toward the bedroom on the other side of the cabin. What they were doing in there was anybody's guess, but, after a bit, out they all came grinning and laughing, even the deputy. The three of them gathered again out on the front porch. I heard the deputy saying things about older neighbors and quiet neighborhoods, and the goons were nodding and agreeing and waiting for him to leave.

The minute the squad car crested the hill and disappeared from view the two goons began their sermon. They spoke to us one at a time. "You shriveled old dick," one of them yelled toward Earl's place, "you go to bed right now and pull the pillow over your Dumbo-sized ears or this'll turn into a night you'll surely regret." Earl's ears don't lay back so well and one evening when he'd had a few he told us he'd taped them back at night all during high school. I probably would've enjoyed an element in the goon's speech—it was the kind of thing a man like Earl needed every now and then—if it hadn't've been for the fact that the two of them were now directing their attention to the cabin across the road, which is owned by the Feenstras, who are as nice as nice can be, and it didn't take Sherlock Holmes to figure out we were next. Letty switched off the tv and all the lights and opened the near window, which we huddled close to. It was like waiting in the basement in Nebraska for a tornado.

But with us the tactics changed. "And how about our two magnolias in their cozy little cottage?" one of them sang out in a sickening-sweet voice. And the other one in singsong said, "In their solitary cabin's solitary bed!" They didn't stop there either.

Letty wound shut the window. She looked at me through the dark and in a whispery voice said, "Don't you listen," and with her huge hands was softly covering my ears.

◆   ◆   ◆

I don't dislike men. The problem is it's never simple. Take, for example, Arthur. I was thirty-five and living in Lincoln, Nebraska, when Arthur moved in next door. I was with Cy at the time. My ex. Cy was an old story. High school football star, teacher's college dropout, beer distributor, borderline alcoholic. He was going slack in a hurry. Nights he spent sipping Scotch and watching the set. I did a little housework and got good at crosswords. Lots of days I never got out of the robe. So I was ripe for Arthur. At first it was just to see if I was alive anymore, but pretty soon I was beginning to take it seriously. I had it bad in fact.

Arthur was married, but his wife worked at Hovland-Swanson, so she wasn't home days, and neither was Cy. For a living Arthur was a steward for this charter airline that toted V.I.P.s wherever in the world they wanted to go next. He'd served Don Ho, the Rolling Stones, and Tab Hunter, just to name a few. Anyhow, one day out of the blue he says he's been transferred to L.A. I went right home and packed. It didn't work out of course, and there I was.

Hewlett-Packard is where I met Letty. We were the only ones in the whole lunchroom who ate alone every day, so we tended to pay attention to each other. She's a big woman, but her lunches consisted of just candy bars and yogurt.

One day I sat down nearby and didn't say anything. Finally I did. "How come you eat so much chocolate?" I said. She smiled at me and said, "Because I used to drink, but now I eat a lot of chocolate instead." She told me about A.A. and made it sound fun. She had red cheeks and a laugh snappy as apples. I liked her.

Letty was pretty well fixed. She had her Hewlett-Packard wage plus a pension from her time in the Air Force, and she had this cabin, though she didn't mention that right off. When finally she did, she hardly looked at me. She was spooning herself yogurt at the time. "My husband and I bought it. For 600 down. Then when the marriage fritzed he took the Corvette and I got the cabin. I thought I would use it more, but I don't."

A guy that would take a car over a cabin interested me. I asked about him. She shrugged. "Before we were married he acted like a human being and afterwards he didn't." Period.

"So how come you don't go up to your cabin more?" I said, getting back to that.

Letty was scraping her yogurt carton, making a real project of it. In a slow careful way she said, "Because the only person I'd want to go with wouldn't want to."

"Who?" I said, because I was really curious, but she wouldn't say, so I said, "Anyhow I'll bet you're wrong. Any man'd be a fool to say no to you." And then, without a thought, I said that I'd be happy to stand in for whoever it was she wasn't asking.

That first weekend Letty had us right off the bat down to the lake fishing out of a rowboat. I'd never fished before, but by the end of the day I'd learned to like it. It was September. Leaves and sticks and shadows floated on the water. As Letty rowed us in that afternoon, they curled around the boat and closed after. I took a deep breath. There was something about the world around Letty that allowed you to nestle down into it and feel the kind of peacefulness I'd spent years trying to learn to live without.

We began spending all our weekends and holidays there. For Christmas, Letty gave me a black silk blouse in a box that said Bullocks Wilshire. "Came from there too," she said. When I put it on, she laughed her snappy laugh and said it was what I'd catch my next man in. I wore it New Year's Eve to the Antlers. That was where at about midnight we began to plot an early retirement so we could move up here permanent.

It only took us five years. That's what Letty said when we unlocked the front door with Mr. Finny at our feet and the car in the driveway full of everything in the world we owned. "It only took us five years." I was forty-one and Letty was a few years older. We were real good friends by then, without any secrets I knew about. The idea was to add a bedroom when we could swing it. But by the time the two yahoos moved in next door a few years later, I'd gotten afraid of trying to sleep without Letty breathing beside me, and the idea of adding a room hadn't been mentioned for ages.

◆   ◆   ◆

I slept poorly the night of the fracas, so when Letty packed up for fishing that afternoon I begged off in favor of a nap. She got Mr. Finny's leash, but didn't leave. "I'm going to say just one thing," she said, "and it's about those rummies next door. They're like a wave, a huge gigantic wave, and if we hold fast it'll pass by and we'll still be here. But if we let go and swim for it, we're goners." She gave me a long look. "You see what I mean?"

I do now, but didn't then, even though I nodded like I did. But any way you look at it, it was a bad move by Letty. In situations like this you just have to assume the best and count on the higher instincts, because as soon as you start to issue warnings it's like you're assuming the worst, which in a funny way helps make the worst come true. Though that's all hindsight, of course, or maybe just a way of making excuses for myself.

Anyhow, after Letty left, I lay down to think what I was going to do, but my ideas went off in ten different directions. Outside, a scraping sound began repeating itself, so I looked out the window and there was the crooner out back, sharpening a knife. I watched him for quite a while. He was the not-ugly one, which for some reason made me think he was the less mean of the two, so I changed my blouse and went over there. The idea was to tell him that Letty and I were just two regular people who lived together under one roof just like him and his buddy did, nothing more or less, and that we all ought to let bygones be bygones.

When I got there, though, I just stood behind him and said, "Hi."

He glanced at me once and didn't say a word, merely kept sweeping the knife over the hone. Finally he held up the knife and in a friendly enough way said, "What kinda knife you think this is?"

"Arkansas toothpick?" I said, trying for humor.

He didn't even smile. "Randall-made Smithsonian Bowie," he said. "Cost me $300 and I had to wait two years to get it."

On the breeze was a faint odor I couldn't place.

"Ever see *The Iron Mistress*," he said, "with Alan Ladd as Jim Bowie?—The knife he uses is this knife. The Smithsonian Bowie."

He straightened his back then squatted again. He hunched forward. I couldn't see the black briefs anywhere in the gap between his pants and his back. I was feeling a little giddy. "I always liked Alan Ladd," I said. "Only he hardly ever smiled."

The crooner smiled, just barely, but a smile all the same. He spat on a second hone of finer grit and began again to work the knife.

"Where's your buddy?" I said.

He glanced up. "We're alone if that's what you mean."

"Except for your girlfriend," I said.

This time his look had an edge to it, but then he relaxed himself. "Yeah," he said, "except for my girlfriend."

"She sick?"

He thought about it. "A little."

He switched sides of the blade with each sweep, slow and steady and almost hypnotizing. There was nothing but the sound of the air moving through the tall pines, and a truck in the distance changing gears, and the even sound of the blade on the stone. Except for the bad smell in the air, everything was nice, and all of a sudden he was looking at me while he worked. In his eyes was this calmness that affected me. He looked at me up and down, in and out of my blouse. It was the silk one Letty gave me, I probably should've mentioned that, and it always made me skittish. I don't know what I was considering. It could've been anything. But suddenly the scraping stopped and I heard him saying, "So speaking of best girls, where's yours?" and whatever I was considering changed.

"Fishing," I said, "and she's not my best girl." It didn't come out like I meant it, but I couldn't think what to say next. That made me cranky, and so did the goon's beginning to polish his knife with a special little cloth he took out of a special little pouch. "Tell me if it's none of my business," I said, "but do you two have a line of work?"

The goon, like he was filling up with importance, raised from his squat. "Bounty hunters," he said, real solemn, and motioned me toward the tin shed they'd built out back.

The shed, it turned out, was where the bad smell was coming from. He opened the door and it got worse. I looked inside. There were furs stretched and tacked on boards and there were dog-shaped slabs of red meat with a sickening glisten to them.

"Coyotes," he said. "Thirty dollars per from a private party. Cash. Been averaging ten animals a day." He was grinning and putting his calm clammy eyes on me. "Your little mountain resort is just chock-full of unafraid coyotes."

I looked at them again. Even their legs were skinned.

He slid his knife along a curve of slick meat, then wiped it on his special little cloth. "So," he said, "how'd you come to find out about my girlfriend?"

"Grapevine," I said. A lie, and my face shows lies, so I threw in some truth. "And we saw you carrying her the night you moved in."

He looked surprised and then he didn't. We were looking at each other like something significant was on the line. I didn't blink. There were footsteps behind me and I still didn't blink.

"The night the deputy visited us he was real interested in the girlfriend," he said. "Which means whoever called in the sheriff's let what they knew of the girlfriend be known." He glanced over my shoulder then back to me. "And here in idle conversation I come to find out you two magnolias know plenty about the girlfriend."

"So guess who we have to feel called the deputy?" the other goon said, joining in from behind me.

"This isn't what I wanted to talk about," I said, turning round. What I remember about the second goon is the togetherness of his eyes. They made him look deficient. "I came to straighten things out," I said, swinging back to the crooner. "We've tried to be neighborly, but when you popped off last night you hurt Letty's feelings."

The crooner smiled. "Those weren't exactly shots in the dark. That was good information. From one of your neighborly neighbors."

I was wondering just who that would have been when the crooner's smile stretched wider. "Here's what I don't get. How a pretty little individual like you gets hooked up with someone shaggy as her."

"Like who?" I said, but the ugly one leaned in and took me out of my thoughts. His jaw worked, his eyes squinched littler and I thought, Here's the guy who can do the worst thing you can think of, and he did.

"What we want to know is who does what?" he said, which I didn't get, but then the one who I'd wanted to think was nice jumped in and said, "Who does the diddling and who does the giggling?"

My face had frozen up, but the rest of me was moving. I felt like I was walking underwater. It took me ages to get to the house. In the kitchen I had to hold my hands one in the other to take the shake out of them. I don't know when I'd felt that scared or after I was through being scared that mad. I felt slapped and wanted to slap back. I couldn't help it, I just stepped out the front door and even though I couldn't see them anywhere I took a speaking position at the gate.

"I've seen you two before," I said in a voice as normal as I could make it. "It was when me and my husband Cy went to Key West, Florida and stumbled into a hotel swarming with these men," I said and felt my voice rising, "young pretty-looking men in little black swimsuits like the kind you two are always sashaying around in as if your parts are a present to see!"

That was the whole spiel. It was plenty.

♦   ♦   ♦

Letty came home that afternoon hauling a big cardboard box. "Fishing was bad," she said, "so we hunted bargains." She'd found a garage sale, and had bought a whole set of blue fiesta ware, which she was spreading out on the table. I wouldn't say anything about them so finally Letty said, "I know what you're thinking. You're thinking, What would the two of us want with a whole set of fiesta ware." That made me feel pretty funny. It was almost exactly what I'd been thinking. I wasn't talking however. Letty studied me, then went back to her dishes. "So," she said without looking up, "what did you do all afternoon?"

"Nothing," I said, too quick, and tried to patch it. "Slept."

Letty held a plate to the light. "Why the blouse?"

I'd forgotten to change. My face was getting hot and I needed to give it a reason. "For you," I said.

I could feel Letty peering into me. It was like she'd taken the lid off and was looking inside.

I said, "I thought you might like seeing me in it tonight after last night." This was a black lie, but once you've stopped telling the truth it's a hard thing to get turned around.

Letty believed me. She wanted to, so she did. She stared out the window toward the goons's cabin. "I was thinking about them today," she said. "I guess I don't have to tell you that whatever they think or say doesn't mean beans."

"Who said it did?" I said.

Letty kept looking out. It was getting dark. "There's something I'm ashamed of," she said. She took a deep breath. "It's that I thought you might've gone over there today. I thought it once while I was out and then again for a minute just now." Her face was changing. She looked at me and made an awful smile to keep from crying. "You didn't though, did you?"

"No," I said, "Why would I?" and before she could answer turned on the set and began a silence between us that lasted till supper.

◆   ◆   ◆

Just to put the record straight, Letty was never overly familiar with me, so I can say to whoever might wonder what went on between us that the answer is almost nothing. But love can take a lot of funny forms. In fact, you could talk me into thinking that it takes nothing but. In my years with Letty, for example, I moved within it, room to room, not giving it a thought until one night two boys called it what it wasn't and gave me doubts.

◆   ◆   ◆

Mr. Finny had his own doggy door, so he could go out to the yard, which was fenced, whenever he felt like taking care of business. That night we used the fiesta ware for the only time we ever did, and then, while we were watching a movie on the cable, Mr. Finny went out for the last time. A half hour passed before Letty realized he hadn't come in, so she went out to call.

Nothing.

I got the flashlight out. The front gate was ajar. We began to walk, then to drive. We would shut off the motor and stand outside listening for the clinking of his chain or his particular bark. This went on for three days. Letty was miserable and, I'll tell you the truth, I wanted him back alive but a couple of times I was so tired I thought it might be a relief to find him a goner on the road just so we could go home and go to bed knowing what the final score was.

On the third night I said, "Letty, do you remember how the other day I said I just napped? I was fibbing. I went over to the goons's to be nice and straighten things out, but they just thought I was silly." I looked at Letty. "I said some things. I think I might've gotten their goat."

The dashboard threw a pale green light and made Letty's eyes look like little caves. I knew something was going on—sadness I thought—but when I put my hand on her arm she pushed it away and in a cold unLettylike voice said, "I knew it."

◆   ◆   ◆

The next day Letty watched the two goons drive off and then walked over there. I followed along. Letty tried their door. It was open.

"Anybody home?" Letty called in. I guess she was thinking about the girl, but nobody answered. Letty eased inside, and, after a second, I did, too.

We began to nose around. Letty headed back to the freezer. I went into the bedrooms. They were both a mess. There were sheets over the windows and their clothes were in cardboard boxes. Somebody had been busy on the only dresser—there was what looked like gunpowder and stuffing and that sort of thing. In the second closet I found the girl they'd carried in. She was the store-window kind. They had her in a blonde wig, khaki pants, and no shirt. There were these huge coconut halves cupped over her breasts with red Christmas bulbs for nipples. I took her over to a socket and plugged her in. One didn't work, but the other one did. It was a blinker. I headed off to the kitchen with the so-called corpse over my shoulder, thinking somehow that it'd put Letty in a calmer frame of mind.

She was standing in the kitchen holding Mr. Finny frozen dead.

"Letty," I said.

She sat down.

Ten minutes went by and I said, "Maybe we should be going."

But Letty went like a zombie to the freezer and came back with the buffalo gun and a box of shells. She loaded two and stood four more in a row on the table in front of her.

I picked up the box. Hi-Power, it said. Triple-wadding, denser patterns, fewer strays. "Letty," I said, "let's leave now."

She wasn't talking. I looked at her and knew she was way past all the regular things people feel. Maybe thirty minutes passed before we heard them at the front door. Letty got her hands around the gun and leaned forward. The goons came in together and made a quick read of things—the dog dead and Letty grim and the shells set out in a row. They began moving inchmeal away from each other, fanning out. Letty pointed the gun and they stopped. "Let me explain," the crooner said, "I can explain. The dog got into one of our traps is what happened. What you've got is just a part-picture."

It sounded lame and anyhow Letty wasn't ready to listen to anything. They could see that. She was pointing the gun and looking harder and harder at the two goons and in return they were looking worse and worse. "Stand close," she said, and when they did she said, "Close your eyes," and they did that, too.

The first shot exploded and the crooning goon's legs crumpled him to his knees, but there was no blood, that was the first clue. The second goon was looking whitefaced at his buddy when the gun went off again and his body just froze there.

After a still moment they began feeling themselves.

I grabbed for the other shells lined up there, and for the box, too, I don't know why. The second goon was looking confused at Letty, as if he couldn't understand how she could've missed.

"Letty, please," I said, but I don't think she heard.

The crooning goon tried to push himself up. "You stay sat," Letty said and he slithered back down. Letty was looking around for the box of shells like she didn't see me take them. The second goon was staring above him at the wall where the shots went.

Letty kept the gun on them. "All I care about now is making you two die in a way that suits you," she said. "Something based on real awfulness." She was looking so weird and serious you had to believe her. "You'll think of killing me first, but you can't because I'm already dead," she said. "A vapor. Know what I mean by that?" They were listening carefully. One of them was even nodding. Letty asked me to get a sack for Mr. Finny and I did and then she put the gun down and we walked out of there and buried Mr. Finny behind the cabin, deep in the ground, beyond predators.

◆   ◆   ◆

That night, while Letty slept, I watched the goons move. They worked fast and kept it quiet. Dark, too. They threw their stuff in the back of their van, then coasted it down the driveway and past Earl's before they fired it up, turned on their headlights and, after lobbing a couple of bottles onto the pavement and letting out a few last whoops, drove off toward somebody else's neighborhood.

I went in to Letty and whispered, "They're gone for good," but she was out like a light. For dinner I'd made her some soup, which she wouldn't take, and then some thick hot chocolate laced with Nytols, which she did.

Word of what happened traveled fast. By nine the next morning Anne Feenstra, who worked years for See's, brought us a platter of homemade coconut creams, maybe two dozen of them. Letty ate them all by noon, and a couple of Baby Ruths besides. Earl came by and cleaned up the last of Mr. Finny's business in the front yard and raked pine needles and without saying anything made himself helpful. Letty avoided me. If I was inside she went out. If I came outside she went in. Her eyes were half-open and wherever she went she stood half-staring off at who knew what. In the afternoon I found my black silk blouse wadded up in the trash under the sink, and I noticed the beer we kept on hand for Earl was gone from the refrigerator.

"We've got us," I said to myself out loud, just to hear it, though I knew when I said it that when it had been true I hadn't really believed it, and now that I did believe it I could see it wasn't true anymore. That night I stayed awake all night with my arm around Letty, but the next night I couldn't stay awake and somehow or other she got away. I woke up and she was gone.

♦   ♦   ♦

The only word I got was a note in Letty's hand that went, *Car's at the bus depot in San Berdoo. Keep busy. Love, Letty.* The envelope was postmarked Amarillo. Amarillo, I thought. Amarillo made no sense at all. Neither did keep busy.

Earl took me down to get the car, but before heading back up the hill we went to Danuvios for Mexican, and after two glasses of beer, Earl, who can be sly, said, "How about before calling it a day I run you by the pound?" As soon as I got out of the car and heard them all yapping I knew I'd been had. I took one who was supposed to be part Shih Tzu. She had a caved-in face and not a lot of pep, but she wouldn't take her eyes off me.

A day or two later Sally Ann Newville came over with a couple of romance novels she said she thought I might like. I doubted that, but I was just sitting with Earl over coffee, so I asked her in for a cup.

"I'd take some Lipton's tea if you had some," she said to me and gave Earl a big smile. I wondered what Earl looked like to her. Anymore all I see when I look at Earl is his Dumbo-sized ears.

"Cookies?" I said.

"Maybe just one." She was looking at my dog with suspicion.

"Her name's Paula," I said. "I don't know why the name. It just came to me." I scooted Sally Ann her tea and cookies.

"Well," Sally Ann said, still looking at the dog, "fleas can't live up at this altitude. That's one good thing."

That got me, that the best thing she could think of to say about my new dog was that fleas couldn't live on her. I went into a slow burn. Said nothing. Earl, however, was taking up the slack. He was being quite a talker. I remember him telling a joke about a wart and a frog that I didn't laugh at. Sally Ann did, extra loud, and afterwards said, "Earl, you're an original!" which of course stoked Earl completely. He kept talking and talking. While she listened Sally Ann took the string from her teabag and began to floss with it. Finally Earl wound down and I said, "Sally Ann, did you ever get a letter about being a space alien?"

Sally Ann said she didn't remember anything like that.

"Letty and I sent it."

Sally Ann got prim and looked at her lap. "I knew that."

I said, "How would you have known that?"

Sally Ann shrugged. Her face was bland as bland can be. It was like a mask of her face. I went fishing. I said, "Those two goons said you talked to them a couple of times."

You should've seen her real face arrive. "Only once."

"They said you said we were dykes." This was a lie, but it didn't really sound like one.

"I didn't say that word," Sally Ann said. "I've never said that word." She smoothed her dress. "And I'm not used to hearing it, especially as a guest in someone's home."

Oh yeah?

"Dyke!" I heard myself yell. "Dyke!Dyke!Dyke!Dyke!Dyke!"—like I was a needle stitching it into her. "There! Now you're used to it."

After she left, Earl, who'd sat sipping coffee through all this, said, "Well, I guess it's safe to say you overreacted."

I said, "Well, that was for Letty." And it was. It was for you, Letty.

Earl went to the stove and poured himself a refill. He put in the condensed milk first, then the coffee, so it never even began black. Letty always began with it black. With one hand she'd start her coffee into a nice easy swirl and then with the other she'd slowly pour in the lightener.

"Cold enough to snow," Earl said, and began picking through the newspaper. He was right. It did snow. It's been snowing. The new dog and I go walking in it. It's a deep dry snow, with a waiting stillness to it, soft and quiet to be in.

MARK JAY MIRSKY

Mark Jay Mirsky was born in Boston in 1939. He grew up in anxious Jewish streets, the son of prominent political parents, one a state legislator, the other a Commissioner of Industrial Accidents in the Commonwealth of Massachusetts. He attended the Beth El Hebrew School, the Sarah Greenwood Elementary School, the Solomon Lewenberg Junior High School, the Boston Public Latin School, Harvard College, and Stanford University. Instructed by Albert Guerard to leave his graduate studies after a year at Stanford, he joined the U.S. Air Force Reserve, as a psychiatric ward technician. He is presently professor of English at the City College of New York. He has published three novels, Thou Worm Jacob, Blue Hill Avenue, Proceedings of the Rabble, *a collection of novellas and short stories, called* The Secret Table, *and the essays,* My Search for Messiah. *His latest novel,* The Red Adam, *was published by Sun and Moon Press in June of 1988. The Jewish Publication Society will issue, under his co-editorship, the anthology* Rabbinical Fantasy, *in 1989. The History of Pinsk, 1503–1940, has tentatively been scheduled for publication by the Harvard University Press under his general editorship. Mirsky is the editor of the magazine* Fiction. *He has received a senior fellowship grant from the N.E.H., editor's awards from the N.E.A. (CCLM), the New York State Council on the Arts, and a CAPS award as a novelist.*

"Pages from a novel, yet these were written long after the first and second drafts of *The Red Adam*, a reflection on the insights of the scholar of Kaballah, Gershom Scholem, into the making of clay men, women. The story comes from a period in my life when childless, I wondered about the act of human creation and the creation which binds us to it, evil as emptiness."

◆　　◆　　◆

Songs of Infancy

From *The Red Adam*

LEAH?

Did I invent her? One always invents out of materials that are given, furnished, *real*, if that word has meaning. Let us say that I found her on the road. Her father and mother, when I asked—wondering at the plaid skirt that showed, spilling from the unbuttoned tan trenchcoat, a pretty girl, sixteen, seventeen years old, her face puckered with a smile, freckles spattered across her cheeks, out with a small suitcase on a backcountry spur early in the morning—did not exist.

"They hung themselves." She told me, almost in the first moment, after I asked her, "Where are you going?"

She answered, "I don't know." That catch, husky, breathless, in her voice, which always made me shiver.

"And your parents?"

"They are dead."

"I'm sorry."

"Why?"

"I have no parents either."

"They hung themselves."

"How did that happen?" And she told me, the bodies hanging from opposite trees in the back of a farmhouse on a backroad in Vermont, further north. A gentleman's farm, for he had inherited something and left a barn full of cows and a child. The story told so easily, quickly, as if she were anxious to be naked before me. We drove on, through the morning, into the afternoon, keeping to the backroads, while she drew the portrait of the private school she was running away from, her eyes moving brightly over the oily leather of my car's upholstery, talking of the money left to her in the hands of a drowsy trustee, making fun of the social pretensions of the girls in an institution she had deserted in the wan New England dawn, wanting now to be free, in the world, she asked me, "What do you do?"

"I think."

"About what?"

"Death."

"Why?"

"I want to live." She put her warm hand over the hairs of my right hand, which rested, ungloved, on the seat. At that moment a buck of unusual size rose out of the trees to the left of the road, sprang just in front of the car and galloped a few yards before jumping off again on the same side, its antlers, hindquarters, disappearing into the brush. I had slowed the automobile down to a crawl and now I braked, stopped the white-walled tires on the black road. "It makes me feel like an animal seeing that," I said, my voice throbbing in my throat.

"I do too," she whispered.

"An animal in heat." My words were barely audible. Her fingers tightened over mine.

"Let's take a walk," I said. And she looked up at me with eyes full of trust, almost of devotion.

"Did you see the bodies?" I asked as we walked through the woods. One does not invent such tragedies. They occur. The anger implicit in a man or woman taking his, her life, reverberates through the lives of their descendants. It touched this girl with an attraction born of pathos and gave to her features, her eyes, the halo of sanctity. She was marked as if by a force of the divine. For a creature of self-disgust like myself, what this girl had undergone gave every gesture the glow of such pathos that it was hard to look at her. I could feel the horror upon her.

To be flesh of the flesh of what she had suffered, that was my ambition since

I could not feel love. I said that to myself. Now, now, I do not entirely believe it.

Or to explain it crudely, I wished in this landscape of delicate church spires and carefully crafted houses, barns, this ideal America, to be the Jew as the gentile sees him in nightmare, the creature covetous for flesh, not for money but for the very pound of skin, life, blood, to be a creature of the libel that even Shakespeare put his lips to, Marlowe embraced, a refraction of that ogre who cries, "I walk abroad o' nights and kill sick people groaning under walls: Sometimes I go about and poison wells. . . ." To be the man who "every moon made some or other mad." O caricature, for it is the Jew who abominates blood, to whom flesh is forbidden unless it is drained, salted, made fit, and to whom mutilation is taboo. Yet, dead to myself, I would walk in the caricature and desire what the nightmare imagined as my opposite.

Did I see it in Leah's eyes, herself as the yielding child, the lamb, Oliver Twist, or better, Olivia, under my fingers, ragged nails . . .

And I thought, in this drama that her thoughts offered me, to feed on innocence and make myself innocent, pure, wash myself in the tears of a little girl's freckled face, feed those tears to the idea to which I prayed, put her trembling heart in the cavity under my ribs.

I became her father, then lover . . . brother.

Why did they die? I asked her over and over. She would only shake the brown tassels of her curls and let her eyes grow moist, or smile up through the mist as if some article of faith were breaking in her chest and I must not ask further. I found the answer only in living with her, feeling her body go hot, cold, come closer, drift away, as I teased, tormented, comforted her. Love, they had died for love, for lack of it, so bitter in the illusion whose neck was broken in that comfortable farmhouse, the very outline in its gables, weathervanes, America held in its most private recesses and cherished dearest that when they found each other with the perfect family, house, income, so bored they were nauseous at the breakfast table, so abhorrent of the flesh opposite them they could not bear its touch at the kitchen sink, let alone under the clammy blankets of the bed; they despaired of life and whatever promise it might have, at the end of that valley of rolling humpbacked peaks spilling down green hillsides. They were too honorable to seek mystery by other means, to cross partners, to masquerade invoking demons, witches, mix themselves up with the veins of anthracite, copper, iron running under the forthright stony soil of the valley floor and lower slopes.

Clay has that knowledge.

Do not let me disgust you too quickly, I who fornicated with a waif I rescued on the roadside. I wanted to reach through her legs, where the cobweb of death had spun, delicate, enticing, into the knowledge of life. And out of the fog that rises from the runnels of water in the ditches by the side of the lane, it was possible to imagine such a girl, to stop, ask her if she wanted a lift, begin the conversation, and give her knees such presence by the afternoon, when a brief moment of sun lighted them up, folded, beyond her thighs indented in the soft leather cushions of the car, that it was only a step more to hearing her voice and hearing the door swing open, as I came round to take her hand, to walk.

We entered the woods. The creature lusting for blood is not in the mythology of the Hebrews. That is a being of the Angles, Saxons, of tribes cousin to their language. It is the Adam, the clay man, who lies half-formed, soulless in the culverts of our dreams, ready to rise and walk the earth. To the state of such a creature I had fallen. I did not break her neck, cup her veins, drink. I thought instead I had found a partner to raise me up: a girl so innocent her life would free me from my condition, an image mired in the sticky net of earth. I would fly up from the dross, I thought.

And I might have. Only she was an image, too.

I tortured, tortured, hoping the spirit would come walking out of the husk, the pure joy, pain, draw my own out, so we could ascend.

Late that afternoon, in the chill New England air, when the cold, hidden sun lit up the dying gold, orange, brown of the leaves under the oak trees by the side of the country road below the embankment which held up a ribbon of asphalt, I rolled up her trenchcoat for a pillow under her head, took off her blouse of white linen, her brassiere, the thin stuff of her underwear, under the joints of those evil oaks. Entering her, I wept, hoping that I was pushing through the doors of creation.

It was I who was entered at that moment. I could not have known it. It is I who deserve your pity.

I was drugged. The lines of her father were drawn over my malleable cheeks, chin, nose. She sank her white teeth into her maker's lips, drew the blood back from his broken neck, drew in the dreams of that last year's afternoon when she might have sunk his despair in her own flesh and saved him. It was her mother in my arms, a woman angry, betrayed, contemptuous.

Was I once human? I found myself crumpled on the sheets, a castoff toy, an abandoned puppet.

How then, when she asked me for children, could I have given them? Everything was in my power but to engender. I thought. I was the subject of magic beyond what I could imagine. I thought I wanted a life beyond earth, which I had come from. Did she want to return me to my elements, seed, water, clay? She wanted. . . . I only know that the thrill of those afternoons, our first meetings, finding, touching, faded; and I woke up beside a strange person, in a house, as an idea, the imagined one.

Who am I? One of those walking the earth, not flesh, not blood, but an image feeling pain? I am the guardian of the woods where two parents swing, hanging from the trees. Far away I can see the kitchen, lighted by a soft lamp, where a girl of twelve sits and does her homework, humming. Come out, I cry, come out to me.

MARY JANE MOFFAT

Mary Jane Moffat entered the Stanford Creative Writing Program in fiction in 1966. After receiving her M.A. in 1968 she taught there until 1971 and again in 1979. Two literary anthologies she edited and introduced have come out from Random House/Vintage: the continuously popular Revelations: Diaries of Women *(with Charlotte Painter) and* In the Midst of Winter. *Since 1976 she has taught the writing of autobiography at Foothill College, in the San Francisco Bay Area, and has lectured widely on this subject. Her latest book is* City of Roses, *a fictional memoir published by former Stanford Stegner Fellow John Daniel, of Santa Barbara.*

"This story, from my collection, *City of Roses,* grew out of an assignment I give my writing students: to thank some figure in our past for a previously unacknowledged gift. The tale is my own myth of origin; for I firmly believe that without Miss Thayer's intervention I might never have learned to read. And thereby never have learned from later blessed teachers—Wallace Stegner, Richard Scowcroft, Tillie Olsen—or have become a teacher myself."

◆　　◆　　◆

Homage to Miss Thayer

FIRST GRADE! THOSE LOVELY lineny books the teacher passed out the first day. I opened mine and saw a smiling family standing on a lawn with a swing outside a white house—just the kind of place where I would have liked to live. There was even a dog. I buried my face in the smell of new paper, wishing to crawl inside and stay forever in that green, sunshiny garden.

From high above my seat in the first row where the teacher stood in a full skirt came her voice: books are not to wipe our noses on. Books are to be read. Tomorrow we will begin to learn to read. Today we will learn how to hold a book and how to turn its pages. We must never touch a book unless our hands are very clean. . . .

And on and on. I felt so downhearted. By tomorrow I was sure the family and their spotted dog would have driven off in the father's black car, lost to me forever. Great slobbery tears fell on my new plaid jumper; my nose ran and I wiped it on the back of my arm.

The voice above me said, didn't I know enough to carry a handkerchief in my pocket? It said I must go to the girl's lavatory and collect myself.

Collect myself? Wasn't I already here?

Those first weeks of 1939 passed into months and by April and my sixth birthday, I still had not learned to read. What I did learn was a runny-nosed sense of wrongness about myself. The high-topped shoes my father insisted I wear for weak ankles marked me as a baby. My green metal lunch box my mother filled with such care every morning before she left for work was wrong; the other children carried their sandwiches to school in paper sacks. My bibbed jumper was wrong. Girls the teacher praised wore pleated skirts with narrow straps that crossed over the backs of their blouses.

The young teacher herself wore, day after rainy day, that same full skirt in a nasty shade of reddish brown. As the smallest child, I'd been assigned the first row seat right under where she stood to instruct us. Perhaps I remember the skirt because it was what I saw the most—that and a view of her nostrils shaped like the black spades on my father's playing cards.

"Look and say," she said, as I stared up beyond that curtain of brown at the glossy chart she pulled down like a window shade. Her long wooden pointer circled a collection of lines that was supposed to mean "car." But to me the *c* was a teacup handle, the *a* a ball leaning against a wall, the *r* a flower with its head cut off and one leaf remaining. All together, in no way did they resemble any automobile I'd ever seen.

I still liked the pictures in the book and the smell and feel of the paper; but the story was moving awfully slowly. Instead of the characters disappearing off the page in the car, it seemed to take weeks for Dick to throw the ball to Spot and for Jane to talk about it: Look, Dick, look. See Spot run.

"Do you read aloud to Mary Jane at home?" the teacher asked my mother in an interview about my lack of progress.

My mother assured her that my father read to me almost every night.

"What kind of books?"

"*Treasure Island*," Mother bragged. "*Swiss Family Robinson*."

"Please ask him to stop," said the teacher gravely. "Those books are too interesting. They impede her motivation."

The black marks on the pages of my books became my enemies. I particularly disliked the letter *g* and others like it that dared to drop below the line, just as at home I had a mad on with certain members of the silverware family. Spoon was a chubby-cheeked child, anxious to please and Knife was a tall guardian knight. But Fork was a cold queen, capable of sudden viciousness. I refused to touch her. "Will she ever learn to eat right?" my father complained when I speared salad into my mouth with a knife.

I "lost" my green lunch box under a juniper bush on the way home from school. I stamped on my plaid jumper and said I would never never never wear it again. More and more, my father said, "I can't stand it when she whines," and left the house, slamming the door behind him.

I asked my mother what "whines" was. She said not to mind, "Your Daddy has a problem with his nerves. But sometimes we both wonder what happened to the nice little girl we used to have."

When called upon to read aloud in class, I made up stories about the family in the primer. Their shiny car had been a gift from a magical boat that last week had arrived in the Portland harbor. (When I had asked my father when we would own a car, he'd said, "When my ship comes in.") I suggested that the reason the ever-smiling mother always stayed home in her apron was because she had a problem with her nerves and couldn't go to work anymore in an office downtown, the way my mother did.

In the midst of these recitations—just as I was warming to my story—the teacher's eyebrows would beetle together and I'd be told to sit down. When I raised my hand to go to the lavatory, the teacher always excused me even though she made the other children wait until recess. I took to spending more and more time in the cool gray stall with its child-sized toilet, contemplating my wrongness to the tune of flushing water.

One afternoon in May one of the girls with the right kind of pleated skirt came to the lavatory to fetch me; my mother had come to visit our class, she told me self-importantly, as if she knew her better than I. I didn't believe her but there my mother was, sitting in the back row behind the tallest boy. I was very proud of her in her smart navy suit and the little hat my father called a pancake—her presence seemed to perfume the chalk-and-eraser air of the classroom with her own special scent of Downtown, a mix of carbon paper and cigarettes and Evening in Paris. I wanted to run and hug her but the teacher told me to take my seat and recite from the lesson of the day in our primer.

The black letters under the picture performed their usual angry act of trying to escape their imprisonment between the lines and I must have performed my usual act of making up some story about the picture, pausing between every word the way the other children did when they read aloud, because the teacher stopped me. I heard her voice above my head say to my mother in the back row, "You see?"

From my bed that night I heard Mother tell Father in her sad-news voice, "The teacher says she's slow. That she may never learn."

I might have remained a victim of the Sight Method of teaching reading then in vogue in the Oregon schools had not my father's "problem with his nerves" worsened. Before the end of the school term, which I was bound to fail, he had to be hospitalized. Mother took me out of school and sent me to spend the summer with an aunt in southern California.

In the fall when I returned, my parents had moved to a flat on upper Broadway near Portland's downtown. I don't know why. Perhaps it was a cheaper rent than the little house we'd lived in on the outskirts. Perhaps it was better for my father's nerves, now that he was working again, not to have to transfer three times on the bus to and from a district I thought was named Hellengon because Daddy always said that he hated living "way out there to hell and gone."

My mother enrolled me in Shattuck school, a block up Broadway from our wood-framed second floor flat. Always an optimist, Mother lied that I would have successfully completed grade 1-A if I'd been able to finish the term at my former school. Until my records arrived, the secretary sent me to the 1-B classroom.

And there I found Miss Thayer.

She was the oldest woman I'd ever seen, with a puff of white hair that caught the light as she handed us our workbooks that first day. She didn't bend over our desks but knelt beside each student as she helped us find our place or fit our awkward fingers around the new slippery pencils; and so I was able to look her full in the face. Her skin reminded me of a bowl my mother treasured on our what-not stand at home: milky and gilded with hundreds of tiny lines that didn't crack the opaline surface. I know, because the second day of class, before she creaked up from her kneeling position beside my desk, I put my hand on her cheek and she let my hand stay there until its curiosity was satisfied.

Unlike my previous teacher, Miss Thayer seemed to be on good terms with the chalk when she wrote on the blackboard—there was never that terrible screech that used to make my back teeth ache. Miss Thayer often strolled to the window as she taught us, as if she knew what marvelous dances the motes of light performed on her cloud of hair and her pink scalp.

She moved among us—from the blackboard to the window to the coat closet where she helped us with our wraps, as she called them—in dresses of soft material and even softer colors, colors as soothing as her voice: lavender, moss-green, robin's-egg blue.

On rainy days, Miss Thayer wore around her shoulders a frothy piece of cloth that matched her hair. I'd never seen its like and one day I lagged behind, at recess, bold enough to ask her what it was.

"It's a fichu, little Miss. Now hurry out and play before the bars get wet again—this spell of sunshine won't last long."

This struck me as wonderfully strange. Why would a fish need a shoe?

At recess the kids still called me a baby because of my high-top shoes but now I could return to the haven of Miss Thayer's room and its faint scent of violet talc. When she called upon me to read I imagined that the printing said that Dick and Jane were bad children who made their father nervous. If they didn't stop whining and running in the house the Red Man—a grinning character who often peeked out from my bedroom curtains at night—was going to come and take them away. Miss Thayer listened to my recitations with considerable interest it seemed to me; at least she shushed the titters of my classmates and always let me finish.

One warm Indian summer Friday afternoon I was startled to see my mother appear in the classroom door just as I was collecting my wrap to go home. In low and anxious tones she spoke to my teacher about my father: something about a breakdown and the state hospital in Salem. Daddy was always complaining about being broke, which I never believed because he looked all in one piece to me; but now maybe it was really true. A picture came into my mind of him all alop, like a puppet with its strings cut.

The next thing I knew I was sitting beside Miss Thayer in her car, rubbing my palms against the flannely upholstery as we drove to the country near Gresham. We walked through a small orchard to her house and she must not have been so very old for she lifted me easily to pick a bright green apple from a tree. I bit into its hardness and felt a tiny thrill of pain. When I looked down at the white meat I saw a drizzle of blood and my first lost tooth. Miss Thayer and I laughed.

She lived with an even older woman—perhaps her mother or a sister, I don't remember. They seemed to enjoy each other's company very much and mine as well. In fact, I remember little of those two days in the country except eating wonderful food that the other woman prepared, the kind of food that takes all day to simmer and stew; and in the mornings homemade bread smeared with apple preserves; collecting wild grasses with Miss Thayer and watching minnows in a creek and brightly asking if they wore shoes, knowing full well they didn't, but pleased at my joke.

But something else must have happened that weekend. On Sunday afternoon when my mother met me at the bus station downtown and we walked hand in hand up Broadway, the neon signs were just jittering on. These bright letters were no longer mysterious enemies. They were simply signals that told me what sounds my lips should make. P: puh, puh, puh—Paramount! M—Mickey Mouse. Sam's Grill. Shoes Repaired. All the way home I read the world to my mother.

N. Scott Momaday

N. Scott Momaday earned his M.A. and Ph.D. at Stanford, and he was on the Stanford faculty for eight years. He has taught at U.C. Berkeley, Columbia, Princeton, and the State University of Moscow, U.S.S.R. He holds numerous awards, including the Pulitzer Prize and the Premio Letterario Internazionale "Mondello."

"'Angle of Geese' was written in workshop with Yvor Winters and included in the Winters-Fields anthology, *Quest for Reality* (1969). 'On the Cause of a Homely Death' was written in 1987. I live at ease with these two poems, so far apart in time. They are among the things of mine I wish to keep."

◆   ◆   ◆

Angle of Geese

How shall we adorn
Recognition with our speech?—
　Now the dead firstborn
Will lag in the wake of words.

　Custom intervenes;
We are civil, something more:
　More than language means,
The mute presence mulls and marks.

　Almost of a mind,
We take measure of the loss;
　I am slow to find
The mere margin of repose.

　And one November
It was longer in the watch,
　As if forever,
Of the huge ancestral goose.

　So much symmetry!—
Like the pale angle of time
　And eternity.
The great shape labored and fell.

Quit of hope and hurt,
It held a motionless gaze
Wide of time, alert
On the dark distant flurry.

◆   ◆   ◆

On the Cause of a Homely Death

Even the echoes are distilled
In dust. Imagine it was age,
And worthy destiny fulfilled,
Not fear, not loneliness, not rage.

HUGH NISSENSON

Hugh Nissenson was born in New York City in 1933. He now lives in New York with his wife and two daughters. He has published two collections of short stories: A Pile of Stones *(1965), and* In the Reign of Peace *(1972). In 1968, he published a book of nonfiction,* Notes from the Frontier. *Nissenson has published two novels:* My Own Ground, *in 1976, and* The Tree of Life, *in 1985, which was nominated for the American Book Award and the PEN/ Faulkner Award. Nissenson was a Stegner Fellow at Stanford University in 1961–62. He taught creative writing at Yale University and Barnard College in 1988. His selected short stories and journals, from 1957 to 1987, entitled* The Elephant and the Jewish Problem, *was published in the United States in 1988. He is working on a new novel,* The Song of the Earth.

"I wrote the first draft of the opening chapter of *My Own Ground* in the south of France. The world it dramatizes derives from the stories my father told me when I was a child. Its themes obsess me, no matter where I set the action: contemporary Israel, nineteenth-century Ohio, or, in my current work in progress, twenty-first-century Mars."

◆　　　◆　　　◆

From *My Own Ground*

IN THE SUMMER OF 1912, when I was fifteen years old, Schlifka the pimp offered me ten bucks to tell him when Hannah Isaacs showed up on Orchard Street in the building where I lived.

"Take it or leave it," he said. "No questions asked."

"Ten bucks?"

"Just say the word."

"Yeah."

We shook on it. I got a whiff of his cigar. "I knew you was my man," he said. "I knew it the first time we met."

We'd met on a Wednesday night, the week before. He was on the stoop when I got home from work at seven. I recognized him by his red hair, parted in the middle, which was slicked down with brilliantine; it shone in the light from the gas jet behind him on the hallway wall. His black-patent-leather shoes were shiny, too; even the high heels. Come to think of it, I noticed them later: after supper, when I went back outside for a breath of air. He stared me down.

"You must be Jake Brody," he said. "The kid from the third floor that speaks English. I heard a lot about you."

"That makes us even."

"You speak real good. How long you been in America?"

"Almost three years now."

"Is that all? You're a smart boy. Good-looking, too," he said. "All you need is a haircut. Never mind. It's nice long. On you it looks good. You ought to get it singed, though, to shape it. I got a wop barber on Mulberry Street who'll do it for a dime. You got a dime?"

"I make out okay."

He said, "So I understand," and wiped the sweat from his face and neck with a handkerchief. He was wearing a stiff shirt with rubber cuffs and no collar. In his right hand he had a walking stick with a gold handle. The rumor was that he had brained a Chinaman on Mott Street with it in a fight over a Polish girl.

"I like a kid with a good head on his shoulders," he said. "Where you from?"

"You never heard of it."

"Try me."

"Umersk."

"You're right," he said. "Where's that?"

"About halfway between Zhitomir and Kiev," I told him. "And you?"

"Me?" He laughed. "I was born the minute I stepped off the boat at Castle Gardens."

He lit a cigar and the flare of the match was reflected in his eyes; they were pale blue. Blowing the smoke from his nose, he said, "They tell me your folks are dead."

"That's right."

"No brothers or sisters?"

"Nobody but me."

"You're better off."

Just at that moment, there was the squeal of the ungreased axle of a pushcart and the jingle of bells from the street.

I said, "I know it," and he laid a hand on my arm. A diamond ring glittered on his pinky. In the street, the peddler cried out in Yiddish, "Buy, Jews, buy!" He sold dried fruit, I remember.

Before he walked off, swinging that stick, Schlifka bought a pound of figs for a dime. "A little something for the girls on Allen Street," he said.

I wondered where he got his information about me. Mrs. Tauber, my landlady, would have spit in his eye, and there was no one else in the building, where I'd lived only three months, who knew I spoke English.

But the next morning, at work, I suddenly thought, I once told Hannah Isaacs, and put my steam iron down on the red-hot stove. A burning coal shot a yellow flame through the grate. In the front room, tailors, basters, and finishers bent over their rented sewing machines. A girl wearing a pleated skirt and a blouse with a high collar made her way down the aisle with a bundle of cut work in her arms. My iron hissed. I thought, Hannele and Schlifka? No, that ain't possible, but it was as if the heat had already fused them together in the back of my mind.

As soon as I got home, I had my supper—a piece of herring on a slice of black bread. The cup of coffee made me sweat. Hannele and her father lived in the back apartment, to the right, on the other side of the stairs. Every time the toilet in the hallway was flushed, I looked out the door. Finally, at about eight, when the water gushed and gurgled again in the pipes, I caught the eye of the locksmith from the second floor who was her old man's best friend. He buttoned up his fly and asked, "Something I can do for you?"

"Is Hannele at home?"

"Hannele's gone away," he said.

That night I waited on the stoop until ten for Schlifka to show up again. It was very hot. Mrs. Tauber was wearing her kimono; Feibush, the greenhorn, was in his undershirt. He had broad shoulders for a Jew. You could tell from the way he kept pulling on his chin that he had recently shaved off his beard.

While I watched the street, they talked in Yiddish with strong Ukrainian accents about Odessa: the Moldavanka district, some park near an avenue lined with poplar trees, Import Square. Mrs. Tauber said, "I miss the sea." An ambulance clanged by, drawn by two white horses; their hooves struck sparks from the cobblestones. Feibush must have asked her something about her husband, because then I heard her say, "No, he's been dead three years," as I got to my feet and went down the stairs.

I started out to buy a hard roll for breakfast in the bakery on the corner of Hester Street; instead I made a left and kept going for another block. I suppose I had hopes of running into Schlifka on his home ground: under the El, on Allen Street, where it was always dark. In any case, I headed uptown. Now and then, in the light from an open store, I could make out a face: a Gypsy, with a gold ring in one ear, who was smoking a cigarette; a bearded Jew. On a fire escape, a girl put down a kerosene lamp with a tin shade. She had long hair. There was a pillow under her arm. The downtown express roared overhead. I passed the Russian steam bath and the shop that sold white linen shrouds, brass candlesticks for the Sabbath, and little bags of earth, tied with string, from the Holy Land. A hot moist wind was blowing. There was a smell of rotten fruit from the gutter.

On the corner of Broome Street, I sneaked upstairs to the Syrian coffeehouse on the second floor. The fat Syrian who owned the joint had tossed me out of there twice that summer before I had a chance to see the belly dancer do her stuff. This time I saw a woman on her knees in the center of a room. Her head was thrown back; a necklace of silver coins dangled between her naked breasts. She squeezed them together. Even now, after all these years, that sticks in my mind.

What completely escapes me is how and where I met Schlifka again. I know it was the following Saturday evening because I have a distinct memory, at one point, of hearing a verse from the hymn that marks the end of the Sabbath through the open window of a shul:

> At the close of the Day of Rest
> Deliver thy people;
> Send us Elijah . . .

It might have been from the old Beth Hamidrash Hagadol on Norfolk Street, the one that used to be a church. Schlifka hummed the tune under his breath and said, "That takes me way back."

"Where to?"

"I already told you. Another life."

"Did you go to shul on Shabbes?"

"Not only that, but I studied Gemara as well."

"Where? In a yeshiva?"

"No, at a Gemara cheder."

"Me too."

"We got a lot in common," he said.

"Were you a good student?"

"By the time I was eleven, I knew the Mesachet Shabbes by heart."

"Then how come you didn't go to a yeshiva?"

"That's a long story," he said. "And very sad. What about you?"

"Mine's a long story, too."

We wound up on Allen Street, opposite the Rivington Street station.

"I got me a room here on the second floor," he said, in front of an open doorway. "This is where I green out my new girls."

A gas jet burned in the hallway; the glass mantel was chipped. There was a dead rat in the big puddle on the black-and-white-tile floor.

A little way up the block, outside a saloon, Schlifka went on, "Gimme a girl, any girl, up in that room for a week or ten days, and I promise you this: when I spit in her face, she'll call it rain. Understand me? No, you can't. You're too young. Well, then, I'll try and put it to you another way."

He thumped me on the chest with the gold handle of his walking stick: the head of a dog with a long muzzle and pointed ears. "Our rabbis teach us to discover our 'shoresh nishama.' You know what that means?"

"Sure."

"What?"

"What's 'shoresh' again in English? It's on the tip of my tongue."

"Root."

"Yeah, that's it. I got it now. It means 'the root of the soul.'"

"That's right," he said. "Very good. For instance, Levi Yitzhak . . . no . . . the Apter, as you know, had the same root as the High Priest in Jerusalem, who was a very holy man. Well, believe it or not, I've discovered mine. It came to me in a flash one night up there in that room with a girl. And you know who it is?"

"No."

"Take a guess," he said. "I'll give you a hint. I seen a bone once, from his thigh, in a show at Coney Island. It was as tall as me."

"I don't know what you're talking about."

"I'm talking about Og," he said, "the root of my soul."

"Who?"

"Og," he repeated. "Don't you remember?" He quoted the Hebrew in an exaggerated singsong voice, "'Behold, his bedstead was a bedstead of iron. And nine cubits was its length, and four cubits its breadth.'"

"I remember," I said. "He was the king of Bashan."

"Right again. And, like the rabbis tell us, he had a thousand wives. As a matter of fact, every girl in that town, on the day she turned twelve years old, became his slave. She went to live in the palace that afternoon. And that very night, apart from her jewelry—which was made from iron, too—she had to strip herself naked and bring the king his supper and a glass of beer. But if he liked what he saw, she didn't last long."

"Why not?"

He bit off the tip of a cigar, spit it out, and said, "A guy that size?"

We burst out laughing together.

"You got a sense of humor," he said. "You're okay. Do you like cigars?"

"I don't know. I never tried one."

"Try one of these. It's a genuine Havana—the best. It set me back four bits."

"For one cigar?"

"Nothing's too good for Schlifka and his pals."

"Are we pals?"

"We could be," he said, giving me a light. "Well, how do you like it?"

"I don't know yet."

"No, don't drag it quick, like a cigarette. Puff on it slow and easy," he said. "That's the way. Now lick the wrapper; that's the leaf on the outside. It tastes good, don't it? That's how you can tell a good Havana. This wrapper is called *Vuelta Abajo*. That's Spanish; it's the best money can buy. Now puff on it again. Enjoy the smell."

"How come you know Spanish?"

"I get around," he said. "Well, how do you like it now?"

"It makes me dizzy."

"That's because you drag on it, like a cigarette."

"Maybe so, but it ain't for me," I told him, tossing it in the gutter.

He laughed again and said, "You make up your mind very fast."

"I know what I like."

"How would you like to make yourself ten bucks?"

"Very much."

"With no questions asked."

"That all depends."

"No," he said. "Not for ten bucks."

He reached into his pocket, pulled out a wad, and peeled off one of the bills. "This is for you," he said. "All you have to do is tell me when Hannah Isaacs comes home to her papa."

"Is Hannah Isaacs one of your girls?"

He stuffed the bill down the front of my shirt and pinched me on the right cheek. There was a gust of wind. A sheet, strung between two fire escapes, flapped above his head. The shiny hair stayed slicked down. After we made the deal and shook on it, the wind changed and I caught a whiff of his cigar.

Kent Nussey grew up in rural upstate New York. He graduated from Houghton College in 1976, and after living in various Canadian cities for several years enrolled in the writers' workshop at Syracuse University where he studied with Raymond Carver and Tobias Wolff. In 1983, he was awarded a Stegner Fellowship in fiction at Stanford. The next year he became a Jones Lecturer and taught fiction there until 1987.

"'Laughter of Young Women' was a reaction to some of my earlier stories. It seemed I'd been writing about situations I hadn't yet but soon would experience. In a way, they were stories of anticipation. When I was about to turn thirty I realized that a great store of characters and places from my adolescence had never made it into my fiction, and that many of them were indeed worthy. This story, then, was a deliberate effort to catch up with myself before the next lurch, leap, or fall."

◆   ◆   ◆

Laughter of Young Women

IT HADN'T BEEN A good day for Bernie. He fell asleep in history class and woke to find he'd been assigned extra homework. Worse yet, Raeleen had to make up a biology lab and couldn't meet him for lunch. In the final study hall of the day some tenth graders threw tiny balls of clay at the back of his head. After school he stayed another hour for band practice. His pitch was consistently flat and the other french horns gave him dirty looks.

It was nearly five o'clock when he stepped into Smitty's Diner with his instrument case. His hands were wet and cold and his hair was plastered back on his forehead with rain. Raeleen was working the counter. A row of squat men in dirty plaid jackets and billed caps watched her move back and forth with the steaming coffee pot in her hand. Their heads turned as Bernie took a stool at the end. His horn tumbled off the foot ledge and whammed against the floor. The men laughed.

"Lover boy's here," said a pie-faced man with a knuckle hooked through a coffee cup.

Bernie looked at the man. The man met his look.

"Leave him alone, Tom," Raeleen said. She refilled the man's cup and moved down the counter to Bernie.

"How was band?" she asked. She crossed her arms behind her back and went up on the balls of her feet as she spoke.

"Horrible. I hate the french horn and I missed my bus."

"You're in one of your moods."

"It's been that kind of day," he said. "When do you get off?"

"Seven, same as always. Can you stay?"

"Naw, Pobjoy socked me with a paper. I have to get home."

"Want a Coke?" she said, turning away.

"All right. No ice."

Bernie watched her stretch for the wax-paper cups. The short white dress inched up her thighs. Bernie glanced quickly at the row of men. They grinned at him.

"Here," said Raeleen, pushing the cup toward him.

In a low, tense voice he said, "I hate this place."

She frowned at him. "You blow everything out of proportion. Everything's a big deal with you."

"This place stinks."

"Look," she said, squaring her shoulders. "I'm not going to let you depress me again. It's a job."

She went to turn a meat patty on the grill. It hissed and a plume of greasy smoke rose above her. The bad air was affecting his head, Bernie thought. He thought he felt a cold coming on.

On the highway he breathed easier, though the rain fell steady and cold. He considered what a dismal affair his life would be without Raeleen. And yet, he depressed her. She'd said it. He felt ashamed. But on the other hand, who wouldn't be depressed, living around here? His gaze took in the unturned fields, broken with outcroppings of rocks and black tree stumps. Brown pools had gathered in the low stretches near the highway. He walked with his head down, his chin tucked into the zippered collar of his nylon jacket. Two cars passed before he turned to show his thumb. In the distance the hills blurred behind a veil of low sky and rain.

The third car was a long fishtailed Pontiac with a toothy grill and round headlamps that glowed in the late afternoon. The car swooped toward him and Bernie shuddered slightly as it slowed and stopped on the gravel shoulder. He ran to it with the French horn case bumping his knee. The door on the passenger side swung open and Bernie ducked in, catching the case between his knees. He'd hardly shut the door before the car was moving again.

"Thanks," Bernie said, and he looked at the driver. She was a young woman, maybe in her twenties, maybe older: in the first glimpse there was no telling. She smiled and accelerated. She wore a blue athletic jacket with a gold patch on the shoulder that said "Bulldogs." Her hair was a bad bleached yellow and her right hand, which held a cigarette away from the wheel, bore a short bluish scar between her thumb and first finger. Bernie wanted to stare at it but the hand moved jerkily between the steering wheel and the ashtray beneath the dash. Little gray ashes sat between the creases of her jeans.

"It's raining like a bitch," she said. "It rains ten months of the year in this fucking state. That's Sherry in back."

Bernie twisted around to nod at the girl behind him. She was younger than the driver, a skinny girl with thin black hair and shadows under her eyes. Her mouth twitched at him but she did not return his nod. Bernie watched the road in front of him.

The windshield was stained with a gray-blue film. The dash was littered with matchbooks that said "State Bank of Fillmore" and "King Edward Cigars."

"Where you headed?" asked the driver.

"Just down to Homer," said Bernie.

"Homer," she said. "That's a waste of a town. That's one nothing place to live. What do you say, Sherry?"

"Homer's a shit hole," said the voice in back. Bernie felt it on his neck, the uneasy air, as if someone were sharpening a straight razor on a strop behind him.

"What say to that?" the driver asked, and before Bernie could answer she said, "What'd you say your name was?"

Bernie took a breath. "Harold," he said.

"Harold," said the driver. "That's a good one."

The girl in back made a short sound. Bernie decided he wouldn't look around again.

"Harold," said the driver. "That's a waste of a name."

Bernie kept his eyes on the countryside, the dreary March harshness of the fields that had barely lost their snow, the grim and infrequent little houses behind sagging barns. Long stretches of brown weeds and mud.

"Hey, don't get us wrong," said the driver. "You smoke? You want a smoke?" She shook a pack of Lucky Strikes at him.

"I don't smoke," he said.

"Ha. That fits. A million guys with habits and I pick the one that don't smoke."

Sherry snorted at the back of his neck.

He felt dizzy. He closed his eyes and angled his thoughts toward Raeleen. There was a fine summer afternoon when he'd happened to see her playing tennis with Tim Moler, captain of the baseball team. Raeleen's long, tan legs flashed in the sunlight as she rushed the net. In the middle of their set Bernie walked home and drove his brother's car to the abandoned quarry and cried and cried, bumping his head in a slow rhythm on the steering wheel.

"So Harold," the driver said. "You got a girl friend?"

Bernie stiffened in the seat and faced her. "No," he said.

"Come on, Harold, what's that look? I bet you got a girl friend back in Fillmore. Am I right?"

"I got girl friends. So what?"

"What do they let you do?"

"What?"

"I said what do they let you do?"

The rain whipped against the windshield and the wipers squeaked softly, back and forth. Bernie made himself laugh, but he didn't answer.

"I mean, do you fuck these girls, or just kind of feel them up?"

Bernie shook his head and looked out the window. They were on the outskirts of his town. They passed the Keystone station and the trailer where Old Man Hardy lived.

"I bet he fucks them," the driver said. "What do you think, Sherry?"

There was a pause and Bernie wondered if Sherry was laughing.

She said, "No, not this guy. He just kisses them. He's a kisser."

The driver laughed.

"I get off here," Bernie said. "I can get out right here."

She steered the long automobile down the main street of his town; Bernie watched Trombley's Town & Country Store and the Homer Inn float on the dingy windows and disappear as if the town were being sucked down a hole behind them.

"I have to get home," Bernie said. "My folks'll yell at me."

"What's the rush?" said the driver. "You got time for a ride."

"I have to get home," he said.

The driver cracked the window and pitched her cigarette. Bernie felt a tiny point of rain blow against his face before she rolled the window shut with a single hard twist. The girl behind him lit a fresh cigarette and expelled a fuggy cloud into the front seat. Bernie blinked and held his breath. He felt nauseous. His knees squeezed the instrument case.

"What's the matter, Harold? You don't look so good."

The driver grinned and tugged her jeans at the crotch. "How about some music?" she said, and she switched on the radio. It crackled and sputtered and a nasal voice sang out of a great distance, "I got it bad and that ain't good. . . ."

The driver fiddled with the tuning. She looked at Bernie.

"So Harold, what's your kind of music? I see you got some kind of instrument there. What do you play?"

Before he could answer she said, "What do you like on the radio?"

"Anything."

"How about your girl friend? What does she like?"

Bernie opened his mouth and the voice behind him said, "I bet I know what she likes."

They laughed, beside and behind him, and the car swerved from the empty highway to a country road running up into the hills. The black bark on the trees shone like ebony and the gray saplings dripped silver rain. Soon it would be dark.

"Where are we going?" Bernie asked.

"You'll find out," the driver said.

The car continued uphill, the big engine laboring. The road was mud and stones and the car lurched over deep ruts. Brown water streamed across the window on Bernie's side.

"This is it," said the voice behind him, and the driver swung the wheel. Bernie fell toward her and caught himself on the dash. The driver laughed and braked. They were in a weedy clearing surrounded by black pines. She killed the engine and gave Bernie a different kind of look. She wasn't smiling.

"You got a long walk home," she said.

Bernie clutched his horn case and threw the door open. He took three strides through the wet grass and then the one with the yellow hair moved in front of him and stood with one hand in her jeans and the other lifted as if to bring everything to a stop. The blue scar seemed to glow and squirm against her skin.

"Hold it," she said. "Behind you."

Bernie turned. The thin, dark girl stood beside the car with her hands on a length of steel or a crowbar or bumper-jack and it wasn't until she sighted him down the bore that Bernie realized it was a shotgun. He gripped the case. The rain fell against his mouth.

"Don't shoot," he said.

The blonde one said, "We got some questions for you, and don't try her. Sherry nails a buck every deer season. She likes to play with that thing."

Bernie's eyes stayed on the shotgun.

"Ask him something," said the thin girl.

"Okay, Harold. Let's see how smart you are. If you get two right answers in a row she may not shoot you where it hurts."

Bernie's knees wobbled. He pushed his free hand against his stomach.

"Question number one," the blonde one said. "Who's the best all-time singer in America?"

Bernie closed his eyes. He imagined Raeleen walking into the warmth of her well-lit house. He imagined her sitting in front of the television with a mug of hot Ovaltine in her hands, the sound of her mother's sewing machine in the next room.

The dark girl took two steps forward and jabbed him in the ribs with the snout of the gun. He gasped and half-buckled but he maintained his grip on the case.

"What about it?" she said.

"I don't know."

"Wrong," said the blonde one. "The answer is Elvis Presley." She stared at him with a pale, steady light on her face. "Question number two," she said. "Who's the second best singer of all time?"

Bernie swallowed. "Male or female?" he said.

She smiled. "Female," she said.

"Wait a minute. I can't think. Just give me a minute," he said.

"Patsy Cline. You aren't real bright, are you, Harold? Are you?"

"No," he said.

She said, "Here's your last chance. Get this one right and you're off the hook. You ready?"

Bernie nodded.

"Here it is. What's the best all-time American song?" The smile vanished again. "You better get this one right. Think about it," she said.

His voice contracted in his throat and a small sound squeaked through his lips.

" 'Duke of Earl,' " the blonde one said. "Answer is 'Duke of Earl.' "

"You lose," said the skinny girl. She pointed the gun at his chest. The rain had soaked her hair flat around her face and behind her ears. The water ran down the black barrel and dripped from the end.

"Ask him something else," she said.

The other considered, grimacing. She said, "All right, I've got one. How old is your girl friend, Harold?"

He heard her repeat the question and he heard himself say, "Seventeen. Same as me."

"What's her name?"

"Raeleen." The sound of his voice shamed him.

"Do you love her?"

They waited. Bernie listened to the rain drilling through the trees. He looked at their peaks silhouetted against the fading sky.

"Answer me," said the blonde one.

"I don't know," he said, and then in the same breath, taking a chance, he said, "Yes, I love her," and he thought he saw the thin girl wince.

The blonde one moved her tongue on her mouth. She said, "Good for you, Harold. Good for you." She moved behind the girl with the gun. "One last question," she said. "What's in the case?"

Bernie glanced down at it. "French horn," he said.

The girls laughed suddenly and loud, as if he'd betrayed the true colors of his soul.

The blonde one said, "I think I'd like to hear a song. How about you, Sherry? Sherry and me want a song."

Bernie told himself that they only meant to frighten him, but the girl held the gun as if she'd used it before.

"Play something," she said.

"Take it out and play a tune."

"Take it out," said the girl with the gun.

Bernie kneeled and fumbled at the clips with numb fingers. He slid the cold mouthpiece into place and stood up with the horn. The pale coil glimmered in the rain.

"That's all there is to it," he said. "I can't play anything out here. I can't."

"Play us a song," said the girl with the gun.

"Play 'Duke of Earl,'" said the blonde one.

Bernie blinked at them. "I can't," he said.

The girl with the gun lowered it to her hip, level with his midsection. Bernie heard a click and her grip tightened.

"All right," Bernie said. "I'll try. But it won't sound like anything."

He snugged his fist into the bell. He drummed on the valves. Then he blew into the mouthpiece. His mouth was tight and dry.

"Play it," said the girl with the gun.

He took a deep breath and fit the small nickel cup to his lips. A few mournful notes blooped out and were swallowed in the rain and gathering darkness. He took another breath and stumbled into a tune, not any tune he'd heard before but something that came to his lungs and fingers from a part of him that was not scared.

"That's not it," said the blonde one.

Bernie faltered and started again, this time with a melody that might have been the one they wanted, as nearly as he could remember it. In flat hollow tones the recognizable rhythm rolled into the dark hills behind the rain. The girls did not move. Bernie closed his eyes and played the chorus again and again.

He heard the blonde girl say, "Good going, Harold. Keep playing."

He heard their feet in the grass and sucking mud but he didn't look and he played the song until the engine roared and the high beams swept his face.

The salesman who stopped for him looked twice when Bernie climbed into the car.

"What's in the case?" the salesman said.

"French horn," said Bernie.

"You look cold. How about I give us some heat?"

Bernie didn't answer but the salesman pushed a switch and almost immediately a stale warmth filled the car. The salesman poured some coffee from a thermos with his free hand. He took a gulp and offered the plastic cup to Bernie.

As Bernie drank the salesman said, "I have a trunk full of vacuum cleaners. I don't suppose your mother's in the market for a good vacuum at a good price?"

Bernie didn't answer. The salesman shook his head.

"You'd think people didn't use them anymore," he said. "Nobody buys around here. I might as well go back to the city."

The heat blew on Bernie's face and hands and he felt the hot coffee working at the knot in his chest. He put his hand over his mouth as if he would laugh. He didn't laugh, he wasn't smiling, but he heard it in himself. Maybe it wasn't even his laughter, but it carried him down the road, a dozen years into the future, and he was with a woman who was not Raeleen, who sat beside him on a large rumpled bed, and he was telling the story about the girls in the Pontiac, how they'd made him play his horn in the rain. He laughed as he told it and the woman laughed and kissed the back of his neck and then he came back to himself trembling in the car, in the night, and he heard the salesman say, "Bud, you mind telling me what this is all about?"

RAYMOND OLIVER

I come from near Boston, of a half-immigrant, half-Anglo family, and have spent goodly portions of my life in the Deep South, the Midwest, California, Germany, England, and France. Educated at Andover, Oberlin, Wisconsin, Munich, and Stanford. Married to the former Mary Anne McPherson, a theologian; two children, Kathryn and Nathan. I am a professor of English at U.C. Berkeley.

"These poems display my attraction to the Long Ago and Far Away, including the Far Away of foreign languages; but they try to convey that romantic attraction in a classical manner—lucidly, in strict form (for that palpable sense of everything locking into place), and without the cult of personality. More recent poems are more compressed and oblique."

Dream Vision

If I could open only one of those days—
December 6, 1160, Oxford?—
Locked in the Mind where all our story stays,
What would I find? A high medieval quaintness?
Tall men at altars, mantled, stony-faced,
As in Autun's façade? Or men with eyes
Like goggles, limbs at funny angles, braced
To hurl their wavy spears, as at Bayeux,
In linen? Parchment peasants from the books,
In skirts and puttees, tending tiny sheep,
Gesturing statically with bishop's-crooks?

I see a snow-filled wood, not, as in Frost,
Lovely, but rough, indifferent, like Montana,
Part of the total frozen forest crossed
Only by fragile trails from far-off hamlets
To towns like Oxford there: no dreaming spires
But tufts of cottage smoke in the early distance.
And here a clearing, where the morning fires
Reek of mere wood for heat, not roasting boar.
And from a thatched and earthy A-frame shack
A man comes forth, just for a moment pausing,

Smiling; in words like Dutch he hollers back
To make a woman laugh. I recognize him.

◆   ◆   ◆

Portuguese

This is no tongue to turn a compliment,
Or twist a curse too graceful to resent,
Or speak in flames grandly of heaven and hell;
Its sound is intimate, like the frying-smell
Of garlic. With liquids like a heavy wine,
It speaks of sweet-loaves, olives packed in brine,
Chestnuts and squash; its consonants
      are blurred,
Nasals insinuating, diphthongs slurred
With overtones, like some ignoble wish;
It is a language of linguiça, fish,
Mary, and Christ—staples on which to fatten
Both flesh and soul. Among the sons of Latin
It seems a country cousin, rich but crude;
Yet one must praise a tongue that savors food
And God with gusto: familial Portuguese,
In whose irregular moods I feel at ease.

TILLIE OLSEN

♦   ♦

Born (1912 or 1913) and raised in Nebraska; a San Franciscan since 1933. Public libraries were her college. She began writing when young, but the necessity of working on everyday jobs and raising four children silenced her for twenty years. Her books, published in eleven languages, are Tell Me A Riddle; Yonnondio: From the Thirties; Silences; *and* Mother to Daughter, Daughter to Mother. *Pieces from them have been anthologized more than 100 times. She has taught or been writer-in-residence at Amherst and Kenyon Colleges, M.I.T., Stanford, and the Universities of Massachusetts and Minnesota. In addition to many awards, including a Guggenheim, she has received five honorary degrees.*

"'Dream-Vision' was not written in my Stanford time. It was lived. Yet—with so much inexhaustible else of those temporal, infinite, eight months—did it plough and seed within me. Through thirty-three years has fed, feeds, comprehension, caring, expression; come tangible, present, in all I have published since—and my as yet unpublished, unharvested."

♦   ♦   ♦

Dream-Vision

IN THE WINTER OF 1955, in her last weeks of life, my mother—so much of whose waking life had been a nightmare, that common everyday nightmare of hardship, limitation, longing; of baffling struggle to raise six children in a world hostile to human unfolding—my mother, dying of cancer, had beautiful dream-visions—in color.

Already beyond calendar time, she could not have known that the last dream she had breath to tell came to her on Christmas Eve. Nor, conscious, would she have named it so. As a girl in long ago Czarist Russia, she had sternly broken with all observances of organized religion, associating it with pogroms and wars; "mind forg'd manacles"; a repressive state. We did not observe religious holidays in her house.

Perhaps, in her last consciousness, she *did* know that the year was drawing towards that solstice time of the shortest light, the longest dark, the cruellest cold, when—as she had explained to us as children—poorly sheltered ancient peoples in northern climes had summoned their resources to make out of song, light, food, expressions of human love—festivals of courage, hope, warmth, belief.

It seemed to her that there was a knocking at her door. Even as she rose to open it, she guessed who would be there, for she heard the neighing of camels.

(I did not say to her: "Ma, camels don't neigh.") Against the frosty lights of a far city she had never seen, "a city holy to three faiths" she said, the three wise men stood: magnificent in jewelled robes of crimson, of gold, of royal blue.

"Have you lost your way?" she asked, "Else, why do you come to me? I am not religious, I am not a believer."

"To talk with *you*, we came," the wise man whose skin was black and robe crimson, assured her, "to talk of whys, of wisdom."

"Come in then, come in and be warm—and welcome. I have starved for such talk."

But as they began to talk, she saw that they were not men, but women:

That they were not dressed in jewelled robes, but in the coarse everyday shifts and shawls of the old country women of her childhood, their feet wrapped round and round with rags for lack of boots; snow now sifting into the room;

That their speech was not highflown, but homilies; their bodies not lordly in bearing, magnificent, but stunted, misshapen—used all their lives as a beast of burden is used;

That the camels were not camels, but farm beasts, such as were kept in the house all winter, their white cow breaths steaming into the cold.

And now it was many women, a babble.

One old woman, seamed and bent, began to sing. Swaying, the others joined her, their faces and voices transfiguring as they sang; my mother, through cracked lips, singing too—a lullaby.

For in the shining cloud of their breaths, a baby lay, breathing the universal sounds every human baby makes, sounds out of which are made all the separate languages of the world.

Singing, one by one the women cradled and sheltered the baby.

"The joy, the reason to believe," my mother said, "the hope for the world; the baby, holy with possibility, that is all of us at birth." And she began to cry, out of the dream and its telling now.

"Still I feel the baby in my arms, the human baby," crying now so I could scarcely make out the words "—the human baby, before we are misshapen; crucified into a sex, a color, a walk of life, a nationality . . . and the world yet warrings and winter."

I had seen my mother but three times in my adult life, separated as we were by the continent between, by lack of means, by jobs I had to keep and by the needs of my four children. She could scarcely write English—her only education in this country a few months of night school. When at last I flew to her, it was in the last days she had language at all. Too late to talk with her of what was in our hearts; or of harms and crucifying and strengths as she had known and experienced them; or of whys and knowledge, of wisdom. She died a few weeks later.

She, who had no worldly goods to leave, yet left to me an inexhaustible legacy. Inherent in it, this heritage of summoning resources to make—out of song, food, warmth, expressions of human love—courage, hope, resistance, belief; this vision of universality, before the lessenings, harms, divisions of the world are visited upon it.

She sheltered and carried that belief, that wisdom—as she sheltered and carried us, and others—throughout a lifetime lived in a world whose season was, as still it is, a time of winter.

✦ NANCY HUDDLESTON PACKER ✦

Nancy Huddleston Packer was born in Washington, D.C., in 1925 and grew up in Birmingham, Alabama. She is a professor of English at Stanford University and the author of three volumes of stories: Small Moments *(University of Illinois Press),* In My Father's House: Tales of an Unconformable Man *(John Daniel Publisher), and* The Women Who Walk and Other Stories *(Louisiana State University Press, forthcoming).*

"A few years ago as I drove along near the Stanford campus, I began to notice women walking alone. I didn't know who the women were, but I was struck by their unconventional dress and by their heedless intensity. This story came out of that observation."

✦　　✦　　✦

The Women Who Walk

IN THE DAYS RIGHT after Malcolm left her, Marian began to notice the women who walked the deserted streets near the university campus. They were a flash of color in the brilliant June sunlight at a distant intersection, a single shape thrusting through the shadows of the giant sycamores along the sidewalk. She did not at first differentiate one from another. She was too absorbed in her own suffering. Images of Malcolm that last day spun through her mind. The thin ankle over the thin knee as he sat on his luggage in the front hall. The silver lighter touched to the black cigarette. Well, Marian, he said. She pulled the car over to the curb and gave herself up to the blurring tears, the sudden thunder in her chest.

Soon, quieter, she looked around the empty streets. Had anyone seen her? She saw in the distance a lonely figure, walking, walking.

Two weeks had passed and she had not yet told the children. She had said, "He's out of town, he's at a conference, he's giving a lecture, he'll be back." One evening as they sat in the dying sun in the patio, Joseph, who was eleven, said,

"When? When will he be back?"

A bluebird squawked in the high branches of the silver maple. "Your father . . ." she began. She felt suffocated by the heat in her throat. Molly began to cry and buried her face in Marian's lap. Joseph grew red and he ran into the house. Later that night, Marian called Malcolm at the backstreet hotel where he had taken a room. "I can't tell them," she managed to say, and quickly hung up.

Next day, Malcolm carried the children away for lunch. After that, each evening he spoke to them on the telephone. On the following Saturday, he took Joseph to a Giants game. On Sunday, he and Molly visited a horse farm in the hills. Marian longed to know what he had said, whether he had spoken of her. But they did not tell her.

Finally she asked. Molly grew somber, hooded, afraid. Joseph became moody and glared at the floor. Molly said,

"Daddy says we're not to carry tales back and forth."

"You're my children," she said.

"His too," said Joseph, "just as much as yours."

She felt an explosion and a wind and a fire, but she sat silent and staring.

The first few weeks, women she had counted as friends called her on the phone, invited her to lunch, came by to visit. From behind the living room curtain, she saw them walk up the drive, often in tennis whites, practicing an overhead slam or a low backhand as they waited for her to answer their knock. When she opened the door, their faces were grave. They sat on the sofa and put their sneakers on the coffee table and frowned and shook their heads in sympathy.

She could not speak of him. She tried to talk of other things, but all paths through her mind led back to the injustice she had suffered, of which she could not speak. The silence soon weighed too heavily on them, and their faces grew round and flat as moons, and pale. They knew they could not help her. They must leave now, they said, but they would return. They wished her well. They were her friends. She heard their tires sighing as they escaped down the street.

They were not her friends. They were the wives of his friends, the mothers of his children's friends, the neighbors who were no more than friends of his house. She had no friends. She would never be able to speak of herself, to share herself with friends. He had exiled her to an island of silence. She stood up and began to move around the room, shifting ashtrays, picking lint from the floor. She felt a restless, angry energy gathering in her.

During the summer, Marian frequently saw the woman in the large black coat walking rapidly on the outskirts of the university or the residential streets bordering the business area of the town. She thought the woman was an older faculty wife who apparently spent her leisure doing good works, carrying petitions door-to-door or collecting for the Cancer Society or the Red Cross.

The woman wore sandals and heavy dark socks, a floppy straw hat, and the black coat. The coat was shaped like a wigwam, with sloping shoulders and a wide skirt that struck her just above the ankles. Marian thought the woman wore it like a burnoose, a protection against the dog-day heat of late August and September. The woman was obviously a character, a throwback to the days when faculty and faculty wives were rather expected to be eccentric. Marian liked her, liked her independence and freedom from vanity. Often Marian waved as she drove by, but the woman never seemed to see her. She kept her eyes down, as if she were afraid she might stumble as she rushed along in her waddling, slue-footed gait.

One hot day in late September as Marian waited for a stoplight, the woman in the black coat started across the street in front of the car. Marian had never seen her so close before. She was much younger than she looked from a distance, about thirty-five or so, Marian's age. And still quite pretty, with a high-bridged, delicate nose and delicate fine lips and a soft-looking pale skin. When she came even with the front of the car, she abruptly twisted her head and glanced at Marian through the windshield. As their gazes met, Marian knew that she had seen the woman before—how long ago, under what circumstances she could not recall, perhaps at a university party, a meeting, at the sandbox or the swings of the city park. She would never forget those startled pale gray eyes.

Marian waved but the woman ducked her head again and hurried on to the sidewalk. Watching her—the hunched tension of her neck and shoulders, the awkward, powerful, rushing gait—Marian felt that when they had met, they had been drawn together in one of those rare moments of intense though inexplicable intimacy. And now Marian longed to recapture the strange, trea- sured feeling.

She drove around the block and pulled into a driveway in the woman's path. She got out and stood leaning on the fender, waiting, smiling. The woman walked straight at her, heedless, but at the last moment, without lifting her gaze from the ground, veered clumsily aside. Marian reached out and touched her shoulder. "Wait," she said. "Don't I know you?"

The woman stopped and after a long moment lifted her head. Her gaze whipped from Marian to the sky to the trees. She pulled her coat collar up around her face. Marian said, "What is it? Can I help you?"

The woman threw back her head, like a colt shying, and opened her mouth. Marian heard the sound—distant, muted—of a strangled voice and she thought the voice said, "I'm so very cold." For an instant the woman stared at Marian, and then she lowered her head and rushed down the street.

Malcolm came late one evening to settle details. He sat in the red leather chair he had always sat in. He looked handsome, tanned, his graying hair tousled and longer than he had ever worn it. When he asked how everything was, he was charming and attentive, his smile warm and pleasing, as if she were his dinner partner. She sat on the edge of the wing chair, her knees close, her hands kneading each other, and told him the lie he wanted to hear. Yes, everything was fine. He nodded at her approvingly, no longer angry and irritated with her.

"Well, now," he began, and leaned forward. She did not want to hear it all just then, and she stood up.

"I'll get some coffee," she said. "Turkish coffee," she pleaded. He sighed and nodded.

She went into the kitchen and turned on the faucet. She waited for her heartbeat to slow. When she heard his footsteps, she busied herself with cups and saucers. He stood in the doorway and gazed around him, smiling at the wall decorated with dinner plates from different countries.

"I always liked that one," he said, pointing at a Mexican plate he had brought to her from Mexico City where he had gone for a conference. But, he hastened to assure her, she needn't worry, all he wanted were a few mementos, keepsakes that had been in his family for a long time. The tintype of his great-grandmother and of course its antique frame and the silver ladle his great-aunt had saved from the Yankees. He smiled. Everything else was hers, absolutely, he didn't want anything else. Nothing.

Nothing? she wanted to ask. Nothing? No memento, no keepsake of our fifteen years together?

"Nothing besides coffee?" she asked. "Some fruit?" She picked up an immense pineapple from the straw basket on the counter. It was just ripe, soft and yellow. He had always loved pineapples. "It's just ripe," she said. "I'll cut it for you." When he shook his head, she held it close to his face. "Smell it," she pleaded.

"I do not want to smell it, for God's sake," he said. For an instant his composure dropped away and she saw what she had remembered all these months: the rigid shoulders, the pinched mouth, the hard, irritated eyes. She could easily drag the sharp points of the pineapple across his face. She watched little specks of blood ooze from his skin, swell into a long thick ruby streamer that marked his cheek like a savage decoration. She put the pineapple down and handed him a cup of coffee. Back in the living room, he sat again in the red chair and put his feet up on the matching ottoman.

Molly and Joseph were already in bed, but when they heard his voice they ran into the living room. Joseph stood in the doorway, smiling quizzically. Molly climbed over Malcolm's legs and onto his lap. He set the coffee down and Molly burrowed under his arm, into his armpit. He stroked her hair. Marian felt an uneasiness, a tension, and then she was suddenly shaken by a yearning—to be held, to be stroked—and she felt dizzy, as if she might faint.

"Run along now," said Malcolm to the children, "and I'll see you Sunday." As the children left the room, he explained. "They're coming to my new place for lunch on Sunday. If that's all right with you?" She nodded. "Did you know I had a place? It's not exactly elegant, but I like it much better than the hotel. I like having a place of my own."

"This is yours." She slid off her chair and dropped to her knees beside him. She pressed her face against his thigh. He did not move beneath her caresses. When she looked up, she saw the prim set of his lips. She stood up.

"Now about the arrangements," he said. "Here's what I thought, but I want you to be thoroughly satisfied."

He pulled a folded-up piece of paper from his wallet. It was covered with words and figures in his neat small handwriting. She saw the words "Insurance" and "Automobile."

"You really should get a lawyer," he said. She seized upon the kindness in his voice.

"Who should I get?"

He drew one of the black cigarettes from the box. He tamped it against the back of his hand and lighted it with his silver lighter. After a moment, he said, "You've got to start making that kind of decision for yourself, you know."

"Don't you see that it's too late?" she whispered.

He stood up, tapped ashes into the ashtray, drank off the last of the coffee, gathered together his cigarettes and lighter and wallet. "You're a perfectly competent woman," he said, "as no one knows better than I. After all," he went on, smiling at her, his voice remote, jocular, false, "you managed to get me through graduate school. I don't forget that. I'll always be grateful for that."

She went to the window and stared out at the darkness. "Then how can you desert me like this?" Her voice was hoarse, choked.

"There's no point going over this again," he said in an exasperated voice. "I know it's right for both of us."

She heard his sigh, the sound of the ottoman scraping over the floor as he pushed it aside, his footsteps brushing across the rug. The sky was cloudless, moonless, starless. The leaves of the eucalyptus shivered. Dark spaces opened within her. She spoke softly to the windowpane.

"Can't you stay just tonight?"

"Now, Marian," he said, moving into the hallway.

"Just to hold me," she whispered, "in the dark, a last time."

"Good night," he called from the front door. Soon the lights of his car vanished into the dark. She stood at the window a moment longer. She felt the agitation rising, the fury, the rush of movement through her body. She felt the hardness gather in the center of her chest and she could make no sound.

The rains came early, and by the middle of November the ground was soggy. For days the sky was close in and gray. Through the autumn Marian had become aware of the woman in white, seen as a flash of light out of the corner of her eye as she drove along. The woman was probably a nurse, cutting through the campus on her way to the university hospital. She was about five nine or five ten and very very thin, like a wraith. She was swaybacked and as she walked she lifted her knees high, her feet far out in front of her, like a drum majorette on parade. The knobby joints between her long thin bones made her look even more awkward and absurd. Yet she walked without self-consciousness, head high, as if she had better thoughts to ponder than the amusement of people driving by in their big cars. This lack of vanity was one of the characteristics shared by the women who walked. That, and the vigorous, almost heedless, way they moved.

Marian had only seen the wraith—as she came to think of her—in the vicinity of the university until a drizzly Sunday afternoon in early December when she saw her on a downtown street. The children had eaten lunch with Malcolm and she had contrived to pick them up. Malcolm lived in a cottage behind a large Spanish house close by the freeway. Often she had driven past and stared down the overgrown path that ran alongside the house. Baskets of ferns and wandering Jew hung from the roof of the little dilapidated porch, and there were bright flowered curtains behind the windows. Though appealing in the way that dark, shabby little cottages sometimes are, the charm of this one seemed utterly foreign to everything she believed she knew of Malcolm's taste. He had always insisted that their house be neat, clean, sparse. Something had changed in him, and she thought that if only she could see inside the place, she might at last understand what had gone wrong between them. And so she had told him that she was going on an errand and since she didn't want the children to return to an empty house, she would pick them up.

But even before she had turned off the ignition, she saw Molly running down the path toward her, and Joseph sauntering behind. Malcolm, in a bright green sweatshirt and jeans, stood on the porch and waved to her as if she were only the mother of children visiting at his house. She was filled with shame at her scheme, and with disappointment at its failure, and then with relief.

Joseph got in the front seat. He looked sullen, moody, as he often did after the Sundays with his father. Molly climbed in back and grasped Marian's ears and said, "Giddap." Marian patted Molly's hands. And she said, "I'll bet anything you had—let's see—bologna on store-bought bread and Coke. And of course Oreos." The thought of Malcolm's providing such a dreary lunch gave her pleasure, and revving the motor she laughed aloud.

"No," said Joseph. He crossed his arms and dropped his head.

"We had chicken with some kind of orange stuff all over it," said Molly. "I didn't like it but that lady said I had to eat it since she made it special."

Joseph turned to the backseat. "You're stupid," he said. "Nobody can trust you, you're a baby."

Marian thrust her foot against the accelerator and the car jumped from the curb, bucked, almost died, caught, sped away. That lady. A woman. No one had told her there was a woman. But who would? Who did she have to tell her anything? Yet she should have known. She was the stupid one. The secrecy. The children's silence. The shabby place with its shabby charm. The ferns. The bright curtains. And behind the curtains, a woman peering out at her, perhaps laughing at her. The rejected wife. The discard. Garbage.

"I didn't mean to tell," said Molly. She patted Marian's shoulder. "I'm sorry."

Marian drove in silence, beneath the immense white oaks, past the fine old mansions, past the run-down rooming houses and flats. No life stirred. Even the downtown streets were empty. The car moved through empty gray streets. The day was cold, damp, dark. She saw a flash of shimmering white. Without thinking, she said,

"One of the walkers."

The woman strutted toward them on her long heron legs. She had on a pale pink jacket over her white dress. As the car drew near Marian saw that the jacket was short-sleeved, that it barely covered the woman's breasts, that it was loose-fitting, flimsy, crocheted. That it was a bed jacket. As Marian stared, the woman turned toward her. Her eyes were narrowed, glittering, defiant. She grinned fiercely.

"What walker?" asked Joseph. He dropped his feet from the dashboard and sat up to see. Marian pressed the accelerator and the car jerked forward and threw Joseph against the seat.

"Never mind. We've passed her." Marian flushed with embarrassment. She felt she had somehow humiliated the woman in front of Joseph and Molly.

"I saw her," said Molly. "She had on pink and white. Joseph just doesn't look."

Joseph spun toward her. "You shut up, you shut up," he said. His voice trembled. Marian touched his shoulder.

"Please don't quarrel," she said.

He pulled away from her hand. "I hate you and Daddy," he shouted. "You don't care about us, you don't care what you do to us."

"Mommy didn't do it, did you?" said Molly. "It was Daddy and that lady."

"He wouldn't have just left," said Joseph. "It was her fault, too."

Hot moisture bubbled into her eyes, and shrill sounds rose into her ears. She pulled the car over to the curb. Now she would tell them. Her fault? Her fault too? Now she would unleash her suffering, she would engulf them in her anguish. She would tell them, she would tell them. She turned to Joseph. His eyelids were slightly lowered and his nose and mouth were stretched down and pinched. She twisted to see Molly.

"Don't," said Molly. "Please don't look like that. Don't cry, please don't cry. You're so ugly when you cry. Please don't."

Marian pressed her fingers into her skull. She held her neck muscles taut. She pushed out her chest and belly to make room for the expanding pressure. They were her children. They were all she now had. She must protect them from misery and pain. From herself. In the rearview mirror, she could make out in the gray distance the comic cakewalk of the woman in white, alone, in the cold.

Over the next weeks, she longed to tell Malcolm that she knew about the lady. She longed to taunt him. How typical, how trite, how sordid. He had deserted his family for the sleaziest of reasons, another woman, a younger woman, probably a graduate student. Malcolm with his dignity and pride. How comical it was. She saw herself pick up the telephone and dial his number. She heard her contemptuous yet amused voice ringing through the wires. Sleazy and comical, she heard herself say.

But she did not call him. She was afraid. His voice would be hard and irritable, and he would say hateful things to her that she could not bear to hear. She imagined his saying, I never loved you, not even at the beginning. She heard him say, I married you only so I could finish my degree. He would infect her memories with doubt and ruin the past for her. He would leave her with nothing. While he had his lady.

Through the winter months, she spent hours at a time daydreaming about Malcolm and his woman. Often, she sat at her bedroom window and watched the rain break against the pane. She believed that if she concentrated hard enough, she would be able to conjure up an image of his woman. But always as the face began to form on the film of the glass, the wind swept the image away.

One day as the outline of the eyes appeared, she leaned close to fasten the face to the windowpane. She saw her own reflection, and she saw that her eyes were more haggard than she remembered, her lips thin, her nose taut. She had grown suddenly old and ugly. She drew back from the windowpane, and as she did, her reflection began to move away from her, as if the image were running to a distant point in the street. She saw her reflection grow smaller and smaller, and then vanish.

She jumped from the chair and rushed into the living room. She must come out of her misery. She had lost touch with the world, gone stale and sour inside herself. Her life had lost its shape. She had no purpose. She had been only marking time, waiting for relief that would never come. She had to build her life again, become a person again.

She sat down in the red chair, Malcolm's chair. No, she thought, it's my chair. She pulled the *New York Times Magazine* from the mahogany rack by the chair. The magazine was six months old. She dumped all the magazines on the floor, the *New Republic, Harper's, The New York Review.* They were all stiff and yellow with age. Malcolm's magazines. He had taken the subscriptions with him, and she had not even missed them. She had read nothing in months.

The blood rose to her head and pounded behind her eyes. She had once been an attractive, interesting woman who kept up, who could talk of anything. Yes, talk so that men listened to her and admired her and desired her. Malcolm had taken all that from her. That, too. Slowly, slowly. Over the years he had frequently said hurtful things to her—that she chattered, that she told everything in boring detail. Hurtful things that made her feel inadequate or silly and that broke her confidence. She had given up, content to let him do the talking, content with the warmth of his brilliance. To please him, she had become a cipher. And when he thought he had completed her destruction, he had deserted her.

But he was wrong: she was not destroyed. Free of him, she was ready to become the attractive woman she had once been. Everything was still there, ready to emerge from the half-life she had lived all these years. She felt that her powers were flooding back to her, washing away her fear of him, her timidity.

Exultant, triumphant, she rushed to the telephone and dialed his number at the university. But when a soft young female voice answered, she could not speak. She heard Malcolm ask, "Who is it, Teddy?" and then "Hello" into the phone. She could not remember what she had intended to say to him. A pressure began, swelled larger and larger until she feared it would explode in her chest, crash through her eardrums, shatter the delicate membrane of her nostrils and eyes. She opened her mouth to let the sounds out, but no sounds came.

Marian had often noticed the woman in the red plastic coat who walked with one hand palm up at her shoulder and the other on her hip. Her white hair was burnished to a metallic sheen and it stood high above her face like a chef's cap. She wore multicolored platform shoes with six-inch heels that threw her forward, and she took quick little mincing steps as if hurrying to catch up with her top before it fell. She was, Marian decided, probably a prostitute.

But prostitute or not, she was a human being and a woman, and a woman obviously mistreated by men. And so seeing her on a drizzly March afternoon walking with the red coat held straight-armed above the elaborate hair-do, Marian decided to give the woman a lift. She drew the car alongside the curb and leaned across the passenger seat to lower the window.

And then she noticed the sores on the woman's bare legs. Some of the sores were black holes with diameters the size of a pencil and some were raw looking with moist crusts and some were fresh, suppurating, leaving faint trails down her calves.

The woman turned. Her face was mottled and skull-like and Marian thought the flesh had already begun to rot back from the bones. Marian felt a hard spasm in her lower belly, as if a steel hand had fastened around her groin. The woman grinned then, a terrible grin of complicity, as if she had anticipated, had desired, now shared the sudden hatred Marian felt surging through her. As Marian reared back from the window and twisted the steering wheel toward the street, she heard a muffled, constricted whimpering, and she knew it was her own.

One Sunday afternoon in June, Malcolm came into the house with the children. It had been nearly a year since he had left; the divorce was final. He stood in the hallway and leaned casually against the wall. He was deeply tanned and his gray sideburns were long and bushy and somehow boyish. He seemed cheerful

and lighthearted, qualities she thought he had long ago given up to his seriousness, his image of himself as a scholar. He wore his new happiness like an
advertisement and he apparently expected her to rejoice with him.

He said, "I've got a plan I know you're going to like."

Her resentment was like a coagulant. As he spoke her blood and her energy
ceased to flow, and she felt sullen, dull, thick.

He told her that he would take the children for July to one of the San Juan
Islands off Seattle. No electricity, he exulted. No cars. No telephone. Just man
against nature, with the necessities flown in, he said, laughing archly. He had
never been there, of course, but—he paused no more than a heartbeat—he
knew someone who had. He began to describe the island, as if he were enticing
her to come along, the cliffs, the immense trees, the wild berries, the birds.

"This will be one of the best experiences of their lives," he said, "and you'll
be free for a whole month."

"Free to do what?" she asked. Her tongue was thick and heavy, and her voice
hardly rose to her mouth.

"See you next Sunday," he called to the children, and waving, waving, he
backed out the front door.

"I'm going to have a shell collection," Molly said.

"There's a lot of driftwood," said Joseph, "so you can carve things and all."

"Teddy says the shells are beautiful and I'm going to make you a beautiful
shell necklace."

"Be quiet," said Joseph.

"I've never been to an island," said Molly. "I wish you could come too."

"Yeah," said Joseph.

After her hot bath, she lay in bed in the dark, staring at the odd shapes the
moon cast against the draperies. The moon on the water and the sandy beaches
and the shadows of trees. The wind blew in her open window and the draperies
billowed. She saw people in the moving folds. Heads. Bodies. Lovers moving
against each other in the dark shadows. Malcolm and his lady. She drew her
hands along her hips, squeezed her breasts between her fingers. No one would
ever hold her, whisper to her in the night. For a moment she feared that she
would scream out in her anguish, and she threw back the covers and sat up on
the side of the bed.

If only she had someone to talk to, to whom she could tell her suffering. She
thought of her parents, both dead, and of the brother she had not seen in years.
The faces of girls she had been close to came to her, and one in particular who
had blond hair in a Dutch boy cut and who had moved away when they were
both eleven. She thought of a boy whose name she could not recall who had
given her chocolates in a heart-shaped box and had kissed her clumsily on the
ear. And of the boy who had loved her in high school and whom she had loved
until she had met Malcolm. All these, and others she might have talked to, were
gone.

She got up to close the window against the wind and she saw a light beneath
Joseph's door. Molly had already deserted her, had said "Teddy" in an affec-
tionate, accepting way. But Joseph, her first-born, suffered, too.

She went to his room. He lay prone on his bed, propped on his elbows, a book open in front of him. She said, "I want to talk to you."

He folded the book over his finger and turned over. He lay back against the headboard. The light from the bullet lamp fell across the side of his face. He looked frail and sad.

She sat down in the desk chair and dragged it closer to the bed. "You're going away," she said, "with them." She held his gaze.

"Mom, please don't," he said. His shadowed face turned away from her. "We're not supposed to talk about the other one. He never talks about you."

"Never? Has he never said anything?"

"All he ever said was he had a right to try to be happy," Joseph said in a soft, fretful, placating voice. He drew his knees up and folded his arms across them and buried his head in his arms. "Please don't talk to me, please," he said.

As he lifted his face to her, his head seemed to rise above the knees, disembodied. As she stared at him, his face grew larger and larger and whiter and whiter. It swelled toward her, a pale disc, like the moon. She got to her feet.

"Sleep well," she said.

She went to the kitchen to make sure she had turned off the oven and the burners. She checked the locks on outside doors. She listened for the sound of a forgotten sprinkler. The house was still and dark and hot. She felt dull and sluggish, and yet excited, too restless to stay inside.

She went into her bathroom and took her old flannel robe off the hook on the back of the door. She got in the car and drove over to the university lake. In the springtime, the students boated and swam and sunned at the lake, and often she and Malcolm had brought the children there to search for tadpoles and frogs. Now, in June, the lake was slowly drying into a swamp.

She sat on the dark bank and breathed in the cool night air. The moon shimmered in the puddles on the lake bottom. It was the end of Spring term and she heard the murmur of student lovers and the rustle of dry leaves. She imagined bodies touching, and the soft delicious look of desire on their mouths and in their eyes. She had known that ecstasy. She remembered the first night she and Malcolm had been together. They had been on Cape Cod. She saw them lying in a little pocket of leafy brush, protected from the wind by an overhanging cliff. She had felt nothing existed but the two of them, and nothing mattered but the act of love they performed.

And in the moonlight, sitting on the damp bank of the swampy lake, she began to cry. Her crying was a moan that returned to her as the sound of soft thunder. And then she saw movement in the shadows of the trees. The students, the lovers, were moving away from her along the shores of the lake. She had driven them away. In her groin was the pain that was like lust, like fear, like hatred. She didn't care what the lovers or anyone thought of her. Her chest swelled with sobs. They seemed to be exploding through her ribs, bursting from her armpits, ripping through her ears and eye-sockets.

She stood up. The streets were empty. She clutched her bathrobe tighter against the suddenly chilly night, and she began to walk quickly, recklessly, in the direction of the moon. As she walked, she felt the power of her thrusting stride, the rising flood of her energy, the release of her torment.

CHARLOTTE PAINTER

Charlotte Painter was a Stegner Fellow at Stanford in 1961–62, and a Jones Lecturer for three years. Co-editor of Revelations: Diaries of Women *(with Mary Jane Moffat), she has based two books on her own diaries,* Who Made the Lamb *and* Confession from the Málaga Madhouse. *She is the author of* Gifts of Age: 32 Remarkable Women, *and two novels,* Seeing Things *and* The Matrix *(forthcoming). She is a professor at San Francisco State University.*

"I am just now completing a novel that I started at Stanford back in 1964, which may suggest I'm trying to set a Guinness record for the longest time ever spent on a novel. But my mind, like that of the middle-aged heroine in this short story, isn't very linear. The fact is that by some circuitous route I finally learned some of the lessons taught me in those days."

◆　　　◆　　　◆

Memory Loss

I WAS STEPPING OUT of some too-tight slacks, surrounded by merciless images of myself in the fitting-room wall mirrors, when a young woman came in and said, "Ms. Harris, how nice to see you."

I didn't recognize her. I said, "Hi there," a shade too brightly.

She piled some things on the bench next to me, placed a few dresses on a hook above. An attendant was hanging garments on a moving conveyance for return to the outside racks. Otherwise, we had the huge dressing room to ourselves.

The merest glimmer of memory stirred, not strong enough to light up her name. Tall and slender, an animated face, high-heeled sandals. Who is she, I wondered? A friend of my son? A former student? She was chattering, anticipating responses. "I love Loehmann's, don't you?"

I looked in the mirror. I could see that I looked much like other women I noticed shopping at Loehmann's, women with a certain slick eye for style, but without the wherewithal, so that they never quite looked put together right. I could see myself clearly in that open try-on room, where all four mirrored walls pressed at me mercilessly, with evidence of lumps and bulges, my belly spilling over, my legs marbled with veins down to my nylon ankle stockings. A dumpy, middle-aged bargain hunter. I did not love Loehmann's.

The price tag of the slacks I was taking off snagged my ankle stockings and I staggered getting free.

"I come here once a week," the girl was saying, "to see what new designer seconds have come in. I haven't seen you in ages." The attendant took the slacks from me and hung them on her return rack.

"I know," I acknowledged. This was just one of many recent lapses—a faintly familiar face, an exchange of pleasantries, while I teetered over a chasm of memory loss. "How have you been?" I asked.

"Wonderful." The mirror drew her eyes. She smoothed an eyebrow with her forefinger, then gazed at my image in the mirror. "You're looking great."

I realized I was hiding behind a garment I had taken from its hanger. "I've got to lose ten pounds," I mumbled. "My figure's a disgrace."

She slapped herself on the behind. "Look at this fat fanny." She slipped a yellow skirt over her head.

"You look much thinner," I guessed. Always a welcome compliment.

I would have asked her name, but on an earlier occasion I did ask and made matters worse. A young woman I couldn't place had stopped me on the street. "I'm Jane," she had said. "Jane." I widened my eyes at the sidewalk, where her name froze like a carving on soft cement. I said, "Oh Jane, I feel so stupid," and waved myself away. Another time I was leaving a movie with my teenage son and his girl friend, before the second feature, a Marx Brothers movie. A young woman waiting in line grabbed my hand, reached out, and startlingly kissed my cheek. "Marian, it's been so long." Too long. I smiled and wrung her hand, grateful for the darkness outside the theater. This young woman had come out into the night to the Mission to see *Duck Soup*. Who would do that? An irretrievable film buff? Someone suicidally depressed? Fortunately, my son and his girl friend had walked ahead and I could wave myself away with: "Imagine bumping into you at the movies!"

And now this—caught in ankle cheaters. All three encounters with women, young women. Did that mean something? Maybe I had reached an age when all young women look alike the way old ladies used to.

The girl was admiring herself in the skirt, a yellow print that she zipped up to her narrow waist. Underneath she had on a navy blue leotard she had worn into the store under Levi's. This skirt would help her image-change, she said: she thought she'd buy it. "You remember my classic Radcliffe clothes. Style was anathema to me."

A graduate student, then? Or a transfer? How long ago in Radcliffe? I imagined her disappointment after the gracious Eastern quads as she trudged our inhospitable institutional State campus, with its Union demonically designed to circumvent large student gatherings of protest, or even community. As she turned to see how the skirt flared, her movement stirred in the mirrors around the room. She was engaging, really, had such a candid face.

She asked, "I've improved a bit, though, don't you think?" She leaned toward the mirror as if for answer. I reflected that if I waited, said nothing, she might fully reveal herself.

"Of course," I assured her. It was safe enough. She was twenty-five or twenty-six, the age when young women always improve. But who *was* she?

"I'm doing a lot of pictures nowadays. Have a tech job in the photography lab. Just a few hours a week. I get to use the darkroom in my spare time."

Photography. Something was trying to melt out of my frozen memory cells. I pulled on another pair of slacks. These had an elastic waistband and might not bind so badly in the waist. Would anything but a robe ever be comfortable again?

"And then on the weekends, I have a waitress job that pays a lot in tips. At Pier 14. Very expensive." All right, I thought, she'd have to have been an English major. Some of the best waitresses in the city had been English majors.

"I get over to your building now and then," she said, "because—oh, you probably know him—" and she named a man, a teaching assistant in our department. She said, "We live together now. He's my new honey."

Suddenly the girl's story broke loose, turning my mind into a hive.

She was Natalie Bunsen. She had come west four years ago after painful experiences in Cambridge. She had told me everything, had written it for me when she was my student. As a teenager, she had had a breakdown. This came about after her mother's second marriage, to a man of wealth who had tried to seduce Natalie. She hadn't used that old-fashioned term, though. She said he tried to get her to make it with him and when she refused he raped her repeatedly. Finally she told her mother what was going on. Her mother's response was to commit Natalie to a private sanitorium and take a trip to Europe with the man. Over the next two years the sanitorium gave Natalie a series of shock treatments. Other women inmates comforted her, she said, kept her alive. She came out of the experience a lesbian and moved to the Coast. When she took my comp course, her hair was cropped straight and she must have weighed thirty pounds more.

Natalie pulled on another garment, a print dress with tiny blue flowers and tinier buttons. Not at all a dress she would have worn before. "It's a Cacharel," she said. "My mother used to buy things like this for me. Maybe I can come round to this sort of thing again."

A few other customers had come into the dressing room. Reflections of women stirred in the mirrors, undressing, pulling garments over their heads, setting them aside, murmuring to one another.

"How do I look in this? Is it too frilly?" A dark, saturnine woman about my age, who also wore ankle cheaters, had turned to us. "I had a color-style analysis, and they told me to wear pink ruffles." She tugged at a polyester knit with a pink ruff around the neck.

I felt helpless. "I'm no judge," I said.

But Natalie moved toward her, straightened the jacket. "No," she said, "the fabric's wrong. But they're right about the ruffles."

I was touched by this charity. The woman snatched the dress off. "Thank heaven you're here. I'll be right back," she said, zipping up her own dress.

"Do you know her?" I asked.

"Not that I know of," Natalie laughed.

Her lively eyes turned reflective. She said, "I read that book you gave me so many times. Countless times."

What book? I betrayed my confusion. Natalie said, "Oh, I imagine you've forgotten. You can't remember every book you give a student, I'm sure. But it was so important to me. *The Yellow Wallpaper.*"

Then I remembered the rest of Natalie's story. She came to visit me in my office. She couldn't do the assignment, she said, which was to write of a childhood experience. The class was all women, quite by chance, and so I had assigned only women's essays and stories. A warm generosity pervaded the group, and many of the women became good friends. "I love this class," said Natalie. "I want to do this paper in the worst way." But her childhood was a blank. She felt disconnected from her past as a result of her treatment at the hospital. I suggested ways she might get at the problem. As we talked, Natalie leafed through a copy of *The Yellow Wallpaper* by Charlotte Perkins Gilman that lay on my desk. It was an extra copy and so I told her to take it, to keep it.

She came back to the office a few days later and said that reading the story of another woman's dissociation had helped her to accept what she'd been through. She began to remember things, to piece together her past. The rest of the term she wrote of the hospital experiences.

At a party we had at the end of the term she told me of a plan. She wanted to take pictures of all the women who had helped her. She would make a personal narrative book, with a picture to accompany stories of women she wanted to acknowledge. "Women taught me to live again," she said. She even had a publisher for it, a women's press. "I'd like to take your picture for it," she said. "Your giving me *The Yellow Wallpaper*—I never realized before how a book can change a life."

I had stalled. I didn't want Natalie to take my picture, for a reason I don't like to admit. I was afraid I might be the only straight woman in the book. It was one thing to accept the sexual preferences of others, but something else to be pegged mistakenly, I told myself. Like getting credit for Greek when my elective was Romance Languages.

Natalie apparently understood my evasion and didn't call about the picture. She didn't come to see me either. We hadn't met again until today, when she had transformed herself into this slender young woman who lived with a man she called her "new honey."

She sat down on the bench with her back to the mirror looking at me with a soft earnestness. "I had forgotten everything, remember? Until you helped me."

I felt a rush of emotion, stammered a denial. "You did it yourself, you know." My own memory failure seemed too trivial compared with what Natalie had been through. Yet it wasn't trivial; to forget was terrible. I tried to think of my lapses as absurdities. I never spoke of them to anyone. I glimpsed myself now, all lumps and veins and nylon ankle stockings. Maybe Natalie would like my picture this way—"Forgetful Lady."

As if reading my mind, she said, "You told me that everybody tends to backslide into forgetfulness."

"I did?"

"Knowledge is a spiral and sometimes it turns, eclipses, and when it spirals back around, we have to relearn on a deeper level what we knew before. I'm *quoting* you."

I glimpsed my face in the mirror; it was flushed, blotched. Sweat had broken out on my nose.

Images of other women in their underthings moved within the mirror. None of the women in the dressing room had figures like Natalie's, I realized. Some were scrawny, most were at least as lumpy as I. They wore bras that did not uplift, stockings that left red bands at their thighs or waists, shoes that pinched.

The woman nearest us had taken off some high-heeled boots; the great toe folded over her others, permanently displaced by tight shoes. These women had riffled through the racks outside, had come into the mutual space of this dressing room with the fruits of their efforts and they spoke to one another, asking opinions that opened up their lives—was this blouse too dressy for the opera matinee? Would Mother ever wear anything this bright? Will this purple attract attention in the office? They offered reassurance, solicitude, encouragement. They had driven from all over the Bay Area out to Daly City, and were trying on something that might enhance their lives, help them to beauty, grace.

Suddenly, I sat beside Natalie on the bench, groping for Kleenex. To my disgust, I was about to cry. Natalie knelt down as if in supplication, speaking softly, elatedly. "You're going through menopause, aren't you? I hope you're not embarrassed. I mean, this is one of the real things women go through, after all. I'll be there before I know it, and can't help wondering what it's like."

I had to laugh. "Don't be in a hurry."

"What I'm trying to say is, *only* women can know anything about a hot flash, for instance. I mean *really*."

I blew my nose. I myself called those surges in temperature that burned up my interest in life simply "flashes." The "hot" part seemed an ultimate humiliation, an aspersion on failed sexuality. Maybe I was also trying to endow the flash with mysticism—a flash, a charge of insight, a revelation. But if it was that, I somehow kept missing the point. Or ducking it. *Duck Soup*. Now I had the name of the young woman going into the movie. Eleanor Barrett, a music student, Nate Barrett's daughter. She was writing a paper about the piano of Chico Marx.

I laughed. Suddenly, I was telling Natalie all about it, that I had forgotten not only giving her the book but had at first forgotten who she was, had trouble remembering everything these days, would get into my car and forget where I was going, to the store and not know what I meant to buy, start a lecture and after a few remarks have to stop to recall the subject. And Natalie was writing now the name of a whiz of an older woman doctor who had been through it all and was saying, "I mean I always think of what you said—you have to try everything, even if it's hard to keep challenging yourself. *You* said that to me."

I shook my head. "I don't remember." Natalie laughed.

As we were getting ready to leave, Natalie said, "I had a lovely dream after that course. I had to go back to the psych ward because they had only let me out on leave. And when I got there, the place was gone. It didn't even exist anymore."

Our gazes crossed and rested on one another's images in the mirror. "Thank you, Natalie," I said.

The dark woman came back with more ruffles. "What about this one?" she asked Natalie. It was a blouse of the same colors, black and pink, in a silk fabric.

"Much better," said Natalie. "Let's see how it looks on you."

The woman dived into it. As her head came through the neck opening, she said, "I know one woman who had her colors done, and she's seeing altogether different people now. The right combination can change your life."

"You better believe it," said Natalie.

GAIL PEREZ

Gail Perez was a Stegner Fellow in poetry at Stanford in 1983. She has taught writing at the University of Wyoming, the University of Santa Clara, and Stanford, and she is at present finishing her Ph.D. at Stanford.

"Both poems were written after my year as a Stegner Fellow. The first was written in Wyoming during moments stolen from grading piles of student essays, the second during long, uneasy California afternoons. They are dedicated to the workshop, Ken Fields, and W. S. Di Piero, the gang on Perry Lane, and the toxic wine at the Nuthouse."

◆　　　◆　　　◆

Thanksgiving Dogs

In the snowbound town, nothing moves
as I walk to the liquor store
but rising smoke and an occasional car
passing with the celebratory clank
of chains. The streets are safe
for my skidding dogs, who pee bright trails
in the snow that even I can follow.
Hunters have filled the alleys with bone
and hide, and now the dogs hunt freely.

If I had an antelope's vision,
I'd see the herds from here. At this hour
the cold descends, a hypothermic
peace on earth; by Venus's rising
they've found the lee of a hill,
eyes viscous, noses wet, at ten below.
Once or twice in the night they rise,
rump hair flaring at a coyote's bark.
The cold continues to descend
to the atmosphere's floor; blue grass waves
in the snow. Antelope, coyote, fox,
breathe and move, fantastic deep-sea creatures,
and, breaking the surface of cold—stars.

I hurry, my hands bright orange.
The dogs lick the ice balls in their feet

and fall in with my step, anxious, glad,
though they alone might survive this night.
I'll buy my rum and walk home slowly,
fuzzy with cold, but wanting to stay
that way, holiday rummy—anything
to grasp a moment that outer world,
perfectly uninhabitable.
I know that blessed difference,
just so much as we imagine it,
shapes these familiar things. The dogs weave
through trees, taking us as close as we
can come to not counting for everything.

◆   ◆   ◆

Lonely for the World

1.
Loneliness is, I know, bourgeois
and isolation, illusion,
but even with you here in bed,
I can't sleep without scanning my maps.
As though matter can't help reflecting,
I must hold the world in my hands,
or trace blue highways on your body,
wondering why we're obsessed
with distance: our anxious spaceshots
beam back the earth's voluptuous curve,
the stars are at war, and only
state of the art invaders connect.
Next door, a rumpus room glows blue
in the global village, nowhere
and everywhere. Satellites
thrust in space ensure we enjoy
the lives of shadowy ancestors,
crackling on wires above the earth.

2.
I visit my neighbor across town.
He's on the kitchen phone. (Ex-loved
ones smile at us, thick as pin-ups
on a convict's wall.) This one, he says,
Madam Rosa, can put us in touch
—that is, with Reagan's astral police,
healing crystals, or muscular sprites
that bend spoons. Backing to the wall,
at attention, vulnerable,
he says, "See my aura?" Wide-eyed,

missing again, I see nothing
but messages from the fruit bowl:
Chiquita, Texsun, Sunmaid.
I'm just another alien.

In the glass door, our doppelgangers
slouch; sex, even lunch, clearly out.
Beyond, a brown man rakes up pods,
another stands by the jacuzzi,
grabbing at loquats. I recall
police flagging down truckloads
of pickers, north of Tijuana:
the straight line of interstate
suddenly alive with men,
women, children. I've got a map,
but my friend says it's my trip.

3.
Years ago, the Feds dumped carloads
of my father's Mexican fruit—
melons carefully wrapped in green
paper—to rot on the border.
Bankrupt, we saw the USA
from darkest Meso-America
to shining New York fruitstands,
knowing what hands, invisible
and yet terribly alive, brought
such riches. When we touch the things
of this world, do we long for these
felt presences, beyond the sad
suburban will to self-fulfillment?
If these workers live in the world,
a broken line for "seldom traveled"
marks the way. It's easy to miss
the turn when electronic
Jesuses, Billy Sundays,
and Swamis point the way inward,
terrible angels, forbidding us
the world we can actually have.

ROBERT PINSKY

Robert Pinsky was a Stegner Fellow in 1964; he came to Stanford from New Jersey. His books of poetry are Sadness And Happiness *(Princeton, 1975),* An Explanation of America *(Princeton, 1979), and* History of My Heart *(Ecco, 1984). His critical books are* Landor's Poetry *(Chicago, 1968), which was written as a thesis under Albert Guerard's direction,* The Situation of Poetry *(Princeton, 1977), and* Poetry and the World *(Ecco, 1988). Pinsky teaches at Berkeley.*

"At the center of my memories of Stanford stands the figure—magnetic, grumpy, magisterial, beloved—of Yvor Winters. He taught me so much, and I resisted him so hard, that some part of me still resists and learns. I hope that 'From the Childhood of Jesus,' because of the couplets and the Christianity, and the way both are twisted by the poem, will serve as an appropriately complicated, and sincere, tribute to Winters in an anthology of Stanford writing."

♦ ♦ ♦

From the Childhood of Jesus

One Saturday morning he went to the river to play.
He modelled twelve sparrows out of the river clay

And scooped a clear pond, with a dam of twigs and mud.
Around the pond he set the birds he had made,

Evenly as the hours. Jesus was five. He smiled,
As a child would who had made a little world

Of clear still water and clay beside a river.
But a certain Jew came by, a friend of his father,

And he scolded the child and ran at once to Joseph,
Saying, "Come see how your child has profaned the Sabbath,

Making images at the river on the Day of Rest."
So Joseph came to the place and took his wrist

And told him, "Child, you have offended the Word."
Then Jesus freed the hand that Joseph held

And clapped his hands and shouted to the birds
To go away. They raised their beaks at his words,

And breathed and stirred their feathers and flew away.
The people were frightened. Meanwhile, another boy,

The son of Annas the scribe, had idly taken
A branch of driftwood and leaning against it had broken

The dam and muddied the little pond and scattered
The twigs and stones. Then Jesus was angry and shouted,

"Unrighteous, impious, ignorant, what did the water
Do to harm you? Now you are going to wither

The way a tree does, you shall bear no fruit
And no leaves, you shall wither down to the root."

At once, the boy was all withered. His parents moaned,
The Jews gasped, Jesus began to leave, then turned

And prophesied, his child's face wet with tears:
"Twelve times twelve times twelve thousands of years

Before these heavens and this earth were made,
The Creator set a jewel in the throne of God

With Hell on the left and Heaven to the right,
The Sanctuary in front, and behind, an endless night

Endlessly fleeing a Torah written in flame.
And on that jewel in the throne, God wrote my name."

Then Jesus left and went into Joseph's house.
The family of the withered one also left the place,

Carrying him home. The Sabbath was nearly over.
By dusk, the Jews were all gone from the river.

Small creatures came from the undergrowth to drink
And foraged in the shadows along the bank.

Alone in his cot in Joseph's house, the Son
Of Man was crying himself to sleep. The moon

Rose higher, the Jews put out their lights and slept,
And all was calm and as it had been, except

In the agitated household of the scribe Annas,
And high in the dark, where unknown even to Jesus

The twelve new sparrows flew aimlessly through the night,
Not blinking or resting, as if never to alight.

◆   ◆   ◆

The Hearts

The legendary muscle that wants and grieves,
The organ of attachment, the pump of thrills
And troubles, clinging in stubborn colonies

Like pulpy shore-life battened on a jetty.
Slashed by the little deaths of sleep and pleasure,
They swell in the nurturing spasms of the waves,

Sucking to cling; and even in death itself—
Baked, frozen—they shrink to grip the granite harder.
"Rid yourself of attachments and aversions"—

But in her father's orchard, already, he says
He'd like to be her bird, and she says: Sweet, yes,
Yet I should kill thee with much cherishing,

Showing that she knows already—as Art Pepper,
That first time he takes heroin, already knows
That he will go to prison, and knows he'll suffer

And says, he needs to have it or die; and the one
Who makes the General lose the world for love
Lets him say, *would I had never seen her,* but Oh!

Says Enobarbus, Then you would have missed
A wonderful piece of work, which left unseen
Would bring less glory to your travels. Among

The creatures in the rock-torn surf, a wave
Of agitation, a gasp. A scholar quips,
Shakespeare was almost certainly homosexual,

Bisexual, or heterosexual, the sonnets
Provide no evidence on the matter. He writes
Romeo an extravagant speech on tears,

In the Italian manner, his teardrops cover
His chamber window, says the boy, he calls them crystals,
Inanely, and sings them to Juliet with his heart:

The almost certainly invented heart
Which Buddha denounces, in its endless changes
Forever jumping and moving, like an ape.

Over the poor beast's head the crystal fountain
Crashes illusions, the cold salt spume of pain
And meaningless distinction, as Buddha says,

But here in the crystal shower mouths are open
To sing, it is Lee Andrews and The Hearts
In 1957, singing *I sit in my room*

Looking out at the rain, My teardrops are
Like crystals, they cover my windowpane, the turns
Of these illusions we make become their glory:

To Buddha every distinct thing is illusion
And becoming is destruction, but still we sing
In the shower. I do. In the beginning God drenched

The Emptiness with images: the potter
Crosslegged at his wheel in Benares market
Making mud cups, another cup each second

Tapering up between his fingers, one more
To sell the tea-seller at a penny a dozen,
And tea a penny a cup. The customers smash

The empties, and waves of traffic grind the shards
To mud for new cups, in turn; and I keep one here
Next to me: holding it a while from out of the cloud

Of dust that rises from the shattered pieces,
The risen dust alive with fire, then settled
And soaked and whirling again on the wheel that turns

And looks on the world as on another cloud,
On everything the heart can grasp and throw away
As a passing cloud, with even Enlightenment

Itself another image, another cloud
To break and churn a salt foam over the heart
Like an anemone that sucks at clouds and makes

Itself with clouds and sings in clouds and covers
Its windowpane with clouds that blur and melt,
Until one clings and holds—as once in the Temple

In the time before the Temple was destroyed
A young priest saw the seraphim of the Lord:
Each had six wings, with two they covered their faces,

With two they covered their legs and feet, with two
They darted and hovered like dragonflies or perched
Like griffins in the shadows near the ceiling—

These are the visions, too barbarous for heaven
And too preposterous for belief on earth,
God sends to taunt his prophet with the truth

No one can see, that leads to who knows where.
A seraph took a live coal from the altar
And seared the prophet's lips, and so he spoke.

As the record ends, a coda in retard:
The Hearts in a shifting velvety *ah,* and *ah*
Prolonged again, and again as Lee Andrews

Reaches *ah* high for *I have to gain Faith, Hope*
And Charity, God only knows the girl
Who will love me—Oh! if we only could

Start over again! Then The Hearts chant the chords
Again a final time, *ah* and the record turns
Through all the music, and on into silence again.

NAHID RACHLIN

I live in New York City with my husband and daughter. I spend much of my day writing and teaching fiction. I look back fondly on the year I held the Stegner Fellowship at Stanford, about ten years ago. Since then I have published two novels, Foreigner *(Norton) and* Married to a Stranger *(Dutton) and several short stories. I have held an N.E.A. grant for fiction and other fellowships and grants. At present I teach at New York University.*

"Last March I was meeting my aunt in Istanbul, halfway between Iran and the United States. We were caught there in a blizzard and confined to our hotel for several days. I met an Arab man, along with other people, stranded in the hotel. The Arab man kept talking about his three wives and how he loved each in a different way. These are the facts about a trip that inspired this story, the rest is fiction."

◆　　　◆　　　◆

Blizzard in Istanbul

RHODA SAT IN THE lobby of the Dilson Hotel's restaurant in Istanbul, sipping Turkish coffee and constantly glancing at the snow churning rapidly outside. The minarets and the blue dome of the mosque across the street had a blurred look. The airport had been closed for two days now, trapping her, and others. It was unprecedented in March for the snow to be so harsh. She was supposed to have been back at her job the day before—she was an English teacher in a private school in Roslyn, Long Island. She was enjoying the anticipation in the air though, the closeness the situation had created between a group of strangers in the hotel. She had come mainly to visit a Turkish friend at Ankara and she was in Istanbul to make the airplane connection back. The trip had gone well, it had been full of unexpected moments. She had liked visiting ancient and exotic mosques and mansions. Friendly people stopped to help whenever she was at a loss. Once pausing in a park to take a picture of her friend, a group of high school boys had gathered around them and asked if they could be included in the picture. After the photograph was taken one of the boys had written down his name so that Rhoda could send them a copy. Another time she and her friend were invited by a woman they met on a bus to have tea. They had gone to the woman's house, on a narrow, cobblestoned street and sat in a room covered by Turkish rugs and handwoven cushions and had tea. The woman had seemed delighted to talk to Rhoda, someone from so far away, and asked her many questions and told her of her own yearnings as a teenager to go to a university in the United States. Now she was married and had four children. She was content enough with her way of life, but, she said, a longing remained. She pointed to a photograph of herself, her husband, and two sons and two daughters set on the top of the mantel. She was a lively, slightly plump woman and wore a lot of gold jewelry. Her husband had a sturdy, robust look. He was smiling into the camera. That had made Rhoda think of her ex-husband, Paul, thin, tall, blond. . . . They had been married for only five years, it was twenty years since the divorce, but still he never quite left her. She was forty-eight years old now, would probably never marry again. She had no inclination to. . . .

She turned to the Greek woman, Irene, and her Greek boy friend, Costa, sitting on the sofa across from her in the hotel lobby. She had met them at breakfast.

"Can you read my fortune?" Rhoda asked, pointing to the thick sediments of coffee left at the bottom of the cup.

"I can tell your fortune better by cards," Irene said. As if she had been hoping for this opportunity she promptly took out a stack of cards from her purse and spread them on the table. "This upside-down bed indicates you're having trouble in love." She laughed. "As for me I wouldn't care. I have another man every week." She winked at Costa. "My husband is always on the ship."

Rhoda wondered at the nature of Irene and Costa's relationship, the open callousness of her remark. Costa did not know any English, but still. Irene provided the answer. "I miss my husband, I just use Costa to pass time." She went on to tell Rhoda that a jealous woman was about to give her trouble.

On the other side of the room groups of people were carrying on lively conversations in different languages. The clatter of dishes from the kitchen, footsteps of waiters coming and going hummed in the background. The scent of spices and potted plants set in various corners were pleasantly mixed.

Two men came and sat next to Rhoda. She had met both of them several times at the hotel. One was from Jordan and the other from Iran. They were both middle-aged and said they were there on business. The man from Jordan, Norooz, was short, had dyed his hair black and had a large, gold tooth in front. He was wearing a checkered gray and blue suit. He had a thick, gold wedding band and a large diamond ring on his fingers. His room was on the same floor as hers and every time he saw her in the hall he paused and asked her questions. Why was she there, why alone, where was her home, how old was she. His eyes probed. Yet when she asked him questions, he was evasive. The man from Iran, Parviz, was thin, tall, had straight, limp brown hair which he had parted neatly in the middle. He wore a tailored navy suit, a beige sweater, and well-polished black shoes. They all began to talk together.

"It's real spring in Teheran right now," Parviz said. In a surprisingly maudlin tone, he added, "I miss my wife and children."

Norooz was looking at Rhoda, intently into her eyes, at her mouth, neck, breasts. "You ought to come and live in Jordan. Men from our part of the world know how to treat women." He had a flirtatious glint in his eyes. "I treat my wives very well."

"How many do you have?"

"Three."

"You see each on a different night?"

"I live in three countries for my business, with one wife in each. I have glass factories in Oman, Saudi Arabia, and Jordan. My first wife was arranged for me by my family, the second was my partner, and the third, . . ," He laughed. "I fell in love with her. I saw her coming out of her house once and I began to pursue her."

"Is she your favorite?"

"Each one has a special place in my heart."

"Three wives are nothing compared to what the kings here had," Rhoda said jokingly. "One of them had as many as four hundred." The day before, in spite of the blizzard, Rhoda had taken a taxi to Topkapi which also contained a labyrinthine harem—with hundreds of small, intricately arranged rooms.

"The Sultan probably wanted to allow for some of his wives getting sick on some days. He had to have four hundred to make sure they go around for a year," Norooz said. He asked suddenly, "Why aren't you married?"

"I was once. It didn't last."

"You want to be free." He looked skeptical. "I like being with people." Leaning forward he said, "That's a nice pendant."

"I bought it yesterday, in the Old Bazaar. It's hand painted." As she had walked through tiny shops set on clusters of narrow, interweaving lanes, she had had the sensation of being in a happy dream.

The waiter came over to take orders for drinks. Outside the air had been darkened by the increasing snow.

"Have you heard the latest news about the weather?" Rhoda asked the waiter.

"Only God knows the answer to that."

He took everyone's order and walked away. A young man wearing a purple hat over his head came and stood near the sofa next to Parviz. "Are you from Iran?"

Parviz nodded.

"So am I." He took a card from his wallet and threw it in front of Parviz. "This is my business card." He paused and then said suddenly, "Can you spare some money? I'll pay you back when we're in Iran. I work for a television station as you see, but all my money was robbed from me in my hotel last night. Someone had come into my room while I was taking a shower. I'm penniless and my plane doesn't leave until Monday."

"You could go to the Iranian consulate and borrow money."

"I went there. They said the consul is stranded in Ankara until Monday because of the snow. Another man from Iran was robbed at the same time as I was, only in his case it was worse. He had his entire savings from years of work, $5,000, in his suitcase and the whole thing was lifted. He's hysterical, staying in his room and crying all the time."

"It's foolish to have kept all that money in cash," Parviz said.

"Yes, of course." In a pleading tone the young man added, "Won't you help me? I promise I'll pay you back. I'm not a beggar." He looked sheepish.

Parviz took out 3,000 lire and gave it to the man. "I can't help in a major way but this will buy your supper tonight."

The man took the money and picked up his business card promptly.

As soon as he left Parviz said, "He's all fake, a good actor. If he really was robbed he wouldn't be so calm about it. He would blush, he would stammer, he wouldn't throw a business card in front of me so cooly. I gave him the money out of weakness. Being away from my family does that to me."

A wistfulness for a strong attachment came over Rhoda. She had many friends and acquaintances but no one in particular. Of course that was what gave her the sense of freedom. She worked hard at school, organized her evenings and weekends the way she liked and took trips abroad on every vacation.

The waiter came over with the drinks. In the streetlights, which had suddenly gone on, Rhoda could see that the snow was still falling relentlessly. The waiter turned to her and said, "See that tree?" He pointed to a large, potted ficus plant. "Every leaf on that plant was put there by God. Every one of the leaves that fall down is in His will. It's in His will to end the snow." He walked away.

Rhoda thought of the taxi driver, taking her to Topkapi, "If it's in God's will we'll get there." They had been passing through a lane so narrow that it was more appropriate for donkeys than cars. Taxis, cars, were slipping down, getting caught in the snow or puddles.

"We all get along so well here," Norooz said. "We're from different countries, different religions, still we sit here together peacefully." He kept looking at Rhoda in an obsessive and furtive way as if there was more to what he was saying than the words conveyed.

A muezzin was calling people to prayers from the mosque across the street. His voice mingled with the sad, romantic Turkish music being played on the radio in the restaurant.

In a few moments Rhoda got up to leave. She was tired and wanted to get to bed early. "See you at breakfast," she said to everyone.

"You're leaving us?" Norooz said.

"I've had an exhausting day."

Norooz looked disappointed as she walked away.

Going up the dark stairway she heard footsteps behind her.

"Can I come with you to your room?"

It was Norooz. His breath smelled of alcohol.

"I have to get some sleep."

"Are you sure I can't come. . . ." He brushed his hand over her hair. "It's so soft and silky," he said. There was a glint of lust in his eyes, so strong as if he had seen her naked.

The space between them was taut. "I'm sorry." She walked up more rapidly, without looking at him.

"I had a clear feeling you liked me." There was something persistent in his tone that made her apprehensive.

"I . . . I don't mind you, I enjoyed talking to you. . . ." Maybe I encouraged him a little too much, she thought guiltily. "I'll see you in the dining room in the morning," she said, walking on.

In her room she shut the door quickly and locked it. The incident had left her upset and restless. She stood in front of the mirror and stared at her reflection. She had streaks of gray scattered through her blond hair and there were fine wrinkles under her eyes. She gave a severe impression, she knew, something that she fought against but it was as much a part of her as her blue eyes and blond hair were. That inner struggle created contradictory signals for others, making her unapproachable to certain people, like the students for instance. She took off the barrette which held her hair back and let it tumble down over her shoulders. That gave her a softer look. Then she put on the rose-colored nightgown she had bought in Ankara and that too added to the softness. This is definitely a better image for me, she thought. If only I could sustain it. Finally she went to bed but she had a hard time sleeping. Through the window overlooking Taksim Square she could see, under the streetlights, the snow falling as rapidly as before. It was as if it was never going to stop. After a while she drifted into dreams. In one dream she and Paul were taking a walk on a wide, tree-lined street. Light flurries of snow were falling through sunlight. There was a mellow mood between them. They were holding hands and talking in soft tones. "You're leaving me for two whole weeks," he was saying.

Then she woke and began to think of Paul. They had met in classes at the University of Michigan in Ann Arbor and then she had followed him to the New York area for him to pursue a career in acting. Before long he had fallen in love with an actress and when she found out about their affair she left him. It was frightening how he had changed during those months before they split. Something gray and cold lay between them. There was absolutely no light in his eyes. No hate, no anger, no love were reflected in them. Just blankness. After the divorce she had many affairs but none of them lasted for very long. Almost all the men were foreigners whom she met on her travels, one from Greece, one from Spain. . . . She met the Spanish man on the hydrofoil going from Algeciras to Tangiers. He was a singer and he had an engagement to perform in a nightclub in Tangiers. He had a great reed-like voice when he spoke and he sang well. Though she enjoyed the brief, intense affairs, she had no urgency to continue with the men for too long. But she liked corresponding with them and had stacks of letters from them that she reread occasionally, enjoying the evocation of their time together. Thinking of the men would fill her with an aching elation. Her friends would say, "How could you stand all these partings?" And sometimes a panicky voice came on inside her, "I'm really all alone in the world." Then she would spend hours thinking of what in her character or background had led to her living like this. Did anyone really choose a way of life, she wondered now. There was something comforting about the Moslems' attitude of attributing everything to fate.

She heard loud knocks on the door. The knocks grew louder. She got out of the bed, put on her robe and went to the door. "Who is it?"

There was no answer. She was about to turn around. Then there were more knocks.

"Who is it?"

"It's me."

Was it Norooz? She unlocked the door, opened it as far as the chain would go and looked out. She saw Norooz standing there in a bathrobe. The front of the robe was open and his chest and belly were exposed. Then, slowly, he began to pull open the rest of the robe, grinning, as if nothing was out of the ordinary. She shrank back, startled.

She thought she should make a joke of it or at least show a sense of humor about it but instead she felt awkward and she giggled nervously. Then abruptly she shut the door. Her hands were shaking, she realized.

"All I want is to show you a good time," he said, knocking again. "We'll get along, I know. I could take you away with me and we'd get married by the Moslem law. . . ."

Guiltily she opened the door again and said, "I don't mean to be rude but this isn't, I'm not up to it. . . ."

She shut the door more gently, put the chain in its notch, and returned to bed. She pulled the phone close to her hand. I'll have to call the desk if he doesn't go away, she thought.

The knocks stopped. She heard footsteps receding. Then she could hear a far-off sound of Turkish music, a song accompanied by cymbals and drums, on a radio. It seemed to come from the direction of Norooz's room.

She lay awake for a long time. She was full of contradictory feelings toward Norooz, both repelled by and strangely drawn to him. In a way she liked his crude openness—it seemed to go along with a certain strength. She imagined being a fourth wife to a man like him in an Arabic country. It would be a sensual, protected existence. It would have been interesting if she could lead a life like that briefly. Her life on Long Island was active, busy, but without indulgences. There was something sparse and constricting about it. It was a long time since she had felt desire or love.

A strong urge came over her to go to Norooz's room. I have nothing to lose. It is probably my last night here. She got out of the bed, put on her slippers she had laid at the bottom of the bed and went out into the corridor. She knocked on the door of his room. The Turkish music had been coming from his room— she could hear the nasal voice of a woman singing.

In a moment he opened the door. He smiled at her, naturally, showing no surprise. "I knew you'd come." He was wearing striped blue and white pajamas. He moved to the side to let her in.

He did not try to carry on a conversation with her, neither did he offer her a drink. He took her hand—for a moment she thought he wanted to dance with her—but he led her onto the bed. She followed as if she were in a dream, the way she had felt in the bazaar. He pulled her robe over her head and then took off his own pajamas. Their bodies intertwined. There was a scent of cologne about his skin that she found arousing and she liked the feeling of his bushy hair against her face.

"I like being with you," he said, caressing her gently. He whispered something that sounded like "I want you to become my wife," and then said, more audibly, "I knew we would get along well."

She felt totally at ease with him as if she could do nothing wrong in his eyes and so she found herself very sure in her movements. On and off she was aware of the woman singing. She had a quick, strong orgasm. She moaned.

He became quiet and still, his breathing deep and regular. She realized he had fallen asleep. Carefully, she disentangled herself from him and got out of the bed. She put on her gown and slippers and went back to her own room. She stood by the window and looked out. The snow had stopped falling. The mosaics of the mosque, the snow-covered branches of the trees, everything she could see was bright and sharply delineated under the moonlight. Illuminated signs around the square, advertising a bank, a tv store, a nightclub, blinked in blue, red, and violet colors. Though it was two in the morning there were people walking on the street. A group of children were playing on the sidewalk, making balls with the snow and throwing them against the lampposts. She had a vivid memory of herself as a child, standing by the window of their house in Grand Rapids, Michigan, and looking at the snow falling outside. She had had an urge to run out and play in the snow but something elusive, yet strong held her back. Then, as if no time had passed, she heard her mother's voice, anxious and distinct, "Watch out, you're going to get hurt."

BELLE RANDALL

Belle Randall was born in 1940, in Ellensburg, Washington, and lives in Seattle. She studied at the University of California (Berkeley) and at Stanford, where she held a Stegner Fellowship. She teaches at Cornish Institute in Seattle and does a prosody workshop at Centrum Writers' Conference. Her works include 101 Different Ways of Playing Solitaire *(University of Pittsburgh Press) and* The Orpheus Sedan *(Copper Canyon Press). Three of her poems are included in the anthology* Contemporary Religious Poetry *(Paulist Press, 1987).*

"'Learning to Write' is what I came to Stanford to do. I was lucky to have Donald Davie as a teacher. Even luckier, the year I came was his first year of teaching poetry writing. Although he had been a professor for years, this was a subject which he was wisely reluctant to 'profess.' As for the poem, the facts of my grade school penmanship instruction are authentic, even to my fifth-grade teacher's name. I was surprised to discover that my own childhood in retrospect looks old-fashioned."

◆   ◆   ◆

Learning to Write

Miss Reedy turns and dims the lights upon
the globe, our little theatre, the rows
of empty desks black ornamental iron
connects, a filigree as intricate
as the exemplary penmanship
I copied on the slanted lid.

At school by rote, at home by heart,
I learned to write, and cut by hand
old flannel nighties into heart-
shaped wipers for a pen whose nibs
splayed beneath the pressure of my hand,
a tool so black, austere and dangerous,
nowadays they'd never issue it to kids.
My middle-finger knuckle swelled
is swollen still, as if the bone itself
enlarged. Over and over I practiced helix
coils and slinky spirals; I tried my name
in backhand styles. My hand improved. My glass

inkwell runneth over. Around the rim
the ink dried to a kind of blood-
brown iridescence like the color of
the bug some clown impaled behind my back.
Into black waters thick with sludge
where a zillion paper planes had dipped
their fuselages, I dipped again,
who did calligraphic flights
of loop the loops in dreams.
                        Thus I learned
Longfellow, longhand. Beneath my arm,
the pages blank, unwrit upon as now
was then. Ephemera, that copybook,
that pen, yet every page, I stumbled on
graffiti bolder boys passed on
to higher forms had gouged no doubt
they thought for good, another era's
hieroglyphics: swastikas,
pin-cushion hearts; scratches and scars, more deep,
more permanent it seemed than ours; engraved
initials in the waves of dark grained wood.

◆   ◆   ◆

Ravelling the Unravellable

Poetry is a picturebook
being read to us
by our mother Death,

A Gordian knot, the untying of which
proves umbilical, a riddle
whose answer is your name.

Look, the little red church
has a cupola
as well as a steeple.

If you don't understand
what walks on three legs now,
maybe you will come to it later on.

We fall asleep. One by one,
the child assigned the part
wakens us with the touch

Of a yellow yardstick wand.

◆   ◆   ◆

Harpo

My brother has a way with words.
"Duck!" he says, "Say the magic word
and a duck comes down
and hits you on the head."

His wiggling brows italicize
the double entendre
that makes you groan
in recognition.

Me, I'm dumb, the speechless one,
the epileptic halfwit
hobo with a harp.

O my heart
your art
is pantomime.

JUDITH RASCOE

Judith Rascoe was born in San Francisco and educated at Stanford and Harvard. In 1973, the Atlantic Monthly Press published her novella and stories under the title Yours, And Mine. *Since that time she has concentrated on writing screenplays:* Portrait of the Artist as a Young Man, Who'll Stop The Rain, Endless Love, *and* Eat a Bowl of Tea, *among others.*

"'A Lot of Cowboys' was written in workshop in 1969 and shortly afterward published in *The Atlantic*. Within a week of publication, Judith Rascoe received three offers to write screenplays. Joseph Strick made her an offer she couldn't refuse, and subsequently she wrote for him the script of *Portrait of the Artist as a Young Man*. She has written screenplays ever since."

♦   ♦   ♦

A Lot of Cowboys

WHEN IT BEGAN TO snow all the cowboys came into town and rented motel rooms with free TV. One of the cowboys said his favorite program was "Bonanza." "It's pretty authentic."

"Aw, shit, what do you know about authentic?"

"Well, I know. I'm a cowboy, ain't I?"

"Well, so am I, and I think 'Bonanza' is a bunch of bull-pucky. Now if you want authentic stuff you ought to watch 'Gunsmoke.'"

"Well, you old cuss, I will show you what's authentic." So the cowboy hit the other cowboy with his fist.

"No fighting in here, so you cut that out," said the motel manager.

"You're right," the cowboys said. They got some ice and some White Horse and some Coca-Cola. The motel manager said to his wife, "By God, you can't tell them dumb cowhands nothing. They mix good scotch with Coca-Cola."

"I knew I never wanted to marry a cowboy," his wife said. "I knew *all* about them. They weren't the fellows for me." She was keeping her eye on a young couple who weren't married; the girl seemed to have made a wedding ring out of a gold cellophane strip from a cigarette package. Looked mean; good thing the poor fellow hadn't married her yet. That night in the bar the motel manager's wife told him he shouldn't marry her.

"Huh?" he inquired.

A number of cowboys went to see the Ford dealer. He turned on the lights in his office and brought out two fifths of bourbon. The cars stood around the showroom like cows around a campfire, reflecting little gleams from the office and little gleams from the street. You could almost hear them sighing.

"Goddamn, that Maverick is a pretty little car," a cowboy said.

"Yeah, yeah," another cowboy said. "But I tell you, I got my eye on a pickup so pretty you'd like to cry. Dark-green gold-flecked. Air conditioning. And I'd hang toolboxes on the side. And maybe—"

He had their attention.

"—and maybe I do and maybe I don't know a Mexican fellow who wants to make me hand-tooled leather seat covers."

"Aaaaooooow-*ha*. WooooooooowwEEEEE."

Also little tsk-tsk-tsk noises. Head shakes. Lip bites. Breaths indrawn.

"Pwuh," said the Ford dealer. He was a classicist. He couldn't stand to think of a hand-tooled Mexican leather seat cover. Of course he was a town fellow.

"When I was in the Army," one of the cowboys said illustratively, "I got me a tailor over in Munich, and I went in and I said—well, I drew him what I wanted, and he made me a suit, *bitte schön!* Mama, oh that were a suit! It had six slantpockets in the jacket. Course, uh, course, I don't wear it too often, you understand."

Oh, yes, they understood!

There were those cowboys laughing like they were fit to be tied.

An old woman living above the Western Auto store stuck her head out the window and listened to the cowboys come and go. The snow was falling slowly, and down the street Stan Melchek was sitting in his car waiting for a speeder. A pair of lights appeared in the distance but it was a big tractor-trailer rig, after all, pulling slowly through town, and its taillights went past the All Nite Truck Café, and the old woman pulled her head back inside and closed the window.

One cowboy lay on one twin bed and another cowboy lay on the other. One cowboy said, "I like Tammy Wynette. I sure get a kick out of her. My favorite record is 'Stand By Your Man.' My little sister sings it just like her. You close your eyes and you don't know it ain't Tammy Wynette singing. She wants me to get a guitar and learn to play and accompany her."

"I wrote a song once," the other cowboy said. "I showed it to this fellow works in Denver, and he said maybe I could publish it and maybe I couldn't."

"Oh, there's money there," the first cowboy said.

"Oh, you better believe it."

"What's on now?"

"'Hawaii Five-O.'"

"Shee-it."

"Well?"

"We sure as hell ain't going to no drive-in tonight."

We had all these cowboys in town because of the snow, and they were mostly drinking whiskey and watching television and talking about cars. It was Saturday night, but you sure couldn't tell it from any other night because of the snow. The Basque Hall advertised a dance, but the group they were going to have didn't have chains or something and anyway called from Salt Lake and said nothing doing, so there wasn't even a dance. Some of the older fellows went to the motel bar and danced, but it was mostly Guy Lombardo, which the bartender's wife favored. Maud, the motel manager's wife, had different ideas; she sat down next to a cowboy she knew and said, "We need to light a fire under some of these old cayuses. Play some of the music the kids like."

"I don't like it," the cowboy said.

"Well, hell, no, *you* don't like it, an old fart like you. Hell, you can't dance that way with one foot in the grave."

"Now, cut it out."

"I'll wash out my mouth, Carl."

"I don't like to hear you talk like that, Maud." His eyes filled with tears. "Honest to Christ, Maud, you was the most beautiful girl I ever saw. You wore your hair the sweetest little way with two little curls in front of your ears, and you wore a green silk dress. You were the sweetest little thing."

"Now, don't start crying here."

"Well, God help me, I can't help it."

"You'll just make me cry too." She had handkerchiefs for both of them. She got another round of drinks. That mean little thing with the cellophane wedding ring was looking, and Maud bet *she'd* never known a real man like Carl. These cowboys were always getting drunk and bawling, and it made her bawl too, to tell the truth.

So, you see, everybody was either in a motel room or in the motel bar, and it was snowing pretty heavily, and then George Byron Cutler drove into town. He was something of a celebrity because his picture was up in post offices, and he was known as G. Byron Cutler and Byron George Cutler and G. B. Cutler, to give only a few of his aliases. He was wanted mostly for mail fraud, but he had also held up a post office and was armed, and considered himself dangerous. He usually wore khaki shirts and trousers, but he wore good boots. Most criminals have a peculiarity like that. Anyhow, George Byron Cutler went to the motel and asked for a room, and then stuck his head in the bar and yelled, "Where's the action?"

"Well, now, I thought you was bringing it," somebody yelled back.

"Well, I was, but she didn't have a friend."

"Well, bring her in."

It kind of fell flat. He winked at Maud.

"Is my old man at the desk?" she yelled.

"Yeah, your old man is at the desk," said a voice behind George Byron Cutler. And so Cutler went on to his room, and about an hour later two sheriff's men came by and said they were looking for him.

"Christ almighty! I got to tell Maud," her husband said. "Don't you do nothing 'til I tell Maud. She won't forgive me if we got a bandido in the motel and she's not here."

"You done us a favor," the sheriff's men said, agreeable. They accepted a Coke apiece. They left snow on the Astroturf. "That's Astroturf," Maud's husband said.

"God almighty," the sheriff's men said.

So Maud's husband went in to get Maud, and she said real loud, "You mean we got a criminal in this here motel? Oh, I don't know why this hasn't happened before. We are the only motel for fifty miles. The only motel you'd stop at, that's to say. Of course there's always Mrs. Oldon's place. You boys don't stop there, you hear?" A lot of coarse laughter greeted this remark, because the cowboys knew that Mrs. Oldon had a prostitute come through in the summer. Every summer she had a different prostitute, and these girls were known as Winnemucca Discards. It was a common joke that only sheepherders went to Mrs. Oldon. "I am feeling like a sheepherder tonight," a cowboy would say, and the reply to that was, "I'd get a sheep instead."

"What sort of a criminal is this fellow?" Maud asked.

"He's a mail fraud," her husband said.

"Sounds like a pansy to me," a cowboy said.

"I want to see the police capture him anyways," Maud said. She rose to her feet, showing a lot of bosom to the assembled, and led the way to the motel lobby, and all the cowboys and even the mean girl with the cellophane wedding ring and her "husband" followed. The sheriff's men were feeling the Astroturf.

"Snowing like all hell," one of the sheriff's men said.

"Is this fellow dangerous?" Maud said.

"Well he is armed and considered dangerous," one of the patrolmen said.

"He's in 211," her husband said.

"Then everybody can see," Maud said. They all looked outside and saw the two layers of rooms, and 211 was pretty well located, being close to the big light and close to the middle of the balcony. The sheriff's men told everybody their names and shook some hands and then went out while everybody watched from the lobby. They went up to 211, and you could see them knock at the door. They didn't even have their guns out.

"He can't be very dangerous if they don't even take out their guns," Maud said.

"It's a Supreme Court rule now," somebody said.

"I don't know how they catch anybody."

Then there was an awful sound like a board breaking and nobody knew what it was at first and then one of the sheriff's men started yelling and all the cowboys and everybody else started yelling, "He's been shot! Jesus Christ, he shot him! Oh, get out of the way." The other sheriff's man started running, and then 211 opened the door and George Byron Cutler stood there with a gun in his hand.

He was shouting something but nobody heard it. Finally a cowboy lying on the Astroturf slid open the double glass door and yelled back, "What did you say?"

"I said I just want to get out of here," yelled George Byron Cutler. "I have killed a man, and I have nothing to lose now."

"Did you hear what he said?" Maud asked somebody. "I would never have featured it."

"Where is that other sheriff's man? Did he shoot him too?"

It turned out the other sheriff's man was back in his car calling for help. And all the cowboys in the motel rooms were calling to find out what was going wrong. Maud got on the switchboard and told everybody, "Don't peek out. God almighty, don't peek out. Just keep your door locked and lie low. He has a gun, and he has killed a police officer."

George Byron Cutler walked toward the lobby with his gun shaking. All the cowboys and women were on top of each other on the floor or crawling away, and a lot of people were crying. Maud said to the switchboard, "Dear Lord, he is coming in here. I got to hang up now. Do not come here. You cannot help us."

Then George Byron Cutler tried to open the lobby door, but it was cold and stuck. He began making faces and pounding at it. "Wait wait wait wait." A cowboy got up real slow and opened the door for him.

"Just stay as you are," Cutler said to everybody. "Give me your money."

"I'll give it to you," Maud said. "But I haven't got much cash."

He thought a long time. Then he told everybody to throw down their credit cards. He took the whole pile of credit cards and put them in his shirt and said, "This will take some time to work out, boys."

Later Maud said she'd thought at first he was scared but he surely showed he was a cool customer.

Then he went out again and they heard a car start and make lots of noise and roar away, and then they heard some more shots, and finally somebody went out and found the cowboys from the Ford dealer's place all standing around the street where George Byron Cutler was lying dead, shot by Stan Melchek.

"I thought at first he was a speeder, but when I stopped him he fired his gun at me."

"I guess you didn't tell him his rights," one of the cowboys said.

"Oh, shut your mouth," another cowboy said. "This fellow has been killed."

Nobody could sleep after that. Maud opened the coffee shop and heated up some bear claws. She sat down with Carl and a couple of the younger fellows.

"Stan Melchek is a cowboy," she said. "He is a cowboy by nature. Those fellows shoot first and ask questions later. That's the code of the West. These big-city criminals don't realize they're out in the Wild West. Out on the frontier here."

"They don't realize," Carl said.

In a very sad voice Maud said, "Well, I guess he learned."

"You don't fool around with a cowboy. You don't fool around in this country," Carl said.

"The cowboy is a vanishing race," one of the cowboys said.

"But he's not finished yet," Maud said.

"Not by a long shot," said one of the cowboys.

WILLIAM PITT ROOT

William Pitt Root currently teaches in the Creative Writing Program at Hunter College in New York. He was a Stegner Fellow at Stanford in 1968–69, a Rockefeller Fellow in 1969–70, a Guggenheim Fellow in 1970–71. His work has also received N.E.A. and US/UK Fellowships. Faultdancing *(University of Pittsburgh, 1986) is his most recent collection.*

"'7 For A Magician' was written as I was about to set out on a reading tour and suddenly felt my poems were too linear. 'Under The Umbrella Of Blood' was my way of celebrating what my fortieth birthday meant to me, a bit grim but to the point. Both, when they came, came quick. Were, that is, live births."

7 For A Magician

For Ray Rice

1.
Out of his black hat
he draws
rabbit after rabbit

and out
of the clear air
breath after breath.

2.
It takes him years
to learn
perfectly the poise
with which to reach
into his own sleeve,
withdrawing
the blaze of silk
it takes a generation
of mulberry leaves
and worms to spin
and the fingers

of strangers
to weave.

For the magician
about to astound
his audience.

For the lady
about to betray
her lover.

For the matador
into whose unborn wounds
first the horns
and scarlet scarf
then the faithful worm
must pass.

Applause.

He bows.

Applause.

She cries out
to the dark.

Applause.

His eyes widen
as the horn sinks in
and in.

3.
Who brushes
the magician's favorite hat?

The rabbit and the dove.

While he tends
to the hutch and scattered nest.

4.
His best makeup
is in our minds,
the hunger
of old locks,

rusted and lost,
to be opened.

Even skepticism
is a prayer
to him,
for whom fire obeys
the moon,
for whom water burns.

Imagine
the key of ice
designed to enter stone,
the lock made of mercury
which is its own pure key.

And look
into the clarified eyes
of just this one
who performs dreams,
who never sleeps.

5.
He brushes his teeth,
blows his nose,
eats with his mouth,
has but one suit of clothes.

He is very much like us,
it would seem,
to us.

6.
After each performance
he disappears.

Outside the stars brighten,
inside
the lights go on.

On the other side of the earth
it is morning
where he shares breakfast
with the chimpanzee,
who asks if it all went well.

They laugh as they eat.

7.
The last achievement
of an ultimate magician
is the proper
care and treatment
of all beings
filling the vast emptiness
of that hat
with which he lives.

♦   ♦   ♦

Under The Umbrella Of Blood

In the shower not ten minutes ago and blind from the vinegar rinse
I was thinking 40, I'm 40
when the stinging reminded me how Turks used to bet on
just how far a headless man could run—
                                    It was orderly, in its way,
with a band of selected prisoners, troops in attendance, distance markers,
a hammered copper plate glowing like the sun at the end of a pole;
as the prisoners one at a time ran past the sword took off their heads
and the plate scorched the neck-stumps shut to keep blood pressure up
so the runners ran farther, each stumbling on under the umbrella of blood
until the disfigured collapse, all legs and loose elbows.

Do you suppose as each head fell staring and revolving
that it could hear the tossed coins clink on the outspread blanket?
Could it see the body running off without it?
As it lay speechless, facing dirt or the sky, as chance would have it,
would it know whether it won or lost for its learned critics?

I wonder, and I rush off to the typewriter wiping my eyes clear,
knowing if I am to get it right
the images under the final downpour must be running
faster than the applauding coins of the world can ever fall.

VIKRAM SETH

Vikram Seth was born in India. While a student in the Economics Department at Stanford he wrote a novel in verse, The Golden Gate. *He has also written a book of poems,* The Humble Administrator's Garden, *and a travel book about a hitchhiking journey across Tibet,* From Heaven Lake. *He was a Stegner Fellow in creative writing at Stanford and later a senior editor at Stanford University Press.*

"These poems (from the book *The Humble Administrator's Garden*) were written while I was an economics graduate student at Stanford. My subject of study (which took me to China for two years) was the relationship between economic and demographic patterns in Chinese villages; this research is referred to in a couple of these poems."

The Humble Administrator's Garden

A plump gold carp nudges a lily pad
And shakes the raindrops off like mercury,
And Mr. Wang walks round. "Not bad, not bad."
He eyes the Fragrant Chamber dreamily.
He eyes the Rainbow Bridge. He may have got
The means by somewhat dubious means, but now
This is the loveliest of all gardens. What
Do scruples know of beauty anyhow?
The Humble Administrator admires a bee
Poised on a lotus, walks through the bamboo wood,
Strips half a dozen loquats off a tree
And looks about and sees that it is good.
   He leans against a willow with a dish
   And throws a dumpling to a passing fish.

The Accountant's House

We go in the evening to the accountant's house.
It is dark and the road is slush.
The fireflies fleck silver.
The ash flicked off by my companion, the barefoot doctor, is gold.

I want to clear up some questions on the income and expenditure account.
His wife and two daughters smile as I come in.
They pour tea. Their son died last Spring Festival.
We smile and discuss electricity fees.

This is my last day here. The Ministry of Education
Has decreed a two-and-a-half-week limit.
I will turn into a pumpkin soon enough
But today there is work, are pleasantries.

The green seedlings outside have been transplanted.
The accountant looks sad and my heart goes out.
No-one knows how he died. He came home from play
And his head was hot, his nose bled, and he died.

Yet they laugh, yet they laugh, these lovely people,
And he clicks his abacus and she gives me a towel and the two girls
Smile shyly, boldly at the stranger and the father
Discussing matters of much importance together.

♦   ♦   ♦

From California

Sunday night in the house.
The blinds drawn, the phone dead.
The sound of the kettle, the rain.
Supper: cheese, celery, bread.

For company, old letters
In the same disjointed script.
Old love wells up again,
All that I thought had slipped

Through the sieve of long absence
Is here with me again:
The long stone walls, the green
Hillsides renewed with rain.

The way you would lick your finger
And touch your forehead, the way
You hummed a phrase from the flute
Sonatas, or turned to say,

"Larches—the only conifers
That blend honestly with Wales."
I walk with you again
Along those settled trails.

It seems I started this poem
So many years ago
I cannot follow its ending
And must begin anew.

Blame, some bitterness,
I recall there were these.
Yet what survives is Bach
And a few blackberries.

Something of the "falling sunlight,"
In the phrase of Wang Wei,
Falls on my shadowed self.
I thank you that today

His words are open to me.
How much you have inspired
You cannot know. The end
Left much to be desired.

"There is a comfort in
The strength of love." I quote
Another favourite
You vouchsafed me. Please note

The lack of hope or faith:
Neither is justified.
I have closed out the night.
The random rain outside

Rejuvenates the parched
Foothills along the Bay.
Anaesthetised by years
I think of you today

Not with impassionedness
So much as half a smile
To see the weathered past
Still worth my present while.

ALAN SHAPIRO

Alan Shapiro, associate professor of English at Northwestern University, was a Stegner Fellow at Stanford in 1975. He has published three volumes of poetry: After The Digging, The Courtesy, *and* Happy Hour. *In addition to being nominated for a National Book Critics Circle Award,* Happy Hour *was selected by the Poetry Society of America as the 1987 winner of the William Carlos Williams Award.*

"During the summer of 1978, I worked as a guard in the microfilm room of the old Stanford library. When no one was around, which was most of the time, I'd spend the better part of each workday reading through microfilm of nineteenth-century editions of *The London Times,* particularly the column called 'The Irish Question,' begun around 1845 in response to the Irish potato famine. The English accounts of what was happening in Ireland provided not only the inspiration for the following poems, but also the idiom and tone in which they're cast."

Randolf Routh to Charles Trevelyan

—September 6, 1846

Dear Sir, the harvest, such as it will be,
will be here soon. Yet we know it is Summer
only by the calendar. The rain
falls in unebbing tides, making each day
a darkness that the light illuminates.
Sir, the reports which come in every day
are not, as you suggest, exaggerations:
from Giant's Causeway to Cape Clear, from Dublin
to Galway Bay, the cold fires of disaster
burn through the green fields and each black plant blooms
luxuriant as an abundant harvest.

The people do starve
                              peaceably, as yet.
But how much longer, how much longer?
                                                    Armed
with spades, a horde of paupers entered Cork—

"So thin," the officer in charge has written,
"I could not tell which ones were men, and which
were spades, except the spades looked sturdier."
They demanded food, and work. And when dispersed,
"Would that the government would send us food
instead of troops," one of them muttered, while
the rest like phantoms in an eerie silence
went off.

        Last week, outside of Erris where
the poor like crows swarm, combing the black fields,
living on nettles, weeds, and cabbage leaves,
women and children plundered a meal cart,
fifteen of them tearing at the sacks;
enlivened rags, numb to the drivers' whips,
too weak to drag the sacks off, or to scream,
they hobbled away, clutching to themselves
only small handfuls of the precious stuff.

Please do not think me impudent. Like you
I feel no great affection for the Irish.
But it is not enough that "we should tell them
they suffer from the providence of God";
or that "in terms of economic law
it's beneficial that the price of grain
should rise in proportion to the drop in wage."
We can no longer answer cries of want
with quoting economics, or with prayer.
Ireland is not, and never can be, Whitehall.
And while they starve, no Englishman is safe.

Sir, you have said yourself, "The evil here
with which we must contend is not the famine,
but their turbulent and selfish character,"
which I half think Nature herself condemns:
today, as if from the Old Testament—
with thunder beating on the iron clouds
which do not bend—the electricity
strikes with the bright and jagged edge of judgment,
while over each blighted field a dense fog falls
cold and damp and close, without any wind.

◆   ◆   ◆

Captain Wynne to Randolf Routh

—December 24, 1846

Dear Randolf, since the shooting incident
my staff is greatly agitated, and

I fear won't hold together for much longer.
They all seem waiting for the right excuse
to go—Tom Webb has gone and his successor,
Mr. MacBride (whom those who still can curse
call Mr. Hennessey), has left already.
Mr. Pratt's resigned, and Mr. Gamble
(the engineer in charge) thinks Millet's life
is threatened, and is going to remove him.

We must resume the works. Though this suspension
be the only armor we possess
against the bullet of assassins, still
something must be done. I have myself
inspected the small hamlets in the parish
and would describe to you what I have witnessed,
but anything you picture to yourself
which still enables you to kiss your wife,
embrace your son, and sleep until you wake,
is not what I have seen, nor what I felt.
But I must tell you something nonetheless.

Since even nettles now have all been eaten,
or buried in the snow—the snow which now
alone must feed the peasants, and keep them warm—
each hamlet is entirely deserted.
I counted fifteen corpses on the road,
like crops the living were too weak to plant:
the only earth upon them was the snow,
a few sticks, and small stones.

                    And no sounds came
from any of the hovels that I passed.
And it occurs to me, in retrospect,
that those poor wretches must have heard me coming
and knowing that (as I must now confess)
I looked upon starvation as disease,
kept quiet as a trap to draw me in,
hoping to sicken me. And I was sickened:

In one small hut I saw six human beings
crouched in a corner in some filthy straw:
four had once been children, but now wore
the anxious look of premature old age;
the other two, their parents I presume,
for though as thin as children, they were taller.
As I approached I realized the father
was the only one alive, for he was moaning
low and demonically, and his legs twitched—

though not enough to move, or move the others
who leant upon him still as if in death
they still cried for the help he could not give.

I hurried off, and faces stared at me
from every window that I passed, faces
whose eyes hunger had magnified, whose lips—
the last soft flesh upon them—were as blue
as the new snow and were speaking God knows what,
soundless as in a dream . . . what were they speaking?
Tell me, Randolf, what words they uttered, words
which every night are riddling my dreams,
which I wake up to; tell me what they mean.

And tell me when the works will be resumed.
Consider, Randolf, what I have recited;
I am a match for almost anything
I meet with here, but this I cannot stand.
Consider it, for something must be done.
And trust I speak sincerely when I say
I hope the winter finds you well, and please
pass on warmest regards to Randolf Junior,
and kiss your dear wife once for me.

                                        Yours, Wynne.

THOMAS SIMMONS

Born in 1956, in West Chester, Pennsylvania, Thomas Simmons moved to Los Altos, California, in 1969. After graduating from Stanford in 1978, he went on to hold a Stegner Fellowship there. He received his Ph.D. in English from U.C. Berkeley in 1988, and is now an assistant professor in the Writing Program at M.I.T.

"'First Sunday of Advent, 1967' came into the world in late 1982 as a three-stanza imagist poem. A failure at birth, it went to a desk drawer while I tried to recover my wits. Four months later, on a hunch, I spun it into its current form. 'Second Person,' written in mid-1987, sounds like a way of saying good-bye to poetry. I can't yet say if this is true. It is true that, as I grow older, I have less confidence in the ability of poems—as opposed to silence—to convey something essential about being human."

◆　　　◆　　　◆

Second Person

Sometimes it becomes necessary
to say good-bye to yourself—
to give up the lifelong study
of centripetal force, to abandon
the center . . .

    Someone is leaving for work.
It is morning, summer.
The sun spreads in the branches
like conscription, many suns.
You are a deserter. The poems
you leave behind are dark leaves.

◆　　　◆　　　◆

First Sunday of Advent, 1967

Today it's nearly dusk
when the snow gathers, finally,
on the lawn, the tired side

of the wind turned white
and settling down.
I watch the steady storm

from my mother's rocking chair
upstairs, all roomlights off.
The house below is quiet.

My father, too, may be staring
out the window, straining to see
the fender of the Chevrolet

he banged up on a tree this afternoon;
he will not speak for hours, or days.
My mother, having trouble reading

in the intricate silence,
lays down her book and glides into the kitchen:
she adds potatoes to the sizzling roast.

Up here it hardly matters what they do.
Through the lulling constancy of snow,
I hear the muffled grunts and spatters

of their need, and still I sit,
a dream apart from love. For who am I
to cry, entranced with the night,

and lost to them as if,
unseeing, I looked down
from the darkness of heaven?

BRETT SINGER

Born in Jersey City, N.J., in 1952, Brett Singer studied philosophy and English literature at Vassar College and held a Mirrielees Fellowship at Stanford in 1975–76. She served as a Jones Lecturer at Stanford from 1976 to 1979 and has also taught writing at Vassar College and Penn State. The author of The Petting Zoo *and* Footstool in Heaven, *she is currently at work on her third novel.*

"Chuck Kinder and Ray Carver stole every bottle of booze in my house, along with my surly roommate's happy birthday cake. Allan Gurganus wore white jumpsuits and kept all his money in paper bags. Alice Hoffman was dark and mysterious and spoke in a Jackie Kennedy voice. Robert Stone introduced me to a couple of former Merry Pranksters, but I couldn't keep up with those boys and I lost them, along with those giddy days of camaraderie, somewhere back in Menlo Park."

♦   ♦   ♦

The Catskills

From *Footstool in Heaven*

"IT BOTHERS ME THAT we can't reach her. *I'll* pay for a telephone if she can't afford one." Sid is rinsing the breakfast plates—French toast and rib-eye steak. A river of maple syrup and blood swirls into the sink.

"She *has* a phone. It's unlisted. No one has her number. Not even Melanie. What do you make of the picture?" Miriam examines a Polaroid Sophie sent by way of reply to their two-page letter. It had been hard to fill two pages— *two* yellow legal pages—with chatty words and no advice. What could she tell her daughter at this point? She was sure psychiatry had done Sophie no good. Miriam knew they had screwed her up—both of them, she and Sid.

She didn't blame Sid exclusively, though how many years had he been gone before he'd really left? The night of her miscarriage he'd been off at the Copa, pounding the table with little drumsticks they gave out for free. And there had been others before Dori. That crazy Anita's mother, Lee. And Gladys had said something in Berkeley about someone named Eve Giletti. Miriam remembered a baby-sitter they'd had in 1961. A tall redhead with bad teeth named Marci, or was it Darci? Sid was supposed to be showing her around the house— emergency phone numbers, extra bottles of soda. Miriam had come downstairs wearing a leopard-print jumper she'd bought that day in Orbach's. She'd taken time with her hair. She was only thirty-two, but she'd felt matronly next to these coltish baby-sitters of seventeen and less. Did they even have hair under their arms? (Yes, yes, Sid would have said. Orange fluff. Like cotton candy.) She'd come downstairs in ballet slippers and there on the stairs to their own rec room—their wreck room—Sid and Darci were kissing. Miriam had slammed the door, whacking the baby-sitter's ear.

Miriam couldn't believe what a nerd, what a clod, she had been in those days. She'd fetched an ice bag for the girl—they still had that same *farshtinkener* ice bag rotting upstairs in a bathroom drawer. And then she'd gone off with her cheater husband to a dinner dance at the JVFW, the Jewish Veterans of Foreign Wars. What could she have been thinking? Slurping down barley soup? Spooning up baby peas? It wasn't that she'd been smiling bravely, putting up some kind of front, patching her marriage for the public. She had merely pretended the kiss had never happened. As if she'd gone down to the basement landing, and seen, instead of her husband kissing the baby-sitter, an apparition, hallucination, the visitation of a ghost.

She remembered the stacks of canned goods lining the way to the basement, food stockpiled to keep them eating during the Cuban Missile Crisis. She remembers how happy those stacks had made her, how secure their amount had made her feel. It would take thirty years to eat up all those canned carrots, those jarred beets, those tinned hams. Why, she could make a hundred baked zitis out of all those cans of sauce—Aunt Millie's from the sixties.

In reality the cans had dwindled remarkably after Sid left. Miriam remembers sending the kids over the bridge to visit their father and his new wife. Her skinny obedient children. Sophie wearing patent shoes, Brian's tender cowlick. They had survived the Missile Crisis only for Sid to abandon them for some skinny bluestocking of twenty-four. She'd seen those girls at Barnard in the forties. They'd wear the same cashmere sweater two weeks in a row, while insecure Jewish girls like herself changed their outfits every ten minutes. She remembers the trunk from her college days. She remembers her father's foreigner's lettering on the genuine leather ID tag he'd bought for her going away. Her Greek fisherman father, dead at forty-six—her sophomore year. Her mother dead two years later in a movie-house fire. Watching *One Way Street* with James Mason and Dan Duryea.

By the time she'd sung at Town Hall with an all-girls' choir, by the time she was graduated from Barnard Phi Beta Kappa, by the time she'd landed a husband—a dentist!—a blond Jew, Yale '50!—Old Eli!—she'd buried both her parents in a small cemetery run by the Sephardim of Northern Ohio.

She'd met Sid in the Catskills at a convention of college choral groups. It was spring of 1947, the air was sweet with apple blossoms, and still with the victory of the Allies. Their hotel was very modest compared to the splendor of Grossinger's down the road. Sid and his roommate, Jody Fox, another Jewish Yalie, had been at the center of everything. Jody was the handsome dark one, and Sid was the gorgeous blond one, and all the women at the convention were determined to have one of them.

They'd all gone over to Grossinger's for the entertainment. Warming up for the comic was a magician named Nick Romancer. Somehow, a tipsy Miriam had ended up the stooge in a trick. He'd pulled a brassiere out of her blouse, a black brassiere with transparent cups. No one had seen such a daring brassiere in 1947. How innocent she had been. How susceptible to Sid. One of the girls who went to Vassar had told her Sid was a famous Lothario, a smooth-talking seducer who'd made every Jewish girl in the class of '49. Big deal, she wasn't impressed by this Sidney Spivack. God, they called him Sid the Kid.

She thought his hair was too long, she thought his gut was a little soft. She thought his tenor was only this side of so-so. When he came to her room in the Gold Mountain at three in the morning, she was fully dressed and reading—of all things—Bertrand Russell's *Marriage and Morals*. She'd come to the door remarkably groomed and perky for 3:00 A.M. She'd been lost in Lord Russell, oblivious to the romantic tendencies of their setting. The apple blossoms in the wind, unchaperoned youth after the war, a supernumerary black brassiere pulled out of her sweater by a swarthy magician named Nick Romancer.

"Can I help you?" she'd whispered. In the next bed Lily Shnee was smiling smugly in her sleep.

Sid had laughed drunkenly and shrugged his arms. "The apple blossoms are falling," he'd said.

"And what do you propose I do? Make applesauce?" Miriam said.

He'd laughed and kissed her lightly then, lightly on the shoulder. No one had ever kissed her on the shoulder before. The convention was ending the next day and Sid was determined to have her by checkout nine hours later. This smart dignified brunette girl reading Bertrand Russell.

"You're very funny," Sid had said.

"Maybe Lily could make room for you in her. . . ." She gestured to her sleeping roommate. She realized she was milking it. He shook his head. This girl was tough.

"Do you want to have breakfast?" Sid had asked.

"By the time I finish this chapter and do my exercises and go to sleep and have a dream and wake up and take a shower. . . ."

"I meant right now," he said thickly.

"You seem to have had enough breakfast for one night," she'd said, smiling. She knew she was losing ground. If she didn't close the door right now. . . .

"There's a coffee shop open across the road."

How much harm could be done at a coffee shop at 3:00 A.M.? No one she knew had lost her virginity in a coffee shop. She'd put aside her Bertrand Russell and gathered up Lily's shawl. She let the big shot take her arm and together they'd walked across the road. In the distance she thought she heard the sounds of Tommy Dorsey or Harry James—the rich people laughing and clicking ice. He'd been right about one thing—the apple blossoms were surely falling. The breezes were wild with delicate petals. McIntosh. Wealthy. Delicious. Winesap. Rome Beauty. Grimes Golden. Northern Spy.

"She looks okay," Sid says, picking up the snapshot of Sophie.

"Who?" asks Miriam.

"Your *daughter*," Sid says, his fleshy arm rummaging in the fruit bowl. "What were you thinking, Mim?" Sid bites into an apple. "These apples are old." He makes a face.

"Older than you know."

GREGORY BLAKE SMITH

Gregory Blake Smith is the author of a novel, The Devil in the Dooryard, *published in 1986 by William Morrow, and in 1987 by Ballantine. He has been a National Endowment for the Arts Fellow and teaches American literature and creative writing at Carleton College.*

"The following story was part of my Stegner application. I remember John L'Heureux phoning me up and asking whether the sonnets that the raccoon writes were Petrarchan or Shakespearean. Raccoonian, I told him; he offered me a Stegner on the spot."

◆   ◆   ◆

Hands

HERE IN NEW ENGLAND we sit in chairs.

It's from my porch rocker that I watch the raccoon. He usually comes at dusk, that time of day half dog and half wolf, when the downturned leaves seem to glow with the sunset and the upturned ones glimmer with moonlight. I watch him pad through autumn weeds while the sweat of my chairmaking dries on my skin. He lingers in the shadows, still woodside, the sun falling further with each moment, and then waddles onto my lawn. He looks like a housecat once the woods are behind him. He tosses a wary look at me and then slowly disappears behind the chair shop. After another minute I hear the enormous crash of my garbage can lid falling on the stones. He doesn't even bother to run off as he used to, dawdling at the wood's edge until it's safe to come back. He seems to know I won't leave my chair.

"A twenty-two," my neighbor Moose says while I pare stretchers. "A twenty-two and then we won't blow the b'Jesus out of the pelt."

I take a few more cuts with my gouge and then ask him how he thinks the raccoon has missed his trap line all this time. He peers at me with that cold menace of old age. He has a white beard that rims his chin like frost.

"It probably don't run my way," he says. "But if you want it trapped I can trap it. It's just a pissload easier to shoot it if it's coming every night like you're ringing the dinner bell. Right here," he says and he goes over to the window just above my workbench and taps at a pane. His fingers are scarred with patches of old frostbite. "We'll take this here pane out. I can rest the barrel on the mullion. If it's close enough I'll get it clean through the head and I'll be richer one pelt and you'll be poorer one dinner guest."

I tell him I'm not sure I want to kill him.

"Him?" he says. "How d'you know it's a *him?"* And he spits on my woodstove so the cast iron sizzles and steams.

Outside, my moaning tree sends up a regular howl.

"Please cut that tree down, Smitty," my sister Jaxxlyn says every weekend when she comes up from New York. "It's driving me positively psychotic."

I tell her it's a poplar. I can't cut it down. I don't use poplar in my chairs.

"But you heat with wood," she says. "Don't you? Don't you heat with wood?"

Not poplar wood I don't, I say. Too soft.

"It's driving me positively psychotic, Smitty."

I say what about New York. What about the car horns and the sirens. She says they don't have trees that moan in New York, Smitty.

Smitty, she says.

My name is Smith. I'm a chairmaker with a tree that's grown itself tight around a telephone pole and a raccoon that's taken a fancy to my garbage. I've never minded the name Smith. I like the ancestral whiff of fashioning and forging in its single syllable. And I don't mind the moaning tree and its outrage over the telephone poles that have been stabbed into the landscape like stilettos, rubbing its insulted bark in the slightest breeze and howling when the wind blows in earnest. But the raccoon has unsettled me and I don't know why. My sister—who hates her last name and is being driven psychotic by my moaning tree—is not bothered by the raccoon.

"I think he's *cute,"* she says, sitting on my porch with me as the fat creature moves from shadow into moonlight and back into shadow. "My friend Flora in the west seventies has a skunk for a pet. You should see him, Smitty! His little claws go clack-clack-clack on the linoleum, you know? Of course he's been desmelled or whatever they do to them. Oh, Smitty!" she says as the garbage can lid crashes on the stony ground. "Isn't that the cutest thing? How does he do it? Just *how* does he do it? Do you leave the lid on loose for him? Is that how he does it?"

Hands, I tell her, and I feel a faint panic at the word. They've got hands. And I hold my own hands up in the gloom, the backs reddish with dusk, the palms silver with moonlight.

When Monday comes I try tying the lid shut with mason's twine. That night there is no aluminum crash and I think: so much for hands, so much for raccoons, so much for half dog and half wolf! The next day I start in on a set of eight Queen Anne chairs, carefully designing the S-shaped legs to Hogarth's line of beauty. But that evening the raccoon comes trotting along the forest floor, hiking up onto my lawn behind the shop. It takes him a few minutes longer, but eventually the harsh, bright crash shatters the dusk. I sit in a stupor. In ten minutes he emerges from behind the shop trundling happily along. He pauses partway to the wood's edge and tosses me a scornful look over his shoulder and then vanishes into the now-dark bushes.

"You might open up a motel," Moose suggests, "seeing as what you already got yourself a rest'rant."

My cabriole legs aren't right. I can't strike the balance between knee and foot. It's never happened like this before. I get out Hogarth's *Analysis of Beauty* and look his *S*'s over, and I print *S S S S S* on my graph paper, write my own name: Smith, Smith, Smith, Smith, but when I go to draft my Queen Anne leg

I can't balance the knee to the foot, the foot to the knee, the *S*'s top orb to its bottom. I spend a whole day at my drafting table, trying, and end up tossing a sheaf of rejected legs into the stove. That night the raccoon dines on pumpkin and old cantaloupe.

I get my bucksaw and my knapsack and my spool of pink ribbon. If I can't work I'll hunt wood, do the felling now and wait until the first decent snow to find the marker ribbons and sledge the logs out with Moose's snowmobile. I plan on a two-day roam, bringing my sleeping bag and some food. At the sight of my bucksaw, my moaning tree groans.

I'm going to forget about raccoons.

I poach my lumber, and maybe that's why I have a feeling of trespassing when I go into the woods, of being where I only half belong. There are stone walls everywhere, built in earlier centuries and now running mute and indecipherable through the forest. Walking, I try to picture perfect *S*'s in the air, but the stone walls distract me. They are like hieroglyphs on the land. From time to time I come across an old foundation, a sprinkle of broken glass in the weeds and a small graveyard a ways off. I find a bottle or two, an old auger, but they look as alien there as I do. Further on, the stone walls are so tumble-down they have ceased to look like walls. There is a feeling of low menace all around.

I mark my wood as I go, but on this trip I keep my eyes open for hollowed trees, for trees with holes, a cicatrix, disease. I climb up several and look inside, peer up the trunk of one, but there's no sign of habitation. That night, lying on dark pine needles, I have a recurring picture of the raccoon back at my house, sitting at the kitchen table in one of my chairs, with knife and fork in hand—perhaps a napkin—eating.

By noontime on the second day I've swung around to where I know there's a stand of tiger maple near a marshy pond two miles from the house. I spend the afternoon carefully harvesting the rare, figured wood, dragging the delimbed trunks down to the pondside and stickering them off the ground so they won't rot. The work puts the raccoon out of my mind. I feel healthy, feel the steel teeth of my bucksaw sharp and vengeful, the rasp of the sawn wood like the sound of defeat. But after the last haul, just as I sit content and forgetful on a stump, I catch sight of a tiny footprint in the soft silt that rings the water. Further on, there's another one.

There's a hush over the pond. The marsh reeds stand like pickets along the shore. Across the way the shadows between the junipers and low laurels seem to breathe in and out. I have a feeling of having been tricked, of having been watched all along. On the water the whirligigs hover like spies. A scarlet leaf flutters through the blue air and lands a foot or so from the raccoon's footprint, then cartwheels slyly until it covers the print. But it's too late. In the west, where my house is, the sun is kindling nests of reddish fire in the blue tops of the spruces.

You've got yourself a comfy den, I'm saying half an hour later after I've found the raccoon's beech tree. I've brought a crotched branch from the pondside for a leg-up, and I'm peering into a yawning hole maybe ten feet off the ground. I say it out loud. I do. I say: leaves and dried reeds, decaying wood for heat, some duck down. You've done all right. Yes, you have. You've done all right.

The trees seem to stir at the sound of my voice. I pull my head out and listen. They sound baffled, outraged. I want to say to them: "Do you think so? Do you think so? So *I'm* the intruder? Do you think so?" But I don't. I just look at the hasty illogic of the shadows. Trees don't come on all fours and pry your garbage can lid off, I say. Even Darwin can't see to that, I say, and I go back to looking inside the raccoon's den.

I'm not afraid he's in there somewhere. I *know* what time of day it is. I *know* where he is. But off to the side, in a decaying burl, something has caught my eye, something shiny and unnatural. I look closer and realize he's got himself a cache of junk, bottle caps and aluminum can rings. Then in the next instant I recognize a piece of old coffee cup I'd broken in the summer, and then too a router bit I'd chipped and thrown out, then an old ballpoint, a spoon, screws.

Are you a user of spoons too, raccoon? I finally say out loud. And screws? And pens? Are you a writer of sonnets? I say.

But even as I talk I hear footsteps behind me on the leaves. I pull my head out and look around, but there's nothing moving, just the vagrant leaves falling. I listen again, hear them coming closer. Is it the raccoon returning? I hang fire a moment and then start hurriedly down the trunk. But before I do I reach in and steal back my old ballpoint. I hide the crotched limb in some bushes nearby.

For the next few days I wonder just how much the raccoon knows. There's no new contempt evident in his regard as he bellies up out of the woods onto my lawn—but he may be a master of his emotions. Jaxxlyn has put a bowl of water out for him. She says she's going to move it nearer to the house each day until the raccoon gets used to being with us. She wants me to do the moving on the weekdays.

My West Hartford client calls and asks how her Queen Anne chairs are coming. I start to tell her about the raccoon. I start to tell her about William Hogarth and beauty and order, about how a man can't work when a raccoon's eating his garbage, about how I've allowed eagle's claws for chair feet in the past, lion's paws too. But this raccoon is asking too much, I tell her. There's a silence on the line when I stop—and then she asks again how her chairs are coming.

"Six inches each day," Jaxx tells me as she gets into her car. "Six inches, Smitty."

Monday I can't work. Tuesday I can't either. Tuesday evening I wander off into the woods again, walk the two miles to the raccoon's tree. Somewhere on the way I know we cross paths. Is he hiding from me? I get the crotched limb out of its hiding place and steal back a screw.

The next morning I get the mating *S*'s of the cabriole legs down perfectly in ten minutes, and by sundown I have all sixteen legs squared up and cut. That night I take the router bit back.

Thursday it's another screw. Friday a piece of china. I'm going great guns on my chairs.

Jaxxlyn doesn't understand why the raccoon won't drink her water. She asks if I've moved it each day. Then she talks to the raccoon from the porch, talks to him so he pauses in his jaunty walk and looks our way. She alternates from a low, cooing voice to a high, baby voice. The raccoon and I exchange looks. He knows, I think to myself. He knows. He can hardly cart things off as fast as I can steal them back. He knows.

For the next week I am a maker of chairs in the daytime and a sitter of chairs at night. I'm a happy man. Only during the in-between hours do I venture through the woods to the raccoon's house and then venture back in the near-dark. I've taken to putting my booty back in the trash can.

My West Hartford lady drives cross-state to see how her chairs are coming along. I let her run her wealthy fingers across the soft wood, up and down the smooth legs. She shivers and says it feels alive still. "Doesn't it feel alive still?" she says.

Back in the woods I take a different route to the raccoon's tree. I figure I might catch him out this time, but it turns out we've merely switched paths, and he's trying to catch me out. I round the pond quickly, the last fall leaves floating like toy boats on the water, and hurry to the bushes where the crotched branch is hidden. The trees are quiet. I throw the crotch up against the treetrunk, climb quickly up, and in the half-light see that the raccoon has taken the ballpoint pen back.

Still writing sonnets, raccoon? I say and I reach in and take the pen back. But just as I do the den bursts into a flurry of fur and claws and teeth. I hear a hiss, a growling sibilance, and just before I fall see two leathery hands gripped around my wrist and a furry mouth set to bite. An instant later I am lying scratched and hurt in the laurel below. Above me the raccoon peers fiercely down at me from his hole. His eyes are black and fanatical, and he seems to say: "All right? All right? Understand? All right?"

Violence! I spit through my teeth, stumbling back through the woods. I don't even try to stanch the blood coming from the punctures on my wrist. *Violence! Violence!*

Moose laughs. He laughs and asks how much the first of my rabies series costs. I'm sitting in his living room feeding bark into his stove. I don't answer him at first. I'm sick and I ache from the shot. Finally I tell him twenty dollars.

"Well, let's see," he says and he sights down the barrel of his twenty-two. "A raccoon pelt brings thirty dollar nowadays. You already used up twenty of them dollars on that shot. But I figure my half is still fifteen. So I figure you owe me five dollar."

I muster enough character to tell him he's getting a little ahead of himself, he's getting a little eager.

"No eagerer than that raccoon's getting," he says. The frostbite on his face crumples with his laugh, as if the skin there were half alive. I sit sullen and witless. I feel wasted. I don't know what to do. The raccoon comes and ravages my garbage.

I lie in bed for two days. When I'm up again I ask Moose for one of his box traps. I tell him I don't want to shoot the raccoon, I want to trap him. And once I've trapped him I want to let him go. He looks at me like this is confirmation of some suspicion he's had about me all along, never mind raccoons, some suspicion he'd had since he met me and my chairs.

"I ain't altogether sure a raccoon will trap so near a house," he says. "Raccoons ain't dumb."

This one will, I say. He's a modern raccoon.

But that night, sitting in my warm chair shop on a half-finished Queen Anne chair, I watch the raccoon stop and inspect the trap, puff at the acorn squash inside and then waddle over to the garbage can. He knocks the lid off with a professional air, but before he crouches into the garbage, he tosses a disdainful look through the windowpane at me and my chair. Behind him the trap sits in a state of frozen violence.

Beauty is the visible fitness of a thing to its use, I say to the raccoon in my dreams. Order, in other words. In a Yale-ish voice he answers back: "Not entirely different from that beauty which there is in fitting a mortise to its tenon."

I wake in a sweat. My wound itches under its bandage.

On the second night, kneeling on the wooden floor in my shop, the chairs empty behind me, I watch the raccoon sniff a moment longer at the squash but again pass it up. This time it's contempt in his face when he catches sight of me through the windowpane. That night the air turns cold.

What do you want? I whisper to the raccoon in my sleep. *What do you want?*

"*What do you want?*" the raccoon whispers back. "*What do you want?*"

On the third night I forsake the chair shop for the junipers, hiding myself long before dusk in the green shrubbery that skirts the forest's edge. It's snowing. The flurries make an icy whisper in the trees overhead. I watch the sun fall through autumn avatars and set in blue winter. The snowflakes land on my eyelashes and melt New England into an antique drizzle. I blink my eyes to clear them and wait with my joints stiffening, my toes disappearing.

By the time the raccoon comes I am iced over, a snowy stump among the evergreens. He pads silently through the snow, leaving tiny handprints behind him on the slushy ground. He doesn't see me. I watch him with frost inside me, my breathing halted, my hands clubbed. He looks for me on the porch, in my rocker, then tries to spy me through my shop window. For an instant he seems stunned by my absence, by the change in things. He turns and peers straight across at where I sit in the frozen junipers. I am certain he sees me, even nod my head at him. For a moment we are poised, balanced, the one against the other. He blinks, acknowledging my presence in the snow, and then with an air of genteel reciprocation, turns and walks straight into the trap.

When I reach him he has his paws up on the trap's sides, the fingers outstretched on the fencing. He peers up at me as if to see if I'll take his hands as evidence after all. There are snowflakes on his eyelashes. When I bend over him our breaths mingle in the cold gray New England air.

BRENT SPENCER

Brent Spencer was born in 1952 and grew up in northeastern Pennsylvania. He holds an M.F.A. from the Iowa Writers Workshop and a Ph.D. from Penn State. His work has appeared in The Atlantic *and elsewhere. He has been a Michener Fellow at Iowa and a Stegner Fellow at Stanford, where he is currently a Jones Lecturer in creative writing.*

"For a while, I ran a farm, thinking country living would give me peace and time to write. But from dawn to dark my days were filled with hauling and hammering, feeding and killing, plowing, planting, and harvesting. I didn't have the energy to write a single word. Years later and a world away, I thought of my old neighbors—the real farmers, not the dilettantes like me—and tried to write about the everyday courage of their lives."

◆　　　◆　　　◆

Night, Sleep, Death, and the Stars

THE FIRST TIME I saw Easy, he was standing in the middle of the road, a one-armed man kicking the big back tire of a tractor, slapping at it with his hat. It was a small tractor, an old gray Ford held together with baling wire and electrical tape. After we rolled it onto the shoulder, I drove him back to his farm.

He had about forty head of cattle on twenty-five acres that sloped into a shallow valley. The top ten acres were fenced off and full of timothy, tall and shimmering in the wind. The rest was pasture and woodland. He didn't seem worried about the tractor. But then, it wouldn't start for some thief any easier than it had for him.

I stayed for supper, though at first Joan, his wife, seemed nervous at having a stranger in her house. Their boy must have been the quietest four-year-old on record. Jimmy. We had chicken, mashed potatoes, and peas, but he would only eat slices of buttered bread.

Easy was the kind of man who likes to run the talk at supper.

"Those cows of mine are stupid on purpose," he said. From the kitchen window, we could see them coming up the lane and crowding together in the holding pen, moaning at the closed barn door. Big dull eyes, and smaller than any cows I had ever seen. They were full-grown yet stood only waist-high.

"All the smarts got bred out so they'd be easy to handle. And being small, they need less acreage. They're the latest thing."

Easy was Frank Nagle. He had brown shaggy hair that looked like he cut it himself, in the dark. He and Joan were thirty, thirty-five. She was taller than Easy by a couple inches. She wore faded jeans and one of his flannel shirts that had seen too much work and washing. The colors were faded and the cloth was limp and threadbare, but that only brought out her beauty. She had a generous look that told you the things you said mattered to her.

Easy rubbed the stub of his right arm. "It was one of those things you warn everybody else about, then all of a sudden you just can't believe it's happening to you."

I could see Joan tense up as she listened to a story she must have heard many times.

"Corn got caught in my picker," he said, "so I went back to unclog it. Forgot to turn the damn thing off. It grabbed my hand, pulled the whole arm in.

"Caddy Leboux, my neighbor, he came running when he heard the screams. He says he found me jammed up against the picker, with my arm being clawed to pieces inside. I was unconscious by then. He says the damn picker wouldn't let me fall. He had to take the son-of-a-bitch apart to get me loose. I got my name because I can do things easier with one arm than most can with two."

"Except when it comes to cleaning up after himself," Joan said.

After supper he and I sat on the back porch and drank like hillbillies, from a big brown crock. Once a month he visited a cousin in West Virginia. He called it his "moon run." Moonshine.

We left the porch light off to keep the bugs away. Barn swallows had built a nest in the space above the fixture. We'd watch them come dipping up the long slope toward the house and then swoop above us to the nest. All evening it was like that, sitting in the dark, drinking Easy's moon.

He wanted to take out a loan so he could fence in more pasture and buy more "mini-cows." Hard work for a one-armed man. Maybe it was that, or the drinking, or just the good feeling I had sitting there, but I offered to stay and help out.

He looked at me a little suspiciously and took a pull from the crock. "If it's money you're after, there isn't any," he said.

"I'm only after food and a place to stay," I said.

He was quiet for a while. Then he said, "Let's sleep on this. See if it sounds good sober."

Next morning he showed me a whitewashed shack about a hundred yards below the house, two rooms attached to a potting shed.

"My idea was to have a place to hide when the Russians drop the bomb. But then Caddy Leboux told me about radiation, so that was that. Now I come down here when Joan kicks me out. I poison my liver and argue with the empty rooms. You fix it up any way you like."

The front room had a moldy cot, a potbellied stove, and a pile of firewood. In the kitchen were a Formica table and two rusty chairs with split, sun-bleached seatpads. The electric stove didn't work, and the sink had no drainpipe, just an open hole to the floor. Canned food was stacked on wooden shelves all around the room—ham, peaches, tomatoes, peas—a whole truckload. I got used to heating cans on the wood stove.

The shack was a wreck, but one wall of the front room had a homemade picture window that looked out over the farm. The light in those fields was pure luxury. Country light. Clean. I'd sit and stare for hours, listening to birds circling through the trees, to wind hissing in the long grass.

Easy and I got on well together, with me doing the heavy work and him dealing with feed suppliers and the bank. His farm was not a money-maker, but he was serious, he had plans. And little by little, we thought, we could turn the place around. Those huge farms you see, they're all science. A small farm like Easy's is a record of the farmer's life. Sometimes it's a record of the failures and mistakes and accidents that make a life. So it was important for us to do things right. The farm was a kind of fresh start for Easy. He had bought it a few years back, when he and Joan married, using inheritance money he hadn't already drunk or gambled away. He liked to say that Joan's love saved his life. It embarrassed me whenever he said that, the sentimentality of it.

The first snow came in early October, right when money was getting scarce. One evening Easy and Joan started yelling at each other and slamming doors. I could hear some of it all the way to the shack, maybe because of the way sound carries over snowy ground. Maybe because misery carries over any ground.

She said, ". . . cows . . . loser . . . farm . . . lunatic."

Then Easy, louder: ". . . beat me . . . I'll be damned . . . " I heard glass breaking. The TV came on loud. Some goofy cartoon voice sang, "Take good care of yourself, like your friend Shamu!" Then the TV went off, and I didn't hear anything for a long time.

A little later I went up near the house to burn some trash. All through the fight, Jimmy was out there playing in the snow, rolling snowballs that kept falling apart. He looked like a small blue astronaut in his snow gear. He was talking and singing to himself, words I couldn't make out. The barrel of trash was in full blaze. I poked at it with a broom handle so it crackled and roared. Sparks shot up in bright showers, and fell on the snow. It was late. It had been quiet for a long time.

When I looked up, Easy and Joan were standing on the back porch. Joan clung to him a little like she was hurt, like he had beaten her and it was all she could do to stand up. She was crying a little with her head against his shirt, stroking his chest. There were tears in his eyes, too. They stood there on the porch in the cold, staring off down the hill. He held her close and kissed her hair without taking his eyes off the darkness. She held him like that to keep him from flying apart.

Easy called to the boy, his voice raw and weak. The boy walked toward them and climbed the back steps slowly.

When you're four years old, I think, the world goes on pretty much without you. You find the safe places where you can. He climbed those stairs like an old man coming home from a long day of field work. His house was safe again, for a little while at least. The three of them went inside. Lights came on upstairs, and after a time went out again. There was nothing left but the night and the snow and flames spraying into the cold wind.

One warm day late in October, I started digging postholes. It was the wrong season for work like that, but we were anxious to get the field ready for the new cows. Digging postholes was something a one-armed man couldn't do. He was off at the Agway and the bank. After a few holes, I went up to the house for a beer. Joan was standing at the sink, her hands in soapy water, just staring out at the farm.

Her windowsill was full of cuttings in jelly jars. Coleus. Wandering Jew. Swedish ivy. We got to talking, like neighbors over a back fence. I don't know what brought us together that day. Unless it was the cuttings, like a sign of hope, the late-afternoon light sloping through the windows, her hair shining in that pale gold light: we make up stories to carry ourselves through the longest nights, and this is mine.

She took my hand and led me upstairs, where we made love like old friends who thought they'd never see each other again. Slow and solemn love. Later, we talked. Easy was her second husband. Frank, she called him.

"I was first married to Big John, Jimmy's father. He was a small, spiteful man with corns on his vocal cords from screaming at wrestlers on the TV."

I was lying on my back, listening to Joan, listening for the sound of Easy's pickup. Already the feelings that had made it all seem so natural were starting to fade. I think she knew that, and that's why she kept talking.

"Big John worked in a heat-treating plant. Anchor chains, gun barrels, camshafts, and the like. Dangerous work. The furnaces would heat up to 1,800 degrees. Sometimes an oil bath would burst into flame and blow out every window in the place. Two men died there, and Big John was one of them. He fell off an I-beam into a vat of caustic soda. When I'm feeling truly mean about the past, I like to say all they could fish out was his rodeo belt buckle. But the truth is he survived, at least for a while. He swallowed some of that slop, though, and died later from pneumonia."

She rolled so she was leaning on her elbow, looking down at me, her loose hair shading her face. She said, "The day I married Frank, my heart was in my mouth. Without him, I would just turn into some kind of character."

When Easy's pickup pulled in, I was back in the field, chopping at the cold ground, feeling cheap and lonely. Joan was sweet and strong, and I loved her in a way that afternoon, but I thought I had ruined all our lives.

I don't know a thing about cattle. Before the snow I'd sit in the shack and watch them graze. Cowbirds sat on their shoulders. Flies swarmed in their eyes. Nothing bothered those cows. Easy was right about how stupid they were. When I ran a water line to the field and attached a noser, it took them all day to learn how to nuzzle the paddle for fresh water.

They'd walk the fence, looking for a break into the wild grapes on the other side. During storms they'd huddle under the lean-to. It was nothing but sapling trunks and sheets of tin, but it was sturdy. Then they found out they could scratch an itch by rubbing against the roof supports. Each day that roof was more and more crooked. Someday, I figured, it would come right down on them.

When Easy couldn't get his price for the cows, he decided to keep them through winter. Lots of farmers did that—kept cattle, siloed grain—waiting for a better market. But there was the extra cost. We had a barn full of hay, a little corn. Feed, though, all that extra Super Fit-n-Fresh—that was expensive. Easy couldn't get his price because the buyers said there wasn't enough meat on the new breed. They said the cows were all bone. But Easy didn't see it that way. He would keep those cows, he said, until he found a buyer who wasn't out to cheat him.

Things began to fall apart when the feed started running out. At night I'd hear the cows groaning and butting the barn door. They wanted to graze, I guess, but they couldn't, not with two feet of snow on the ground and more falling all the time.

Pretty soon the grain was gone. I pitched plenty of hay to them, but they needed more than that to keep up their body heat. They kicked at the pens when they saw the hay dropping down. Big whucking kicks that splintered wood. Later, as they passed the silo on their way to the field, they licked the feeding auger, but when they saw it was no use, they stamped the ground, tails switching like whips.

One evening a couple of weeks later I noticed some of them hadn't come back to the barn. Three of them were lying against one another in the lean-to. They didn't seem to have the strength to make it up the hill. That night the temperature dropped to twenty below. By morning they were dead.

For days I couldn't look at them. I hoped the drifting snow would cover them up, but no. The other cows wouldn't go near the lean-to. More died, in the field, in the lane that went down to the field, in the barn. He had gone to all the feed suppliers in the valley, but his credit was stretched to the limit and the bank wouldn't give him a break. He just sat on the porch all day in the cold, drinking his cousin's home brew and staring at the cows as if they had betrayed him.

It was one of those days when the sun is so bright and the cold so cutting that you can hardly stand it. I had just stepped out of the shack and was waiting for my eyes to adjust to the glare. Jimmy was out there, beside a red plastic sled loaded with kindling, a piece of rope, a few handfuls of snow, other trash. He stared up at me.

"He says to give you this."

The note said, "Let's fall by The Farmer's and do some damage."

Jimmy was almost crying, his voice like a prayer: "You're hurting my shadow."

I stepped away from him. His small shadow lay sprawled on the snow, its chest caved in by my footprints.

When I got to the house, Easy was coming out the door.

Joan followed, saying, "You were my hope against hope. Do you hear? I thought . . . but look at us, Frank. Look at us."

Jimmy had followed me up the hill. Now he emptied the heavy sled onto the snow, singing quietly to himself.

Easy threw things into the back of his pickup—rope, stray lumber, a sack of rock salt. I think he wanted to hear what she had to say but didn't want her to know it.

He said, "Don't lay it all on me, Joan." He said her name as if it were a dirty word. He stomped around the truck, kicking it, banging his fist against it. We climbed into the cab and he yelled, "I'm bitched! I'm bitched!"

Joan was at my window. I rolled it down. "Talk to him, Evan," she said. "Knock some sense into the pigheaded cripple." She pushed off the truck and went back into the house. Easy pumped the gas hard and swung into the road.

When we were away from the house, he looked at me and broke out laughing. "Pigheaded cripple! God, I love that woman!"

At The Farmer's Inn we drank a few beers and threw some darts. Easy's shots kept hitting the wall.

He said, "It's a rag-arm, but it's the only arm I got. Let's say you won. Anyway, the soup here's a killer, and I'm hungry."

A few farmers were sitting around with their caps pushed back on their heads, sipping beers and rubbing their chins. They nodded at Easy as if they knew his trouble but weren't going to be the ones to bring it up.

"Sure, my head's hard," Easy said to me. "I'm a pigheaded cripple! After this is all over, I'm going to have to get me a new nickname. Pig. That'd be it, I guess."

He unpinned his sleeve and reached up inside to scratch his stub. "You know what I miss?" he said, looking down at his empty sleeve, his voice softening. "I had the prettiest little dragon tattoo. Right about here." He touched the sleeve where his forearm had been. "Isn't that the damndest thing? I miss my tattoo."

The old woman behind the bar brought us two bowls of split pea. She was wide in the hips and took her time.

Easy said, "This is a good bar. Never saw a single unruly drunk here. Gerry, here, is really something. She saved me many times in the bad old days. Helped me face up to my weaselly ways."

The old woman wrapped her bar rag around Easy's neck and pulled his head back against her stomach. He laughed. She slowly bent over and kissed his forehead, like a blessing.

As I ate my soup, I thought about Joan and that afternoon months before. "You don't know me very well, Easy," I said.

"I know your work," he said. "You learn a thing about a man when you see him work. That's enough for me."

"I could be some kind of escapee," I said.

"I thought of that, at first, when you wanted to stay on. But then I thought, what've we got to steal?"

I laughed and he said, "You married, Evan? I know it's none of my business, but you have a look. You married?"

"Not in the eyes of the law," I said.

"Not in the eyes of the law. Now that's sad as can be. When you came to the farm, I figured you were broke down. Joan said your car looked fine to her, and I said no, it was more than that. That's all we needed to know. She trusts you the same as me."

"You shouldn't trust me," I said. "Easy," I said, "people do things. They don't mean to, but they do them. Later they're sorry, but the harm is already done."

"You planning on robbing us after all?" he said, scraping at the green sludge on the bottom of his bowl.

"You're not listening to me. I've done something I'm ashamed of, and I have to tell you."

Easy looked up then and sipped his beer, his eyes going over me.

"A little while ago," I said, "I was working in the field. I went to the house for a beer. Joan and I got to talking."

"That woman is a great one for talking. Sometimes she's quiet for days. And then it's like a dam burst—everything just rushes right out."

"Easy," I said, and for the first time it seemed like a foolish name to say.

"She takes her time thinking about a thing. She'll talk about it only after she has it figured out in her mind. She's deeper than me, and I admire that."

"Easy, something happened between Joan and me that afternoon."

"I know," he said quietly. "You spent time together." He was looking down at the rings of wetness his bottle had made on the tablecloth. He ran his hand through his shaggy hair. He looked tired.

"I'm sorry, Frank."

"Only Joan calls me Frank," he said. "Nobody else."

I said, "I wish it never happened. I wish we didn't have this standing between us."

"When Joan told me, first I was mad. Then I cried. I thought she was leaving me. But she said it was just something that happened, naturally, between friends. She doesn't lie to me, Evan. I know enough to listen to her. I'm not that pigheaded. I used to be a drunk and a runaround. I know that life—do the worst and don't get caught. Joan settled me down. She opened my eyes. If you're sorry because you hurt me, well, that's one thing. To that I say, I'll live. But if you're sorry it happened, that's something else. I don't really think you are. Do you?"

I don't know how to account for the calm in some people. Easy was a one-armed man watching his life fall apart. I was the stranger who stole his wife away one afternoon. But we spent hours in The Farmer's, talking and laughing about bills that were past due, money beyond our reach, and the string of useless postholes I had dug.

By the time we got home, the evening was setting in. We stood awkwardly near the steps of the side door. He gripped my shoulder. There was a lot of strength in that hand. Then he moved his rough palm up against the side of my neck and held it there.

"Oh, Evan," he said. He said it like a lover, the way a woman says your name in the dark when the stars are right, making you forget how much you fear her.

I said, "Easy, this afternoon, before we left, I heard Jimmy out here. You know how he sings all the time? Well, I finally heard what he's singing: 'Cows are brown, cows are gray, cows are in the field all day.'"

Easy looked off at the dead cattle lying in the field and shook his head. "That's not fair to him. He shouldn't have to see that. What have I been thinking?"

Earlier that day, as Easy and Joan argued, Jimmy stood quietly chanting his song. His wagonload of junk was the most important thing in his life at that moment—an empty cigarette pack, a saucer, old clay pots and medicine bottles...

"We got unfinished business, Evan."

After hooking up the backhoe, I drove the tractor down the icy, rutted lane running along the far edge of the farm. Easy rode behind, with one foot on the axle and the other on the backhoe, so I drove slow. The tractor almost shook itself apart as it lurched and slid over the hard ground. Twice the engine died, and in the silence I could feel the presence of the dead cattle lying in the field beside us. The clouds were faint scraps of shadow far away, and the stars were beginning to show.

They lay in the dark field like mounds of freshly turned earth. Heavy black birds strutted back and forth over the bloated carcasses, their broad, oily wings snapping viciously.

Halfway down the lane I yelled to Easy over the engine's roar, "Let's dig it in the woods, okay?"

He nodded a few times, but I'm not sure he heard me. I wanted the grave to be hidden, so I drove to a clearing deep in the woods. It was darker there and felt colder, despite the windbreak of pine, cedar, and laurel. Easy walked off into the trees. He must have figured he wouldn't be much help, and that probably embarrassed him.

I set to work on the grave, but every time I brought the backhoe against the icy ground, the tractor's engine strained and choked and nearly died. I gave it a little more gas and shifted into the lowest gear. Nothing worked.

Finally, cold and angry, I yanked the prong of the throttle toward me, ripping it over the metal notches on its scale. The engine roared with the rich gasoline, the backhoe bit into the ground, but then sour black smoke began to pour from the engine, the roar became an aching metal shriek, and the whole thing shuddered into silence.

I jumped down, cursing myself and the tractor. My feet were cold, my breath came in plumes. The stars glowed weakly over the bristle of trees at the edge of the clearing.

Easy called to me from deeper in the woods. I thought he was yelling at me for burning out the engine, but he wanted me to bring the wire cutters.

I climbed over some fallen trees and stepped across a narrow, frozen stream. I couldn't move quickly, because of the rocks and roots hidden beneath the snow.

Easy was standing near the border fence, rubbing the back of his neck and moaning a little. One of the cows had become caught in the barbed wire that ran between Easy's place and Leboux's.

Easy said, "At first I thought it might be a boulder, the woods are so dark. Then I saw it clear. Then I knew."

The cow had tried to push its head between the top two strings and step through, but it had fouled itself and fallen into the wire. The posts on either side strained and creaked with its weight.

Easy said, "I feel so awful. This is all my fault."

"It was an accident, Easy. It just happened, that's all."

The cow had not died right away. It must have struggled against the sharp wire with the last of its strength. Blood stood as thick as jelly in the long, twisting grooves the wire had cut into its flesh. The carcass was pitched forward, with its head hanging just a few inches above the dark, crusty snow. A frozen yellow beard of drool hung from its mouth.

One string of wire had caught the long jaw, holding it like a strap. One hind leg was strung up so it barely touched the ground. The other was splayed and twisted in midair by the wire. Both forelegs were bent and bound against the stomach.

"We got to cut it free," Easy said.

"It's dead. What good will that do?"

He turned to me. His face was rashy and swollen from the cold. "We can't leave it like this," he said.

I set the metal jaw of the snip against the wire, near the cow's head, and bit into it. The wire sprang into spiky coils as the body fell forward onto the ground.

The cow was still alive. It gave a long screaming moan of pain, and then struggled to stand. One hind leg was still hung up in the wire. The other kept slipping on the snow. Its eyes were wide and white. I could see its fat black tongue behind its bared teeth. Then it slammed its bloody head back into my chest.

Easy said, "Oh my God, my God. . . . "

The cow screamed again, a rising groan of terror. It tried to shake its hind leg free but couldn't. Just then its forelegs buckled and the cow crashed down for the last time, one eye rolling in its socket, then trembling, then congealing to ice. The cow lay there on the bloody snow, finally dead.

There was nothing we could do. We left the tractor and the cow, and made our way back through the woods toward home. When we got to the stone wall at the edge of the field, we sat down. Easy kneaded his stump and stared.

He said, "What was I thinking when I bought those cows? They're none of them any good."

My lungs burned and my ribs ached from where the cow had hit me. I said, "That tractor's a piece of junk, too."

"That tractor's a '49 Ford. It's a classic," he said. "You just got it all gummed up."

"I think I ruined it," I said.

"No, no. We'll just give it a good swift kick in the morning. That's the thing about a classic."

"I hope you're right," I said. "I hope we can get them buried."

The shadows of clouds crossing the moon floated over the field.

"This is a terrible thing," Easy said. "I sure messed things up good. Some farmer I am. Some kind of farmer."

"Look," I said. "You can see the house from here." About a mile uphill, we could see the porchlight glowing weakly. It was like the sudden light you find sometimes in deep woods. All you expect is darkness and shadow. Then a shaft of moonlight spills onto the ground just where you were going to set your foot. It's a small thing, but it makes you think you should keep walking.

Overhead, the night hardened around its cold stars. Maybe there were things he could have done. He could have sold off some acreage or unloaded the cattle at any price. But there really wasn't time. And anyway, that didn't matter. The only thing that mattered was the way he and Joan stood on the back porch that night, clinging to each other, while out there in the dark their dreams were dying.

What happens happens. The day rises and the night falls. Troubles turn on you before you bat an eye. "Should have" and "could have" don't count. Your house is in flames and the world is made of ice.

Easy stood and said, "I'm never going to be the same."

But he was wrong. He would be all right. Easy would let the small things save him. Days of sun and sweet breezes. Late afternoons full of birds streaming into the trees. And other shadows on other nights, as deer climb down from the high ground to the stream in moonlight.

TIMOTHY STEELE

Born in Vermont in 1948, Timothy Steele attended Stanford as an undergraduate; he later held a Stegner Fellowship and a Jones Lectureship at Stanford. His collections of poems are Uncertainties and Rest *(L.S.U., 1979) and* Sapphics Against Anger and Other Poems *(Random House, 1986); his honors include a Guggenheim Fellowship and a Lavan Younger Poets Award from the Academy of American Poets.*

"I wrote 'Aurora' and 'Pacific Rim' early in 1987. At the time, they seemed very different poems: the first was an impersonal hymn in rhyming trimeters, the second a more personal piece in blank verse. Looking back, however, I see that both are about human consciousness, that miracle to whose development and preservation teachers, fiction writers, scholars, and poets are equally devoted. Thanks to the Writing Program, people from all these groups have had at Stanford the chance to share this devotion with each other and perhaps to grow more thoughtful, better natured, and less dogmatic as a result."

Aurora

Your sleep is so profound
This room seems a recess
Awaiting consciousness.
Gauze curtains, drawn around
The postered bed, confute
Each waking attribute—
Volition, movement, sound.

Outside, though, chilly light
Shivers a puddle's coil
Of iridescent oil;
Windows, sun-struck, ignite;
Doves strut along the edge
Of roof- and terrace-ledge
And drop off into flight.

And soon enough you'll rise.
Long-gowned and self-aware,
Brushing life through your hair,

You'll notice with surprise
The way your glass displays,
Twin-miniatured, your face
In your reflective eyes.

Goddess, it's you in whom
Our clear hearts joy and chafe.
Awaken, then. Vouchsafe
Ideas to resume.
Draw back the drapes: let this
Quick muffled emphasis
Flood light across the room.

◆   ◆   ◆

Pacific Rim

Unsteadily, I stand against the wash
Flooding in, climbing thigh, waist, rib-cage. Turning,
It sweeps me, breaststroking, out on its swift
Sudsy withdrawal. Greenly a wave looms;
I duck beneath its thundering collapse,
Emerging on the far side, swimming hard
For the more manageable, deeper waters.
How the sea elevates! Pausing to tread it
And feather-kicking its profundity,
The swimmer wears each swell around his neck,
And rides the slopes that heave through him,
The running valleys that he sinks across,
Part of the comprehensive element
Washing as well now the Galapagos,
The bay at Wenchow, the Great Barrier Reef.

Why, then, this ache, this sadness? Toweled off,
The flesh is mortified, the small hairs standing
Among their goosebumps, the teeth chattering
Within the skull. A brutal century
Draws to a close. Bewildering genetrix,
As your miraculous experiment
In consciousness hangs in the balance, do
You pity those enacting it? The headlands'
Blunt contours sloping to the oceanside,
Do angels weep for our folly? Merciful,
Do you accompany our mortality,
Just as, low to the water, the pelican
Swiftly pursues his shadow down a swell?

ALAN STEPHENS

Born Greeley, Colorado, 1925. Service in Air Force, 1943–46. B.A. and M.A., University of Denver, where studied with Alan Swallow. Ph.D., University of Missouri, 1954. Taught at Arizona State, Tempe. Stanford Writing Fellowship, studying with Yvor Winters, 1956–57. Since 1959, teaching at U.C. Santa Barbara, acquiring, with age, increasing respect for intelligence of young people. Married, three sons, two grandchildren.

"Luis Buñuel tells us in his memoirs that now, when he leaves a place that has become a part of him, he says good-bye to it, adding, 'I'll never see you again, but you'll go on without me.' 'To My Matilija' was written as a variation on that sentiment. (The poem required a sequel when earthmovers appeared on the cherished scene; yet, had they not, we know that the feelings, too, are a river that may change, or be changed, beyond recognition.)"

♦   ♦   ♦

To My Matilija

Where the canyon walls
Close in, and the air cools,
And the little green trout flick and hover
In the clear green pools
Between the falls:
Where that sturdy solitary, the slate-gray dipper, year round, sings
Till the steep stone rings
Is where I'll go, still unforgiving
Of others' and my own poor past
(How keep my mind clear and not curse
Doings that make life worse?)—
And be, Matilija, your lover
When I am dead, and at long last
Won't have to make a living.

♦   ♦   ♦

As for the agony
Clenching in me:
My own and others' imperfection,
Killing delight. . . .

On those clear pools my own reflection
Is broken light.

And in that steep stone cleft
What will be left
Of me is not the middling lover
Here, of a wife
With whom he gladly would live over
A second life—

Nor that one who'd begun
A better son,
Friend, father, in his own thinking,
Than he became—
So maimed in the doing (heart here sinking)
And yet the same.

Say all these disappear
Into the sheer
Fire of that anger—what's remaining?
Stranger, the sight,
Say, of the tall slim pale wild oats leaning,
In the late light,

Beautiful, on a stony rise
Before your eyes,
While you stand making out a crossing
Down where the stream
Slips roaring through boulders, and the spray's tossing,
And the alders gleam:

At such a moment, here
I'll come, tho' not appear,
But be coincident with your seeing
The shining scene
And in that moment have my being,
Unhuman, and serene.

◆   ◆   ◆

Martial of Bilbilis

Nothing in Rome escaped his glance, he understood
  This touchy sort of verse,
And mixed the poor ones with the good:
Your even book, he said, is worse.

Old and fed up, this son of Bilbilis went home,
    A harsh hill town with a cold
   River below, that shipped to Rome
   A lot of iron, a little gold.

ROBERT STONE

Robert Stone grew up in New York City, joined the Navy, attended N.Y.U. for a time, and later became one of Ken Kesey's "Merry Pranksters." A Stegner Fellow at Stanford in 1963, his novels include Children of Light *(1986),* A Flag for Sunrise *(1981), the National Book Award winner* Dog Soldiers *(1974), and* A Hall of Mirrors *(1968), Stone's first novel, from which the following passage has been taken.*

"For Robert Stone, writing *A Hall of Mirrors* was a way of coming to terms with personal and political upheavals, as he makes clear in his *Paris Review* interview: '*A Hall of Mirrors* was something I shattered my youth against. All of my youth went into it. I put everything I knew into that book. It was written through years of dramatic change, not only for me, but for the country. It covers the sixties from the Kennedy assassination through the civil rights movement to the beginning of acid, the hippies, the war. . . . One way or another it all went into the book.'"

The California of the Mind

ONE FLIGHT DOWN, HE came upon a bearded man in blue farmer's coveralls who was lying across the landing, balanced on an elbow. The man looked up at him with bright madman's eyes.

"Man," he said as Rheinhardt started for the lower story, "how you makin' it, man?"

"Good," Rheinhardt said. "How you makin' it?"

The man laughed a mock Negro laugh and ground his strangely white front teeth together. "Bad," he said, "bad news makin' it. You have a cigarette?"

The door of Bogdanovich's opened and a girl came out to them. She was about twenty-five, dark and slim with small black eyes and a pale long face; she reminded Rheinhardt for all the world of a homosexual yeoman who had once propositioned him at the Anacostia Naval Air Station.

"We have cigarettes in here, Marvin," she told the bearded man.

Rheinhardt looked at her. She was wearing a khaki officer's shirt and trousers with brown sandals.

"I've got some," Rheinhardt said. "Do you want one too?"

Marvin took a cigarette and laughed his Negro laugh again, baring his teeth at the girl.

He looked at them and saw that all—Bogdanovich, the girl, Mad Marvin—

were displaying what dear Natasha liked to call Philosopher's Eye; they were teaheads and they were quietly blasted. He felt a sudden rush of affection for them on Natasha's account.

"What was your scene?" Bogdanovich asked him softly.

"Oh, well . . ." Rheinhardt said. "New York."

"Of course," Bogdanovich said, with the manner of one who had graciously turned a compliment. Rheinhardt bowed.

"Tell me," he asked them, "did you know Natasha Kaplan?"

"Of course," Bogdanovich said.

"Of course," Marvin said. "I did."

"No, truly, man, did you know my Natasha?"

"Why not?" Marvin asked. Everyone looked thoughtful.

"She's in Wingdale," Rheinhardt told them.

"Ah," they said, and nodded approvingly.

"You were in Wingdale, Marvin," the dark girl asked, "did you know her?"

"When I was in Wingdale," Marvin said, "Listen—when I was in Wingdale—" he closed his eyes and moved his head from side to side. "There was nothing... there was nothing—that I knew!"

Everyone nodded again.

"But in the mountains—in the mountains, man—I knew all of it."

"Yes," Bogdanovich said.

"Truly," Marvin said. "Believe it."

"Of course," Bogdanovich said.

Marvin looked from face to face and stopped at Rheinhardt. "Man," he said, "that wasn't the California you know. No mufflers. No titty-tatty. No ogla bee. No gasoline-smell greasetrap taco stand plastic supermarket shit. No fatwoman drive-ins. No polite killer cops. No oregano salesmen. No Northbeach. No Southbeach. No Beach Beach. It wasn't like that, man—you think it was?"

"No," Rheinhardt said. "It couldn't have been."

"It couldn't have been," Marvin said soberly. "It could not have been. And it was not."

"It was a California of the mind," the girl said.

"My God," Bogdanovich said stepping forward in wide-eyed astonishment, "what a California that would be!" As they watched, he raised his hands to describe a box and held them palm facing palm. "Look," he told them, "that's your mind, dig? And here it's all gray, it's all nowhere, it's just dry and barren and terrible trips. But here, dig—at the western end there's a curving beach and white surf rolling up on it. And there's blue and purple islands and high cold mountains and forests with a carpet of pine needles. And orange juice in the clear desert."

"And orange juice in the desert!" the dark girl sighed. She put a hand to her mouth and moaned with longing.

"At that place, man. At the end of that dry hairiness, on the other side of the skeletons and the windies and the terrible salt flats, at the further edge of the bad trips—that's the California of the mind. Suddenly you find it there!"

"Yeah," Marvin said. "Tell more. Tell more!"

"Well, man, there's nothin' but miles of it ocean and prairie and rangeland and all of San Francisco and fair L.A.—all in the mind. And canyon creeks with trout and Herefords and velvety green hills of the mind, green and sweet smelling."

"Yeah," Marvin said.

"And fishing boats of the mind," the girl said.

"And abalones of the mind. And glider contests of the mind."

"Motorcycles of the mind. Chinatowns of the mind."

"And Chinamen of the mind."

"And wine of the mind," Rheinhardt said.

"Oh, shit yes, man!" Marvin said ecstatically, "and wine of the mind."

"Oaklands of the mind."

"And Watsonvilles of the mind."

"And cliffs and seals and sulfur baths of the mind. At the western end of your mind, man. All of it, man."

"And beautiful people," Marvin said.

"Beautiful people," the dark girl said, sighing again with longing.

"Yes," Bogdanovich said.

"We had raccoons," Marvin said. "At night—raccoons."

"Raccoons of the mind," Rheinhardt said idly.

"Fuck that," the girl said.

"Yeah," Marvin said. "Raccoons are groovy, but not so groovy are the raccoons of the mind."

"Oh," the girl said, shuddering now and moaning with revulsion, "the dirty raccoons of the mind."

"That's the worst kind of raccoons there are," Bogdanovich told them with a scholarly air. "The ravagey little raccoons of the mind."

"Are they in the mind's California?" the girl asked fearfully.

"No," Bogdanovich said, "the raccoons are actual raccoons."

"Thank God," the girl said.

Rheinhardt closed his eyes and saw the furry creatures of the night before—cavies of the mind. "How did you get down here?" he asked Bogdanovich.

"Who knows?" Bogdanovich said.

"How?" Marvin said. "Why does anyone come to California, man. The sea, the sky, the air, man!"

"This isn't California, Marv," the girl said gently. "This is Louisiana here."

Marvin started to his feet in alarm. "Louisiana," he cried. "Louisiana! Holy shit, man, that ain't no place to be! We gotta get out of here."

"Louisiana is where New Orleans *is,* man," the girl explained. "There's no way around it, actually. California was another time."

"That's right," Marvin agreed. "That's what it's all about, right?"

"Right," the girl said.

"Say," Rheinhardt said after a moment, "where can a man score around here?"

"Score what?" Bogdanovich asked him.

"Score what?" the girl said in a small voice.

"Yeah," Marvin said, "what is that—score?"

They looked at him angrily.

"Everything's cool," Rheinhardt said. "I'm not fuzz or anything. I'm just looking to score a lid."

"We don't know too much about that," Bogdanovich said. "Next to nothing."

"Hey Bogdan," Marvin said. "How come you always say that lately—next to nothing—what kind of a groove is that?"

"Well, I don't know," Bogdanovich said, turning away from Rheinhardt, "it's something people say. It sort of makes a picture."

"It sure does," Marvin said. "Like there's her and there's you and there's me and there's nothing. So I'm next to nothing."

"That's what I'm trying to convey, dig?"

"I'm always next to nothing," Marvin said. "Nothing is with me night and day."

"Marvin is an outsider," Bogdanovich explained.

"I see," Rheinhardt said. "Well I'll see you all later."

"Where are you off to?" Bogdanovich asked him.

"I thought I'd take a walk around."

"I'm going to the laundry. You want to walk me?"

"Sure," Rheinhardt said.

They left Marvin and the girl to listen to the *Pastoral* again and went out into the street. There were people out now, walking up from the bus stop at the French Market. The late afternoon fruit vendors pushed their carts before them calling their buyers with cries that were part Sicilian patois and part field holler.

"Trawberries . . . *tutti cuam'*."

They bought a bag each from an old man with dyed sideburns.

"Thanks, dad," Bogdanovich told him.

Chewing the huge sweet berries, wiping the rich juice from their mouths, they walked to Decatur Street.

"Oh, man," Bogdanovich said. "Strawberries."

Down at the levee the longshoremen were changing shifts, the bars and wine barrel rooms were full. Passing the Harbor Bar they saw a small fat Cuban bring his fist down on the glass topping of a pinball machine and look with triumphant malice at the shattered glass and the streaks of blood on his arm.

"*Chingo su madre*," he said. Groans and curses came from farther inside. A jukebox in the barrel house at the corner of St. Philip was playing "Walk Don't Run."

Bogdanovich took a running step across the sidewalk, and whirled to face Rheinhardt—fierce-eyed and brandishing the strawberry bag. "*Chingo su madre*," he said snarling. And he smiled. "I wish I could do that."

"Your mother?" Rheinhardt asked cautiously.

"Oh, no no no man," Bogdanovich said. "My mother! My poor old mother! No, I mean I wish I could take on the world and say—*Chingo su madre!*"

"I wish I could too," Rheinhardt said.

"But if I did the world would say—What? The world would say WHAT WAS THAT ABOUT MY MOTHER?"

"Then you would have had it," Rheinhardt agreed.

"The world would shake and crack and open up and down I'd go, man, and the world would say—THAT'S FOR WHAT YOU SAID ABOUT MY MOTHER."

"Thus conscience doth make cowards of us all," Rheinhardt said.

Linda Svendsen received a B.A. from the University of British Columbia, Vancouver, an M.F.A. from Columbia University, and was a Stegner Fellow at Stanford during 1980–81. Her fiction has appeared in The Atlantic *and other periodicals, and has been included in the* O. Henry Prize Stories 1983, The New Generation, *and* Best Canadian Stories 1980, 1981, *and* 1987. *Her first collection of stories will be published by Farrar, Straus & Giroux.*

"A white lie sparked this story. My brother, who'd lost custody of his kids and who'd been drinking, invited my sister's children to a distant beach. My sister, concerned about safety, made an excuse. When she told me this she started to cry, and then I did, because it was hard to see our brother hurt, and hurting himself, and to deny him the joy and respite of a simple picnic, with nephew and niece, one summer afternoon. In a workshop that fall, I wrote out of an almost wild need to heal—if not him, or her, then myself. Sometimes it felt like prayer."

◆   ◆   ◆

Who He Slept By

FIRST OUR MOTHER, ALTHOUGH I can't swear. Some summer afternoon, hot in Montreal, after a cool wipe and a quick caress of talcum, she might have lain down beside him on a blanket in shade, or in the darkest room in the house, Venetian blinds tight. Anyplace that would ease the chafing. Ray's eyes would close and she'd talk to her baby. *Who's a muggy boy? Who's my sticky? Who's a little heat wave?* She wouldn't nap; with her tongue, she might worry an ice cube into a suggestion of snow, and study Ray and wonder if he'd contract rashes she'd never heard of or seen. She was always on the lookout for treachery, crawling or flying or freakish.

The coolest spot may have been under the grand piano. After settling Ray, she would practice her winter repertoire. Softly, "Silver Bells," "Frosty." (When I was a child she did this too, exerting a maternal power over weather. *Listen, I'll put a bite in the air.* And after her concert, the room seemed somehow lighter, chillier.) Maybe this was when he acquired a predisposition for ladies' feet and ankles, and later, when he could view the keyboard, for fingers and flexible wrists. "Watch her tickle those ivories," he'd say when he was older.

Ray's father prospected for asbestos. When he was away, staking claims, Mum probably carried Ray into their wide double bed. She watched him breathe; she said she could watch her babies breathe for hours. Anticipating their eventual arch, she traced his eyebrows with a finger dampened by saliva. Even if I was blind, she'd say, I could pick my baby out of an orphanage. She could honestly assert this, not only because she knew Ray's shape and weight, but because her scent upon him was implicit, perfect.

They would sleep facing each other, a human palm apart. If dreams leave the body in breaths, as evil spirits enter in sneezes, who knows what his gentle inhalation drew.

I don't know; in 1940 I was not alive. When there are no early memories, I invent them or go without. In Ray's case, my brother's, I do a little of both. When I was six, he was twenty. I turned twenty, he was thirty-four. He had always been old enough to invent me.

Our mother believed what little she read. When she first moved to Quebec, before Ray's birth, she noticed that all the bridges were named Pont. On the West Coast a different name existed for every crossing—Lion's Gate, Capilano, Patullo. She thought it must be so disorienting for the French with this Pont Bridge, Pont Bridge everywhere.

Then, at a particularly somber birthday supper, Ray's, a few years ago, our mother mentioned the report of an American doctor. She urged this newspaper filler into the realm of premonition and hindsight through her tone of voice. She altered its impact, the same way she had influenced seasons, raised and lowered temperatures, when we were children. "He says that who you sleep by determines your dreams. That's something to consider." Then she presented Ray's lit cake and asked him to make a wish.

In 1959, Ray was nineteen, two fathers wiser, and working as a spare at Vancouver Wharves. His first girl friend, Velma, worked in a beauty parlor doing manicures and shampoos. One Sunday they drove to Spanish Banks and Mum sent me along. She must have read that sibling responsibility curbed passion.

As soon as their towels kissed sand, they sent me on errands. After delivering their fish and chips, I made a separate trip for each condiment. Salt, ketchup, vinegar. They sent me for 7-Up, straws, ice cream and extra napkins, for the transistor radio baking on the dashboard.

"Go look for shells," Ray said when I came back from the parking lot. "Go dig a hole to China."

Velma was usually very friendly. Skinny and quiet, she would bring spoils from the salon: Adorn, nail hardeners, hairnets that would strangle goldfish. She would let me hold the heated towel while she shampooed Ray's hair; this act usually took half an hour. She moved her hands every imaginable way, assuaging with fingertips and knuckles, tapping, tugging, scratching his head as if seeking entrance. And then rinses. Egg yolk, flat beer, lemon rinse for highlight, baking soda for manageability, and vinegar for purity. She wrapped the towel around his head and they shuffled to his bedroom to use our mother's hair dryer. Velma would leave me with a new shade of polish and instructions. Always stroke away from yourself, she told me.

At the beach that day, I squirmed closer to her oiled body. When I grew up I wanted to dye my hair her color.

"Go pick up litter," Ray suggested. "Make yourself useful to society."

"Raymond," Velma said.

He handed me a dime. "Treat yourself to the trampolines."

"Where?"

"Across from the fish and chips."

"I don't want to jump."

"I'll make you want to jump."

I bounced with other kids, flags of noisy color, in the air. At the peak of each jump, I scanned the beach, trying to distinguish Ray and Velma from the other sunbathers. But they blended with all the other bodies and I stretched out, flat, on the trampoline. Through the straps, I stared at the puddles below and knew that the ocean was quietly escaping. Then the guy yelled that my time was up.

Velma was pushing back Ray's cuticles with a coffee stirring rod when I returned.

"Back already?"

I didn't answer him.

"Want to be buried in sand, Adele?" He used my name when he meant business.

"No."

Velma suggested we all go in the water, but Ray said I had to remain on shore to frighten beach burglars. I started to cry. Some teenage gals, two towels over, volunteered to guard the site if they could change the station on our radio. Ray said, "O.K. But Adele, stay in the shallow part."

I stood in water up to my knees, listlessly filling a bright yellow pail with the waves I met, then emptying them out.

They went far beyond my depth. Velma hoisted herself onto Ray's shoulders, her thighs clenched around his neck, and he sang "Blow the Man Down," something nautical. They laughed and splashed, Velma shielding her hair with a free hand, protecting a recent tint. I saw Ray toss Velma into the water and push her shoulders under the surface. Then her head. Everything suddenly seemed silent, as it had when I'd looked below the trampoline, and then Velma emerged, gasping, and started paddling toward me.

"You dink," she called at Ray.

Ray floated on his back.

When he joined us on shore, afterwards, Velma looked up at him. "What gets into you?"

He said he was only teasing, couldn't she take a joke, didn't she know he was the Purple People Eater.

They didn't talk. Ray turned his face in the other direction, toward the Pacific Ocean. I packed wet sand into my pail, turned it upside down, and eased out castles. I dug narrow moats around them until I was bored.

I thought Ray was asleep. Velma's hand rested on the small of his back, her nails bright as the buoys bobbing in the distance. Crouching beside him, I avoided his cheek and then carefully lifted the eyelid; I wanted to see his eye drifting and vulnerable. But his eye, unmoving, gazed directly at me. He wasn't really asleep; he was pretending.

A mermaid cupping her blue breast: Ray and our cousin Jackson had identical tattoos on their forearms. They also longshored together.

After rinsing cargo sulphur from their eyes and showering, they spent their evenings fishing for diversion. They parked on mountaintops for optimum short-wave reception and once tuned in Hong Kong. Witnessed demolition derbies and sometimes crossed into Washington state where bars served until dawn. They met sullen Haida sisters at hotels near the harbor, loved them rude and slow, and asked for Indian burns. Ray saved brassieres that he and Jackson identified by cologne and sweat rings—"Sue in October. C." He kept the collection in his glove compartment.

The winter of 1964, Ray and Jackson sat home with girl friends and Cheezies to watch hockey. After the playoffs, Jackson became engaged to Pat and decided to enlist with the RCMP. "Jackson's going to be a Dudley," Ray commented. "A Do Good."

At Jackson's wedding, that June, Ray acted as usher. He was supposed to be the best man, but Jackson's brother had pulled the longer straw.

Ray started drinking before the ceremony, bracing his breakfast juice with white rum. After our mother and stepfather departed, he offered me a taste. "You're old enough to be corrupted."

"I like it," I said.

"Drink up."

On our way to pick up Ray's date, Nadine, I honked the horn indiscriminately and Ray made a few U-turns. He turned the tightest U's. We had devoted the previous afternoon to folding Kleenex into frail blossoms, and attaching them to the car as if they grew there naturally. I climbed over the seat when Ray opened the front door for Nadine. Do something about those rolling bottles, he told me, and I placed my white patent shoes upon them. Nadine never complimented the car; she spoke in serious tones about her Arabian's fetlock.

Nadine lived in Shaughnessy, the rich section of Vancouver, and worked for a travel agency, Funseekers. Twice a year, she holidayed in Waikiki. Twice a week, she performed her equestrienne routines. Ray attended her events at the Agrodome and would sometimes allow me to come. Children under twelve were admitted free.

I liked listening to Ray watch her. He predicted her moves, her strategies with doting accuracy. *Watch her bite flank with that spur. Now she's neck reining. She knows where to put her weight.* The horse responded to the slightest suggestion of her thigh; Ray was correct. Even her tongue moistening her lips seemed to indicate a specific command—I could sense that. She wore boots and her nails were as blunt as her conversation, and she kept them that way intentionally; if they were longer, they would hamper grooming. She always seemed to be looking ahead to the next obstacle, past it.

When the judging was concluded, Ray met her at the stables. Once he had pushed a finger, sideways, across her mouth. "Chafing for a bit?" he'd asked.

She had slapped his hand. "Smarten up." Then smiled, apologetically.

She smiled often at the reception; congratulated Jackson and Pat. In the receiving line, Ray usurped the position of best man and stood beside Jackson, embracing every woman. "Ray the Ush," he introduced himself. Nadine politely joined my parents and me. I asked her opinion about a television series starring a talking horse; she said she'd never heard of it. Smiling vaguely, she stared at Ray.

Ray waited until the second chorus of "Telstar" before cutting in on Jackson and Pat's first dance as newlyweds. He spun the laughing Jackson across the floor and then they returned to Pat, giggling and pale, enfolding her in their arms. The three clung to each other in the spotlight.

Later I saw Ray and Nadine attempting the beer-barrel polka; she led. I wanted to twist with my brother, who had taught me, but he declined. "Got to save my strength for the garter," Ray said. "Go ask an uncle."

When Jackson tossed the garter and Pat her bouquet, neither Ray nor Nadine was present. I hoped: elopement, riding lessons under Nadine's expert guidance, saddle sores I would never mention. At the gift table, I was appraising three toasters, deciding which ones I'd return, when my mother accosted me.

"Where's your brother?"

We searched the cabaret; our parents knew he was not in exemplary driving condition. Exhausted, they chose to assume that Nadine had commandeered the wheel and that the couple were safely at home, sipping coffee and comparing test patterns. Nothing else.

Ray's car was not parked in the street.

I couldn't sleep; I knew where they were. At the stables, measuring each other's height in hands, or snuggling in straw and being nuzzled by long-nosed horses with white stars or blazes. Except for his socks, they probably had taken off all their clothes, hung them on nails, and kissed. I fell asleep picturing a soft foal watching them, whinnying, and forgot to slide the wedding cake under my pillow.

Jackson called in the morning. He told us that Ray had spent the night with him and Pat, at their apartment, and had just left. He said they had fried eggs and talked until five, about women, the waterfront, unions, and then passed out on the living room rug, side by side.

Twelve years later, Jackson stood as godfather to my son. He wore the distinctive red jacket of the Mounted Police. We reminisced about our weddings and he mentioned Ray's impromptu visit, how understanding Pat had been. Jackson laughed. "Ray just wanted to talk. He wanted to talk about how hard it was to be a man." Then he looked at me, sober, as if for corroboration.

Ray spent two weeks in southern California and peripheral Mexico, a town called Dos Reales, early in 1966. Although he had just earned his forklift operator certificate, he was restless and discontented at the piers. His friends convinced him to travel and so he worked weekends, night shift, double time, time and a half. He saved.

I still have his postcard of Alcatraz, obscured by fog, with some scribbled message about the Birdman. And I clearly remember his tan, next to our winter skins, making him seem like a strange guest when he returned.

We were looking at my slides of Europe, a few years ago, when he mentioned this trip. Ray and I were thirty-five and twenty-one, old and comfortable enough to talk openly. I had just admitted that the true story wasn't revealed in the photographs, and told him about making love with a Danish boy on the hovercraft between England and France. He listened, then asked if I wanted to hear about south of the border.

Dos Reales: he breakfasted at the poolside, tequilas, and decided to walk to the main part of town. He was amazed that donkeys still carried sacks of avocados, amazed that poinsettias still grew wild.

A procession of twenty women, veiled in black, crept by him. Hands stroked rosaries, and their knees must have been scratched raw by the rocky paths and highways. Somebody explained that it was Lent and these women had traveled miles on a pilgrimage of repentance. Ray was amazed that people still practiced devotion.

In town he browsed for souvenirs—a poncho for Mum, a sombrero for our stepfather. A young boy no older than fourteen, whose voice had just begun to change, asked Ray if he would like to converse with his sister. Hesitantly, he added, ten American dollars. Very pretty tits.

"*Mañana*," Ray replied, and strolled away. But the boy persisted and soon Ray thought some Mexican pussy might not be a bad idea. The market was crowded and hot; it had been a while.

Ray understood they would go to a hotel or the back of some cantina. Instead, the boy took him to a squat adobe house, near the beach, and introduced him to Capulina.

"*Gracias,* Mister Ray," she said.

She was only twelve, with hair falling below her waist, hiding tiny moles on her back. She invited him into her bedroom and he noted the sagging cot, the Crucifix over the door, a pastel of the Virgin on Capulina's trunk. She got on her knees.

He told me he stayed with her all that afternoon, woke and ate a late supper with her aunt and brother, then spent the entire evening. She wanted to learn English, he said. So he counted numbers on her slender fingers and he taught her nouns—earlobe, hard, cut-offs, bruise.

He marveled at the tininess and tirelessness of her hands and mouth. He watched her bathe his feet and slip her tongue around the toes and soles. During the night she slept on top of him, a full smaller shadow.

Months after that, he worried he may have caught something incurable: a desire for skilled little girls.

I shut off the projector and we sat there.

"It was great," he said, then reminded me. "You were twelve years old then too, Adele."

Ray married Bonnie, who did not deliver the promise of her name. Bonnie of the backcombed hair, who teased herself into an optical illusion six inches taller and wore slippers so fuzzy her feet looked shocked. She worked at the stationery store and her envelopes arrived as frequently as advertising flyers. While Ray seduced her, she courted our family. Greetings from Bonnie, forever. Just a note to say; from Bonnie's abode to yours. Cards with sickly elves and pictures of wheat bending in the wind. She made me skeptical of good intentions.

Bonnie bore this thoughtfulness and legibility into the bedroom. I knew Ray had slept with her because her name would be generously written, if not all over him, somewhere. Where the watchband had been, Bonnie, or on the jugular, Bonnie, or on the big toe.

He loved her; it was obvious. He spent evenings folding sheets with her at the laundromat, making corners meet perfectly. He visited a butcher with her and bragged about pricing cuts, the economics of freezing. While she struggled with sit-ups, he secured her feet and watched her unfailing chin rise toward him. He paid for her fillings, stopped seeing other women, and worked steadily, after a drinking suspension of three months. The kitchen table in his apartment was strewn with Bonnie snaps; and there were a select few by his bed, signed.

Ray slept with Bonnie for five years, 1968–1973, more in sickness than in health. Early in their marriage, he must have made the mistake of tactless or embellished confession. Perhaps, after a brisk shower together and a slower drying out, when talk comes easily, she had inquired about the aquatic woman nestled on his arm. The past. And Ray, confident in her sympathy, had told her about Velma, little Capulina, the skittish horseback rider. About Jill at Hertz; Faye, whom Bonnie had focused upon in our parents' movies of a New Year's Eve. Weights, textures, techniques—inventive, intuitive, or the idealistic blend.

Consequently, Bonnie convinced herself of his infidelity. An excursion for cigarettes indicated a cheap trick. Lilacs, and he was wooing a florist. The waterfront raised possibilities: stowaways, overtime, empty warehouses. At noon, she delivered his lunch, sandwiches and a cold beer, to the docks, sniffed his clothes and kissed him.

To pacify her, Ray stayed home and watched television; she became jealous of soap women, and accused him of fantasizing. Once she thought she caught him jerking off to an erotic commercial.

Ray worked on graveyard shift. He hoped her sleep might be a respite for them both. In the morning he found her crumpled on the couch, curled and defenseless. She was still dressed in her clothes of the day before and had covered herself with an old car coat. In her grogginess, she asked him, "What am I going to do?"

Ray looked into her red eyes. "You have to trust," he said.

He drank more often; she paged him at bars and tailed him in her car. "You must not love me because you drink," she said.

He said, "I drink because I love you."

One night he hit her; knocked her across the kitchen and against the stove. She called the police and Ray was arrested for assault. Disheveled and quiet, she bailed him out the next morning and dropped charges. Ray guessed she suspected the policewomen.

During the next year, Bonnie innovated a series of terminal illnesses that demanded Ray's time and sobriety. He chauffeured her to X-rays, ECGs, blood tests, check-ups. Brain tumor, varieties of cancer, acute murmurs. The doctors were indefinite; she gave herself six months every three months, until her pregnancy.

I visited Ray and Bonnie for a weekend and helped them prepare the baby's room. We painted the walls an undersea hue, a muted aquamarine, and sanded the floors. Diapers, rubber pants, a white basket holding ointments and pins— Ray showed me these as if they were rare discoveries. Bonnie showed us how she would pant during labor.

She miscarried. I don't like to think how or why. Ray didn't sleep in their bedroom when she was in the hospital; he stayed in what would have been the child's room, wrapped in a sleeping bag.

When she was released, Bonnie didn't call Ray as they'd arranged. She took a taxi home instead, dropped off her suitcase and gathered some things, then proceeded to Ballantyne pier.

It was a drizzling Vancouver day and Ray was driving a tractor in the huge hold of a ship, the *Argo*. He leveled hills of salt, pushing them into the loading apparatus. Bonnie ignored the trespassing and danger signs, the foreman, and walked up the gangway, then along the dock to Ray's hold. She screamed to him, sixty feet below, and when he didn't hear, because of the noise of the motor and conveyor belts, she unpacked her bag and pitched the layette into his line of vision. She threw diapers, bibs, a terry giraffe, a rattle.

He quickly shut off the engine and asked her what in hell she was doing.

And she wept, because he wanted her pregnant so he could fuck other women, because her baby had gone to Limbo.

Ray met Maria at a hotel near the grain elevators. She was a barmaid. She gave him free rum, soon followed by room and board. I saw them together only once, at the dinner our parents gave for Ray's birthday. I was majoring in anthropology and pondered Ray and his amour with the biases of a 1974 sophomore. I studied them as I would have a culture on the verge of extinction.

Ray wore discount chic: a shiny polyester shirt with sunsets sinking on the pockets. Maria wore some sort of a baseball cap and a neck brace, because of an old car injury. She was blonde and Portuguese and her voice was husky from two decades of cigarettes. They both spoke the same language. "Adele, hang loose," they said. "Don't be so uptight."

Ray had been laid off from work and Mum asked about his unemployment insurance. He hadn't applied for it. He blamed his laziness on a dose of mononucleosis that had lasted thirty-four years. Sooner or later, he expected compensation. "I live on her tips until then," he said. "I live on her cupcakes," he said to me, conspiratorial. It slowly hit me that my brother might be an asshole.

Maria spoke to me in the basement, where I was killing time stacking coasters. She put her hand on my arm: her nails were chewed halfway to the moons, and the skin that should have been exposed to the air was painted with gloss.

"You're a smart girl, your brother tells me. He's very proud of you. Do you care for your brother very much?"

I nodded, and she kept on running her sentences together.

She told me she loved Ray very much and that soon they might put a down payment on a camper van, but she was concerned about him. Maria said she'd been taking Somas for her neck spasm since the accident, and the pills were disappearing. She hoped Ray wasn't stealing them. He was so tired lately. He couldn't even get it up anymore, said his penis was crooked since birth.

"I don't want to hear this," I said.

She laughed. "Oh, you're so young. Soon you'll be seeing men."

"I already do." My tone was too defensive, revealing the boys' level: awkward and goal-oriented sex.

"Good for you, Adele." She looked sad, as if I'd snubbed her. "Have fun," she said, and walked back upstairs.

Unashamedly, I added Ray to a list: read books outside your field, defrost fridge, call your brother. Sometimes I invited him for lunch and heated up frozen pizza.

I was up late studying for finals when Ray phoned from Maria's apartment. "Adele," he said. "I can't wake her up."

I'm living in Osoyoos now, a village in the interior, and expecting my second child. Up north, my husband works on the DEW, or Distant Early Warning, Line for two months at a time. He tracks the sky for the unexpected: a missile, satellites precarious in their orbits, space debris.

Ray visits occasionally: it's only a day's drive from Vancouver. Whenever he disagrees with Gretel, about every six weeks, he arrives with three cases of beer and says, "Know any smart teachers? Any practical nurses?" By Sunday after-noon, he's anxious to reconcile with his so-called kumquat. I've never met Gretel; she supposedly was a champion swimmer, butterfly stroke, and Ray threatens to bring her Commonwealth medals to prove it. She works in a delicatessen now and keeps their larder stocked with sausages and cheeses. He never mentions Maria.

Ray and I discuss the waterfront, how boring the job is and what little it means. I try to make him part of an international scheme, show him his place in the promise of Canada, how he implements growth: the potash and sulphur from the prairies fertilize Japanese fields, wood chips from our forests provide paper for China, coal turns steel mills in South America, and grains feed the drifting continents. I worry about being condescending and don't even convince myself.

He changes the subject. "You have it good," he begins. "A house, credit, the kid."

He loves Graham.

The last time Ray stayed, a few weeks ago, he wanted to take Graham, who is two, and me back with him to view an air show. He'd seen it the previous year and described all the loops, spins, and formations. Riding on the wing. Skydiving.

"Adele, you've got to see the Blue Angels."

"I know."

"And you should see the Snowbirds, too. They're Canadian."

He mentioned that admission was ten bucks per car, so the more bods the better. Gretel would make sandwiches.

I had to make an excuse, because I couldn't tell him that I was too frightened to drive with him. He drives recklessly; Graham is two; I'm expecting. And I thought, how can I let him down?

We stayed up late and watched the pornographic French films on the CBC. Staying up late with Ray; it was something I had always begged to do as a child. I had faked nightmares and coughs, bit my own arm, anything. Now his companionship was a given.

"I'm beat," I said, before the credits. "Goodnight."

"Sweet dreams, kid," he said.

I covered up Graham and heard Ray pulling out the hide-a-bed.

I slept by my brother once. When I was thirteen and he was twenty-seven, we drove to Medicine Hat to visit Jackson and his wife. Our mother insisted I accompany him; I could read maps and watch for careless deer. Plying Ray with the companionship of a little sister, she protected him from dangers: night driving, night drinking.

The first hundred miles we sang old jingles together, about Brylcreem's "little dab" and the Polaroid Swinger, "it's not like a camera, it's almost alive." Ray took a picture of me by a model of the Ogopogo, a monster in Okanagan Lake. After that, when mountains stood in the way of radio, I read, and read by glaciers, Rocky Mountain goats, and foothills; I missed all the natural phenomena. We spoke at gas stations and burger stands. In Calgary, while searching for access to the Trans-Canada, Ray said that his father, now an oil man, might live there somewhere.

At chapter breaks, I counted how many pages to the end. At the end of a book, I estimated the distances between stops.

On the return trip, we were caught in a prairie storm. Hailstones the size of watch faces pelted the car and Ray couldn't see more than a few feet beyond the headlights. We checked into a small hotel in a town where the power had failed; two separate rooms. We requested a double with single beds but that wasn't available.

I didn't undress. I looked out the window at the new lightning, sheet lightning I found out later, and wondered if I was grounded. People who were struck by lightning often disappeared, I knew.

I knocked on Ray's door. "I'm scared," I said.

Ray had already been asleep. He was only wearing his shorts, and his face was creased from the pillow. "Crawl in," he said.

Pulling up the sheet, I laid on top of it and settled the other blankets, those on my side, over me. I wanted to maintain our respectful distances. Ray was too tired to notice this peculiarity. He turned over on his stomach and was soon breathing evenly.

I watched the flashes outside the window, each one a shock, illuminate his ribs, spine, the globe of his head, and I saw the town suddenly light up again in unfamiliar neon. I heard the thunder, moving east, and I slept soundly, safely.

HELEN PINKERTON TRIMPI

*Helen Pinkerton (Trimpi) has published three collections of poems (*Error Pursued, *1959,* Poems 1946–1976, *1984, and* "The Harvesters" and Other Poems on Works of Art, *1984) and edited translations of the odes of Pindar. Her critical and scholarly work includes several essays on modern poetry, scholarly articles in American studies, and the recently published* Melville's Confidence Men and American Politics in the 1850s. *She is lecturer in English at College of Notre Dame in Belmont, California, and in 1988 was visiting professor at the University of Alberta.*

"These two poems belong to a series of short poems on works of art that was begun in 1983 and is still in progress. The form is a nine-line stanza, occasionally doubled or tripled. The structure is meditative: description, meditation, and colloquy. It should not be necessary to have seen the work of art to comprehend the poem but knowing it should add to the understanding."

◆   ◆   ◆

On Rembrandt's Self Portrait (1658) in the Frick Museum

A luminescence thrusts aside the dark
To mold a hand and lip more real than mine—
Solid in presence, searching to contain
Or say some word, if only by suggestion.
All of your faces ask some question: Paul,
Bathsheba, Aristotle, old Dutch merchants,
Titus, Tobias; your many differing selves,
So constant in contemplative inquiry.
Is that your truth, simply to ask a question?

◆   ◆   ◆

On G. B. Tiepolo's Etching "Adoration of the Magi" (1753) in the Stanford Museum

Plump cherubs ride the star-rays down to see
The Gentiles honor gentle Mary's child,
A tomb his seat, hay-thatch his canopy.

The oldest kneels. A younger waits. A third
Obscurely muffles his face in folds. Time past,
Time present, and Time future hint the Word,
Its timelessness, but fail to solemnize
The mood, as unpretentious as the child—
As you, Joseph, with sleepy, steadfast eyes.

Born in New York City in 1928, I came to Stanford as an undergraduate in 1946, and, after getting a Harvard doctorate, returned here to teach in the English Department in 1957. I have worked primarily in classical, medieval, and renaissance literatures—with some attention to their permutations in the seventeenth through the twentieth centuries.

"'The Desert House' describes, first, the landscape and way of life beside Camelback Mountain outside of Scottsdale, Arizona, at the turn of 1940; and second, a return to that house, now a resort hotel, to find how fragile the desert had been in the face of urban encroachment. 'For the Living' is in memory of Arthur Yvor Winters as teacher and friend."

◆　　◆　　◆

For the Living

To the memory of A. Y. W.

To know that one who died still lives
Is his bequest: for we, the living,
Live by a knowledge of his giving,
And we, the dead, forget he gives.

◆　　◆　　◆

The Desert House

Scottsdale, 1936–43: 1968—for Abbie

They built the house together.
Pepper and palmtree, olive and sharp mesquite,
Transplanted, slowly root, while, undelayed,
　　The seasons in the absent weather
Slip into light as shadows into shade.
The deep adobe walls dispel the heat.

　　Paths edged with tile and mortar.
Portico, lawn, and fountain—the curving spout,
A madonna's hands—guesthouse and lighted pool;

A courtyard where the servants quarter.
Beyond a sun-hat, bowl, and garden stool
A four-foot wall has kept the desert out.

    Workmen quietly chalking
The terrace brick: too distant to enquire,
She watches through the flowers that she arranges
    The child and gardener closely talking.
The clarity which rims the palest ranges
Hides nothing to compel her to desire.

    Each luminous relation
Offers the closer objects in its snare,
Till she, in quest of nothing, only waits.
    And all space narrows to duration:
What is to happen she anticipates
As recompense for what had not been there.

    The present, shy transgressor,
Touches and leaves her, and with the empty light
In memory or foreign silence rests:
    The past and future repossess her.
They sell the house—an inn, now, where as guests
We note those renovations which are slight.

    Heavy doors from the missions,
High-glassed and dowelled, still almost touch the tile
On changeless thresholds into changing halls.
    The old lines vanish in additions:
Where they converged once from the swirl of walls,
Suspended like a floating compass dial.

    Lies true the fast-moored fountain.
With tiny gardens cottages displace
The sage and greasewood, room on drifting room;
    The white drives, rising, mark the mountain;
New seasons circle in the civic fume.
Traveling, shadowless still, without a trace.

SCOTT TUROW

Scott Turow was a Mirrielees Fellow at Stanford from 1970 to 1972, and a Jones Lecturer there from 1972 to 1975. A practicing lawyer, he is the author of One L *(1977), about his law school experience, and* Presumed Innocent *(1987), a novel.*

"This story, written during my second year as a writing fellow, was inspired while I was driving my wife, Annette, to work one morning. Beside a stoplight, I saw a young girl and boy. She was all in white and beyond control with laughter, but her merriment did not spread to him. He was sober, concerned. I imagined that it was she that worried him."

◆　　　◆　　　◆

Some Things Promised, Some Things Dreamed

"WHAT," HE ASKS, "WHAT are you thinking?" He sits in his chair under a lamp, a book on his lap. "When I was fourteen—"

Her fists beat down. *"Fif-*teen."

"If you go in the kitchen," he says, "you will find a calendar, and on that calendar you will see that it is April. You were born in May. *May.* So unless you have started counting like the Chinese, you are fourteen, and when I was fourteen girls did not go to parties which lasted until one o'clock in the morning. Boys or no boys."

"Daaaddy," she moans thrusting forward her small face, the chin lividly blemished, her features still too clouded for him to be certain that when they emerge any week now, any day, it will be in close imitation of beauty. "I didn't say they would be there. I just said they might sort of drop in. Like crash—y'know?"

"Jennifer, where do you get these ideas? Where—"

He cuts himself off and watches her. Her fists thresh again in the air. She twists, shrugs, winces, murmurs. "Shit."

Where? He looks down to his book and reads a sentence and sighs. "Ask your mother, Jennifer."

"I'm not *ask*-ing anybody. I'm *tell*-ing you. And I already told her and she said to tell you."

He rubs his own chin and says, "Well, things sure are different."

"*Thank God*," she answers and picks up her saddle bag purse from the coffee table and slams out the door.

He is thinking about his daughter.

"You gonna do it?" Bo asks her.

"I don't know," she says, "I'll tell you later."

"Whatever you say, chicken." Bo is sixteen and tall and very well-muscled. He is black and Jennifer is white. He lives on the other side of town by the freeway and the factories and Jennifer thinks he is mysterious: she thinks he is the most mysterious person in the whole mysterious world. Her parents met him once and did not say a word against him. Not a word for him either. Now she lies when she goes out with him. They will find out, she knows. They will find out and make a big stink. About lying. Not the boy himself, Jennifer. About lying. She doesn't care. Hard cheese, she'll say when they find out, makes tough shit. They will look at her as if to ask where she got something like that. From Bo. But she won't tell them that.

"Quiet," she says to him. "Where are we going?"

Bo remains leaned against the lamppost, scuffing a shoe on the pavement. Large stucco homes roost behind their smooth lawns across the street.

"Everybody's gonna be at Stanley's for a while," she tells him. "You wanna go there?"

"Uh uh," says Bo.

"Come on," she says, "it'll be cool. Sondra had her palm read this afternoon. At least she said she was going to. It costs $25 and she still had to get some more from her father. But I'll bet she did. Don't you wanna hear? I think it'll be cool."

Bo kicks the lamppost once.

"Well, whatta you wanna do?" she asks.

"Nothin," Bo says.

"Nothing? Oh, I don't wanna just wander around having a shitty time. Come on. Let's go to Stanley's. Come on."

She walks past him and Bo takes hold of her bottom through the long floral print dress.

"Bo!" She wheels, raising her purse to the height of her shoulder.

Bo is laughing, his arms crossed over his chest to contain himself. "Let's go to my house," he says.

"Later," she answers and loops her purse once through the air. She walks off on her toes, exactly like Leslie Caron did in *Gigi* which is a movie she saw on tv last week.

Everybody is at Stanley's, Howie and Gary and Vicky and Ricky and Rudy and Sondra. They are in the pine-sided basement rec room, smoking cigarettes and listening to Stanley's parents' stereo. Sondra is in the center of the circle talking about her palm reading.

"Did you get all the bread from your father?" Gary asks.

"Most of it," says Sondra, "but I was saving up. My aunt sent me a nightgown for my birthday and I cashed it in at Saks."

"Well, what happened?" asks Rudy.

Sondra tells them: that an old black lady dressed like a gypsy came out from behind a curtain and read her fortune in her palm. She told Sondra that she would go far away sometime in the future, and her life would be filled with mystic surprises. She told Sondra her life line was long.

"How neat," Vicky says.

"And she does her own horoscopes too. Reads the stars herself," Sondra says. "She believes in fourteen signs and they're all screwed up. I'm a Pisces instead of a Taurus. Isn't that something?"

"Oh wow," Ricky says.

They all talk about their signs, what they might become on the gypsy's chart. Stanley Kruger moves over and tries to get between Bo and Jennifer. Accidentally he puts his hand on Jennifer's back. He leaves it there.

Howie says his brother in college smoked some great grass when he was home for the weekend. Howie says he can get some, almost for sure.

"My sister smoked some that was soaked in DMT," Sondra says.

"Oh, that's a bummer," Howie tells her.

Jennifer looks at Bo. He lies on the floor, supported on an elbow, eating continuously from a bowl of raisins. He has on gold pants and a white T-shirt and his muscles ripple beneath the shirt-sleeve.

Stanley Kruger moves his hand around to Jennifer's side. She leans away quickly. She reaches to the bowl of raisins and throws one at Stanley. Everyone laughs. Stanley throws a raisin back at Jennifer and everyone begins shouting and throwing raisins at everyone else. Somebody knocks over a table and the parakeet screeches as it beats its wings wildly in its cage and Stanley shouts for them all to stop and help him clean up before his parents get home.

"Wasn't it neat throwing all of those raisins?" Jennifer asks. They are walking toward the intersection.

"Sure," says Bo.

"Oh, it *was* neat," says Jennifer.

"We goin to my house?" Bo asks.

"Sure," says Jennifer.

"You gonna?"

Jennifer grabs her purse with both hands and runs to the stoplight.

Jennifer is doing it for the fourth time, stepping off the curb with her arms rigid before her, her eyes dead ahead, tranced. She does not flinch as the headlights grow brighter. The oncoming traffic jams to a halt spilling a vortex of warm wind around her as she continues in the crosswalk.

Bo sits on the opposite curb, holding her purse. She laughs when she reaches his side, looks back quickly at the stopped cars, and laughs harder. "Isn't that great?" she asks. "Isn't that wild?"

Bo seems to shake his head.

"Oh, Bo," she says, "you're *so* uptight." She takes her purse from him. "Why don't you ever say anything? You just sit there like a lump."

Bo stands up.

"Honestly. Everybody thinks you're really neat, and you never say a *thing* to them."

"Ah," Bo says, "they're just kids."

"But they like you."

"We goin to my house?"

"Sure," Jennifer says, "why not?"

They go to Bo's house. They go whenever his parents are not home. Bo cuts her a piece of chocolate cake in the kitchen but Jennifer does not eat it because of her complexion. Then they go to Bo's room. There are photographs on the walls, pin-ups and action snaps of a football team. Bo sits on his bed and she sits on Bo's lap. "You gonna do it?" Bo asks.

She chews on a strand of her hair. "I don't know," she says finally. "Maybe I'll do something else you want me to."

Bo rolls his eyes and throws his arms out and falls back against the wall.

"We oughta take some precautions, y'know," Jennifer says, smiling slightly. The word makes her feel important. "Have you ever thought of that? It could happen, y'know."

Bo looks the other way.

"Well," Jennifer says and stalks to the center of the room. She waits for him to say something but he doesn't. He never does. That is Bo. "Do you wanna break up?" she asks at last. "Is that it?"

"I didn't say that."

"We could still be friends," she says. "Vicky and Ricky were going together and they're still friends. You saw."

"Hmm," Bo says, in a way that reminds her a little of her father.

"Well, is that what you want?"

Bo sits up. "Stanley Kruger sure would like that."

"Stanley Kruger? That's really funny, that really is. Ha. Stanley Kruger." Excited, she laughs to prove how funny that is. Sometimes Bo frightens her, but there is something wonderful about his saying Stanley's name. It makes her like him again. She comes near to the bed. "Well," she says.

"Well," says Bo.

"Well, I have to get home pretty soon."

"Father waitin?"

"Always," answers Jennifer languorously and sits down on Bo's lap again.

"What now?" his wife asks as he puts down the phone. She is at the head of the stairwell, behind the bend so he cannot see her.

"That was Helen Kruger. She said Jennifer and a few of her friends made quite a mess over there. They found Stanley trying to clean it up."

"Oh my God," his wife says.

"Helen said she thought we should know. Bless her."

"Oh my God," his wife says again. "Where does it come from? Tell me. Did we teach her to act like that?"

"Where does it come from?" he asks himself and goes back to his book, his chair. The bedroom door closes solidly upstairs and the large house settles around him. The plants waver faintly on the mantel; the collie's claws click audibly as he moves around out on the porch. Where does it come from? Out of the air, he supposes, out of the times. There is too much turmoil now in all regards, everything pushed to extremes. Jennifer is like a worm, digesting what she cannot burrow through. And just as blind. Last week his wife displayed to him the items she had pilfered from Jen's drawers. Butts which did not look like cigarettes. A book that might have embarrassed Kinsey. He thumbed a few pages before he made up his mind: just getting used to the idea of boys and girls. "You shouldn't worry," he told his wife. She snapped the book back and asked him, "Who else should?"

That is the point, he guesses; he cannot pretend he has much choice. It is his assignment now to worry, to wonder. Not that he doubts Jen, not really, though he's unsure she'd say the same of him. The simplest things he can no longer ask her, questions a physician puts with ease twenty-five or thirty times a day: Where does it hurt exactly? What is the nature of the pain? Don't you think you should be a bit more careful? He stares up at the lamp as if its radiance is some kind of clue to what she might answer, and suddenly, for no reason he could name, recalls the time when Jennifer was seven and swallowed every pill in a bottle of aspirin and ran all over the house hitting her head on the walls. Unable to let her from his grasp an instant, he sat up with her all night, even shaved the next morning with her still crooked beneath his arm. Remembering that, the man in the mirror and the small form shaped to his body like some peculiar growth, he feels a longing so pronounced it seems to turn his heart to polished stone, and when he looks into the room once more he is stunned again by the sheer size of everything he cannot know, what she is doing now, what she is thinking, that girl, that daughter, his child.

"Come on," she says nudging Bo, "come on." They are both naked and Bo has fallen asleep. With the weight of him upon her, she has remained awake, staring off at the pictures on his walls. Her parents came suddenly into her head a moment ago. Her heart felt liquid, and a laugh, unuttered, tickled like a cough in the back of her throat. Now she does not want to be here. She pushes his elbow again. "Come on, I've gotta get home." He blinks once into her eyes then rolls off.

He walks her halfway home and leaves her under the streetlamp. The night is dry and still and Jennifer strolls on alone, twirling the purse. They didn't do it. They did something else, but Bo tried to get funny and she had to give him a good poke. Her tits still tingle. Maybe she loves Bo, but she doesn't have to do everything he wants. He was mad about Stanley. There are a lot of nice things about Stanley. Like the way he gets embarrassed. When she threw that raisin at him, he turned red from top to bottom. Nobody noticed, but she did. Stanley is always embarrassed. If she bumps him in the hall at school or wrestles, he can't stand it. Bo never wrestles. He never gets embarrassed, but last week she saw Vicky goofing around with him. She didn't get all upset. She's not going to. Bo didn't even look at Vicky tonight. Not once.

Her father is still sitting in the chair when she comes in.

"Did you have a nice time?" he asks.

"Hello, Daddy," she says. "Yeah, OK," and cocks her head, squinting. "Man, you sure didn't read much of that."

He tips up the book. "I suppose I didn't. I was thinking. What did you do tonight?"

"Nothing."

"Just nothing?"

"Kind of wandered around. Whatsa matter with your book?"

"It's actually quite interesting," he says. "The Punic Wars."

"Yicch. Yeah, I can see what's wrong with it." She thumbs through a magazine on the coffee table. "Where's Ma? Asleep?"

"That's right." He closes his book and sits forward. "Jen, let me ask you something. Are you feeling OK lately? Have you been upset?"

"Man," she says, "Ma sure is a big sleeper." When she looks up, her tiny eyes are hard and direct.

"Yes, she is," her father says softly. He raps his knuckles on the closed cover of the book and the dull sound carries thinly through the living room. Finally, he sets the book down on a small table beside him. "Well, Jennifer, there is one thing we must talk about. Mrs. Kruger called before. I'm not going to let her upset me, but she said that a bunch of you apparently got a little out of hand over at her house. She said it looked like a tornado when she came in."

"So?" Jennifer asks, flipping the pages of the magazine.

"So I've been wondering for one thing where you were. You said you were going to Ricky's, not Stanley's."

"I said *Vicky's*—and we just went to Stanley's. Everybody wanted to. Who cares?"

"And where did you go from there?" he asks.

"I dunno." She squints at a picture in the magazine. "We got something to eat. What difference does it make?"

"It makes a difference to me, Jennifer. How would you like it if some lady told you that your child had been tearing her house apart? What am I supposed to say to Mrs. Kruger?"

"Oh." Jennifer sits down on the coffee table and faces her father. "She's a bitch," Jennifer says. "She complains about everything."

She's right of course; he can't help smiling. "You mean someone's worse than me?" he asks quietly.

"You're not such a pill."

"Oh, I'm not?" He laughs at that, the idea, the word, his daughter. "I'm not a pill," he tells himself aloud. "Well, how about giving this not-pill a hug before you go to sleep?"

"I guess." She stands slowly, hooks her chin over his shoulder, her chest lightly against his.

He wraps his arms around her, and finding himself halfway to tears squeezes hard, kisses her temple and resists her sudden attempt to draw back. "It's a rotten time for growing up, Jen," he says, still hugging. "It's a hard time, but I think it's all going to come out all right. I really do. I'm not making you any promises, but that's what I think."

She wrestles away. "Honestly, Daddy, whatsa *mat*-ter with you? There's nothing wrong. Nothing."

"I know, Jen," he says, feeling he's lived his whole life to be valiant like this. "Sometimes I just say things. It's your silly Daddy. Your not-pill Daddy. That's all."

"Jesus," she says, "sure is," then picks up her purse and kisses him so swiftly he cannot feel it before she starts upstairs.

In the hall her mother's snores echo. Outside her room, Jennifer touches her fingertips to her lips. When she enters, she rubs each breast, taps her chin, her stomach, again her lips, again each breast. She thinks about the evening, about Bo, and those headlights which seemed to pull on her like tides, and in that same sensation of movement through water, the way she eased from her father's arms. She thinks about Sondra's gypsy whom she imagines with a red bandana and a gold tooth and a spidery brown hand motioning outward, outward, as if there really were a sea nearby, an ocean wide and fathomless and black. She thinks about it all, and a sudden dwelling shiver drags down to the bottom of her spine; she shuts her eyes and lets her purse slip to the floor and wraps her arms about herself. She does not have much time.

STEPHANIE VAUGHN

I was born in Ohio. I entered kindergarten in an Army school in the Philippines and graduated from an Army school in Italy. In between, we moved around the United States, but we always went back to Ohio. Twice we went there to live, and many times we went there for a month or two in between postings to military bases. Where we went in Ohio, people said "crick" instead of "creek" and ate pickled pigs' feet. Now I keep meeting people who spent the first twenty years of their lives in Ohio, but they tell me they are really from California or Massachusetts. I live in Ithaca, New York, but I'm really from Ohio.

"Before I wrote the first sentence of this story, I wrote fifty pages of nothing at all. In mid-project, I took all the pages to John L'Heureux, who was teaching the fiction seminar that quarter, and we rummaged through them looking for readable paragraphs. There weren't any. 'This is superb!' he said. 'This is excellent!' he said. 'Just keep writing!' Eventually, I hit that first sentence, whose candor gave me, very quickly, the whole story, and I threw out the other fifty pages. Thank you, John L'Heureux, for your shrewd and hopeful enthusiasm."

◆   ◆   ◆

My Mother Breathing Light

MY MOTHER CANNOT SAY the word "cancer." A year ago, after an operation to remove a tumor at the juncture of her small and large intestines, she used the word "blockage" to explain what the problem had been. "The doctors have found a blockage in my intestines," she told relatives who came to visit as she convalesced on the porch. "Now that it's gone, I can finally eat again, thank God."

My Aunt Ruda took me aside and said, "I want you to tell me the truth about your mother. Is she talking about an ulcer, or what?" Aunt Ruda is my mother's sister-in-law. When I visit every summer, at the end of my teaching year, she has a new inventory of details about other people's medical problems—grotesque incisions, ruined arteries, fatal blood clots, irradiated wombs. Aunt Ruda is overweight, fat with the stories of other people's grief.

"Gemma, you mustn't tell anyone what the operation was really for," my mother said to me, and I saw the fear skate across her eyes, cold in the blue light of the kitchen's fluorescent bulb. "If any of your aunts and uncles find out that it was something really serious, they'll keep asking how I am." I understood then how a question about one's health can be like a sheath on a sword, hiding the real question—"When will you die?"

Now we visit as we always have the first night I am home in Ohio. We sit in front of the television in separate chintz-covered chairs, our feet propped on a shared footstool, a box of chocolate buttercreams on the table between us. This year, however, I have come home early to deal with what my mother says is a "new wrinkle." For one year, she has led a healthy, normal life. She has gained weight, she has bought new clothes. She has visited me in California. But two weeks ago, during a quarterly checkup, something unexpected appeared in the X-rays.

"You look healthy," I tell her. "You look wonderful."

"I feel fine," she says. "I can eat anything."

We invent a dessert menu for the next week. Chocolate mousse, peach Melba, apple spice cake, banana-cream pie, cherries in cognac. In the muted light of the television screen we feel safe.

Usually in June there is a milky haze lying among the wooded hills and the steaming crops—young corn, ripe wheat, silvery middle-aged oats. Today, the landscape surprises us with its sparkle and clarity, as if we have driven into the center of a crystal prism. I can see the way a slender leaf of corn ripples along its center vein. I can see the fanning seed head on a stalk of yellow wheat.

"Ironwort, tiger lily." My mother gives me back names from my youth, identifying the wild flowers that lean frailly away from the edge of the road.

When I was a child, I suffered from frequent kidney infections, which my mother called "attacks." It was not until years later, when I casually used the term during a college physical examination, that I recognized its benign absurdity. "An attack?" said the doctor. "A kidney *attack?*" At once, I saw the image it must have called up, of a scowling cartoon kidney, with thin arms and mitten-shaped hands carrying muggers' weapons. Now we drive back through the Ohio countryside. We are on our way home from the university hospital, where a second opinion has been offered on the spot that showed up on the X-rays of my mother's liver. She calls the spot a "development," as if it is something promising, like a housing project. Her hands move quickly as she talks. The backs of them are tanned from her work in the garden. The palms, flashing white as she speaks, remind me of the undersides of maple leaves exposed in a wind. With her hands my mother can make small houses, a street intersection, a car going out of control.

"Well, it just went poof," she said once, explaining to my father and grandmother where the grocery money had gone and why we were having hot dogs once again for our Sunday dinner. "Like that," she said, and her hands described baroque scrolls of smoke above her dinner plate. It seemed to me that with her hands she might produce, out of the imaginary smoke, an emerald bird, inside of which would be a golden egg, inside of which would be a lifetime supply of grocery money.

My father, ever mindful of my education, cast a meaningful eye my way and said, "Although a hot dog on a bun is not the feast we had all hoped for this afternoon, let us remember that it contains more protein than the average Chinese person eats in a week."

"I am not Chinese," my grandmother said, looking sideways at my mother. "I am a Protestant."

"I'll need time to think about this new development," my mother says now. "I'll need time to plan." My father has been dead for five years, and my grandmother three. Not long before he died, my father moved the family, without consulting anyone, from a large house on the edge of town to a smaller one near the center. He was thinking ahead to their old age, he told me. The smaller house was near drugstores and supermarkets, and closer to the hardware store he ran. It was near the hospital in case of emergency. The Christmas after he bought the house, he drove me into the countryside to discuss the future.

"These are the insurance policies, this is the will." He handed me thick brown envelopes. "This is the key to the safe-deposit box. Do not let your mother sell that house when I am gone. It is in a good location for old people." I had been home from college only two days, but already I felt like a child again, inarticulate and fearful. I felt the old speech rhythms return, the truncated syntax, the vague euphemistic vocabulary, and a sense that there were always secrets to be kept from someone else in the family.

"You're still alive," I said. We walked down a slope to a pond, sliding on the crusted snow.

"I've arranged it so that your mother will not be able to get her hands on all of the money all at once," he said.

I thought of her back at the house, wrapping presents with my grandmother. I thought of how pleased she had looked as my father and I left the house, suspecting, perhaps, that we were going to collect a surprise Christmas present. Instead, we stood at the edge of the pond as the sun went down, and defined the limits of her future: where she could live, how much she could spend, who would die first—as if her life were a geometric pattern, something that could be drawn with ruled sides and with perfect arcs spun off the tip of a compass.

The sun slid behind a row of fir trees, and the pond glowed lavender near the shadows of the opposite bank. "The ice is too thick this winter," my father said. "There's no light at the bottom of this pond. The water plants will die and then the fish will die, too." He spoke matter-of-factly. It was not his pond. "If we don't have a thaw, the farmer will have to come out here and drill holes to save the fish." He paused and looked at me. He seemed about to suggest a lesson in life. "It's a good thing we do not live in the country," he said. "Your mother and grandmother think they would like to live in the country, but it is better for them to live in town."

The following summer, he died. Two winters later, my grandmother died, not long after falling on the ice in front of our house. There was a step she had forgotten about, at the juncture of our walk and the city sidewalk. It was not a badly designed step—just one that, in her old age, she had overlooked.

Aunt Ruda knows that something is up. Every day for the last two weeks, my mother has been going through closets and trunks and throwing away things that once belonged to my father and grandmother. Old shoes, shirts, dresses, sweaters, cheap jewelry, soured cologne still in its Christmas box, gun magazines, clippings of inspirational pieces from Christian newsletters. Ruda stands on the porch and frowns at the seven garbage bags sitting by the curb.

"She's selling the house, isn't she?" Ruda says. My father was Ruda's brother, and now she takes a proprietary interest in the house on his behalf. "If she moves into the country, she'll never be able to get out of her drive in winter."

"I don't know what she's doing," I say truthfully.

In a spiral notebook, I have made an orderly list of the decisions that must soon be made about my mother's chemotherapy treatments. Where will she have them—in California, with me, or in Ohio, near Ruda and the other relatives? Should a registered nurse be engaged? Should a housekeeper be brought in? My mother ignores the notebook and moves through the house in a distracted way, bumping into furniture. "This house is too small," she tells me. "It was designed for short people." She has decided to remodel the kitchen, and she presses me for advice. "Do you like harvest green or that yellow color?"

"I don't know." I am impatient with her, anxious to deal with the crisis at hand. She pretends that this is like any other summer, that once, a year ago, she was sick and gaunt but now she is well again. It is early July and the serious heat is here, moist and languid, settling upon the town like sleep. In the evenings, we drive into the cooler countryside in search of air-conditioned rural restaurants. My mother eats hearty meals—mashed potatoes and gravy, fried chicken, buttered corn. I think about her liver struggling to sort out the proteins, the fats, the poisons. Something must be done. She lingers over the menu, wondering whether to order liver and bacon, liver and onions, or chicken livers in wine and sour cream. Watching her, I wonder whether this is an unwitting irony or part of a secret plan to attack the diseased cells with surrogates. Suddenly I can imagine them, the bad cells, as cartoon cousins to my evil kidney, planning their defense with small knives and guns and miniature cannons.

Under her bed I find a stack of new books, optimistic in their clean dust jackets. "Mind Over Matter." "Long Life and Nutrition." In the mornings, when she thinks I am reading the newspaper on the porch, she goes into the kitchen and blends a viscous concoction of raw eggs, goat's milk, brewer's yeast, honey, kelp, bananas, wheat germ, cooked rice—everything she has ever heard was good for one's health. I am a spy in the house. In her desk I find a brochure describing a health spa in Mexico where inoperable patients are given a vegetable diet and coffee enemas. In her purse I find a newspaper clipping about a Catholic shrine in Indiana, where blind people are able to see again and arthritics stand up straight. Her disease is becoming a secret that each of us keeps from the other. At night, after she has gone to bed, I read about the side effects of chemotherapy. I discover that one of the chemicals used in what is called "chemotherapy" is similar to the fuels used in jet airplanes.

"Rachel has a secret," my grandmother said to my father at the dinner table that Sunday as they sat before their hot dogs and wondered why the grocery budget, so carefully calculated by my father, was so badly mismanaged by my mother. It was true. My mother did have a secret. Since her marriage, she had never had a job, and now she had decided to go to work. She had decided to become an American Fragrance Lady, selling cosmetics and perfumes door to door. For weeks she had been taking a few dollars from the various household budgets in order to raise the capital for the initial investment. She invited me along the day she went to collect the merchandise from the regional representative. I was fourteen years old and already beginning to talk in the superior way my grandmother and father had, but still she took me into her confidence. On my lap I held the huge envelope of fugitive dollar bills.

"Maybe I'll let you take a few of the products around to some of the high-school girls," she said, already imagining the empire we would build.

"She always had secrets when she was a kid," my grandmother continued. "She used to steal money from my purse."

"That was me," I said. "I stole quarters." It was a joke, a diversionary tactic. My mother smiled faintly.

"You stole from your grandmother?" my father said.

"So did Rachel," my grandmother said. "This is a wonderful family."

"Oh, for heaven's sake," said my mother. She left the room and returned carrying the American Fragrance display case, which she placed on the table and snapped open to reveal the rows of glittering bottles. They were made of heavy glass in red, blue, and opaque white, and were cast in the shapes of the Liberty Bell, Independence Hall, and other national monuments. I think there was a moment, as she lifted a red bottle in the shape of the Lincoln Memorial and held it to the light of the window so that it sparkled like a gemstone, when she actually thought my father might be pleased by the prospect of his wife's going from door to door of his friends and neighbors and his customers at the hardware store.

Without looking at her, he picked up the mustard knife and said, "If you have a private matter to discuss with me, we will discuss it after dinner." I didn't hear the conversation. I imagine it was brief and sensible. My father would have been organized and logical, using a legal tablet to calculate the triviality of her projected profits. He would have reminded her that she did not have, after all, the aggressive personality of a saleslady. Perhaps he made fun of the products, their ludicrous shapes, their dubious smells. Perhaps he simply said no. I never saw the display case again. My mother never set out into the neighborhood dressed in a suit and the heavily applied makeup prescribed by the American Fragrance regional representative.

"I don't have fifteen hundred dollars a week," my mother is saying. She says it so sharply that it sounds like an accusation. "Do you have fifteen hundred dollars a week?" I am young and healthy. I grew up an only child in a family of three adults. Tap lessons, ballet, clarinet, piano, Western-saddle riding lessons, English-saddle, a college education, graduate school, a job in California. I am the one who escaped this house. All morning she has sat on this porch and torn photographs out of old albums, ripped them into halves and thrown them in a plastic garbage bag by her feet. I awoke earlier than I usually do, and when I came downstairs I saw her there, through the gauze of the living-room curtains, seated near the trellis of honeysuckle vines. I watched as she held the pictures before she tore them up. They trembled in her hands like caught animals. It seemed to me that she was destroying my own past, pictures of herself with me, my father, my grandmother. Something must be done. I decided to force the issue. I went out to the porch and asked where—exactly where and how—she would like to begin treatment for the spot on her liver, which was not a development but a cancer. She put the albums aside and closed the garbage bag with a twist tie. She gave me a long, stern look, as if I were an adversary, and said, "Switzerland."

Switzerland? What was in Switzerland?

"A place where they give you mineral baths and chemicals that don't make you sicker than you already are."

"All right," I said. A place in Switzerland was better than no place at all. "Let's look into it."

She already had. The place in Switzerland would cost fifteen hundred dollars a week, plus air fare. Our medical insurance would cover most of the treatment if the clinic were in America, but it was not. I thought of the American Fragrance venture and wondered whether she was thinking of it, too—of how the sale of a thousand little Plymouth Rocks and Empire State Buildings might have bought her, if not health, then at least the rarefied air and the beguiling sunlight on the side of an Alpine mountain.

"Do you have fifteen hundred dollars a week?" she says again.

"Fifteen hundred dollars for a mineral bath?" I say it too quickly, too callously, my own hysteria turning to flippancy. "Can't you find a mineral bath in America?"

She stands up. Her hands are fists. "I don't want to lose my hair," she says. She walks past me to the other end of the porch and says it again. "I don't want to lose my hair. Do you want your own mother to lose her hair?" And now suddenly the stiffness leaves her body, the accusation melts in the summer heat. She returns to the far end of the porch and studies the honeysuckle vines which she planted six years ago, when my father bought the house. She reaches up and begins to unwind a runner that spirals toward the ceiling of the porch. "If you let them grow straight up, they'll just droop from the roof and look sloppy," she says. She begins to rewind it along a horizontal piece of lath. Her fingers are so long and supple in the green light that she seems to be winding her own hands into the latticework. "I'm going to phone your Aunt Ruda for some advice," she says at last. "She knows all about doctors and diseases."

While she is on the phone, I hurry through the photo albums and the garbage bag to see what can be salvaged. Here is a picture of my mother and father, looking younger than I am now, at the seashore. Here is one of the four of us in our best clothes in front of my father's hardware store. I want to weep. I see that my mother's target has not been the family, as I had imagined. It has been merely the pictures of herself which are blurry or unflattering. All morning she has labored on the family photo albums like an editor, expurgating the ugly likenesses of herself in order to leave an attractive vision for me when she is gone.

My mother went to bed early this evening. She sleeps ten hours a day now, taking care of herself. I watched television until two in the morning. On a talk show there was a woman who researches death. She has made a living by talking to people who are dying or who have nearly died. She has asked them what the approach of death is like. She told the talk-show host that what she learned should make everyone hopeful and happy. "We never die alone," she said. In all the case histories she studied, the dying people reported that they were with a loved one who had already preceded them in death. The heart-attack victims in surgery, the drowning victims called back from death by mouth-to-mouth resuscitation, the badly mutilated victims of automobile accidents, the weak and frail and palsied in their hospital beds—all of them, she said, reported that they were in the presence of loved ones who came through the dark to be at their sides. The woman was a doctor, middle-aged and passionate. She spoke with a German accent, surely the voice of science. I moved closer to the television and listened carefully, wanting to believe her.

Now the screen is foggy blue, and I can hear the deep sighs of my mother's sleep float in the stairwell. I think of how at nine o'clock she rose from the chintz-covered chair and went up the stairs with a fierce, eager step, the hem of her white robe rippling behind in a satin fury, like water swooshing uphill. "Don't forget the lights," she said. "Electricity costs money." And that simple injunction, which I have heard all my life, smoothed out the fabric of our terrible day. Don't forget the lights, don't let the screen door slam, don't tramp snow across the carpet—this is the language that circumscribes domestic life, making it compact and manageable. I snap off the television and turn off the lights—this one between the chintz-covered chairs, this one by the sofa, and this one on top of the newel post—grateful for the small instruction which tells how to end the day. If my mother could choose the loved ones who would meet her at death's threshold, I wonder whether she would choose my father and grandmother, the people who established the narrow pattern of her life and handed down the judgments.

It's come to this—a linen-covered table, shrimp salads in a country club. Ruda brought us here to meet the "medical counsellor," a youngish woman who wears a silk dress and too much jewelry. I can see that she makes my mother feel awkward, almost obsequious, yet cautiously hopeful. My mother handles her silverware with too much care, as if the knife and fork had razor tips. On the way here, Ruda cheered us up with cancer success stories. There was one about a man who laughed himself into good health while he was locked in a hotel room with a movie screen and prints of all the Three Stooges films.

"Is this woman a psychiatrist?" I asked. "Is she an M.D.?"

"She's a professional," Ruda said. "She's studied at an institute." Ruda says she does not feel well herself. She has high blood pressure, and heart attacks run in the family, she reminds us.

"I always like to have the family here on the first session," the counsellor says. She puts a hand on Ruda's arm and a hand on mine. "I want you to close your eyes and think of this image. It came to me in a dream last night when I knew I was going to meet you." Her voice is like Muzak—an uninspired hum, too sweet. Ruda closes her eyes and bows her head, as if in prayer. My mother looks at me quickly. She did not expect dream therapy.

"The image is a bowl of pink crystals. Can you see them? Translucent and pure. I want you both to imagine that you are eating these crystals every day. I want you to say to yourselves, 'I am eating the wholeness of crystals, and they are faith, hope, and responsibility.'"

My mother looks at me again, anxiously. Ruda's eyes are still closed; so are the counsellor's.

"I have trouble picturing a bowl of pink crystals," my mother says.

I remove my arm from the counsellor's hand. "How about a bowl of chocolate buttercreams?" I say.

My mother says to the counsellor, "I know my daughter and Ruda already have those things without trying to pretend."

When I was about six, I nearly died of a kidney infection. It was very cold outside, perhaps twenty degrees below zero. On the inside corner of my bedroom window a frond of ice bloomed and unfurled across the glass. I was feverish, my face felt like burning paper. I got out of bed and laid my cheek against the ice. My mother took me to the hospital in an ambulance. It was night and we were alone. My father was in another state on business, and my grandmother had not come to live with us yet. My mother carried me out to the ambulance herself and sang a little song as someone placed ice packs around my body. She sang the little tune, and made up words in her soft, airy voice as she went along. "We're going on a little trip, and everything will be all right. We're going on a little trip, we're not afraid of the night." It was cold in the ambulance. She leaned over me as she sang, and put her hand on my forehead. I could see her breath misting white in the darkness and it seemed to me that she was exhaling light.

The weather has been peculiar this summer—first the clear days in June and now a fog in early August, as a cold front sweeps across the state and the warm ground sends a mist into the air. It is after midnight, and my mother and I are walking arm in arm along the sidewalk under the maple trees. A while ago, she got out of bed and came downstairs to find me in front of the television. "You can't sleep, either, can you?" she said. "Neither can I." She made us cups of hot cocoa, as if I were the young child again, and she the young mother. "You'd think we could sleep now that it is cooler," she said.

I watch her breath as we walk—white puffs of light which seem to phosphorize the air around us.

"Actually, what I'd like to do sometime is go to Japan and have a meal at one of those places where you get the soup with the fish eggs," she is saying. "Or maybe to China, where they bring the soup to the table with the chicken feet still in it."

I nod. It is not too late to sell the house. We could fly around the world. We could eat grape leaves in Greece. We could eat camel ankles in Ethiopia. "They're very frugal, those people," I say. "They can make anything tasty." I imagine the two of us seated serenely before a small meal in a house in the Himalayas, where the Hunzas, who live to a hundred but have no term for old age, feast on apricot blossoms in the spring.

"Your grandmother never liked foreigners. They weren't Christian enough for her, but I've always thought they were probably as happy as we are."

The word "happy" surprises me. All summer I have regarded us as miserable. My mother stops under a halo of light. The fog hangs among the trees like veils of trailing lace. She smiles. "Well, if it's going to be this cold in the summer, I just wish for your sake we could be cold someplace fun, like Bavaria." She pulls the sweater together in front of her breasts and hugs herself. It is late and she is tired. We have walked too far. I reach out to touch her, to offer the support of my arm around her shoulders, and she leans easily against my body, as if I were the mother, strong, cheerful, controlling a small bubble of space in which there is no time, only light and warmth. I recall the German woman doctor on television, earnest and importunate, making the plea for faith: We never die alone. A car skids on rain-slick pavement, an airplane dives into the sea, a hospital bed defines at last the perimeter of a mortal life—yet we are never alone. Embracing my mother, I seem to embrace belief itself. Suddenly, I want us to be back at the house, rooting through the refrigerator for leftover chicken and sweet tomatoes—a Midwestern feast.

"It's all right," I say to my mother, holding her close in the fog. "Everything will be all right."

SARA VOGAN

Sara Vogan was born in Pennsylvania and is now hoping to achieve semi-native status in California. Her first novel, In Shelly's Leg, *is about a bar in Montana that sponsors a woman's softball team.* Scenes From The Homefront *is a collection of her short stories. Her second novel,* Loss of Flight, *is about a psychiatrist who makes house calls. She received an M.F.A. from the University of Iowa, a Stegner Fellowship at Stanford, and two N.E.A. grants.*

"All writers tap into certain themes over and over again. I find the natural world surrounding us is often in counterpoint to our daily lives, lives filled with broken romances, lost connections, soured ambitions, wars. The theme of women and war has always been important to me, not the women who go off to fight, but the ones who have to wait through it, work around it, and absorb the consequences of it."

◆　　◆　　◆

The Confession of the Finch

A FINCH HAS NO true way to prepare for death. Like cats, we treasure nine lifetimes. Death is a secret we must discover while we live. All my gypsies have readied themselves in some way before death and I am like a gypsy vampire, living only through these women's souls. On some mornings, just as the sun rises and the air is pink with the smell of dew, I want to forget I have lived with eight gypsy fortune-tellers. I want to be surprised by death; it is supremely sexual. This gypsy is my ninth fortune-teller. When she dies, I die too.

I would like to die in the traditional manner, listening to sad violins and ringing tambourines. I want the magical chanting, the touching of the jewels and beads. I want the wailing of old men and children at the moment our souls become part of the air. But we will die alone, my last gypsy and I. We have no clan to protect us, no *voivode* to break my gypsy's little fingers, to toss the coins upon her breast. There will be no women to dress her in the five skirts and prepare her for her meeting with *O Deloro*. And worse, perhaps this gypsy will die in her home, upon her bed. If this should happen her soul will be trapped. And mine will too.

I know little of the beliefs my last gypsy has chosen to call her own. But I know death is more elaborate than life and the mysteries of her new religion will affect us somehow. One of the mysteries is the ritual of confession, as foreign to gypsies as bones in a wooden horse. Because of this, I cannot see my gypsy's thoughts in the confessional. This is the cornerstone of our misunderstanding. As a true believer in *O Deloro,* I have no need for another god. My last gypsy needs both her gods. I am sure this will be our undoing.

This is my attempt to confess her life since no one can know a gypsy more intimately than her finch. This is our plea for mercy.

She has been my saddest gypsy. I don't think she ever learned to laugh and her dreams torment her. I know everything about her life because I chose her long before Natalia died. I was curious about this marked gypsy and knew the moment when my last gypsy fortune-teller was conceived in the Portuguese village of Ponte de Sor. She spent her gestation upon waters. My gypsies are people of the land, the deserts. For a gypsy to lose sight of land is an omen of death. But this gypsy began to bloom first on the river Soraia to the port of Lisbon, then on the freighter across the stormy Atlantic to New Orleans. The soul of a gypsy who quickens on the water can be gifted with a unique sight.

As a dark-eyed child she prowled the levees of New Orleans, watching boats ply back and forth with a look in her eyes as if she might know her own future, as gypsies never can. When she was eight her mother ordered the left eyetooth removed and replaced with a gold one, a tiny ruby set in the middle. "You will always be rich," her mother told her. "And if we are ever parted I will be able to find you by your smile." It was the curse of the long days upon the ocean. Gypsies should never be separated. The power of their magic is strongest when bound to a clan.

I could not go to her, could not save her, until Natalia died because finches can fly only from death to life. When she, my last gypsy fortune-teller, was placed in a Catholic orphanage and her parents and their caravan moved on, I could not help her. I could only watch as this first mistake, this sin against our tradition, fell upon her shoulders. Her parents wished to be Americans, not gypsies, and that desire cursed us all.

My last gypsy fortune-teller remained in that orphanage three years and during this time her soul became a cinder. The gift of blooming upon waters was lost to her and replaced with a small gold cross. I watched with the eye of my heart as her magic and power drained out of her as the soul of a dying man seeps from his left foot.

She does not remember the day I found her flying on the white wings of another gypsy's death, the music of the funeral still lingering in my ears. But she recognized me for the sign that I am and we left the orphanage, although she refused to surrender the small gold cross. She believed I would lead her to her parents, although they had long been dead. Her father, a bearleader, and her mother, a silversmith, died shortly after they took factory jobs in Chicago. They said they were Armenians, unskilled workers. To deny you are gypsy brings certain death. They did not believe a European curse would find them in Chicago.

My last gypsy fortune-teller still dreams of her parents and often touches the tiny ruby in her tooth as a talisman. The image of her parents is as pure as on the day they left her. High young color, the firm cheekbones. She refuses to let them age in her mind, to allow them the gray that lines her own hair or the dimness of her cataract eyes. My gypsy fortune-teller imagines her mother asking strange women to smile.

She is the only gypsy fortune-teller I have known as a child. Her flower is the orange Aureus crocus, the symbol of the springtime of her soul, just as Natalia's flower was the white Calla lily since I did not fly to her until Natalia was in her sixties.

In puberty, not yet to her full height or dimensions, my last gypsy fortune-teller would sleep with men. They believed she could read their dreams. But when she slept with them the men all had the same dream. They dreamed of her childlike body resting in their hands. A small garden grew at her feet, phlox, aster, lupine. She walked the length of their life lines and her feet placed tiny burns upon their palms.

My last gypsy is cursed. Her father abandoned her; she had no *voivode* to arrange for her marriage. She never became pregnant, which is the deepest sadness for gypsy women, a sign she has had carnal commerce with a vampire. And although she has met other gypsy women, they treated her as an outcast. She never fell in love, as three of my other gypsies did. Her heart never stirred when she awaited a man's arrival; she felt nothing when the men left. She stopped sleeping with men when she had to get glasses and at that time began to wear her kerchief tied at the nape of her neck, after the fashion of married women. The glasses she wore only in secret, those plastic-framed lenses I am the only one to have seen. It is not traditional to wear glasses to see the future.

It was in the orphanage where the dreams came upon her, dreams unlike any I have ever seen before. You can know the secret places in the hearts of women when you watch them dream. I have seen the dreams of centuries, watched the truly mystical dreams of fortune-tellers in India and Eastern Europe. This, my last gypsy fortune-teller, dreams of Christ. He talks to her, shaking a bony finger and clutching his robes around him in embarrassment. In her dreams he becomes an old man, then a child, then the child's own father. My last gypsy fortune-teller's only sexual dream is of the Jew who made the nails for Christ's crucifixion.

A finch must honor and protect his gypsy. But she has betrayed her tradition, and I am afraid for her. My gypsy has lied, three lies that even she does not understand. Gypsies cannot lie for the sake of their immortal souls. And this, my last gypsy, is Catholic. What her Catholic god will do to her for lying, I do not know. But I do know what will happen to a gypsy who tries to deceive O *Deloro*. I know her fate after death. A finch must know many things to be of service to his gypsy.

She told the first lie just after she received her glasses and stopped sleeping with men. I remember this date as the moment our future was sealed. It was a sultry night in August 1967. This boy, as thin in his body as in his spirit, was going to war in the Annamese Cordillera. He wanted his cards read and the cards were clear. The life card was the Three of Wands who stands on the edge of a cliff looking out over a golden bay at the purple sunset. There are three small sailboats on the sea, proceeding to the Land of the Dead. The Three of Wands stands with his back to the reader; two of his wands are behind him and he carries one wand as a staff for his journey. This boy would die. But worse, as his life unfolded before us we could see his soul was as inconsequential as the little floating boats. Born of a loveless marriage, as were both his parents, this boy had only the spark of a soul. There was not enough spirit to give him a good life in these times or to have him reborn. He would die without a mark on his body and leave hardly a ripple in the world. Even his parents would soon forget him. His death would be a failure of spirit.

My gypsy fortune-teller saw his cards as clearly as I did and looked into his eyes and saw how little light they contained. The Nine of Swords, grieving on his sarcophagus, crossed this boy's Three of Wands. Failure. Death. The boy twisted his hands, running his nails across them as if they itched, and we could tell from the hands his faint desire for the life he had not experienced in this world but hoped to find in the cards. Staring directly into the Tarot, my gypsy fortune-teller said: "You will see foreign lands and sleep with women whose language you will not understand." We knew this boy would die a virgin. But as she turned up the final card, which could only be Death, my gypsy said: "This card gives you power at a moment when you will need it most. Through this card you will find unique knowledge, a knowledge that comes to each of us but once in our lives."

"I won't get hurt?" The boy braided his fingers like willow sticks on the ends of his hands.

"No." This was not a lie. But she had given him his fortune as if Death had been reversed, the sign for Change. "After that moment you will be a different person."

Lying, for a gypsy, scars the soul. My gypsy fortune-teller should have given this boy the opportunity to prepare for his journey to the world of the spirit. Instead, she led him to believe he would live. It was a gift to him he could not use. His death now becomes one with my gypsy's, and she will not be able to prepare for her own.

The night this boy died I saw his death near the banks of the Ia Drang river. I watched him sleeping and knew he was not dreaming. When the bomb went off and the sky lit up over his bunker I saw the red cape of the Three of Wands, the thin heart bleeding inside this boy's body. Since he was not dreaming there was nowhere for his spirit to escape. He drew one last breath and the spark of his soul flickered out. But I saw my gypsy's dream: The Jew making the fourth nail that should have been placed in Christ's left foot, the nail that has doomed us to wander. I watched my gypsy touch herself, her hands moving smoothly over her aged body. She dreamed she was a young girl again, men in her bed dreaming the same dream. The Jew forged the fourth nail in the fire and its heat filled my gypsy's body and covered her brow with sweat. The next day she went to confession.

It was over two years before she lied again. It was in the autumn. This boy had presence; I could tell by the roll of his hips when he walked, the pride he carried along his spine. He would be an instrument of the devil, O Bengh, the Evil One. There was the faint odor of cordite around him. His eyes folded in on themselves, like an Oriental's. This boy was too proud to accept his place in the universe. He would be reborn, but as some malevolent thing, perhaps a knife with a life of its own.

For a gypsy, to lie to an instrument of O Bengh brings grief to the graves of your ancestors. Her parents, long dead although she won't believe me, will be quartered in ever finer pieces, each strip of their bodies divided in half, and in half once again, and again, until my gypsy dies by the knife she has created.

This boy wanted his palm read, and the blind man who sells newspapers across the street could feel the shortness of the life line. He would die by the hands of those close to him, not an accident and never discovered. He would remain unburied until his next life, as a sword or a knife, had revenged itself on my gypsy.

"Will I die?" the boy asked, and I could sense the stiffening along his spine, his pride in his belief he knew the answer.

My gypsy lied. "You will be in power a long time." And then I watched her as she made the sign of the cross from her forehead to her breast. She reached over and crossed the boy also. During that moment, the wind ceased to hum and all the colors vanished from the room.

It was many months later, in the full moon at the end of a fading season when this boy stood in a rocky outcropping near the summit of Chu Mnang Mountain. The moon made the night shine like noontime, and this boy saw his shadow stretched upon the ground. At his feet lay the gnawed bones of a macaque, killed the night before by an oriental tiger. This boy watched the shadows of four men and saw the blue glint of their M-16 rifles pointed at his heart. His last thought was of my gypsy and how she had promised him power and a long life.

That night, in my gypsy's dream, the Jew appeared to her again. In the fire of his forge he honed the first two nails for Christ's palms. From rough iron spikes he beat the hot metal into sheets thin as paper and the colors turned from red to blue, blue to yellow, and the golden yellow finally became silver. With his tongs, the Jew held up the silver sheet of beaten metal and shaved off four thin needles. My gypsy, in her sleep, cried at the sight of the silver, at the perfect roundness of the needles, their points dripping blood. She shed tears for the delicacy of their elliptical eyes. Seeing her tears, the Jew placed the needles in her hands and scorched each of her palms with the shape of a cross.

The next morning my gypsy discovered the tears of her sleep had clouded her sight. She saw this world as nothing more than shadows. The Jew had taken from her the true colors of this world and given her colors no mortal has seen. She now knows the exact shade of death, the color of music, the tone of the air, and the hue of thoughts.

She spent that whole day kneeling in confession, her mind closed to me who could only know the ache in her knees on the velvet cushion, the stiffness in her hands folded in prayer for long hours. That evening she got drunk, as gypsies seldom do, and told a blonde woman with no soul to never believe gypsy fortune-tellers because they sleep with vampires.

It has been six years since she told the last lie. It was in November and she lied to a young man who had a wife and two small babies. This young man is not dead. He neither sees nor speaks, hears or moves. He is kept in a hospital with only his thoughts for companionship. His dreams are shrouded in clouds. It is hard to know how long he will live, but I am afraid when he dies, we will die too.

Since we will die together, I want to experience her, this, my last gypsy fortune-teller. I experienced Lenore, my second gypsy, whose flower was the pink bleeding heart since I came to her when she was a young woman still living in the Carpathian Mountains. Night after night I took each hair of her woman's beard in my beak, my wings beating fine music and clear air between her thighs.

I kept my eyes open as my head and glassy wings pulsed through her body. When she would release me, my wings grazed her teeth and I felt her hot breath on my feathers. Like a cat, I could inspect her. My eye leveled with the curvature of her ear; my beak slipped between her toes. I could move beneath the curls of her hair. During long nights together I discovered the thin, liquid space between her heart and her ribs. I saw her soul had the brightness of a perfect emerald and sat slightly to the left of her breastbone.

I have not experienced all my gypsy fortune-tellers. Some were married, some fell in love. When they died they chose to commingle with spirits of their own kind. But I experienced Natalia at the moment of her death. Far above me in the dark channels of Natalia's dying body I saw the violet of her soul as it faded like a gem without light. She died with her mouth open, as if laughing, and I continued my flight to this, my last gypsy fortune-teller. I have never experienced her but I will do so to honor her because in all our years together she has had no one but me.

The third young man wanted both his cards and his palm read, as if one could cancel out or reassure the other. His life card was the pretty Ten of Cups, the sign for repose of the heart. A man and a woman, arms around each other's waists, are waving good-bye to a rainbow of chalices. Their backs are to the reader and nearby their children play without concern. His cross card was the gray Four of Swords, a Knight upon a sarcophagus, his hands folded in prayer. Three swords hang above him beneath a stained glass window framing a woman and child. One sword lies beneath him. Exile. The Hermit's repose.

We watched his life unfold before us, the happiness of his childhood, the good marriage to a gracious wife. It was perfect balance: the idyll of his young life against the hardships of his maturity. His final card was the Seven of Cups, a black-cloaked figure standing with his back to the reader, his arm reaching for strange chalices of vision he will never hold.

The young man's palm revealed his life line broken in eighty-six places, a smooth hand that suddenly becomes painfully discontinuous until the life line disappeared like rain into the earth. This young man was right to have both his cards and his palm read. There was no mistaking his future.

My gypsy lied. "You will live to be eighty-seven," she said. But his life line revealed he would survive eighty-six deaths.

I have tried keeping count because this is my gypsy's third lie. With this lie she has assumed all the pain she tried to spare this boy. If I can count for her, as I am now trying to confess for her, perhaps in some way *O Deloro* will forgive us. Indecision was her sin, playing faith against her heritage, hoping one would counteract the other.

The counting is complicated. He had twelve childhood accidents, eight close brushes with death before this boy stepped on the mine in the Phu Yen province near the village of Tuy Hoa. I wonder if each subsequent operation, eleven, signifies another escape from death or does each time the body falters, the spirit fails, count as one. I am uncertain. This young man could be six beats from death or thirty-five.

My gypsy's punishment has already begun. The night this young man stepped on the mine she dreamed her last dream. It was the Jew again but he neither spoke nor moved. He hung on a cross, crucified by three delicate silver needles.

A fourth was placed in his heart. My gypsy did not know whether he was alive or dead, but she removed him from the cross and placed him in her womb. She secured the four silver needles in her heart. She has had no dreams since then, six years. A gypsy who does not dream has no power.

When her soul quickened upon the Portuguese waters I believed she would make special use of her unique sight. I wanted her to become a *phuri dai,* a wise and revered woman respected by her clan. I thought she might have miraculous visions and be worshipped by our people as we worship the Black Virgin. Instead, we will die alone, no tambourines ringing, no violins. If her fingers are not broken we will be trapped in her grave forever.

Finches are gifted with sight only year by year. We see and contain all of the past but our vision into the future is renewed only on the first full moon of each new year. By Christmas my gypsy will be totally blind. Her cataracts are as clouded as cotton patches over her eyes. I pity her, my last gypsy fortune-teller, caught between two worlds without believing in or understanding either of them.

At times I will move papers or dishes so her sightless eyes can guide her hands to familiar places. I keep careful watch on the knives. Before Christmas I will experience her. I will be the last thing she will see. On the full moon I will rise from her mouth. I am afraid we will all be dead by the new year.

CHARLES WASSERBURG

Charles Wasserburg was born and grew up in Pasadena, California. He has been both a Stegner Fellow and a Jones Lecturer in poetry at Stanford.

"This poem was substantially rewritten at Stanford in one of the writing workshops. The painter referred to in the early going is Domenico Ghirlandaio, the Florentine artist and teacher of Michelangelo."

◆　　◆　　◆

The Provinces

I.
The walls jut toward us, cut away
to show the saint's last hour,
his bedside mourners kneeling
and marbled in fading colors.
Perspective magnifies:
behind the resurrection
of a solemn child, a drunk
pitches from a window,
a boy rolls a hoop.
Even the portrait's thick-lidded
ham-pink buyer prays
beneath the child, with skylarks
lofting in gold above
the painter himself, who stands
fist on hip—the scene
behind him dwindling—watching us.

I spend awhile watching back,
then leave the church. Later,
my highschool students ask
about the Rolling Stones
who, I explain, are British.
One girl wants to see
Detroit. *Why?* Because
The Blues Brothers come from there.
In turn naive, I say
I like Fellini and Dante
and they shake their heads: "it's not

like that," they grin, "Thank God."
After class I drift
along the river walkway
smelling the tang of brickdust,
loving the way the walls
tinge peach at sunset, and try
remembering that Lorenzo
loved all this and still
appreciated
the proper, thorough treatment
of suspected enemies:

"the said alleged had the soles
stripped from his feet which
were then put over a fire
until the fat ran. They then
stood him up and made him walk
over rock-salt, so that he died of this."

Pigeons rock on the updrafts,
a stairway lifting skyward
in alleys I walk between
palace and gallery.
On Via Duomo crane jaws
drop and drop below
the ditch edge, dragging up
cobbles and knots of piping,
as I sit reading in a bar
about a man who scraped
his dining room paint, finding
a fresco underneath.
All night as shoppers slip
around the roar of tractors,
work continues: huge
between blue-white spokes
of arc lamps, the piping
swings in the jaws of a crane,
black and gorgon-tangled.

At noon, the winter sky
goes gray as steel hinges
on the old prison doors.
Without the summer babble
only the guards' conversation
echoes among the statuary
into the courtyard, whose silence
makes me realize
that where a fountain stands
some kneeled to the chopping block.

Those students may be right,
the way this "shitty province"
walls them in with old ideas
and older complications,
where even the drunks who lounge
inside the wineshop know
the English teacher's visiting
the divorcee next door,
and wink at us
when we come down her stairs.
Returning home on streets
where even guttered garbage
freezes into artifact,
I've started to believe
their visions of my home
in songs the radio plays,
someplace far away
from the deads' marble weight,
only an engine's hum,
the sky behind us and ahead
an unambiguous blue.

II.
Concrete riverbeds slip beside the bus,
    narrow into gullies and rise
toward hills flickering with manzanita. Their tops
    lift stucco mansions toward the sun.
A bridge swings over the bus roof like a boom
    into a junkyard where a factory once smoked.
Everything has shifted—the land, and then
    the past that I looked forward to:

"Dear Chuck:
I'm writing from this place (Impact) because
I started shooting dope again
and I tried everything to stop. I'll be
the first to admit my life's a mess.
One time I saw a calendar and realized
I didn't know March had passed.
I am writing this so you will know how I feel.
I really am trying to get better
and want to know what's going on outside,
so write me, please."

I think I don't know him now, though once we drove
    with our friends, flooring it toward the desert.
I remember hitting Highway 10, the houses
    thinning out to scattered trees,

the trees to scrub and sand, the car nearly
   gliding over the purple suds
of wildflowers, no traffic on the road.
   We stared outside, forgetting family
or names of places we passed and spoke with ease—
   Alta Loma, San Gabriel, Cajon—
names someone had used before we came
   so we would know how they had felt:
"our saint is Gabriel. We know this canyon."

WILL WEAVER

I was born in 1950 in northern Minnesota and grew up on a dairy farm. My family life was Scandinavian plain style, no tv or movies, so I spent my youth haying, hunting, and reading. Early on I sensed that the Great Novels had much in common with farming: both presented the elementals of birth, season, character, and death; both required a personal response. From the farm I went to the University of Minnesota. A story about deer hunting brought me to Stanford in 1976. Red Earth, White Earth *was published in 1986, and a collection of short stories is forthcoming in 1989, both from Simon & Schuster.*

"The following story illustrates, I think, a recurring theme in my fiction, something E. M. Forster called 'the effect of land on character.'"

♦　　　♦　　　♦

From The Landing

THE SUMMER I WAS seven years old and of no real use to my father—hay bales were too heavy, tractors too tall—my grandfather came almost daily to take me fishing. But whenever his gray Ford slowed at our driveway and its wheels crunched gravel in their turning, I ran away.

That July morning I ran to the garden, down its rows of sharp-leaved sweet corn, shielding my face with my arms, until I reached the shady center where the dirt was damp and cool. I hunkered there out of sight. In the yard my grandfather's Ford coasted to a halt; its engine sputtered and died.

In the silence pigeon feet scraped atop the metal dome of the silo. A calf bleated in the barn. Around me, mosquitos whined faintly like tiny, faraway planes taking off, as they rose up from the damp stalks and roots toward the heat of my body.

The Ford's horn tooted.

I squatted lower still, crouching there, hoping my grandfather would start his engine and drive away, drive up the road to my cousin Bobby's farm—take Bobby fishing, not me.

The Ford's radio came on. Music, some faint country western song, began to play off the wide face of the barn and into the garden. Mosquitos lit on my ankles, my shoulders, my neck. I swore at them. I swore at the music, at old men who can wait all day—and again at the mosquitos which finally drove me from my hiding place.

As I crossed the garden I picked up a hoe. I'd been working, hadn't heard my grandfather drive in. But the hoe was unnecessary, for behind the steering wheel my grandfather sat staring straight ahead through the windshield to the fields beyond; he didn't turn. Atop the Ford, three cane poles were tied to the roof. Three red and white bobbers, clipped to black lines, swayed slightly in a breeze I could not feel.

I came alongside the car.

"Hey Buddy!" my grandfather said. His face lit up as if either he or I had been away somewhere, as if two days were a long time. He switched off the radio.

"Hi Gramps," I said loudly.

He looked at the hoe. "What you digging, Buddy?"

"Hoeing," I said. "It's not a shovel, it's a hoe." I held it up close to his face. He leaned forward. His watery blue eyes squinted first at the hoe, then across to the garden.

"Finished?" he asked.

"Supposed to do four more rows," I said.

He blinked at the garden. "Those weeds will be there tomorrow," he said. "Right now we better pick up Bobby and go, else our minnows will die."

My cousin Bobby lived on the next farm south but he was nowhere to be seen. I searched our bale forts in the hayloft. I peered inside the empty calf hutches beside the dairy barn. I eased into the silo room and squinted between the vinegary-smelling stacks of wooden doors. I slipped into the milkhouse and sprang behind the big stainless steel bulk tank. No Bobby.

Back in the yard I paused for a moment to look around. Some scruffy white hens were easing back to their sand-scratching spot in front of the machine shed; they kept clucking and looking around. I circled behind the building to the scrap iron pile. I slowed among the junked cornpickers, the half-combines, the black piles of old tires. I found Bobby curled up inside an old tractor tire like one white bean in a big black pod. I leaned into the tire and grinned down at him. "Grandpa's here—" I said.

"Doubledamn!" he shouted. His voice circled inside the tire and came at me from behind. It sounded like his father's voice. Bobby was a year older than me. He had blonde hair like me but was thicker in his chest and shoulders, and sometimes he got to drive the little Allis Chalmers tractor all by himself.

Bobby scrambled out of the tire. He went to the corner of the machine shed and peeked around it into the yard. "Damn," he whispered. He looked back at me and folded his arms across his chest. "I ain't going," he said.

I shrugged.

The Ford's horn tooted.

"You better tell Grandpa, then," I said.

Bobby was silent. "You tell him for me." He stepped one step toward me and raised a fist. "Tell him you couldn't find me," Bobby said.

I shook my head no.

Bobby stared at me; he lowered his fist.

"I'll let you drive the Allis," he said.

I thought about that for a while. Then I shook my head no.

He raised his fist again.

I closed my eyes and braced myself.

Bobby swore again.

When I opened my eyes he was staring back toward the yard.

The horn tooted again.

Bobby turned to look at me. For a long moment we stared at each other—then we broke for the yard. Dust flew, chickens scattered as we ran, but Bobby beat me to the back seat and slammed the door and locked it. I had to sit in front.

"Ready boys?" Grandpa said.

"Sure—" Bobby called from the back. He giggled, then hissed in my ear. "I'll come to your funeral. I'll sit in the first pew, but there won't be no open casket."

"I wouldn't even come to yours," I said. "Nobody will."

"Nobody's who's dead already, you mean," Bobby said.

"Shut up," I said. We spoke without turning our heads or moving our lips.

Grandpa brought up the rpms and let out the clutch—the Ford jerked ahead.

"Christ, he started in third!" Bobby said.

"So third is better than reverse," I said.

The Ford swung wide onto the lawn, then found gravel again, and we were on our way. Across the driveway a yellow oats field stretched away west; midfield, between windrows of grain, two pickups sat parked beside the red Massey-Ferguson grain swather. The swather's reel stood high in the air like an upraised aluminum fist: breakdown. My father and my Uncle Karl lay under the swather with only their legs sticking out. On the yellow oat stubble the swather was a big hub and their legs were the spokes of a broken wheel.

The Ford drew even with the field. Grandpa didn't notice the machinery or the pickups and the men on the ground did not look out toward the road.

"Crappies are biting over on Boulder Lake, boys," Grandpa said.

"Triple damn," Bobby groaned. "You know what that means," he said in my ear.

I knew. The highway.

"You coulda told him you couldn't find me—" Bobby said. He kicked the seat hard from behind.

Grandpa felt the kick. He turned. "Boys!" he said, "steady now." Then he looked back to the road. He drove with his head tilted back, his arms straight out to the steering wheel. "Crappies big as dinner plates," he said in his faraway driving voice.

We drove on gravel, and as we neared the highway I began to watch Grandpa's eyes and the stop sign swimming up red. His eyes kept staring straight on down the road. I put my hands on the dashboard. Finally I said, "Stop sign, Gramps."

With his right hand Grandpa lifted his leg onto the brake. The Ford came to a halt with a scrape of gravel on asphalt. I let out a breath. The Ford's front bumper hung on the white center stripe, and a passing motor home swung wide and tooted its horn. A wall of air rocked the Ford.

"You want me to take the front seat?" Bobby said.

"Why? What's the matter?" I said. I grinned out of sight from Bobby, who swore again.

Grandpa waited at the intersection. "Say when, Buddy," he said to me.

The crappies schooled but were not hungry. Our three white bobbers swam sideways, then in small circles, but never dipped beneath the surface. Bobby and I gave up casting and fished straight over the side of the boat. We took turns threading minnows onto Grandpa's hook; it took him so long, bent over the hook and minnow like he was sewing something, that we helped him so we didn't have to watch.

"Okay," Bobby said, and swung Grandpa's baited hook out and away from us. Bobby checked his wristwatch and looked at the sun. He looked at me. I looked away, toward my bobber. It was moving away from the boat, toward the landing. I set the hook hard but there was nothing there.

"Tomorrow," Grandpa said to us, "they'll bite tomorrow."

On the way home Bobby had to take the front seat, and I lay full length in the back. The rear seat was deep and soft and scratchy and smelled like dog. I watched the green tops of spruce trees flash by the window, then change to blue sky as we turned onto the highway. I smelled water as we passed a swamp, pigs from a farm.

Bobby's side of the seat tilted back an inch. "A little more to the right Gramps," Bobby said.

A big semi-trailer's air horn blasted over us and its slipstream shuddered the Ford.

Bobby let out a breath and swore again.

I didn't look up. By the passing smells and the flow of treetops against blue sky I kept track of where we were. Three more miles. I closed my eyes.

"Curve," Bobby said to Grandpa. I felt Bobby's seat tilt back again.

I kept my eyes closed until the Ford slowed and gravel chattered in the wheel wells. Bobby whirled in his seat and punched me hard in the chest.

"What'd you do that for!" I said. It hurt.

Bobby grinned down at me. "Just for the hell of it," he said. He kept grinning down at me.

"Watch the damn road," I said.

"Hey, made in the shade!" Bobby replied. Then he said, "You shoulda seen that semi—a big Peterbilt with a flat front—I swear it was big as a barn!" He spread his fingers and pushed his open palm straight at my face.

I swatted his hand away. "We're not home yet," I said, "you'd better—"

Suddenly the Ford scraped and tilted. So fast. When we hit I went onto the floor, onto the minnow pail, and I felt rocks slamming underneath, grating on the muffler and tailpipe. Bobby shouted and I saw his arms grab for the wheel. Then we were stopped.

There was silence. Crappie minnows flipped and twisted in a pool of water on the floor. My shirt was wet.

"Boys," Grandpa said slowly, "what have we done?"

He began to open his door.

"No—not that side," Bobby shouted.

I peeked up over the side of my window. The Ford hung on the slanted shoulder of the road. Below were cattails and water in the ditch. I scrambled to the high side of the Ford.

"This way, Gramps!" I shouted close to his ear. We pulled him over to Bobby's seat.

Grandpa squinted out his window. I knew he could see only sky. "Boys—we got too far over," he murmured.

Bobby and I looked at each other. Bobby began to giggle. I did, too.

"Somebody better go for help," Grandpa said.

"Me," Bobby said immediately. He eased out his door, dropped to the ground, then sprinted off down the road. His tennis shoes kicked up dust. Bobby's dust hung in the sunlight even when he was out of sight over the hill, like part of him had stayed behind.

Twenty minutes later a pickup came fast down the road. My father drove. Bobby rode standing up in the rear. I waited outside the car, and soon the truck braked hard, its dust rolling over me and then onto the Ford where Grandpa waited. The men, and Bobby, hurried forward. A smudge of oil streaked my father's forehead. He wore dark green, dusty coveralls with some silvery box-end wrenches jammed in the front pockets; the wrenches clanked as he walked and their dark eyes swayed.

"What the hell happened here?" my father said. He looked at the car, then to my grandfather, who had remained in the front seat, the rider's side.

Grandpa was silent for a moment. "Cut it too close, I guess," he said slowly.

"He can't drive worth a damn anymore," Bobby said, jerking his head at Grandpa. I waited for my uncle to nail Bobby for swearing, but nothing happened. Though none of us stirred, I felt Bobby take some kind of step away from me. Or me from him. One of us moved.

"He almost killed Buddy and me!" Bobby said. "Every time we go with him he almost kills us."

No one said anything.

My father turned to stare at me. Then he looked at his own father, then back to me.

"Buddy?" my father asked.

I looked down. I shrugged. "We got too far over, that's all."

"Hell, that's not all—" Bobby said. "Today we almost got hit by a motor home, then by a semi. If we didn't help him drive he couldn't drive at all!"

My grandfather stared at Bobby. He was reading Bobby's lips. Bobby looked straight at him. Bobby's face was red and he swallowed, but he still kept staring straight on.

My father turned to me. "How long has this been going on?" he said slowly.

I looked down.

"Buddy?" my father repeated.

"What's been going on?" I said.

"You helping him drive."

Bobby answered for me. "All this summer. Most of last summer, too."

My father knelt to look at me straight on. "Buddy, you should have said something," he said. He looked up to his own brother, my uncle. "We get busy, I know, but still you should have told us." His face had gone white.

I looked down. My eyes and throat burned. The shapes around me—the truck, my father, small stones on the road, the silver eyelets on my own boots—wavered and swelled and shimmered. I wiped my eyes.

Uncle Karl turned to my grandfather. "Well the damn fishing trips are over. If you can't drive on the right side of the road you shouldn't be driving at all."

My grandfather stared a long time at the men; at Bobby. Then he leaned over and removed the ignition keys. He stared at them in his hand for a moment, then slowly held them out the window. The keys caught sunlight as they fell.

Years later I saw Bobby and his wife only occasionally. Bobby had stayed home to take over his father's place and two more of my uncles' farms. There was not enough land for everybody to farm, but that was all right by me. I was a teacher by then and I lived a hundred miles away with my own wife and kids. I came back to the farm three or four times a year to help my father put up wood or just to walk the fencelines and look for birds and animal tracks. I always brought my children along; I wanted them to know what a farm was like without them having to live on one.

Those trips back were when I saw Bobby. We didn't have much in common anymore, only the past. So once a year, usually in July, we went fishing together. We took Bobby's boat down to Little Moon, the lake closest to the farm. No weekend trip to Canada, nothing like that. Just one evening on a lake.

That night, Bobby's chores ran late and the sun was already low and orange before we pushed off from the landing. The lake was a plate of blue. Disturbed, the water around the boat gave off a chill and a reedy smell, yet the sun was warm on my neck and shoulders. Across the lake two loons swam just beyond the reed point where the water dropped off.

Bobby didn't start up the Evinrude. He rowed, and then we drifted and we fished the shoreline. We sat at opposite ends of the boat and cast shiner minnows toward the bank, then jigged them slowly toward deep water. The minnows wavered, glinting, across green moss, then blue water, then broke through to daylight and air where they spun off bright droplets as we cast them again.

Bobby and I didn't talk much. On a lake at sundown with a rod and reel in your hands, there wasn't much that needed saying.

Two mallards came in low and set their wings.

Bobby said, "Old Gramps would have dropped those two."

"You've got that right," I said.

We cast again.

Then Bobby said something about Grandpa's Winchester twelve gauge, and we got to talking more. We spoke about that gun. About the old Allis Chalmers. The '39 Ford.

We fell silent for a few casts. The air and water blued toward each other.

Then Bobby said, "Sometimes I think old Gramps might still be fishing."

I didn't know quite what he meant. "Maybe so," I said.

We cast again.

"If it weren't for me, he'd still be fishing," Bobby said. "That's what I meant."

I was silent.

"That day when we got off too far with the Ford," Bobby said. His back was to me.

"I remember that day," I said. I chuckled once. Bobby didn't laugh.

He reeled his minnow up from water, and sat staring at it for a long time. A clear bead of water stretched from the tail of his minnow.

"He never drove his car after that day," Bobby said.

I didn't say anything.

Bobby said, "He just sat there in his chair in his living room and shriveled up and died."

I slowed my reeling.

Bobby turned to me. "Sometimes I think I killed him," Bobby said softly. "That was the day I killed my own grandfather."

"That's crazy," I said. "You don't want to think that."

Bobby kept staring at me but beyond me as well. Then he shook his head and focused his eyes on me. "Nothing is crazy," he said. "Everything is crazy and nothing is crazy."

We stared at each other for a long moment. I was the one who looked away. I felt Bobby's eyes on me, then we cast our minnows at the same time. That's when I began to talk. I felt it was my duty. I told Bobby that somebody had to say it, how our grandfather was endangering us and everybody else on the road. How the driving couldn't have gone on forever.

At first Bobby was silent. Occasionally he nodded. After a while he said things like, "Maybe so," or, "I guess I can see that."

The air shaded from blue to purple. We kept casting, and slowly Bobby began to talk, at first about our grandfather, then, slowly, about other things. I talked, too. As we cast our minnows into the shortening light, the shrinking depth of field, with each swing of our arms we threw off some thin layer of our bodies until an hour later only our voices were left in the dark. After that we fished by the faint, reflected starlight, by the habits of our hands.

We spoke of our kids.

Our jobs.

Our wives.

Our jobs again.

Things we wanted to do with our lives but hadn't done. Bobby said he had always wanted to go to Alaska and catch a king salmon. "Just one king salmon would do it," he told me.

I said I wanted to go to Brazil, to Rio de Janeiro and the Carnival there. I wanted to wear one of those tall costumes and dance the samba.

Bobby laughed at that.

Everything there was to say about ourselves, that night we said it. We only stopped talking when one or the other of us cast—when the brief whistle of a rod split the air. We paused as line whispered off the reel, clear monofilament line reaching into the dark, unwinding to a moment of silence just before the minnow, somewhere far out there, kissed down on water.

We fished until car lights angled yellow through the trees and bounced sharply toward the landing. The beams cast their light onto the water, then halted. A car door slammed. Someone moved between the beams, one of our wives, we couldn't tell which one, and began to call out for us. Our names came across the water, then again in echo from the dark shore behind. Someone from the landing stood there calling to us, asking if we were still out there? If we were all right.

WILLIAM WIEGAND

William Wiegand was a Fellow at Stanford in the mid-fifties. He stayed for his Ph.D., and later taught at Harvard, and then at San Francisco State, where he is chair of the Creative Writing Department. His published novels include At Last, Mr. Tolliver; The Treatment Man; The School of Soft Knocks; *and* The Chester A. Arthur Conspiracy.

"Some people have wondered how you can teach anyone to be 'creative.' If you can't, maybe it's best to teach it as you would algebra. Just remain professional. I know I always am."

Pathetic Fallacy

WHEN HOLMBERG REACHED THE top of the steps across from his office, he heard the sound of a typewriter from the department secretary's office down the hall and knew that his student, Miss Marcy, must be batting away at her short story as she had promised. The corridor itself was deserted. It was the last day of the spring semester, finals were over, and most of the students had already left town. Even some of the secretaries were gone. Miss Marcy had already informed him that her friend, the secretary for the freshman program, was going to be away, and that therefore Miss Marcy would use the secretary's office in which to write her final story for his course. Miss Marcy and all the secretaries were friends; Holmberg supposed Miss Marcy was friends with almost everybody.

As he sat down in front of his desk, he looked ahead to an afternoon of almost unbearable tedium. It was only ten minutes after two, and he had given Miss Marcy until four-thirty to finish her story. That would give him half an hour to read it, enter her course grade on the record sheets, and then get the sheets over to the registrar's office before they closed at five. He already knew what grade he was going to give Miss Marcy—a C; but he did not know what he was going to give Alice Cole. That was why he had come in a little early: to think about it. At the moment it probably didn't make a damn bit of difference to Alice Cole what grade she got in English 177; as far as he knew she hadn't even regained consciousness since her accident. Holmberg fiddled with a pencil. The picture of himself sitting there in the office debating whether or not to bestow an A on the poor girl as (what?) a consoling gesture would have struck anyone of intelligence as self-important, and possibly morbid.

Down the hall, the typing broke off suddenly: perhaps Miss Marcy was reaching for a thought. Happily, the sound resumed almost at once. He did not have much doubt Miss Marcy could knock off thirty pages in a few hours if only she set her mind to it. As he reached over to turn on the desk lamp, he noticed that she had left him something. She was already off to a good start. A few pages of manuscript, which he had not seen, were lying on the desk, and from the idiotic width of the margins, he knew they were Miss Marcy's.

There was a note clipped to the upper leaf: "Dr. Holmberg: Here are the first five pages of my story. I am working in the secretary's office and will bring them in to you five pages at a time until I reach the thirty I owe you. That way you can keep up with me and I will not keep you unduly." A new paragraph: "I saw Alice this morning but she did not recognize me." Another new paragraph: "Thank you very much for extending the deadline for me." The signature was typed in: Marilyn M.

He lifted the note and began reading the story.

> They say that springtime is romance time, but they are wrong. When bare trees shiver against a clouded sky and the moon spreads silver elegance across the world, then is the real romance time. It is a gay time and a rain-splattered bright time, and it is in the magic city where you find the romance time . . .

It was a relief to find that at least the story wasn't about Alice Cole.

He took up his pencil and started to mark the page. Over "they" in the first sentence he wrote, "Who are 'they'?" He had written it before over other "theys." In the second sentence, he marked "p.f." over "bare trees shiver." That meant "pathetic fallacy," something he had spent a whole hour lecturing about one day last month. He underlined "silver elegance" and "romance time"; he was going to mark them "cliché," but then decided that that wasn't what they were. They were just bad. Quickly, he read down the page to see if he could think up some catch-all comment to put in the wide vertical margin. "Trite," maybe.

> . . . I was in love then. It was one of those beach romances; you know the kind. You love him and you love him hard because it is summer and summer is the don't care time. You love him hard, and when autumn cries on the lonely beach, you forget him because autumn is now and the summer's children are gone.

Probably it was hopeless. He put down the pencil and lighted a cigarette. The typing had stopped. Presently Miss Marcy was standing in the doorway.

"Well, here's five more," she said.

She seemed, as she always did, to have sewed all her own clothes, and to have mismeasured them. She had no style. She was too tall and her hair was too short. She had been raised, he supposed, by a society of middle-aged people who were volunteer workers in a charity home. Sometimes he thought she had reached him from a time warp.

Nevertheless, he smiled at her. "You seem to be forging ahead famously."

"I'm using a kind of conversational style," she said. "You've probably noticed."

"I haven't read very far yet."

She crouched a little, regularizing up her five pages of copy by squaring them against the surface of the desk. "It's dreadful of me, isn't it, to be dashing off practically the whole semester's work like this at the last minute? Even after the last minute: you were so nice to give me the extra day."

"Are you feeling better?" he asked.

"I'm over the original shock of Alice's accident," she said. "Are you?"

He looked down. "Over the shock? Not entirely, I guess."

Miss Marcy said: "Alice thought you were a fine, fine teacher, you know. She always said you were the greatest person . . . I hope it doesn't embarrass you to hear that."

Holmberg did not say anything.

Miss Marcy focused her eyes a little distantly on the window. "Remember that time in class," she said, "when you started to read Alice's story, and she stopped you and said, 'Oh, please don't read that!' Do you know why she stopped you?"

"Not exactly."

"There was something very personal in it. About a boy in the class she was having an affair with. She was afraid it might hurt his feelings."

"Oh."

"Anyway, she appreciated your reading that story by Flannery O'Connor instead."

Holmberg said, "You haven't spoken to her at the hospital? I mean, she's not conscious, is she?"

"No," Miss Marcy said, "she probably won't recover consciousness at all. Her mother's arrived from New Jersey, you know."

Holmberg shook his head.

Miss Marcy looked at him levelly. "She was that kind of girl, wasn't she? She didn't want to hurt anybody."

"Most of us don't want to hurt anybody," Holmberg said.

Miss Marcy blinked a little. "Well, you know what I mean." She had moved around behind him, looking over his shoulder to see what marks he had made on the first page of her story.

"How is it so far? What's that 'p.f.' for?"

Holmberg turned.

"Pathetic fallacy."

"Oh, but it isn't!" she exclaimed. "It's a direct refutation of pathetic fallacy. If I'd said springtime *is* romance time, then it would be p.f. But I'm saying springtime is *not* romance time; that's the whole point."

"It's still a little gushy," Holmberg said.

"Is it?" Miss Marcy blinked again. "I'll tone it down." She moved back around the desk, smiling very brightly. But she lingered once more in the doorway. "You know," she said, "the boy wasn't hurt at all."

"What boy?"

"The boy who was driving the motorcycle Alice was on. He just banged up his knee a little."

Holmberg didn't say anything; in fact he looked back down at her story as though anxious to get back to it. She hung on another moment, then she said, "Well, back to the salt mines." In a moment he heard her typing again.

Probably, he decided, he had been abrupt with her. What she wanted, no doubt, was a long, melancholy conversation about Alice and how she never wanted to hurt anybody. Such a conversation might make her feel better, but it would only make him feel worse. He was ready to think about Alice, but not to talk about her with Marilyn Marcy. What Marilyn desired of him was to conduct a seminar with her on the ironies of the situation. Like wasn't it ironic that the boy wasn't hurt? Wasn't it also ironic that Alice scarcely knew this particular boy (as he had heard), indeed that she probably had no feeling for him at all? Wasn't there a story there somewhere? With Dr. Holmberg's help, Marilyn would learn what to feel.

For lack of anything else to do, he took the grade report sheet out of the top drawer of his desk, clicked out the tip of his Papermate pen, and gave Alice Cole an A. He felt at once foolish, futile, idiotic. It was not that Alice did not deserve an A, but he knew he probably would have given her a B, except for the accident. The A was after all his gesture. He didn't want to hurt anybody either. Not Alice, who "thought he was the greatest person." Not Alice's heirs either, if that was all they were to have of Alice. Still, he felt cheap doing it, like a funeral director who tries to bear himself respectfully toward the corpse and toward the corpse's relatives. It was not only false, it was pointless.

Holmberg refolded the sheet. Almost he was growing accustomed to his students getting killed or badly injured in highway accidents. It happened so damned often, in fact, that he had to caution the other students against writing stories about the subject. He told them that since such accidents came out of the blue, they had no demonstrable connection with human purpose. For instance, when McCafferty turned his MG over on the hill road and it rolled all the way down the mountain: it was just that McCafferty had missed the turn. Or when Arnold Whatshisname ran over his fraternity brother, who was throwing up along the shoulder of the road: Arnold was amiably drunk, he didn't mean to do it. Nobody was feeling anything one way or the other. Or Alice. She was taking a ride on the back of a motorcycle, and nobody wanted to hurt anybody. Holmberg rejected the idea of unconscious complicity; he did not believe they were deep-dyed sadists or masochists.

Alice herself, for example, had written with real acuity about that boy in the class, yet she had managed to avoid hurting him. "Oh, please don't read that," she had said, thereby controlling the consequences of what she felt. It was a mature way to respond. He could almost hear her saying it.

Forty minutes later, Miss Marcy reappeared with Pages 11 to 15. She seemed somewhat chastened, and Holmberg wondered if it would be kindness to tell her to stop, that he would accept what she had already written and call it enough. But he decided that she might only start blinking at him again as though he had rejected her.

"You ought to take a five-minute break," he said in a friendly tone. "Get a cup of coffee for yourself."

She had wandered over to the window, a little dormer thrust into the crook of the eaves. "No, thanks," she said. "I'll barely get finished as it is." Her eyes were so mascaraed, *she* was beginning to look like a corpse.

"You'll make it," he said encouragingly.

Her voice was very mournful. "It's raining again," she said. "Is that pathetic fallacy?"

"Life and literature aren't the same," he said cheerfully. "They're two different things."

For some reason she looked aggrieved at the news. "I never heard it put that way," she said.

He had been trying to lighten the mood. Now he leaned back and put his hands behind his head. "Oh, when I'm off duty, Marilyn, I say some wild things."

Momentarily, she responded with a coquettish look. But that was out of habit; what his informality really did was give her confidence to return to the subject she wanted to talk about.

"Do you still have Alice's last stories?" she asked.

He conceded that he did. "The last two."

"Are they good?"

"Pretty good. It's been over a week since I read them."

Miss Marcy said: "You know, her mother would like to have them."

"All right," Holmberg said. "Her mother can have them."

"May I take them over after I'm finished here?" Miss Marcy asked. "I'm going straight over to the hospital and it might make her mother feel better, a little, since she spoke of wanting them—"

The girl was swaying slightly, not as though she were faint, but as if she were possessed by something. More than a bit irritated, Holmberg thrust back his chair and pulled open a desk drawer; he had no doubt that Miss Marcy wanted Alice's mother to want the manuscripts. He handed them to the girl at once, and said: "Now I think you'd better try to forget about this all, Marilyn. If you feel you can't, I'll understand." He looked up at her. "In fact, I think it might be better if you called it a day and—"

"Oh, no!" she said. "I don't want you to think that I'm using Alice to get off. I hope that's not what you think!"

Holmberg said that he didn't.

"I can't help reverting to the subject," she went on. "It's on my mind."

"I understand."

"And I *do* appreciate your waiting so patiently!"

Holmberg picked up Pages 11 to 15, hoping the move might get rid of her. She seemed calmer all at once, reassured and reassuring. Before leaving, she snatched up Alice Cole's manuscripts. In the doorway she said, "You'll find I've toned down my style. It's much more straightforward now."

As soon as she had vanished, Holmberg raised his eyes to stare at the wall for the full fifteen seconds it took her to get down the hall. Then the familiar rattle of the machinery began again, and his eyes went back to the page.

> "You don't make yourself very clear." He reached into his shirt pocket for a cigarette and inhaled deeply, blowing a stream of smoke that fanned itself out across the windshield in rolling curls.

> "OK, have it your way." He reached down and flicked the light

switch, attracting the attention of a car hop. She nodded her
head and then entered the building to leave the tray.

"That blonde in the front seat is Jane Slater, Bud's sister. He
graduated when you did, didn't he?"

"Yeah. She's grown up quite a bit. A very cute girl." He gazed
past her shoulder out the window.

A small knot of fear made her stomach contract, and she added
tensely, "Here comes our coffee."

Holmberg stared again at the blank wall. I can't go on, he thought, I'll go on.
In Miss Marcy's margin he wrote, "This is at least less gushy."

About twenty minutes later, sitting with his arms folded, he noted the first
long interruption in the steady echo of the typewriter. He had long since
completed reading and marking the last page she had given him, then had let
himself become mesmerized by the remarkably rhythmic vibrations from down
the hall. The sense of the absurdity of her creative process and his critical
process had, more or less, left him. Still, he couldn't concentrate on any other
reading.

In the extending intermission he quickly began to wonder if he shouldn't go
down and check up on her. It was not Miss Marcy's habit to lapse silently into
thought. The one thing she might be doing in the stillness was reading Alice
Cole's manuscripts. If she had left for the restroom, he would have heard her
footsteps. For a moment, he continued to stare at the little square of wet foliage
framed in the dormer window, thinking about Alice Cole's stories and her nice
eastern wit and the precision of her feeling, when a terrible thought suddenly
struck him.

Miss Marcy's typing resumed at the same moment. The thought he had was
a memory, vague it still was, that in one of Alice's stories she had written a sharp
and satirical portrait of her mother. It was one of the things he had most
respected in the story. But it would be cruel to let her mother see it. He recalled
it quite clearly now. The character was drawn as a transparent social climber.
She appeared only once in the story, at the side of a country club swimming
pool. She sat in a cane chair and kept adjusting the strap on her bathing suit.
No one could miss the tone Alice took toward her.

That the character was based on her own mother, Holmberg could not doubt.
It was too charged not to be. Also, there was other evidence. The father in the
story was a banker as, Holmberg had learned, Alice's father was. The daughter,
the Alice-figure, was a projection; but it too was unmistakably Alice—humorous, faintly restless, just a bit better-looking and more glamorous than the real
Alice was.

Holmberg got at once to his feet. He would have to get the manuscript back.
He might be able to remove just the country club scene. If they noticed some of
the pages were missing, he could say that they were lost. He could say something.

He moved down the hall toward the sound of Miss Marcy's typing. If he was
lucky, he could get back the story without any explanation to her. Otherwise he

would have to enter a conspiracy with the silly girl. She would revel in it: a conspiracy of kindness. He could hear her telling her friends: "Dr. Holmberg and I were afraid of hurting Alice's mother." The idea of her being able to couple his name with hers as it suited her maudlin fancy appalled him. For an instant, he even felt it physically, and he slowed his step. Then he proceeded more softly. He hoped she had not heard him coming.

When he reached the door to the secretary's office where she was, he lingered in the doorway, looking around for the manuscripts. Miss Marcy's back was toward him. She had not broken the even rhythm of her typing. Her purse was behind the typewriter on the table where she worked, and he quickly saw that that was where Alice's stories were. It was a big brown shoulder bag. The manuscripts were sticking out one corner under the flap.

"Getting impatient?"

Miss Marcy had spoken to him without turning. Her hands hung suspended over the keys, as though they had stopped out of courtesy to him, not because they couldn't have gone on while she was talking.

Holmberg said: "No, I'm not impatient. When everything fell silent a moment ago, I thought maybe you hit a snag."

"I'm suffering ribbon trouble," Miss Marcy said. "The ribbon won't wind right. It's all shredded and strained. It's plumb tuckered out." She reached him some pages back over her shoulder. "In a minute, I'm going to have to go downstairs and get a new one."

He took the pages.

Miss Marcy said: "This story should round off very nicely at thirty."

The wrists quivered and flexed, the fingers dove once more at the keys. Holmberg looked again at the purse on the table, then turned around and left the office.

For many minutes Holmberg sat behind his desk, waiting. He did not read Pages 16 through 19. For a long time there was no break in the sound of the rolling sea, but, patient for his opportunity, he kept his ear sharp. It was not Alice's mother he was protecting. He knew that much. It was Alice. He gave less than a damn about Alice's mother.

When the lull came, the loud silence, he felt calm and prepared. It was too early for Pages 20 through 25. He listened for the sound of her steps, and when they came, as he had anticipated, they did not move in his direction. He could hear them going the other way down the stairs.

If it was only to the restroom, he knew very well she would take her purse with her. But if not, if she was going for the ribbon, it gave him his chance and he would take it. He waited until the click of her heels was reverberating from well down the stairs. He did not hurry down the corridor, he walked grimly. At the door of the secretary's office, he hardly glanced at the stairway from which she would be returning. Inside the office, he saw at once that her purse was there. Next to it lay the two sprocket wheels from inside the typewriter joined by a ribbon as strained and shredded as Miss Marcy's soul.

Holmberg opened the purse and took out the story he wanted. At the same time, he heard footsteps again at the bottom of the stairs. They were unquestionably Miss Marcy's. Evidently she had gone to fetch the ribbon out of the supply closet. Holmberg closed the purse, leaving the second manuscript sticking out of the corner. He got out of there, hurrying this time. He made it to his office without too much to spare.

In his chair again, he waited for the typing to resume. Miss Marcy was obviously having difficulties changing the ribbon. He was breathing a little hard. He had no immediate plan how he would get the story back into her purse after he had removed the country club scene, but perhaps something would come to him.

Finally, after many minutes, he could hear her rewinding the new ribbon, and when the typing started up again at once, he knew he was safe from interruption. Slowly, he began turning the pages of Alice Cole's story. Now and then he read a sentence or two. At one point he erased an especially sardonic comment he had earlier written into the margin. The story was better than he had remembered it.

When he had gone through the entire manuscript, however, without finding the country club scene, he grew puzzled. One more time he glanced over the story, page by page. Then, of course, he realized what had happened, and it made him feel cold and angry, and, worst of all, insensitive. He had misremembered where Alice had put her mother. It wasn't in this story at all. It was in the one still in Miss Marcy's shoulder bag.

At ten minutes to four, Miss Marcy returned to Holmberg's office. She laid several more pages on his desk without making any comment. He did not look up at her. He had a book open on the desk in front of him.

Presently, Miss Marcy said: "You know, Dr. Holmberg, I've been thinking. Wouldn't it be nice if a bunch of us got together, maybe along with the school magazine, and put out a special memorial edition of Alice Cole's stories?"

Holmberg did not raise his eyes.

"Probably," she went on, "we could get hold of more than just these two stories. I mean, we'll probably find her earlier work among her things. If she dies. Among her effects."

Holmberg lowered his head further. If her eyes happened to notice the manuscript of Alice's on his desk, he would not have registered it. He did not care anymore.

Miss Marcy said: "Would you happen to know if the stories she wrote earlier in the term are in her possession? Did you hand them back to her?"

Holmberg said: "Miss Marcy, I think I've had enough."

Miss Marcy blinked at him.

"Pardon me?"

"I say I think I've had enough. Go home. This story you're writing is rot. How can you hope to write anything decent under these conditions and with your mind dwelling so morbidly on another subject?" She blinked again. "Besides," he said, "you're asking too much of me. You haven't any right to expect me to sit here all afternoon patiently waiting for your sausage machine to grind out five pages by five pages of work that you've had all semester to complete. It's absurd. I mean it. Go home."

Miss Marcy began to cry.

Holmberg watched the tears gather in her eyes, then he looked quickly away.

She wept silently at first, then suddenly she broke into heart-rending sobs. She sank into the chair beside his desk, and sitting there on the very front edge of it with her right arm on his desk and the fist of her left hand clenched against her mouth, she wept and wept until he thought she would never stop. At last, he reached over and patted her hand once.

"All right," he said softly. "It's all right."

"I can't help it. I'm sorry . . . I'm sorry."

It was a long time before she stopped. The mascara ran out of her eyes in two long black streaks down her cheeks. Holmberg patted her hand again. She seemed to be quieting down.

She said: "I guess I'm not crying because of what you said."

She rubbed her cheeks with the heel and palm of her hands.

"No, I think I know that," Holmberg replied. "But I should have said it more gently." For himself, he tried to understand why he hadn't. In a way, it seemed that in her need she had driven him to it. But that didn't entirely explain why he had yielded.

"Oh, I think I feel better now," Miss Marcy said at last. "I feel better. I wasn't really over the original shock till now."

"I understand."

She got to her feet.

"Don't you feel better too?" she asked curiously.

"I wonder," Holmberg said.

But after she left for the restroom, he admitted it to himself. It had been primitive as a soap opera, and exactly the opposite of everything he had stood for all semester. Nevertheless, he admitted it again: he felt better. And why? Because he must have been sick of himself, sick of fine judgments and all the protocol he knew for emotions. So he had made her cry, as though tears lent an authenticity that words hadn't been able to do. Not *her* words. And certainly not his either. It was disgraceful.

Presently, he heard the clackety-clack of the typewriter again. He went down the corridor and was surprised at what he found: Miss Marcy hunched over the infernal machine, having resumed. She heard him come in, but she didn't turn around. On the window, drops still rolled down the pane.

"I feel so much better," she said, "that I'm going to finish it whether you stay around and read it, or not."

After a moment, Holmberg said, "Well, it's true that there are a few things I can do in the meantime."

What he did was ask for Alice's other short story from the shoulder bag, and while Miss Marcy typed, he worked on it for a while. He cut out two pages from the manuscript, then x-ed over some connective material, and put new numbers on the pages. At last, he restored it to the cavernous handbag.

Sidelong, Miss Marcy glanced at him. "Is it all right now?"

"Everything's reassembled," Holmberg said.

While she was finishing, he put on his raincoat and took the grade sheet, which he protected between coat and sweater, over to the registrar. Without thinking very hard about it, he had left Alice with her A, and to Miss Marcy he gave a C plus. Then, dripping, he returned to his office and waited for her story to be completed.

TOBIAS WOLFF

Tobias Wolff was born in Alabama and grew up in Washington state. After four years in the Army he attended Oxford University and subsequently worked as a reporter, waiter, high-school teacher, and night watchman before receiving a Stegner Fellowship at Stanford in 1975. His books include the novel The Barracks Thief, *winner of the 1985 PEN/Faulkner Award, and two collections of stories,* In the Garden of the North American Martyrs *and* Back in the World. *A memoir of youth,* This Boy's Life, *will be published by Atlantic Monthly Press in January, 1989.*

"'Hunters in the Snow' was an important story for me. I wrote it during my time at Stanford, after a series of false starts on a novel that wouldn't work. The encouraging reactions of John L'Heureux and Ron Hansen, to whom I first showed 'Hunters,' gave me heart to do what I wanted to do anyway, which was write more stories."

◆　　　◆　　　◆

Hunters in the Snow

TUB HAD BEEN WAITING for an hour in the falling snow. He paced the sidewalk to keep warm and stuck his head out over the curb whenever he saw lights approaching. One driver stopped for him but before Tub could wave the man on he saw the rifle on Tub's back and hit the gas. The tires spun on the ice.

The fall of snow thickened. Tub stood below the overhang of a building. Across the road the clouds whitened just above the rooftops, and the street lights went out. He shifted the rifle strap to his other shoulder. The whiteness seeped up the sky.

A truck slid around the corner, horn blaring, rear end sashaying. Tub moved to the sidewalk and held up his hand. The truck jumped the curb and kept coming, half on the street and half on the sidewalk. It wasn't slowing down at all. Tub stood for a moment, still holding up his hand, then jumped back. His rifle slipped off his shoulder and clattered on the ice, a sandwich fell out of his pocket. He ran for the steps of the building. Another sandwich and a package of cookies tumbled onto the new snow. He made the steps and looked back.

The truck had stopped several feet beyond where Tub had been standing. He picked up his sandwiches and his cookies and slung the rifle and went up to the driver's window. The driver was bent against the steering wheel, slapping his knees and drumming his feet on the floorboards. He looked like a cartoon of a person laughing, except that his eyes watched the man on the seat beside him.

"You ought to see yourself," the driver said. "He looks just like a beach ball with a hat on, doesn't he? Doesn't he, Frank?"

The man beside him smiled and looked off.

"You almost ran me down," Tub said. "You could've killed me."

"Come on, Tub," said the man beside the driver. "Be mellow. Kenny was just messing around." He opened the door and slid over to the middle of the seat.

Tub took the bolt out of his rifle and climbed in beside him. "I waited an hour," he said. "If you meant ten o'clock why didn't you say ten o'clock?"

"Tub, you haven't done anything but complain since we got here," said the man in the middle. "If you want to piss and moan all day you might as well go home and bitch at your kids. Take your pick." When Tub didn't say anything he turned to the driver. "Okay, Kenny, let's hit the road."

Some juvenile delinquents had heaved a brick through the windshield on the driver's side, so the cold and snow tunneled right into the cab. The heater didn't work. They covered themselves with a couple of blankets Kenny had brought along and pulled down the muffs on their caps. Tub tried to keep his hands warm by rubbing them under the blanket but Frank made him stop.

They left Spokane and drove deep into the country, running along black lines of fences. The snow let up, but still there was no edge to the land where it met the sky. Nothing moved in the chalky fields. The cold bleached their faces and made the stubble stand out on their cheeks and along their upper lips. They stopped twice for coffee before they got to the woods where Kenny wanted to hunt.

Tub was for trying someplace different; two years in a row they'd been up and down this land and hadn't seen a thing. Frank didn't care one way or the other, he just wanted to get out of the goddamned truck. "Feel that," Frank said, slamming the door. He spread his feet and closed his eyes and leaned his head way back and breathed deeply. "Tune in on that energy."

"Another thing," Kenny said. "This is open land. Most of the land around here is posted."

"I'm cold," Tub said.

Frank breathed out. "Stop bitching, Tub. Get centered."

"I wasn't bitching."

"Centered," Kenny said. "Next thing you'll be wearing a nightgown, Frank. Selling flowers out at the airport."

"Kenny," Frank said, "you talk too much."

"Okay," Kenny said. "I won't say a word. Like I won't say anything about a certain babysitter."

"What babysitter?" Tub asked.

"That's between us," Frank said, looking at Kenny. "That's confidential. You keep your mouth shut."

Kenny laughed.

"You're asking for it," Frank said.

"Asking for what?"

"You'll see."

"Hey," Tub said, "are we hunting or what?"

They started off across the field. Tub had trouble getting through the fences. Frank and Kenny could have helped him; they could have lifted up on the top wire and stepped on the bottom wire, but they didn't. They stood and watched him. There were a lot of fences and Tub was puffing when they reached the woods.

They hunted for over two hours and saw no deer, no tracks, no sign. Finally they stopped by the creek to eat. Kenny had several slices of pizza and a couple of candy bars; Frank had a sandwich, an apple, two carrots, and a square of chocolate; Tub ate one hard-boiled egg and a stick of celery.

"You ask me how I want to die today," Kenny said, "I'll tell you burn me at the stake." He turned to Tub. "You still on that diet?" He winked at Frank.

"What do you think? You think I like hard-boiled eggs?"

"All I can say is, it's the first diet I ever heard of where you gained weight from it."

"Who said I gained weight?"

"Oh, pardon me. I take it back. You're just wasting away before my very eyes. Isn't he, Frank?"

Frank had his fingers fanned out, tips against the bark of the stump where he'd laid his food. His knuckles were hairy. He wore a heavy wedding band and on his right pinky another gold ring with a flat face and an "F" in what looked like diamonds. He turned the ring this way and that. "Tub," he said, "you haven't seen your own balls in ten years."

Kenny doubled over laughing. He took off his hat and slapped his leg with it.

"What am I supposed to do?" Tub said. "It's my glands."

They left the woods and hunted along the creek. Frank and Kenny worked one bank and Tub worked the other, moving upstream. The snow was light but the drifts were deep and hard to move through. Wherever Tub looked the surface was smooth, undisturbed, and after a time he lost interest. He stopped looking for tracks and just tried to keep up with Frank and Kenny on the other side. A moment came when he realized he hadn't seen them in a long time. The breeze was moving from him to them; when it stilled he could sometimes hear Kenny laughing but that was all. He quickened his pace, breasting hard into the drifts, fighting away the snow with his knees and elbows. He heard his heart and felt the flush on his face but he never once stopped.

Tub caught up with Frank and Kenny at a bend of the creek. They were standing on a log that stretched from their bank to his. Ice had backed up behind the log. Frozen reeds stuck out, barely nodding when the air moved.

"See anything?" Frank asked.

Tub shook his head.

There wasn't much daylight left and they decided to head back toward the road. Frank and Kenny crossed the log and they started downstream, using the trail Tub had broken. Before they had gone very far Kenny stopped. "Look at that," he said, and pointed to some tracks going from the creek back into the woods. Tub's footprints crossed right over them. There on the bank, plain as day, were several mounds of deer sign. "What do you think that is, Tub?" Kenny kicked at it. "Walnuts on vanilla icing?"

"I guess I didn't notice."

Kenny looked at Frank.

"I was lost."

"You were lost. Big deal."

They followed the tracks into the woods. The deer had gone over a fence half buried in drifting snow. A no hunting sign was nailed to the top of one of the posts. Frank laughed and said the son of a bitch could read. Kenny wanted to go after him but Frank said no way, the people out here didn't mess around. He thought maybe the farmer who owned the land would let them use it if they asked. Kenny wasn't so sure. Anyway, he figured that by the time they walked to the truck and drove up the road and doubled back it would be almost dark.

"Relax," Frank said. "You can't hurry nature. If we're meant to get that deer, we'll get it. If we're not, we won't."

They started back toward the truck. This part of the woods was mainly pine. The snow was shaded and had a glaze on it. It held up Kenny and Frank but Tub kept falling through. As he kicked forward, the edge of the crust bruised his shins. Kenny and Frank pulled ahead of him, to where he couldn't even hear their voices any more. He sat down on a stump and wiped his face. He ate both the sandwiches and half the cookies, taking his own sweet time. It was dead quiet.

When Tub crossed the last fence into the road the truck started moving. Tub had to run for it and just managed to grab hold of the tailgate and hoist himself into the bed. He lay there, panting. Kenny looked out the rear window and grinned. Tub crawled into the lee of the cab to get out of the freezing wind. He pulled his earflaps low and pushed his chin into the collar of his coat. Someone rapped on the window but Tub would not turn around.

He and Frank waited outside while Kenny went into the farmhouse to ask permission. The house was old and paint was curling off the sides. The smoke streamed westward off the top of the chimney, fanning away into a thin gray plume. Above the ridge of the hills another ridge of blue clouds was rising.

"You've got a short memory," Tub said.

"What?" Frank said. He had been staring off.

"I used to stick up for you."

"Okay, so you used to stick up for me. What's eating you?"

"You shouldn't have just left me back there like that."

"You're a grown-up, Tub. You can take care of yourself. Anyway, if you think you're the only person with problems I can tell you that you're not."

"Is something bothering you, Frank?"

Frank kicked at a branch poking out of the snow. "Never mind," he said.

"What did Kenny mean about the babysitter?"

"Kenny talks too much," Frank said. "You just mind your own business."

Kenny came out of the farmhouse and gave the thumbs-up and they began walking back toward the woods. As they passed the barn a large black hound with a grizzled snout ran out and barked at them. Every time he barked he slid backwards a bit, like a cannon recoiling. Kenny got down on all fours and snarled and barked back at him, and the dog slunk away into the barn, looking over his shoulder and peeing a little as he went.

"That's an old-timer," Frank said. "A real graybeard. Fifteen years if he's a day."

"Too old," Kenny said.

Past the barn they cut off through the fields. The land was unfenced and the crust was freezing up thick and they made good time. They kept to the edge of the field until they picked up the tracks again and followed them into the woods, farther and farther back toward the hills. The trees started to blur with the shadows and the wind rose and needled their faces with the crystals it swept off the glaze. Finally they lost the tracks.

Kenny swore and threw down his hat. "This is the worst day of hunting I ever had, bar none." He picked up his hat and brushed off the snow. "This will be the first season since I was fifteen I haven't got my deer."

"It isn't the deer," Frank said. "It's the hunting. There are all these forces out here and you just have to go with them."

"You go with them," Kenny said. "I came out here to get me a deer, not listen to a bunch of hippie bullshit. And if it hadn't been for dimples here I would have, too."

"That's enough," Frank said.

"And you—you're so busy thinking about that little jailbait of yours you wouldn't know a deer if you saw one."

"Drop dead," Frank said, and turned away.

Kenny and Tub followed him back across the fields. When they were coming up to the barn Kenny stopped and pointed. "I hate that post," he said. He raised his rifle and fired. It sounded like a dry branch cracking. The post splintered along its right side, up towards the top. "There," Kenny said. "It's dead."

"Knock it off," Frank said, walking ahead.

Kenny looked at Tub. He smiled. "I hate that tree," he said, and fired again. Tub hurried to catch up with Frank. He started to speak but just then the dog ran out of the barn and barked at them. "Easy, boy," Frank said.

"I hate that dog." Kenny was behind them.

"That's enough," Frank said. "You put that gun down."

Kenny fired. The bullet went in between the dog's eyes. He sank right down into the snow, his legs splayed out on each side, his yellow eyes open and staring. Except for the blood he looked like a small bearskin rug. The blood ran down the dog's muzzle into the snow.

They all looked at the dog lying there.

"What did he ever do to you?" Tub asked. "He was just barking."

Kenny turned to Tub. "I hate you."

Tub shot from the waist. Kenny jerked backward against the fence and buckled to his knees. He folded his hands across his stomach. "Look," he said. His hands were covered with blood. In the dusk his blood was more blue than red. It seemed to belong to the shadows. It didn't seem out of place. Kenny eased himself onto his back. He sighed several times, deeply. "You shot me," he said.

"I had to," Tub said. He knelt beside Kenny. "Oh God," he said. "Frank. Frank."

Frank hadn't moved since Kenny killed the dog.

"Frank!" Tub shouted.

"I was just kidding around," Kenny said. "It was a joke. Oh!" he said, and arched his back suddenly. "Oh!" he said again, and dug his heels into the snow and pushed himself along on his head for several feet. Then he stopped and lay there, rocking back and forth on his heels and head like a wrestler doing warm-up exercises.

Frank roused himself. "Kenny," he said. He bent down and put his gloved hand on Kenny's brow. "You shot him," he said to Tub.

"He made me," Tub said.

"No no no," Kenny said.

Tub was weeping from the eyes and nostrils. His whole face was wet. Frank closed his eyes, then looked down at Kenny again. "Where does it hurt?"

"Everywhere," Kenny said, "just everywhere."

"Oh God," Tub said.

"I mean where did it go in?" Frank said.

"Here." Kenny pointed at the wound in his stomach. It was welling slowly with blood.

"You're lucky," Frank said. "It's on the left side. It missed your appendix. If it had hit your appendix you'd really be in the soup." He turned and threw up onto the snow, holding his sides as if to keep warm.

"Are you all right?" Tub said.

"There's some aspirin in the truck," Kenny said.

"I'm all right," Frank said.

"We'd better call an ambulance," Tub said.

"Jesus," Frank said. "What are we going to say?"

"Exactly what happened," Tub said. "He was going to shoot me but I shot him first."

"No sir!" Kenny said. "I wasn't either!"

Frank patted Kenny on the arm. "Easy does it, partner." He stood. "Let's go."

Tub picked up Kenny's rifle as they walked down toward the farmhouse. "No sense leaving this around," he said. "Kenny might get ideas."

"I can tell you one thing," Frank said. "You've really done it this time. This definitely takes the cake."

They had to knock on the door twice before it was opened by a thin man with lank hair. The room behind him was filled with smoke. He squinted at them. "You get anything?" he asked.

"No," Frank said.

"I knew you wouldn't. That's what I told the other fellow."

"We've had an accident."

The man looked past Frank and Tub into the gloom. "Shoot your friend, did you?"

Frank nodded.

"I did," Tub said.

"I suppose you want to use the phone."

"If it's okay."

The man in the door looked behind him, then stepped back. Frank and Tub followed him into the house. There was a woman sitting by the stove in the middle of the room. The stove was smoking badly. She looked up and then down again at the child asleep in her lap. Her face was white and damp; strands of hair were pasted across her forehead. Tub warmed his hands over the stove while Frank went into the kitchen to call. The man who had let them in stood at the window, his hands in his pockets.

"My friend shot your dog," Tub said.

The man nodded without turning around. "I should have done it myself. I just couldn't."

"He loved that dog so much," the woman said. The child squirmed and she rocked it.

"You asked him to?" Tub said. "You asked him to shoot your dog?"

"He was old and sick. Couldn't chew his food any more. I would have done it myself but I don't have a gun."

"You couldn't have anyway," the woman said. "Never in a million years."

The man shrugged.

Frank came out of the kitchen. "We'll have to take him ourselves. The nearest hospital is fifty miles from here and all their ambulances are out anyway."

The woman knew a shortcut but the directions were complicated and Tub had to write them down. The man told them where they could find some boards to carry Kenny on. He didn't have a flashlight but he said he would leave the porch light on.

It was dark outside. The clouds were low and heavy-looking and the wind blew in shrill gusts. There was a screen loose on the house and it banged slowly and then quickly as the wind rose again. They could hear it all the way to the barn. Frank went for the boards while Tub looked for Kenny, who was not where they had left him. Tub found him farther up the drive, lying on his stomach. "You okay?" Tub said.

"It hurts."

"Frank says it missed your appendix."

"I already had my appendix out."

"All right," Frank said, coming up to them. "We'll have you in a nice warm bed before you can say Jack Robinson." He put the two boards on Kenny's right side.

"Just as long as I don't have one of those male nurses," Kenny said.

"Ha ha," Frank said. "That's the spirit. Get ready, set, *over you go*," and he rolled Kenny onto the boards. Kenny screamed and kicked his legs in the air. When he quieted down Frank and Tub lifted the boards and carried him down the drive. Tub had the back end, and with the snow blowing into his face he had trouble with his footing. Also he was tired and the man inside had forgotten to turn the porch light on. Just past the house Tub slipped and threw out his hands to catch himself. The boards fell and Kenny tumbled out and rolled to the bottom of the drive, yelling all the way. He came to rest against the right front wheel of the truck.

"You fat moron," Frank said. "You aren't good for diddly."

Tub grabbed Frank by the collar and backed him hard up against the fence. Frank tried to pull his hands away but Tub shook him and snapped his head back and forth and finally Frank gave up.

"What do you know about fat," Tub said. "What do you know about glands." As he spoke he kept shaking Frank. "What do you know about me."

"All right," Frank said.

"No more," Tub said.

"All right."

"No more talking to me like that. No more watching. No more laughing."

"Okay, Tub. I promise."

Tub let go of Frank and leaned his forehead against the fence. His arms hung straight at his sides.

"I'm sorry, Tub." Frank touched him on the shoulder. "I'll be down at the truck."

Tub stood by the fence for a while and then got the rifles off the porch. Frank had rolled Kenny back onto the boards and they lifted him into the bed of the truck. Frank spread the seat blankets over him. "Warm enough?" he asked.

Kenny nodded.

"Okay. Now how does reverse work on this thing?"

"All the way to the left and up." Kenny sat up as Frank started forward to the cab. "Frank!"

"What?"

"If it sticks don't force it."

The truck started right away. "One thing," Frank said, "you've got to hand it to the Japanese. A very ancient, very spiritual culture and they can still make a hell of a truck." He glanced over at Tub. "Look, I'm sorry. I didn't know you felt that way, honest to God I didn't. You should have said something."

"I did."

"When? Name one time."

"A couple of hours ago."

"I guess I wasn't paying attention."

"That's true, Frank," Tub said. "You don't pay attention very much."

"Tub," Frank said, "what happened back there, I should have been more sympathetic. I realize that. You were going through a lot. I just want you to know it wasn't your fault. He was asking for it."

"You think so?"

"Absolutely. It was him or you. I would have done the same thing in your shoes, no question."

The wind was blowing into their faces. The snow was a moving white wall in front of their lights; it swirled into the cab through the hole in the windshield and settled on them. Tub clapped his hands and shifted around to stay warm, but it didn't work.

"I'm going to have to stop," Frank said. "I can't feel my fingers."

Up ahead they saw some lights off the road. It was a tavern. Outside in the parking lot there were several jeeps and trucks. A couple of them had deer strapped across their hoods. Frank parked and they went back to Kenny. "How you doing, partner," Frank said.

"I'm cold."

"Well, don't feel like the Lone Ranger. It's worse inside, take my word for it. You should get that windshield fixed."

"Look," Tub said, "he threw the blankets off." They were lying in a heap against the tailgate.

"Now look, Kenny," Frank said, "it's no use whining about being cold if you're not going to try and keep warm. You've got to do your share." He spread the blankets over Kenny and tucked them in at the corners.

"They blew off."

"Hold on to them then."

"Why are we stopping, Frank?"

"Because if me and Tub don't get warmed up we're going to freeze solid and then where will you be?" He punched Kenny lightly in the arm. "So just hold your horses."

The bar was full of men in colored jackets, mostly orange. The waitress brought coffee. "Just what the doctor ordered," Frank said, cradling the steaming cup in his hand. His skin was bone white. "Tub, I've been thinking. What you said about me not paying attention, that's true."

"It's okay."

"No. I really had that coming. I guess I've just been a little too interested in old number one. I've had a lot on my mind. Not that that's any excuse."

"Forget it, Frank. I sort of lost my temper back there. I guess we're all a little on edge."

Frank shook his head. "It isn't just that."

"You want to talk about it?"

"Just between us, Tub?"

"Sure, Frank. Just between us."

"Tub, I think I'm going to be leaving Nancy."

"Oh, Frank. Oh, Frank." Tub sat back and shook his head.

Frank reached out and laid his hand on Tub's arm. "Tub, have you ever been really in love?"

"Well—"

"I mean *really* in love." He squeezed Tub's wrist. "With your whole being."

"I don't know. When you put it like that, I don't know."

"You haven't then. Nothing against you, but you'd know it if you had." Frank let go of Tub's arm. "This isn't just some bit of fluff I'm talking about."

"Who is she, Frank?"

Frank paused. He looked into his empty cup. "Roxanne Brewer."

"Cliff Brewer's kid? The babysitter?"

"You can't just put people into categories like that, Tub. That's why the whole system is wrong. And that's why this country is going to hell in a rowboat."

"But she can't be more than—" Tub shook his head.

"Fifteen. She'll be sixteen in May." Frank smiled. "May fourth, three twenty-seven p.m. Hell, Tub, a hundred years ago she'd have been an old maid by that age. Juliet was only thirteen."

"Juliet? Juliet Miller? Jesus, Frank, she doesn't even have breasts. She doesn't even wear a top to her bathing suit. She's still collecting frogs."

"Not Juliet Miller. The real Juliet. Tub, don't you see how you're dividing people up into categories? He's an executive, she's a secretary, he's a truck driver, she's fifteen years old. Tub, this so-called babysitter, this so-called fifteen-year-old has more in her little finger than most of us have in our entire bodies. I can tell you this little lady is something special."

Tub nodded. "I know the kids like her."

"She's opened up whole worlds to me that I never knew were there."

"What does Nancy think about all of this?"

"She doesn't know."

"You haven't told her?"

"Not yet. It's not so easy. She's been damned good to me all these years. Then there's the kids to consider." The brightness in Frank's eyes trembled and he wiped quickly at them with the back of his hand. "I guess you think I'm a complete bastard."

"No, Frank. I don't think that."

"Well, you *ought* to."

"Frank, when you've got a friend it means you've always got someone on your side, no matter what. That's the way I feel about it, anyway."

"You mean that, Tub?"

"Sure I do."

Frank smiled. "You don't know how good it feels to hear you say that."

Kenny had tried to get out of the truck but he hadn't made it. He was jackknifed over the tailgate, his head hanging above the bumper. They lifted him back into the bed and covered him again. He was sweating and his teeth chattered. "It hurts, Frank."

"It wouldn't hurt so much if you just stayed put. Now we're going to the hospital. Got that? Say it—I'm going to the hospital."

"I'm going to the hospital."

"Again."

"I'm going to the hospital."

"Now just keep saying that to yourself and before you know it we'll be there."

After they had gone a few miles Tub turned to Frank. "I just pulled a real boner," he said.

"What's that?"

"I left the directions on the table back there."

"That's okay. I remember them pretty well."

The snowfall lightened and the clouds began to roll back off the fields, but it was no warmer and after a time both Frank and Tub were bitten through and shaking. Frank almost didn't make it around a curve, and they decided to stop at the next roadhouse.

There was an automatic hand-dryer in the bathroom and they took turns standing in front of it, opening their jackets and shirts and letting the jet of hot air breathe across their faces and chests.

"You know," Tub said, "what you told me back there, I appreciate it. Trusting me."

Frank opened and closed his fingers in front of the nozzle. "The way I look at it, Tub, no man is an island. You've got to trust someone."

"Frank—"

Frank waited.

"When I said that about my glands, that wasn't true. The truth is I just shovel it in."

"Well, Tub—"

"Day and night, Frank. In the shower. On the freeway." He turned and let the air play over his back. "I've even got stuff in the paper towel machine at work."

"There's nothing wrong with your glands at all?" Frank had taken his boots and socks off. He held first his right, then his left foot up to the nozzle.

"No. There never was."

"Does Alice know?" The machine went off and Frank started lacing up his boots.

"Nobody knows. That's the worst of it, Frank. Not the being fat, I never got any big kick out of being thin, but the lying. Having to lead a double life like a spy or a hit man. This sounds strange but I feel sorry for those guys, I really do. I know what they go through. Always having to think about what you say and do. Always feeling like people are watching you, trying to catch you at something. Never able to just be yourself. Like when I make a big deal about only having an orange for breakfast and then scarf all the way to work. Oreos, Mars Bars, Twinkies. Sugar Babies. Snickers." Tub glanced at Frank and looked quickly away. "Pretty disgusting, isn't it?"

"Tub. Tub." Frank shook his head. "Come on." He took Tub's arm and led him into the restaurant half of the bar. "My friend is hungry," he told the waitress. "Bring four orders of pancakes, plenty of butter and syrup."

"Frank—"

"Sit down."

When the dishes came Frank carved out slabs of butter and just laid them on the pancakes. Then he emptied the bottle of syrup, moving it back and forth over the plates. He leaned forward on his elbows and rested his chin in one hand. "Go on, Tub."

Tub ate several mouthfuls, then started to wipe his lips. Frank took the napkin away from him. "No wiping," he said. Tub kept at it. The syrup covered his chin; it dripped to a point like a goatee. "Weigh in, Tub," Frank said, pushing another fork across the table. "Get down to business." Tub took the fork in his left hand and lowered his head and started really chowing down. "Clean your plate," Frank said when the pancakes were gone, and Tub lifted each of the four plates and licked it clean. He sat back, trying to catch his breath.

"Beautiful," Frank said. "Are you full?"

"I'm full," Tub said. "I've never been so full."

Kenny's blankets were bunched up against the tailgate again.

"They must have blown off," Tub said.

"They're not doing him any good," Frank said. "We might as well get some use out of them."

Kenny mumbled. Tub bent over him. "What? Speak up."

"I'm going to the hospital," Kenny said.

"Attaboy," Frank said.

The blankets helped. The wind still got their faces and Frank's hands but it was much better. The fresh snow on the road and the trees sparkled under the beam of the headlights. Squares of light from farmhouse windows fell onto the blue snow in the fields.

"Frank," Tub said after a time, "you know that farmer? He told Kenny to kill the dog."

"You're kidding!" Frank leaned forward, considering. "That Kenny. What a card." He laughed and so did Tub. Tub smiled out the back window. Kenny lay with his arms folded over his stomach, moving his lips at the stars. Right overhead was the Big Dipper, and behind, hanging between Kenny's toes in the direction of the hospital, was the North Star, Pole Star, Help to Sailors. As the truck twisted through the gentle hills the star went back and forth between Kenny's boots, staying always in his sight. "I'm going to the hospital," Kenny said. But he was wrong. They had taken a different turn a long way back.

AL YOUNG

Born on the Gulf Coast in 1939, Al Young grew up in Mississippi, Detroit, and the San Francisco Bay Area, where he lives. Widely acclaimed and translated, he is the author of numerous screenplays, magazine articles, and more than fifteen books of poetry, essays, and fiction, including Sitting Pretty, Seduction By Light, *and* Heaven: Collected Poems, 1958–1988.

"'Straight, No Chaser' relates a violent urban incident I witnessed during the summer of 1960, when I lived in Manhattan and made it my business to frequent jazz clubs. The story is selected from *Kinds of Blue*, the second volume of my musical memoir trilogy in which music and memory mix."

◆　　◆　　◆

Straight, No Chaser

Thelonious Monk, 1960

THOSE WERE NIGHTS WHEN the Baroness would pull up in her shiny, other-worldly Bentley to fetch Thelonious and motor him away between sets at the Jazz Gallery. The scene was simply not to be believed unless you happened to be there to see it for yourself as I was for as many nights as my lean, practically nonexistent budget would allow. Somehow I never worried about money. It came my way in dribbles, but mostly it went. It went for foolishness, and foolishness was a staple for me in those summery times when I was so much older than I am now.

Foolishness sustained me. Foolishness was rambling around the whole of Manhattan, mostly on foot, but also on buses and by subway. I went it alone and I ran in crowds, thinking it possible, as a matter of course, to hear all the music there was, see all the films, read all the books, meet all the people and, in my idler moments, write reams and reams of prose and magical poems to celebrate the wonder of it all and, naturally, just to keep my writing chops up. Oh, and there were languages to learn, and girls; long philosophical chitchats into the night, and entire days whiled and gladdened away in Hoboken and Brooklyn; ferryboat rides to Staten Island, funky weekend parties, airy beach parties on Long Island, tuning in nightly to radio bard Jean Shepherd, wanderings through museums, hanging around the docks and parks, crashing in strange friends' and friendly strangers' rooms and apartments, learning new things on guitar and ways of deepening and stretching the singing voice, sitting at a Village curb with Dennis Rosmini (guitar Dick Rosmini's pint-sized cousin) and sketching on cheap paper with cheap pencils the disappearing world as it zoomed and wobbled before our eyes. Am I romanticizing? Am I licensing myself to poeticize what, after all, were only quotidian, dissolving events in the formative era of a simple-minded kid whose head and eyes and ears and nervous system all needed shrinking at the time? Perhaps I am. But that's only because this was the way I lived it when and while it seemed to be happening—these things, these foolish things that continue to remind us of ourselves when we're in the magical process of becoming ourselves.

And Thelonious Monk was as much a part of me then as he is now. All kids who listen to Monk's music seem to love it at once. It's a childlike music; compelling and attractive in a fundamental way. There's no way, really, to put this all in language (spoken luggage), but when has being at a loss for words ever stopped a writer?

On one of those nights, one crazier than usual, I spent a rapt three sets at the Gallery with my guitar buddy Perry Lederman and with Gordon Hope, a drinker with writing ambitions. We had put away a gang of ale and cheese, crackers and onions over at McSorley's Irish Saloon, and now we were checking out Monk who had Coltrane with him just then. It was also a night when Steve Lacy was sitting in with the group on soprano saxophone. Charlie Rouse was the other horn man. Actually, Monk and Trane were being featured separately as a double bill, but Trane's energy level was such at the time that he managed to ease in on Monk's sets with no apparent strain.

The setup was fascinating. Lacy had just recorded his first album on Prestige, which included the Monk compositions, "Bye-Ya" and "Trinkle Trinkle." For formal reasons, Monk had Lacy sit all by himself off to one side of the little stage, and when it came his turn to solo, Lacy would stand and play while the rest of the band provided him with serious, intensive backing. It was like a microcosm of the kind of situation you'd expect to run up against in Johannesburg or in Monk's native South Carolina, but not at the Jazz Gallery.

I don't know why that detail of spatial arrangement registered with me so deeply. Black soloists, after all, had long been featured with white bands as island performers, you might say; in fact, it had become something of a tradition. I could tell, though, that Monk appreciated Lacy's playing and ideas. That Steve Lacy had also chosen Monk as an inspirational ace and mentor must have accounted for his presence on the bandstand at all. It never left my mind, however, that bop itself had been pioneered by ingenious musicians, some of whom had as their express purpose the creation of a music white players weren't going to be able to steal. And, for a time anyway, Bird and Diz and Monk and others like them managed to pull the wool over the white boys' ears, and some colored ears too. Fletcher Henderson's arrangements had helped float the Benny Goodman band to glory; Sy Oliver had cut the kindling and stacked the logs for the Tommy Dorsey band's success; Glenn Miller had borrowed his reedy, lead-clarinet-above-the-saxophones sound from the lesser-known Negro band of Eddie Durham, and on it went.

This is how the rest of that night went at the Jazz Gallery with its cozy decor of abstract expressionist paintings: Perry sat there stunned set after set, drifting into the music from a folk music and country blues perspective. Gordon kept disappearing into the john to sneak little nips of gin from a half-pint he'd packed. The minute the last set ended, Monk disappeared. He didn't dance offstage the way he'd later do nightly once he landed a long-running gig at the Five Spot; Perry, who wasn't a smoker yet, rushed outside for air. I had no idea where Gordon had gone, but since he was basketball-player height, I figured he wouldn't be that hard to locate. Monk, I imagined, would be outside the club at curbside, climbing into the Bentley with the doting, glamorous Baroness Pannonica Rothschild de Koenigswarter at the wheel. To the press she was the Jazz Baroness, but to a tight coterie of musicians she was Nica. Monk had written his lovely "Pannonica" for her, and she had inspired Horace Silver's sultry "Nica's Tempo" and other jazz compositions. It was in her apartment that Charlie Parker had died.

I rushed out into the leafy, downtown summer night, blinded by its artificial brilliance. And that's when I saw it. That's when I glimpsed the scrawny black man being chased, hounded by a pack of white hoods. I blinked and then saw him drop to the pavement, scroonched up in the fetal position with nothing on but briefs, occasionally flailing his arms and kicking to ward off blows. He was bleeding and kept groaning.

"This is what he gets," one of the hooligans busy kicking him shouted to the crowd. "This is what he gets for goosin a girl in the park!"

The assailants were scuzzy-looking, sallow and ugly, like hooligans every-where. And, like their movie counterparts, they were playing to the flashing camera minds of the crowd gathered at curbside. "For goosin a girl in the park," they shouted. It was a litany.

They kept saying it, all six or seven of them, as if it justified their every savage move: "For goosin a girl in the park, for goosin a girl in the pahk, fuh goozin a goil in da pahk, f'goozin a guheeeyull innapahk, f'goozinagoilinnapahk, f'goozinagoilinnapahk!!!"

What goil? What pahk? What offense justified any of this? Right away—the music forgotten, the notion of getting another look at Monk and Nica dissolved, the whereabouts of my pals shattered into glassy bits and pieces of meaning like the night with its thousand eyes—I wanted to pull a gun, anybody's from anywhere, and blast them all away, slowly, each by each, as the flames of my anger inched toward insanity—Choom-Choom-Choom-Ka-pyowww! Thunk! Fight fire with fire!

In instant replay slow motion, unknown back then, I can almost chart this pitiful event frame by frame. Suddenly there Gordon stood, cursing and on the verge of exploding, right there on the curb. In real time it was all coming at me so fast I didn't know where start finished or where ended began. Hatred heated the moment. A big old American car was waiting with the engine running and a nervous driver, ready to make the getaway. At first I stood transfixed, trying to size up the scheme. What had really happened? Who was the girl? Who was the young man being stomped before my eyes? Had it all begun in Washington Square Park? When? How? What were we looking at? "Quit it, stop!" I screamed.

Without thinking, I pushed my way through the crowd toward the victim. I didn't know what I could do, but I knew I had to make my way to the front line and let whatever was going to happen happen. The minute I reached the curb, the thugs turned tail and raced into the street to squeeze inside the getaway car, one of them yelling out one last "That's-what-he-gets-f'goozinagoilinnapahk!"

I turned to see Gordon moving toward me from out of the crowd. He looked practically sober with concern and fright. "Al," he said, "thank God, you're OK. I thought it was you they were kicking the shit out of!"

The two of us automatically got to work at once and, with Gordon taking the man's arms and me lifting him by the feet, we lifted the bruised, bleeding man from the gutter and stretched him out on the sidewalk. Someone must have already phoned the police because in no time we heard a siren and could see the twirling colored lights approaching the nightclub. That's when Charlie Rouse, a mainstay with Monk's band, walked out of the Jazz Gallery, his saxophone in hand. He strolled to the curb and looked down at the victim impassively.

"What happened?" some latecomer asked from the crowds.

Rouse shook his head slowly from side to side and said, "Humph! I reckon the cat musta fell down. Yeah, he musta fell down."

Gordon got down on his knees and put his ear to the man's face and heart. "He's still breathing," he announced. "But they sure did do a number on him, poor guy."

Perry popped up then from out of nowhere. He said, "If I had me a gun I'da shot the muthafukkas. This is Mafia shit, that's all it is, but I'da shot 'em!"

The cops arrived and dispersed the crown and cleared the way for an ambulance to park. We were all told to stand back and to go home, the authorities were going to take care of it.

The three of us took the subway to our respective digs, and we spent a lot of time talking about the crazy, disgusting wrongness of it all.

"I'm gonna get me a gun," Perry kept saying. "Can't believe I grew up around here and still don't have a gun. You gotta protect yourself against shit like this!"

Gordon sipped from his bottle and said, "Yeah, that's some terrible stuff. I'm just glad it wasn't one of us."

I don't remember what I said, but I do remember how passive and resigned the crowd had been, and I couldn't get it out of my mind that this had taken place in New York City, in the liberal, permissive ghetto of Greenwich Village; not in Alabama, Mississippi, or the Georgia backwoods.

"Who were those guys doing the kicking?" I asked Perry.

"Local Italians," said Perry. "They never have liked all these outsiders coming into the Village, and Negroes in particular. I'm telling you, man, you better pack yourself some heat!"

What a way to end a night of beautiful, exciting music!

The subway sped uptown to our separate but equal worlds, each of us locked into the pain and anger of that night.

Later I heard that there were repercussions; that a black gang known as the Chaplains—the very ones reputed to have once challenged the New York Police Department to a rumble in Central Park—poured into the Village in taxicabs and got out dressed in suits and ties, toting neat little business-like attaché cases. Inside those valises were bicycle chains, knives, pipe wrenches, and other urban artillery. The way I heard it was that the Chaplains—whom many whites called the Mau Mau Chaplains—proceeded to avenge the brutal beating that'd taken place outside the nightclub by slashing out at any white man who even *looked* street tough.

Although I come from a family of pistol-packing southerners, right on down to my elderly grandmother and aunts, I never felt comfortable with guns. But Perry did, indeed, get himself a gun, and that's another story. They actually sent the Baroness up the river on a narcotics possession rap. Steve Lacy, like dozens of American jazz artists, moved to Europe. John Coltrane and his music flourished, even to the point of inspiring one devoted cult to build a church around it. Monk quit playing in the 1970s; simply stopped with no explanation and died in 1982. A year later, Gordon died of chronic alcoholism. Charlie Rouse seems to still be on his feet, alive and well and working, with no sign yet of falling down. And, as you can see, I lived long enough to get this down onto paper, knowing well that—like notations jotted on musical score paper—it'll go on being strictly dead stuff, an artifact, until another human being runs it through that most marvelous of instruments, imagination, and transforms the look of it into sound by breathing sense and meaning and feeling back into these blues.

PATRICIA ZELVER

I took my A.B. and my M.A. at Stanford. I have published two novels and a collection, A Man of Middle Age and Twelve Stories. *My stories have appeared in* The Atlantic, Esquire, Shenandoah, The Ohio Review, Ascent, *and* The Virginia Quarterly, *and in the O. Henry Awards collection of prize stories, and other anthologies.*

"I came back to Stanford in 1946 to study under Dick Scowcroft and Wally Stegner. It was an exciting time. The veterans were back, writing their war novels. Well-known authors—Katherine Anne Porter, Elizabeth Bowen, Walter Van Tillburg Clark, and Stephen Spender among them—came to talk, to hold seminars, and to join our parties. Much later, one of the Fellows, William Abrahams, became my editor."

♦   ♦   ♦

The Little Pub

IT WAS JANUARY. NIGHT fell abruptly, shrouding the oak-studded hills of Vista Verde in deep shadows. Only a few lights were visible from the picture window where Mrs. Jessup stood having her Happy Hour, her first—or was it her second?—vodka martini in her hand. She stood at the window in her house on La Floresta Lane, looking at the lights far below. They were the lights, she said to herself, of the Little Pub. The lights of the Little Pub twinkled cheerily in the darkness. Smoke would be curling out of its chimney in tidy loops like the chimney smoke in a child's drawing. Big Bill has lit a fire, she thought. Perhaps I should call Ruff and walk down there. But would we be able to find our way in the dark? There were no sidewalks and no street lights in Vista Verde, very different from Chestnut Hill, where she and Mr. Jessup had lived before moving here. The lights were visible from the house, but would they be in the darkness, on the lane? Probably not visible, she decided. Probably we would lose our way. And, anyhow, I have the cards to finish. First things first, she told herself. Sacrifices are always entailed whenever people put first things first, as they must if they want to do things worthwhile.

That morning Mrs. Jessup had driven to the city to attend a Seminar for Executive Wives at the Hyatt Regency, sponsored by Mr. Jessup's corporation. It had been an extremely rewarding session. A Social Anthropologist had spoken to them on "Developing Inner Resources Through Creativity." Or was it a Social Psychologist? She must try to remember to tell Mr. Jessup when he returned.

Distinctions of that sort were important to him, and rightly so, though she was not absolutely sure why.

The Social Anthropologist or Social Psychologist had traced the forces which made up the Modern World. The old-fashioned sort of Community Life, which was extolled in magazines and films and on TV, and about which so many people were foolishly nostalgic, was archaic—a thing of the past. It was particularly a thing of the past for dynamic men who set high goals for themselves. The world, not just their tiny community, was their milieu; mobility their Life Style. It was important, he said, to face facts. But this did not mean that their wives need lack fulfillment. It was, he had pointed out, really up to them. There were endless avenues open in which to be creative. He had enumerated some of these open endless avenues—foreign language lessons; decorating and art and gourmet cooking courses; working as a docent in a museum; volunteering to help the handicapped; entertaining graciously; bringing up children; graciously volunteering to entertain graciously; even, and perhaps most important of all, providing a serene and loving atmosphere for the executive husband. They—the executive wives—should think of their job as a part of a Team Effort. Sacrifices were, of course, entailed, but sacrifices were always entailed whenever people did things worthwhile. The rewards would be their own personal growth and their husbands' gratitude.

Mrs. Jessup had explored most of these avenues at one time or another, but she had not explored them lately. For the last six months, ever since they had moved into Vista Verde, she had really stopped exploring altogether. Almost the moment she had the furniture arranged and the new curtains up, Mr. Jessup had told her, in his proud, quiet way, that another Transfer was in the air, this time a very important one; the Chairman of the Board was about to retire, and he was in line for this position. It would be—now was—the culmination of his career. She had therefore done nothing in the way of exploring or making new acquaintances, and for this reason she was grateful to the Social Anthropologist–Psychologist for reminding her of what he called her "potential." As the wife of the Chairman of the Board, Inner Resources Through Creativity would be more useful than ever.

After the seminar, she had gone to the city's largest stationery store and searched through the cards, hoping to find a more original one than the ones she had sent so many times before. She had not succeeded, and had to hurry home in order to be there when Mr. Jessup, who was at a conference at the Airport Hilton—or was it the Airport Sheraton?—would phone her. There was three hours' difference, and with three hours' difference he always called at three o'clock to be present at the Happy Hour before the conference dinner. On the way, she had been struck by an idea. Perhaps she could make a card herself? During an art class she had taken once, in a past exploration of avenues, she had learned how to make a block print with a raw potato. Various designs and messages occurred to her. Cartoon figures? An old-fashioned script? Black and white? Colors? She had suggested the idea, somewhat shyly, to Mr. Jessup when he phoned.

"Make one?" said Mr. Jessup. "What did you have in mind?"

"I don't know yet. Something humorous, maybe. I thought it might be fun."

"Oh, let's keep it kosher," Mr. Jessup said.

"You mean, buy a card?"

"It seems to me you have enough to do, just addressing them," he said thoughtfully.

As soon as he hung up, Mrs. Jessup drove down to the Vista Verde Shopping Center, below their house, and bought the simplest card she could find. It was then almost four. She had called Ruff to feed him, but Ruff had crawled out from under the fence again, and was gone.

The nice young Vista Verde patrolman will bring him back, Mrs. Jessup said to herself.

Whenever Mr. Jessup was out of town, the private patrol car stopped by in the early evening, and the nice young man rang her doorbell and asked her if everything was all right. This was something Mr. Jessup insisted upon. Mrs. Jessup didn't mind because she liked the young man. He reminded her, somewhat, of her younger son, an engineer, now married and working in Saudi Arabia. She also liked the nice relationship the young man had with Ruff. He either brought Ruff back from the shopping center, where he liked to go, or, if Ruff came to the door with her, he would pat Ruff's gray fat back, while Ruff wriggled all over in ecstasy.

"I guess you can't be too lonely with old Ruff," the young man would say.

"Ruff is a good companion," Mrs. Jessup would tell the young man. "Of course, if a burglar came, he wouldn't be much help."

"Oh, we all know Ruff. He'd show the burglar around the house," the young man would say.

"Would you care to come in and have a drink?" Mrs. Jessup had said once.

"I'd sure like to, Ma'am, but we're not allowed to, when we're on duty."

"Of course, how silly of me," said Mrs. Jessup.

"Now, you take care of yourself, Ma'am. Just call us if you've any problems."

"Thank you, it's good just to know I can," Mrs. Jessup said.

The view from the picture window was of the wooded hills, now black shadows against the sky. Except for the lights of the Little Pub in the distance, you would never guess there were other homes around. The Vista Verde Neighborhood Association reviewed the plans of each house before it was built to be certain that no one's view was obstructed. The ad for the Jessup house, which was running in the Vista Verde *Crier* now, was similar to the ads the real estate people had run the last six times they had moved:

> Spanking new executive mansion in exclusive neighborhood.
> Secluded, three-acre, wooded retreat. AEK. Pool, three-car ga-
> rage. Country Club.

Except for the lights of the Little Pub, one might think one was stranded, alone, perhaps the last person alive in the whole world. Mrs. Jessup had once read a book like that; the memory of it still made her feel funny. She mixed herself another cocktail at the wet bar, then she went into the kitchen and opened the oven and looked at the frozen Stouffer cheese soufflé she had put in before her first drink. Then she returned to the living room window. If she did not have the other cards to do, she decided, she would definitely call Ruff and walk down there; they would, somehow, find their way in the dark. How pleasant it would be, if she did not have the cards to do, to sit in her favorite chair beside the Little Pub's fireplace—the old, sprung, cracked leather chair—or was it the old, sprung, chintz chair? It didn't matter. The chair was not the important thing. What was important was the general ambience.

The general ambience of the Little Pub was very agreeable. The credit for this went to Bill. Big Bill, the regulars called him. Mrs. Jessup was a bit too reserved for this; it was not her style. She left off the "Big" and addressed him simply as "Bill." Bill called her "Sugar."

"The usual, Sugar?" Big Bill would say to her, when she had settled herself down in her favorite chair.

She would smile—a bit coquettishly—and nod. With anyone else, she might have been offended, but not with Big Bill. Big Bill, she thought, could call the Duchess of Windsor "Sugar" and get away with it. He had such a nice, easy manner with the ladies, and everyone else, too, for that matter.

"One vodka martini on the rocks for my little Sugar," Big Bill would sing out, as he mixed the drink himself. This was a little joke they had together. He would then bring the drink on a tray to Mrs. Jessup, and present it with a comical flourish. "And what is Ruff's pleasure?" he would say, looking down at Ruff.

Mrs. Jessup would laugh. This was another joke she shared with Big Bill.

Mrs. Jessup sipped her cocktail and thought about the Little Pub. About her chair, the crackling fire, about Big Bill. About the general agreeable ambience.

"I'm leaving, Mr. Jessup is being transferred," she would tell him.

She could imagine Big Bill's regret at hearing this. "He's Chairman of the Board," she would say. "It's quite an honor, of course, but I shall miss the Little Pub."

Big Bill would, undoubtedly, present her with a drink on the house; perhaps he would even toast her and Mr. Jessup's future. Certainly he would ask about Ruff. "What about Ruff?" he would say. "How does he feel about this?"

"I'm afraid Ruff doesn't care much for Transfers," Mrs. Jessup would tell him. "The last one made him so upset I had to give him some of my tranquilizers."

Mrs. Jessup looked at her watch. It was five-thirty, almost time for the patrolman to bring Ruff home. In the meantime, it was pleasant to think about the Little Pub.

At the Little Pub you were surrounded by people of all ages and sexes. People of all sexes, including men. Yes, even though she was no longer nubile, as they said somewhere—perhaps in Japan—though she was of a "certain age," as they said in Scandinavian countries—or was it France?—or "over the hill," as the common folk saying went, she still enjoyed a room with men, now and then, on a lonely evening during the Happy Hour.

She liked, she thought, the way men looked. The way their jackets scrunched up in back, and their trousers wrinkled at the crotch; the way they talked, sometimes in monosyllables or little grunts. Their laughs—their hearty men chuckles—she liked this, too. There were, of course, men in her life. The check-out clerk at the Vista Verde market, the pharmacist, her doctor, the hardware man, the nice young patrolman; Mr. Tanaguchi, the gardener. She had an especially warm relationship with Mr. Tanaguchi, who possessed an amazing understanding of plants. It would be resourceful—even creative—to go to the phone, right now, and call him up and invite him and Mrs. Tanaguchi over for a cocktail. But what if Mr. Tanaguchi didn't drink? Or, suppose he drank only sake? She had no sake in the house. Or—worst of all—suppose Mrs. Tanaguchi, whom she had never had the pleasure of meeting, misunderstood her warm relationship with Mr. Tanaguchi? No, this particular avenue was not open; she could not be the cause of any embarrassment to Mr. Tanaguchi.

The doorbell rang. Mrs. Jessup went to answer it. The young patrolman was standing on the doorstep. Mrs. Jessup smiled at him. Just seeing him there gave her a nice feeling.

This time the young man did not smile back. His face, she noticed, was serious, actually quite pale. Could he be ill? Mrs. Jessup wondered.

"Ma'am, I have something to tell you," he said. His voice was not as hearty as usual, and he cleared his throat nervously. "Maybe you'd like me to come in, and you can sit down?"

Mrs. Jessup led him into the living room. She sat down, but the young man remained awkwardly standing.

He cleared his throat again. "It's about Ruff, Ma'am. I don't know exactly how to say it, but—we found him this evening. He was run over by a car on the road. I'm afraid there was nothing we could do. He was already—gone."

Mrs. Jessup's first thought was of the young man. How kind he was! How apologetic! But it was not his fault. Silly old Ruff was always digging out from under the fence and roaming around, which was against the Vista Verde leash law. Mrs. Jessup tried very hard to think of something to say to cheer him up.

"Dogs," she said after a moment, "are incapable of sacrifice."

The young man looked at her in an odd way. He seemed almost frightened, the way he stood there, clutching at his cap. Mrs. Jessup was determined to get her point over in order to reassure him.

"Dogs enjoy an old-fashioned community life, they are foolishly nostalgic," she said. "New neighborhoods—new and unusual odors and noises—fill them with a kind of frenzy. They forget their house-training, chew things up, dig under fences—and get run over! They lack inner resources and are not at all creative!"

"Mrs. Jessup, I have Ruff's body out there in the truck. I didn't know . . . Do you want us to take care of it, or would you prefer to?" He was stammering slightly, backing toward the door as he spoke.

Mrs. Jessup pretended not to notice his nervousness. Instead, she considered his words carefully. It would be nice, she thought, to bury Ruff in the back yard, with a little monument of some sort over his grave. "Ruff—A Good Dog." Something like that. But she could not expect the people who bought the house to keep up a grave. "It would be very kind of you—to dispose of it," she said.

The young man put out his hand, and Mrs. Jessup shook it. "Take care of yourself, now," he said, and left hurriedly.

Mrs. Jessup returned to the picture window. Should she go down to the Little Pub, she wondered, and tell Big Bill about Ruff? "Ruff is dead," she would say. It was important to face facts. It was important, too, to stop thinking about the Little Pub. There was no Little Pub. This was another fact that needed to be faced. No Little Pub existed in Vista Verde, and never would. Imagine the Neighborhood Association permitting such a thing! It would be against the zoning regulations, which did not allow Commercial Uses—only executive-style houses with proper setbacks and shake roofs on three acres. Worst of all, a Little Pub would attract Undesirable Elements. Undesirable Elements, sitting in old squashed leather—or chintz?—chairs (it did not matter), smiling co-quettishly at Big Bill, letting Big Bill call them "Sugar."

One could not have that. She finished her drink and went into the kitchen and took out the soufflé and put it on the dining room table in its foil container. It was limp and sticky, but she managed to get most of it down. Then she went into the den and began, again, upon the cards.

"Helen and Bill," she wrote, filling out the blanks, "are moving to *4 Old County Lane, Greenwich, Connecticut.*" There was a drawing of a doormat, and under that it said, "The Welcome Mat is Out."

She finished all of Mr. Jessup's list, which Mr. Jessup's secretary had sent her from his office. Tomorrow, she would begin the list of their friends. It was now ten-thirty. She made herself a nightcap and took it into the bedroom with her and flipped on the TV. She lay in bed, watching the middle of an old movie, sipping the drink, and thinking how surprised and grateful Mr. Jessup would be that she had accomplished so much in his absence.

ACKNOWLEDGMENTS

Grateful acknowledgment is made to the following authors and publishers for permission to reprint copyrighted material included in *The Uncommon Touch*. All selections are reprinted by permission.

Edward Abbey, "Fire Lookout," copyright ©1979, 1989 by Edward Abbey. First published in *Abbey's Road* (E. P. Dutton, 1979); also appears in *Slumgullion Stew* (E. P. Dutton, 1984).

Katharine Andres, "With the Potters," copyright ©1979 by *The New Yorker* Magazine, Inc. First published in *The New Yorker* (1979) and reprinted by permission.

Peter S. Beagle, "Come Lady Death," copyright ©1963, 1978 by Peter S. Beagle. First published in *The Atlantic Monthly* (1963).

Leslee Becker, "Twilight on the El Camino," copyright ©1987 by Leslee Becker. First published in *The Iowa Review* (1987).

Wendell Berry, "History," copyright ©1985 by Wendell Berry. First published in *Collected Poems* (North Point Press, 1985) and reprinted by permission of North Point Press.

Thomas Bontly, "Re-Encounter," copyright ©1989 by Thomas Bontly.

Edgar Bowers, "The Stoic: for Laura von Courten," copyright ©1973 by Edgar Bowers; "From William Tyndale to John Frith," copyright ©1973 by Edgar Bowers. Both first published in *Living Together* (David R. Godine, Publisher, 1973).

Blanche McCrary Boyd, "My Town," copyright ©1987 by Blanche McCrary Boyd. First published in "Voice Literary Supplement," *The Village Voice* (1987).

Nora Cain, "Drunkard's Path," copyright ©1983 by Nora Cain; "Darting Minnows," copyright ©1983 by Nora Cain; "Grief Quilt," copyright ©1983 by Nora Cain. All first published in *Sequoia* (1983).

Michelle Carter, "Sister," copyright ©1988 by Michelle Carter. First published in *Epoch* (1988).

Raymond Carver, "Errand," copyright ©1987, 1988 by Raymond Carver. First published in *The New Yorker* (1987); also appears in *Where I'm Calling From* (Atlantic

Reginald Gibbons, "Eating," copyright ©1986 by Reginald Gibbons; "No Matter What Has Happened This May," copyright ©1986 by Reginald Gibbons. Both first published in *Saints* (Persea Books, Inc., 1986) and reprinted by permission of Persea Books, Inc.

Ivy Goodman, "In Twos," copyright ©1986 by Ivy Goodman. First published in *Fiction 86: Gargoyle Magazine* (1986).

Hannah Green, "The Sphinx and the Pyramid," copyright ©1966 by *The New Yorker* Magazine, Inc. First published in *The New Yorker* (1966) and reprinted by permission.

Charles Gullans, "The Wall," copyright ©1989 by Charles Gullans; "The Aglaonema," copyright ©1989 by Charles Gullans.

Thom Gunn, "The Reassurance," copyright ©1987 by Thom Gunn; "Sacred Heart," copyright ©1988 by Thom Gunn. "The Reassurance" first published in *Critical Quarterly* (1987); "Sacred Heart" first published in *The Paris Review* (1988).

Allan Gurganus, "It Had Wings," copyright ©1985 by Allan Gurganus. First published in *The Paris Review* (1985).

Donald Hall, "Ox Cart Man," copyright ©1976 by Donald Hall; "My Son My Executioner," copyright ©1955 by Donald Hall. "Ox Cart Man" first published in *Kicking the Leaves* (Harper & Row, 1978) and reprinted by permission of Harper & Row Publishers, Inc.; "My Son My Executioner" first published in *Exiles and Marriages* (Viking, 1955).

James Baker Hall, "Organdy Curtains, Window, South Bank of the Ohio," copyright ©1988 by James Baker Hall; "Sitting Between Two Mirrors," copyright ©1988 by James Baker Hall. Both first published in *Poetry* (1988); both also appear in *Stopping On the Edge to Wave* (Wesleyan University Press, 1988) and reprinted by permission of Wesleyan University Press.

Ron Hansen, "Nebraska," copyright ©1987, 1989 by Ron Hansen. First published in *Prairie Schooner* (1986); also appears in *Nebraska* (Atlantic Monthly Press, 1989) and is reproduced here by permission of the Atlantic Monthly Press.

William J. Harris, "Modern Romance," copyright ©1977 by William J. Harris; "Hey Fella Would You Mind Holding This Piano a Moment," copyright ©1974 by William J. Harris. "Modern Romance" first published in *In My Own Dark Way* (Ithaca House, 1977); "Hey Fella Would You Mind Holding This Piano a Moment" first published in *Hey Fella Would You Mind Holding This Piano a Moment* (Ithaca House, 1974).

Jeffrey Harrison, "The One That Got Away," copyright ©1988 by Jeffrey Harrison; "The Otter in the Washington Zoo," © copyright 1988 by Jeffrey Harrison. "The One That Got Away" first published in *Poetry*; both appear in *The Singing Underneath* (E. P. Dutton/NAL Penguin, Inc., 1988) and are reprinted by permission of E. P. Dutton, a division of NAL Penguin, Inc.

Robert Hass, "Palo Alto: The Marshes," copyright ©1973 by Robert Hass; "Meditation at Lagunitas," copyright ©1974, 1975, 1976, 1977, 1978, 1979 by Robert Hass. "Palo Alto: The Marshes" first published in *Field Guide* (Yale University Press, 1973) and reprinted by permission of Yale University Press; "Meditation at Lagunitas," first published in *Praise* (The Ecco Press, 1979) and reprinted by permission of The Ecco Press.

Ehud Havazelet, "Solace," copyright ©1988 by Ehud Havazelet. First published in *North American Review* (1987); also appears in *What Is It Then Between Us?* (Charles Scribner's Sons, 1988) and is reprinted with the permission of Charles Scribner's Sons, an imprint of Macmillan Publishing Company.

Kathryn Hellerstein, "A Universal Language," copyright ©1987 by Kathryn Hellerstein; "My Great Poem," a translation of the Yiddish poem "Mayn groys lid," by Malka Heifetz Tussman, copyright ©1988 by Kathryn Hellerstein. "A Universal Language" first published in *Tikkun* (1987); "My Great Poem" first published in *Yiddish* (1988).

Mary Jane Moffat, "Homage to Miss Thayer," copyright ©1986 by Mary Jane Moffat. First published in *City of Roses: Stories from Girlhood* (John Daniel Publisher, 1986).

N. Scott Momaday, "Angle of Geese," copyright ©1969 by N. Scott Momaday; "On the Cause of a Homely Death," copyright ©1987 by N. Scott Momaday. "Angle of Geese" first published in *Quest for Reality* (Swallow Press of Ohio University Press, 1969).

Hugh Nissenson, excerpt from *My Own Ground*, copyright ©1976 by Hugh Nissenson. First published as part of *My Own Ground* (Farrar, Straus & Giroux, Inc., 1976) and reprinted by permission of Farrar, Straus & Giroux, Inc.

Kent Nussey, "Laughter of Young Women," copyright ©1985 by Kent Nussey. First published in *Crazyhorse* (1985).

Raymond Oliver, "Dream Vision," copyright ©1982, 1989 by Raymond Oliver; "Portuguese," copyright ©1982, 1989 by Raymond Oliver. "Dream Vision" first published in *Threepenny Review* (1982); "Portuguese" first published in *Entries* (David R. Godine, Publisher, 1982) and reprinted by permission of David R. Godine, Publisher.

Tillie Olsen, "Dream-Vision," copyright ©1984 by Tillie Olsen. First published as part of *Mother to Daughter: Daughter to Mother* (The Feminist Press, 1984).

Nancy Huddleston Packer, "The Women Who Walk," copyright ©1980 by Nancy Huddleston Packer. First published in *Southwest Review* (1980); also appears in *The Women Who Walk and Other Stories* (Louisiana State University Press, 1989).

Charlotte Painter, "Memory Loss," copyright ©1985 by Charlotte Painter. First published by PEN Syndicated Fiction Series, 1985.

Gail Perez, "Thanksgiving Dogs," copyright ©1984 by Gail Perez; "Lonely for the World," copyright ©1989 by Gail Perez. "Thanksgiving Dogs" first published in *Sequoia* (1984).

Robert Pinsky, "From the Childhood of Jesus," copyright ©1988 by Robert Pinsky; "The Hearts," copyright ©1987 by Robert Pinsky. "From the Childhood of Jesus" first published in *Verse* (1988); "The Hearts" first published in *The New Republic* (1987).

Nahid Rachlin, "Blizzard in Istanbul," copyright ©1988 by Nahid Rachlin. First published in *Fiction* (1988).

Belle Randall, "Learning to Write," copyright ©1989 by Belle Randall; "Ravelling the Unravellable," copyright ©1989 by Belle Randall; "Harpo," copyright ©1989 by Belle Randall.

Judith Rascoe, "A Lot of Cowboys," copyright ©1970 by Judith Rascoe. First published in *The Atlantic* (1970); also appears in *Yours, And Mine: Novella and Stories* (Atlantic Monthly Press, 1973) and reprinted by permission of Little, Brown & Co.

William Pitt Root, "7 For a Magician," copyright ©1974 by William Pitt Root; "Under the Umbrella of Blood," copyright ©1984 by William Pitt Root. "7 For a Magician" first published (as "For a Magician") in *Harper's* (1974); also appears in *Invisible Guests* (Confluence Press, 1983); "Under the Umbrella of Blood" first published in *Under the Umbrella of Blood* (Mesilla Press, 1984).

Vikram Seth, "The Humble Administrator's Garden," copyright ©1985 by Vikram Seth; "The Accountant's House," copyright ©1985 by Vikram Seth; "From California," copyright ©1985 by Vikram Seth. All first published in *The Humble Administrator's Garden* (Carcanet Press, 1985).

Alan Shapiro, "Randolf Routh to Charles Trevelyan," copyright ©1981 by Alan Shapiro; "Captain Wynne to Randolf Routh," copyright ©1981 by Alan Shapiro. Both first published in *After the Digging* (Elpenor Books, 1981).

Thomas Simmons, "Second Person," copyright ©1989 by Thomas Simmons; "First Sunday of Advent, 1967," copyright ©1983 by Thomas Simmons. "First Sunday of Advent, 1967" first published in *The New Republic* (1983).

Brett Singer, "The Catskills," copyright ©1986 by Brett Singer. First published as part